The CHARLES ELIOT NORTON LECTURES for 1938-1939

SIGFRIED GIEDION

SPACE, TIME

AND ARCHITECTURE

the growth of a new tradition

CAMBRIDGE, MASSACHUSETTS
HARVARD UNIVERSITY PRESS
FOURTH EDITION, ENLARGED
1965

ML '66 | 5 2 2 | 39/1

PRINTINGS
first, March 1941
second, August 1941
third, February 1942
fourth, April 1943
fifth, July 1944
sixth, June 1946
seventh, June 1947
eighth (second edition, enlarged), November 1949
ninth, January 1952
tenth (third edition, reset and enlarged), January 1954
eleventh, October 1956
twelfth, September 1959
thirteenth (fourth edition, enlarged), January 1962
fourteenth, April 1963
fifteenth, November 1965

PRINTED
in the United States of America

Library of Congress Catalog Card Number 62–14459

FOREWORD TO THE THIRTEENTH PRINTING

On the occasion of this thirteenth printing the question arose whether a second volume, concerned with developments during the last twenty years should not be added. More than enough material is available. But I have abstained from following this suggestion. One reason was that I feel *Space, Time and Architecture* is an entity in itself which, with all its shortcomings, should not be disturbed.

Instead, I have permitted myself to add a short introduction. I have never ceased to be interested in the formation of the man of today, nor have I ever lost contact with contemporary architecture and planning, and from time to time I have given accounts of it: *A Decade of Contemporary Architecture* (Zürich, 1954), showed — in the form of an anthology — what happened to architecture during the disturbed years between 1937 and 1947. In 1954, when Walter Gropius was awarded the international prize for architecture at the Biennale of São Paolo, Brazilian officials asked me to recount his life's work. *Walter Gropius, Work and Teamwork* (1954) is to some extent a record of the beginnings of contemporary architecture in Germany. *Architecture, You and Me* (Cambridge, Massachusetts, 1958), subtitled "a diary of a development" gives an account of my attitude towards evolving problems since 1937.

To these publications may be added the anonymous activity of teaching in Zürich and Harvard where — in addition to other courses — a long series of seminars on "The Human Scale" has been closely connected with contemporary urban and architectural development.

To gain insight into contemporary man and contemporary architecture the most direct methods have not always proved

v

the most rewarding. The frame has had to be constantly enlarged. I have never had a preconceived plan. I have followed problems as they developed. Only when looking backwards, can I see how each was foreshadowed by the previous one. I let myself be led by the evolving problems just as a sculptor is led by his material.

Space, Time and Architecture was concerned with contemporary man's separation between thinking and feeling — with his split personality — and with the unconscious parallelism of methods employed in art and science.

In *Mechanization Takes Command* (New York, 1948) I tried to show how this break between thinking and feeling came about, and how every generation has to find its own solution to the same problem: how to bridge the gap between inner and outer reality by reestablishing the dynamic equilibrium that governs their relationships.

This still seemed too small a frame to encompass the psychic structure of the man of today. The question which at present comes everywhere to the fore and which cuts increasingly deeper into the marrow of this century, is the relation between constancy and change. In other words — as a result of bitter experiences — we are concerned to know what can be changed and what can not be changed in human nature without disturbing its equipoise. I have been closely concerned with this problem for more than a decade. Contemporary art was born out of an urge to go back to elemental expression. The artist plunges into the depths of human experience, just like the psychologist. The artist shows that an inner affinity exists between the expressions of primeval man and contemporary man with his longings to become aware of his buried depths. This led me to the third step of my research, to the problem of *Constancy and Change* in primeval art and in the architecture of the first high civilizations, which is to be issued in two volumes of the Bollingen Series: *The Eternal Present: The Beginnings of Art* and *The Eternal Present: The Beginnings of Architecture.*

Zürich, Doldertal, December 1961   S.G.

vi

FOREWORD TO THE FIRST EDITION

Space, Time and Architecture is intended for those who are alarmed by the present state of our culture and anxious to find a way out of the apparent chaos of its contradictory tendencies.

I have attempted to establish, both by argument and by objective evidence, that in spite of the seeming confusion there is nevertheless a true, if hidden, unity, a secret synthesis, in our present civilization. To point out *why* this synthesis has *not* become *a conscious and active reality* has been one of my chief aims.

My interest has been particularly concentrated on the growth of the new tradition in architecture, for the purpose of showing its interrelations with other human activities and the similarity of methods that are in use today in architecture, construction, painting, city planning, and science.

I have found it preferable, in order to arrive at a true and complete understanding of the growth of the new tradition, to select from the vast body of available historical material only relatively few facts. *History is not a compilation of facts, but an insight into a moving process of life.* Moreover, such insight is obtained not by the exclusive use of the panoramic survey, the bird's-eye view, but by isolating and examining certain specific events intensively, penetrating and exploring them in the manner of the close-up. This procedure makes it possible to evaluate a culture from within as well as from without.

In keeping with this approach, the bibliographical apparatus has been reduced to a minimum. For those interested in further study and research in the subject, the necessary information is given in footnotes. No general bibliography has been provided. Its addition, in view of the theme and design of the book, would simply have swollen the volume by some fifty extra pages without at the same time affording scientific completeness.

Space, Time and Architecture was written in stimulating association with young Americans — an outgrowth of lectures and seminars which I gave as Charles Eliot Norton Professor at Harvard University. The problem of its composition was to transmute the spoken word of lecture and discussion into the quite different medium of the printed page. For the lectures the English version was prepared by Mr. *R. Bottomley.* Mr. *W. J. Callaghan* and Mr. *Erwart Matthews* made the English translation of the book, which was completed at Cambridge, Massachusetts, in the Spring of 1940. . . .

ZÜRICH, DOLDERTAL, JUNE 1940   S. G.

FOREWORD TO THE THIRD EDITION

Jacob Burckhardt and Heinrich Woefflin never touched their books once they were written; they let others "improve" later editions. Jacob Burckhardt, in reference to a late printing of his *Cicerone*, once remarked to his students, "I can really recommend this book to you; nine tenths of it have been re-written by others."

Indeed, books are born of a particular moment; it does no good to revise them later. For the eighth printing (second edition) of *Space, Time and Architecture* we have merely added some new illustrations, scattered here and there throughout the book; some pages on "Gustave Eiffel and His Tower"; some additional notes on the works of Robert Maillart; and a chapter on Alvar Aalto.

Since for the tenth printing (third edition) *Space, Time and Architecture* had to be reset, we have had an opportunity to add some new chapters, particularly in Part II. The chapter on "Perspective and Urban Planning" outlines the formation of urban elements during the Renaissance, including some of the contributions of the great masters, such as Bramante's Court of the Belvedere in the Vatican, Michelangelo's Capitol, Leonardo's preludes to regional planning. The chapter on "Sixtus V and the Planning of Baroque Rome" evaluates the work of the first modern town planner, as it grows out of Rome's medieval and Renaissance background.

A chapter on "Mies van der Rohe and the Integrity of Form," one on "Gropius in America," and some indispensable remarks on "Le Corbusier's Development since 1938" have been added in Part VI.

ZÜRICH, DOLDERTAL, JUNE 1953   S. G.

CONTENTS

ILLUSTRATIONS IN INTRODUCTION

ILLUSTRATIONS

xxi

xxiv

INTRODUCTION **ARCHITECTURE IN THE 1960'S:**
HOPES AND FEARS

CONFUSION AND BOREDOM

At the moment a certain confusion exists in contemporary architecture, as in painting; a kind of pause, even a kind of exhaustion. Everyone is aware of it. Fatigue is normally accompanied by uncertainty, what to do and where to go. Fatigue is the mother of indecision, opening the door to escapism, to superficialities of all kinds.

A symposium at the Metropolitan Museum of New York in the spring of 1961 discussed the question, "Modern Architecture, Death or Metamorphosis?" As this topic indicates, contemporary architecture is regarded by some as a fashion and — as an American architect expressed it — many designers who had adopted the fashionable aspects of the "International Style," now found the fashion had worn thin and were engaged in a romantic orgy. The current fashion, with its historical fragments picked at random, has infected unfortunately many gifted architects. By 1960 its results could be seen everywhere: in smallbreasted, gothic-styled colleges, in a lacework of glittering details inside and outside, in the toothpick stilts and assembly of isolated buildings of the largest cultural center.

A kind of playboy-architecture is *en vogue:* an architecture treated as playboys treat life, jumping from one sensation to another and quickly bored with everything.

I have no doubt that this fashion born out of an inner uncertainty will soon be obsolete; but for the moment its effects can be rather dangerous, because of the world-wide influence of the United States.

In *Architecture, You and Me* I pointed out the difference between the nineteenth- and twentieth-century approach to architecture. We are amidst the formation period of a new tradition, which is still at its beginning. I remarked then that there is a word we should refrain from using to describe contemporary architecture. This is the word "style." The moment we fence architecture within a notion of "style," we open the door to a formalistic approach. Contemporary movement is not a "style" in the nineteenth-century meaning of form characterization. It is an approach to the life that slumbers unconsciously within all of us.

In architecture the word "style" has often been combined with the epithet "international," though this epithet has never been accepted in Europe. The term "international style" quickly became harmful, implying something hovering in mid-air, with no roots anywhere: cardboard architecture. Contemporary architecture worthy of the name sees its main task as the interpretation of a way of life equivalent to our period. There can be no question of "Death or Metamorphosis," there can only be the question of evolving a new tradition, and many signs show that this is in the doing.

SIGNS OF THE EVOLVING TRADITION

An easy pandering to popular taste in architecture has been tried several times since the optical revolution around 1910. These trends came and went. And the playboy attitude of 1960 will vanish too. There are definite signs that the process of developing a new tradition is continuing in spite of temporary disturbances.

A period terrified that mankind may destroy itself at any moment is simultaneously impelled by a frantic desire to found new cities such as has not occurred since the thirteenth century.

Another phenomenon is that contemporary architecture has become enriched, both in architecture and urbanism, by contributions from countries from the rims of Western civilization, first from Finland and Brazil and lately from Japan.

The directions in which architecture will develop have become increasingly clearer during the last fifteen years: strengthening of its plastic tendencies and strengthening of conditions for its further evolution.

There is universal agreement that the values lost to our period must be restored: the human scale, the rights of the individual, the most primitive security of movement within the city. Behind this desire stands the unchanging constancy of human life which demands fulfillment. In earlier periods it was relatively simple to create settlements in which man was not too far removed from his need for contact with the soil. Today nothing is harder than to fulfill the simplest needs of life. The heavy weight of mechanization and all that follows in its train have entailed enormous complications that make it almost impossible to adopt any simple lines of direction.

As a result the questions which preoccupy us today tend to demand a global solution. Large-scale planning has long since moved from making plans for an individual city or region to the realm of mass production.

But despite the complicated situation of the present day, the unchanging values of life remain. Independent of all obstructions which impede its fulfillment the uppermost question is: *How do we wish to live?* The present state of urban planning indicates the current trends.

URBAN DEVELOPMENT

The future way of life consists in the recovery of the intimacy of life. A rise in population from ten thousand to ten million gives one an almost physical revulsion. A horror of mankind arises from the enormous heaping up of human beings. Overfilled cities have perforce led to a bankruptcy of life. An irrepressible desire for more concentration is again perceptible, despite all decentralization.

Formerly poets and painters retired into isolation. Today research laboratories and the offices of large organizations or insurance companies flee from the great metropolitan cities to barricade themselves with an undisturbed green belt of privacy.

A feeling of uneasiness and dissatisfaction with the urban situation has crept over the whole earth: schemes to displant urban centers, so that the city can expand without strangling its ancient compact center, exist for nearly every major city, from Helsinki to Athens in Europe and in the old and new capitals of Asia and Africa — Baghdad, Khartoum, Islamabad, and Chandigarh.

Chandigarh is paramount among newly founded capitals for placing its government center at the head of its urban body and not in its womb as was the custom in the walled towns.

I. LUCIO COSTA. Plaza of the Three Powers, Brasilia, 1957. *Sketch from the pilot plan.*

Brasilia solves the same problem by placing the government center — the plaza of "the three powers" (legislative, executive, and judiciary) — at the tail of its aeroplanelike plan.

The idea of placing a government center at the head of a city is not new, but it had to be re-invented. It was inherent in another form in the Château de Versailles. We considered the constituent fact embodied in Versailles to be the direct confrontation of a large building complex — including the ministries of France — with nature. Today I would also stress that the city behind it could have expanded at will. If the urbanists of the nineteenth and twentieth centuries could have understood early enough the new message of Versailles, the situation today would be radically different; but, because of the inertia of human decisions, the world waited till it stood before a nearly insoluble situation.

The center within the city, renewed or even newly created, is by no means at an end. It depends upon the circumstances. Stockholm is creating a place for a large new center. In

Boston several university professors planned a new center over an old railroad yard. If built, it would have been a highly needed landmark for the whole country.

As far as the placing of volumes in space is concerned, the much earlier Rockefeller Center still remains the most impressive, though a farsighted scheme prepared in Philadelphia has been developed as far as circumstances have permitted.

Ten years ago nobody would have expected the renewal boom in the United States. It is proceding much more quickly than the knowledge of how to accomplish it architecturally.

New ideas for urban development now come from Japan. To diminish the overcrowding and the congestion within a city like Tokyo, proposals have been made to create new land by building out into the bay. The horrifying growth of Tokyo during the last twenty years to an agglomeration of eleven millions provided the incentive for this idea. Different schemes use different modern techniques. In one project ferroconcrete pillars, anchored at the bottom of the sea, are proposed as foundations for high-rise buildings; another proposes enormous ferroconcrete rafts upon which the buildings will be placed. Kenzo Tange's plan for Tokyo (1960) is the most comprehensive. His structures, built on stilts, are in the Venetian tradition and, if one likes, could be traced back even to the primeval lake-dwellers. It is only astonishing that it has taken such a long time for modern construction methods to be proposed for this purpose.

Everything becomes clearer by comparison. To confront the amount of urban exploration of the last twenty years with what was done during nearly a century before is really astonishing.

In the first edition of *Space, Time and Architecture* we posed the question: Destruction or transformation of the city? Frank Lloyd Wright's desire to see the complete destruction of the city has not been followed up. We now see the way before us, though it still has to be implemented: the reconquering of intimate life, the human scale, the planning for growth. There are many other problems. But we can see the way.

The city will not disappear. It has been an ineradicable phenomenon since the very beginning of higher civilization. But its form is changing. Today all development moves in the direction of making the aspect of major cities more rural and smaller rural agglomerations more urban.

UNIVERSAL ARCHITECTURE

In the last quarter of a century Europe has not been the only source of breezes freshening the development of contemporary architecture. A universal civilization is in the making but it is by no means developing internationally upon an equalized basis.

It has in common a space conception, which is as much a part of its emotional as of its spiritual attitude. It is not the independent unrelated form that is the be-all of architecture today but the organization of forms in space: space conception. This has been true for all creative periods, including the present day. The present space-time conception — the way volumes are placed in space and relate to one another, the way interior space is separated from exterior space or is perforated by it to bring about an interpenetration — is a universal attribute which is at the basis of all contemporary architecture.

To this can be added another factor which is of no little importance and which lies at the basis of the best contemporary architecture. The radiance this emanates is generated by the respect it has given to the eternal cosmic and terrestrial conditions of a particular region. Instead of being regarded as hindrances these have served as springboards for the artistic imagination. It has often been remarked that the painting of this century has again and again driven boreholes into the past, both to renew contact with fraternal strivings and to draw new strength from these contacts. Just as in architecture, this is not achieved by adopting the forms of the past but by developing a spiritual bond.

This penetrating into the cosmic and terrestrial elements of a region we have termed elsewhere the "new regionalism."

Through the aid of contemporary space conception, through the aid of contemporary means of expression, a dialogue with unchanging constants can be reopened.

The manner in which the new regionalism is expressed by a creatively oriented architect depends entirely upon his actual tasks and their especial needs. These are different in the Near East and in the Far East, in Finland and in Brazil. Beneath the general shelter of the contemporary space conception a polyphonic architecture can develop.

The individual differences of architecture together with a similar over-all attitude provide one of the hopeful indices of the whole development.

UNIVERSAL ARCHITECTURE AND REGIONAL DEVELOPMENT

Structures imbued with creative force suddenly arose, first in Finland, as noted in this volume, and then in Brazil. Each country made its own regional contribution. Strongly democratic Finland showed how contemporary architecture can be simultaneously relaxed, regional, and universal. Brazil, constantly menaced by Latin American upheavals, introduced a grandeur of line and form in a series of glittering façades and astonishingly impressive projects.

The latest surprise has been the entry of Japan into the main stream of contemporary architecture, announcing for the first time the voice of the Far East. Before this moment traditional China and Japan had provided incentives for the West during the eighteenth century — Rococo — and, more profoundly, during the nineteenth century when Japanese woodcuts helped to release the imagination of the Impressionists.

But the situation today is quite different. The Japanese contribution is no longer confined to work in an age-old tradition. When, in 1953, I wrote a foreword for the Japanese translation of *Space, Time and Architecture* I felt it in some way a duty to point out that we of the West no longer adhere to a creed of production for production's sake and that the civilization which is now in the making may lead to a cross-fertilization of West and East. The West is again becoming conscious of something the Japanese civilization never forgot: the continuity of human experience. The rejuvenation of Japanese architecture is nurtured by elements which have persisted throughout its own tradition. This rejuvenation did not occur of itself. The creative impulse came from certain young Japanese architects who found their inspiration in 35 Rue de Sèvres, working in the atelier of Le Corbusier.

The emergence of contemporary architecture in Japan came later than one might expect. It might seem that Frank Lloyd Wright's Imperial Hotel in Tokyo (1917–1922) would have released the new movement. But it was not so. The Imperial Hotel was not conceived in a contemporary Japanese spirit. It was closer to the Chinese influence in Japan. Though this hotel survived so marvelously the earthquake of 1923, it could not — with its lavish ornamentation — give the necessary impetus for a new move forward.

The means for Western and Eastern spirits to come together had to be different. The key lay in the hands of young Japanese architects — Maekawa, Sakakura and others — who had found their way to Le Corbusier's atelier. Here they discovered what they needed. Le Corbusier is more closely connected than others to that Eternal Present which lives in the creative artefacts of all periods.

Except for a short interlude, the Japanese — in contrast to Western man — never severed themselves from times past. They have had no incentive to imitate former "styles," since the past is constantly alive. The simplicity of their homes, despite all refinements, remains primeval. Their contemporary use of concrete beams and stilts appears simultaneously age-old and new-born.

There is now a long line of young Japanese architects, of whom Kenzo Tange, who once worked in the office of Maekawa, has attracted the greatest attention. Their secret is a close contact with the living past and an eagerness to reach out into the future.

CONSTRUCTION AND ITS SPATIAL IMPLICATIONS

In the nineteenth century, structural engineering gave expression to desires which lay slumbering in the subconscious of the architecture of that period. In this century things are different. Architecture is now in the van and often asks more from the engineer than he can yet accomplish.

Structural engineering grew out of new methods of calculation and new developments in the manufacture of ferrous metals. In calculation, all structural parts were conceived as linear elements — forces obliged to follow and act in a prescribed direction — so that their behavior could be measured and controlled in advance. These forces were guided through beams, trusses, and arches as through a pipe line. Prefabrication and standardization naturally became involved in this procedure. The Eiffel Tower is the most famous example of its early application.

A peak of development was reached just before 1890 with brilliant bridges spun in mid air, the Eiffel Tower, and the Palais des Machines of 1889. Simultaneously the modern skyscraper was born in Chicago. Its construction, based on prefabricated linear elements, has been continually perfected up to the present day. The highly complicated procedures for calculating pre-stressed concrete beams also, to some extent, follow nineteenth-century linear methods.

Twentieth-century structural engineering is moving along a different path. The tendency to activate every part of a structural system instead of concentrating the flow of forces into single lines or channels continues to grow. Such systems can expand with full liberty in all directions. This results in certain difficulties. The forces cannot be easily controlled: often they evade precise calculation. Only tests by means of models and mock-ups can help. Construction merges with the irrational and sculptural.

This development required a more flexible material than straight-line steel trusses. About 1900 reinforced concrete was sufficiently developed for shell construction to be possible.

In this book we show the bridges of Robert Maillart because they have a pure beauty to eyes trained by contemporary art. This beauty was not arbitrary. Maillart was one of the first to conceive and to develop the idea of using surface tension in the flat or curved slabs of his bridges and mushroom ceiling, eliminating all linear elements. Freyssinnet and Maillart built their eggshell vaults about 1930.

Maillart once said he had got his inspiration from a steam boiler. The directive of a spatial distribution of forces throughout an entire structure has now been extended in many fields. E. Y. Galantay, one of my former Zürich students, now Visiting Critic in Architecture at Harvard, has prepared an approximate record of these tendencies: in the design both of automobiles and of railroad rolling stock, separation of the supporting chassis and the supported box is replaced by a self-supporting stressed-skin body. A move from open-truss to stressed-skin bodies in airplane construction presents the most spectacular development, but shell construction also occurs in shipbuilding. Large-scale thin-shell dams (as developed in France) are slowly replacing the heavy arch and buttress types. Even furniture design begins to follow this trend. The single-legged chairs of Eero Saarinen, who died so prematurely, are pure shell structures.

Since the death of Maillart in 1941, shell structures and space frames have continued to develop an astonishing richness and versatility and to offer more and more possibilities to kindle architectural imagination.

Shapes, formerly possible only with the use of the lightest materials, can now be made in shell concrete. The earliest forms of shelter reappear: the nomad's tent, the hanging roof used in prehistoric Russian settlements, the baldachin and other canopies. Even the principle of the hammock is employed in a network of concave roofing, and the principle of the drum appears in pre-stressed concrete.

A bewildering multitude of possibilities can arise from combinations of rotational shells with a single or double curvature or complicated spatial forms such as hyperbolic paraboloids arising from straight generators. Also cables — the most flexible of building materials — in prefabricated concrete acquire symptomatic importance.

The lightness and great flexibility of form offered by shells are now, for the first time in the history of vaulting, accompanied by no lateral stress. The structural system is equilibrated within itself. Shell construction appears ever more strongly to be the starting point for the specific solution of the vaulting problem for our period.

This does not mean that linear structural elements have been discarded. They continue to be used both in large and in small constructions. They have been developed further by great engineers, such as Pier Luigi Nervi, who uses prefabricated linear elements in spanning his large vaults and domes. In his Turin Exhibition Hall of 1961 — one of Nervi's most daring experiments — he strives for a more complicated spatial organization by the use of huge free-standing columns of different heights, which radiate fanlike structural fingers. A certain dichotomy arises between the form of these isolated structural members and the total boxlike enclosure with its flat ceiling. It may be that this building represents both the peak and the end of a long development.

The way ahead lies with a freer use of shell construction such as has been developed by Candela in Mexico, the architect-engineer Catalano, now at Massachusetts Institute of Technology, and, above all, Torroja in Spain. Eduard Torroja, who died prematurely in June 1961, was a profound theoretician as well as a great artist who sometimes, as in the structure of the Madrid Racecourse (1943), seemed to reach the point where construction acquires the organic power of nature. The Tachira Club of Caracas, Venezuela (1957), one of his latest works with S. Vivas, has the lightness and overwhelming grace of a moving sail.

DIFFERENT APPROACHES TO THE PAST

We have always regarded the past as something not dead but an integral part of existence, coming to understand more and more the wisdom of the Bergsonian saying that the past gnaws incessantly into the future.

It all depends on how one approaches the past. One way is to regard it as a useful dictionary from which one can select forms and shapes. The nineteenth century did this, using the past as a means of escape from its own time by masking itself with the shells of bygone periods.

The fashion of the 1960's is more refined. It only flirts with the past, nibbling at random details — pointed arches, renaissance porticoes, cupolas — giving them a surrealistic flavoring, so as to achieve a "poetic" expression.

The creative artists of this period have taken another way: poets, painters, sculptors, and architects alike. In their work, past, present, and future merge together as the indivisible wholeness of human destiny.

Early in this century the paintings of the great masters used means of expression — abstraction, transparency, simultaneity — which are close to those of primeval art. This did not represent a sudden, quickly devaluated, fashion. It was the outcome of an unconscious parallelism, arising from an urge to probe into the elemental, the irrational, the sources of symbolic expression. It was born of a desire to counteract the damages of mechanization. This can only be noted briefly here but is treated extensively in my book *The Eternal Present: Volume I: The Beginnings of Art.*

This attitude toward the past emerges in the work of leading architects, not in the adoption of shapes but in the expression of inner affinities. In the monastery of La Tourette by Le Corbusier (1959), everything seems radically changed in formal expression: the customary placement of the cloister, the plastic thrust of the spire, and the church, which are all welded together with the building. Yet La Tourette was inspired by French monasteries of the thirteenth century. In it their spirit continues to live.

Another example of this approach is the reintroduction of the patio in contemporary architecture. The patio, the inner court, the secluded part of a dwelling, has been known since the private houses of Ur, built around 2000 B.C. Roman country houses had a whole series of interior courts, serving specific functions. José Luis Sert, some years ago, reintroduced the patio for worker's settlements in Chimbote, Peru, to give the people some needed privacy and distance from their neighbors. By this means, Sert — maybe with some memories of Moorish-Spanish patios — achieved a spatial generosity together with a highly compact plan.

The approach to the past only becomes creative when the architect is able to enter into its inner meaning and content. It degenerates into a dangerous pastime when one is merely hunting for forms: playboy architecture.

THE PRESENT STATE OF ARCHITECTURE

Many architects are disturbed by the sculptural tendencies evinced in much of today's architecture: the Ronchamps Pilgrimage Chapel (1955) by Le Corbusier; the Sydney Opera House (1957) by Joern Utzon; the Tokyo Festival Hall (1961) by Kunio Maekawa. Architecture is approaching sculpture and sculpture approaches architecture. What do these symptoms mean?

To recognize and evaluate what is happening today and where we now stand needs a longer perspective than the immediate historical past. It may be advisable to project the present happenings against the large screen of historical developments. We see them in the light of the prejudices we were born with. Among these is a belief that architectural space is synonymous with hollowed-out space, with interior space. This belief is based on the development of the last two thousand years. Since the days of Imperial Rome, the formation of interior space has been the major problem of the art of building. This experience of architectural space is so familiar that it requires a very considerable effort for us to become aware of its relative nature, as I have said in *Architecture, You and Me* (p. 119) and elsewhere.

II. KUNIO MAEKAWA. Festival Hall, Tokyo, 1961.

But another space conception exists which has an equal right to recognition. This persisted throughout the first high civilizations — Egypt, Sumer, and even Greece. In all of these, the shaping of interior space was not regarded as of great importance. From the point of view of later times it could be said that their builders neglected or disregarded it. They remained beginners in finding solutions to the vaulting problem because they never gave it the high symbolic importance it acquired in later periods.

Again, it was the masters of modern painting who sharpened our eyes so that we could recognize that these Archaic high civilizations had their own conception of space, which led them to such supreme achievements as the placement of the triad of pyramids at Giza and the assemblage of temples upon the Acropolis at Athens.

At the dawn of history, man's relations with the cosmos had not yet been severed. One of the expressions of this relation was a setting of volumes in boundless space. Vaults then received no light. They signified darkness, the motherly womb of the earth. This situation, basic for what is happening in architecture today, is developed in *The Beginnings of Architecture* (*The Eternal Present*, volume II).

Forms are not restricted to their corporeal limits. Forms emanate and model space. Today we are again becoming aware that shapes, surfaces and planes serve not only to model interior space. They operate just as strongly, far beyond the confines of their actual measured dimensions, as constituent elements of volumes standing freely in the open. It is not just the size of the pyramids or the never-surpassed perfection of the Parthenon that is significant. It is the interaction between volumes which gives full orchestration to the first architectural space conception.

Today we have again become sensitive to the space-emanating powers of volumes, thus awakening to an emotional affinity with the earliest origins of architecture. Today we again realize that volumes affect space just as an enclosure gives

III. LUCIO COSTA. Plaza of the Three Powers, Brasilia, 1957–60.

shape to an interior space. We can turn to the work of a sculptor for an expression of this contemporary awareness of the relations between volumes of different form, height, and position. For twenty years Alberto Giacometti experimented with the interplay of primitive forms: from his design *Pour une Place* of 1930 and the *Palace at 4.0 a.m.* of 1932 to a small bronze group *Passers-by on a Square*, in 1948. The bodies of these passers-by are dematerialized to the utmost, yet they are so formed and placed that they fill the space between and beyond them.

In contemporary architecture I think the first planned relations of volumes in space can be found in Le Corbusier's project for the City Center of Saint Dié (1945). Here the different buildings are designed and placed in such a way that each emanates and fills its own spatial atmosphere and simultaneously each bears an intimate relationship with the whole.

Today architects constantly face the task of placing volumes of different height and form in mutual relationship. But the talent to do this has become rare, maybe because the shaping of interior space has for so long been regarded as architecture's supreme task. Even the marvelous urban courts and squares of the late baroque, with their surrounding walls, are a form of interior space, roofed by the open sky.

The situation now is fundamentally changed. The enclosing walls have disappeared. High towers must be related with low buildings. Squares without walls are developing. One of the first plans of this type is the triangular Plaza of the Three Powers in Brasilia (1957–60), where the dominating complex of senate, congress and administration buildings enter into a free relation with lower structures — the presidential palace and the high court of justice — at the corners of the triangle. There are no walls: "le jeu savant des volumes dans l'espace."

Architecture and Sculpture

That architecture is approaching sculpture and sculpture is approaching architecture is no deviation from the development of contemporary architecture.

One of the features of this evolving tradition is the simultaneity of freedom and involvement. Through this the volume has reacquired the significance it possessed at the dawn of civilization. It has again become an active emanating body. This is one of the reasons why buildings like Ronchamps Chapel or the Tokyo Festival Hall are so strongly modeled. The shaping of Ronchamps constantly reminds one of the interconnection between inner and outer space, as well as with the entire landscape which Le Corbusier calls "acoustic space."

During the first phase of the present development painting stood in the foreground. Now, in the second phase, it is sculpture.

With good reason, warnings have come from many sides that the example of Ronchamps in the hands of an average architect can be a disastrous influence. The secret of Le Corbusier's work is that he is also a painter and a sculptor. These gifts are normally divided today between different personalities. The average architect rarely knows how to place volumes and even less how to sculpture them. Sculptors, on the other hand, have developed this sensitivity. But there is no connecting bridge between them and the architects. Normally it is only when everything about a building has already been decided that an artist is called in and offered some spot to "decorate."

Following this principle, even the best and most carefully selected artists can never achieve more than a museum display. An integration is impossible. After several such bitter experiences most of the best sculptors have resigned and returned to their workshops. There is but a faint hope that the necessary humility will develop so that architect and artist can work together from the very beginning. Yet this presents the only way forward.

The Vaulting Problem

During the last two millenia, each period has created its own form of vaulting interior space: the Roman, Byzantine, Romanesque, Gothic, Renaissance, Baroque. Each specific form of vaulting has almost become the symbol of its age.

We are still at the beginning of a period. It is far too early to make any definite statement in view of the multitude of different vaulting possibilities offered to architects by the engineers of our time. It is possible, in contrast to earlier periods, that many forms may develop simultaneously.

One possibility is that ceiling and floor may mirror one another like mussel shells, as in Naum Gabo's early design for the assembly halls of the Palace of the Soviets (1931). Le Corbusier's outstanding proposal for the assembly hall of the United Nations in New York (1947), which would have created one of the most exciting interior spaces of our period, also moves in this direction.

IV. LE CORBUSIER. Pilgrimage Chapel, Ronchamps, 1955.

The greatest possibilities are offered by shell concrete vaults.
Up to now the center of a vaulted ceiling has always been
indicated by its point of highest elevation. But now ceilings
are able to become concave and their center can occur at the
lowest point: Ronchamps (1955), Berlin Conference Hall
(Stubbins and Severud, 1957). This is psychologically not
unimportant. The interpenetration of inner and outer space,
fundamental at the beginning of the new tradition, has become
transposed into a more refined form. The concave ceiling
rises up to the encompassing walls, indicating by this that it
does not stop there but extends further. At Ronchamps a
narrow rim of glass separating ceiling and wall underscores
this intention. The ceiling rests upon the walls like a descending bird.

The hyperparaboloid space frame offers a new starting point
for the spatial imagination. Whether of wood or of shell
concrete its balance is always contained within itself and its
hovering impression derives from its inner constitution. This

development is treated in more detail in *Architecture, You and Me*.

The Revitalization of the Wall

To become a constituent element of a volume, the wall had first to be cleansed of all decorative eruptions of the nineteenth century. There had to be a rediscovery of the aesthetic values of the pure surface plane whose expressive power had been lost since Egyptian times.

In terms of space conception this rediscovery tore the massive traditional house apart. It was in the early twenties that Doesburg, van Eesteren, Rietveldt and Mies van der Rohe achieved this transformation. The house became dissected into flat rectangular planes.

This rediscovery of the surface plane was fundamental. It formed the basis on which a second phase could be developed. This second phase also embodied the plane as an inherent element. It was diametrically opposed to the use of the wall as a backdrop for the attachment of reliefs: an attitude which finds its prototype in late Hellenistic, almost free-standing, reliefs (Altar at Pergamon). What concerns us in this second phase is the plastic integration of surface and modeling. This is the hallmark of present-day reliefs as well as of architectural-sculptural treatment of the wall. The nature of primeval reliefs, embedded in the rock, and of the sunken reliefs of Egypt, embedded in stone, is given new life.

Contemporary interest in sculpture and in the plastic possibilities of architecture results in an increasing interest in mural reliefs on the part of the sculptor and in the revitalization of the wall on the part of the architect. Artists pioneering in this field, even before 1920, included Lipschitz, Duchamp-Villon, Marcel Duchamp. Among others a big impetus was given about 1950 by Mirko's beautiful relief portals in the Fosse Ardeatine, Rome (1953), a monument to shot prisoners of war; by Henry Moore's brick reliefs growing out of a brick wall, Rotterdam (1955); and by the entire work of Etienne Hajdu.

As in the case of Ronchamps, there is every reason to be aware of the danger bound up with the architectural revitalization of the wall. It has already thrown a beguiling cloak over the playboy fashions of the 1960's. One can observe everywhere a tendency to degrade the wall with new decorative elements.

This is not the basic purpose. Architecture is fundamentally concerned with the revitalization of the wall from within. Le Corbusier must again be cited as the pathfinder. In his Unité d'Habitation, Marseilles (1945), a plastic modeling of the wall was already fulfilled. Its surfaces are interwoven with large-scale rhythms of horizontality and verticality. The glass walls of the apartments retire behind a perforated screen.

In his Chandigarh Secretariat (1952–56) the revitalization of the wall acquires the strongest expression it has yet received. This results from a sculptural use of construction elements, such as vertical parapets and vertical and horizontal *brise-soleils*. The delicate vertical expansion joints which separate the Secretariat's four divisions, subtly articulate the entire 254-meter building. The whole consists of four distinct parts and the section for the Minister acquires an especial charm through the plastic differentiation and variation of its massive and perforated elements. But the most daring feature of this structure is the 40-meter high ramp building, with its great unbroken plane surfaces, which shoots forward at a sharp angle, like a pointing finger. The contrast of a filagree-like articulation of the walls with the large planes of this slender ramp structure brings the wall surfaces of this building into an inspirited tension.

TO SUMMARIZE

It is easier to understand what is happening in architecture today when it is set into a wider frame of architectural reference. To summarize briefly: There are three stages of architectural development. During the first stage — the first space conception — space was brought into being by the interplay between volumes. This stage encompassed the architecture of Egypt, Sumer, and Greece. Interior space was disregarded.

V. LE CORBUSIER. The Secretariat, Chandigarh, 1952–56.

During the second space conception, the formation of architectural space was synonymous with hollowed-out, interior space. Despite several profound differentiations, this second space conception encompassed the period from the Roman Pantheon to the end of the eighteenth century.

The nineteenth century forms an intermediary link. A spatial analysis of its buildings indicates that elements of all the different phases of the second stage are simultaneously intermingled (Paul Frankl). But the earlier spatial unity vanished more and more. Buildings which most truly represented the period were ignored.

The third space conception set in with the optical revolution at the beginning of this century which abolished the single viewpoint of perspective. This had fundamental consequences for the conception of architecture and the urban scene. The space-emanating qualities of buildings could again be recognized, freed from the restrictive bounds of wall barriers.

There is an affinity with the first space conception. At the same time the supreme preoccupation of the second space conception — the hollowing out of interior space — is carried further. New elements are introduced: a hitherto unknown interpenetration of inner and outer space; an interpenetration of different levels above and below the earth, brought about by the effect of the automobile, which has forced the incorporation of movement as an inseparable element of architecture. These have resulted in the space conception of this period which forms the backbone for its evolving tradition. We are still passing through the convulsions of its formative years. Many detours can be expected. But the great lines have already been traced.

PART I HISTORY A PART OF LIFE

INTRODUCTION

Unknown in the United States and using a language that is foreign to me, I must seek the shortest way to direct contact with an American public. The way of personal contact is always the shortest route to understanding, not merely in personal but in general matters. Let me begin then by saying a few words about where I come from and where I intend to go — for these facts have a bearing upon the discussion that follows.

Heinrich Wölf-flin: contrasting periods

As an art historian I am a disciple of Heinrich Wölfflin. In our personal contacts with him as well as through his distinguished lectures, we, his pupils, learned to grasp the spirit of an epoch. Wölfflin's incisive analysis made clear to us the true meaning and significance of a painting or a piece of sculpture.

He delighted in contrasting one period with another. He employed this method most effectively both in his teaching and in his books — in his *Renaissance and Baroque* (1889), in *Classical Art* (1899), in which the fifteenth century is opposed to the sixteenth, and even in his *Principles of Art* (*Kunstgeschichtliche Grundbegriffe*, 1915), which had just appeared when I studied under him at Munich. Many of his pupils have tried to emulate this method of contrasting styles, but none have achieved the same depth and directness.

Late Baroque and Romantic Classicism

In my own first book, *Late Baroque and Romantic Classicism* (Munich, 1922, written as a thesis), I tried to follow Wölfflin's method. The periods contrasted were the end of the eighteenth century and the beginning of the nineteenth, both periods of classicism. The Louis XVI style formed in shape and structure the end of late baroque tendencies, with classicism serving as its framework. The classicism of the beginning of the nineteenth century found its most significant outlet in that country of romantics, Germany. In the architecture of the time the trend toward an individualistic isolation of rooms from each other was nowhere so strongly marked as it was in Germany — in the work of K. F. Schinkel, for example. This was the true architectural equivalent of the individualism of the romantic poets.

I called this period one of romantic classicism. Classicism in both periods was only a coloring — a transitory fact, as I would say now. The essential characteristic of this time was that, beneath the classic exterior, the baroque inheritance had begun to disintegrate and nineteenth-century tendencies had begun to appear.

The problem which fascinated me was how our epoch had been formed, where the roots of present-day thought lay buried. This problem has fascinated me from the time I first became capable of reasoning about it until today.

Heinrich Wölfflin was the pupil of Jakob Burckhardt, and succeeded him as professor at the University of Basle when he was only twenty-seven years old. He later taught with great success at Berlin and Munich. Wölfflin always laid stress on the wide view taken by Jakob Burckhardt and often quoted Burckhardt's words not only in his lectures but also in conversation. Thus the Swiss historical tradition formed the basis of our instruction in the science of art. But I am afraid that many of us did not grasp the significance of Burckhardt — a significance which reached beyond his *métier* — until much later.

Jakob Burckhardt (1818–1897) was the great discoverer of the age of the Renaissance. He first showed how a period should be treated in its entirety, with regard not only for its painting, sculpture, and architecture but for the social institutions of its daily life as well.

Jakob Burckhardt: the integral treatment of a period

I shall mention only one book in this connection, his *Civilization of the Renaissance*, which first appeared in 1860. The English translation was produced in 1878. An extremely well-informed review of it appeared in the *New York Herald* for October 20, 1880. Burckhardt, who normally shrank from praise, was so pleased with this review that he wrote "Bravo!" at the bottom.

In *Civilization of the Renaissance* Burckhardt emphasized sources and records rather than his own opinions. He treated only fragments of the life of the period but treated them so skillfully that a picture of the whole forms in his readers' minds. Jakob Burckhardt had no love for his own time: he saw during the forties an artificially constituted Europe which was on the verge of being overwhelmed by a flood of brutal forces. The

South at that time appeared to have withdrawn from history; for Burckhardt it had the quiet of a tomb. So it was to the South, to Italy, that he turned for refuge from all those things for which he felt hatred and disgust. But Burckhardt was a man of great vitality, and a man of vitality cannot entirely desert his own time. His flight to Italy produced the finest traveler's guide that has ever been written, his *Cicerone* (1855) — a book which has opened the eyes of four generations to the unique qualities of the Italian scene. His *Civilization of the Renaissance* aimed at an objective ordering of factual material, but in it his greatest efforts are devoted to uncovering the origins of the man of today. John Ruskin, Burckhardt's immediate contemporary, also hated the age and sought to draw the means for its regeneration from other periods (though not those which preoccupied the Swiss historian).

Contemporary artists: significance for historical method

But I owe as large a debt to the artists of today as to these guides of my youth. It is they who have taught me to observe seriously objects which seemed unworthy of interest, or of interest only to specialists. Modern artists have shown that mere fragments lifted from the life of a period can reveal its habits and feelings; that one must have the courage to take small things and raise them to large dimensions.

These artists have shown in their pictures that the furniture of daily life, the unnoticed articles that result from mass production — spoons, bottles, glasses, all the things we look at hourly without seeing — have become parts of our natures. They have welded themselves into our lives without our knowing it.

My activities have brought me into friendly contact with the architects of our day. We have sat together in small groups about many tables in Europe, from Stockholm to Athens — not to discuss problems in art or matters of specialized detail but to determine as clearly as possible what directions housing, town planning, or regional planning had to take. This close and continual contact granted me the privilege of seeing architectural problems in their nascent state.

THE HISTORIAN'S RELATION TO HIS AGE

The historian, the historian of architecture especially, must be in close contact with contemporary conceptions.

The historian and contemporary conceptions

Only when he is permeated by the spirit of his own time is he prepared to detect those tracts of the past which previous generations have overlooked.

History is not static but dynamic. No generation is privileged to grasp a work of art from all sides; each actively living generation discovers new aspects of it. But these new aspects will not be discovered unless the historian shows in his field the courage and energy which artists have displayed in their use of methods developed in their own epoch.

History dynamic rather than static

Architects have imitated other periods, taken over their special shapes and techniques, in the hope of escaping from transitory work and achieving a timeless rightness. And after a short time their buildings have become lifeless masses of stone, in spite of the incorporation into them of details from works of eternal beauty. These men possessed the exact contrary of the "Midas touch" — everything they put their hands on turned to dust rather than to gold. Today we can see why. History is not simply the repository of unchanging facts, but a process, a pattern of living and changing attitudes and interpretations. As such, it is deeply a part of our own natures. To turn backward to a past age is not just to inspect it, to find a pattern which will be the same for all comers. The backward look transforms its object; every spectator at every period — at every moment, indeed — inevitably transforms the past according to his own nature. Absolute points of reference are no more open to the historian than they are to the physicist; both produce descriptions relative to a particular situation.

History is changed when touched

Likewise there are no absolute standards in the arts: the nineteenth-century painters and architects who thought certain forms were valid for every age were mistaken. History cannot be touched without changing it.

The painters of our period have formulated a different attitude: *lo spettatore nel centro del quadro.* The observer must be placed in the middle of the painting, not at some isolated

5

observation point outside. Modern art, like modern science, recognizes the fact that observation and what is observed form one complex situation — to observe something is to act upon and alter it.

The historian's relation to the present

Historians quite generally distrust absorption into contemporary ways of thinking and feeling as a menace to their scientific detachment, dignity, and breadth of outlook. But one can be thoroughly the creature of one's own period, embued with its methods, without sacrificing these qualities. Indeed, the historian in every field must be united with his own time by as widespread a system of roots as possible. The world of history, like the world of nature, explains itself only to those who ask the right questions, raise the right problems. The historian must be intimately a part of his own period to know what questions concerning the past are significant to it. Apart from this approach, history remains a wilderness of blank happenings in which no creative work is possible. Only dead chronologies and limited special studies will be produced. The historian detached from the life of his own time writes irrelevant history, deals in frozen facts. But it is his unique and nontransferable task to uncover for his own age its vital interrelationships with the past.

The historian cannot in actual fact detach himself from the life about him; he, too, stands in the stream. The ideal historian — out of the press of affairs, *au-dessus de la mêlée*, surveying all time and all existence from a lofty pedestal — is a fiction.

The historian, like every other man, is the creature of his time and draws from it both his powers and his weaknesses. By virtue of his calling he may survey a larger circle of events than his average contemporary, but this does not lift him out of his own historical setting. It is even to his advantage to be forced from his academic chair occasionally and made to participate in the common struggles of the moment. For direct contact with life and its necessities sharpens his abilities to penetrate the jungle of printed records to the unfalsified voices of the real actors.

It is the task of the historian to recognize the truth through all its disguises.

6

Unfortunately the historian has often used his office to proclaim the eternal right of a static past. He has gone further and has used arguments based on past happenings to restrict and distort the future.

THE DEMAND FOR CONTINUITY

For planning of any sort our knowledge must go beyond the state of affairs that actually prevails. To plan we must know what has gone on in the past and feel what is coming in the future. This is not an invitation to prophecy but a demand for a universal outlook upon the world.

The need for a
universal outlook

At the present time the difficult field of town planning seems to resist all handling. In times when a universal viewpoint existed no genius was required to produce urban treatments of high quality whose influence long outlasted the period of their creation. Achievements brought about for a specific purpose and a specific social class proved serviceable in a quite different period for different purposes and different groups. This was possible simply because the original creation came out of a universal point of view.

Today the urge toward such universality is deeply felt by everyone. It is the reaction against a whole century spent in living from day to day. What we see around us is the reckoning that this shortsightedness has piled up.

This living from day to day, from hour to hour, with no feeling for relationships, does not merely lack dignity; it is neither natural nor human. It leads to a perception of events as isolated points rather than as parts of a process with dimensions reaching out into history. The demand for a closer contact with history is the natural outcome of this condition. To have a closer contact with history: in other words, to carry on our lives in a wider time-dimension. Present-day happenings are simply the most conspicuous sections of a continuum; they are like that small series of wave lengths between ultraviolet and infra-red which translate themselves into colors visible to the human eye.

The destructive confusion of events in the world at large today is so great that the movement toward universality is clearly visible in the field of science and scholarship. The desire for similarity of methods in the separate sciences — including the social sciences — in philosophy, and in art, becomes more and more definite. Already the demand for a universal outlook upon the world has made itself felt in the college: intellectual connections between the various faculties are consciously being developed.

Everybody knows that we have far more means of bringing change under farsighted control than any of the peoples of earlier times. It is the new potentialities at our disposal which are the key to a new and balanced life for enormous numbers of men.

The desire for universality is an expression of the need we feel to master and coördinate these new potentialities.

It is always dangerous to assume that one's own time has an exceptional importance. Even so, the years through which we are living seem to constitute a test period for mankind, a test of man's ability to organize his own life.

CONTEMPORARY HISTORY

The need for a historical background

A wider survey of the whole domain of human activity is the unmistakable need of the century. It is in this connection that history can play an important role. One of the functions of history is to help us to live in a larger sense, in wider dimensions. This does not mean that we should copy the forms and attitudes of bygone periods, as the nineteenth century did, but that we should conduct our lives against a much wider historical background.

Consequences of living from day to day

In the part of contemporary history we shall be concerned with, the most important developments are the changes that have come about in daily life.

The eternal complaint of the nineteenth century was that all the dignity had gone out of ordinary life. And ordinary life did lose its dignity from the moment it was put on an exclusively day-to-day basis. People lost all sense of playing a part in history; they were either indifferent to the period in which they lived or they hated it. When they compared themselves with the people of other periods their activities seemed unimportant and without significance, either good or bad.

The same feeling produced an extreme disregard for the immediate past — for contemporary history, that is. Unconsciously, in their matter-of-fact constructions, the men of the nineteenth century were producing the constituent facts from which the future was to take its structure. They did not see this, however; indeed, it is sometimes not recognized today. The result was not merely the neglect of contemporary history but something still worse — the wanton destruction of the objects and the records which were essential to its understanding. Later periods will be forced to leave great gaps in their accounts of the modes of existence of the nineteenth and twentieth centuries and the origin of these. *Indifference to the immediate past; its effects*

On every hand we hear the complaint that essential documents have been lost through sheer indifference to our own tradition. The town planner, for example, cannot find the detailed accounts of the evolution of great cities which he needs in his researches. The virtues and defects of the various types of cities — governmental centers, sea ports, factory towns — cannot be compared, simply because there has been no steady and unified research. The fact that research has been so irregular means that the historian anxious to complete a survey such as this one must sometimes fall back on his own investigations. The danger of overemphasis is, of course, always present. *On town planning*

The history of nineteenth-century industry has suffered heavily from our indifference to our own tradition and is full of gaps. The extremely interesting development of tools, for example, can be seen only from the few surviving nineteenth-century hardware catalogues. For the most part these catalogues of the thirties, fifties, and seventies have been lost. There are only a few places where these irreplaceable documents have been preserved; the library of the Victoria and Albert Museum in London is one of them. *On the history of nineteenth-century industry*

The period in America when complicated trades abandoned handwork and changed over to machine production is a unique one, without counterpart elsewhere in the world. I myself visited a great factory outside Boston where clocks and watches were first assembled from standardized parts shortly after 1850. (This principle later found its most extensive use in the manufacture of automobiles.) The early products of this factory were mentioned by some European observers of the seventies. I wanted to see examples of them and to study the early catalogues of the company. There were no old catalogues at all — the company destroyed them, on principle, when they were three years old — and the only old watches were those which had come in for repairs. There was, on the other hand, a large, valuable, but historically unimportant collection of European watches.

The oldest mail-order house in the country, with an annual business of $500,000,000, is located in Chicago. I went there to see what changes had been made in articles of daily life since Civil War times. The company possessed some material — incomplete, however — and very properly kept it in a safe.

The Otis Elevator Company in New York had comparatively full records of their products — and the literature dealing with elevators is none too precise — but even here material dealing with the earliest beginnings had not been preserved.

On architecture In the 1880's, when European architecture seemed given over to a future of muddle, indecision, and despair, a new architecture was growing up on the American prairies. From 1880 to the time of the Columbian Exposition of 1893 the "Loop" area in Chicago (its business quarter, that is) was the center of architectural development not merely for the United States but for the whole world.

It may be that after a few decades the skyscraper automatically becomes a sort of blighted area and must be torn down. It may be that the Marshall Field wholesale store — one of Chicago's finest buildings and Henry Hobson Richardson's best work — had to be destroyed to create a parking lot. It may be that there was no other direction for a highway except one that will eventually lead over the site of the Adler and Sullivan Auditorium, with its unique theater interior. It may be that John Root's Monadnock Block — the most celebrated of the early skyscrapers — cannot be protected

10

against the advance of the subway system. Whether or not this assault upon the recent past is unavoidable does not concern us here.

It does concern us, however, that there is no particular feeling for what is being destroyed. Chicago seems quite unaware of the significance of the Chicago school. I went searching in Chicago for pictures of the interiors of its great hotels and apartment houses in the eighties, buildings which in their whole organization foreshadowed many present-day developments. One photographer told me that he had destroyed thousands of plates picturing these interiors; he needed the space, and was aware of no reason why they should be preserved. For the past few years several institutions in Chicago have been endeavoring to preserve material of this sort. It is doubtful, however, whether their endeavors are enough to stop the losses that constantly occur.

These remarks have been made simply to indicate the widespread indifference to the immediate past, to the century out of which our period grows and derives the basic elements for its own life.

THE IDENTITY OF METHODS

Our period is a period of transition. The tangle of different tendencies continuing from the past or pointing to the future, tendencies which mix confusedly and interpenetrate at every point, makes our period seem to lack any definite line of advance. To some it presents the appearance of a chaos of contradictory impulses. An eminent French sociologist wrote recently that "we see around us nothing save tumult, aimless agitation, hesitant opinions, vacillating thoughts."

Our period one of transition

We must not forget, however, that this particular transition period has lasted for a whole century. It has made itself felt in each country at the same rate and in the same proportion as the disorder which the process of industrialization produced everywhere.

Ever since the opening of this transitional period, our mental life has been without equilibrium. Our inner being has undergone division. This state of the contemporary spirit has been recognized often enough, but its consequences have not been drawn.

If chaos had for its only definition the coexistence of tendencies contradictory to one another, our period would certainly deserve to be called chaotic. But we believe that these contradictions are merely surface ones.

There is this remarkable circumstance which we can observe today: sciences which differ widely in their objects are beginning to resemble each other in their methods. A continued and extensive search for exact knowledge is at the bottom of this growing resemblance. It is being recognized in all quarters that the ideas which we have taken over from the past are both too complex and too crude.

A transition period may affect two observers in very different ways. One may see only the chaos of contradictory traits and mutually destructive principles; the other may see beneath all this confusion those elements which are working together to open the way for new solutions. It is not a simple thing to decide between two such judgments, to determine which has emphasized the essential marks of the time. We need some objective guide to what is going on in the depths of the period, some sign by which we can determine whether or not its dispersed energies are being brought into united action. A comparison of the methods which govern its major activities, its thinking and feeling, may afford us such an objective criterion.

Have science and art anything in common? John Dewey, in his *Art as Experience*, points out that "compartmentalization of occupations and interests brings about separation of that mode of activity commonly called 'practise' from insight, of imagination from executive doing, of significant purpose from work, of emotion from thought and doing." Each of these activities is then assigned "its own place in which it must abide. Those who write the anatomy of experience then suppose that these divisions inhere in the very constitution of human nature."

It is just such an evolution which lies behind the doubt as to whether science and art have anything in common. The question would not be raised except in a period where thinking and

12

feeling proceed on different levels in opposition to each other. In such a period, people no longer expect a scientific discovery to have any repercussions in the realm of feeling. It seems unnatural for a theory in mathematical physics to meet with an equivalent in the arts. But this is to forget that the two are formulated by men living in the same period, exposed to the same general influences, and moved by similar impulses. Thought and feeling could be entirely separated only by cutting men in two.

We have behind us a period in which thinking and feeling were separated. This schism produced individuals whose inner development was uneven, who lacked inner equilibrium: split personalities. The split personality as a psychopathic case does not concern us here; we are speaking of the inner disharmony which is found in the structure of the normal personality of this period.

Separation of thinking and feeling

What are the effects of this inner division? Only very rarely do we encounter a master in one field who is capable of recognizing workers of the same stature and tendency in another. Contemporary artists and scientists have lost contact with each other; they speak the language of their time in their own work, but they cannot even understand it as it is expressed in work of a different character. The great physicist may lack all understanding of a painting which presents the artistic equivalent of his own ideas. A great painter may fail entirely to grasp architecture which has developed out of his own principles. Men who produce poetry which is purely an expression of this time are indifferent to the music which is contemporary in the same sense and to the same degree. This is our inheritance from the nineteenth century, during which the different departments of human activity steadily lost touch with one another. The principles of *laissez-faire* and *laissez-aller* were extended to the life of the spirit.

The split personality

Throughout the nineteenth century the natural sciences went splendidly ahead, impelled by the great tradition which the previous two hundred years had established, and sustained by problems which had a direction and momentum of their own. The real spirit of the age came out in these researches — in the realm of thinking, that is. But these achievements

The split civilization

were regarded as emotionally neutral, as having no relation to the realm of feeling. Feeling could not keep up with the swift advances made in science and the techniques. The century's genuine strength and special accomplishments remained largely irrelevant to man's inner life.

This orientation of the vital energies of the period is reflected in the make-up of the man of today. Scarcely anyone can escape the unbalanced development which it encourages. The split personality, the unevenly adjusted man, is symptomatic of our period.

Unconscious parallelisms of method in science and art

But behind these disintegrating forces in our period tendencies leading toward unity can be observed. From the first decade of this century on, we encounter curious parallelisms of method in the separate realms of thought and feeling, science and art. Problems whose roots lie entirely in our time are being treated in similar ways, even when their subject matter is very different and their solutions are arrived at independently.

In 1908 the great mathematician Hermann Minkowski first conceived a world in four dimensions, with space and time coming together to form an indivisible continuum. His *Space and Time* of that year begins with the celebrated statement, "Henceforth space by itself, and time by itself, are doomed to fade away into mere shadows, and only a kind of union of the two will preserve an independent reality." It was just at this time that in France and in Italy cubist and futurist painters developed the artistic equivalent of space-time in their search for means of expressing purely contemporaneous feelings.

Some less spectacular duplications of methods in the fields of thought and feeling also date from this period. Thus new basic elements designed to permit the solving of problems that had just been recognized were introduced in construction and painting around 1908. The basic identity of these elements will be discussed in Part VI, "Space-Time in Art, Architecture, and Construction."

Nineteenth-century popularization of the sciences: emphasis on results

Only a small part of the full range of the sciences can be mastered by a single man. Their specialized inquiries and complicated techniques of research make any far-reaching competency impossible. But, even apart from this impossibil-

14

ity, we move in a different direction today in seeking to arrive at a general outlook. It is no longer specific scientific facts and achievements that call for popularization, as was the case in the nineteenth century. Then even the greatest scientists felt it necessary to acquaint the public with what was being done in their fields. In the thirties of the nineteenth century Michael Faraday in England and François Arago in France were greatly concerned with increasing popular knowledge of the sciences. Faraday's chair during his lifetime was associated with the Royal Institution in London, a society founded in 1799 for "the promotion and the diffusion and extension of useful knowledge." To the present day the weekly evening meetings of this rather exclusive society are attended by members only (white ties obligatory) in Faraday's old lecture theater in Albemarle Street, London. Faraday himself introduced in 1826 a special course for juvenile auditors which until the present day has been delivered every year at Christmas time.

François Arago, the well-known physicist who discovered fundamental laws of electricity and who was a pioneer in the undulatory theory of light, was most celebrated for his gift for treating difficult subjects — such as astronomy — in a popular manner. In his courses at the observatory in Paris, he spoke to an audience unacquainted with mathematics. The larger part of the fourteen volumes embracing his work is devoted to such popularizing.

University extension in the modern sense, introduced in the seventies of the nineteenth century at Oxford and Cambridge, grew out of these efforts to popularize scientific results.

Today a leading scientist — a "Secrétaire perpétuel de l'Académie," such as Arago was, for example — would not make the popularization of scientific research one of his chief concerns. Other problems are more important today. The methods of science are of more concern to us now than any of their separate results.

The problem of today is not to popularize science. What our period needs much more than this is to gain an understanding and a general view of the dominant methods in different fields of human activity, recognizing their differences and their likenesses.

The scientific education of our day is designed to produce extreme specialists. That there is, on the other hand, an urge toward interrelation cannot be denied. Yet there is no institution to help us understand the interrelations that exist between the different sciences or between the sciences and the realm of feeling.

Knowledge of scientific method more important today

A general contemporary understanding of scientific method is more important for our culture as a whole than widespread knowledge of scientific facts. It is through their increasing similarity of method that the various activities of our times are drawing together to constitute one culture. Some grasp of the way in which different sciences resemble each other in the employment of similar methods is needed for insight into contemporary life as a whole.

But science is not an activity which goes on independently of all others. Each period lives in a realm of feeling as well as in a realm of thought, and changes in each realm affect the changes in the other. Each period finds outlets for its emotions through different means of expression. Emotions and expressive means vary concomitantly with the concepts that dominate the epoch. Thus in the Renaissance the dominant space conceptions found their proper frame in perspective, while in our period the conception of space-time leads the artist to adopt very different means.

Economics and politics have been taken as points of departure for explanations of the structure of a period in all its aspects. The influence of feeling upon reality, its constant permeation of all human activities, has been largely disregarded or felt to be of negligible importance. In tracing the interrelated developments in art, architecture, and construction through the period we have selected, it is precisely the influence of feeling which we shall emphasize.

Cosmological background of the baroque period

Our culture has a structure different in many of its aspects from the cultures that grew up in pre-industrial periods. In the baroque period, for example, Leibnitz arrived at the discovery of the calculus from a starting point in philosophy. He moved from a general — one might say a cosmological — outlook to this particular discovery.

16

With our inheritance from preceding generations, we are obliged to adopt a different starting point and follow another route. We must take our departure from a large number of specialized disciplines and go on from there toward a coherent general outlook on our world. It is beside the point whether or not this route is more difficult, more precarious, and less certain to end in success than the path that lay open to Leibnitz. It is the route that present realities force us to take. Unity, for us, will have to come about through the unintended parallelisms in method that are springing up in the specialized sciences and the equally specialized arts. These are the indications that we are nearing a spontaneously established harmony of emotional and intellectual activities.

Our culture rooted in specialization

In both contemporary science and contemporary art it is possible to detect elements of the general pattern which our culture will embody. The situation is a curious one: our culture is like an orchestra where the instruments lie ready tuned but where every musician is cut off from his fellows by a sound-proof wall. It is impossible to foretell the events that will have to come before these barriers are broken down. The only service the historian can perform is to point out this situation, to bring it into consciousness.

The degree to which its methods of thinking and of feeling coincide determines the equilibrium of an epoch. When these methods move apart from each other there is no possibility of a culture and a tradition. These are not deliberations remote from our subject: we shall soon see that it was just this unfortunate schism between its thought and feeling which struck down the magnificent power of the nineteenth century. Out of such a schism come split personalities and split civilizations.

TRANSITORY AND CONSTITUENT FACTS

It is not the historian's task to tell the public what pleases or displeases him personally. That is a private affair which loses all its interest in the telling. The historian is not required to correct an epoch in the light of his own opinions. He has to explain it, to show why history took a certain direction. The

Fact and interpretation in history

people who lived in a period can best tell us, out of their own inner feelings, whether its development was happy or unhappy.

The voices which come to us out of the fortunes or misfortunes of an age furnish indispensable testimony. No man of a later time, however great the impartiality which distance from the events has brought, can approach the direct and certain feeling for a period which belonged to those in the midst of the struggle — a struggle which involved their destiny. Words uttered out of the needs of the time are the historian's real guides, and it is from them that he must draw his explanation of the period. The true critique of an age can only be taken from the testimony of that age.

Entirely objective judgment with no trace of personal bias is, on the face of things, quite impossible. Nevertheless, the infiltration of the personal must be reduced to a minimum. The historian is not solely a cataloguer of facts; it is his right, and indeed his duty, to pass judgment. His judgments must, however, spring directly from his facts.

The historian cannot speak with the direct authority of a contemporary, but he has a breadth of outlook which the contemporary inevitably lacks. He sees facts which were hidden from the people of the time he studies. He can tell more or less short-lived novelties from genuinely new trends. The facts of history fall into one or the other of these classes, and it is the business of the historian to distinguish accurately between them.

Constituent facts: recurrent and cumulative tendencies

Constituent facts are those tendencies which, when they are suppressed, inevitably reappear. Their recurrence makes us aware that these are elements which, all together, are producing a *new tradition*. Constituent facts in architecture, for example, are the undulation of the wall, the juxtaposition of nature and the human dwelling, the open ground-plan. Constituent facts in the nineteenth century are the new potentialities in construction, the use of mass production in industry, the changed organization of society.

Transitory facts: sporadic trends

Facts of the other sort — equally the work of the forces moving in a period — lack the stuff of permanence and fail to attach themselves to a new tradition. At first appearance they may have all the éclat and brilliance of a firework display, but they have no greater durability. Sometimes they are interlaced with every refinement of fashion — the furniture of the Second Empire in France is an instance. These we shall call transitory facts.

Transitory facts in their dash and glitter often succeed in taking over the center of the stage. This was the case with the experiments in historical styles that went on — with infinite changes of direction — throughout the whole nineteenth century. The entire output of official painting was a transitory fact of that period, almost wholly without significance to the present day.

A period may be dominated by transitory or by constituent facts; both alternatives are open. There is, however, no doubt which of these two classes of trends is the more likely to produce a solution of the real problems of the age.

It is in this field that the historian is not only free to use his judgment but obliged to. To make the not always obvious distinction between transitory and constituent facts is his own personal responsibility.

ARCHITECTURE AS AN ORGANISM

We are looking for the reflection in architecture of the progress our own period has made toward consciousness of itself — of its special limitations and potentialities, needs, and aims. Architecture can give us an insight into this process just because it is so bound up with the life of a period as a whole. Everything in it, from its fondness for certain shapes to the approaches to specific building problems which it finds most natural, reflects the conditions of the age from which it springs. It is the product of all sorts of factors — social, economic, scientific, technical, ethnological.

Architecture as an index to a period

However much a period may try to disguise itself, its real nature will still show through in its architecture, whether this uses original forms of expression or attempts to copy bygone epochs. We recognize the character of the age as easily as we identify a friend's handwriting beneath attempted disguises. It is as an unmistakable index to what was really going on in a period that architecture is indispensable when we are seeking to evaluate that period.

In the great architectural masterpieces, as in every great work of art, the human shortcomings which every period exhibits so liberally fall away. This is why these works are true monuments of their epochs; with the overlay of recurrent human weaknesses removed, the central drives of the time of their creation show plainly.

But if architecture is the result of so many conditions, is it either proper or possible to examine it out of its context, as a finite organism in its own right?

Architecture as an independent organism

An architecture may be called into being by all sorts of external conditions, but once it appears it constitutes an organism in itself, with its own character and its own continuing life. Its value cannot be stated in the sociological or economic terms by which we explain its origin, and its influence may continue after its original environment has altered or disappeared. Architecture can reach out beyond the period of its birth, beyond the social class that called it into being, beyond the style to which it belongs.

Continuing tendencies

When a Roman baroque architect of the late seventeenth century invents the undulating church façade we can account for the invention in various ways. This was the time of the Counter Reformation; means were demanded of focusing all the attention of the people upon the Church. Or we might invoke economic factors and attribute the undulation of the wall to the constricted streets of Rome and the economy of front which they made necessary.

Both factors were no doubt involved. The undulating wall, however, was used later on, when these factors were no longer operative, in the great dwelling complexes of the eighteenth and early nineteenth centuries. The undulating wall, once invented, became a constituent fact in architecture, and continued to work in the realm of architectural knowledge after the Counter Reformation and Roman late baroque had both come to an end.

The château of Versailles admits of a purely sociological explanation. Or, again, the shapes that compose it and the plan-

20

ning of its rooms can be analyzed in the light of the historical styles from which they derive. The Italian and Dutch influences in the great gardens can be disentangled. All these studies result in a picture of the time, taken from various angles, which is certainly informative and interesting. They overlook, however, the constituent facts, the lasting tendencies, which made their first appearance at Versailles.

In a modern work of art it is the relationships between the elements in the composition that are decisive in determining its character. Modern science likewise seeks to fit the objects of its study into a relational scheme. It is not the qualities which make these objects unique among others that are of interest but rather the ways in which they function in their environment. History is always the last of the sciences to develop a method in harmony with its own period. Nevertheless, a modern history seems to be taking form which is following the direction art and science have already adopted. The historian nowadays seems more concerned with the links between periods, the lines of force which persist and develop through several periods, than with those special aspects which separate each period from every other.

Search for historical interrelations

In the arts, periods are differentiated by the "styles" which became fixed and definite in each stage of development. And the study of the history of styles was the special work of nineteenth-century historians, a work most skillfully carried through. But it may be that the links and associations between periods — the constituent facts — are more important to us than self-enclosed entities such as styles.

When we consider the château of Versailles, for example, what we find most interesting in it is that here, for the first time, a great dwelling complex (equal to a small town in size) was placed in direct contact with nature. This had never been done before on such a large scale. The juxtaposition of residences with nature was one of the constituent facts that grew out of the period of Louis XIV. A century later, this pattern for living was adopted in town planning for a completely different social class in another country.

The associations and interrelations of events are what matter most to us. We know that there are no isolated or spontaneous

21

happenings, and we look always for the connections between them.

Parallel between the history of art and the history of science

Even though architecture is inseparable from life as a whole, it is still possible to write a history of architecture in which it is regarded as an independent organism. The case is no different from that of mathematics or physical science. The evolution of mathematical knowledge is discussed ordinarily without reference to the social background against which it took place — this in spite of the fact that there is a baroque mathematics, as well as a baroque physics. The integral calculus is a perfectly consistent outgrowth of the baroque universalistic point of view. It is no coincidence that in this period two investigators hit upon it simultaneously, though the most promising of previous efforts in this direction invariably stopped short of a solution. And the two discoverers developed distinctively baroque schemes in other fields — Newton in his universally active laws of gravitation, Leibnitz in the monad's internal relationships to the entire universe. But it would not occur to anyone to stress the baroque origin of the integral calculus. It is independently a part of the whole body of mathematical knowledge, and its most significant aspect is the role it played in the evolution of mathematics.

The human factor obviously plays a much larger part in architecture than it does in science; the two are not entirely comparable. Nevertheless there is a history of architecture, and there are developments which are influenced by architectural considerations alone and can be evaluated solely in architectural terms. This history from baroque to nineteenth-century times has its stormy moments and its full share of dramatic episodes.

Lessened importance of stylistic variation

If it is the general line of evolution which interests us — the development which runs through different periods, social orders, and races — then the formal and stylistic variations which mark the separate stages will lose some of their importance. Our attention will shift to the history of architecture as an enterprise with a continuous and independent growth of its own, apart from questions of economics, class interests, race, or other issues.

Architecture is not exclusively an affair of styles and forms, nor is it completely determined by sociological or economic conditions. It has a life of its own, grows or dwindles, finds new potentialities and forgets them again. The view of architecture as a growing organism is particularly useful in the study of American architecture. In this field concentration on styles, on particular outlets or manifestations of the life of architecture, leads us nowhere. The fundamental line of development that runs through the different periods, ignoring stylistic fashions, is the only way of escape from complete confusion. Styles and their variations form a baffling maze, with all its alleys stopped.

From the beginning, styles in America were imported. They were not developed in the country but came here full-grown. None of them in the nineteenth century — romantic, Victorian, Tudor, Gothic revival — is representative of the American spirit, whose adventures and changes went on outside their narrow limits. The manor houses of the romantics, the Victorian villas, even the doorways and columns of colonial dwellings — charming as they are — mislead rather than inform us about that spirit. The elements of American architecture have their sources elsewhere.

PROCEDURE

We intend to see how our period has come to consciousness of itself in one field, architecture. To do this we must understand the architectural inheritance of our period, the knowledge which had been continuously evolved in the preceding periods. These periods do not have to be examined in their entirety. It will be enough to see how a new space conception appears in the early Renaissance with the revival of the direct and disinterested study of nature. Two and a half centuries afterward, in late baroque times, this conception is given a new boldness and flexibility.

The architectural inheritance

Our next concern will be the ways in which outer space was organized, first in the South and then (in the seventeenth century) in northern countries — France and England. These developments, employing the architectural experience which had accumulated since the Renaissance, raised town planning and the organization of space on a large scale to new heights. Throughout the eighteenth century this tradition in urbanism spread and developed. All over Europe we encounter examples of its ability to bring separate and often already existent elements into splendid, coherent, and surprising unity. At that time, just before industrialization set in, town planning was advancing toward solutions which artists of our day are once more attempting — with the changed approach which new needs and new knowledge dictate.

Importance of construction and town planning

The fact that we are considering architecture as an organism makes it natural for us to examine both its beginning and its end, construction and town planning. And it will be easier for us to deal with our subject if we can, so to speak, use two handles to pick it up by. At all events, it will be necessary for us to give more attention to construction and town planning than would be the case if we were writing a history of styles.

Construction as the subconsciousness of architecture

It would be a mistake to look at modern engineering constructions only through the eyes of the engineer or to see in them only efficient adjustments to useful purposes. Their technical aspects will not concern us so much as the general methods that appear in them and their content of feeling — prophetic of architectonic expressions which come later.

In the nineteenth century, as in all periods when methods of production are changing, construction was particularly important for the architectural knowledge which lay hidden in it. The new potentialities of the period are shown much more clearly in its engineering constructions than in its strictly architectural works. For a hundred years architecture lay smothered in a dead, eclectic atmosphere in spite of its continual attempts at escape. All that while, construction played the part of architecture's subconsciousness, contained things which it prophesied and half revealed long before they could become realities. The constituent facts in the nineteenth century can often be found in construction when the ruling architecture gives no clue to them. It is construction and not architecture which offers the best guideposts through the century.

Architecture has caught up with construction very gradually. Our own period has been slowly finding the ability to express in architecture what construction has for a long while been mutely signifying in its abstract language. This process moved so slowly that around 1900 on the Continent most of the buildings from which the modern development stems lacked all connection with human residence. They were factories, stock exchanges, warehouses, and the like. The building schemes which represent the first solutions in the manner of the present day were set forward in a neutral atmosphere, one far removed from the range of intimate personal feelings.

Architects today are perfectly aware that the future of architecture is inseparably bound up with town planning. A single beautiful house or a single fine residential development accomplishes very little. Everything depends on the unified organization of life. The interrelations between house, town, and country, or residence, labor, and leisure, can no longer be left to chance. Conscious planning is demanded.

In a single building something extraordinary may be sought after and achieved. The whole body of a city, however, shows beyond dispute the state of the architectural knowledge of a period. It shows the extent to which the period was capable of organizing its own life.

In Europe during the nineties a demand for morality in architecture arose in many different countries. As van de Velde puts it, people saw that the reigning architecture was a "lie," all posturing and no truth, and that greater purity of expression was needed. This means that, besides the urge to find new ways of expression suitable to the times, there was the more general urge to bring artistic expression into harmony with the new potentialities born of the age. Or we might say that the desire grew up to reconcile methods of feeling with methods of thinking.

We shall observe the development which the demand for morality set under way through some close-ups of a few of its critical stages. The whole process is bound up with the progressive awakening to the potentialities inherent in modern construction: with the iron-skeleton building in Belgium of the nineties, for example, and with the ferroconcrete skeleton in France around 1900.

Significance of the Chicago school of the eighties

Architecture gradually threw off its confusion and indecision in the face of the new building tasks of the century. It saw its way clearly first as regards those buildings which stood half-way between "neutral" industrial constructions and the human residence, with its inescapable associations of feeling. Thus the gap between bare construction and architecture in the grand manner is first bridged in the Chicago business buildings of the 1880's. The architecture of the Chicago school shows with astonishing clarity the urge to use constructional discoveries expressively that is a keynote in this period.

Frank Lloyd Wright

It was the Chicago atmosphere that made it possible for a phenomenon like Frank Lloyd Wright to appear during the nineties. During his stay in Chicago, Wright reached solutions of the dwelling problem which furnished the basis for further developments in Europe at the hands of the post-war generation. These men resumed the problem at the point where Wright had left off.

The new space conception in painting and architecture

Up to 1910 architects tried many ways of arriving at a new feeling for space — the basis and the strongest impulse for original architectonic creation. They could never quite break through. Only the narrow gates of "fitness for purpose" and "rejection of historical styles" were open to such endeavors.

Around 1910 an event of decisive importance occurred: the discovery of a new space conception in the arts. Working in their studios as though in laboratories, painters and sculptors investigated the ways in which space, volumes, and materials existed for feeling.

The speculations of the mathematical physicists seem very far removed from reality and from practical affairs, but they have led to profound alterations in the human environment. In the same way the experiments of the cubists seemed to have little significance for any kind of practice — even for architecture. Actually, however, it was just such work which gave the architects the hints they needed to master reality in their particular sphere. These discoveries offered architecture the objective means of organizing space in ways that gave form to contemporary feelings.

Our interest is confined to the reflection in architecture of the process by which the period has moved toward self-

26

consciousness. We shall follow the development only to that point when architecture achieves a clear mastery of means of expression natural to our time. This point is reached about 1926 or 1927.

In the field of town planning we shall consider only those places where the furthest advance was made at a given period. The London squares (1800–50) illustrate the continuation into the nineteenth century of late baroque urban forms. The *rue corridor*, an outstanding fact of nineteenth-century urbanism, has its first large-scale development in Haussmann's transformation of Paris (1850–70). The evolution to the city of today is summarized in the step-by-step development of Amsterdam that has continued from 1900 until the present time.

Stages in nine-teenth-century town planning

In town planning we cannot ignore the developments that are still in progress. Town planning, always the last branch of architecture to reach full growth, has begun to arrive at new conceptions only quite recently — since about 1925. We shall try to assemble the fragmentary and dispersed work that has been done and derive from it some insight into the tendencies which are still evolving.

Contemporary tendencies in town planning

The history of architecture could be treated by sketching, in very broad strokes, all the great variety of movements and the masses of facts connected with them. But in attempting to determine the extent and the nature of our period's consciousness of itself, it is more helpful to examine rather carefully cross sections of decisive stages in the history of architecture. We prefer to deal with fewer events more penetratingly, in close-up view. A few facts seen clearly enough may lead to a knowledge of something more important than the isolated facts themselves: the inner structure of architecture at the stage of growth which it has reached in our time.

Choice of events and figures

There are some individual artists whom we shall also scrutinize at close range, men like Borromini, Labrouste, Berlage, Gropius, Le Corbusier, men in whom the spirit of an age crystallizes. In each case we shall examine only those of their works which are most helpful in understanding the period.

Often we can learn more about the way in which nineteenth-century life developed from forgotten and unsuccessful figures of the period than we can from its great official celebrities. Simple utilitarian structures reveal more of its essential spirit than magnificent edifices intended to have an immortal appeal. The anonymous products of industry, unpretentious articles of daily use, often show more creative force than luxurious and immensely expensive furnishings.

Significance for history of objects of daily use Picasso once wrote, "The artist is a receptacle for emotions, regardless of whether they spring from heaven, from earth, from a scrap of paper, from a passing face, or from a spider's web. That is why he must not distinguish between things. *Quartiers de noblesse* do not exist among objects." The historian has to take the same attitude toward his material: he wants to know the truth about life, and he must take it where he finds it. It will not do for him to study only the highest artistic realizations of a period. Often he can learn more about the forces that shape its life from the common objects and utensils which are the undisguised products of its industry.

PART II OUR ARCHITECTURAL INHERITANCE

Why a knowledge
of our architectural
inheritance is
necessary

With no clear perception of the relation in which it stands to the past or of the route by which it must advance into the future, the life of any period will be lived on an aimless, day-to-day basis. Our time has suffered severely from this short-sighted, *laissez-faire* attitude, and from the complete lack of planning that is its result.

But it is plain that a revolt against this myopic outlook is under way, in science, art, and industry. There is a growing demand for a wider survey of all realms of human activity.

It is in this connection that history has an important role to play. History can reveal to our period the forgotten elements of its being, just as our parents can recover for us those childhood and ancestral peculiarities which continue to determine our natures though they are not to be found in our memories. A connection with the past is a prerequisite for the appearance of a new and self-confident tradition.

THE NEW SPACE CONCEPTION: PERSPECTIVE

Florence as the
workshop of the
modern spirit

Jakob Burckhardt in *The Civilization of the Renaissance* asserts that "the most elevated political thought and the most varied forms of human development are found united in the history of Florence, which in this sense deserves the name of the first modern state in the world. . . . That wondrous Florentine spirit, at once keenly critical and artistically creative, was incessantly transforming the social and political condition of the state, and as incessantly describing and judging the change." But Florence around 1400, at the beginning of the *quattrocento*, was important not merely as the home of political and social experiments; it was also the place where the *esprit nouveau* of the Renaissance broke through most strongly. It was this peculiarly Florentine temper that made it the "unique city — the most important workshop of the Italian and, indeed, of the modern European spirit."

The Renaissance ferment which was working in Florence showed itself under the widest variety of forms. We shall consider only one of the new developments in which it resulted: a new conception of space. At the start of the fifteenth century,

30

in Florence, this conception was translated into artistic terms through the discovery of perspective. Throughout the following five centuries perspective was to be one of the constituent facts in the history of art, the unchallenged canon to which every artistic representation had to conform.

In linear "perspective" — etymologically "clear-seeing" — objects are depicted upon a plane surface in conformity with the way they are seen, without reference to their absolute shapes or relations. The whole picture or design is calculated to be valid for one station or observation point only. To the fifteenth century the principle of perspective came as a complete revolution, involving an extreme and violent break with the medieval conception of space, and with the flat, floating arrangements which were its artistic expression.

Linear perspective and the growth of modern individualism

With the invention of perspective the modern notion of individualism found its artistic counterpart. Every element in a perspective representation is related to the unique point of view of the individual spectator.

This principle came as an entirely new invention, but seldom has a new invention been so much in harmony with a basic feeling of an epoch. From the time of its discovery no hesitation can be observed in its application; it was used at once with complete confidence and sureness. Artists and scientists elaborated its secrets with a readily understandable excitement and pride. Their feeling toward it appears in the enthusiastic exclamation of the painter Paolo Uccello, "How sweet is perspective!"

Perspective was not the discovery of any one person; it was the expression of the whole era. We shall encounter a similar situation later, when we come to discuss cubism. There, too, we shall find a whole movement arising in response to the new space conception developed in our time, rather than a single inventor. In both cases the significant thing is the mixture of art with science, but the two worked together far more closely in the development of perspective. Indeed, one rarely sees so complete a unity of thinking and feeling — art and science — as is to be found in the early fifteenth century. There was not only the important identity of method in these two spheres, but a complete union of artist and scientist in the same person.

No single inventor of perspective

31

Unity of thinking
and feeling in the
Renaissance:
Brunelleschi

Brunelleschi (1377–1446), one of the great initiators of perspective, was just such a figure. He began his career as a goldsmith and a student of ancient languages, and went on to become at the same time a great architect, sculptor, engineer, and mathematician. We have no right to say that such extreme versatility was possible only in earlier times. In a certain sense, it is possible in any time when specialists do not rule independently, but are included within a unified conception of life. It is, in fact, one of the secrets of the high degree of perfection of Renaissance work that it was not divided among limited specialists. Thus Brunelleschi, when he undertook the task of building the dome of the cathedral at Florence, could set about it as, simultaneously, a daring architect and a bold constructor. He projected a cupola which was double-shelled, like earlier Oriental constructions. The vault was erected without scaffolding, built freely up into the air to a height of around ninety feet. In its boldness as an engineering work this dome is comparable to the bridges of the French engineer, Eiffel, which were constructed straight out into space.

Do we realize, in comparing our own period with this one, what it means to find a single man uniting the capacities needed for executing both the most audacious engineering works and the finest sculpture? Yet such a union of talents is to be seen in nearly all the great artists of the Renaissance. Leonardo da Vinci represents a type, not an exception. And the tradition that the scientist and the creative artist are combined in the same person persists throughout the seventeenth and eighteenth centuries.

In the Renaissance the longest step forward was taken during the ten years between 1420 and 1430.

Masaccio, the painter, was the youngest of the great Renaissance masters, and the most advanced. Born with the new century — in 1401 — he was a true incarnation of the Renaissance spirit. The history of painting in this period would certainly have been different but for his early death at the age of twenty-seven. Brunelleschi, the architect, was nearly twenty-five years older than Masaccio, and to a great extent shared the Gothic spirit of the fourteenth century. Donatello, the sculptor, was eighteen years older than Masaccio; he too had to break away from Gothic ways of feeling, and succeeded in doing so through his astonishing naturalistic genius. The fact that, among these three, the painter was the first to attain to the new vision of his time is by no means unparalleled. We shall see, further on, that modern painting anticipated modern architecture in much the same way.

Masaccio's "Fresco of the Trinity" (*fig.* 1) in Santa Maria Novella at Florence was executed when he was about twenty-five years old. Painted during the twenties of the *quattrocento*, it was rediscovered in the late nineteenth century and exists today in a badly damaged condition. The Trinity fresco has long been famous for its naturalistic portraits of the founders of the church that contains it. It is the first example of an endless series of paintings of this type. But it is of much more significance to us that the whole composition is encircled by a majestic barrel vault. The point of origin from which its perspective is calculated is taken very low, so that the vault may be seen in all its grandeur. This fresco, painted at a time before any Renaissance interior had been completed, represents what seems to be the first successful expression, in architectonic terms, of the Renaissance feeling that underlay the development of perspective. It reveals a surprising use of the newly discovered elements in combination with absolutely circumscribed tectonic surroundings. Its impressiveness was undeniable; even Vasari — familiar with daring perspective treatments of space — admired the way in which this painted vault pierced the flat surface of the wall.

It is possible that Masaccio was taught perspective by Brunelleschi; it has even been argued that Brunelleschi himself may have executed the perspective architecture of the Trinity fresco. It was quite common in the *quattrocento* for painters and sculptors to employ qualified specialists for this part of their work. But Masaccio's barrel vault is not a part incidental to the whole composition; it is not a simple background. Instead it dominates the entire picture. At the time it was painted Brunelleschi was occupied with the building of the portico of the Innocenti and with the sacristy of San Lorenzo. Not even in his last works did he ever use the vault in this way; he always kept some attachment to medieval modes. The

2. LEON BATTIS‑TA ALBERTI.
S. Andrea, Mantua, 1472–1514. *Almost five decades after the Trinity fresco, the longitudinal barrel vault was used in the interior of this church. Even in the exterior, the desire to use the receding barrel vault led to its employment at the most unexpected points.*

Trinity fresco with its heavy coffered vault has the greatness of a triumphal arch. The cheerful expression beloved by early Renaissance taste and present in all the works of Brunelleschi is absent. In its place there is the Roman gravity of a later age.

The longitudinal barrel vault that Masaccio painted was to prove the great solution to the vaulting problem that confronted the architects of the full Renaissance and baroque periods. It does not appear in concrete form before the church of San Andrea at Mantua (*fig. 2*), in 1472 — nearly forty-five years after Masaccio's death. This church, with its severe vaulting, is the architectural realization of the ideal prefigured in Masaccio's painting. It is likewise significant that San Andrea was designed by a member of Masaccio's generation, by

The barrel vault from the Trinity fresco to St. Peter's

←
1. MASACCIO. Fresco of the Trinity, Santa Maria Novella, Florence, c. 1425. *The longitudinal barrel vault which Masaccio painted not only fulfilled the aim of perspective by receding deeply into space but also anticipated the chief vaulting problem of the Renaissance builders.*

another man born just as the *quattrocento* began: the Florentine humanist and architect, Leon Battista Alberti (1404–1472). Even in the exterior the desire to use the receding barrel vault led to its employment at the most unexpected points.

Bramante's "illusionistic" choir in Milan — a work of small size but great influence — is one of the steps leading from Masaccio's fresco to St. Peter's in Rome. A continuous line of development connects the Trinity fresco, Bramante's choir, and the immense baroque nave of St. Peter's — its culminating point.

Bramante's illusionistic choir (*fig.* **3**) in the church of Santa Maria presso San Satiro (1479–1514) is actually only a small niche. It was half built up and half painted, in order to produce the greatest possible effect of depth with the space at the artist's disposal. For us it has importance as one of the steps leading from Masaccio's fresco to St. Peter's.

Carlo Maderno executed the central nave of St. Peter's (*fig.* **4**), along with its side chapels and façade, during the ten years

3. BRAMANTE. Illusionistic choir in Santa Maria presso S. Satiro, Milan, 1479–1514.

1. CARLO MADERNO. Nave of St. Peter's, Rome, 1607–17. *The most majestic solution of the Renaissance vaulting problem. Earlier stages leading up to this solution appear in the San Gesù and many other Roman churches.*

between 1607 and 1617. Following the orders of a new pope, he altered Michelangelo's scheme for its ground plan, changing it from a Greek into a Latin cross. We are told that the change was made to afford more room for the congregation and to take up the entire site of the Early Christian basilica and some additional space as well.

Nevertheless, the scale for this enterprise had already been set by Michelangelo in the height of the pillars for the central dome which he had built. Michelangelo had envisaged a concentration in one place of all the artistic energies represented in the cathedral: they came together in his cupola in one great explosion. The later generation of Maderno and his pope enlarged this conception longitudinally, in accordance with late baroque desires for a long and unbroken expanse. The impression that the spectator receives on entering St. Peter's derives from the superhuman dimensions of this new nave.

Its height exceeds a hundred and fifty feet — equal to that of the early skyscrapers. Its width is relatively small, but Maderno knew how to keep the onlooker from becoming conscious of this. The fully developed art of the baroque period and its control over space appear in the way this is done: the side chapels, almost imperceptibly, expand the actual dimensions of the nave and impart a new power to it.

Masaccio's Trinity fresco marks the discovery of the majesty and strength which can be expressed through simple and grand elements. Carlo Maderno's nave in St. Peter's differs from Masaccio's painted vault both in its dimensions and its complexity. But these differences only sum up the possibilities that were latent in the vision which had come to the fifteenth-century master.

The generation which immediately followed Carlo Maderno carried this unfolding to further and more special results. But before we deal with these we shall turn to some of the architectural works already executed in which the spirit of the early Renaissance first showed through.

The new feeling in early Renaissance buildings

The first building in which the Renaissance spirit appears is Brunelleschi's loggia on the front of the Spedale degli Innocenti at Florence. The Spedale degli Innocenti, or the Foundling Hospital, was built at the order of the silk-weavers' guild, of which Brunelleschi, as a goldsmith, was also a member. Between 1419 and 1424 he constructed the nine arches in the center of the building.

The Spedale degli Innocenti

Since this first Renaissance building was intended for a practical community service, it did not have to conform in its appearance to the dignified and impressive standards that held for edifices of state — buildings which are often found to reflect the taste of the previous period. Thus Florentine palaces preserved their resemblance to Gothic closed fortresses up to the middle of the fifteenth century. In the Foundling Hospital Brunelleschi had an opportunity to open up the closed, fortress-like block of the house. He did this by means of a round-arched porch, pleasant in its graceful lightness.

The upper wall of the Innocenti is not rusticated, but is kept a flat surface, with sparsely distributed windows. A Renaissance preference is revealed on the outside by the entablature which bisects the whole surface of the wall horizontally.

But the hospital's chief distinction is the portico, and the most interesting feature of the latter is the manner in which the vault is treated. The diagonal Gothic cross ribs have disappeared; a light coved vault, resembling wind-filled sails, replaces them. Binding arches are used for marking distinctly the boundaries between each vault and the one next it, thereby enforcing the Renaissance demand for the complete independence of every section of a design.

There is no direct connection between classical architecture and Brunelleschi's Foundling Hospital. It has often been remarked that the chief features of Brunelleschi's architectural style are closely related to buildings which he saw every day in Florence — to the Baptistery, to San Miniato, and to the Badia of Fiesole. All these are in the tradition of medieval architecture from the eighth to the twelfth century. The coved or hemispherical vault which Brunelleschi used with such great sureness in his churches and in the Innocenti — and which was always the vaulting motif he preferred — was likewise unusual in antiquity. It was, however, quite common in Byzantine architecture, especially for loggias and the entrance halls of ecclesiastical structures. There was a comparatively close connection between Florence and Byzantium in Brunelleschi's time. Recent researches have also made it plain that some other early Renaissance treatments of the vaulting problem owe more to the Middle Ages and to Byzantium than they do to classical antiquity.

Relation to Byzantine architecture

Brunelleschi's Pazzi Chapel (*fig.* 5) is the first Renaissance structure in which the interior as well as the exterior is of monumental size and character. It was begun in 1430, some ten years after the Innocenti, and when Masaccio was already dead. The chapel itself was finished in 1442; its decoration was not completed until 1469. Brunelleschi replaced the spherical vaults used in the Foundling Hospital with barrel vaults arranged transversely, instead of receding as they do in Masaccio's Trinity fresco. (Transverse barrel vaults are to be found in

The Pazzi Chapel, Florence

5. BRUNELLESCHI. Pazzi Chapel, Florence, begun in 1430. *The barrel vaults are placed transversely, not receding as in Masaccio's Trinity fresco. Bold display of the wall as a flat surface.*

Byzantine and Syrian architecture.) These vaults, together with the dome over their place of intersection in the middle, produce a flat impression rather than the depth-penetrating perspective which was sought by Masaccio and the later Renaissance.

The interior; difficulty in working with a new space conception

The interior of the Pazzi Chapel forms the starting point for all Renaissance churches of the centralized type. It is developed by the addition of compartments whose geometrical form can readily be grasped, all clearly marked off by stone framework in contrasting colors. It has all the inimitable freshness of a new birth, but the two small barrel vaults, in their cautious dimensions, show that confidence in the new vision had not yet been attained. When contrasted with Masaccio's Trinity fresco, for example, the handling of the vaulting problem shows — in all that involves the newly introduced shapes — a noticeable timidity. It is from cases such as this that we learn how difficult it is for the human spirit to plunge into a new conception of space. The Brunelleschi who shows hesitancy here is the same man who, as long as he was working within the familiar Gothic tradition, threw himself into the most daring enterprises. A complete confidence appears in his design for the Cathedral of Santa Maria del Fiore in Florence, with its immense dome over a system of radial ribs.

One feature of the exterior of the Pazzi Chapel requires mention here: the bold manner of displaying the wall as a flat surface. (The small roof which it exhibits today is a later addition.) This wall, with its delicate subdivisions, has nothing to support; it is like a screen. The emancipation of the wall that appears here is important for the whole future. The wall taken simply as a surface will soon be the subject of important architectural innovations. The flat surface of the outer wall

PERSPECTIVE AND URBANISM

Prerequisites for the Growth of Cities

Like plants, human settlements require certain conditions for growth; but human community life depends upon far more intricate conditions than the plant. What is common to both is that there are periods which favor growth and other periods which hinder growth.

A city is the expression of the diversity of social relationships which have become fused into a single organism.

The conditions that influence its growth can be of a widely dissimilar nature. Cities have arisen in periods of dictatorship, when the despot has power to compel everyone to build in conformity with a single design. They have also arisen in periods of purposeful communal energy.

The despot has the advantage of his capacity for rapid and ruthless action; but since his sovereign will is bound to ignore the imponderable laws which stimulate human coöperation, a city built under a dictatorship can never acquire the essential quality of organic diversity.

41

In cities that have been developed by the united efforts of their citizens, everything — even to the last detail — is permeated with a wonderful strength. Never since the democratic way of life first found expression in Greece in the fifth century B.C. has so much loving care been lavished on the development of cities, or space been so amply provided for gatherings of the populace; nor has the spot where the people's decisions were enunciated and carried into effect ever dominated the town's physical and moral structure so effectively as did the agora in these early Greek cities. Perhaps the only later towns which could sustain comparison with them in such respects are some of those founded in the midst of Europe in the twelfth to fourteenth centuries, whose dogged struggles against temporal or spiritual feudal overlords laid the foundations of modern democracy.

At the dawn of the Renaissance, the principal city-republics of Italy — Venice, Siena, and above all Florence — already had their struggles for democracy behind them. But exaltation of the individual ego now began to supersede the old team spirit of the Middle Ages, and paved the way for the absolutism of the seventeenth century. An age so imbued with the supreme importance of personality was not likely to be one known for the building of new towns.

The Star–Shaped City

It is not easy to arrive at a definite conclusion regarding the nature of urban planning in the Renaissance town. Compared with the immense creative urge manifested in every other field, city planning seems at first sight strangely devoid of that vigorous and imaginative grasp of the subject which is so overwhelmingly evident in painting and sculpture.

How can this be explained?

In contrast to the collective spirit of the Gothic period, the complex organism of a city with its manifold social indentations was foreign to the Renaissance — to the period in which perspective was invented, where the whole picture is calculated

42

from a single focal point, from the viewpoint of a single static observer.

The Renaissance was hypnotized by one city type which for a century and a half — from Filarete to Scamozzi — was impressed upon all utopian schemes: this is the star-shaped city. From a symmetrical fortified polygon, radial streets lead to a main center. This is the basic diagram. The central area is either left open, as in the completed city of Palmanova (1593), or contains a central tower — a central observation post — from which the radiating streets are seen in shortened perspective.

The influence of firearms

Certainly the sharply faceted conformation of these six-, eight-, nine-, and twelve-pointed stars was decisively influenced by the introduction of gunpowder. In the Middle Ages a close circuit of protecting walls with towers rising above the battlements at appropriate intervals had been adequate. Now the encircling wall is transformed into a series of regularly indented bastions (*fig.* **6**) from which flanking fire can be directed upon the attacker.

6. FRANCESCO DI GIORGIO. Wedge-shaped bastions from his "Trattatto di Architettura." *These bastions, which enabled the defenders to rake the ranks of the attacking forces from whatever side they might approach, are said to have been invented by Francesco di Giorgio.*

43

The centralized
building and the
star-shaped city

The polygon and star shapes of the *città ideale* result from the
fortification system of the Renaissance: but this is not the
decisive influence. In the background of the star-shaped city
stands the Renaissance theory of the centrally organized
building. This conception dominated Bramante throughout
his life, and it is known that the combination of a domed
structure with radiating chapels was the architectural problem
which more than all others piqued the interest of Leonardo

7. VITTORE CARPACCIO. S. George and the Dragon, between 1502 and 1507.
*As is so often the case in Venetian pictures, the most important part of the composition is
not the subject matter but the display of a large spatial expanse. The centralized church
in the background is more dominant than the main actors in the foreground. No piazza
of such grandiose conception and dimensions was ever built by Carpaccio's contemporaries.*

da Vinci. The central building in the midst of a star-shaped
city fulfills the same role — that of a symbolic observer standing at the focal point. The central building recurs persistently
in the painting of the period. We need only to mention a
well-known early work of Raphael in the Brera, the "Sposa-
lizio" or "Marriage of the Virgin" (1504), where a polygonal
temple soars right up to the top of the frame and dominates

the whole composition, while from the short flights of steps surrounding the temple wide expanses of dark marble paving radiate into perspective distance on every side. The drawing of Vittore Carpaccio (*fig.* 7) may serve as one of many other possible examples.

Medieval origins

The star-shaped *città ideale* of the Renaissance is really the rationalization of a medieval type [1] in which the castle, cathedral, or main square forming the core of the town is encircled by anything from one to four irregular belts.[2] The tree-like plan of Bagnacavallo in Italy (*fig.* 8) shows the organic manner in which a similar situation was handled in the Middle Ages. The difference is that what the Middle Ages brought about organically in a number of different ways the Renaissance proceeded to freeze into a rigid formal pattern from the outset. The medieval city is characterized by expanding belts of streets; the Renaissance, by streets that radiate directly from the center.

Filarete (1400–69)

The star-shaped town is the creation of the *quattrocento*. It was first elaborated soon after the middle of the fifteenth century by the Florentine Filarete (Antonio di Pietro Averlino), who was followed some twenty years later by the Sienese architect, sculptor, and painter Francesco di Giorgio Martini. Although that great animater Leone Battista Alberti had discussed the possibility of building an "ideal city" in the tenth book of his "De Re Aedificatoria," written about 1450, it was left to Filarete to fill in the details and work out a definite scheme. Filarete wrote his "Trattato d'Architettura"[3] between 1460 and 1464, when he was in the service of Francesco Sforza and while he was engaged in building the large Ospedale Maggiore in Milan which was badly damaged in the Second World War. Since this treatise was intended as propaganda,

[1] Information about other still earlier examples of this type of town will be found in L. Piccinato, "Origini dello Schemo Urbano Circolare nel Medioevo," *Palladio*, vol. V. no. 3 (Rome, 1941); and in *Urbanistica*, XVI (Rome, 1947), 124–136.

[2] Various examples are given under "Urbanistica Medioevale" in L. Piccinato's *Urbanistica dall' Antichita ad Oggi* (Florence, 1943), and on p. 298 and following of the second edition of G. Giovannoni's *Saggi sulla Architettura del Rinascimento* (Milan, 1935).

[3] This was first published in Vienna in 1890 by W. von Oettingen, in *Quellenschriften für Kunstgeschichte und Kunsttechnik*, under the title "Antonio Averlino Filarete's Tractat über die Baukunst." There is also an illustrated edition published under the title *Filarete, Scultore e Architetto del Secolo XV*, edited by M. Lazzaroni and A. Muñoz (Rome, 1908).

8. Bagnocavallo, a medieval town of Roman origin. *The streets grow like the annular rings of a tree and not on the radial system of the ideal cities of the Renaissance. Their irregularities are caused by the natural formation of the ground.*

9. FILARETE. The site of the star-shaped city "Sforzinda" about 1460–64. *The geometrical pattern for this city is placed in a mild Italian "valley surrounded by hills through which the river 'Inda' flows," described by Filarete in his second book.*

lita didetta ualle domanda come sichiamaua quello fiume chedorreua
perlomezzo didetta ualle & lui dusse chesichiamaua sforzindo & laualle
sichiamaua inda ilperche molto mipiacque & accepti laproferta chedeteo
gentile huomo maueua fatta & cosi insua compagnia anda uedendo questo
sto sito & questa ualle nella quale non era gia terre grosse mamolte uille

Ilfiume sforzindo
Lauualle inda

Come to detto lo rinostetro questo plntamento ilquale o riquadrato in
quadri piccholi tuglipotresti intendere grandi & piccholi atuo senno maio
clinitendo diquesta misura cioe diquattro stadij praoschetto quadro dx fare
che almodo nostro mezzo mglio pquadro Siche uedendo questo tupuoi fa
pere quanto mene cessere grande per lacutn ouuoi dure mglia o uuoi
due stndij ouuoi due braccia tu sai quanti stadij o uno mglio & su
quante braccia e lostadio molnprucha & sapenai quanto ella circundo
& quanto elle percgni uerso Co cosi allarngione diqueste misure massisi

11. FILARETE. "Sforzinda," the star-shaped
city with its radial road pattern. *Sixteen main
streets radiate from the central piazza to the eight city
gates and the eight corner towers. Midway, each street
crosses an open square, eight of which have a church in
the center.*

it took the form of a dialogue between a Tuscan architect
(Antonio Filarete) and a Renaissance prince (Francesco
Sforza). The building of an ideal city, to be called "Sforzinda," was proposed and described in great detail, from the
prince's palace and the cathedral down to the quarters to be
alloted to merchants and artisans, and not forgetting the pris-
ons. In plan Sforzinda was to be a symmetrical eight-pointed
star: "The outer walls should form a sixteen-sided figure and
their height be four times their depth. The streets should
lead from the gates to the center of the town where I would
place the main square, which ought to be twice as long as it
is wide. In the middle of it I would build a tower high enough
to overlook the whole surrounding district" (*figs.* **9–11**).

The idea of the *città ideale* was probably received by Filarete
from Leone Battista Alberti, but it first took on a plastic form
in the hands of that consummate all-round artist Francesco di

Francesco di
Giorgio Martini
(1439–1502)

Giorgio Martini (1439–1502). In the third book of his treatise on architecture [4] he is preoccupied with the development of the star-shaped city. The original star plan has already become altered to a regular star-shaped polygon with a projecting bastion at each of its exterior angles. Francesco di Giorgio, being a Sienese, had been familiar from birth with a town built on a steep hill, and for that kind of site he suggested a second plan resembling a clerical skullcap, with spiral roads corkscrewing up to the summit. In a third and most important type of plan — a type adopted by most of his successors and one which influenced Evelyn's plan for rebuilding London after the Great Fire of 1666 — he compressed a severely rectangular pattern of streets opening out of a number of big public squares into yet another polygonal mold. Francesco di Giorgio was at pains to make plans for the *città ideale* suitable for widely varied conditions. He was, moreover, quite clear in his own mind that the city planner need only establish the main lines of the plan and leave it to life itself to make adjustments where necessary.

Vigevano:
Piazza Ducale
(1493–95)

The time at the disposal of Italian despots of the late fifteenth century was far too limited for them to become involved in such long-term ventures as the erection of an ideal city. One of the few cases before 1500 where there is a faint reflection of Filarete's "Sforzinda" is in the little town of Vigevano, which lies with its medieval castle twenty miles southwest of Milan. Here, in 1452, Ludovico Sforza ("il Moro") was born, the great Maecenas to whose court came Leonardo da Vinci and Bramante. Long before he had become Duke of Milan, Ludovico Sforza decided to embellish his birthplace by modernizing its towering medieval stronghold into a Renaissance palace — partly by Bramante himself — and by building a wide and regular open square, approximately to the dimensions 1:2 advocated by Filarete. In this way Vigevano's Piazza Ducale came into being, built as it were at one stroke within the shortest possible time, 1493–95.

---

[4] The *Trattato di Architettura Civile e Militare di Giorgio di Martini* was first published in Turin in 1841. See also R. Papini, *Francesco di Giorgio, Architetto*, 3 vols. (Florence n.d., circa 1946). Volume II contains good illustrations from the whole field of his work, and also an index to the contents of the *Trattato*.

12. Vigevano: Piazza del Duomo, 1493–95. *A rare example of an early and rapidly completed Renaissance square. It is surrounded by arcades as in the new towns built in the thirteenth century. The fourth side is occupied by the baroque façade of the cathedral. The tall "Tower of Bramante" overlooks law buildings that surround the square, which was created by Ludovico il Moro rather as an approach to his castle than as a center of local activity. It is interesting that, despite the contemporary Renaissance theories of the square as a focusing point for radial streets, this square looks more like an enclosed courtyard.*

13. Vigevano: Main Entrance to the Piazza del Duomo. *The picture shows the arches through which the main street enters the square surmounted by a sham façade to maintain the continuity of the wall surfaces. This view is of the entrance from the outside looking toward the cathedral: in the former illustration the entrance arches and sham façade can be seen in the center.*

The whole program is certainly reminiscent of Filarete: there is a tower "high enough to overlook the surrounding district," the palace of the prince, and even the rudiments of some radiating streets. But the 180-foot tower and the dominating palace (now crumbling away as a barracks) stand apart from the arcaded square, which contains only the medieval church with a seventeenth-century façade along its fourth side. Ludovico expropriated and scrapped, under severe legislation,[5] the buildings that had formerly occupied this area. It was a good instinct that obliged him to work so quickly, for he had little time to enjoy the results of his endeavor. Within a few years he was defeated by Francis I and became a prisoner in France, and never returned.

Ludovico Sforza considered the Piazza Ducale as part of a grandiose access to his palatial castle. Yet the square remains strictly isolated, and the great tower (the so-called Tower of Bramante) looms up strangely behind the regular arcaded wall of the square, only two and a half stories high.

It seems that one of the secrets of a good public square or gathering place is the simplicity of its architectonic elements. This simplicity is evident in the stoa, the *Wandelhalle*, and the agora as well as in the heavy arcades of medieval cities such as the thirteenth-century squares of the fortified towns in Southern France and, here, on the verge of the early Renaissance, the lightly swinging arcades of the Piazza Ducale. Above these distinctly articulated arches the walls are broken by sparsely distributed, round-headed window openings. At one time the entire wall surface was overlaid by playful Lombardesque frescoes, but now only a few faded fragments remain of this colorful mockery of architecture. The square itself still holds its reposeful human dignity even though its role has become that of a car park, flooded incessantly with cycles, motor scooters, and tourists.

The many-sidedness of Renaissance man

One of the most convincing explanations of the immense creative energy of the Renaissance is that it consciously developed the whole man instead of training him as a specialist in a single field. Universality is the secret of its wealth of all-round talent and the glowing fullness of life which confronts us in its works.

[5] *L'Arte*, V (1902), 249.

Francesco di Giorgio was certainly a man of this sort. In the treatise on which he worked throughout a generation, while dealing with the wide scope of his own experience he refers also to the Greek philosophers. These are not superficial quotations, for he consciously followed the Aristotelian method of proceeding from the general to the particular.

Francesco di Giorgio was a celebrated fortress engineer; for the Duke of Urbino alone he built nearly seventy strongholds. His versatility as an architect is well known. He ended his career as the master builder of Siena Cathedral. The extent of his experience is reflected in some of the building schemes in his treatise which are well in advance of the development of his time. These designs provide a refreshing contrast both to the sixty-odd dreary projects which the younger Vasari (Vasari *il giovane*) worked into stillborn plans for ideal towns a century later and to those produced somewhere about the same time by that otherwise rather interesting architect Bartolomeo Ammanati.[6]

How natural it was for the painter Francesco di Giorgio to blend imagination and reality is shown by several of his *cassone* paintings (paintings on wooden chests) of ideal squares and streets. These pictures not only express the subtlety of a Sienese painter but also contain new architectural concepts. There is a narrow picture of a "Piazza Ideale" now in the Walters Collection at Baltimore (*fig.* **22**) in which there is a very interesting treatment of different levels; the surprisingly modern spatial setting of the plastic elements reveals the experience of a practiced sculptor. It is to Francesco di Giorgio, incidentally, that we owe the delicately modeled bronze angels on the high altar of Siena Cathedral, which rank among the most distinguished sculptures of the period immediately before Michelangelo.

---

[6] The rich and largely still unstudied collection of architectural drawings in the Uffizi includes the "Città Ideale del Cavaliere Giorgio Vasari Inventato" as well as Bartolomeo Ammanati's frigid designs. It is only fair to add that among the latter's endless repetitions of columned courtyards he at least shows some interest in making provision for various crafts. No hint can be found in any of these designs that the great development of Baroque was close at hand, or that they are the designs of the man who was at this very time building the florid Palazzo Ruspoli on the Corso in Rome.

This Sienese painter of delicate annunciations and madonnas became a stern rationalist as soon as he took up his T square and set about the plan of a town. When he presupposed a special case, such as a town with a river running through the middle of it, the river would be forced into a straight channel and crossed by bridges at mathematically regular intervals (*fig.* 14). In the Windsor Castle collection there is a very sketchy plan of Florence drawn by Leonardo da Vinci in which he remodels Florence upon a chessboard pattern: the River Arno — as in the Francesco di Giorgio drawings — becomes as straight as a bowstring (*fig.* 15). These two artists stood close to one another in point of age. They met in 1490 at Milan, where they had been called in to give expert advice on the construction of the dome of the cathedral. We know that Leonardo felt that he had much in common with Francesco di Giorgio and held him in esteem.

The Renaissance did not envisage the complete overall replanning of towns, but it took a passionate interest in the development of certain urban architectural elements.[7]

The origin of Renaissance porticoes

Most of the piazzas built during the Renaissance were surrounded by arcades. Although of Roman origin (as may be seen at Ostia), it is probable that they were reintroduced into Italy, by way of Venice, from Byzantium, whose streets, often arcaded on two stories, had long been famous. But, even if not with historical accuracy, arcaded piazzas have been chiefly identified with the Renaissance. Michelangelo himself proposed to arcade both the Piazza della Signoria at Florence and the square in front of St. Peter's.

The stately open squares of the Renaissance often took hundreds of years to complete, and the noblest of all — the Piazza di San Marco with the Piazzetta in Venice — remained unfinished for nearly five centuries.

The rigidity of the star-shaped city

As has already been pointed out, the *città ideale* merely systematized a preëxisting medieval type. Both were based on the exigencies of defense. In Italy, towns with elected municipalities had usually been sovereign city-states, and a wall-girded city was a symbol of political independence. Since the princi-

---

[7] Volume X of the *Enciclopedia Italiana* contains a good selection of illustrations of the *città ideale* on page 490.

14. FRANCESCO DI GIORGIO. Polygonal city crossed by a river, c. 1490. *The river is forced into a rigidly straight channel crossed by bridges at mathematically regular intervals.*

15. LEONARDO DA VINCI. The city of Florence changed into an "ideal city." *Florence is remodeled upon a chess-board pattern and the River Arno becomes as straight as a bow string.*

ple of self-government broke down during the Renaissance, it is clear that the star-shaped towns were only meant to serve as fortresses.[8] The frontier stronghold of Palmanova, some sixty miles northwest of Venice, was famous as the classic example of regularity until well into the Baroque period: nine-pointed ground plan, hexagonal central piazza as the meeting

---

[8] It is significant that in a more northern country Vauban should have adopted a star-shaped plan for the fortress-town of Saarlouis as late as 1681.

place of six radial roads. It was built by Vincenzo Scamozzi, the architect of the Procuratie on the south side of the Piazza di San Marco, of which he built several bays. Scamozzi is the last of the Renaissance theorists, with his *Idea dell' Architettura Universale*, published in Venice in 1615, just before his death.[9]

The hundred and fifty years which elapsed between Filarete's *Trattato* and Scamozzi's *Idea* saw no notable changes, for the polygonal town was far too rigid a type to lend itself to progressive evolution.

Town planning and the conception of space

From the particular visual angle of that age the star-shaped town was a perfectly logical concept, for Renaissance perspective is based on a strictly limited range of distance and demands a measurable point of optical arrest. In Francesco di Giorgio's Piazza Ideale (*fig. 22*) an arch of one of the town gates is set in the extreme background as a sort of ultimate target for the eye. No one gave nobler expression or grander scale to this sort of design than Michelangelo, in a work of his later years, the Porta Pia at Rome.

Baroque perspective, on the other hand, was based on a limitless field of vision. Hence typical towns of the late Baroque period, such as Versailles (second half of the seventeenth century) and Karlsruhe (about a hundred years later), have nothing to do with the star-shaped plan. The palace of the ruler stands boldly between town and country, dominating — at least in the optical sense — limitless space.

[9] Scamozzi described his own *città ideale* in his second book. Julius von Schlosser's *Materialen zur Quellenkunde der Kunstgeschichte* — more particularly Part II, "Frührenaissance" (Vienna, 1915) and Part VI, "Die Kunstliteratur des Manierismus" (Vienna, 1919) — is an invaluable source of information on the architectural theorists of this period.

PERSPECTIVE AND THE CONSTITUENT ELEMENTS OF THE CITY

It would be misleading to judge Renaissance town planning simply by these successive versions of the *città ideale*. The idea of the town as an entity in which the interactions of thousands of separate existences can be coördinated was foreign to the temper of that era. None of the great Renaissance artists has left us a plan for a new kind of town — neither Bramante, nor Michelangelo, nor even Leonardo, from whose vision, which so often leapt forward centuries in time, it might almost have been expected.[1]

What was new in Renaissance civic design must be sought elsewhere, in the thorough mastery of some of a town's constituent elements. In that field Bramante and Michelangelo opened up hitherto unknown possibilities. Intermediate between the fruitful age of Gothic, with its communal ethos, and the absolutism of Baroque, in the realm of town planning the Renaissance is a preparatory period. The fifteenth century in northern countries was still wholly Gothic, but in Italy the position is complicated. Although perspective was creating a new attitude of mind, the Gothic tradition lived on in many ways and influenced the implementation of city improvements, particularly in the public squares.[2] In a sociological sense Italy and the northern countries by no means stood in such marked contrast to one another during this transitional period.

---

[1] In a celebrated letter to Ludovico il Moro, Duke of Milan, which probably dates from the plague of 1485–86 in that city, Leonardo da Vinci expressed a desire to see towns made more sanitary, so that their inhabitants would no longer have to live "packed together like goats and polluting the air for one another." He proposed building ten towns for the Duke, each for a population of five thousand. These were to be "situated on rivers regulated by locks. . . Within them light, air and cleanliness shall prevail." Among Leonardo's drawings preserved at Windsor Castle there are plans of existing towns but none of any *città ideale* (*I Disegni Geografici, conservati nel Castello di Windsor*, edited by M. Baratta (Rome, 1941).

[2] Evidence of the persistence of the Gothic tradition in major civic undertakings can be found in a large number of the many public squares that were laid out in North-Italian towns during the *quattrocento* — the Piazza del Santo in Padua, the Piazza Grande in Parma, the realignment of the Piazza del Campo in Siena (fig. 21), the Piazza Principale in Piacenza, and so on. A good selection of these are illustrated on pages 268–280 of the second edition of G. Giovannoni's *Saggi sulla Architettura del Rinascimento* (Milan, 1935).

The modeling of large volumes

The Renaissance learned to handle large volumes and to shape them into new forms. Palaces often thrust aside the homes of the townsfolk, streets, and squares. But their builders discovered how great expanses of wall could be opened on to the street. This was something antiquity had never achieved, though here and there it sometimes allowed glimpses of the street from one or two windows. These Renaissance palaces gazed wide-eyed upon the world without as if they were seeking to appraise it just as with the new medium of perspective. Although Gothic elevations are often loopholed by fenestration to a considerable extent, the windows remain islanded, lost in a vast expanse of walling, as in the thirteenth-century Palazzo della Signoria at Florence.

At the zenith of the Renaissance, however, about 1500, we find windows ranged upon windows, each treated as a separate feature and accentuated by a pediment, pilasters, or columns, yet rhythmically articulated to one another.

The Palazzo Farnese

Nowhere can the changes undergone by the wall surfaces be more plainly perceived than in the Farnese Palace at Rome, which Cardinal Alessandro Farnese began in 1514. Antonio Sangallo the younger designed this building and carried it out up to the roof cornice, but Michelangelo, among others, added to it after Sangallo's death in 1546 — that is to say, at the very end of the late Renaissance. Sangallo's volumes overwhelm the capacity of the site, exemplifying the exaggerated individualism of the Renaissance mind. The incredibly pretentious magnificence of this residence for a single man points to the imminence of Baroque.

Alessandro Farnese started to build himself a palace as a cardinal, and finished it as Pope Paul III. He portrays the transition from individualism to absolutism. Michelangelo knew how to express this sculpturally. Sangallo had already emphasized the central window with two concentric arches,[3] but Michelangelo set to work in quite a different manner. In

---

[3] As illustrated by C. de Tolnay in his "Beiträge zu den späten architektonischen Projekten Michelangelos," *Jahrbuch der Preussischen Kunstsammlungen*, vol. 51 (1930).

salient contrast to the alternating triangular and segmental pediments over the windows on either side, he placed an architrave over the dominant central window where the whole emphasis could be concentrated on a huge shield carved with the Farnese coat of arms and surmounted by the papal tiara. This monumental window seems to await the arrival of the great overlord who is about to show himself to the populace.

On the garden front the Palazzo Farnese faces the Via Giulia, which Bramante had traced, and the Tiber. Michelangelo felt there was need for more open space round the huge bulk of the palace. He proposed a bridge across the river so as to include the Villa Farnesina and the Trastevere quarter in the way that was later adopted for the approaches to many French châteaux.

The Renaissance did not treat the street as a unity even where it would have been quite easy to do so. Scenically, the Renaissance street consisted of a number of individual buildings set down at random on separate sites; and this holds good from the late *quattrocento* up to the sixteenth century. Francesco di Giorgio's fine paintings of streets and squares (*figs.* **16, 22**) show no two houses alike. Even the porticoes of the houses which so clearly call for uniform treatment are not continuous; each house has its separate arcade. Even much later, as can be seen in the frequently reproduced stage set of Sebastiano Serlio about 1550 — which is not designed simply to produce a perspective effect — the street is still an agglomeration of heterogeneous buildings.

The street in the Renaissance

Thus when Donato Bramante (1444–1514) laid down the alignment for the first new street in Rome, the kilometer-long Via Giulia,[4] at the behest of Pope Julius II, he did not envisage continuous frontages, for he intended to place his Palace of Justice, with its massive quoins and corner towers, foursquare along part of this street. The Palace of Justice was begun in 1506, but after the death of Pope Julius II the work stopped. A few Cyclopean blocks of stone built into some nearby houses

Bramante's Via Giulia in Rome

[4] Ceccarius, *Strada Giulia* (Rome, 1941). Straight and still broader streets were not uncommon in newly founded twelfth- and thirteenth-century towns north of the Alps, e.g., Berne.

give an idea of the extent to which this building would have disrupted the Via Giulia.[5]

All the more surprising, therefore, is the architectural uniformity of the short street in Florence originally known as the Piazza degli Uffizi on which Giorgio Vasari erected administrative buildings for the Medici between 1560 and 1574. The continuous, lightly bracketed triple cornice seen with the sym-

16. FRANCESCO DI GIORGIO. Piazza and Street of an Ideal City, Detail. *The Renaissance did not treat the street as an architectural unit, even when it would seem almost obvious to do so. In Francesco di Giorgio's fine painting no two adjacent houses are alike.*

metrical outline of the roof above make this a masterpiece of perspective in depth (*fig.* **17**). This regular planning of the

[5] Domenico Gnoli, "Il Palazzo di Giustizia di Bramante," *Nuova Antologia*, April 16, 1914.

Uffizi would have been almost inconceivable but for the example Vasari's master, Michelangelo, had given him in the group of buildings then under construction on the Capitoline hill in Rome.

Vasari's indebtedness to Michelangelo appears even in details, such as the use of alternating piers and pairs of columns, but instead of being dynamically backed against the piers, as on the Capitol, Vasari's columns are spaced out at regular intervals. It is known that Vasari showed his designs to his master in Rome, so Michelangelo had his hand in the design.

Bramante and the Open Stairway

Besides their bold handling of the surfaces of walls facing streets and squares, Renaissance builders went to great pains

17. GIORGIO DI VASARI. The Uffizi, Florence, 1560–74. *In the latest development of the Renaissance, the Mannerist painter Vasari achieved a masterpiece of perspective in depth in the short street of the Uffizi by means of continuous horizontal lines: the projecting roof, the three cornices, the steps. This view is taken from the arch of the loggia which closes the vista toward the Arno.*

to bring horizontal surfaces lying on different planes into spatial relation with one another. This they achieved by the device of imposing monumental stairways left open to the sky.

18. JACOPO BELLINI. The presentation of the Virgin in the Temple, c. 1440.
The subject-matter and the figure of the Virgin Mary are only a pretext for the artist's real intentions. From the stone floor in the foreground, where the observer is placed, up to the immense barrel vault of the spacious church, numerous figures are dotted about at different levels, in a supreme effort to conquer perspective in depth. The stairway zigzagging backward and forward is the early attempt of a painter to convey perspective in depth in terms of architecture.

19. ÉTIENNE DU PÉRAC. Tournament in Bramante's Cortile del Belvedere, 1565. *This engraving was executed shortly after Pirro Ligorio had finished the building of the Belvedere Court by the addition of the Nicchione and left-hand corridors. A few years later, Bramante's conception, already altered by Ligorio, was annihilated by Sixtus V, whose high library wing cut the court in two. From then on worldly feasts were forever banished from the Vatican. In contrast to Jacopo Bellini's drawing, the observer has chosen here an all-embracing viewpoint high in the air, revealing the High Renaissance control of perspective in depth and creating a setting particularly suited to worldly pleasures in festivities.*

Bramante used these flights of steps as a means of incorporating expanses of outlying space within his composition, and thereby introduced a new element into urban architecture.

Building in terraces goes back to very remote times in the East, and pyramidal flights of steps which formed the plinths of temples or processional approaches to sunken courts are a conspicuous feature of hieratic architecture in Pre-Columbian America.[6] Neither terrace formations nor monumental stairways were, of course, new in themselves, but Renaissance builders used both in an entirely new manner.[7] This, though evident at the outset, is still more clearly manifested in their later work.

Jacopo Bellini
(c. 1440)

A silverpoint drawing in Jacopo Bellini's sketchbook, which dates from about 1440, shows the purpose that a stairway was intended to serve (*fig.* **18**). A barrel-vaulted church crowns the highest of three successive terraces ascended by a stairway which zigzags back and forth from one level to another up to the open church front. These terraces, like the numerous figures dotted about the foreground and background, reveal the designer's object: to produce an impression of perspective in depth.

Bramante's stairways in the forecourt of the Belvedere

Donato Bramante of Urbino was the first architect to introduce monumental stairways as a formative element through which space could, as it were, be embodied in the design of buildings; and the place where he first realized this embodiment was the garden forecourt of the Belvedere at the Vatican (1506–13). The buildings of Bramante around 1500 display for the first time the new grandeur which the atmosphere of Rome and the patronage of the humanist Pope Julius II brought into the work of the artists. These influences are seen in Raphael, and even to some extent in the towering genius Michelangelo himself. Bramante evinces a new sense of power in his control of the unprecedented dimensions he was called upon to handle at St. Peter's after 1506. Though less ambitious, his handling of the Belvedere's forecourt is no less masterly.

---

[6] P. Kelemen, *Medieval American Art* (New York, 1943), vol. II, plates 4 and 7.

[7] To the best of my belief no investigation into the treatment of stairways in the Middle Ages (notably in Italy) has yet been undertaken.

The Belvedere is a small papal summer residence which stands on an eminence some three hundred meters distant from the Vatican Palace. In 1506 Julius II entrusted Bramante with the task of combining these two buildings in a comprehensive architectural vista. The Pope had already set up some classical sculpture in the forecourt. He now directed that the whole intervening area be remodeled in the new majestic Roman manner. As the culminating point of his vista at the upper

20. The Cortile del Belvedere after Bramante's death. Detail of a fresco in the Castello S. Angelo, Rome, 1537–41, attributed to the Mannerist painter, Perino del Vaga. *This fresco shows the grandeur of Bramante's modeling of exterior space better than any of the well-known representations of the Cortile. The unfinished architecture helps one to understand how, in Bramante's hands, the open stairway and ramps, the working with levels on different planes, became a new element of urban design.*

end, on the front of the Belvedere, Bramante erected a monumental screen with a huge niche in the middle after the manner sometimes adopted in villas under the Caesars; and at the lower end, in front of the Vatican, a semicircular arena. Terracing enabled him to establish a formal relation between the new buildings with their triple tier of loggias.

63

Here we are concerned with this stairway as an agency by means of which spatial areas have been articulated and woven into a spatial unit.[8]   A wide flight of steps leads from the first to the second level, where it divides into two branches under the retaining wall to gain the topmost garden and with it the Belvedere (*fig.* **20**).   As secluded as the garden of an immense medieval cloister, everything was here devised for courtly pleasures.   Nearly fifty years after Bramante's death, when the vast ensemble had been finally completed, the marriage of one of Pius IV's nephews provided a fitting occasion for inaugurating the Cortile del Belvedere.   Étienne du Pérac's engravings have perpetuated the splendor of those sumptuous feasts and tournaments (*fig.* **19**).   But the Cortile was not destined to remain for long as Bramante had remodeled it. In 1589, Sixtus V wrecked the unity of the design by building a new library athwart the middle of its parterres.   That great town planner destroyed many monuments of ancient Rome, but this was his most destructive act.

Later on, the monumental stairway, of which Bramante's stately ascent to the platform of the Belvedere had been the prototype, became the noblest pediment that could be added to a church (S. Maria Maggiore).   Eventually the monumental stairway became an almost independent structure whose role was to merge planes lying at different levels into a single field of space (the Scala di Spagna, 1721–25, which connects S. Trinità dei Monti with the Piazza di Spagna).   In late Baroque interiors we find large staircases — the symbol of movement — used to create cavernous voids which have no parallel in the history of architecture.

Michelangelo and the Modeling of Outer Space

Michelangelo's "Capitolina" in Rome

In the Area Capitolina, the great square in which stood the Roman Capitol, Michelangelo showed how to achieve a balance between carefully molded masses — the spatial relationship of great volumes.   When he took this work in hand in 1536,

---

[8] There is a good detailed description in M. L. Gothein, *A History of Garden Art* (London, 1928), I, 227–231.   See also James S. Ackerman, "The Belvedere as a Classical Villa," *Journal of the Warburg and Courtauld Institutes*, XIV, Nos. 1–2 (January–June 1951). I am indebted to Professor Ackerman for fig. 20.

toward the end of the Renaissance, he had already reached the zenith of his fame as a painter and sculptor: the ceiling of the Sistine Chapel, the tomb of Pope Julius, and the Medici Chapel in Florence all lay behind him. Thus his architecture is the fruit of his ripest years. Giovanni Lorenzo Bernini, whose colonnade in front of St. Peter's so marvelously completes Michelangelo's conception and who seldom spoke good of others, said, "Michelangelo was great both as sculptor and painter: but divine as an architect." Bernini's closing words find an eternal echo in the Area Capitolina, where Michelangelo's plastic genius created a sublime spatial symphony out of a jumble of medieval remains.

This square, now called the Piazza del Campidoglio, occupies the cliff-top site of the ancient Capitol which overhung the Forum Romanum. It is a complex consisting of three buildings, the square itself, and a broad-ramped stairway called "la Cordonata" which leads down to the town. The whole complex faces toward the medieval city, and closing the approach is the modest town hall, the Senatorial Palace, flanked on the right by the Palace of the Conservatori and on the left by the Capitoline Museum, the world's oldest collection of antiquities.

Michelangelo lived to see only a part of his great branching stairway finished in front of the Senatorial Palace. Both the other buildings were begun after his death. Yet in spite of certain modifications introduced during the course of their construction, which continued until well into the seventeenth century, the plans and dispositions Michelangelo had got out in 1546 (reproduced in the engravings of Du Pérac, 1568 and 1569) were adhered to in essentials.

The great stairway was not yet built when Charles V made his triumphal entry into Rome in 1536. He had to clamber up to the Capitol from the other side — from the Forum — to which the Area Capitolina was oriented in Roman times. "La Cordonata" is a ramped stairway — an inclined plane built up of sloping treads. Those mounting the wide, shallow steps to the platform above are constrained to a slow and measured ascent. The bronze equestrian statue of Marcus Aurelius which Michelangelo transferred from the Lateran

21. Siena: Piazza del Campo, paved in 1413. *The huge, shell-shaped public square in the center of Siena is set between the three hills upon which the city is built. Admirable use is made of the natural slope to give the Public Palace its dominating position. Eleven streets run out from the square, and the white marble stripes of the pavement shoot out like rays from a light-house at the focal point of the community.*

22. FRANCESCO DI GIORGIO. Piazza of an ideal city. *The interesting treatment of different levels, and the surprisingly modern spatial setting reveal the experience of a practiced sculptor. The human figures scattered here and there show that he saw columns in space, varied planes, and sculptures, all in relation to moving people. These are problems that in our period are again coming to the fore, as can be seen in certain aspects of the work of Alberto Giacometti.*

23. MICHELANGELO. The Capitol, Rome, begun 1536. *This photograph, taken from the height of the Senatorial Palace, gives some idea of Michelangelo's spatial conception: the sunken oval; the equestrian statue in the center of a twelve-pointed star that explodes like a firework; the majestic Cordinata, which leads down to the medieval city. The three buildings that surround the square give evidence of its trapezoidal form, even though they are seen only as fragments.*

comes into sight in the center of the square. As an effigy it is as nobly simple in its disdain of all heroic gesticulations (as Stendhal remarked) as the unassuming pedestal Michelangelo designed for it.

None the less its lonely sky-girt position commanding the axis of the stairway from the very center of the square proves that the master who confidently handled such unprecedented voids as the dome of St. Peter's could treat the nicest graduations in plane with the same unerring sureness.

The wedge-shaped piazza of the Area Capitolina narrows toward the balustrade where the stairway debouches. No particle of the ground is left unconsidered. Michelangelo places an oval within the wedge-shaped square. This oval is slightly recessed and is ringed around by two steps, whose curving shadows define the formal ambit of the statue's emplacement. The ground itself swells gently upwards toward the pedestal. This spot is called the *caput mundi*, and its curving surface has been likened to a segment of the terrestrial globe.[9]

What an excitement has now infected those quiet stripes of marble which in the *quattrocento* used to cover the surfaces of the most distinguished squares, such as the rounded piazza at Siena! Now the stripes radiate out in fingerlike beams from Marcus Aurelius on his pedestal to form a twelve-pointed star of flattened intersecting curves.[10] Their fantastic pattern enflames the whole frenzied interplay of contrasts: oval, trapezoid, the background of Roman and medieval tradition, the subtly shifting interplay of Baroque light and shadow that models the walls,[11] the grandiose gesture of the great stairway — all combine to form a single all-embracing harmony, for the relation of each to each and of the whole to its parts has

---

[9] C. de Tolnay, "Beiträge zu den späten architektonischen Projekten Michelangelos," *Jahrbuch der Preussischen Kunstsammlungen*, vol. 51 (1930), p. 26. This statement may be compared with H. Sedlmayr's prompt attack on it which will be found on pages 176–181 of the same publication for 1931.

[10] In 1940, over four hundred years after Michelangelo had designed it, the original star-shaped paving at last replaced the meager pattern which was substituted after his death.

[11] None of the photographs so far published bring out the extraordinary dynamic quality of this composition, but the reader may be referred to Plates 50–75 in Armando Schiavo's *Michelangelo Architetto* (Rome, 1949).

been consummately affined. One understands Vasari's statement: "Whatever he set his hand to, Michelangelo worked miracles." [12]

In the "Last Judgment" and the tomb of Julius II Michelangelo had already replaced the static emptiness of *quattrocento* space with a dynamic space of his own. This he also achieved in the Capitol.

Our mental picture of the Renaissance begins to evaporate. That "extremely divergent opinions as to Michelangelo's precise historic significance" [13] should have prevailed among scholars ever since Jakob Burckhardt is understandable enough, for Michelangelo was one of those infrequent geniuses who bridge periods in art which do not necessarily succeed one another chronologically. John Constable and J. M. W. Turner, if of minor stature, belong to this same exceptional order of men in that they form the link between the painting of the late Baroque and that of nineteenth-century France. Michelangelo was an admixture of Gothic and Baroque. He connects the worldly universality of the Baroque with the spirituality of the Gothic. Life and death to him were one and the same: from the day of his birth every man is doomed to carry the seed of death hidden within him. In 1555 he wrote to Vasari, "I have never expressed an idea which was not molded in the lineaments of death." [14] That is the utterance of a medieval craftsman, not of a Renaissance artist. Yet he was always powerfully attracted to the problems of movement,[15] had the urge to experiment with its artistic and physical potentialities, which, being inherent in Western man, permeates the Gothic just as it does the Baroque.

The architectural significance of the Capitol can be rapidly summarized. It is a development of Bramante's use of terraces at the Belvedere into an element of urbanism. It is a comprehensive composition in depth — piazza, stairway, city — and

Michelangelo as a bridger of styles

The architectural significance of the Capitol

---

[12] C. de Tolnay, *Werk und Weltbild des Michelangelo* (Zürich, 1949), p. 90.

[13] C. de Tolnay, "Beiträge zu den späten architektonischen Projekten Michelangelos," p. 47.

[14] C. de Tolnay, *Werk und Weltbild des Michelangelo*, p. 59.

[15] Cf. my *Mechanization Takes Command* (New York, 1948), pp. 14–30, in the chapter on Movement.

at the same time a preparation for the great axis emanating from a single building, the Senatorial Palace: something the ancient world had never sought to realize.   In the Area Capitolina, Michelangelo was able to carry out some, though not all, that he had vainly planned for the Palazzo Farnese.   Later, in the hands of the French, the axial vista was studied with assiduity and, proudly termed "la culte de l'axe," became the vertebrate principle of eighteenth-century town planning.

What Is the Real Significance of the Area Capitolina?

None of Michelangelo's notes about the Capitol exist, so there is free scope for conjecture as to what was in his mind when he planned this proud civic monument to the purely nominal remnant of autonomy which the citizens of Rome could still lay claim to.   What could his private feelings have been when he built it?

In 1530 the city-republic of Florence lost its former independence to the Medici despot Cosimo I.   Michelangelo had taken an active part in the defense of his native city against the Medici Pope Clement VII.   Following the death of the Pope, who was his personal enemy, Michelangelo left Florence in profound antagonism to the new regime in 1534 and spent the last thirty years of his life as a voluntary exile in Rome. After the death of Antonio Sangallo the younger in 1546, he became the city's master builder.   Although he was then over seventy, every important building was entrusted to him: the dome of St. Peter's, the Farnese Palace, the whole comprehensive layout and design for the Capitol.

Charles De Tolnay, whose *Michelangelos politische Anschauungen* shows profound insight into the master's political beliefs, quotes a sonnet [16] which reveals all the gnawing bitterness he felt even so late as 1545.   That sonnet makes his own statue of Night in the Medici Chapel say:

> *Non veder, non sentir, m'è gran ventura;*
> *Però, non mi destar, deh! parla basso!*

(*Speak softly that I wake not, for this one sovereign boon I crave: to see and feel no more!*)

---

[16] On page 32.

The significance of the Capitol would appear to be analogous to that of this sonnet. In neither does Michelangelo express himself directly, but deliberately chooses to speak through a seemingly impersonalized mouthpiece. Could he really have raised the Capitol to glorify a shadowy vestige of power? Should we not rather see in it a passionate longing to retrieve the lost freedom of his native Florence, a dream wrought out and made manifest in stone?

The whole of Michelangelo's work reflects his own tragic conception of life. Even in planning his layout he knew how to give succinct expression to the conflicting motives that actuate every human being and every true democracy — the need to preserve the rights of the individual while safeguarding those of the community. What he had derived from his youthful experience in Florence was brought to reality in the Rome of the Counter Reformation, a Rome in which there was no freedom and no democracy. So his Capitol is both a symbol of the vanished liberties of the medieval city-republics and a memorial to the tragic dream of its creator.

The supine imagination evinced by our contemporary attempts to devise new features in town planning, such as civic centers, is invariably condoned on the plea that we no longer have a manner of life it would be possible to express. What Michelangelo has mirrored in the Area Capitolina is the baffling irrationality of historical events and the enigmatic omission of any direct relation between effect and cause. Once more we realize that a great artist is able to create the artistic form for a phase of social history long before that phase has begun to take tangible shape.

LEONARDO DA VINCI AND THE DAWN OF REGIONAL PLANNING

The sketches Leonardo used to make of his observations, whether they concern mechanical spinning devices, helicopters, proposals concerning traffic regulations, or surveys for regional planning, all appear today as distant glimpses into ages yet unborn. In a manuscript now in possession of the Institut

24. LEONARDO DA VINCI. The River Arno and its regulation by a canal. *Bold proposal to make the Arno navigable by building a broad canal in a curving sweep over all differences of level, to link Florence with Pistoia. Reproduced by gracious permission of H.M., The Queen, Windsor Castle.*

de France,[1] proposals for separating pedestrian from wheeled traffic at different levels and a scheme for delivering produce to householders by barges along canals controlled by locks have been interpolated between hydrodynamic studies and drawings of cranes, engines of war, and systems of fortification.

These are flashes of insight into technical possibilities, but little more; there is no trace of comprehensive town planning in any of them. The fragmentary scheme for Florence now

---

[1] *I Manoscritti e i Disegni di Leonardo da Vinci,* vol. V, "Il Codice B. (2173) nell' Instituto di Francia" (Rome, 1941).

in the collection at Windsor Castle is merely a project for regularizing the River Arno so as to make it flow in a dead straight line through the middle of the town — a plan which treats Florence as if it were yet another *cillà ideale*. No buildings are shown, and the streets bordering the river are ruled out into chessboard squares (*fig.* **15**). Leonardo's interests lay in other directions.

25. LEONARDO DA VINCI. Scheme for draining the Pontine Marshes, 1514. *This project has never been completely carried out to this day, though, seventy years later, part was begun by Sixtus V, on the lines planned by Leonardo. Reproduced by gracious permission of H.M., The Queen, Windsor Castle.*

His hydrodynamic studies deal with scientific problems that for the most part were not solved until centuries later. For instance, he investigated the conditions which cause whirlpools; he had realized that water moves faster on the surface than at lower levels. At eighteen he was already concerned with representing the whirlpools in the river in the landscape which he had to paint for his master Verrocchio's picture "Baptism of Christ."[2] Leonardo always tried to investigate

---

[2] L. H. Heydenreich, *Leonardo* (Berlin, 1943), p. 267. Heydenreich's broad outlook with its inseparable interrelation of the artistic and the scientific work of Leonardo offers perhaps the best introduction to Leonardo's work.

the hidden, dynamic, forces in the inorganic and organic sphere, in the microcosm and in the macrocosm. As no one else, he could fill his drawings of plants with a feeling of dynamic growth.

Of all the natural forces, however, Leonardo was most interested, as he himself expressed it, "in the nature and movement of water," which was the only motive power available at the time. From his hydrodynamic studies he is led step by step to formulate definite plans based on a comprehension of the physical structure of a region — a rationalized standpoint characteristic of Renaissance enlightenment. To these belong his accurately surveyed projects for irrigating the Po valley and for building a network of canals between Milan and the North Italian lakes, of which he actually had trial sections excavated. During the time he lived in Rome under Pope Leo X and did not paint a single picture (1513–14), Leonardo drew up an impressive hydrographic plan for draining the Pontine marshes, an undertaking that was only partly carried out by Sixtus V at the very end of his reign (*fig. 25*). The boldness of another proposal of his to make a river navigable by building a broad canal in a curving sweep eighty kilometers long over all differences of level is, so far as we know, unsurpassed even by the canals constructed during the nineteenth century. In a sepia pen-and-ink drawing as arresting as any of his pictures, Leonardo plotted out the line of a canal that would bypass the Arno, link Florence with Pistoia, and rejoin the river lower down its course (*fig. 24*).[3]

Regional planning must have an insight into the conditions of a certain area in order to permit coördinated planning of the use of land and organization of human activities. The detailed inquiries necessary today are far removed from the cosmological approach of Leonardo, who tried to survey and organize the natural forces of a whole region so as to serve human purposes. Nevertheless, all of Leonardo's plans were

[3] Mario Baratta, *I Disegni Geografici*, pl. 5 on right; Mario Baratta, "Leonardo da Vinci negli Studi per la Navigazione dell'Arno," *Bolletino della Società Geografica Italiana*, serie V, vol. VI (1905), pp. 739–761 and 893–919; Kenneth M. Clark, *A Catalogue of the Drawings of Leonardo da Vinci in the Collection of His Majesty the King at Windsor Castle* (2 vols., 1935).

the fruit of painstaking analysis of each of the various problems he had to contend with. For all its volcanic turbulence, his was a zealously inquiring age. Out of its tumultuous urge to leave no field of knowledge unexplored there emerged the first conscious attempts at regional planning: seed which, though foredoomed to fall on stony ground, held more latent promise than all those geometric plans for ideal new cities that never looked beyond the immediate orbit of their own day.

SIXTUS V (1585–1590) AND THE PLANNING OF BAROQUE ROME

Rome, Paris, and London — the most important foci of western civilization — created the prototypes of the large cities of to-day. Rome, however, is unique. There had been cities in earlier periods with a million or more inhabitants, focusing points of vast empires and cultures. But when these fell, their nerve centers disintegrated completely. They had never a chance to rise again. Even Rome — after its name had been given to a world-wide empire — sank for a thousand years after its overthrow into a languishing decline.

Rome: the unique city

But by 1500 Rome had risen anew, and for the next one and a half centuries it became the center, first of artistic developments, then of town planning. It was on Roman soil that the Renaissance reached its zenith and it was here that the Baroque means of expression were formulated, which penetrated the whole of western culture, halting neither at territorial nor at religious frontiers.[1]

To anticipate: In Rome the urban scale of the Renaissance was shattered once and for all. In place of the limited, wall-girded, star-shaped city, a new development of great importance was heralded during the five years' reign of Sixtus V.

---

[1] Christopher Wren's St. Paul's Cathedral in London (1675–1716) has been shown by recent research in England to have been based on a good grounding in Baroque architecture. George Baehr's protestant Frauenkirche in Dresden, which was unfortunately destroyed by bombs in the Second World War, was one of the finest of the Baroque churches.

It was in Rome that the lines of the traffic web of a modern city were first formulated, and were carried out with absolute assurance.

The development of Rome by non-Roman artists

There are other reasons also why Rome is unique among cities — reasons which are perhaps less easily grasped. The Holy See is supported by no world empire. The Papacy is an international religious power. The citizens of Rome, being subject to the papal dictatorship, had little say in the development of their city. Nevertheless here was created one of the most sumptuous achievements of civic design, Baroque Rome, which, even today, dominates the entire face of the City.[2]

From the Renaissance onwards, the development of Rome was almost entirely the work of men who came in from outside — artists, bankers, merchants and manufacturers. When the Popes moved from the Lateran to the Vatican, the district around the Basilica of St. Peter was gradually built up as the *Borgo Nuovo*, and in the middle of the fifteenth century Pope Nicholas V (1447–1455) was struck with the idea of creating here a huge isolated and impressive ecclesiastical residence. This scheme, which was never carried out, was planned by the Florentine, Leone Battista Alberti.

About 1500, when rebuilding started in earnest and the Popes became the greatest builders in the world, Julius II, a Rovere from Urbino, and Leo X, a Medici from Florence, called in their compatriots — Bramante and Raphael from Urbino and Michelangelo from Florence — to carry out their grandiose schemes: and the employment of designers from other cities continued even in the time of Baroque Rome.

There is no clear reason for this curious state of affairs. It can only be said that Rome itself did not produce many outstanding artists either during the Renaissance or during the Baroque period. But there is no doubt that the atmosphere of the Eternal City and the vast scale of the Papal undertakings kindled the imagination of the visiting artists and inspired them to create works of such majesty as exist in no other city of that period.

---

[2] Naturally this is bound up with the pervading presence of antiquity. Before the "hollow luxury" of the buildings of the late nineteenth century it is better simply to close the eyes.

Rome, like Paris in recent times, became a gathering place for contemporary talent. A continual process of interchange took place. The talent of the outsiders — the foreigners — was heightened by the atmosphere of the city: in turn their creations gave the city a new polyphonic expression.

Within the Roman phenomenon there lies a hope for a still intangible future, for a time when it may become indispensable for the existence of the western world to create a new form of central administration inspired by spiritual principles. Baroque Rome shows that this does not necessarily result in a deadening of all achievement to a colorless monotone, a drab international gray. On the contrary it demonstrates that the interaction of a diversity of forces can produce a new vitality.

The Medieval and the Renaissance City

It is not possible to see Sixtus V's master plan for Rome in its true setting without at least a glance at the legacy he had received from the Middle Ages and the Renaissance. Sixtus did not tinker with fragmentary remedies. He left medieval Rome untouched and concentrated his energy, from the very first, upon new adventures.

The reawakening of Rome from its lethargy of the Middle Ages is as much a historic marvel as the rest of its destiny. In other parts of Europe (and in the north of Italy since the eleventh century) there had been a remarkable resurgence of city life. Rome still slept. Though the spiritual might of the Pope was never more powerful than during the Middle Ages, the city of Rome led but the existence of a shadow. In Baroque Rome churches sprang up like mushrooms, but in Medieval Rome there were no new cathedrals that could stand even a distant comparison with those of the self-governing cities of the north. It was the same with the population.

The comparison often made of Rome's thirteenth-century population — estimated at 17,000 — with that of Venice or London or Paris shows its immense shrinkage.

26. GIOVANNI BATTISTA FALDA. Medieval Rome, from the Castello S. Angelo to the Bridge of Sixtus IV (detail from map, 1676). *Falda's map shows very distinctly how the principal part of medieval Rome lay cramped within a fold of the Tiber dominated by the Castello S. Angelo with its new wedge-shaped bastions. Falda even depicts the subterranean corridor which connected this papal treasure-house, prison, and place of refuge with the Vatican. The Ponte S. Angelo, which since the days of Hadrian had crossed the river on the axis of the fortress, and the Piazza di Ponte at the bridgehead now became the hub of the main arteries of the medieval city. The radiating pattern of streets emanating from this square, which was completed under Paul III (1534–49), is the first of its kind.*

$\rightarrow$

27. The Planning of Baroque Rome by Sixtus V. *This diagrammatic map attempts to show the plans of Sixtus V in relation to what existed before his time. Streets laid out for Sixtus V are marked by heavier lines; the limit of medieval Rome is shown by shading, and the outline of Rome under Marcus Aurelius by the line of the Aurelian wall. It becomes obvious that Sixtus V planned his streets as organically as a spine, strengthened by structural connections wherever these were demanded by the Roman topography.*

THE PLANNING OF BAROQUE ROME BY SIXTUS V
1585-90

NICOLAUS	V	1447-55
SIXTUS	IV	1471-84
JULIUS	II	1502-13
LEO	X	1513-22
PAULUS	III	1534-50
JULIUS	III	1550-55
PIUS	IV	1559-66
PIUS	V	1566-72
GREGOR	XIII	1572-85
SIXTUS	V	1585-90
PAULUS	V	1605-21

The situation changed slowly with the return of the Popes
from their exile in Avignon, their new settlement in the Vatican, and the rise to the papacy of the worldly-wise Medicis and
members of other mercantile families, or of descendants of
condottieri such as Julius II.

The scarcely usable medieval kernel of Rome was a district
wedged into a fold of the Tiber opposite the Castello S. Angelo.
It was noted for its insalubrious climate and, for this reason,
had been left undeveloped throughout the period of the
ancient Roman Empire. Medieval Rome had spread out from
this center slowly and chaotically in the directions of the
Capitol and of the Theater of Marcellus,[3] near the Tiber.

Transformation of the city began outside the medieval kernel
in the Borgo Nuovo, the area that connected the Vatican with
the Castello S. Angelo. This castle served the Popes as treasure
house, prison, and place of refuge in times of invasion or revolt.
Its dominating position is obvious in Giovanni Battista Falda's
map (*fig.* **26**), which also shows the parallel Renaissance
streets of the Borgo Nuovo.

The Ponte S. Angelo — the bridge on the axis of the castle —
now became the most important entry into the central area
and gave its name to the Renaissance business center. Here
was the papal mint and here assembled the foreign banking
houses and great mercantile organizations such as the Chigi,
the Medici, and the Fuggers from Augsburg. Here, in fact,
was the Wall Street of Renaissance Rome, and in this small
district decisions were made that sometimes affected the monetary, diplomatic, and ecclesiastical fate of the whole of
Europe.

From the time of Nicholas V, the Popes were occupied with the
formation of the piazza at the bridgehead — called the "Forum
Pontis" in Bufalini's map of Rome (1551) and "Piazza di
Ponte" in Falda's map of 1676.[4] At the time of the Renais-

---

[3] Piero Tomei, *L'Archittetura a Roma nel Quattrocento* (Rome, 1942).

[4] The best introduction to the study of the development of Rome is afforded by the
excellent reproductions, published by the Vatican Library, of the principal sixteenth-,
seventeenth-, and eighteenth-century maps of the city. These are, for the time of
Julius III, the map by Leonardo Bufalini (1551); for Rome before Sixtus V, Du Pérac–
Lafréry (1577); for Rome after Sixtus V, Antonio Tempesta (1593); for Rome during

80

sance this square becomes a focal point from which, directly or indirectly, radiate the main arteries through the medieval city. These streets bear proud names. The Via Peregrinorum,[5] by piecing together a number of short lengths of irregular medieval lanes, finally led to the Theater of Marcellus. The Via Papalis, which carries an even more splendid name, makes an equally tortuous connection with the Capitol and further on with the Lateran. A third important through connection is the Via Recta — in part of ancient origin —[6] which, not without some difficulty, makes a connection with the later-formed Piazza Colonna and the Corso or Via Lata (*fig.* **27**).

The Via Peregrinorum, Via Papalis, and Via dei Coronari were all partly of medieval origin and partly composed of fifteenth-century improvements. In his Papal Edict of 1480, Sixtus IV, the *Restaurator Urbis*, commanded that all building projections and street obstructions be cleared away. This was the most important single act of improvement in the urban condition of the city.

It was during the late Renaissance that the Popes, in especial Paul III (1534–1549), successfully completed their work around the Piazza di Ponte by establishing short and direct connecting streets from the piazza to the medieval and Renaissance roads across the city. This pattern of short but radiating streets is the first of its kind. It included the Via Paolo, leading to Bramante's Via Giulia, and the Via di Panico, which, a short way along its route, connects with the Via dei Coronari.

Finally one of the most important through routes of Renaissance Rome, the Via Trinitatis, had its source at the Piazza di

The streets of the Renaissance city

---

the Baroque, Giovanni Maggi (1625) and G. B. Falda (1676); for Papal Rome before its decline, G. B. Nolli (1748). Bufalini's map, a woodcut, is the first drawn on the basis of a precise pattern of streets; Tempesta and Falda are outstanding for their clarity of presentation; Nolli, like Bufalini, uses the modern method of depicting streets and the delightful handicraft of this engraving approaches a work of art. For more detailed information see C. Scaccia-Scarafoni, *Le Piante di Roma* (Rome, 1939).

[5] Piero Tomei, "Le Strade di Roma e l'Opera di Sisto Quarto," *L'Urbe*, II (1937), July, pp. 12–20.

[6] Its most famous section, the Via dei Coronari, named after the sellers of rose wreaths, is today almost a slum. Anyone who retraces Ludwig von Pastor's walk, after a lapse of little more than a generation, cannot but be shocked at the speed with which decay has followed upon neglect and disfigurement of the buildings. See L. von Pastor, *Die Stadt Rom zu Ende der Renaissance*, 3rd edition (Freiburg, 1916). This little book describes in great detail the condition of Rome before the time of Sixtus V.

28. G. F. BORDINO. Sketch plan of the streets of Sixtus V, 1588. *This contemporary sketch plan of the work of Sixtus V reduces his street planning to a simple system of connections between holy places.*

Ponte by means of the northbound Strada di Tor di Nona. The Via Trinitatis was begun by Paul III and continued by Julius III (1550–1555). It is shown on Leonardo Bufalini's map of 1551 as a long straight line, traversing for the most part still unbuilt sections of Renaissance Rome, and terminating near the Renaissance church of S. Trinità dei Monti at the foot of the Pincio hill, where it enters into the sphere of activity of Sixtus V.

Sixtus V and his Pontificate

The papal throne

Only members of the nobility and the ruling houses of Italy were usually elected to the papal throne. There were, however, exceptions, even in a period such as the end of the sixteenth century, when the steadily increasing privileges of the nobility had usurped the medieval rights of the populace. Hence it was possible for Sixtus V, a man from the lowest

29. Sixtus V's Master Plan of Rome, 1589. *This fresco in the Vatican Library is oriented from northwest to southeast. Medieval Rome and the Vatican are both cut away by the arch of the Library door, so that the view is concentrated upon the undertakings of Sixtus V. The picture is dominated by the straight line of the Strada Felice which runs from the Piazza del Popolo on the left, past S. Trinità dei Monti to S. Maria Maggiore and then further on to the Lateran. Obelisks and columns project from their squares, and the fountains of the Acqua Felice can also be seen in the middle distance to the left, on the Strada Pia.*

stratum of society, to be invested with the highest dignity of spiritual and temporal power to which a mortal could aspire. It says much for the inner strength, vitality, and instinct of the Catholic Restoration that it had the courage at this very dangerous moment to elevate a man such as Sixtus V to this office — a man who, regardless of his ancestry, was clearly born for action.

Sixtus V was the papal title chosen by the Franciscan mendi- Life of Sixtus V
cant friar Felix Peretti, who had entered his order at the age of thirteen. He had been a member of the church from the very beginning of his conscious existence, just as an artist or a scientist with an inner vocation belongs to art or to science long before his brain is fully developed.

Peretti's father, a small tenant farmer and gardener of Dalmatian stock, filled with visions of the future destiny of his son, gave him the name of Felix. This name Sixtus V, in contrast

30. Rome: The area between the Coliseum and the Lateran, from the map of Du Pérac Lafréry, 1577. *The country-like character of the hill districts shortly before the time of Sixtus V is clearly shown, as well as the haphazardly winding roads. In the map the Lateran is to the left and S. Maria Maggiore, in its country setting, can be seen on the right. It is also clear that the Via Gregoriana, built by Gregory XIII, consisted of one short straight stretch between the two churches. The difficulties faced by Sixtus V in forming the Strada Felice between S. Maria Maggiore and the Pincio can be well understood from this map.*

to other Popes, never laid entirely aside. He bestowed it upon two of the projects that lay nearest his heart: the Strada Felice, Rome's grandiose northwest–southeast highway, and the Acqua Felice, the water system which brought life to the hills of the southeast.

The Pope must be wise and the Pope must be aged, for it is not intended that he should reign too long. This requirement gave rise to a tragic conflict for each of the great Popes, between his desire to carry out his schemes and the limits imposed by death. The life of Sixtus V illustrates this tragic situation. He had a swift and splendid career up to the rank of cardinal:

84

31. Rome: The area between the Coliseum and the Lateran, from the map of Antonio Tempesta, 1593. *This map, made shortly after the time of Sixtus V, cannot easily be compared with the other because of their different orientation. Even so, it is at once apparent that immense changes had occurred within these few years. A straight road now leads from the Coliseum to the obelisk before the Lateran Palace and from there a straight line (the improved Via Gregoriana) runs right across the map to S. Maria Maggiore (off the map to the left). This, Sixtus V's favorite church, was also connected by a straight route (part of the Strada Felice) to S. Croce (at the top of the map). Close to the Coliseum great building activity can be observed as the countryside becomes covered with houses.*

his theological erudition was profound; his religious zeal limitless; as a Lenten preacher he was awe-inspiring. As Friar Felix he was, at thirty-five, the pitiless inquisitor of the Republic of Venice. When he acquired the purple robe at the age of forty-eight he assumed the title of Cardinal Montalto, the name of the village where he had entered the Franciscan order, close to his own birthplace, Grottammare. After the death of his protector, Pius V, the Cardinal was ignored during the whole of the reign of Gregory XIII, who was very coldly

32. S. Maria Maggiore and the Villa Montalto, from the map of Antonio Tempesta, *1593. S. Maria Maggiore with its monastic buildings stood alone upon a deserted and waterless spot on the Esquiline Hill when the Cardinal Montalto (later Sixtus V) purchased the site for his Villa Montalto in 1581. In Tempesta's map the wall-girdled estate with its "palazzotto" and tower and two avenues of cypress trees is clearly shown, as well as the newly created square and the obelisk before S. Maria Maggiore, while, behind the church, Sixtus V's new road to S. Lorenzo pierces through the Aurelian wall. The Strada Felice is not easy to discern, since Tempesta felt obliged to curve it to depict the rugged nature of the land.*

disposed toward him. Sixtus V was sixty-four when he was elevated to the Papal throne, and sixty-nine when he succumbed to malaria within the walls of his unfinished Quirinal Palace.

Just five years and four months were allotted to this great organizer for the immense tasks he desired to accomplish —

33. S. Maria Maggiore and its obelisk, 1587, from the fresco now in the Collegio Massimo. *This fresco once decorated the buildings that Sixtus V erected along the outer wall of his estate for his household staff. In the foreground is an early high-wheeled carriage, and to the left the young trees bordering his estate, in all their tender fragility, planted by his own hands.*

34. The obelisk today, from the opposite side. *This view of the obelisk, taken from S. Maria Maggiore, looks down the Strada Felice toward the Pincio.*

in politics, in administration, in town planning. Nowhere is his race with death more apparent than in the incredible rapidity with which he carried through his building program. Again and again his architect, Domenico Fontana, remarks that nothing could be accomplished quickly enough to please his beloved lord.

At the outset of his reign, Sixtus V completed the Strada Felice in less than a year (1585–86), and at the end his enormous determination enabled the cupola of St. Peter's (which had hardly been touched for a quarter of a century) to rise within twenty-two months (1588–90). Giacomo della Porta and Domenico Fontana, who were responsible for carrying out Michelangelo's designs, had eight hundred workmen on the job, day and night, weekdays and holidays.

From the death of Pius V the Cardinal Montalto had had long to wait for action: thirteen years — the best years of his life.

VEDUTA DEL GIARDINO DELL' EMINᵐᵒ SIG. CARDINALE PAOLO SAVELLI PERETTI VERSO SANTA MARIA MAGGIORE.
1. Aspetto del Palazzetto felice . 2. Giardini secreti . Architettura del Caual: Domenico Fontana . 3. Teatro è fontane auanti il Palazzo felice 4 Fontane di leoni apprefso G. Jac de Sandrart

35. The Villa Montalto in the late seventeenth century. *The gardens with their directional vistas as they were laid out by Sixtus V, a century ahead of the square parterres of the Renaissance. The avenues of cypress stood until they were devoured in the railway age by the growth of the city planned by Sixtus himself.*

During all these years he had stood aside, ignored by Gregory XIII and banned from active life. He discovered at this time a place of retreat — an environment in which he was content to live and to rest forever. It was a deserted and waterless spot on the Esquiline hill, remote from any habitation [7] but adjacent to his beloved church of S. Maria Maggiore. The Cardinal bought the site in 1581 and with Domenico Fontana

[7] A. von Hübner, *The Life and Times of Sixtus V* (London, 1872), I, 225 ff.

36. DOMENICO FONTANA. The Transportation of the Chapel of the Sacred Crib. *The removal of the entire chapel, which contains the remains of the Sacred Crib, from its former place within S. Maria Maggiore to the new chapel that Sixtus V built for his own tomb and that of his benefactor, Pius IV, was a most precarious undertaking and revealed Fontana's great capacity for feats of engineering.*

created there the Villa Montalto, an estate with a very large garden and a small country house, surmounted by a tower, which he named the Palazetto Felice (*fig.* **32**).

The development of this estate was one of the happiest coöperative enterprises between architect and client in history. This exceptionally happy union was based on deep inner affinities. Domenico Fontana,[8] like his master, possessed a talent

---

[8] Domenico Fontana was one of the first architects who came to Rome from the far north — from Melide on the Swiss side of the frontier lake of Lugano. It is interesting to note that Fontana's nephew, Carlo Maderno, builder of the nave of St. Peter's, and Francesco Borromini, a nephew of Maderno, all came from nearby villages and belonged to the same clan. See Ugo Donati, *Artisti Ticinesi a Roma* (Bellinzona, 1942).

for precise and efficient organization. Sufficient evidence of this is shown in his own description of the precautions he took in the transportation of the Vatican obelisk. Less spectacular, but even more precarious, was the movement of the relics of the sacred crib in S. Maria Maggiore to the new mausoleum he had erected (*fig.* **36**). Fontana belonged to the artistically mediocre generation of architects between Michelangelo and the rise of Roman Baroque. His taste was as flavorless as that of his master. The Lateran, the Quirinal, and the wing he built of the Vatican are among the dullest palaces of Rome, but the collective interaction of his work produced an urbanism that had no parallel at that period.

Fontana's Palazetto on the Montalto estate was equally insignificant, but the layout of the garden (*fig.* **35**) with its long vistas was a century ahead of the square-patterned gardens of the Renaissance. At Montalto the son of a tenant farmer had found a piece of land that was entirely his own, and here his long-suppressed yearning for contact with the soil came to the fore. As Cardinal and Pope he gave the utmost care to the cultivation of his property, planting cypress and olive trees with his own hands. On one of the frescoes, in a new wing that he added later, now preserved at the Collegio Romano, these new young trees appear behind a wall in all their fragility (*fig.* **33**).

Simultaneous
planning

Here, in seclusion, the Cardinal Montalto spent most of the last four years before he ascended the papal throne. Perhaps the most impressive aspect of his activity as Pope is the simultaneity with which he was able to carry out his great works, from the very day of his appointment. The power to accomplish his master plan in so limited a period was acquired during the years of contemplation he spent upon the very spot on which he started. The synchronization of the work was carried out with the unfailing surety of a general staff plan. Baron Haussmann effected the transformation of Paris step by step, *réseau* by *réseau;* Sixtus V began everywhere at once, with an astonishing simultaneity.

A scrupulously kept notebook is still preserved recording the minute transactions of the mendicant friar Felix Peretti. The Pope Sixtus V determined to introduce the same order into the social and financial affairs of the Papal State. He was successful in both. In a short time he had broken up the gangs of bandits and aristocrats which had worked together to terrorize the people both within and outside the city,[9] and during his short reign the papal treasury at the Castel S. Angelo increased twentyfold. The measures he took, in every field, touched the fringe of cruelty. He combined the rigid morality of his puritan contemporaries with the pitilessness of the Catholic inquisitors. In the words of the Grand Duke of Tuscany, construction was handled as recklessly as men.

At the same time that he was establishing order in the country, Sixtus V was carrying through his *magnanime imprese*, his "grandiose enterprises" as Domenico Fontana called them. In the first year of his reign, work was started upon the Strada Felice and completed the same year; the task of moving the obelisk in front of St. Peter's was begun; a beginning was made upon the viaducts and canals for the Acqua Felice, the Lateran Palace and Basilica, the clearing of the Trajan column, and the drainage of the Pontine marshes (with two thousand workers). Besides all this, work was proceeding at a frantic pace on the development of his own estate and of the sumptuous chapel of S. Maria Maggiore. This account may serve as sufficient illustration of the simultaneity of his urban planning.

The Master Plan

In the domain of town planning, Sixtus V was one of those rare men who are able to organize, assemble the facts, and execute the scheme. He took over the work of his predecessors, integrated it with his own plans, and pointed the way for future development. He allowed nothing to stand in the way of the realization of his plans. Only death itself could check — all too soon — his unbridled energy.

Already, before the time of Sixtus, a strange phenomenon had taken place in Rome. Instead of developing, as most cities do, from east to west, modern Rome had grown from west to east

Rome grows from West to East

---

[9] Hübner, *Sixtus V*, gives details of this struggle, I, 275, 284, 293.

— or, more exactly, from northwest (the Vatican) toward the more salubrious hill regions of the southeast.

Between 1503 and 1513, Julius II had laid out two straight streets on either side of the river Tiber: the Lungara on the right bank, the Via Giulia on the left. His successor, Leo X (1513–1521), planned the Strada Leonina (Via Ripetta), the most easterly of the three streets that radiate from the Piazza del Popolo. Paul III (1534–1549) was responsible for its counterpart, the Via Babuino; while the central, axial, street, the Via Lata (today the Corso) was already in existence as the ancient entry into Rome from the north. It is typical that two of the few Renaissance churches of Rome that stand here — S. Maria del Popolo and, on the summit of the Pincio, S. Trinità dei Monti — were completed under Sixtus V.

Now the development takes an energetic leap toward the southeast. From the deserted Quirinal hill Pius IV (1559–1565) shot a straight line across two kilometers to Michelangelo's unexcelled Porta Pia (1561). This street, first named after him the Strada Pia, is now the Via del Quirinale and the Via XX Settembre. Here we are already amidst the sphere of Sixtus V's scheme. Lastly, the immediate predecessor (and opponent) of Sixtus V, Gregory XIII (1572–1585), straightened out rather fragmentarily, the old road that connected S. Maria Maggiore with the basilica of S. Giovanni in Laterano (*fig.* **30**).

Ecclesiastical impulse for Sixtus V's planning

At his accession to power, the Franciscan Pope, Sixtus V, thus found a series of fragmentary developments extending, in chronological order, from west to east. He was able to bring all of them together into a unified scheme — his master plan. The first impulse for this new transformation was, above all, an ecclesiastical one. Road connections should link all the seven main churches and holy shrines which had to be visited by the faithful during the course of a day's pilgrimage. Behind this enterprise can be seen the Counter Reformation and the newly awakened vitality of the Church. The desire of Sixtus — as expressed by Pastor — was to make the whole of Rome into "a single holy shrine."

To the clergy and pilgrims, Sixtus' plan appeared as a simple street connection between the holy places. There is a poem of praise to the works of Sixtus V, written by the archbishop of Avignon, Bordino, in Latin hexameters (1588) [10] — at a time when the work was still under way. It is illustrated by a rudimentary sketch-plan (*fig.* **23**) in which only the main churches and their connecting streets are shown. These streets form a star radiating from the basilica of S. Maria Maggiore to the various churches, *in syderis formam*. The star-like plan has given rise to misunderstandings concerning the real purpose of the scheme — which was, in fact, of an entirely different nature from that of the star-shaped city of the Renaissance.

Unfortunately our search for the architect's original plans has been without success. Maybe they never existed. In Domenico Fontana's work on the projects he carried out under Sixtus V, he makes only a few brief remarks "on the streets opened by our lord." Yet these are the first expressions of the point of view which has determined the layout of the streets of a modern city. This is sufficient reason for some of Fontana's passages [11] to be included here. He begins by describing the general problem:

"Our lord, now wishing to ease the way for those who, prompted by devotion or by vows, are accustomed to visit frequently the most holy places of the City of Rome, and in particular the seven churches so celebrated for their great indulgences and relics; opened many most commodious and straight streets in many places. Thus one can by foot, by horse, or in a carriage, start from whatever place in Rome one may wish, and continue virtually in a straight line to the most famous devotions."

The lines of the roads were carried through, regardless of the many difficulties that were encountered, overcoming all natural obstacles and tearing down whatever was in the way. At the same time, Sixtus was well aware of the marvelous diversity of the Roman topography, and he made use of its "various and divers perspectives . . . to charm the senses of the body."

[10] Giovanni Francesco Bordino, *De rebus praeclare gestis a Sixto V* (Rome, 1588). This book is very rare; there are however copies in the Library of the Palazzo Venezia in Rome, in the British Museum, and in the Bibliothèque Nationale.

[11] The following quotations from *Della Trasportatione dell' Obelisco Vaticano et delle Fabriche di Nostro Signore Papa Sisto V, fatto dal Cav. Domenico Fontana, Architetto di Sua Santita*, Libro Primo (Rome, 1590), have been kindly translated by Dr. James S. Ackerman.

"Now at a truly incredible cost, and in conformity with the spirit of so great a prince [Sixtus], has extended these streets from one end of the city to the other, without concern for either the hills or the valleys which they crossed; but, causing the former to be leveled and the latter filled, has reduced them to most gentle plains, and charming sites, revealing in several places which they pass, the lowest portions of the city with various and diverse perspectives; so that, aside from the devotions, they also nourish with their charm the senses of the body."

In a few words Fontana presents the basic intentions of Sixtus. Two thirds of the city of Rome lay within the Aurelian walls. Of this portion the hill areas, which had the best climate, were practically uninhabited, and, indeed, barely habitable. Nothing was there except "some church towers, dating from the Middle Ages, projecting from among some anciently revered basilicas. The whole deserted region seemed destined forever to be the abode of prayers and silence. The only habitations were cloisters and a few scattered hovels." [12]

It was these hills of ancient Rome, open to the winds of the Campagna, and stretching from the Pincio in the northeast to the Esquiline, Quirinal, Viminal, and Caelius, that Sixtus wanted again to make accessible. To accomplish this, he immediately set to work to change a simple assembly of roads into a multiple urban transport system.

"The wish is now serving to refill the City, because, these streets being frequented by the crowd, houses and shops are being built there in the greatest profusion, where formerly one was impeded by the many turnings of the road."

Following the practice of the Middle Ages when founding new cities, Sixtus encouraged building activity by granting various privileges. One of his biographers [13] records that Sixtus' own sister, Donna Camila, who was shrewdly aware of commercial advantage, built some shops which she rented profitably on a part of the Esquiline near S. Maria Maggiore.

---

[12] Pastor, *Die Stadt Rom zu Ende der Renaissance*, p. 102.

[13] Hübner, *Sixtus V*, II, 137 f.

The change in the city was so great and so rapid that a priest on returning to Rome after the death of Sixtus remarked that he could hardly recognize it any more: "Everything seems to be new, edifices, streets, squares, fountains, aqueducts, obelisks."[14]

The greatest pride of Fontana was the Strada Felice, which bore the name of the Pope, and which was started and completed within one year, 1585–86. This great street (now the Via Agostino Depretis and the Via Quattro Fontane) slopes down hill from the obelisk before S. Maria Maggiore, then climbs up to the summit of the Pincio and the church of S. Trinità dei Monti, which Sixtus dedicated in 1585,[15] and which thus becomes linked to S. Maria Maggiore upon the Esquiline hill. The final stretch, which was never completed, was intended to lead downwards again to the obelisk in the Piazza del Popolo. This is clearly shown in the fresco in the Vatican (*fg.* **29**). The Spanish Steps, planned by Sixtus as a link between the lofty S. Trinità dei Monti and the heart of the city — by means of the Via Trinitatis (today Via Condotti) — had to wait until the eighteenth century to be built.

On the far side of S. Maria Maggiore, the Strada Felice continues in an undeviating straight line to the church of S. Croce in Gerusalemme. In the second half of the nineteenth century this stretch of the road was to serve as the backbone of one of the most wearisomely dull districts of Rome, and various names were then given to different sections of the road. Fontana speaks of the Strada Felice as follows:

"The most celebrated is the street called Felice, which originates at the church of Santa Croce in Gerusalemme, passes the church of Santa Maria Maggiore, and then continues on to the Trinità dei Monti from where one descends to the Porta di Popolo: which in all comprises a distance of two miles and a half, and throughout straight as a plumb line and wide enough to allow five carriages to ride abreast."

[14] "Lettere di Angelo Grillo, Venezia, 1612," quoted by Antonio Muñoz, *Domenico Fontana* (Rome, 1944), p. 39.

[15] The obelisk before this church was erected in 1789 by the classistic Pope Pius VII.

A road along which five carriages could drive abreast — in other words, a five-lane road — must have seemed somewhat extreme to the Romans, for this was at the beginning of the change-over from horse and sedan chair to coach and carriage.[16] Sixtus scarcely ever forgets to include in his frescoes one of the primitive carriages of the period, with open front and back, as a reminder of the improvements he had brought about in such a short span of time.

Sixtus' plan not
star-shaped

Fond as Sixtus V was of the area around S. Maria Maggiore, he never thought of making the Basilica the center of a star-shaped street pattern, as in the "ideal cities" of the Renaissance. His was no paper plan. Sixtus V had Rome, as it were, in his bones. He himself trudged the streets the pilgrims had to follow and experienced the distances between points, and when, in March 1588, he opened the new road from the Coliseum to the Lateran, he walked with his cardinals all the way to the Lateran Palace, then under construction.

Integration of
new and old

Sixtus V spread out his streets organically, wherever they were demanded by the topographical structure of Rome. He was also wise enough to incorporate with great care whatever he could of the work of his predecessors. Sometimes he improved upon their work, as in the straightening of Gregory XIII's Via Gregoriana (*fig.* **28**) or the raising and leveling of the Strada Pia. He traced his own Strada Felice to form a most happy conjunction with the Strada Pia.[17] The angle at which they cross is not quite a right angle, but Domenico Fontana placed four fountains here, fed by the waters of the Acqua Felice, so that the deviation disappeared and the importance of the crossing was emphasized. The spot has added interest from the vistas afforded in each direction: Michelangelo's Porta Pia; the obelisk of S. Maria Maggiore; the giant late-Roman statues of the Two Horse Tamers at the Quirinal near by; and, continuing the perspective of the Strada Felice, up hill and down dale to S. Trinità dei Monti and the Pincio.

---

[16] L. von Pastor, *Sisto V, il Creatore della Nuova Roma* (Rome, 1922), p. 15.

[17] This junction proved extremely valuable after 1870, when the building up of this quarter came into full swing following the confinement of the papal authority to the Vatican and the sequestration of the papal lands.

Sixtus V integrated his new web of streets not only with stretches of existing roads, but also with the needs of the city itself. The fresco that he had painted on the ceiling of the Vatican Library in 1589 is far from exact either in scale or completeness, but, by giving an indication of what Sixtus V would have done if time had given him the chance, it conveys the idea of his master plan better than the maps of what was actually carried out (*fig.* **29**).

Master-plan fresco in Vatican Library

On the left-hand side of the fresco is the obelisk at the Piazza del Popolo. The straight line of the Strada Felice runs up to the obelisk of S. Maria Maggiore and continues on to S. Giovanni in Laterano. From here a connection is outlined to the distant church of S. Paolo fuori le Mura (St. Paul's Outside the Walls) and, in the opposite direction, to the nearby S. Croce in Gerusalemme. The stretch connecting the Lateran and the Coliseum has already been mentioned.

Returning to S. Maria Maggiore, we find another road leading directly to S. Croce in Gerusalemme, and — particularly interesting for this period — a connection to S. Lorenzo fuori le Mura which would not have stopped at the old Roman town wall. Finally, contact with the old city is secured by the Via Panisperna, leading directly to Trajan's Column and the Piazza S. Marco (Venezia). A web of cross streets interconnects these main arteries.[18] If time had permitted, Sixtus V would have redeveloped the whole of Rome with streets, squares, water supply, and buildings.

Rome had been unable to create proud civic cores expressing civic spirit in monumental terms such as were built in Florence, Siena, and Venice. The squares of Rome were off back streets, such as the Piazza Navona which followed the outline of Domitian's stadium. These squares were used for markets or carnivals, but they possessed no buildings of social significance. Even the Capitol, for all its architectural grandeur, occupied a rather isolated site. Sixtus V gave a far more energetic impulse than any Pope before or since to the creation

Squares and obelisks

[18] Excellent information on the realization of some of the work of Sixtus V can be found in the *Avvisi di Roma*, some of which were published by L. von Pastor, *Geschichte der Päpste*, X (Freiburg, 1926), 591–609, and in I. A. F. Orbaan, *Sixtine Rome* (London, 1910).

37. G. F. BORDINI. The Antonine Column and the beginning of the Piazza Colonna, 1588. *Sixtus V placed his obelisks as though with a divining rod at points where marvelous squares would later grow up. Here he cleared the Antonine Column and the space around it from the debris of centuries, fixing the boundaries that achieved their architectural form only in the late seventeenth century. In Bordini's engraving the primitive character of the contemporary buildings can be seen more clearly than in the Vatican fresco. Even at the present day the Piazza Colonna holds its position as the center of Rome.*

of squares all over the city. Many of these were related to churches, but not by any means all.

In front of his own buildings — the Lateran and Quirinal — and wherever his streets came together, Sixtus V made provision for ample open space, sufficient for much later development. An example is the large area he reserved in front of the Diocletian Thermae and bordering his own estate of Montalto which developed into the Piazza delle Terme, the square of the nineteenth-century railway terminal. By clearing around the Antonine Column and tracing the outline of the Piazza Colonna (1588) he created the present-day center of the city. Trajan's Column near the Coliseum with its enlarged surrounding square was a link between the old city and the new.

38. G. F. BORDINI. The obelisk before St. Peter's shortly after its erection, 1588. *The transportation of this obelisk, as well as the removal of the Sacred Crib in S. Maria Maggiore, are typical of the virtuosity and great interest shown in difficult mechanical exploits during the late sixteenth century, and foreshadow the later work of Galileo.*

Like a man with a divining rod, Sixtus V placed his obelisks at points where, during the coming centuries, the most marvelous squares would develop. Of all his enterprises, the most sensational and spectacular for more than a century was the dismantling, transportation, and reërection of the obelisk before St. Peter's (1585–86). It was the only obelisk that still stood upright where the Emperor Caligula had placed it at the *spina* of Nero's circus. Since Nicholas V, the Popes, and especially Gregory XIII, had considered moving and reërecting the obelisk, but nobody dared to attack the problem of taking it down and transporting it.

Italy at the end of the sixteenth century had a highly developed technology and interest in machines and mechanics, and Sixtus V had the necessary daring. Yet much more important than the sensational reërection of the obelisk is the new artistic significance Sixtus V gave to the Egyptian symbol of sun rays as a space-absorbing medium. The instinct for civic design of the Pope and his architect is demonstrated again in their selection of a new site for the obelisk at just the right distance from the unfinished cathedral: it was as though Bernini himself had pre-selected it as the magical center for his colonnades.

The last of the four obelisks that Sixtus was able to set up was given perhaps the most subtle position of all. Placed at the northern entrance to the city, it marked the confluence of three main streets (as well as the often projected but never executed final extension of the Strada Felice). Two centuries later the Piazza del Popolo crystallized around this spot. The only other obelisk to occupy such a dominating position is that in the Place de la Concorde in Paris, set up in 1836.

The Social Aspect

Sixtus V was the first of the modern town planners. From the beginning he was aware of the city as a complex organism, and knew that the beauty of open squares and wide streets had to be buttressed by social implementation.

The Acqua Felice   The very day that he entered the Lateran as master, he made the decision, we are told by Domenico Fontana,[19] that he would provide a water supply — the Acqua Felice — for the hill areas of the city, which had lain deserted since the destruction of the Roman aqueducts built by Alexander Severus (A.D. 222–235). Sixtus V intended to conduct water to the very highest points of the Roman hills — the Esquiline, Caelius, Viminal, Capitoline, and Pincio. The main difficulty was that there was only a very small fall from the springs that he had purchased near Palestrina, sixteen miles away; and the topography seemed to make it impossible for the conduit to be laid in a straight line. The problem was solved by carrying the conduit for seven miles along a high arched aqueduct and for seven miles under ground. Within eighteen months the work was

[19] Muñoz, *Domenico Fontana*, p. 42.

successfully accomplished. It was an exciting moment for Sixtus V, wondering whether the flow of water would reach the Quirinal and other places. But by October 1586 water was running in the gardens of the Villa Montalto, and in 1589 it gushed from all the twenty-seven public fountains.[20]

Other Popes had restored the aqueducts that served the lower parts of the city, and Gregory XIII had had the intention of carrying out the same venture as Sixtus V, but he had been frightened by the technical difficulties and the high costs and had never got further than preliminary negotiations.

On the fresco at the Vatican Library, the monumental entry of the Acqua Felice into the city is marked by the three-arched Moses Fountain (1587) which juts out, very white and out of proportion, on the Strada Pia (*fig.* **39**). Even in the seventeenth century this fountain was considered as being in very bad style (*pessimo stile*) [21] and it is scarcely conceivable that such mediocrity was possible only two decades after the death of Michelangelo. The real purpose of this fountain can be seen in another of the Vatican Library frescoes (*fig.* **42**); it is not intended as a show piece. It is a reminder that this part of Rome had had no water for over a millennium, but above all it is a social institution. The Egyptian lions are spitting water for the use of the passers by; the three large basins serve as water reservoirs for the local inhabitants; the marble barriers are there to protect them from pollution by animals, while to the right is a special basin for the use of horses and cattle.

Near to the Moses Fountain, on what is now the Piazza delle Terme, Sixtus V installed a public washing place with two long basins (*fig.* **44**) "for everybody who wanted to clean dirty laundry." He further provided an enclosed space containing a covered wash house "for bad weather and where women could stay without danger of being bothered by anybody (*alcuna sorte di persone*)." [22] This sixteenth-century establishment re-

Social establishments

---

[20] Pastor, *Päpste*, X, 426–433; A. D. Tani, *Le Acque e le Fontane di Roma* (Rome, 1926), p. 49 ff.

[21] See the biography of Domenico Fontana in G. Baglione, *Le Vite de' Pittori, Scultori, ed Architetti* (Rome, 1642).

[22] Fontana, *Della Trasportatione dell' Obelisco Vaticano* (2d ed., Naples, 1604), pt. I, fol. 88.

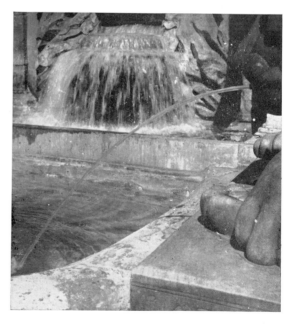

40. Basins of the Moses Fountain. *Even today the basins of the fountain are in constant use by the local inhabitants.*

41. Drinking-water fountain. *The Egyptian lions still spit water for the thirsty passers-by.*

39. The Moses Fountain, 1587. *This three-arched fountain with Moses in the center symbolizes the triumphal entry of the Acqua Felice into the hill areas of Rome, which had been without a water supply for more than a thousand years.   The large basins of the fountain were designed for practical use as a water reservoir for the local people, while a special trough was provided on the right for the use of animals.*

minds us of the hesitating experiments at erecting public laundries in England around 1830 and in France under Napoleon III.

The largest basin of water that Sixtus offered to the people of Rome was a basin for the rinsing of wool, planned as an encouragement to the woolen industry.   It was made over in the eighteenth century into the theatrical Fontana di Trevi.

When Sixtus V came to power, he found the treasury exhausted and the city full of beggars and unemployed.   He dealt with

42. The Moses Fountain beside the Strada Pia, 1616. *Here, too, Sixtus V provided a square which, under the special circumstances, served both a practical and a social function.*

43. The Moses Fountain today. *This square, created almost entirely by Sixtus V, retains its original character.*

44. The wash house at the Piazza delle Terme, fresco in the Collegio Massimo. *Here two long basins were installed for the use of all who wished to clean their linen. Covered wash houses for bad weather and greater privacy were also provided.*

this problem by building poorhouses and by employing thousands of workers upon his program of public works. But these measures did not prove sufficient, and he decided to develop export trade by reviving (of course by foreigners) the old Roman wool and silk industries. He made a law that mulberry trees must be planted everywhere, and one of his last schemes was for the transformation of the Coliseum into a wool-spinning establishment. There were to be workshops on the ground floor and dwelling apartments for the workers in the upper story (*fig.* **45**). "He had already begun to excavate the earth and to level the street, working with seventy wagons and a hundred laborers, so that if the Pope had lived only one year more" [23] the Coliseum would have become the first worker's settlement and large-scale unit of manufacture.

There is no doubt that Sixtus V's extraordinary passion for town planning stands out spectacularly from among his other achievements. In other ways than in the somewhat naive inscriptions upon obelisks and slabs of marble his name is deeply engraved upon the face of Rome.

The greatness of Sixtus V

Sixtus V was clearly aware of the great complexity of modern urban planning. This is the reason for the striking assurance with which he attacked the most diverse urban problems at one and the same moment, but this simultaneity in urban planning is only one of the facets of this great organizer. There

[23] Fontana, *Della Trasportatione* . . . (2d ed., Naples, 1604), pt. II, fol. 18.

45. DOMENICO FONTANA. Sixtus V's plan transforming the Coliseum into a factory for wool spinning, 1590. *During the last year of his reign Sixtus V made plans to transform the Coliseum into a colony of workshops for wool spinners, where they could have their living quarters in the upper stories and working areas on the ground floor.*

were not many quiet hours during the pontificate of Sixtus V. The church was again in danger, and the disturbing political background could not be ignored. Germany was divided and in disorder; France was on the verge of becoming Protestant; Mary, Queen of Scots, had been decapitated, the Spanish Armada destroyed, and England lost forever to the faith. Most wearisome of all were the never-ending controversies with the arrogant and ambitious Philip of Spain, which, Pastor believed, Sixtus V paid for with his life.

Against this uncertain political background, Sixtus V attempted to fashion Rome as a world capital where the Pope would reside as eternal arbitrator of the balance of power between temporal states. This did not happen. Rationalism forced development into another direction. But the religious faith of Sixtus V had inspired him with an optimism that enabled him to accomplish the seemingly impossible. One cannot plan cities if one does not believe in life.

46. FRANCESCO BORROMINI. San Carlo alle Quattro Fontane, Rome, 1662–67. Exterior. *The whole wall translated into undulating movement. The undulating wall — first used by Borromini in S. Filippo Neri, Rome — is one of the constituent facts in late baroque architecture.*

THE LATE BAROQUE

The manner in which Renaissance modes shaded off into baroque, the way in which the new shapes became more and more evident until they were wholly transformed by the architects of the late seventeenth century — all this is quite familiar.

Universal outlook of the baroque period

107

In the hands of the baroque builders, the Renaissance shapes were no more than the primitive elements of architectural composition. In just the way that Bach would transpose a simple melody into a great new harmony, elaborate and subtle, these architects transmuted the forms developed in the Renaissance. The interiors they produced are marked by an inseparable union of two kinds of interests usually encountered separately: they are at once the products of purely mathematical speculations of a high order of complexity, and completely visionary or mystical imaginative creations. The same union of two such different spirits appears in the work of a baroque master of another medium, Blaise Pascal (1623–1662). At sixteen he had written a classic work on conic sections; he went on to study the cycloid curve, to develop the theory of probability, and to do pioneer work in physical science. Pascal's religious mysticism had its roots in such speculations. "The eternal silence of these infinite spaces terrifies me" comes out of his work on the mathematical implications of infinity, and leads up to his feeling for the insignificance of man without God.

The last phases of the baroque development are the true inheritance of the epoch out of which we grow. We shall have to consider first the Italian products of the baroque era, and then go on to see what the north of Europe adds to these results.

"Baroque" indicates a period rather than special shapes

It may perhaps be advisable — in view of the history of the term — to offer the prefatory comment that "baroque" does not apply exclusively to an overdecorated building in Mexico or Spain. For more than fifty years the history of art has used "baroque" to designate the period beginning with Michelangelo and continuing until the eighteenth century, and even beyond in some fields — town planning, for example. "Late baroque" would date a work as after 1660. The baroque age lasted therefore about as long as the Gothic. Its name, curiously enough, has had much the same fate — thus "Gothic" up to the nineteenth century remained a synonym for the barbarous or the uncouth. In some contemporary English histories of architecture, baroque is still taken to mean a "debased" form of art. But the work of Heinrich Wölfflin had taught us, even before 1890, to appreciate the early Roman baroque that begins with Michelangelo. The German architect, Cornelius Gurlitt, soon performed the same service for the late baroque of nearly all countries. More recently, the excellent Viennese school of history has covered the late period with great thoroughness. "Baroque" has by now an accepted meaning in the field of art history, as referring not to a special shape but to a whole period.

The distinguishing mark of the baroque age is the method of thinking and of feeling that prevails in it; its outstanding feature is the development of a specific kind of universality. In our field, this manifests itself as a new power to mold space, and to produce an astonishing and unified whole from the most various parts. But it is worthy of note that, in all departments, baroque methods and ways of feeling survive until the disintegration produced by the industrial age sets in and brings with it a temporary destruction of the universal point of view.

In the late seventeenth century we find the baroque universality working with the infinite in the field of mathematics as a basis for practical calculations. In painting and in architecture the impression of infinity — the infinite in a linear sense, as an indefinitely extended perspective — is being used as a means for artistic effect. Thus, early in the century, the Dutch landscape painters introduce an "atmospheric infinity" into their works; somewhat later the Roman architects succeed in realizing the same mystical feeling of endlessness — often in astonishingly small churches — through a simultaneous exploitation of all the resources of painting, sculpture, architecture, and optical theory. With the French landscape architects of the late seventeenth century there appears the artistic employment of the infinity of nature (although much the same kind of thing had been done previously, on a smaller scale, in Italy and in Holland). For the first time in history their gardens incorporated great highways as essential parts of an architectonic expression, and were placed by this means in direct and obvious relation with the unending extension of space. Versailles, with the impressive open road leading from it to Paris, is the great example of such creations. These gardens, in their total effect, stood as models of the baroque universe, and retained its aspect of infinity.

Perspective and baroque notions of infinity

THE UNDULATING WALL AND THE FLEXIBLE GROUND PLAN

Francesco Borromini, 1599–1667 [1]

Borromini's San
Carlo alle
Quattro Fontane

There is an interval of nearly two hundred and fifty years between the flat surface of the entrance wall of the Pazzi Chapel and the last work of Francesco Borromini: the façade of San Carlo alle Quattro Fontane (St. Charles of the Four Fountains) in Rome, 1662–67 (*figs.* **46** and **82**).

The flat surface of the outer wall of the Pazzi Chapel represents a clear succession of equal compartments, each of them closed within itself. The wall of Borromini's San Carlo alle Quattro Fontane expresses movement. The individual compartments are no longer marked off from each other; a continuous chain of interrelations runs through them all and comes to a focus in the center of the structure to produce the impression of an upward straining.

The statue of San Carlo Borromeo, to whom the church is dedicated, stands in a niche above the central porch. An angel is placed on each side of the statue; their wings arched over its head help to accentuate the figure's upward gaze. This ascending motif is continued through the whole façade until, above the vertically elongated medallion, even the surmounting balustrade melts away into a molded gable, which focuses and concludes the upward-surging impulse.

The undulating
wall

Rome at this time was a medieval town, with narrow streets and little space between its buildings. The façade of San Carlo alle Quattro Fontane, in its extraordinary concentration, is no larger than a single pier of St. Peter's. But the façade of this church embodies a conception which was of great influence on the time that followed. Not merely a single form but the whole wall has been translated into undulating movement; the wavelike surface that resulted was Borromini's great invention. It is an invention which did not reappear merely as a means of

---

[1] The work of Francesco Borromini embraces problems which are among the most complicated in the history of architecture. We treat it only in so far as it concerns our architectural inheritance.

110

attracting the attention of passers-by in the small Roman streets. It is present again, in astonishing form, in the English "crescents" of the late eighteenth century, and it persists, in a somewhat altered way, in contemporary architecture.

If the intentions behind this undulation of the wall were simply decorative, they would not demand our attention. Such an attitude toward it might even justify the opinion of Jakob Burckhardt, who angrily observed that the façade of San Carlo looked like something that had been dried in an oven. But our present-day point of view springs out of conditions very different from those that operated in 1855,[2] when Burckhardt wrote his *Cicerone* — which still remains unexcelled as a guidebook to Italy. Nowadays it is easy for us to see the force that appears in the whole structure, in the stressing of the progression and regression of the wall through the hollowing out of niches and the building up of contradistinguished parts. There is to be seen here a real molding of space, a swelling and receding that causes the light to leap over the front of the church. Francesco Borromini succeeded in creating, through purely architectonic means, and in the open air, something which is equivalent to the mild chiaroscuro of his contemporary, Rembrandt, at work on his own last paintings at this same time.

Several historians have found sources for Borromini's treatment of the wall in antiquity. It is possible, but by no means certain, that Borromini knew a contemporary etching of the

Does the undulating wall appear in antiquity?

---

[2] The rediscovery of Francesco Borromini began with Cornelius Gurlitt's *Geschichte des Barockstils in Italien* (Stuttgart, 1887): "All who have still not lost courage for the invention of new means of expression to meet the new tasks . . . in construction will find a congenial spirit in Borromini" (pp. 365–366).

The systematic study of Borromini was first undertaken by the "Vienna School" after 1900. Its leader, Max Dvořák, published a short article on Borromini's work on the restoration of St. John Lateran in 1907: "Francesco Borromini als Restaurator," *Beiblatt zum Kunstgesch.*, Jahrb. der K. K. Zentralkommission (Vienna, 1907), I, 89ff. Oscar Pollak, one of Dvořák's circle, published a biographical study of Borromini in Thieme-Becker, *Allg. Lex. d. bild. Künstler* (Leipzig, 1910), vol. IV. The influence of Borromini's work was pointed out by A. E. Brinckmann, *Die Baukunst des 17. und 18. Jhdts. in den romanischen Ländern* (Berlin, 1915). The standard biography is Eberhard Hempel's *Francesco Borromini* (Vienna, 1924), which contains a full bibliography. Hans Sedlmayr's *Die Architectur Borrominis* (Berlin, 1930) contains complicated "structural analyses" of his work — sometimes very instructive, sometimes overpointed.

47. FRANCESCO BORROMINI. San Carlo alle Quattro Fontane. Interior: the dome, 1634–41.

rock temples at Petra in Asia Minor.[3] But these temples (El Chasne is the best known) are cut into the stone face of a mountain, the wall does not undulate, and all of their elements — the columns, the broken gables, the "sentry boxes" — are isolated one from the other. It seems much more natural to suppose that Borromini started with the flat church façade used since Alberti's Florentine Santa Maria Novella and that he molded all its parts into conformity with his vision.

The comparison with the *Kuppelsaal* of the Piazza d'Oro at Hadrian's villa near Tivoli is more interesting.[4] This late Roman Empire interior has a ground plan determined by eight segments of a circle, with columnal screens alternately convex and concave. The entire hall is set down in the middle of a great square chamber. But here as in other ancient build-

[3] Sedlmayr suggests that Borromini knew these second-century temples through this source, and that he was also familiar with Roman painted wall decorations (*op. cit.*, p. 59).

[4] Sedlmayr, *op. cit.*, pp. 56–57.

ings there is no undulation of the wall in the sense of an unbroken flow of movement that carries through its length. In
the Piazza d'Oro there is no continuity of movement: there are
breaks where the wall sections meet. Its treatment is the reverse
of that appearing in the Temple of Venus at Baalbek, where
concave entablatures were built onto a circular central part.

The undulating wall of Borromini's invention gave flexibility
to stone, changed the stone wall into an elastic material. The
undulating wall is the natural accompaniment to the flowing
spaces of the flexible ground plan.

San Carlo was built for the Spanish order of Discalced Trini-
tarians out of their small means, and was the property of
their monastery. Borromini does not achieve his effect through
ornament and decoration. On the contrary, he is very sparing
with both, as a glance at the small cloister would show.[5] This
court with its severe forms is an example of creation through
purely architectonic means. Its out-curving edges offer another instance of Borromini's power of infusing new life into
all forms, even into the Palladian motif.

Treatment of traditional forms: the court of San Carlo

Borromini built the cloister and the interior of the church
nearly thirty years before he completed the façade — in the
interval between 1634 and 1641. The interior is thus one of
his earliest productions. It is left almost entirely dark; on this
account the way in which the light bursts into it through the
lantern is all the more effective. The light shimmers over the
curious combination of geometrical forms which are cut into
the underside of the dome. As Borromini handles them, these
forms give the dome an appearance that suggests the cellular
structure of a plant (*fig.* 47).

The interior: the dome

Borromini's treatment of an interior space is best shown in
Sant' Ivo (*fig.* 48), the church which he built for the Sapienza (the
University of Rome). He began work on the church in 1642,
one year after finishing the interior of San Carlo, but it was
not completed until twenty years later. Sant' Ivo is situated
at the back of the Renaissance court of the Sapienza. Borromini knew perfectly how to fuse together into an integral
whole the loggia of the Renaissance court and the receding

Borromini's Sant' Ivo, Rome

[5] Cf. Hempel, *op. cit.,* Pl. 13.

48. FRANCESCO BORROMINI. Sant' Ivo, Rome, 1642–62. Ground plan. *Built within the Renaissance court of the Sapienza, Sant' Ivo is fused with it into an integral whole.*

façade of his own church. His addition to it brings a new and vital movement into the quiet Renaissance enclosure. Even the sensation of movement achieved through the unusually formed cupola, one full of new invention, is not in any way disturbing.

Its union of geometry and imagination

The interior of Sant' Ivo exhibits in its wall the same flexibility that marks the outer wall of San Carlo alle Quattro Fontane. Every motif that is introduced is continued throughout the entire building, to the very topmost part of the dome. But the average onlooker probably notes only the wonderful animation and movement. The artistic impulse of its creator can be grasped without analysis of the complicated space conception involved; indeed, the eye cannot pick out the simple mathematical basis of the ground plan. A six-pointed star — Borromini's favorite motif — is the invisible kernel from which the plan grows. But this governing form is hardly more obvious on the plan than the skeleton is in a healthy animal: one can only detect it by a sort of X-ray examination. (The reproduc-

114

tion of Borromini's plan given here has had some of its lines strengthened to reveal the star basis more distinctly.) [6] The star is formed by the intersection of two equilateral triangles. Berlage, the well-known Dutch architect, and some other investigators have shown that many medieval buildings are also based on this pattern. The six points where the sides of his pair of triangles intersect each other are used by Borromini as the master coördinates in his design. From the ideal hexagon which they bound he molds the six niches that transfer the movement of the main elements of his composition upward into the shell of the golden-starred dome. In this way the dome is intimately bound up with the whole interior (*fig.* **49**).

Up to that time, domes had always been round or oval. To cut out sections along the perfect circle of the dome, to continue the movement of a design by treating it as though it were flexible, must have had the same stunning effect upon Borromini's contemporaries that Picasso's disintegration of the human face produced around 1910 (*fig.* **50**). A cross section of Sant' Ivo (*fig.* **53**) reveals what such treatment accomplished in its case: the movement of the whole pattern made up by its design flows without interruption from the ground to the lantern, without entirely ending even there. Borromini, of course, did not have at his disposal the means that enabled Eiffel to bring about the complete interpenetration of inner and outer space achieved in his great tower at Paris. But Borromini, by leading the movement which penetrates every division of the building's inner space on and out through its topmost spiral, is making an approach to the same problem.

Flexibility in the modeling of the interior

The lantern which surmounts the church,[7] with its coupled columns, boldly curved cornice, and the fantastic spiral which replaces the usual cupola cap, resembles some organic growth. The culminating spiral carries a narrow pathway which leads to its top (*fig.* **51**).

Motion transmitted to architecture

---

[6] The complicated organization of the interior space of Sant' Ivo has received various explanations. Some authorities hold that the interior was developed out of a simple prism with an equilateral triangle for its base — other volumes being added on to this in the manner of Peruzzi's early Renaissance plan. Others hold that it was developed through the interpenetration of two such prisms, which together would form a six-pointed star. Cf. Sedlmayr, *op. cit.*, p. 70.

[7] It has been compared to the Temple of Venus at Baalbek.

Now, in our day, when the transition between inner and outer space can be completely effected, it is no wonder that projects appear which spring from the same spirit as that toward which Borromini groped. A clear expression of the same kind of feeling appears in a monument projected by the Russian constructivist painter, Tatlin, in 1920. Like Borromini, he employed the spiral form, with its inherent movement (*fig.* **52**).

Relation to our period

Borromini, like most of the great baroque artists in Rome, came from the far north of Italy. He began as a stonemason employed in the work on St. Peter's. This was his calling for many years, and throughout his life he remained in personal contact with the actual working of materials. But he was also a sculptor, and one of the greatest of the baroque age, although he produced neither brilliant portrait busts nor figures of saints melting away in mystical-erotic ecstasy. Indeed, he did no sculpture at all in the normal sense of the word. He expressed himself — like some modern masters — in abstract spirals, in the wire sculptures on the tops of his churches. But he was, above all, a sculptor of buildings, expressing himself

Borromini as a sculptor

←
49. FRANCESCO BOR–ROMINI. Sant' Ivo, Rome. Interior of dome. *The continuous inner surface of the dome is broken up. It is made to transmit the movement which runs throughout the whole elevation.*

50. PICASSO. Head. Sculpture, c. 1910. *Borromini's intersection of the continuous inner surface of the dome must have had the same stunning effect upon his contemporaries that Picasso's disintegration of the human face produced.*

118

52. TATLIN. Project for a monument in Moscow, 1920. *This, like the Eiffel Tower and some other monuments of our time, is a contemporary realization of the urge toward the interpenetration of inner and outer space.*

←

51. FRANCESCO BOR-ROMINI. Sant' Ivo, Rome. Lantern with coupled columns and spiral. *Culminating point for the movement that penetrates the whole design.*

53. FRANCESCO BOR-ROMINI. Sant' Ivo, Rome. Section through interior.

most fully through an inseparable union of mathematically elaborated ground plans with fantastically hollowed spaces, in structures of which it is hard to say where architecture stops and sculpture begins.

Borromini's chief interest was always the molding of space. He worked with wavelike lines and surfaces, with the sphere (*fig. 54*), with the spiral, and with still more unusual shapes in the wire sculptures on the points of his towers. In his hands all the inherited forms took on a new flexibility. He took nothing for granted, and almost from the beginning of his work he was accused of cultivating the bizarre and allowing himself too great liberties.

Significance of the undulating wall

By his treatment of the wall and the ground plan Borromini gave a new flexibility to architecture. He infused movement into the whole body of architecture. The undulating wall, the sections cut out of the dome of Sant' Ivo, the cupola ending in a spiral toward the sky, are all means working toward the same end.

54. FRANCESCO BOR–ROMINI. Sant' Ivo, Rome. Detail. (Pantheon in the background.) *These cement-like globes are of marble dust molded over an iron armature.*

120

Borromini's influence spread all over Europe and was absorbed into architectural knowledge even in that part dealing with town planning — this in spite of its condemnation by French and English academicians all through the eighteenth century and far into the nineteenth.

For two centuries Borromini figured as a man who had no feeling for the majestic simplicity of antiquity, but in actual fact he was intimately related to the past. He was not an imitator of shapes or façades and did not use history as a substitute for imagination. This revolutionary made careful studies of Gothic frescoes — drawings which still survive. Max Dvořák, who did some of the earliest research on his restoration of St. John Lateran, was astonished at the pains Borromini took to preserve fragments of the old church wherever it was possible, incorporating them into his own work.

Borromini's contact with history

Like every great creator, Borromini preserved connections with the past. He did not imitate the shapes of bygone epochs; he made them part of his own creations. Much as we try to do today, he found in his relations with history a source of power for further development.

Guarino Guarini, 1624–1683

The last phase of late baroque development appears at Turin in the northwest of Italy in the work of Guarino Guarini. Guarini, a Theatine monk and a distinguished savant, was born at Modena just a quarter-century after Borromini and Bernini. He first came to Rome at the time Borromini was at work on the interior of his San Carlo alle Quattro Fontane. The normal course of his calling as a Theatine monk later brought him to Messina in Sicily as professor of philosophy. He designed several churches here, all of them destroyed in the last earthquake. In 1662 he was transferred to Paris, where he taught theology. He began to build another church in this city. This effort was even more unfortunate than his Sicilian enterprises; gutted by fire while it was under construction, the building was never finished.

Guarini, architect and mathematician

Guarini's travels brought him into contact with the Gothic churches of France and the Moorish mosques of Cordova in Spain. He was a complete cosmopolitan. Although he never lost touch with his own country and his own time, he had an awareness of history in all its aesthetic manifestations.

Nothing is more characteristic of this late baroque period than the frequency with which it displays mathematician, empirical scientist, and artist combined in one person. There is an astonishing unity subsisting between methods of thought and of feeling; more precisely, there is a direct connection between artistic and mathematical knowledge. Whenever a new conception appears in mathematics it at once finds an artistic counterpart. Thus the integral calculus, taking definite shape at the end of the seventeenth century, found its architectural equivalent in the complicated treatments of space that appeared at the same time. Guarini's own career is a perfect illustration of the intimate relation between art and mathematics in the late baroque. He was not only an architect and a scholar; he was likewise an eminently talented mathematician. His published work reveals him as anticipating, to a considerable extent, the discovery of descriptive geometry made a century later by Gaspard Monge (1746–1818).

Palazzo Carignano: undulating wall and flexible ground plan

Guarini's most important work was done at Turin, where he lived from 1666 until his death. He was a *prepositus* or abbot of the Theatine order and, at the same time, an engineer in the service of the Duke of Savoy. It was at Turin that he built his finest churches and palaces. One of the latter, his Palazzo Carignano (1680), is an example of the way in which his architectural creations took on a flexibility that was nearly equal to that of Borromini's work. This palace, with its convoluted front and the molding of its staircases, certainly influenced palace architecture of a later period in southern Germany. The large, vaulted entrance hall, elliptical in shape, forms the kernel of the design for the Palazzo Carignano. The elliptical movement of the hall is communicated to the two wings of the staircases on its right and left, and is carried from them into all parts of the undulating outer wall. But, in spite of the architectonic vigor Guarini shows in this work, the arrangement of the interior of the building makes no approach to a

55. GUARINO GUARINI. San Lorenzo, Turin, 1668–87. Section through the cupola and the lantern, with intersecting binding arches.

solution of those strictly residential problems confronting architects of the time. All the force of Italian architecture in this period was being expended upon the interiors of churches. To put it rather more technically, all this unbounded imagination was given over to the molding of huge interior spaces. The

56. GUARINO GUARINI. San Lorenzo, Turin. Cupola with intersecting binding arches. *Architectural vision pushes to the limit of constructional resources in striving to produce the impression of infinity.*

57. GUARINO GUARINI. San Lorenzo, Turin. Ground plan.

generalization holds true in Guarini's own case; he produced his masterpiece in the church of San Lorenzo (*figs.* **55** and **57**), at Turin (1668–87).

San Lorenzo: infinity expressed through architectural means

San Lorenzo was built for Guarini's own order. The basic form of the church is that of a solidly walled square. The dome is circular. Between the ground floor and the cupola there is inserted an octagon with its sides bent alternately in and out in

124

58. Mosque al Hakem, Cordova, 965. Dome of one of the Mih'rabs. *First use of the binding arch as a constructional device.*

a complicated manner which serves to make the transition to the upper elements. The intention of Guarini was to satisfy by architectonic means the baroque feeling for mystery and infinity. The baroque period felt strongly attracted to constructions which seemed to defy the force of gravity. All the arts — including even the use of colored lights — were exploited to produce this exciting impression. In Rome there was a chapel where the lantern in the dome was borne aloft on the shoulders of sculptured angels. In San Lorenzo, Guarini uses purely architectonic means to put gravity at defiance. He proceeds conventionally until the ring of the cupola is reached; there he plunges at once into the realm of fantasy. Intersecting binding arches are carried from one point to another on the ring like a network woven by some giant spider. They cross each other to form a kind of filigree-work star with an octagon-shaped opening in its center. In this way the impression is produced that the lantern above the arches is magically suspended in mid-air. In reality it rests on the octagon formed by their intersection (*fig.* **56**).

The impression of unlimited space has been achieved not through the employment of perspective illusions or of a painted sky but through exclusively architectural means. The dazzling light that penetrates the star-shaped filigree has the effect of dematerializing its surroundings. This is one of the rare cases where a feeling of infiniteness is produced by architectonic means alone.

Relation to tenth-century works: the mosque at Cordova

It is safe to assume that the dome of San Lorenzo would never have been conceived had Guarini not seen the domes of the Mih'rab — the praying niche — of the mosque Al Hakem in Cordova (*fig.* **58**). These domes were constructed toward the end of the tenth century — to be exact, in 965. The same method of construction was employed in the domes that Guarini used in San Lorenzo. They, too, were built on a square base, with a system of binding arches intersecting overhead to form an eight-pointed star, on which the suspended lantern rests.

The cupolas of the praying niches in the mosque at Cordova are the earliest known specimens in which the binding arch is given a constructional function. It has even been asserted by some French historians that it was this Moorish invention which suggested to Gothic builders of a century and a half later the possibility of replacing the solid vault by a framework of ribs in stone. But the dimensions of these Moorish domes are humble in comparison with Guarini's daring masterpiece. As far as I could ascertain, the binding arches of San Lorenzo are composed of long, massive stone beams, a dangerous and laborious method. In fact, the architect of San Lorenzo asked from construction almost more than it was prepared, at that date, to give. No later architect dared to follow the precedent Guarini set in this church. With San Lorenzo the technical possibilities of the age were exhausted, just at the moment when the vision of further architectural advances was beginning to dawn. We find ourselves quite spontaneously driven to think how easy the solution of such a problem would be with the means available to modern construction. But we must reject such reflections as absolutely unhistorical. The dome of San Lorenzo presents the case of an architectural vision that goes to the very end of constructional resources. The situation today is just the reverse. There are available to us constructional possibilities which we have not been able to exploit to anything like their full extent.

South Germany: Vierzehnheiligen

Of the northern countries, only South Germany and Austria, including Bohemia, adopted the complicated space conceptions of Borromini and Guarini. Germany has always been known architecturally as the land of late phases — of late Gothic, late Renaissance, late baroque. In southern Germany especially, the best examples of these periods are to be found.

Belated development in Germany

The late baroque of South Germany in the eighteenth century [8] does not possess the constituent force which Borromini's work spread far beyond his own time. It arose in a country cut up into small principalities, many of them ecclesiastical. It marks the close of a development reaching back to roots in Italy and France, to which it gave a new and exciting expression. It flowered throughout the Catholic lands of South Germany — Franconia, Baden, Bavaria — Austria, Bohemia, and parts of Switzerland. Its largest outgrowth is to be found in Franconia and Bavaria, and also its ripest solutions. These are like full-grown fruits just before they drop from the tree, with all the charm and flavor of a perfect maturity, that final ripening before the beginning of decay. They fulfilled, all unconsciously, their task of closing the period. Instinct with the joy of life, finding expression therefore in terms of spatial imagination, utilizing at the same time the whole orchestra of the arts, they were ultimate and crowning masterpieces.

---

[8] The rediscovery of the German baroque may be credited to Cornelius Gurlitt, whose *Geschichte des Barockstils und des Rokoko in Deutschland* (Stuttgart, 1889), prepared the way for an understanding of this period. The small booklet by Wilhelm Pinder, *Deutscher Barock* (Leipzig, 1911), with excellent introduction and choice of illustrative materials, helped much to popularize it on a large scale (more than 100,000 copies were sold). That the baroque is not characterized simply by superficial ornament but has its own spatial and artistic qualities was recognized in England only in the thirties.

59. BALTHASAR NEUMANN. Vierzehnheiligen (Church of the Fourteen Saints), 1743–72. Façade. *Influence of secular architecture visible in the rows of windows; continuation of Borromini's undulating wall.*

In the fifteenth and sixteenth centuries Franconia had already shown its artistic power by producing such figures as Albrecht Dürer and Veit Stoss. At that time the social background was one of free cities and free citizens, as in Nuremberg. In the eighteenth century the background was an ecclesiastical one, the Counts of Schönborn, who at this time were for the most

60. BALTHASAR NEUMANN. Vierzehnheiligen. *Detail of the undulating wall of the façade.*

61. BALTHASAR NEUMANN. Vierzehnheiligen. Horizontal section. *The usual dome has been done away with. Its place is taken by the space in which the four variously shaped (spherical and ellipsoidal) vaultings meet: those of the nave, the choir, and the two short transepts.*

129

62. BALTHASAR NEUMANN. Vierzehnheiligen. Interior. *The altar is pushed forward into the nave of the church. Light pours in from all sides through great windows of clear glass.*

part the ruling bishops or archbishops of the ecclesiastical principalities of Mainz, Speyer, Bamberg, and Würzburg, being throughout the century the influence under which churches, cloisters, and residences were built.

We shall take from this late period the late work of a late master — Balthazar Neumann (1687–1753) and his Pilgrim's Church of the Fourteen Saints, known as the Vierzehnheiligen.[9] Neumann was in the service of the Schönborns, for whom he built the castle of Würzburg, with the great spatial refinement of its interior evident in every detail from the wide Italian staircase to the concentrated chapel like a jewel transmuted

---

[9] Richard Teufel, *Die Wallfahrtskirche Vierzehnheiligen* (Berlin, 1936); Hans Eckstein, *Vierzehnheiligen* (Leipzig, 1939).

130

63. BALTHASAR NEUMANN. Vierzehnheiligen. *Warped-plane binding arches.*

into space. He grew up in the German part of Bohemia, where he became familiar with the Italian baroque churches. He also traveled in France, and we know that he had in his library Guarini's *Architettura civile* (first edition, Turin, 1686; second edition, 1737), which contained Guarini's principal buildings. In addition, Guarini's ideas had in part made their way northward through the work of German-Italian architects such as Lucas von Hildebrandt, who built the Belvedere in Vienna.

The Church of the Vierzehnheiligen, standing high on a mountain top overlooking the broad valley of the river Main, is the quintessence of Neumann's architectural experience (*figs.* **59–61**). Construction began at the very end of baroque ecclesiastical architecture, in 1743, and was not completed until 1772, long after Neumann's death. The church has a comparatively

Influence of palace architecture

simple exterior in the shape of a cruciform basilica and a slender façade with two towers of the sort that are so familiar in northern countries, though not in Italy. An Italian visitor would likewise be astonished to find this front pierced by many large windows in story formation, testimony to the influence upon church design of the northern châteaux, both French and German. Here, in other words, is an instance of a secular influence upon an ecclesiastical building. The statues in niches are almost wholly eliminated in this limestone front, and instead large windows are cut through the undulating wall.

Interior The *interior* (*fig.* **62**), however, follows more closely the late Italian baroque. It does not continue the complicated constructional treatment of Guarini's domes, nor has it Borromini's plastic intensity. All is lighter and without tragic notes. Yet there is also the use of intersecting and interpenetrating spaces. The ground plan (*fig.* **61**) is worked out on a basis of intersecting circles and ovals, curiously shifted from their usual positions. In a church of this cruciform type, the central crossing is customarily covered by the dome. Here, however, the dome, the most important part of the church, has been completely done away with. Its place is taken by the space in which four variously shaped (spherical and ellipsoidal) vaultings meet: the nave, the choir, and the two short transepts. The interpenetration of the complicated volumes of these vaults requires the use of binding arches formed in warped planes. Their unusual curves reveal the systematic way in which the different spaces are blended into one another. No single particle of space remains separable from the others. The necessity of passing on from each subdivision to the other parts of the scheme that includes it produces the final impression that the whole interior is in motion. The warped-plane binding arches (*fig.* **63**) that establish these relations consist of curves of the third degree — that is, of curves developed in three dimensions, not capable of being embraced in a flat surface, as circles are. It is interesting to note that in this period such three-dimensional curves could be calculated by the aid of the integral calculus.

In the late baroque churches of Italy, the cupola was often left in semidarkness, but here, in this white Church of the

Fourteen Saints, light is permitted to pour in from all directions. Certainly in no earlier period had light been allowed to flow into an ecclesiastical building in such dazzling effulgence. Plain glass, without any decoration, was used for the large windows, so that they might carry out their function — the letting in of light — entirely without hindrance.

The principal force at work in this church is not preëminently architecture — as in the constructions of Borromini and Guarini — but rather a magnificent balance between architecture, sculpture, and painting. In the atmosphere in which Neumann worked, the different arts had grown up in perfect association. Indeed, the secret of this late eighteenth century was the production of a most effective unification of all the arts. The architects of the eighteenth century knew all the hidden secrets of architectural effect. Despite their letting in of light as never before, because of this perfect unity of the arts they kept the mystic power to impress. They could use natural lighting as brilliantly as the most inspired theatrical producer today uses footlights and limelight.

It should perhaps be remembered that these magnificent churches were created just at the time when the Protestant workmen of Birmingham and Manchester were inventing their first cotton-spinning machine.

THE ORGANIZATION OF OUTER SPACE

The Residential Group and Nature

The work of the baroque architects was both continued and supplemented in France during the late seventeenth century. French contributions appear especially in two fields: in the development of more highly refined types of human residence, and in the organization of outer space.

The role of France

The decisive influence upon developments in France, which had just become the leading European country, was the complete supremacy of a secular government. Absolutism was in

Influence of secular absolutism

133

the saddle, and, as a corollary, the personal life of the monarch had become the center of all social life.

The feminine influence

But in addition a new power was making itself felt, a power of the greatest importance and one which did not affect the Roman baroque: the feminine influence. The growing demand for a better organization of human residences, for greater comfort, *commodité*, was intensified by the novel importance of women in French society. These two factors, of course, worked together. In 1665, for example, Louis XIV asked the Pope to permit Lorenzo Bernini, his greatest architect, to come to Paris and draw up a plan for the new Louvre. Bernini's design was rejected — with all possible politeness, of course, but not because it was too theatrical, as the usual explanation has it. An eighteenth-century architect gives us the real reason: "Bernini ne pouvait se prêter à entrer dans tous les details de ces distributions, de ces commodités qui rendent le service d'un palais commode." In other words, Bernini failed to show a grasp of the complicated problems set by a palace building where women played an important role; he quite lost sight of the ladies. The part that women play in the development of French architecture from this period onward is a very important one.

Court ceremonies

The elaborate routine of court ceremonies is another major conditioning circumstance. These changes in French social life dictated a more complicated arrangement of rooms in great houses. A new delicacy and refinement appears in their treatment. At the same time changes are made in the designs of furniture, especially as concerns such pieces as are intended for sitting and lying: these become better accommodated to women, and to love-making.

Refinements in residences of the nobility

At this period in France the general type of dwelling was being transformed; the château was replacing the villa of Italian style. The town mansions of the nobility and of high state officials, buildings like the Hôtel Lambert which Louis Le Vau built at Paris in 1650, showed a highly developed dwelling culture that had arisen out of the special requirements of French life. But very soon the growth of this culture was to be impeded. The importance of the great nobles, the wealthy financiers, and the chief state functionaries alike was eclipsed by the demands of an absolute king.

134

In keeping with this change, the royal château — placed outside the city — became both the social and the architectural center. It dominated the town behind it and the natural terrain that spread out before it. The idea of locating the château midway between town and country had originated in Italy considerably earlier. Michelangelo, for example, when building the Palazzo Farnese in Rome, had conceived the fantastic notion of throwing a bridge across the Tiber as a means of prolonging the axis of the palace far beyond the other side of the river.

It was not the French king, however, but Fouquet, the greatest financier of his time, who was the first to carry this open style of château construction to its logical conclusion, in the château of Vaux-le-Vicomte. This château was built by the architect Louis Le Vau just past the middle of the seventeenth century, 1655–61 (*fig.* **64**). It was comparatively modest in size, but it faced an immense park, the work of André Le Nôtre. The château is built on the principle of the French pavilion. The steep roofs with their tall chimneys are reminiscent of Gothic tower-caps; they are in abrupt contrast with the cupola and its lantern of the middle pavilion. We can well imagine the kind of impression this mixture of building styles must have made on Lorenzo Bernini, who was in Paris at the time the château was erected. Nevertheless, Vaux-le-Vicomte was the first instance of a dwelling designed in close unity with nature, with a park on a grand scale. It embodied this great experiment years before it was adopted, and carried much further, at Versailles. But, as is well known, Fouquet paid a heavy price for his daring. His château and park excited the envy of the King, who would not tolerate rivalry in any direction. Louis XIV accordingly commanded the architect Le Vau and the park designer Le Nôtre to build the palace at Versailles, in all its vaunting splendor — and he put Fouquet in prison for the rest of his life. The incident is not an isolated fact; it represents one stage on the way to absolute rule. The power and prestige of great nobles and the great financiers had to be broken to make Louis an absolute monarch.

64. LOUIS LE VAU. Château Vaux-le-Vicomte, 1655–61.

65. LOUIS LE VAU and JULES HARDOUIN–MANSARD. Versailles. *The château, the garden, and the boulevard.*

136

The château of Versailles symbolizes the supplanting of the ecclesiastical authority of a pope by the secular absolutism of a king. It took Louis XIV nearly half a century (1661–1708) to erect Versailles in all its magnificence. He began the work when he was twenty-two, firmly rejecting the suggestions of his minister Colbert, who advised him to complete the residence of his ancestors, the Louvre in Paris. Of another generation than Colbert, Louis cared neither for the old palace nor for his capital city of Paris. Bernini, then nearly seventy years old, had been brought all the way from Rome to Paris and had been presented by Colbert with a complete list of the requirements for a royal residence. But all this was quite in vain; Louis XIV had other ideas.

Versailles

In particular, the notion of mastering nature, *forcer la nature,* fascinated the King. Louis XIV detested the narrow streets of Paris. A dislike of large cities was, indeed, one of the characteristics of baroque absolutism everywhere. Even when new towns were founded in connection with the new palaces, they failed to prosper. This was to prove true in the case of Versailles, as well as in those of Mannheim and Karlsruhe. But, in any event, Versailles and the idea of creating a new mode of life that would be unrestricted by the confines of a city preoccupied Louis intensely for more than thirty years — this in spite of the fact that it was an unprecedented thing for a ruling monarch to desert and neglect the capital of his country.

Absolutism's dislike of large cities: *forcer la nature*

The Versailles of Louis XIII's day had been a mere hunting-seat, built on a low hill which was surrounded by woods. It was at first merely enlarged. But these alterations — carried through by the architect of Vaux-le-Vicomte, Louis Le Vau — did not suffice; larger dimensions were necessary. During the years 1668–74 a new conception took shape, a conception gigantic in scale (*fig.* **65**). The great U-shaped, central block faces the park. Jules Hardouin-Mansard elongated the front of the palace by building a long wing at right angles to each end of the U. The left wing (1679–82) was built for the royal princes; the right wing (begun in 1684) was built as an office building for the various French ministries. (It was in 1683, when he decided to house the administration of France in his

The hunting-seat of Louis XIII the center of France, 1668–74

137

own palace, that Louis XIV proclaimed Versailles as his official residence. The proclamation almost caused a revolt in Paris.)

The two long wings combined with the ∪ of the central block resulted in an open style of construction that had been hitherto unknown. The whole structure, complex and enormous, served three functions: it housed the King, the royal family, and the ministries of France. Building activity on these immense residential quarters was carried on at its greatest intensity in the years from 1668 to 1684; thirty thousand men were employed on the work. The interval in question corresponds exactly to the rise of the absolute monarchy. At the same time, Roman baroque architecture underwent the last phase of its development in the work of Borromini and Guarini.

Juxtaposition with nature

What is the significance of Versailles? What is the important constituent fact it embodies? It is the close contact it effects with nature. An immense complex of buildings, more than two thousand feet long, has been directly confronted with nature; the grounds are a real part of the structure itself, and form with it a whole of great power and grandeur.

The constituent facts in Versailles

Lorenzo Bernini had not been permitted to carry out his project for the Louvre; nevertheless, when Louis XIV began the new enlargement of Versailles in 1668, Roman grandeur, *grandezza*, scored a success. Straight lines and flat roofs replaced the crabbed medieval silhouette. In the simplicity of a long straight line, used without deviation, there lies a tremendous courage and self-assertiveness. The whole edifice is the architectural response to a new sociological demand: the demand for a new setting for the personal, the ceremonial, and the governmental life of an absolute king. The major functions combined under its one roof have already been noted. Less important ones were likewise provided for; the salons, for example, for all their mythological names, were actually intended for gambling, dancing, and musical entertainments.

The form for a new mode of living

But the interesting thing is still the manner in which great complex buildings for social, residential, and administrative purposes have been welded together and closely juxtaposed with nature (*fig.* **67**). Versailles is important not because of

66. Versailles. Great court, stables, and highway to Paris. *Engraving by Perelle.*

67. Versailles. The gardens, the "Tapis verts," the Grand Canal, and the terraces. *Engraving by Perelle.*

its royal splendor but because it clearly reveals the solution to a problem of living. Nature had been mastered before by man's will, but never before had so large a community been housed under one roof, in open country, away from any big town.

The highway as an architectonic means

Versailles has a highway linking it with Paris (*fig.* **66**). It starts from between two buildings overlooked by the great court; it ends in Paris in the Champs-Élysées and the Louvre. The beautiful curving constructions which give its commencement at Versailles such power and dignity are — almost incredibly — the royal stables. The accentuation of the highway by means of these stables emphasizes the approach to the château. The highway, in other words, has been incorporated into an architectonic expression, is an essential part of it.

The plan of the gardens anticipates later town planning

The baroque will to master the illimitable is best shown by the other side of the palace. The ground slowly declines from the terrace with its ornamental pools. The eye is led by the long lawns — the *tapis verts* — to the Grand Canal, cruciform in shape, with a length of one mile (*fig.* **67**). In the time of Louis XIV it was graced by gondolas and other luxury craft. Beyond the Grand Canal, the view fades into an endless countryside. The woods and shrubbery of the enormous park — its area is one-fourth the area of all Paris — spread out to the right and to the left. Provision was made here for every sort of leisure activity, for sports, for hunting, for festivals, for lovemaking. The woods are dotted with round clearings from which paths emerge like the rays of a searchlight. These circular areas with their radiating pathways or roads will find a place in eighteenth-century town planning.

Louis XIV as "the open-air king"

The extensive and carefully ordered natural setting for the château of Versailles was the background not only of these great new buildings but of the new kind of living that had been developed there. The old myth that Versailles was a kind of vast and sumptuous mausoleum in which Louis XIV was confined like a royal mummy has been destroyed by history. Louis Bertrand, one of his biographers, presents a picture which contradicts the old, familiar, and inaccurate one. He calls Louis "the open-air king" and tells us of those hunts on which he went alone, twice every week, into the forests of

140

Versailles, making hunting his excuse for solitude. From the windows of his bedchamber in the palace he had an unbroken vista of forests and green meadows — a view which, of course, is spoiled today. The constituent facts that are presented by Versailles, the trends that were to be continued in later periods, were not bound up in its royal splendor. They lie in the new ways of living for which it provided a form. An enormous structure, almost a small town in itself, had — together with the life that went on within it — been brought into close contact with nature.

Single Squares

At the time when baroque architecture flourished in Rome, cities all over the world were crowded and lacked space within the walls that surrounded them. The first large open space within a city — in contrast to the enclosed Renaissance square — was the Piazza Obliqua (the "Oval Place") of St. Peter's in Rome (*fig.* **68**). It was built just after the middle of the seventeenth century. Its graduated areas are embraced within the fourfold colonnades of St. Peter's as though by a giant pair of pincers, and linked by them with the portico. Three elements are combined here: the oval plaza, the rectangular plaza, and the body of the church with the dome that crowns it. Bernini had intended to close the opening of the Piazza Obliqua with another colonnade, leaving two narrow entrances. The plan was never executed, however.

Bernini: the Piazza Obliqua, Rome

André Le Nôtre had designed Vaux-le-Vicomte five years before the appearance of Bernini's colonnades for St. Peter's. The work of both men sprang from an urge to dominate wide spaces that manifested itself all over Europe at this time. But Bernini's colonnade is unique in the precision of its modeling, which is calculated to the last inch. The exactitude involved can be fully appreciated only during those church festivals when the Oval Place is filled by the crowds awaiting the papal benediction. The plaza slopes gently downward to the obelisk in its center; it then rises, in slightly inclined terraces and long steps, to the enormous portico. Bernini's architectural mastery

141

68. LORENZO BERNINI. Piazza Obliqua, St. Peter's, Rome. *Lithograph, 1870. Crowds awaiting the papal benediction.*

is revealed when the onlooker, awaiting the blessing, discovers that he can overlook all the great congregation, in addition to seeing everything that takes place on the terraces immediately in front of the church.

Paris under Louis XIV: late start in building squares

What did the north have to offer in comparison with work like this? Paris had the *grands boulevards* with which Vauban, the great engineer of Louis XIV, replaced the city walls when he tore them down. Grass-covered earthworks, more suited to "modern" defensive needs, were thrown up farther outside the city. The first great square of Paris was the Renaissance Place des Vosges (1612). Louis XIV did not build his first square until thirty years after Bernini's colonnades of St. Peter's, and twenty-five years after the beginning of his reign. This was the Place des Victoires (1685–87). It had the form of a circle flattened on one side, and was quite modest in its dimensions. But it was the first circular *place* in Paris intended as a meeting point for streets.

142

The first really large public square built in the Paris of this period was the Place Vendôme, constructed at the beginning of the eighteenth century. It is worthy of note that the Place Vendôme was not built until after the completion of Versailles. The architect of Versailles, Jules Hardouin-Mansard, now had time for work on the important *places* in Paris itself. His first plan in 1699 provided for a simple rectangle; later its corners were cut off, and the new sides that were thus developed were bent outward. Seventy years earlier, Borromini had used the same treatment in the small cloister-court of San Carlo alle Quattro Fontane. But the most significant development in Paris, one which could not be valued truly at the time, was the highroad that was carried directly across the countryside to connect the axis of the château of Versailles with the axis of the Château du Louvre. To this day, the Champs-Élysées follow exactly the plan originally laid down by Louis XIV and continue to provide the only sufficiently broad exit from Paris.

The eighteenth century is a century remarkable for the laying-out of squares. Just as the name of Louis XIV is associated with the building of palaces and gardens, so the name of Louis XV, who succeeded him, is linked with the construction of new town squares and public places. The plan of Paris drawn by Patte in 1748 (*fig.* **69**), which shows all the *places* of the city, both those already in existence and those merely projected, shows at a glance the great amount of such construction under Louis XV. Probably the best-known single example is the Place de la Concorde, designed by Jacques-Ange Gabriel and constructed in 1763. We shall soon have occasion to discuss its significance.

Series of Interrelated Squares

In many towns series of squares or plazas were laid out, not as a mere succession of mutually independent units but in such a way that all together they constituted a rhythmical progression. A compelling and thoroughly self-conscious desire for unity governed their location and the manner in which streets

69. PATTE. Plan of Paris, 1748, with projected and executed squares. *This plan clearly demonstrates the mid-eighteenth century endeavor to organize open spaces — squares — of every shape in all possible locations. Very few of them were ever executed.*

were made to radiate from them. Often whole towns were made to conform to a predetermined scheme of this sort. Karlsruhe, Germany, which was founded in 1715, is one instance. When whole towns were treated in this fashion as architectural units, already existing buildings frequently had additions made to them so that they would fit harmoniously into the system of relations the new scheme established.

The three *places* of Nancy

Among all such series of squares, the most pleasing is that formed by the three *places* of Nancy, the capital of Lorraine. Nancy was at one time the residence of Louis XV's father-in-law, the exiled king of Poland, Stanislas Leszinski. Its three *places* (*fig.* **71**) were built by Héré de Corny between 1752 and 1755, just one century later than Bernini's colonnades. The first *place* (Place Stanislas) — with the Hôtel de Ville (*fig.* **70**), which antedates it — is connected through a triumphal arch with the oblong Place Carrière. The charming rococo wrought-iron work of Lamour forms a transparent screen between the

144

70. HÉRÉ DE CORNY.
Three interrelated squares at
Nancy, Place Stanislas, 1752–55.
View.

71. HÉRÉ DE CORNY.
Three interrelated squares at
Nancy. *Plan. New elements
were used in these squares to bring
already existing features into a
new, inspiring, and vital spatial
unity.*

145

72. HÉRÉ DE CORNY. Palais du Gouvernement with oval colonnades, Nancy.

two. Avenues of trees and symmetrical rows of houses lead on to the third of these squares, the Place Royale. The Palace of Government which faces the Place Royale is another building that was already in existence when the plan for these *places* was being made. The building was made to fit into the whole new composition by the addition of an elegant colonnade to the square. This colonnade around the *place* repeated the motif already present in the arches of the Palace of Government (*fig.* **72**).

Synthesis of separate elements

An immense fund of architectural knowledge is revealed in each one of these squares. It appears equally in the way the heights and proportions of the buildings are regulated and in the handling of the materials used. Walls, transparent iron-work, fountains, trees, colonnades — all these materials are used with instinctive correctness. It is in this that we find the secret of the architecture of the middle eighteenth century: each element is coördinated with all the others; isolated phenomena are synthesized to form the most effective whole.

At the same time that the three squares at Nancy were being constructed, a small town existed in England which was the product of an equal wealth of architectural knowledge, although it had grown up to meet quite different purposes — Bath. In eighteenth-century England, to "take the waters" at Bath's hot springs was a fixed part of social routine; Bath was "the rallying place of good company and social intercourse." There was no church or castle to which the town had to conform. Bath was built for the entertainment of an anonymous and mixed society. It attracted the aristocracy, artists, men of letters, and — as Oliver Goldsmith relates — types still more various: "Clerks and factors from the East-Indies, loaded with the spoils of plundered provinces, planters, negrodrivers from our American Plantations, agents who have fattened in two successive wars, brokers and jobbers of every kind, *men of low birth.*" This sketch might have been written in the late nineteenth century, rather than in the eighteenth.

Bath: new development of the health resort

73. JOHN WOOD THE YOUNGER. The Circus, 1764, and the Royal Crescent, 1769, Bath. *Air view.*

74. JACQUES–ANGE GABRIEL. Place Louis XV — Place de la Concorde, Paris, 1763. *Here nature and an open square are juxtaposed, the same principle as that involved in the Royal Crescent, Bath.*

The Circus and the Royal Crescent

Bath was built for the new bourgeois society by a man who was "at once architect, builder, speculator and an artist" — John Wood. His son and successor, John Wood the younger, completed the Circus in 1764, and in 1769 built the famous Royal Crescent, in which thirty houses are joined together in the shape of an open ellipse (*fig.* **73**).

The Royal Crescent is comparable, in many respects, to Jacques-Ange Gabriel's Place Louis XV (Place de la Concorde), completed six years earlier (*fig.* **74**). The latter remains, despite all changes, the most beautiful of Parisian *places*. It owes its charm to the fact that its single boundary wall permits a country view in the midst of a city: the gardens of the Tuileries are to the left, the Champs-Élysées lie on the right, and the Seine is directly in front. Here is the opinion of a contemporary, the Abbé Laugier, who was already capable of discerning the intention behind this highly developed piece of town planning: "Entourée de jardins et de bosquets, elle ne presente que l'image d'une esplanade embellie au milieu d'une campagne riante. . . ." Quite simply, this *place* is made an integral part of the outlying landscape.

75. JOHN WOOD THE YOUNGER. The Royal Crescent, Bath, 1769. *The broad lawn in front of the Royal Crescent slopes down toward the floor of a valley.*

The single boundary wall of the Place de la Concorde is left open in the center. In this manner the street — the Rue Royale — which leads from this opening (to terminate in a church built at a later date) becomes the axis of the *place* itself.

The Royal Crescent at Bath (*fig.* 75) has no axis and no central opening leading out to a church or a château. Nothing blocks the view from it; there is no building, whether representative of secular or ecclesiastical authority, to which it stands in a servile or dependent relationship. There is only a broad lawn which slopes gently toward the town, and the countryside beyond lies at its front. A completely open view has been attained through a concentration of many individual lodgings. Thirty small standardized houses have been fused into a single unit to produce the Crescent, and its monumental impressiveness derives from the fact that these standardized units are added together without any separations. Not until our own time do we encounter similar undertakings. For example, Gropius' 1937 scheme for eight-story apartment houses to be erected at St. Leonard's Hill — a park near Windsor — tends in the same direction. The wide expanse of the grounds, with their trees and meadows, is retained unbroken by concentrat-

The Royal Crescent: a self-sufficient residential complex

149

ing individual apartments into three eight-story buildings. In this way there is an open view for each tenant. Contrasted with such schemes as the Royal Crescent and that of Gropius, the health and holiday resorts of the nineteenth century, with their rambling hotels and private houses, present the chaotic appearance of a mining camp.

Eighteenth-century Bath was built on speculation; the elder John Wood began building there in 1727. The Place Vendôme in Paris (1701) likewise was the work of speculators for the major part, as were the London squares and crescents with their high architectural standards. Many of the best English architects in the eighteenth century and at the beginning of the nineteenth — men like the Adams, John Nash, Soane, and others — were at one and the same time builders, artists, and speculators. For all that, this architecture manifests discipline and the working of a vigorous tradition. There is only a fragmentary knowledge of the part speculation has played in the development of architecture. And yet the extent of that influence would be worth knowing, not merely for architectural reasons but also for the sake of discovering both the initiative and the destructive roles of the speculator.

Nancy and Bath were not the only towns, nor Paris the only great city, in which town planning attained such astonishing proficiency. The same expertness was displayed throughout eighteenth-century Europe. Thus the basic principle common to the Place de la Concorde and the English crescents and terraces — the blending together of residences with their natural surroundings — likewise governed Valadier's adaptation of the Piazza del Popolo in Rome. Giuseppe Valadier (1762–1839) was, according to the *Enciclopedia italiana*, "the first figure in modern Italian architecture who carried out town planning, together with the preservation of green spaces, as a science." Valadier's choice of forms certainly makes him an architect of the classical revival, but the scheme for this great square, with regard to the space conception on which it rests, follows the late baroque tradition in town planning.

Some knowledge of the condition of the Piazza before Valadier began his alterations is necessary if his work is to be appreciated. The test of the town planner is his ability to instill

76. Piazza del Popolo, Rome. *Engraving by Tempesta, 1593. The Porta del Popolo, the Renaissance church of Santa Maria del Popolo, the obelisk, and the gardens of the Pincio.*

77. Piazza del Popolo, Rome. *View toward the twin churches of Rainaldi.*

order into the diversified complex that confronts him at the start.

Until the age of railroads, the Piazza del Popolo (*fig.* **76**) was the main entrance to Rome for all visitors coming from the north. It was here that the stranger received his first impressions of the papal city. He entered the square through the

The Piazza del Popolo in the seventeenth and eighteenth centuries

151

Porta del Popolo, which had been restored and redecorated during the seventeenth century on the occasion of the visit of Queen Christina of Sweden to Rome. Facing him on the far side of the *piazza* there appeared — as the first symbols of Rome's special importance — Carlo Rainaldi's twin churches of 1662 (*fig.* **77**). With their identical cupolas and porticos, they were like ecclesiastical sentries guarding the three main arteries of the city, which since antiquity have radiated from this spot. Isolated in the center of the *piazza* stood the Egyptian obelisk which had been placed there at the end of the sixteenth century. On the left there was only the simple Renaissance façade of Santa Maria del Popolo, the church attached to the Augustinian monastery where Martin Luther once stayed. The gardens of the monastery rose to the heights of the Pincio. On both sides of the square there was the same combination of high walls and insignificant buildings. These, together with the plain drinking troughs for animals that were placed in it, gave the whole *piazza* the air of being a suburb. This was the situation that Valadier faced in 1794 when his first scheme for the *piazza* was prepared and published. The final scheme, however, was actually carried out between 1816 and 1820, the years when building activity in the squares of Bloomsbury was at its height [10] (*fig.* **78**).

Valadier's scheme (executed 1816–20) Valadier touched none of the monumental buildings in or around the square; he tore down, however, all walls and buildings that had no importance. He transformed the greater part of the gardens of the Augustinian monastery into a public park, giving access to the Pincio. Through this park he led a winding ramp which provided for the passage of vehicular traffic between the *piazza* and the Pincio. Upon the heights of the Pincio itself, Valadier built a terrace, giving it a large substructure whose proportions were related to his other buildings lower down (*fig.* **80**). Thus, despite its being on a much higher level, it fits within and makes a unity of his whole spatial composition. It is possible to see from figures **79** and **80** how successful Valadier was in bringing together into a new relationship buildings of quite different styles and periods.

[10] An excellent study of the Piazza del Popolo, by Rowland Pierce and Thomas Ashby, is contained in *Town Planning Review*, vol. XI, December 1924.

78. GIUSEPPE VALADIER. Scheme of the Piazza del Popolo, Rome, 1816. *This is the final scheme followed in the actual rebuilding.*

79. Piazza del Popolo, Rome. Section through the different levels and ramps. *Drawing by Edward W. Armstrong, 1924.*

In addition to these works, Valadier erected a few residential units bordering the *piazza* and built two elegant hemicycles which served — as they still do — to guide traffic. Beyond this, he provided very carefully for the introduction of landscaped areas into the whole design. This careful infiltration of greenery is characteristic of all such work at this time. He further planned to leave the west side of the square permanently unenclosed and free of buildings so that the

Innovations by Valadier: infiltration of greenery, regulation of traffic, relation of different levels

153

80. Piazza del Popolo, Rome. *View from the Pincio terrace, showing the different horizontal levels involved and their relations to the vertical planes in the Piazza. Valadier here touches upon a fundamental conception of our time: the relation between horizontal and vertical planes as a basis for aesthetic response.*

view might lead out upon a wide green area as it does in the Place de la Concorde and in the Royal Crescent at Bath. Today this area is occupied by broad avenues and tall houses.

The Piazza del Popolo has remained to this day one of the most "modern" in appearance of all the great squares. To a certain extent this is due to the thoroughgoing fusion of buildings and park. Its air of modernity is owing much more, however, to the way in which different levels are brought within the same composition. The series of *places* built at Nancy in the middle of the eighteenth century had exploited the relations that can be made to hold among the vertical surfaces of buildings of different heights. In the Piazza del Popolo, Valadier embodies a hovering sensation in the total effect produced by his design

154

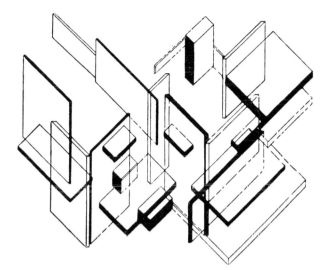

81. THEO VAN DOESBURG. Relation of horizontal and vertical planes, c. 1920.

by bringing into relation with each other two horizontal areas of different levels: the terrace on the Pincio, and the *piazza* proper. A proportion in three dimensions — not merely in two, as at Nancy — is developed.

Interrelated horizontal and vertical surfaces

We have seen how Borromini, in striving to lead the movement of a design through the space of the interior into outer space, anticipated a concern of modern architecture. Valadier's *piazza* touches upon another fundamental conception of our time: the relation between horizontal and vertical surfaces as a basis for aesthetic responses of a special sort. That this is one of the constituent facts in modern architecture, one of the tendencies determining its character, cannot be doubted. A drawing made about 1922 by the Dutch painter, Theo van Doesburg, shows a conscious recognition of the presence of this tendency (*fig.* **81**). Doesburg, one of the most stimulating of the influences upon present-day architecture, made this drawing solely to demonstrate the fact that interrelations between planes are basic means of expression in architecture. The drawing shows the mutual relationships between hovering vertical and horizontal plane surfaces.

To avoid misunderstanding, it may be worth repeating that neither Borromini nor Valadier worked with space con-

155

ceptions identical with those of today. The exact ways in which they differ will be discussed later. But the historian always finds it both interesting and important to note early beginnings of movements that only much later come to a full realization.

82. FRANCESCO BORROMINI. Undulating wall of San Carlo alle Quattro Fontane, 1662–67. *This late baroque invention, the undulating wall, reappears in English town planning toward the end of the eighteenth century.*

Previous to the turbulent and overwhelming onset of industrialization, a high standard existed for housing on both simple and luxurious scales. The principles of town planning were a matter of common knowledge to everyone connected with architecture. When a period succeeds in developing its natural culture, and when this culture is supported by a long tradition, works of the highest quality can be produced by anonymous

156

artists as well as by distinguished ones. For example, it happens that we do know the name of the architect who built the Lansdowne Crescent at Bath toward the beginning of the nineteenth century, but it is a name of no importance for history.

83.   Lansdowne Crescent, Bath, 1794. *Its serpentine windings follow the contours of the site.*

Lansdowne Crescent lies high above the town of Bath (*fig.* **83**). Its three serpent-like windings give it an organic aspect which is strengthened by the way in which they follow the accidental rise and fall of ground to catch as much light and sun as possible. This crescent embodies two of the constituent facts of the preceding centuries. Borromini's use of undulating walls (*fig.* **82**) to bring an unexpected movement and flexibility into

The constituent facts in Lansdowne Crescent, Bath (1794)

157

the narrow Roman streets reappears in the serpentine curves
of its outline.   Its second predecessor was Versailles, the first
great building to be set at the front of an immense park instead
of in the midst of a city's narrow streets.   The manner in
which this great residential group was placed in direct contact
with nature, and the effect of unhampered freedom that resulted, made it the guide for all later experiments.   A similar
freedom characterizes Lansdowne Crescent.   The combination
of movement, surprise, and openness makes its houses exactly

84.   Bath and its crescents.   *Air view.   Near the center are the Royal Crescent and the
Circus; below and to the left is Lansdowne Crescent.*

what every residence should be: the adequate background for
leisure.

During the last few decades, endeavors have been made to
reconquer and to extend the lost knowledge of town planning
which works like Lansdowne Crescent exhibit.   The task is
difficult, what with all the complications attendant upon new
technical developments.   Nevertheless it cannot be evaded.

The sort of solution to this problem that is possible to us today
can be seen — to take only one example — in Le Corbusier's

scheme (1931) for the improvement of Algiers (*fig.* **85**). Le
Corbusier makes use of skyscrapers which have the "organic"
outlines of the crescents at Bath. Like the latter, they are
adjusted to the rise and fall of the ground, although the variations of level are much more extreme than those encountered
in the English town. The individual apartments in these skyscrapers each take up two stories, and are so arranged that
their tenants have considerable control over the interior layout. The plan provides for access to terraces and hanging

Relation to the
present: Le
Corbusier's undu-
lating skyscrapers

85. LE CORBUSIER. Scheme for skyscrapers in Algiers, 1931. *Late baroque space
conceptions came very near to contemporary solutions like this one.*

gardens from every apartment, and all of them would command a magnificent view of the city, the sea, and the sky.

Town planning is always the last department of architecture
to reach full development. It frequently attains maturity
only when a period is nearing its close; this was the case in the
late baroque. Late baroque town planning brings together the
artistic inheritance of four centuries, but it was not at once
applied to residences of all classes. Versailles, the first great
experiment in placing a large residential and administrative

Late eighteenth-
century town
planning;
long tradition

159

block in contiguity with nature, was built for the use of court society and the ministerial staff. Bath marks the point when a middle-class development is given the same treatment; Charles Dickens, for example, lodges Mr. Pickwick in the Royal Crescent at Bath. At the end of the century this type of residential development had become a general mode of expression in architecture, had been taken up by architects whose names never came into prominence. By the early nineteenth century the squares and crescents of London extended the baroque tradition of a juxtaposition of nature and human residences to the housing of still lower classes, and made it no longer the exclusive privilege of wealthy people.

Sudden break
But just at this time there came a sudden break. The kind of town planning that was summed up in contemporary architectural knowledge and concretely exemplified in Bath did not suit the new conditions created by industry. With its demands for dignity and proportion it represented only an obstacle to a time of chaotic expansion, when towns and industrial centers were growing up with uncontrolled speed. Factory towns like Manchester and Birmingham have been scenes of architectural disorder from the day of their inception. From the first onset of the new forces of industry, the knowledge upon which town planning rests was lost with terrifying rapidity.

This disorganization spread from the industrial towns to the old capital cities. A new and deadly influence was at work; the pursuit of wealth through the new increase in the power of production became an end in itself. This led on the one hand to the appearance of slums, and on the other to the building of large and formless mansions. Leisure vanished; no one had the time to live gracefully; life lost its equilibrium. The result was a deep spiritual uncertainty — and the more uncertain of himself man became, the more he tried to bolster up belief in the rightness and stability of things through the creation of buildings in the grand, pseudo-monumental manner.

But there is one branch of architecture where deceit is impossible, and that is town planning. Town planning can spring only from the full life; it is possible only when the different levels of human activity have attained a certain unity and equilibrium.

160

PART **III** **THE EVOLUTION OF NEW POTENTIALITIES**

We have hardly the right to compare our century with the nineteenth so far as boldness and urge toward the unknown are concerned. But what will the final judgment on this period be?

Here the historian comes up against questions of destiny. The final judgment on the nineteenth century cannot be passed today. The main outlines are not settled; transitory and constituent facts are confusingly intermingled.

Some think that we stand at the beginning of a great tradition. Others, seeing the disaster around them, think that we are at the utmost end of an age. The evaluation of the nineteenth century depends upon which of these is right.

If our culture should be destroyed by brutal forces — or even if it should continue to be terrorized by them — then the nineteenth century will have to be judged as having misused men, materials, and human thought, as one of the most wretched of periods. If we prove capable of putting to their right use the potentialities which were handed down to us, then the nineteenth century, in spite of the human disorder it created and in spite of the consequences which are still developing out of it, will grow into new and heroic dimensions.

For these reasons the evaluation of the nineteenth century is inextricably connected with the destiny of our culture — that is to say, with our own destiny.

In treating the nineteenth century we should arrive at unsatisfactory results if we adopted the approach we used for the previous period. A sufficiently comprehensive insight into the period could not be derived from nineteenth-century monumental architecture — which remains, moreover, an incompletely explored subject. The sorting-out of good buildings is still to be done; the history even of transitory developments is not understood. We shall concern ourselves instead with the evolution, during this period, of new architectural potentialities, an evolution that proceeded anonymously and was born out of the depths of the age.

Industrialization as a Fundamental Event

The Industrial Revolution, the abrupt increase in production brought about during the eighteenth century by the introduction of the factory system and the machine, changed the whole appearance of the world, far more so than the social revolution in France. Its effect upon thought and feeling was so profound that even today we cannot estimate how deeply it has penetrated into man's very nature, what great changes it has made there. Certainly there is no one who has escaped these effects, for the Industrial Revolution was not a political upheaval, necessarily limited in its consequences. Rather, it took possession of the whole man and of his whole world. Again, political revolutions subside, after a certain time, into a new social equilibrium, but the equilibrium that went out of human life with the coming of the Industrial Revolution has not been restored to this day. The destruction of man's inner quiet and security has remained the most conspicuous effect of the Industrial Revolution. The individual goes under before the march of production; he is devoured by it.

The heyday of the machine and of unlimited production is heralded in the eighteenth century by the sudden appearance of a widespread urge toward invention. In the England of 1760 this urge had gripped people in all strata of society. Everyone was inventing, from unemployed weavers, small hand workers, farmers' and shepherds' sons like the bridge-builder Telford, to manufacturers like Wedgwood and members of the nobility such as the Duke of Bridgewater (whose tenacious labor was responsible for the creation of the English canal system). Many of these inventors did not even take the trouble to protect their discoveries by taking out patents on them. Many, far from drawing profit from their inventions, were even persecuted because of them. Profit-making and unfair exploitation belong to a later period.

We must, in fact, take care to avoid the delusion that this activity had its source only in material ambitions or in the desire to shine. Its actual source lay much deeper and was one that had for a long time been artificially denied outlet. But at this date the urge to invent could no longer be stemmed. When,

86. Automaton: writing doll, made by Pierre Jaquet-Droz, Neuchâtel, about 1770.

France as in France, it was kept from entering into important regions of practical activity, it was only diverted, not destroyed. It manifested itself then in the creation of odd mechanical contrivances and of marvelous automatons, lifelike mechanical dolls capable of performing the most amazing feats, from walking to playing musical instruments and drawing pictures. Some of these automatons, in the ingenuity and precision of their workmanship, even succeeded in anticipating the principle of the modern automatic telephone — for example, the "writing doll" made at Neuchâtel about 1770 by Pierre Jaquet-Droz. This doll (*fig.* **86**) still exists in a perfectly workable condition.

Invention, carried on in this way by men of all nations and all walks of life, led to the industrialization of almost every human pursuit. But this movement which was to give the nineteenth century its essential character is scarcely reflected at all in its official architecture. We should never be able to perceive the real nature of the period from a study of public buildings, state residences, or great monuments. We must turn instead to an examination of humbler structures. It was in routine and entirely practical construction, and not in the Gothic or classical revivals of the early nineteenth century, that the decisive events occurred, the events that led to the evolution of new potentialities.

But life is complex and irrational. When its evolution is blocked in one direction it seeks another (and often an entirely unexpected) outlet. The development of modern industry is essentially material. Nevertheless, in following its material urge, industry unconsciously creates new powers of expression and new possibilities of experience. These possibilities at first remain bound up in quite matter-of-fact enterprises that do not in any way enter into the intimate and personal lives of men. But, slowly and gradually, the new potentialities become a part of private and individual life. Thus a devious line of development leads from innovations in industrial buildings of all kinds — mines, warehouses, railroads and factories — to the private home and personal life. The history of this metamorphosis is, in large measure, the history of the nineteenth century. Finally these potentialities come to be realized for what they are in themselves, apart from considerations of utility. The architecture of today stands at the end of such a process. Consequently, to understand it, we are obliged to survey in considerable detail developments in regions which seem far removed from aesthetic feeling.

Industry and private life

IRON

Iron, as everyone knows, is far from being a new material; its use dates back to prehistoric times. It was employed only sparingly, however, in the great buildings of classical antiquity. Both the Greeks and the Romans preferred bronze, because of its greater resistance to weather. Neither had the Renaissance much faith in iron as a building material. Thus we find Leon Battista Alberti, the Florentine architect and theorist of the *quattrocento*, recommending materials which are ready for use in their natural state in preference to those which must be prepared by the hand and art of man — *hominum manu et*

Iron before industrialization

165

arte. Even the iron rings which Michelangelo used to hold together the cupola of St. Peter's must be considered merely as fastenings. Even as late as the Victorian period, iron was still regarded as suitable only for fastenings by those men who — like John Ruskin — hated industry. Poor resistance to exposure and lack of classical precedents in its use were not the only reasons why iron played such a small part in construction of every kind. There was also the difficulty that it could not be produced except in relatively small quantities.

Iron as a new material

The moment its production was industrialized, iron took on an entirely new importance. In order to produce the metal industrially, an understanding of its molecular arrangement was requisite. But neither the equipment nor the knowledge essential to the study of the molecular structure of materials was available before the last quarter of the eighteenth century. The history of iron as a substance in wide use is accordingly a part of the history of chemistry, physics, and research into the comparative strengths of materials. Such studies, in making the industrial production of iron possible, converted it into what amounted to a new natural material. And the availability of iron furthered in turn the sciences responsible for it.

Initial setbacks to industrialization in France

England was the birthplace of the whole Industrial Revolution. The desire to advance from manual to industrialized production existed in other countries as well — in France, for example. But the preliminary experiments undertaken in these countries were all singularly unsuccessful, whether they concerned the building of bridges or the industrialization of silk weaving. An instance in point is the failure of the attempt that was made in 1755 to build a cast-iron bridge across the Rhone. It was more than twenty years later that the first cast-iron bridge in England was finally erected over the river Severn. The French effort proved premature and had to be given up simply because it was impossible to cast iron into members of the requisite dimensions.

Conditions in England

Conditions in England were quite different from those prevailing elsewhere. At the end of the seventeenth century the wooded areas of England had been seriously diminished. As a result, attention turned to pit coal as a fuel that might possibly make up for the increasing scarcity of wood and charcoal.

166

Mineral fuel had already supplanted wood to some extent. By the end of the seventeenth century it had become the normal fuel for heating the home, and had even come into pretty general use by tradespeople, bakers, brewers, sugar refiners, cloth weavers, and coppersmiths. During the century its use was increased fourteen-fold. And of course in the eighteenth century demand for it was still further increased by its employment in the iron industry. By this time the use of mineral fuel had come to be regarded by everybody as the natural and ordinary thing. When Abraham Darby in the first half of the eighteenth century began experimenting with the blast furnace in the production of iron, he used coke and not charcoal.

Early Iron Construction in England

It often happens in England that one family dominates a certain trade or industry for several generations. The Darbys occupy this position in the opening stages of the industrialized production of iron. The first Abraham Darby leased an old furnace at Coalbrookdale in 1709, and it was here that the Darby family later succeeded in smelting iron ore with coke instead of charcoal for fuel. The first printed account of these operations appeared in 1747. About 1750 he turned to the use of coal, employing it to turn out pig iron of a quality that could be forged into bar iron. Mass production of iron was now possible, and this advance from manual production of the metal was to change the face of the whole world.

The new material was at first employed only in making machines. When John Smeaton, the great engineer who was one of James Watt's antagonists, used cast-iron utensils for the first time (in 1755), he spoke of this application of cast iron as "a totally new subject." But with Abraham Darby the third, the time had come when cast iron could be used for a variety of entirely new purposes. In 1767 the first iron rails were cast, and at the beginning of the third quarter of the century the first cast-iron bridge was erected over the Severn.[1]

The production of iron industrialized

---

[1] John L. and Barbara Hammond, *The Rise of Modern Industry* (London, 1925), p. 136.

The Severn Bridge (*fig.* **87**) represents one of the boldest experiments in the use of the newly available material. The idea for it seems to have originated in the year 1773 with John Wilkinson, "the ingenious iron-master" (who also invented the cylinder-boring machine which made it possible for James Watt to build a really efficient steam engine), and with the third Abraham Darby. The bridge, executed during the years 1775–

87. ABRAHAM DARBY. The first cast-iron bridge over the river Severn, 1775–79. *Span, one hundred feet; height, forty feet.*

79, consists of a single arch, with a span of 100.5 feet and a rise of 45 feet, made up of five cast-iron ribs. The whole arch is nearly a semicircle in shape. Since the Severn is subject to floods, the bridge had to be very strong. It was manufactured at Darby's Coalbrookdale works, the only plant which was capable of casting arches of such large dimensions and composed of only two members.[2]

[2] William Fairbairn, *On the Application of Cast and Wrought Iron to Building Purposes* (London, 1854), p. 201.

No artistic ambitions were involved in the design of this bridge, and, as architecture, it represents no very great achievement. In these respects it admits of no comparison with the Church of the Fourteen Saints, which had been completed only a few years earlier. But if the church stands on the highest level reached by architecture in its period, it also stands at the end of that architectural tradition. None of its features points

88. Sunderland Bridge, 1793–96. *Single arch of 236 feet. This comparatively large span was achieved by adapting methods of stone construction to work in iron.*

ahead into the future. This simply constructed bridge, for all its lack of interest as a work of art and even as a problem in architecture, opens a path for developments of great importance.

The Sunderland Bridge

The Sunderland Bridge (1793–96) was one of the most daring experiments in construction of its time (*fig. 88*). As early as

Thomas Paine
as inventor

169

1786 Thomas Paine, the famous American political writer, showed Benjamin Franklin the model of a bridge built on a novel system of his own. Franklin, seeing the difficulty of carrying out work on such a system in America, where industry had hardly begun to develop, advised Paine to take it to Eng-

89. HUMPHRY REPTON. Pheasantry for the Royal Pavilion, Brighton, 1808.

land and provided him with recommendations.[3] But in England, as everywhere else, Paine had no luck. His experimental bridge at Paddington (London) left him badly in debt. His name fell into disrepute — and no doubt his political opinions contributed something to this process. Finally his patents

---

[3] Richard Blunck, *Thomas Paine* (Berlin, 1936), p. 115 et seq.

were unscrupulously appropriated by a company directed by Rowland Burdon. Using Paine's plans, Burdon built the Sunderland Bridge and took to himself all the credit for its construction.[4]

This bridge at Sunderland had a single arch of a span of 236 feet. (The Severn Bridge had been only 100 feet.) The six ribs forming the arch were composed of cast-iron panels which acted as voussoirs. A series of 105 such panels made up each rib. In this manner stone vaulting was adapted to iron construction. To make a continuous girder of this span was beyond the capabilities of the time.

90. JOHN NASH. Royal Pavilion at Brighton, 1818-21.

Robert Stephenson's verdict on this bridge, delivered in 1856, is so much to the point that we shall quote it. Stephenson was the constructor of the Britannia Tubular Bridge (1849), the most famous bridge of its time and the outcome of three years of laboratory research. Stephenson has this to say of Paine's work: "About the year 1790, Thomas Paine proposed to construct cast iron arches in the form of voussoirs, and with characteristic energy put his views to the test by constructing an experimental arch of 88 feet span . . . at Paddington. . . . His daring in engineering does full justice to the fervour of his political career — for successful as the result has proved . . . we are led rather to wonder at, than to admire a structure

Robert Stephenson on the Severn Bridge

---

[4] Blunck, p. 22.

171

91. VICTOR LOUIS. Théâtre-Français. *Iron roofing, 1786. The form of the girders reveals an instinctive knowledge of the moment of inertia, which had not as yet been given scientific formulation.*

which, as regards its proportions and the small quantity of materials employed . . . will probably remain unrivalled." [5]

The fascination of cast iron

In this period cast iron — like chromium plate around 1930 — was a new and fascinating material which could not be employed too much. Its unexplored possibilities quickened everybody's imagination. It was such an attitude that led John Wilkinson to want a cast-iron mausoleum, and even a cast-iron coffin. The imaginative possibilities in this technical advance were soon seen to affect architecture also. The association of the new material with exotic birds that appears in a design for a pheasantry with a cast-iron frame shows the imaginative flights that ironwork suggested (*fig.* **89**). Humphry Repton, a famous English landscape gardener, included this aviary in a proposed design for the Royal Pavilion of Prince Regent George at Brighton which he submitted in 1808. It was John Nash, the architect of Regent's Park and Regent Street in London, who finally built this royal pavilion in 1818. A fantastic creation in Indian style, it had a great bulbous cupola over the middle section. The cupola was built over a cast-iron framework that weighed sixty tons [6] (*fig.* **90**).

[5] Robert Stephenson, in *Encyclopaedia Britannica* (Boston, 1856).

[6] John Summerson, *John Nash* (London, 1935), p. 162.

92. The Granary, Paris, 1811. *Bellangé and Brunet used methods of wood construction here, just as the English used methods of stone construction in their first cast-iron bridges. One of the first buildings in which the architect and the engineer were separate persons.*

Early Iron Construction on the Continent

On the Continent iron was first used for building purposes as a roofing material. The timberwork roofs of theaters and warehouses were continually catching fire and burning like tinder. As soon as hand-wrought iron became available in sufficient quantities, attempts were made to prevent such fires by its use. An early effort of this kind came in 1786 with the construction of a wrought-iron roof for the Théâtre-Français in Paris (*fig.* **91**), by the celebrated theater builder, Victor Louis.[7] The elegance and boldness required in the use of iron in a building of this type was to remain continuously characteristic of iron construction in France. The same qualities are exhibited by French work for more than a century after, until iron construction reaches its classic height in the Paris exhibition of 1889.[8]

Elegance of first French uses: Théâtre-Français (1786)

---

[7] Some years before this, Victor Louis produced the last great theater of the *ancien régime* at Bordeaux, one in which spatial relations of the different parts are handled with masterly skill. Victor Louis had some excellent etchings made of this theater. Cf. S. Giedion, *Spätbarocker und romantischer Klassisismus* (Munich, 1922), p. 184.

[8] The elegance of this construction has long been admired; cf. Charles L. Eck, *Traité de l'application du fer, du fonte, et de la tôle* (Paris, 1841), p. 50.

The iron roofing of the Théâtre-Français deserves notice for a more specific reason. The entire construction is counterbalanced in such a way that it needs only comparatively thin walls for its support. As some French theorists have pointed out, the form of its girders reveals an instinctive knowledge of

93. MARC SEGUIN. First French suspension bridge, of wire rope, over the Rhone, near Tournon, 1824.

the moment of inertia, which had not as yet been given scientific formulation.

Cast-iron cupola of the Granary, Paris (1811)

The wooden cupola of the Granary at Paris — covering the circular court — was destroyed by fire in 1802. In 1811 it was replaced by an elaborate construction in iron and copper (*fig.* **92**). The architect Bellangé and the engineer Brunet collaborated in its erection. This was one of the first works in which the architect and the constructor were not the same person. The building shows little more than an adaptation of old constructional methods to the new material, a clever substitution of iron ribs for the woodwork normally used. Nevertheless, the Granary was much admired when it was completed. Napoleon I even found time to assist in its opening. Drastically altered, it survives as a part of the present Bourse de Commerce.

94. Golden Gate Bridge, San Francisco, 1933–37. *The longest single-span suspension bridge. Dimensions: over-all length, 9,200 feet; length of main span, 4,200 feet; width of roadway, 60 feet.*

It was not until about 1850, in the cast-iron cupola of the rotunda of the British Museum, that cast-iron ribs extending from the ground to the top were used in the construction of a large building. In this example papier-mâché was employed in covering the interior of the dome. About this same period — in 1855–63 — the old wooden dome of the United States Capitol in Washington was replaced by a dome with cast-iron ribs. Its peristyle rests on an octagonal base and was interlaced with complicated iron constructional members. Truss girders

Use of the cast-iron cupola in England and the United States were required in the peristyle and the dome to help support the intricate marble profiles on the outside of the whole structure. It is interesting to note how the conventions of the period led, in the case of this important American building, to a mantling of the iron construction by the architecture of the exterior surface.

Seguin's suspension bridge over the Rhone (1824)

The wire-cable suspension bridge goes back to the early nineteenth century. The first French example was built over the Rhone, near Tournon, in 1824 (*fig.* **93**). Marc Seguin, its constructor, was a nephew of Montgolfier and had already invented the tubular boiler which made long railway runs possible. The North American suspension bridges provided models for Seguin's work at Tournon. These bridges were suspended on hemp or rawhide ropes; Seguin used wire cables instead. This was the first time wire rope had been employed for such a purpose in Europe, and Seguin made careful scientific tests of its strength before starting his project. The new material made possible constructions of an extreme elegance and lightness. More than four hundred bridges of this type were eventually erected.

Later examples

In America, Seguin's principles were applied on a larger scale by John Augustus Roebling in his bridges over the Monongahela River at Pittsburgh, 1846, and the Niagara River, 1851–55, and in the Brooklyn Bridge, on which the preliminary work was begun in 1868. And this principle — the transmission of all stresses to a continuous, elastic cable running the length of the structure — still forms the basis for the most daring bridges built today. Seguin's bridge, incidentally, is still in use, although only pedestrian traffic is permitted on it nowadays.

The suspension bridge was continuously developed throughout the nineteenth century as wider spans were demanded and traffic volumes increased. More elaborate constructional applications of this apparently limited principle of elastic suspension were made, until fantastic spans were attained and voids were bridged that had hitherto seemed outside the range of human powers.

Often these bridges are set amidst landscapes of almost cosmic dimensions, and constitute with them new wholes on a more

176

95. FONTAINE. Galerie d'Orléans, Palais Royal, Paris, 1829–31. *A gathering place for elegant society and the precursor not only of such large galleries as the Galleria Vittorio Emmanuele, Milan (1865–67), but also of the glass and iron halls of the great exhibitions. Destroyed in 1935.*

than human scale. The Golden Gate Bridge (*fig.* **94**), the longest single-span suspension bridge in the world, crosses San Francisco Bay against an overwhelming background of sea and rock.[9]

Iron and glass are the two materials whose conjunction in nineteenth-century architecture led it to new solutions. They were first brought together in any considerable structure by Fontaine, some five years after the wire-cable bridge was developed. Fontaine (who, with Percier, founded the Empire style) in his later years (1829–31) used wrought iron to construct the glass roof of the Galerie d'Orléans, a part of the Palais Royal in Paris (*fig.* **95**).

Golden Gate Bridge, San Francisco

Galerie d'Orléans (1829–31)

[9] Erected during the years 1933–37, it has the following dimensions: length over all, 9,200 feet; length of main span, 4,200 feet; width of roadway, 60 feet (accommodating six auto lanes). The capacity of the two cables is 430,000,000 pounds.

177

96. ROUHAULT. Greenhouses of the Botanical Gardens, Paris, 1833. *The prototype of all the large iron-framed conservatories. In contrast to Paxton's English conservatories of the period, the rigidity of these high pavilions is derived solely from the use of cast-iron columns and beams.*

Earlier examples of such galleries in London made an altogether different use of glass. The Royal Opera Arcade, built in 1790 in conjunction with the old Her Majesty's Theatre, has circular openings cut into the vaulting. The light from the hidden glass roof pours into the building through these apertures. A distinctly different impression was created by the Galerie d'Orléans, an impression of freedom and openness as though one were out-of-doors, yet shielded from the elements.

Situated at the end of the inner garden of the Palais Royal, the Galerie d'Orléans was the gathering place of elegant society. It was destroyed in 1935, when the Palais was remodeled, and an open colonnade was put in its place. With its destruction, one of the most charming specimens of early nineteenth-century architecture disappeared, the precursor not only of such large galleries as the Galleria Vittorio Emanuele, Milan (1865–67), but also of the glass and iron halls of the great exhibitions.

The first large structure consisting simply of an iron framework and glass panes was a French conservatory, *les serres des jardins du Musée d'histoire naturelle (fig. 96)*, the greenhouse of the botanical gardens at Paris. Built by Rouhault in 1833, this greenhouse was the prototype of all large, iron-framed conservatories. The unusually large panes of glass, combined with the unrestricted influx of light that the elimination of wood made possible, caused this building to be named "the glass gardens," the *jardins de verre*. Rouhault's conservatory, which is still standing, has an interior volume of nine thousand cubic meters. It is made up of two superimposed quarter-section barrel vaults (where the lower temperatures are maintained), situated between two pavilions fifteen meters high which house the tropical plants. In an article written in 1849 a contemporary — the architect Gottfried Semper — tells of a much more ambitious plan for these gardens. Prior to the overthrow of Louis-Philippe in 1848, there existed a fantastic scheme for completely covering the Botanical Gardens with an immense portable glass roof which could be removed during the summer.

Conservatory of the Jardin des Plantes

FROM THE IRON COLUMN TO THE STEEL FRAME

Perhaps the most characteristic feature of nineteenth-century architecture is its addiction to "period pieces." All the important buildings, all those edifices from which the spectator imagined himself to gain a serious aesthetic impression, appeared in elaborate historical dress. The theoretical issues which received most attention at the time were those raised by the various "revivals" — now classical, now Gothic. Advances in building technique seem to have brought with them only the practical problems involved in using new methods to produce old effects. But even at that early date there were people who saw that no genuine and distinctive tradition could emerge from the medley of inherited forms that overlaid the architecture of the period. A hundred years ago critics spoke

"Period pieces" in nineteenth-century architecture

of "the Harlequin dress of architecture," and indicated with that phrase a disease which is still malignant in our day.

Submerged tendencies

Nevertheless, beneath all the masquerade, tendencies of lasting importance lay hidden and were slowly gathering strength. The architecture of the present is a continuation of these tendencies: it is the product of a great stream of development that has covered a whole century. The common opinion that contemporary architecture owes its foundation to a few innovators appearing around 1900 is both mistaken and superficial. The seeds of this new architecture were planted at the moment when handwork gave place to industrialized production. Like so many other aspects of our civilization, it owes its distinctive character to influences stemming from the Industrial Revolution.

Isolation of architecture from technological advances

But why is it that these tendencies, so important to the future, are to be discovered almost nowhere except in the utilitarian structures of the nineteenth century? Why was their effect upon its official architecture so slight? We should of course expect technological advances to make themselves felt first in the field of industrial construction, but this is not a complete explanation. The Industrial Revolution may have begun in science and technology; that is no reason why it should not have acted upon the arts as well. We have already seen how, in baroque days, new scientific discoveries — even the most abstract and mathematical ones — immediately found their counterparts in the realm of feeling and were translated into artistic terms. In the nineteenth century the paths of science and the arts diverged; the connection between methods of thinking and methods of feeling was broken. The mutual isolation of these two kinds of enterprise, far from being a consequence of their different natures, is a phenomenon peculiar to the nineteenth century and responsible for much about its culture that is otherwise incomprehensible.

The historical posturing of nineteenth-century architecture is simply a special case of this separation, manifested in this field in the schism between the architect and the engineer. The architects of Gothic times did not merely employ the new engineering knowledge; they saw in it possibilities for expressing the aims, emotions, and outlook peculiar to their age. Similarly, the progress of mathematics brought something more into baroque architecture than new instruments of calculation. In both cases new inventions were, so to speak, humanized; emotional and intellectual advances paralleled each other. The situation with regard to those nineteenth-century buildings which were expressly meant to symbolize the spirit of the century is exactly the opposite. Structural iron, for example, was simply a new tool enabling one to erect pseudo-monumental exteriors in the old modes. The new tool, of course, by its very employment reduced these "revived" forms to the status of false fronts.

But as long as scientific and technological advances were used in architecture without being absorbed by it, the engineer remained subordinate to and detached from the architect. The architect, on the other hand, was left isolated from the most important movements going on in the world about him. Until he succeeded in coming to terms with the changed environment, until he recognized the architectonic possibilities in modern constructional methods, no new tradition relevant to the age could develop. It was out of those technical innovations which appear only behind the scenes in nineteenth-century architecture that the architecture of the future had to grow. Construction was, as it were, the subconsciousness of architecture; there lay dormant in it impulses that only much later found explicit theoretical statement.

Hence the interest these apparently trivial developments, these timid introductions of new materials and new methods, have for the historian. Tendencies still living and active in our day, the constituent facts of contemporary architecture, trace back to just such unpretentious beginnings, often of the most unexpected nature. The present chapter, in discussing the development leading from the cast-iron column to the steel frame, will be concerned with it from the point of view we have just advanced. This evolution is important as a particular instance of the way in which, over the hundred years from 1780 to 1880, new architectural potentialities grew out of strictly technical discoveries.

Early appearance
of the cast-iron
column (*c.* 1780)

The cast-iron column was the first structural material produced by the new industrial methods to be used in building.
As early as 1780 — even before the introduction of steam
power — such columns replaced wooden posts as roof supports in the first English cotton mills. The size of the
new machines demanded large rooms with a minimum of
obstructions.

The history of these mills has not yet been thoroughly investigated. One of the rare reports on such buildings — the source
of the illustration we shall discuss next — confesses that "the
buildings have been treated merely as structures, no attempt
being made to probe into their fascinating history. The
'dates' of the various factories have been reduced to an average 'period' rather than a conclusive and accurate date of
actual erection." [1] A typical late eighteenth-century factory
at Bolton shows how the attic stories of existent buildings were
converted to house the newly invented cotton-spinning machines (*fig.* **97**). This factory had been erected with the kind of
heavy wooden framework that had been in use since Gothic
times. At first the machinery was installed only in the attic;
the timber roof trusses — soon to be replaced by trusses of
cast iron — left enough space down the center for the installation of the long spinning frames. Later on, the use of cast-iron
pillars made it possible to install machinery on all the floors.

These masonry buildings (a type which reappeared in Massachusetts when New England began to be industrialized) had
the wide windows of late baroque structures. Standing amidst
unspoiled rural surroundings near the rivers from which they
drew their power, they present an appearance quite different
from factory districts of the steam age. A factory near Manchester, built in 1783, illustrates this stage in the development.
This particular mill was among the first to have iron pillars in
its interior. It is still in operation, and still uses auxiliary water
power.

---

[1] *Official Record of the Annual Conference of the Textile Institute* (Bolton, 1927), pp.
41 ff.

97. Wooden attic of factory, Bolton, England, c. 1800. *The heavy wooden roof trusses left the whole center line of the attic clear for the long spinning machines.*

98. Attic story with cast-iron roof framework, c. 1835. *The cast-iron roof framework represents a later advance; its invention has been credited to J. B. Papworth in 1821. We mention Papworth later as one of the earliest designers of "garden cities" (about 1827).*

The attic of a cotton-spinning factory about 1835 (*fig.* **98**), with its cast-iron roof trusses, shows how room was made for the newly invented self-acting mule spinning frames. The necessity for rooms of very large dimensions is apparent. In this case the spinning frame had to be set up parallel with the long axis of the loft.

Combination with other materials; widespread use Iron pillars were used in combination with stone, brick, and timber alike. Somewhat later, the cast-iron girder and the brick-arch floor were used in mill construction. But for more than a century the cast-iron column played a major role in building of every sort, in all parts of the world. It was used

99. Early use of cast-iron columns, London bookshop, 1794. *Lackington's "Temple of the Muses," Finsbury Square: "The internal arrangement of the building is perfectly novel, . . . the capaciousness of which may be readily conceived from the circumstance of the Weymouth mail, with four horses, having actually been driven around it at . . . its first opening. This room . . . is supported by pillars of iron." ("Ackerman's Repository of Arts," April 1, 1809; courtesy of Mrs. Albert C. Koch, Cambridge, Mass.)*

for a countless variety of architectural purposes during the entire nineteenth century. In the Crystal Palace and in thoroughly workaday market halls, in libraries and in greenhouses — even in the first skyscrapers built in Chicago — the cast-iron pillar furnished the principal means of support. To some extent in England but much more often in America, the cast-iron column was used, during the forties, to form the façades of buildings and to erect structures from prefabricated parts.

As a new material which still had something of the fabulous about it, cast iron even found a place in the Royal Pavilion at Brighton. It was used liberally in this extraordinary edifice, sometimes for purposes of display. John Nash, the Royal Architect, was not one to hesitate in delegating to others the

100. JOHN NASH. Royal Pavilion, Brighton, 1818–21. *Red drawing-room.*

work of designing, but, according to Summerson, he personally designed the "intricate carpentry and ironwork which supports the ceiling" [2] (*fig.* **100**). This was in 1818. So far as I know, it was the first time that cast-iron columns had been used in a formal interior. Nash leads these columns freely through the space of the drawing room. Twenty-five years later Henri Labrouste made a similar undisguised use of iron columns in the small reading room (*La Reserve*) of the Bibliothèque Sainte-Geneviève in Paris. When some contemporary

[2] *John Nash*, p. 162.

architects — around 1925 — proposed doing the same thing, they met with great opposition.

The Royal Pavilion at Brighton was the center of great festivals; in it cast iron as a material for the architect found a setting very remote from labor or affairs. The enormous kitchen (*fig.* **101**) had in its center four slender cast-iron supporting columns, each fantastically elongated and bearing a palm-leaf

101. JOHN NASH. Royal Pavilion, Brighton. *The kitchen.*

Use in the oval garden of the Paris Exhibition of 1867

capital at its top. The unusual slenderness of cast-iron pillars and columns opened up the possibility of new and strange proportions in architecture. Almost fifty years later, in the oval garden in the middle of the main building of the Paris exhibition of 1867, just such exotically slender cast-iron columns were placed in direct association with the palm trees of the South (*fig.* **102**).

Miscellaneous
new uses

We can easily find important witnesses to testify that cast iron soon came to be an approved material for everything from steam engines to churches. Thus Thomas Tredgold, one of the first scientists to interest himself in the possibilities of this material, writes in 1823 that "it is used for the principal supports of churches, theatres, manufacturies, warehouses, and for the main parts of engines." And Tredgold goes on to give some of the reasons for this popularity: "improvements in the processes of its manufacture had made it cheap even in comparison with timber, and . . . it gave a certain protection against fire such as wooden beams could not offer." Thus the reign of cast iron in the nineteenth century was founded upon its fire-resistant qualities, its cheapness, simplicity of manufacture, and resistance to heavy loads. These advantages were

102. Paris Exhibition, 1867. *Oval garden in the center of the main building. Cast-iron columns figure throughout the century, but their use reached its high-water mark around this period. Catalogues of Paris hardware manufacturers offered them in every imaginable shape for Haussmann's great works of transformation.*

enough to assure the domination of the cast-iron pillar until the eighties of the last century, when the steel frame was developed in Chicago.

But there was another reason for the use — and misuse — of cast iron: it is a material which can easily be given any desired shape. The catalogue of a French hardware manufacturer of about 1860 has hundreds of pages devoted to cast iron used for all sorts of purposes. It was even employed in quite abominable imitations of sculptures by the great masters. The

Protean character of cast iron: misuse in mass production

cast-iron pillars, columns, and balustrades for which Haussmann's rebuilding of Paris created a demand were available in finished condition in every conceivable shape. Indeed, the cast-iron column — used without precision or restraint — became one of the symbols of the nineteenth century. As late as 1889 Vierendeel, the great Belgian engineer, still had reason to write, referring to the Paris exhibition, that "the enormous danger of this sort of support lies in its revolting vulgarity." The charm that lay in the proper use of the material was lost in a hopelessly misdirected mass production.

103. Aquatint of Telford's proposed cast-iron bridge over the Thames, London, 1801.

TOWARD THE STEEL FRAME

Telford's project
for London Bridge
(1801)

Two other early examples of the use of cast iron in construction must be mentioned. Both date from the very beginning of the nineteenth century. The first, the Telford and Douglas design for London Bridge, was made in 1801 but never executed (*fig.* **103**). This elegant and well-known design is for a really colossal work in cast iron, a bridge with a rise of 65 feet and a single span of 600 feet. Even five decades later Robert Stephenson's Britannia bridge fell short of this span. Nevertheless the design for London Bridge could have been carried out at the time it was made, since Telford, adopting the system proposed by Thomas Paine in 1783, suggested building it like a stone arch out of a number of small wedge-shaped sections.

The cotton mill of Philip and Lee, built at Salford, Manchester, in 1801, is the second example (*fig.* **104**). This mill surpasses all others of its time in the boldness of its design. It represents the first experiment in the use of iron pillars and beams for the whole interior framework of a building. The erection of this factory was an event of the first importance in the history of modern construction. This truly extraordinary feat for builders of that date — a feat which in time came to be almost forgotten — was accomplished by Boulton and Watt's Soho foundry. The inventor of the steam engine was then concentrating most of his attention upon a machine for making portrait statuary, and was meditating retirement from active business.

The original drawings for this mill, which have never before been published, are in the Boulton and Watt Collection of the Birmingham Reference Library. The plate shows the ground plan and the elevation of the Salford mill. The building is a large one, about 140 feet long and 42 feet wide; its height of seven stories is extraordinary for this early date. As the ground plan shows, there are two ranges of iron pillars set on each floor. For the first time, iron beams are used in combination with these iron columns. These beams, the first of the I-section type, extend across the building from wall to wall at regular distances. The Scottish engineer, William Fairbairn, praises this first employment of the I beam as an example of intuitive recognition of the most efficient shape in advance of the calculations that would prove it to be such. (A similar instance of the instinctively correct solution of an engineering problem has already been encountered in the iron roof of the Théâtre-Français of 1786. Its wrought-iron girders were adjusted to the moment of inertia, even though the theoretical basis for such an adjustment did not exist until much later.) The drawing also shows how the floors of the mill were built up from brick arches, brought to a level surface by a layer of rough concrete.

The second drawing gives a cross-section (*fig.* **105**) of the width of the building. It shows the special foundations provided for the iron columns of the ground floor, and the junctions between the cast-iron columns and beams of the first two floors.

Salford factory by Boulton and Watt (1801): its advanced construction

Combination of iron beams and iron girders

Appearance of the I-section girder

Use of concrete

189

Precision of detail

The third drawing shows the construction of the hollow cast-iron pillars, each of which had an outside diameter of nine inches. This extremely careful treatment reflects the experience acquired by Boulton and Watt in the making of steam-engines (*fig.* **106**). The details of the assembly of pillar and socket (on the right-hand side of the plan) show a precision that had been learned in machinery construction.

Fairbairn on the Salford mill

As Fairbairn remarked in 1854, this experiment at Salford was "the pioneer of that system of fireproof structure which now distinguishes the manufacturing districts of this country. For a quarter of a century this mill was a model for similar buildings. From 1801 until 1824 little or no variation took place in the form of beams." The reason for this was that time was

104. WATT and BOULTON. Working drawings for the first seven-story mill with cast-iron beams and columns, Salford, Manchester, 1801. *The first building ever designed or executed with a metal skeleton — cast-iron columns and beams — enclosed in the outer masonry walls like the works of a watch in its case.*

105. WATT and BOULTON. Working drawings for the first seven-story mill with cast-iron beams and columns.

106. WATT and BOULTON. Working drawings for the first seven-story mill with cast-iron beams and columns. *Sections of a cast-iron column.*

needed to enable experiment and calculation to overtake Watt's astonishingly farsighted structure. The type of building represented by this seven-story mill of 1801 with its cast-iron skeleton surrounded by outer walls of masonry became the standard for warehouses throughout the century and was adopted for some advanced public buildings as well. Watt's Salford experiment was the first step in the development of the steel frame which was finally to appear in Chicago during the eighties.

191

107. WILLIAM FAIRBAIRN. English refinery, c. 1845. *Cross section. Developments moved very slowly during the first half of the century, with no important changes in the methods used by Boulton and Watt. In this Fairbairn refinery there are simply certain technical refinements.*

108. WILLIAM FAIRBAIRN. English refinery, c. 1845. *Ceiling construction.*

Fairbairn improves on Watt's construction in the forties

William Fairbairn himself laid a large share of the groundwork for further advance. A builder of ships and bridges as well as industrial structures, the experiments with tubular iron which he completed in 1846 at his laboratory in Manchester made possible the building of the Britannia Tubular Bridge, the most famous of its time, and encouraged the building of still larger spans later on. The decisive change in methods of industrial construction that is to be observed shortly before the middle of the century owes much to other experiments conducted by this able engineer. Before this time, as he writes, "we had little or no knowledge of the superior resisting powers of wrought iron in the shape of beams: . . . our knowledge of [its] properties may be considered as still very imperfect and confined within exceedingly narrow compass." [1]

In his attempts to make his buildings fireproof Fairbairn was led to employ a remarkable principle of construction. The eight-story, flat-roofed refinery which he built during the middle forties introduces wrought-iron as well as cast-iron members (*fig.* **107**). Wrought-iron I-section girders joined with iron tie bars are here supported by cast-iron pillars. Instead of the brick-arch floor, thin wrought-iron plates are used; running from column to column, they are bent in the segmental form of an arch and then filled to floor level with concrete (*fig.* **108**). The jump from such a building to the building of ferroconcrete

---

[1] William Fairbairn, *The Application of Cast and Wrought Iron to Building Purposes*, p. 152.

is not very great; the time had not yet arrived, however, for this suggestion to be taken up.

The use of iron as a structural material was further increased by the invention of machinery for producing rolled iron and steel joists. The American railroad builder, Robert Stevens of Hoboken, went to England in 1830 to buy locomotives. During his visit he tried to make rolled-iron railroad tracks, finally succeeding in this endeavor, despite its many difficulties, in a South Wales rolling mill. Rolled-iron I beams did not come into use until much later, however. The architect Boileau wrote in 1871 that a combination of exceptional circumstances led to the introduction of rolled-iron beams in France. This was in 1845 at Paris; a strike of masons, the high price of timber, the fear of fire, and the demand for wider spans led a foundryman named Zorès to roll the first wrought-iron joist sections produced in France. They did not appear in England until still later.

Introduction of rolled-iron beams

Important preliminary work for later construction was carried out in the show windows of stores, where, as industrialization continued, ever-larger glassed surfaces were needed. The manuals of iron construction that were published from the fifties to the nineties are filled with instructions for supporting the brickwork of the upper stories on iron girders. These iron columns were the only structural elements of the building visible behind the wide display windows. In view of the fact that the set-back pillar is used in so many modern buildings, a continuous account of the evolution of this practice would be most interesting. It was from these store windows that we first learned how to use large glass areas in dwelling houses.

Show windows lead to larger openings in the wall

James Bogardus

The beginnings of the skeleton construction of the present day are met with as early as 1848 in the home of the skyscraper, the United States. The decisive step was the substitution of iron columns for the masonry of the outer walls as a means of support for the floors of a building. An early example of this type of construction is a five-story factory that was erected in New York in 1848. Its builder was the man who invented this

James Bogardus: the cast-iron skeleton and Renaissance shapes (1848)

109. JAMES BOGARDUS. Design for a factory, 1856, showing the resistance of cast iron.

method of construction, James Bogardus (1800–74). American department stores, warehouses, and office buildings of the period between 1850 and 1880 were based on this system of building. Using prefabricated parts, Bogardus erected these buildings in every section of the United States. According to the *New York Herald* of April 14, 1874, he even delivered an immense building to Santa Catalina, near Havana, Cuba. Excellent examples of these buildings still exist in most American cities. Some particularly fine specimens (warehouses and office buildings) are to be found in the river-front area of St. Louis. One of them, located at 7911 North First Street, is particularly interesting for the uncompromising way in which large areas of glass are introduced into the front wall. All have value as monuments not merely for the step forward in construction which they represent but for the restrained and sober quality of their architecture. This type of building is undoubtedly one of the chief sources of a specifically American architectural style. But in spite of its contemporary importance and its very real merit the work of Bogardus is almost unknown today.

194

James Bogardus' best-known building was executed in Franklin Square on Pearl Street in New York for the famous publishing house of Harper and Brothers, in 1854 (*fig.* **110**).   A
single glance reveals the way in which Bogardus transformed
the outer wall into a surface almost entirely of glass.   The
combination of wide expanses of glass with iron columns and
arches in the Venetian Renaissance style is a perfect illustration of the spirit of his time.   Bogardus himself gives a quite
explicit statement of that spirit.   In a booklet bearing the title,
Cast Iron Buildings: Their Construction and Advantages, by
James Bogardus, "Architect in Iron" (New York, 1858), he
impersonally relates that "Mr. Bogardus first conceived the
idea of emulating [the rich architectural designs of antiquity]
in modern times, by the aid of cast-iron."   This was in the
year 1840.   (This small but important publication has fallen
into such obscurity that it is not mentioned in the sketch of
Bogardus in the *Dictionary of American Biography.*)

Like many of his eighteenth-century precursors, Bogardus
believed cast iron to be a material capable of satisfying all the
demands of both the engineer and the artist.   He would have
liked to apply his system to the building of dwelling houses
as well as commercial structures (*fig.* **109**).   He apparently felt

110.   JAMES BOGARDUS.   Harper & Brothers' Building, New York, 1854.

111.   JAMES BOGARDUS.   Project for the New York World's Fair, 1853.   *The amphi-theater was twelve hundred feet in diameter.   The three-hundred-foot tower was intended to house a passenger elevator.   In a circle of this size, straight girders — capable of resale afterwards — could be employed.*

that the exclusion of his methods from the residential field was due to mere chance.   "Mr. Bogardus firmly believes," we read on page 14 of the booklet, "that had his necessities required him to construct a dwelling house rather than a factory [this method] would be now as popular for this purpose, as it is for stores."   And he planned fantastic houses so designed that even "with the greater part of their ironwork removed . . . or destroyed by violence . . . they will yet remain firm."

Bogardus' unexe-cuted scheme for the New York World's Fair of 1853: original and farsighted

James Bogardus' most imaginative work was the project which he submitted for the first of the American world's fairs, held at New York in 1853 (*fig.* 111).   He advanced as the chief recommendation for his scheme its great economy — the total cost would be only two hundred thousand dollars — and "expressed a conviction that the whole structure would be worth very considerably more when dissected, for ordinary purposes, than in its present form, owing to the economy in reproducing so large a number of identical parts from the same pattern."   With future dissections in mind, Bogardus proposed building a great circular amphitheater twelve hundred feet in diameter.

196

A circle as huge as this could be assembled from straight girders, easily disposed of afterwards.[2]

Bogardus' plan called for an immense coliseum in cast iron.
The exterior wall was sixty feet high, with arches and columns
running in series about it to mark off the separate stories. A
three-hundred-foot tower rose in the center of the enclosure
"to serve the double purpose of a support for the hanging roof
of sheet-iron suspended from it by rods in a catenary curve,
and also as a grand observatory."[3] Such supporting rods of
catenary curvature were standard practice in suspension
bridges. Bogardus planned to install an elevator in this tower
to carry spectators to its top.

The shapes that figure in this design were borrowings from
traditional styles, but the structure as a whole was amazingly
advanced, a daring prevision of future developments. This
building would have been as original a document for the fifties
as the French exhibitions from 1867 on were for their period.

The building actually erected for this fair had no historical
importance, and the other plans entered in the competition
were either undistinguished in quality or inappropriate to the
site. This includes even the scheme submitted by Joseph
Paxton.[4]

The career of James Bogardus was a most interesting one. He
began his active life as a watchmaker and an inventor of great
fertility. He had to his credit a new kind of pencil, the lead of
which was always sharp, the engraving machine that produced
the first English postage stamps, a deep-sea sounding machine,
and a variety of other devices. He was, in fact, a classical
exemplar of a type of inventor peculiar to the beginning of the
nineteenth century, when men were trying to invent, in one
great rush, everything that had *not* been invented in the past.

Bogardus as a type
of inventor

---

[2] The main building at the Paris exhibition of 1867 had two hemicycles built on at its
ends. When the building was torn down at the close of the exhibition, it was very
difficult to find a market for the curved ironwork used in these hemicycles. The American
foresaw this situation, but his project had been forgotten by that time, and remained so
until the present day.

[3] B. Silliman, Jr., and C. R. Goodrich, *The World of Science, Art, and Industry* (New
York, 1854), p. 4.

[4] *Ibid.*, pp. 1–3.

It was a time when it was common to find a single person conducting experiments in the most widely separated departments of industry. The contrast with the Renaissance is striking. Then the ideal figure was the "Universal man," the person who could unite in his own life the greatest number of different *kinds* of activity, the man who was at once artist, scientist, engineer. In the early nineteenth century the ideal was the man who could do all things in one field of industry, the watchmaker-ironworker-engineer type represented by Bogardus.[5]

The St. Louis River Front

Anonymous commercial buildings of the fifties

Commercial buildings with cast-iron fronts, and often with cast-iron skeletons as well, sprang up all over the United States between 1850 and 1880 — the so-called "cast-iron age." Bogardus is simply the best known of their many builders. Whether he was the first to introduce this type of structure is something which cannot be determined at present. The lack of documents makes even a general survey of these buildings impossible — and many of them were astonishingly fresh and straightforward in their design, showing a direct grasp of the functions that had to be fulfilled. They were often erected by the foundries which produced their parts, with no architect taking a share in the work. The owners of these foundries, unlike James Bogardus, had no Italian travels behind them and no desire to inaugurate a Renaissance revival in cast iron.

St. Louis during the fifties

From this anonymous development we select a complete district comprising about five hundred buildings — the central river front of St. Louis. For more than a century after its founding in 1764 as a headquarters for the fur trade, St. Louis was the leading trading center for the entire trans-Mississippi West. Its most prosperous decade came in the 1850's: steamboat traffic was at its height; the gold rushes to California and Colorado were under way; and new lands in the Missouri Valley had just been opened. At this time St. Louis is believed to have been the third steam port of the country, and by 1870 it was the fourth largest city in the United States. The river front was the city's old business area, and most of it was built

Decline after the Civil War

_____

[5] James Watt and the Brummels are other instances of this same type.

198

up during this flourishing period.[6] Building began after the great fire of 1849 (the year of the California gold rush, for which St. Louis was one of the crossroads) and continued until the outbreak of the Civil War. During the post-war years St. Louis steadily fell off in importance, while Chicago went on to take its place as the great mid-western market. Finally, "with the entry of the eastern railroads over Ead's Bridge in 1874 and the decline of the steamboat, the commercial center of the city shifted and left the old river front in decline."[7]

The half-deserted river front has survived as a witness to one of the most exciting periods in the development of America. Some of its commercial buildings — fur and china warehouses, Pony Express offices, ordinary business blocks — exhibit an architecture far in advance of the ordinary standards at the time of their erection.[8]

[6] I owe these data to Mr. Charles E. Peterson, Senior Landscape Architect in the National Park Service, who is one of the architects at work on the Jefferson National Expansion Memorial being erected in this area.

[7] *The Old St. Louis Riverfront, An Exhibition of Architectural Studies in the Historic Area of the Jefferson National Expansion Memorial* (St. Louis Public Library, 1938), p. 17.

[8] The importance of preserving nineteenth-century documents leads us to mention a specific problem which is now being worked on.

Forty blocks of the St. Louis river front have recently been taken over by the United States government as the site for a Jefferson National Expansion Memorial which will extend along the bank of the Mississippi. The first step in the work will be the razing of this historic quarter. It was in connection with this memorial project that research was made into the dates of erection of these buildings and that they were systematically photographed — unusual happenings at this date.

The National Park Service has decided to preserve the fronts of some of the most important of these buildings. The proposal was made to set up these façades in the courtyard of a new building.

I visited St. Louis in August 1939 on the kind invitation of Mr. Peterson and inspected the district just before the pickaxes went to work on it. It seemed to me that the building at 523–529 North First Street at the extreme northern end of the site, could be preserved intact. (Cf. *St. Louis Post-Dispatch, St. Louis Star-Times, St. Louis Daily Globe-Democrat*, Aug. 10, 1939.) The best examples from elsewhere in the section could be moved into this block. All of them could be fitted out as they were when the river front was at its peak — complete with Pony Express office, stock in the warehouses, and the typical stuffed animals under glass domes that stood in the windows of the old fur-trading establishments.

Some one of these buildings could even be used as a museum of the history of the Mississippi region. It would be possible to display its relations with the past and the present, and with the whole United States — north and south, east and west. George Henri Rivière of the Musée du Trocadéro produced a similar re-creation of a Burgundian village for the Paris exhibition of 1937. It told the story of a community in a manner which was full of life. Is it actually so very difficult to realize that commercial buildings of the nineteenth-century are as important witnesses to a period as any seventeenth-century château?

112. St. Louis, river front. Cast-iron front of 523–529 North First Street, c. 1870–71. *The building has been variously a wholesale boot, dry goods, and clothing store. It has been exempted from the demolition work going on in the river-front area.*

→

113. St. Louis, river front. Cast-iron front of Gantt Building, 219–221 Chestnut Street, façade dating from 1877. *Originally a lawyer's office, it later became a wholesale stationer's. The façade is being removed by the National Park Service for future museum use.*

These commercial buildings are of various architectural types, but even when they adapt motifs of stone architecture to cast iron they are not without a certain French elegance. The building at 523–529 North First Street (*c.* 1870–71, *fig.* **112**), at the very end of the Memorial area, should be preserved just as it is.[9] Another fine specimen is the five-story brick warehouse at 7–9–11 North First Street. Its upper stories are bound together into two pairs by slim columns. Its flat surfaces are reminiscent of the shapes of the simplified Romanesque style which later became so celebrated at the hands of Henry Hobson Richardson. Beyond this there are such simple constructions as the building at 109–111 North First Street, which we shall later find occasion to compare with one of the first modern dwellings in Europe, the Horta house in the Rue de Turin of 1893.[10] These structures carry the simplification of the front so far that the iron columns and lintels become scarcely more than the crosspieces in a great casement window spread across the whole façade. For this treatment, and for its

[9] Mr. Peterson has since written me that this is being done.
[10] Cf. Fig. 177.

200

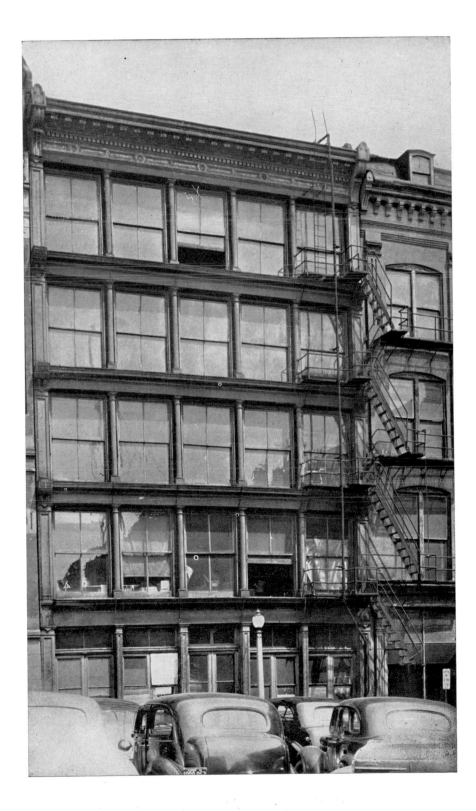

excellent proportions as well, the Gantt Building (1877) at 219–221 Chestnut Street (*fig.* **113**) deserves to be known as one of the finest in the whole period.

Early Skeleton Buildings

First building
of skeleton
construction:
France, 1871

The first building of true skeleton type was the chocolate works constructed in 1871–72 by Jules Saulnier at Noisiel-sur-Marne, near Paris (*fig.* **114**). The factory rests on four piers set into the bed of the Marne, whose current supplied the power for its machinery. The building itself is erected upon four hollow iron girders, each square in section. The building whose base these girders constitute is the first to employ the principles of skeleton construction, the first, that is, in which an iron skeleton is made to carry the whole weight. This skeleton can be seen on the surfaces of the walls; the latter, made of hollow brick, function merely as filling. The diagonal iron stiffeners show clearly that Saulnier derived a part of his inspiration from methods used in wood construction.

Plane surfaces and
the new structural
means coincide

All contemporary buildings intended to have any formal or stately character had their walls overloaded with decoration. The walls of this chocolate works are plane surfaces. As Saulnier himself explains, the construction was responsible for this: "The system of construction used for the façades produced a surface entirely plane from top to bottom, with no projections either horizontal or vertical." [11] European taste in the early seventies nevertheless required some concessions on Saulnier's part. Although he scrupulously preserved the flat surfaces that followed from the logic of his method, the brickwork defining them embodies a pattern in varicolored tiles.

We can see in this building how the flat and unornamented surfaces of present-day architecture appeared simultaneously with the new structural means (*fig.* **115**). Moreover, this took place in spite of the fact that monumental architecture in the late nineteenth century was developing along entirely different lines, in a direction which led to an overdecorated confusion. And it is not the case that a desire to build cheaply was re-

---

[11] *Encyclopédie d'architecture*, 1877, p. 92.

114. JULES SAULNIER.
Menier Chocolate Works,
Noisiel-sur-Marne, 1871–72. *Iron skeleton. So far as we know, the first skeleton building in the modern sense of the word, with the outer walls reduced to functioning simply as curtains.*

115. JULES SAULNIER. Menier Chocolate Works, Noisiel-sur-Marne, 1871–72.
This factory is built over the river Marne, on four great iron floor girders supported by stone piers set into the river bed.

sponsible for the simplicity of the factory at Noisiel. Saulnier's type of construction was considerably more expensive than any other.

No influence on the development of the American skyscraper

The plans of this chocolate mill were published several times in great detail by the best-known French reviews — all of them available in American libraries. It is very curious, accordingly, that Saulnier's work should have remained completely unknown in the United States, as it seems to have done. One would have expected this first example of skeleton construction to have played a considerable part in the development of the skyscraper.

L. S. Buffington as the inventor of the skyscraper

The stages leading up to the American skyscraper are not known with any exactitude. As E. M. Upjohn remarks, "At least three cities — New York, Chicago, and Minneapolis — have sought the honor of being the birthplace of the skyscraper, and several architects have laid claim to distinction as its inventor." [12] The claims of the Minneapolis architect, Leroy S. Buffington, have been advanced more often than any others. They were certainly urged quite strongly by Buffington himself, who claims to have invented the skyscraper in 1880, deriving his inspiration from Viollet-le-Duc's *Lectures on Architecture*, which appeared in translation at about that time. The passage that aroused his interest occurs in volume II of the *Lectures*, on pages 1–2, where Viollet-le-Duc remarks that "a practical architect might not unnaturally conceive the idea of erecting a vast edifice whose frame should be entirely of iron, . . . preserving [that frame] by means of a casing of stone." The possibilities of a building with a "frame of iron . . . clothed with masonry" having been suggested to him, Buffington — so he relates — looked through all the material available in public libraries for an account of such a structure, but without finding any. That being the case, he was quite justified in supposing the system of skeleton construction which he finally developed to be entirely original. [13]

---

[12] E. M. Upjohn, "Buffington and the Skyscraper," *Art Bulletin*, XVII (March 1935), 48–70.

[13] The late William B. Mundie's opinion on Buffington's claim may be of interest. Mr. Mundie was a younger partner of William Le Baron Jenney. I am indebted to Mr. E. C. Jensen of the architectural firm of Mundie, Jensen, Bourke & Havens for the opportunity of quoting these excerpts from one of Mundie's unpublished papers:

116. WILLIAM LE BARON JENNEY. Home Insurance Company, Chicago, 1883–85. *The first skyscraper actually erected upon modern principles of construction. Ten stories high and fireproof, it permitted the maximum amount of light in every office.*

Nevertheless, although Saulnier's methods differ in several respects from those which Buffington proposed, the French constructor had anticipated him in one essential point: he had erected, almost a decade earlier, a building whose outer walls were supported *exclusively* by wrought-iron girders. The mill at Noisiel was, essentially, an iron frame clothed in masonry.

"I feel at a loss just how to approach this claim of Mr. Buffington's for himself as inventor, and the City of Minneapolis as the birthplace of skeleton construction. From my viewpoint it should be ignored, but it has been given such widespread publicity and the Patent Office did issue letters patent calling it an 'invention,' under the name of 'Iron Building Construction,' Patent No. 383,170. Inventor L. S. Buffington. Date May 22, 1888. That cannot be ignored, but it can be controverted."

After some details of the legal controversies between Jenney and Buffington, Mr. Mundie goes on to observe, "All he patented was the use of said construction (which was then well-known) in connection with his laminated steel plate column, composed of plates of steel riveted together side by side, and breaking joints, thus forming a solid steel column from bottom to top. This column being solid was so extravagant that no one ever had a desire to use it. Parties who called to interview Mr. Jenney about the patent, who afterwards proved to be Buffington's attorneys, were told by him that if they could find anyone using that extravagant column, they certainly could be prosecuted for using it, but no architect or engineer of any scientific knowledge would be guilty of using it; in skeleton construction it was worthless."

William Le Baron
Jenney's Home
Insurance Building
(1883)

It is well known that the first skyscraper actually built (and not merely planned) along modern principles of construction was the ten-story building of the Home Insurance Company (*fig.* **116**) of Chicago (1883–85). The commission for its design was given to William Le Baron Jenney in 1883. The Home Insurance Company demanded a new type of office building which would be fireproof and offer the maximum amount of light for every room.[14]

To summarize: a period of slightly more than eight decades lies between James Watt's seven-story cotton factory of 1801 with its iron columns and iron beams and the first iron-framed sky-scraper. It is a curious fact that a similar eighty-year interval between the discovery of an important new principle and its assimilation into everyday life is to be encountered in other fields. For example, just this length of time intervened between Volta's discovery of galvanic electricity in 1800 and the first transmission of electric power in the eighties.

Elevators

The first elevators

At the time when James Bogardus was proclaiming that his new cast-iron buildings could "be raised to a height vastly greater than by any other known means . . . and the greater their height, the firmer they would be," [15] the first mechanical elevators were being invented in Boston and New York. Like nearly all inventions of this period, elevators were first intended to serve industrial purposes only.

James Bogardus proposed to install "a mechanism for hoisting observers to the top by steam power," [16] in the three-hundred-foot central tower of his projected building for the New York World's Fair of 1853. Though the very word had

---

[14] Its construction is noteworthy for the fact that it includes not only cast-iron columns but also a few of the first Bessemer steel girders ever used in a building. This was thirty years after Bessemer had made public the process of making steel which he had invented. Other branches of industry had adopted it almost at once; thus it came very soon to be used in the manufacture of railroad tracks and the armor plate for battleships. Further details of this celebrated building can be found in any history of the skyscraper.

[15] James Bogardus, *Cast Iron Buildings.*

[16] Silliman and Goodrich, *The World of Science, Art, and Industry,* p. 4.

206

117. ELISHA GRAVES OTIS. The world's first safe elevator. 1853.

118. ELISHA GRAVES OTIS. Passenger elevator at the time of the Civil War.

not yet come into use, Bogardus here proposed what would have been the first passenger elevator in the world.

The first completely satisfactory elevator was the work of Elisha Graves Otis of New York (*fig.* **117**). The world's first safe elevator was produced when he attached a safety device to the ordinary hoisting platform. This elevator received its initial showing and demonstration at the Crystal Palace Exposition in New York in 1853. In each demonstration Mr. Otis stepped onto the platform, which was then hoisted above the ground. As the hoisting rope was cut, the elevator came to a stop, whereupon Mr. Otis made the historical remark: "All safe, gentlemen!" A recent check of the archives of the Otis Company revealed that there are no surviving designs of this first elevator. We know only its approximate type from sketches of machines of a slightly later period.

119. Eiffel Tower, elevator to the first platform, 1889.

First passenger elevator: New York, 1857

What is considered to have been the first passenger elevator was installed by Otis in a department store on the corner of Broadway and Broome Street, New York, in 1857.[17] The next passenger elevator was installed in the old Fifth Avenue Hotel in 1859. Its inventor was a Mr. Tufts of Boston, and the device bore the name of "Vertical Screw Railway." Contemporary pictures of these "railways" are also lacking; sketches from about the period of the Civil War survive, however, to give an idea of the principles employed in their design (*fig.* **118**).

First European elevator: Paris Exposition of 1867

The first European elevator, so far as we know now, was not built until 1867, when one was installed at the great Paris exhibition of that year. A hydraulic elevator exhibiting all the ungainliness of some primordial monster, it transported visitors from the grandiose Galerie des Machines to the corrugated iron roof of that immense hall. From these roof terraces the visitors saw spread out below them not only the great city of Paris but a whole new world of glass and iron.

[17] I am indebted to Mr. G. C. Bebb, advertising manager of the Otis Elevator Company, for this date, which corrects a common error.

It is pleasant to relate that the first elevator for a structure of modern skyscraper proportions was built to serve no commercial or narrowly practical purposes. It was destined for a structure which sprang out of the vision rather than the daily needs of man — the Eiffel Tower. The Eiffel Tower, indeed, falls outside the usual connotations of the word "building": it might better be regarded as at once the manifesto and the monument of that Iron Age which embraced the second half of the nineteenth century. An unusual traffic problem was solved by constructing a whole system of elevators. Four large, double-decked elevators ran from the ground to the first platform (*fig.* **119**), a height equal to that of Notre Dame; two more ran from the terrace to the second platform, a height equal to that of the dome of St. Peter's; the rest of the ascent was made in two stages by means of a pair of hydraulic elevators operating on a sort of shuttle system. The total ascent to a height of a thousand feet took only seven minutes, and 2,350 passengers could be transported to the summit every hour.[18] This was achieved in 1889.

First elevator system on a great scale: Eiffel Tower, 1889

THE SCHISM BETWEEN ARCHITECTURE AND TECHNOLOGY

We have already spoken in somewhat general terms of the gap that opened in the course of the nineteenth century between science and its techniques on the one hand and the arts on the other, and hence between architecture and construction. The previous chapter should lend support to the contention we made then that the seeds of the architecture of our day were to be found in technical developments little regarded at the time of their appearance. The present chapter will handle this topic in more detail. We shall deal with the question of the time at which this schism became evident, and the manner in which recognition of its existence led to the demand for a new architecture. Contemporary utterances will enable us to show that from this situation developed many questions the answers

[18] These details are to be found in a contemporary pamphlet of great interest: Gaston Tissandier, *La Tour Eiffel de 300 m.* (Paris, 1889), p. 68.

209

to which are still being sought today. Finally, in separating the constituent facts from the episodic trends of the nineteenth century, we shall be able to fill in many of the gaps in the history of our own development, gaps of whose existence we have often been unconscious.

Effect of the revival of the École des Beaux-Arts (1806)

In the year 1806 Napoleon founded the École des Beaux-Arts, thereby reviving an institution of the *ancien régime*. The program of the École, covering the whole field of the plastic arts, maintained that unity of architecture with the other arts which had been both complete and spontaneous during the baroque period. Unfortunately, the school was administered in such a way that bad results soon followed. It fostered a constantly increasing isolation of the arts from the conditions of ordinary life. From the beginning of the century two opposed attitudes, each extreme and each represented by an official institute, face each other in France; the École des Beaux-Arts is confronted by the École Polytechnique.

École Polytechnique (1794), the gathering point for new forces

The École Polytechnique had been founded during the French Revolution, in 1794 — three years after the *Proclamation de la liberté du travail*, the document which abolished the legal hindrances to the growth of modern industry in France. The École Polytechnique was an *école spéciale*; it offered a uniform scientific preparation for the higher technical schools — *l'école des ponts et chaussées, l'école des mines, l'école de l'artillerie*, etc. The great mathematicians, physicists, and chemists of France acted as instructors, men like Monge, Lagrange, Berthollet, Chaptal. The École Polytechnique had the important function of combining theoretical and practical science. That it directly influenced industry is beyond question. In the first decades of the century it became a center for those interested in political economy and sociology and above all for the Saint-Simonists, whose membership included the creators of the large-scale industries and the railroad systems built up in France around the 1850's.

Discussions

The separate existence of an École des Beaux-Arts and an École Polytechnique in itself points to the schism between architecture and construction. A survey of the architectural journals of the nineteenth century will reveal that the two questions most debated at the time grew out of the dissension between these schools. These questions can be stated as follows:

1. Along what lines should the training of an architect proceed?
2. What is the relation of the engineer to the architect? What special functions are proper to each?

All the other controversies and discussions regarding architectural form are of minor and transitory importance in comparison with the issues these two questions involved.

École Polytechnique: the Connection between Science and Life

The immense influence of the École Polytechnique in the first three decades of the nineteenth century can be attributed to the fact that it quite consciously set itself an enormous task; in it, for the first time, the attempt was made to establish a connection between science and life, to bring out the practical applications to industry of discoveries in the mathematical and physical sciences. Jean-Antoine Chaptal, the great chemist and industrialist who was minister of the interior under Napoleon I, laid down this aim for the École at the beginning of the nineteenth century. He insisted that science must climb down from its pedestal and lend a hand in the work of creating a new world.

The architect and the constructor

It was Rondelet — the theorist whose work on the Panthéon in Paris prevented its collapse — who first insisted that scientific techniques had an important role to play in architecture. His *Discours pour l'ouverture du cours de construction à l'école spéciale d'architecture* (1816) argued that constructional methods had to be allowed much more influence upon the character of a building design than had hitherto been given them. From this time on, the engineer slowly encroaches more and more upon the province of the architect. All unconsciously, the constructor during the nineteenth century played the role of scout for the architect. The new expedients which he kept pressing upon the architect continually forced the latter to

Unconscious influence of construction

venture upon unexplored paths. He broke down the architect's ritualistic and artificial formalism, hammered brusquely upon the door of his ivory tower. And it remains one of the chief functions of construction to furnish architecture with the stimulus and incentive for new growth.

The Demand for a New Architecture

With the quickening of the advance of industry in the middle of the nineteenth century there becomes evident a feeling on the part of the architect that his privileged position is menaced and the traditions of his art outmoded. That anxiety grew in intensity with the progress of industrialization. But contemporary statements of this feeling are of more interest than any abstract deductions we might make concerning it. Let us first quote some evidence of the hopes for a new architecture that the appearance of the new potentialities aroused.

1849: "A new architecture which will take us out of the sterility of the past and the servility of copying is what everybody demands, and what the public waits for." [1]

1849: "The new architecture is architecture in iron. Architectural revolutions always follow social revolutions. In the interim periods few changes are to be seen, no matter how long these periods may be. Men insist upon remolding the old forms until a radical upset wipes the slate clean of banal schools and ideas.

"There are great periods in architecture just as there are great geological periods: a new race of plants or animals only appears after the disappearance of the old. In architecture it is the same: The race of old authorities in architecture had to be superseded — just as the mastodons were superseded — in order to make room for new kinds of artists who will not preserve the traditional prejudices of the old schools.

"But, you may say, where shall we find masters clever enough? We should not tell you to seek these people among old masons whose hands have been so long occupied with stone and mortar that it is safe to presume that their brains also move in an

---

[1] César Daly, *Revue générale de l'architecture*, 1849, p. 26.

212

equally restricted orbit. To create what is new, you must have young people." [2]

1850: "Mankind will produce a completely new architecture out of its period exactly at the moment when the new methods created by recently born industry are made use of. The application of cast iron allows and enforces the use of many new forms, as can be seen in railway stations, suspension bridges, and the arches of conservatories." [3]

1867: Toward the end of the Second Empire, César Daly once more laments the continued influence of old traditions: "One perceives the eclectic atmosphere enveloping the world; all organs of respiration absorb it and, mixed with our blood, it acts on heart and brain." [4]

1889: Two decades later the situation had scarcely improved. Every time new and unusual constructions appeared to stimulate the imagination by their boldness, the old cries went up again. Even the novelist Octave Mirbeau — not in general given to urge on the march into the future — realized after seeing the Eiffel Tower and the Galerie des Machines that "while art cultivates *l'intimisme* or attaches itself to the old formulas with its gaze still fixed on the past, industry moves forward and explores the unknown. It is not in the studios of the painters and sculptors that the revolution so long awaited is preparing — it is in the factories!" [5]

The Interrelations of Architecture and Engineering

There grew up before the eyes of the world in the years after 1850 the iron constructions of the great exhibitions. In them the methods of engineering entered the field of architecture; with that entrance the question of the relation between archi-

Reflection on contemporary utterances

[2] Jobard, "L'Architecture de l'avenir," *Revue générale d'architecture*, 1849, p. 27.

Jobard was an engineer, the first director of the Musée de l'Industrie at Brussels, and one of those scientists most interested in the new processes and materials developed in industry. Jobard did not confine himself simply to invoking the appearance of a new architecture of iron and glass. For example, he suggested a type of structure with double walls filled with glass panes which would permit air-conditioning of the interior. The space between the panes was to be filled with hot air in the winter, cold air in the summer.

[3] The romantic poet Théophile Gautier, in the newspaper *La Presse*.

[4] *Revue générale d'architecture*, 1867, p. 6.

[5] Octave Mirbeau in *Figaro*, 1889; cf. also *Encyclopédie d'architecture*, 1889/90, p. 92.

tect and engineer was raised and became ever more vexing and urgent. For more than sixty years that question was agitated by various theorists.

1852: "Far be it from me to pretend that the style pointed out by our mechanics is what is sometimes miscalled an economical, a cheap style. No! It is the dearest of all the styles! It costs the thought of men, much, very much thought, untiring investigation, ceaseless experiment. Its simplicity is that of justness; I had almost said, of justice.

". . . the mechanics of the United States have already outstripped the artists, and have, by their bold and unflinching adaptation, entered the true track and hold up the light for all who operate for American wants, be they what they will.

"By beauty I mean the promise of function.

"By action I mean the presence of function.

"By character I mean the record of function." [6]

1867: "Is it the fate of architecture to give way to the art of engineering? Will the architect be eclipsed by the engineer?" [7]

1877: In this year the question entered the Académie, when a prize was offered for the best paper discussing "the union or the separation of engineer and architect." Davioud, one of the architects of the Trocadéro, won the prize with this answer: "The accord will never become real, complete, and fruitful until the day that the engineer, the artist, and the scientist are fused together in the same person. We have for a long time lived under the foolish persuasion that art is a kind of activity distinct from all other forms of human intelligence, having its sole source and origin in the personality of the artist himself, and in his capricious fancy." [8]

1889: "A long time ago the influence of the architect declined, and the engineer, *l'homme moderne par excellence*, is beginning to replace him. . . . It will not be [arbitrarily chosen] shapes

[6] Horatio Greenough, the American sculptor, in *The Travels, Observations, and Experiences of a Yankee Stonecutter*; cited by Nancy Wynne and Beaumont Newhall, "Horatio Greenough: Herald of Functionalism," *Magazine of Art*, XXXII (January 1939), 15.

[7] César Daly, *Revue générale d'architecture*, 1867, p. 6.

[8] *Encyclopédie d'architecture*, 1878, p. 67.

which will form the basis of the new architecture: in urban planning, in the real application of modern construction, the taking into account of the new situations which must be reckoned with will lead us to the shapes so long sought in vain. But, you will say, what you propose are the methods of engineering today. I do not deny it, for these are correct." [9]

1899: Thirty years after César Daly's anxiety with regard to the future of architecture one of the founders of the *art nouveau* sees quite clearly that "there is a class of men from whom the title of artist can no longer be withheld. These artists, the creators of new architecture, are the engineers.

"The extraordinary beauty innate in the work of engineers has its basis in their unconsciousness of its artistic possibilities — much as the creators of the beauty of the cathedrals were unaware of the magnificence of their achievements." [10]

Van de Velde already recognized that the engineer promised the regeneration of architecture and not its destruction. It is still the case — as much so as when van de Velde wrote — that the latest works of the engineers embody possibilities of aesthetic experience not as yet exploited, which have still to find their place in architectonic expression. There are, for example, those fantastic, single-columned shelters built in France to protect freight while it is being transshipped, those curving Swiss bridges which are formed out of thin slabs of ferroconcrete, and various other strikingly original constructions elsewhere, which embody unexplored potentialities for architecture.

1924: "The century of the machine awakened the architect. New tasks and new possibilities produced him. He is at work now everywhere." [11]

Such an opinion — one that is shared by the whole generation of architects to which Le Corbusier belongs — marks the solution of the break between the architect and the engineer.

[9] Anatole de Baudot, at the first International Congress of Architects in Paris, 1889.
[10] Henri van de Velde, "Die Rolle der Ingenieure in der modernen Architektur," in *Die Renaissance im modernen Kunstgewerbe* (Berlin, 1901).
[11] Le Corbusier in *L'Esprit nouveau* (Paris, 1924), no. 25.

On the whole it is true that contemporary architects have succeeded at the end of a century of struggle in drawing abreast of construction. New tasks await architecture today. It must now meet needs other than the strictly rational, other than those which are pragmatically determined. A living architecture must also succeed in satisfying those subrational, emotional demands which are deeply rooted in our age.

HENRI LABROUSTE, ARCHITECT–CONSTRUCTOR, 1801–1875

Labrouste born
with the new
century

Until now we have had to dissect practically anonymous constructions to find the first signs of the new developments which life, almost unconsciously, was bringing about. Toward the middle of the nineteenth century, we encounter for the first time in this period a man who unites the abilities of both the engineer and the architect: the architect-constructor Henri Labrouste. Henri Labrouste was born in Paris in 1801. In the same year Telford offered his project for London Bridge, a plan calling for a colossal structure in cast iron. It was also in 1801 that James Watt's Soho foundry built the first cotton mill to embody cast-iron beams and pillars in its interior construction.

Wins *grand prix
de Rome;* sees stay
in Italy as an
estrangement
from life

Labrouste was educated at the Académie des Beaux-Arts and was one of its outstanding pupils. When he was twenty-three, he was awarded the *grand prix de Rome*, which made it possible for him to spend five years at the Villa Medici in Rome. During those five years he came to see antique Rome as something more than a monument or an arsenal of beautiful forms on which a student might draw. He took toward it very nearly the attitude of an onlooker of today; what astonished him was the skill in construction everywhere visible in these works. While, as pensioner of the Academy, he was studying Roman aqueducts and examining the temples at Paestum, he sought always to grasp the spirit behind each construction, *l'organisme de chaque construction.*[1]

[1] Labrouste did not make the usual picturesque reproductions of ancient monuments. He approached them with the sharp eyes of an engineer or an archaeologist. His draw⹀

216

For all that, he ended by regarding his stay in Italy — meant as the highest reward to talent — as a systematic estrangement from life. He preferred studies dealing with problems arising out of his own time. Significantly enough, the last project which he sent to the Academy from Rome was a design for a bridge, one appropriate to stand on the frontiers of two friendly countries.

Labrouste, belonging to that generation which arrived at its maturity around 1830 and seemed to include among its members the most vigorous characters in the century, shared its feeling that social, moral, and intellectual life all alike demanded renewal. In the summer of 1830, when he returned to Paris, he found the routine of the Academy unchanged. He wrote to his brother Theodore on July 12, 1830: "What should I say to you about the École? Its programs of courses are always uninteresting and badly organized; its pupils lack enthusiasm. And even the master of an *atelier* would exhaust himself through futile efforts on programs like these. . . . Architecture must not be circumscribed within studies like those actually pursued at the École des Beaux-Arts. Reforms are called for — what master will have the courage to make the pressing cause of our art his own?" [2]

During this same summer he opened his own *atelier*, a school of design opposed to the principles of the Academy, in which he instructed the progressive youth of France. Once again a letter to his brother (written in November 1830) will give some insight into his methods of instruction:

"I am working prodigiously and — what is harder — I am making my pupils work.

"I have drawn up several schedules of study to drill the beginners in something useful: I want them to learn to compose with very simple means. It is necessary for them from the

---

ings of the temples at Paestum were the source of much controversy at the French Academy. He was among the first to discover traces of the colors which had originally overlaid the buildings and attempted reconstructions of them. During the late fifties the questions raised by the use of polychromy in ancient art occupied many architects in various countries — Schinkel, Hittorf, Gottfried Semper, and others.

[2] *Souvenirs d'Henri Labrouste, Notes recueillies et classées par ses enfants* (Paris, 1928; privately printed), p. 24.

start to see the direction of their work so that they may arrange its parts according to the importance which they can reasonably be given. Then I explain to them that solidity depends more on the way materials are put together than upon their mass, and — as soon as they know the first principles of construction — I tell them that they must derive from the construction itself an ornamentation which is reasoned and expressive.

"I often repeat to them that the arts have the power of making everything beautiful, but I insist that they understand that in architecture form must always be appropriate to the function for which it is intended.

"Finally, I am happy to find myself in the midst of these young comrades, who are attentive, full of good-will, and resolved to continue along the path which we are following together." [3]

First large commission when he had passed forty

The Academy waged a bitter war against the so-called "rationalistic school" which Labrouste headed. This official opposition had its consequences. On the occasions when Labrouste set foot on a building plot it was to inspect the work of other architects. The winner of the *grand prix de Rome* had to wait more than twelve years for a chance to show his talents in an executed work of importance. It was not until he was past forty that Labrouste was commissioned to build the Bibliothèque Sainte-Geneviève in Paris (1843–50).

Bibliothèque Sainte-Geneviève, Paris

In the library of Sainte-Geneviève he made the first attempt to use cast- and wrought-iron construction in an important public building from the foundations to the roof. Sainte-Geneviève was, in addition, the first library building in France designed to be a complete and independent unit. As in the English mills and warehouses, the iron construction is enclosed in the stonework of the exterior like the works of a watch in its case. Thick masonry outer walls still remain, but all structural members — columns, beams, and roofing — are of iron (*figs.* **120, 121**).

Iron skeleton in the interior

The framework of the long, double-naved reading room forms, with that of the roof, a single structure. Labrouste achieved an

---

[3] *Ibid.*

120. HENRI LABROUSTE. Library of Sainte-Geneviève, Paris, 1843–50. *Section through the reading room and the wrought-iron framework of the roof.*

121. HENRI LABROUSTE. Library of Sainte-Geneviève, Paris, 1843–50. *Plan.*

astonishing thinness in the barrel vaults by extending an iron network along them; this network at the same time afforded a base for the plaster covering of the vault. This construction recalls the eggshell-like reinforced concrete vaults in the dock buildings at Casablanca which the French architect Perret constructed in 1916. But Labrouste's chief accomplishment in this library rests in the manner in which the iron construction is balanced in itself, so that it puts no stress on the walls. The achievement of just such a hovering equilibrium became the chief task for engineers in the second half of the nineteenth century.

The Bibliothèque
Nationale, Paris,
his masterpiece

Labrouste reached his full development with the building of
the Bibliothèque Nationale in Paris, begun in 1858 and completed after his death.[4] The increase in the production of
books during the nineteenth century made the provision of
sufficient space the main problem in library building. The
stacks took up more and more room. In earlier times, stack
and reading rooms had been identical; now they had to be
separated. There is no library which solved the problem this
situation created so elegantly as Labrouste's Bibliothèque
Nationale.

Difference from
British Museum

In it Labrouste departed from the example set by his English
contemporary in the same field, Sydney Smirke (1798–1877).
Smirke designed the monumental and frequently imitated
circular reading room in the quadrangle of the British Museum.
But the circular outline of this room left only the remnants of
the quadrangular space whose center it occupied available for
the stack rooms. The inspiration for such an arrangement
came not from the architect but from Sir Anthony Panizzi, the
principal librarian of the British Museum and the creative
force behind much of its development. Panizzi was also responsible for having the reading desks placed along lines
radiating from a central observation point. The library of the
British Museum is worthy of note in another respect; its circular dome is constructed from top to bottom of iron and was
the first of its kind.

Sydney Smirke, its designer, remains an interesting figure in
the architecture of the time. Though overshadowed by his
brother, Robert, he did important work in the design and
equipment of club buildings. His work on English club
interiors is one of the points from which the evolution
of modern furniture proceeds. He also designed those
chairs in the British Museum reading room which are still
unique, in point of comfort, among the great libraries of
the world.

The reading room
in the Bibliothèque
Nationale

The reading room (*figs.* **122, 123**) which Labrouste designed
for the Bibliothèque Nationale was square and contained
sixteen cast-iron pillars. Immediately behind it was the

[4] Cf. Michel Roux-Spitz, "La Bibliothèque nationale de Paris," *L'Architecture d'aujourd'hui,* vol. IX, no. 3 (March 1938).

122. HENRI LABROUSTE. Bibliothèque Nationale, Paris, 1858–68. *Reading room.*
Sixteen slim cast-iron columns; spherical vaults, each with a round opening at the top so
that all the desks are equally well-lighted. It is typically nineteenth-century in the way its
architectural shapes are borrowed from a variety of earlier periods.

**123. HENRI LA-
BROUSTE.** Biblio-
thèque Nationale,
Paris, 1858–68. *Ground
plan.*

large stack room known as the *magasin central*. He thus
set the example of giving the stack room, the real heart
of a modern library, the important position which it deserves. The reading room in its construction follows the
line Labrouste had already taken in the library of Sainte-
Geneviève: the iron construction is enclosed by the massive walls. The tall, slender columns (one foot in diameter

221

124. HENRI LABROUSTE.
Bibliothèque Nationale, Paris,
1858–68. *The stacks (magasin
central). Four stories above ground
and one below, all surmounted by
a glass ceiling. The gridiron floor
plates permit the light to penetrate to all parts of the stacks.*

125. HENRI LABROUSTE.
Bibliothèque Nationale, Paris,
1858–68. *The stacks (magasin
central). Light pouring through
the gridiron floor. Floor plates of
this open design seem to have been
used first in the engine rooms of
steamships. Here they serve a
purely utilitarian function, but
at the same time they contain the
germ of new artistic possibilities.*

126. HENRI LABROUSTE.
Bibliothèque Nationale, Paris,
1858–68. *The stacks (magasin
central). Detail of gridiron floor
and banisters.*

and thirty-two feet high) impart an airy lightness to the room.

Shapes borrowed from various periods

The columns are connected with each other by means of semi-circular girders which come together to form nine light, covered vaults reminiscent of those in Brunelleschi's Foundling Hospital at Florence. Labrouste's spherical vaults are built up of thin plates of faïence earthenware; there is a round opening in the top of each after the manner of the Roman Pantheon. In this way excellent lighting for every reading desk is assured. These details are mentioned only to show how the space conceptions of all periods are mixed together in nineteenth-century architecture.

Manner of using the gridiron floor plates

But Labrouste's masterpiece is the *grand magasin* or stack room (*fig.* **124**) built along the same axis. The *magasin central* has four stories above ground and one below, and was built to accommodate 900,000 volumes. In the recent renovation of the library Labrouste's excellent work in its construction was adjudged to be in perfect condition, and was left completely undisturbed. The whole area was covered with a glass ceiling. Cast-iron floor plates in a gridiron pattern permit the daylight to penetrate the stacks from top to bottom.[5] Floor plates of this open design (*fig.* **126**) seem to have been used first in the engine rooms of steamships. No doubt they were introduced into library buildings with purely practical ends in view. Nevertheless, observing them in our day, we recognize in the manner in which light penetrates the grillwork of the iron floor the germ of new artistic possibilities (*fig.* **125**). This hovering play of light and shadow appears as an artistic means in certain works of modern sculpture as well as in contemporary architecture.

Labrouste took great care to provide for efficient communication between all parts of the *magasin central*. The different stories are connected by bridges so that one can go from one section to another by the shortest route. These bridges, quite apart from their obvious utility, give a certain effect of power

---

[5] Labrouste had been anticipated in this feature of his design. Panizzi not only conceived the plan for the circular reading room of the British Museum but also the idea of using gridiron floor plates in its stack rooms. This was in 1852. Cf. Arundal Esdaile, *National Libraries of the World* (London, 1934), pp. 10, 27.

to the room. Light stairways with gridiron treads permit easy access to all the books. Except for the bookshelves, all the construction is of iron.

In view of the fact that the stack rooms were not open to the general public, Labrouste could proceed quite freely in their design and was not impeded by popular taste. He made good use of this freedom. He dispensed with all applied decoration. There is in its stead an astonishing sureness of expression, resulting from a perfect fitness for purpose which only the hand of an artist could achieve.[6]

Reasons for uncompromising development in stacks

In this room — one never meant for public display — a great artist unfolded new possibilities for architecture. It is true that the Crystal Palace of some years before was a much more spectacular and imaginative structure. In the *magasin central*, however, Labrouste had been set a problem in architecture that was detailed and specific. Using the means possible to an architect of his day, Labrouste solved it in a manner that bears the stamp of a timeless rightness. If there is a Pazzi Chapel to be found anywhere in contemporary architecture, it is here.

The *magasin central* connects with the main reading room through a large arched opening (*fig.* **127**). Labrouste had the audacity that was needed in his day to erect a large glass screen in this opening, so that the magazine of books stored in the stacks could be glimpsed from the reading room. This was an early use on a large scale of the transparent areas so dear to our modern architects (*fig.* **128**).[7] Labrouste, as though a little afraid of his own daring, partially covered his glass partition with heavy red-velvet drapery.

Henri Labrouste is without doubt the architect of the middle nineteenth century whose work possessed the most significance for the future. His time, of course, dictated the use of Renaissance or classical shapes, and he used them with the greatest artistic distinction.

---

[6] The stack rooms behind the circular reading room of the British Museum used similar gridiron floor plates (as we have just seen), but nothing was achieved by their use beyond an efficient organization of this part of the library.

[7] John Nash had used a glass partition to shut off the south end of the principal corridor of Buckingham Palace. But he interlaced this glass partition with ornaments, in the baroque manner. Cf. Henry D. Roberts, *A History of the Pavilion at Brighton* (London, 1939), Fig. 25.

127. HENRI LABROUSTE. Bibliothèque Nationale, Paris, 1858–68. *Glass wall between the stacks (magasin central) and reading room. Early use of large areas of glass in the interior of a permanent public building. The heavy velvet drapery suggests that Labrouste was somewhat alarmed by his own daring.*

128. Glass wall of the Garage Rue Marbœuf, Paris, 1929. *After Labrouste's early recognition of the possibilities of glass, it came increasingly into use throughout the century, ending in immense panes like these whose framework has to be suspended from overhead bridge girders.*

But it was in his methods, in the way he analyzed and executed a task in building, that he stood far in advance of his times and of his colleagues. In spite of this, no studies of this architect have appeared since his death. We have no precise knowledge of the wearisome struggle with the Académie in which he was involved after 1830, or of the resistance he encountered that made a full realization of his ideas impossible. Perhaps the details still lie buried in the archives of the Académie. Some years ago I tried to learn more about the planning and development of Labrouste's most important work, the Bibliothèque Nationale. A search of the Building Department of the Bibliothèque Nationale itself disclosed that Labrouste's plans had been lost.

NEW BUILDING PROBLEMS — NEW SOLUTIONS

In the nineteenth century, buildings which owe nothing to the past begin to appear. Their new lines originate in the new demands presented by big towns, multiplied means of communication, and an ever-expanding industry. All these buildings have one thing in common: they are intended solely for a periodic use that involves rapid distribution of large volumes of merchandise. It is no accident that this type of construction should embody the solutions to the main architectural problems of the century. Because these unpretentious buildings contain the seeds of so much that followed, we must treat them at considerable length.

Market Halls

One of the new problems that were arising first finds a solution in the great public markets, three examples of which will be given. The earliest of such structures to require discussion here was the market hall of the Madeleine, built in Paris in 1824 (*fig.* **129**). The grace of its slender cast-iron columns is reminiscent of Pompeian mural paintings. The lightness of the construction is unbroken by any purely decorative additions. This is one of the earliest examples of the attempts nineteenth-century engineers were making to develop methods of construction which would combine elegance with economy of material.

Hall of the Madeleine, Paris, 1824

The market which was built in London in 1835 to replace the old Hungerford Fish Market represents a somewhat greater advance, so far as construction alone is concerned. A detailed description of the new Hungerford Fish Market (*fig.* **130**) appeared in the *Transactions* of the Institute of British Architects in 1836.[1] On sanitary grounds, the use of lumber in this building had been forbidden. The cast-iron construction dictated by this provision is particularly noteworthy for the wide roof span of thirty-two feet, with its straight line. It has all the elegance of a much later period. "The chief particularity in the construction," according to the report of 1836, "is

Hungerford Fish Market, London, 1835

---

[1] I (1836), 44–46.

129. Market Hall of the Madeleine, Paris, 1824. *One of the earliest examples of the attempts of nineteenth-century engineers to combine elegance with economy of materials.*

130. Hungerford Fish Market, London. *Metal roof, 1835. Particularly noteworthy for its wide roof span (thirty-two feet) with its straight line.*

the absence of any tie or lateral abutment." Already we find the planes of the roof given an inward slope, so that rain water might be carried away through the central columns.

Les Grandes Halles, Paris, 1855

The Grandes Halles of Paris, begun in 1853, had both a more interesting origin and a greater future influence than either of the structures we have just discussed. This market, the first designed to serve a population in the millions, was a part of Haussmann's great transformation of Paris. The Grandes Halles consist of two groups of pavilions connected by covered passageways. Their designer, Victor Baltard, is not by any means to be regarded as one of the great architects. His initial attempt — a stone pavilion that was built in 1851 — aroused a public disapproval so clamorous that Haussmann, then newly appointed prefect, ordered it pulled down.

228

131. VICTOR BALTARD. Halles Centrales, Paris. *Interior. Begun 1853. Baltard had to be forced to use iron in his second attempt (the first — in stone — was a disastrous failure). "Du fer! Du fer! Rien que du fer!" Haussmann insisted.*

It was only direct commands by Napoleon III and Haussmann that induced the academic Baltard to turn to iron construction in his second attempt (*fig.* **131**). Napoleon III, greatly impressed by the recently built Gare de l'Est, had decided that a similar umbrella-like shelter was all that was required in the projected market hall. "Ce sont de vastes parapluies qu'il me faut, rien de plus!" And the prefect Haussmann thundered at Baltard. "Du fer! Du fer! Rien que du fer!" The final design that Baltard produced under this pressure was a derivative patch-work of other men's plans; for all that, it had an important influence on future work.

The new version, all iron and glass, once again amazed Napoleon III when Haussmann brought it to him — this time for different reasons. "Is it possible," he asked, "that the same architect designed two such contradictory buildings?" Haussmann replied, "The architect is the same, but the prefect is different."

The project actually realized in the Grandes Halles is less interesting than two designs which were rejected. The first was the work of Hector Horeau (1801–1872). Hector Horeau was one of those architects who never know the satisfaction of

Unexecuted projects: Hector Horeau

229

FAÇADE LATÉRALE

Quai

Quart du Pavillon

Soubassement

Façade sur le Petit côté.

Coupe sur le Petit côté.

Echelle du Plan général.

Echelle des Plans, Façades et Coupe.

132. HECTOR HOREAU. Project for the Grandes Halles, 1849. *Rejected designs were much more advanced. The three-hundred-foot span in Horeau's project was not practicable until decades later. The principle used here was employed in the main building at the Paris exposition of 1855.*

fulfillment. His projects — all on a grand scale — could not be executed. Mathematical theory had not yet progressed to a point where the calculations required for such buildings could be carried through; it was still impossible to build spans as large as those included in his plans without using tie bars, or to turn out such large iron trusses. His plan for the Grandes Halles (1849) shows an immense hall with a span of three hundred feet, calling for enormously thick walls to take the heavy lateral thrust. It was not until decades later that such an intention could be achieved. Nevertheless, figures like Horeau — men who see the right way before it can be trodden — are not useless; they give the first impulse to what later becomes reality.[2]

Eugène Flachat

The second rejected design was the work of Eugène Flachat (1802–1872), a contemporary of Horeau and of Labrouste.

---

[2] A plan submitted in the Crystal Palace competition in 1850 won first prize for Hector Horeau. It was a sort of basilica with five naves (fig. 147), not to be compared with Paxton's later design.

Elévation du Pavillon principal sur la Rue de Rambuteau.

Echelle des Elévations et de la Coupe.

Demi Elévation latérale.   Demi Coupe parallèle à la Rue de Rambuteau.

133. EUGÈNE FLACHAT. Project for the Grandes Halles, 1849. *This project, using the Polonceau tie system in a span of 260 feet, could have been executed at the time. It was a most pleasing and functional solution to the problem.*

Flachat belonged to the most forceful generation of the nineteenth century, that of 1830, which included De Lesseps, the builder of the Suez Canal, Victor Hugo, the painter Eugène Delacroix, and Auguste Comte, the prophet of the scientific era. It was Flachat who, overcoming widespread resistance, built the first French railroad in 1837. He designed docks, warehouses, ports and canals, projected transatlantic steamship companies, and planned a tunnel through the Alps.

That Flachat was a follower of Saint-Simon is by no means irrelevant to this recital. The Saint-Simonists took it as axiomatic that "la Société toute entière repose sur l'industrie," and were almost alone in foreseeing the scale and the extent of the progress that industry was embarking upon. The Grandes Halles (*fig.* **133**), in its magnitude and social function, was a typical part of that new age the Saint-Simonists felt themselves destined to call forth. In submitting a plan for it, Flachat was animated by the same spirit that stood behind his other more grandiose proposals.

The design itself, like Horeau's, features a very wide span — one of 260 feet. It could, nevertheless, have been executed with the means available at the time. The Polonceau tie system is employed, and, with its minimum of support and widely spread horizontal lines, the plan achieves a most pleasing and functional solution to the problem posed.

Department Stores

Products of industrialization

The department store is a product of the industrial age; it results from the development of mass production and from the loss of direct contact between producer and consumer that was one of its consequences. The department store has no equally large forerunner in the past. In this respect it is like the market halls, railway stations, and exhibition buildings of the nineteenth century, and the object it serves is the same: the rapid handling of business activities involving huge crowds of pedestrians. Like these other buildings, the department store arises out of the growth in the population of cities, the heightened tempo of living, and the demand for cheaper goods.

The name "store" rather than "shop" points to the conditions of its origin; it is more a storage place in the normal sense of that word. The early stores in Paris during the sixties, for example, were known as *docks à bon marché*; they were simply places where goods were kept in quantity for cheap retail sale. To be fit for such a purpose, a department store — like a library stack room or a market hall — must offer a clear view of the articles it contains, a maximum of light, and ample facilities for communication. All these requirements could be met with the new means open to the builder.

Uncertainty as to their beginnings

The economists tell us that "it is fairly certain that the department store originated in Europe, probably in Paris, and antedated American department stores by several years. The Bon Marché has often been credited with being the first department store in the world." [3] Lack of interest in research work into the origins of such contemporary institutions makes it impossible to speak more exactly than this. The origins of the American department store are particularly obscure; no one has definitely determined when and where the first store of this kind was opened. We can only outline the general types out of which this important institution of our economic life has evolved.

Origin as a building-type

Even previous to the forties "commercial buildings," as they were called, were erected in such business centers as Boston,

---

[3] R. H. Nystrom, *Economics of Retailing*, 3rd ed. (New York, 1932), pp. 1–7.

THE WASHINGTON STORES,
In William Street. between Fulton & John Sts. New York. Erected 1845.

134. Washington Stores, New York City, 1845. *A row of stores all under one roof; separate units could be thrown together to house a single establishment.*

St. Louis, and New York. These buildings comprised a row of stores all under one roof and so arranged that two or more units could be thrown together to house a single establishment. Most of them were built on speculation, and the builders rented the individual stores to both retail and wholesale dealers. The "Boston Commercial Buildings," the St. Louis river front warehouses and wholesale places, and the "Washington Stores" (1845) in New York (*fig.* 134) are all typical of this stage in the development. The department store as a building type traces back to these "commercial buildings."

As a business institution the American department store evolved from those establishments which first made cheap ready-to-wear clothing available to the masses. In the forties Boston — flourishing trading-center for the New England area — had one of the largest of these enterprises. This was Oak Hall (*fig.* 135), a concern whose annual turnover was about five hundred thousand dollars.

Origin as a business institution: the ready-made clothing trade

The American stores which grew up from beginnings like these took on a character very different from that of the early European concerns. European stores specialized in dry goods; they did not deal in ready-made clothing.

Difference between American and European department stores

135. Oak Hall, Boston, c. 1850. *Ready-made clothing. One of the ready-made clothing concerns which were precursors of the department store in America.*

The majority opinion among economists is that genuine department stores do not appear before the sixties.[4] It seems to me likely that they started at an earlier date. We know — and this is one of the few exact dates available in these matters — that the first installation of a passenger elevator in a department store was made in 1857, in a building on the corner of Broadway and Broome Street, New York City [5] (*fig.* **136**).

The American department store building derives from the big seven- or eight-story warehouses which were so common during the second half of the nineteenth century. The many-storied English warehouse which the Manchester engineer, William Fairbairn, built in 1845 was an early example of such a building.[6]

Somewhat later, James Bogardus used a system of construction in cast iron which made it possible to erect relatively

[4] Nystrom, *op. cit.*, p. 134.

[5] Cf. p. 208.

[6] Cf. p. 192.

136. Broome Street, New York, 1857. *The first department store to house a passenger elevator. The building is typical of these early establishments.*

137. John Wanamaker Store, Philadelphia, 1876. *A freight shelter transformed into an immense, single-story dry goods store.*

tall buildings of the warehouse type from prefabricated parts. The A. T. Stewart store in New York — believed to be the first large department store — is a structure of this kind. The original building, now a part of the Wanamaker establishment, is still in existence. Completed and first occupied in 1863, it had two stories in the basement, five stories above ground, an attic, and six elevators.

The immense stores erected in Chicago in the late eighties, with their great unbroken areas of floor space, continued to follow the warehouse type. Examples from this period in Chicago are the Leiter Building of 1889 (built originally for single offices and now owned by Sears, Roebuck & Company) and "The Fair" of 1891 — both by William Le Baron Jenney.[7]

A peculiar solution in Philadelphia (1876)

One large store departed from the warehouse pattern — John Wanamaker's "Grand Depot" at Thirteenth and Market streets, in Philadelphia — but even this building was another type of storage place (*fig. 137*). The Grand Depot, opened as a department store in 1876 (the year of Eiffel and Boileau's Magasin au Bon Marché), was originally a freight depot of the Pennsylvania Railroad. It had served as a freight shelter for over twenty years before Wanamaker hit upon the daring idea of transforming it into an immense, single-story dry goods store.[8]

The Grand Depot had more than two acres of floor space. A circular counter ninety feet around occupied the center of the building. From this counter there radiated a series of aisles which were intersected by other aisles and counters that were concentric with the big counter in the middle.[9] The layout resembles that used for the Paris exhibition of 1867.

The Magasin au Bon Marché, Paris, 1876: constructed by Eiffel

The first modern glass and iron department store with a free influx of natural light throughout was the Magasin au Bon Marché in Paris. It was in complete contrast to the warehouse type with its superimposed, artificially lighted stories. At the time of its building in 1876, it was regarded as a model of elegance.[10]

The Bon Marché was the work of the engineer Eiffel (later to construct his famous tower) and the architect L. A. Boileau (the son of one of the great French pioneers in the use of iron in architecture).

[7] Cf. pp. 368–372.

[8] J. H. Appel, "Reminiscences of Retailing," *Bulletin of the Business Historical Society*, vol. XII, no. 6 (December 1938).

[9] Cf. *The Golden Book of the Wanamaker Store* (Philadelphia, 1911), p. 52.

[10] There were many older department stores in Paris; the Magasin au Bon Marché itself had been founded a quarter-century earlier, in 1852.

Boileau felt that thick walls were unsuited to buildings of this type; "only pillars of small diameter are permissible." And he goes on to remark that these pillars "should be no more than the hors d'œuvre of the construction." [11] The ground floor of the building already shows the use of large glass surfaces set in unbroken series. A glass shelter is carried in a continuous line along the whole front of the store above the show windows and reinforces the impression produced by the areas of glass they contain.

The corner of the store is built out, like a pavilion, reminding one of the round towers of the French châteaux. Later examples were unable to break away from this precedent. A similar treatment appears in Paul Sédille's Magasin Printemps, Paris, of 1881–89. Even Louis Sullivan's Carson, Pirie, Scott store in Chicago, built around 1900, reflects in the shape of its corner the persistent memory of the pavilion.[12]

Corner of store built out like a pavilion

The mark of the great constructor Eiffel is visible in the treatment of the interior of the Bon Marché. Its area of more than thirty thousand square feet is divided into a series of courts of various shapes, each covered by a large glass skylight. The passage from court to court is simplified by the presence of lofty iron bridges or *passerelles* like those Labrouste had used, nearly two decades earlier, in the stack room of the Bibliothèque Nationale (*fig.* **138**).

Never before had light flowed into a store in such bright streams. A true glass architecture had been erected over the framework of the building (*fig.* **140**). The creative fantasy of the nineteenth century can be felt in its combination of glass skylights, aerial bridges in iron, slim iron columns, and the curious ornamental shapes so characteristic of the period. For all this variety, there is a seriousness and simplicity about the Magasin au Bon Marché taken as a whole. The architectonic pomp and boastfulness later called upon to attract and seduce the masses is avoided here.

Seriousness and simplicity

The great masses of light which enter the building through its refined and even airy construction anticipate one of the chief

Relation to contemporary work

[11] L. A. Boileau, *fils*, "Les Magasins au Bon Marché," *Encyclopédie d'architecture*, 1880, p. 184.   [12] Cf. pp. 386–388.

138.   EIFFEL and BOILEAU. Bon Marché, Paris, 1876. *Iron bridges in the interior. The creative fantasy of the nineteenth century can be felt in this combination of glass skylights, aerial bridges in iron, slim iron columns, and the curious ornamental shapes so characteristic of the period.*

139.   EIFFEL and BOILEAU. Bon Marché, Paris, 1876. *Ground plan. Area, thirty thousand square feet. The "perforated" interior space is typical of French buildings.*

concerns of contemporary architects.   Five decades after Eiffel's construction of the Bon Marché, the same joy in the play of light through space perforations is to be found in Le Corbusier's interiors and exteriors and in the way he makes the two interpenetrate.

140.   EIFFEL and BOILEAU. Bon Marché, Paris, 1876. *Glass roof over skylight.*
This glass architecture was invisible from the street.   The moment the nineteenth century
feels itself unobserved and has no longer to make a show, then it is truly bold.

Eiffel's imaginative approach to technical problems can be seen in the exterior forms of the high glass roof which is built over the skylights of the courts.   The ordinary spectator never sees this part of the building.   The communicating *passerelles* are fantastically balanced over the inclined planes of this tent-like glass roof.[13]   The moment the nineteenth century feels itself unobserved and is no longer conscious of any need for making a show — then it is truly bold!

Boldness of the nineteenth century where it is unobserved

From this time onward the undisguised shapes with their natural content of feeling that mark the rear and unobserved portions of railroad stations and factories begin to make themselves felt in the front walls of buildings.

[13] The very early photograph made at the time of the erection of the building shows that even then people felt something unusual had been accomplished here.

141. Winter Garden and Assembly Room, Paris, 1847. *Joseph Paxton may well have been inspired for the idea of his Crystal Palace by this once celebrated cross-shaped building, which, standing between Rond Pont and the present Avenue Marbœuf, changed the simple glass house into a social meeting place containing ballroom, café, reading room, and paintings on sale along the high glass walls. "The magnificent building," observed Loudon's En-clopaedia of Gardening in 1850 (pp. 93–94), "is supposed to be one of the largest and finest in Europe . . . extreme length 300 feet, extreme breadth 180 feet, extreme height 60 feet."*

Different ways to solve a new building problem

Comparing nineteenth-century department stores in France and America we may observe how a new building problem — apparently governed solely by practical considerations — is brought to a different solution in different countries.

In America, as we have just seen, the department store followed the warehouse type: one unbroken floor area was built on top of another. In France the light court and "perforated" interior space appear even before Eiffel in department stores of wooden construction (*fig.* **139**). The Eiffel and Boileau Magasin au Bon Marché reveals very clearly a tendency inherent in French architecture. The urge to hollow out interior spaces to the greatest extent possible appears in French buildings from Romanesque times onward. It is visible in those daring Gothic choirs which seem to have been left almost too fragile to stand, and in the latest works of our own day. The audacity of French engineering is only a modified expression of this same trend.

142. First Industrial Exposition, Champ-de-Mars, Paris, 1798.

THE GREAT EXHIBITIONS

The exhibitions

In the second half of the nineteenth century, with industry undergoing its greatest expansion, industrial exhibitions afforded truly creative architecture its best opportunities. Toward the end of the century, when industry had come to be taken as a matter of course and was no longer looked upon as new and marvelous, they lost their creative force. New problems had emerged in the meantime which demanded new solutions.

Facilitated comparison of products

The exhibitions were born almost simultaneously with modern industry; they appeared at the time when the shift from handwork to machine production made itself obvious. Throughout that period people in many countries were working feverishly to invent new machines and new processes. The chief purpose

241

of the early exhibitions was to bring together the results of this work, to display the new discoveries side by side, and thus to facilitate their comparison and adoption. The development of industry in all its branches was accelerated by these exhibitions, in which every sphere of human activity was represented: the implements, methods, and products of mines, mills, machine shops, and farms were on display, together with work in the fine and the applied arts.

The industrial exhibition embodied a synthesis of the as yet unformulated aims of the nineteenth century. It foretold the transformation that was to be effected in man as well as in industry, in human feelings as well as in human surroundings. The exhibitions were a part of the march of industry and were bound up in its destiny.

Two periods in the history of the exhibitions

The history of the exhibition is divided into two periods. The earlier of these periods opens and closes in Paris; it begins with the first industrial exhibition ever held — that of 1798 — and ends with the Paris exhibition of 1849. The exhibitions of this initial period were made possible by the collapse of the guilds in 1791, and were all purely national in character.

The first period, national exhibitions: Paris, 1798

The *première exposition des produits de l'industrie française* was opened on the Champ-de-Mars in Paris in September 1798 (*fig.* **142**). It inaugurated an exhibition movement which was to lead to some of the outstanding achievements of the nineteenth century. The start made at Paris in 1798 was a very modest one. There were some luxury articles displayed, but the precedent for nearly all future exhibitions was set by the central position given to articles of daily use: watches, wall paper, cloth, and cotton yarn — yarn which "was carded and spun by means of machinery," as the catalogue was careful to state.

There were only a hundred and ten exhibitors at this first exposition, but this does not detract from its importance. It was primarily intended as a sort of people's festival, in celebration of the freedom from guild restrictions that the Revolution had brought. This festive motive accounted for its location in the Champ-de-Mars, the scene of all national celebrations since the fall of the monarchy. It was the *proclamation de*

242

la liberté du travail in 1791 that first gave every citizen the right to follow whatever trade he desired. What was more important, this proclamation, in according a new liberty to production, gave official encouragement to a progress of industry and invention from which everyone expected great things. "Ces arts n'avaient pas pu encore se developper à cause des entraves sans nombre. Mais la liberté les vengerait. . . . Sous l'égide de la liberté, les arts utiles étaient appelés à un brilliant avenir."

The second period occupies the latter half of the nineteenth century and owes its force to the principle of free trade. In this period the exhibition takes on a new character; it becomes international in its scope. The national exhibitions of industry during the first half of the century had followed upon the abolition of the legal obligation to belong to a guild. Something else was demanded for an international exhibition: there was no reason to bring together products from all over the world unless there existed at the same time the possibility of selling to the whole world. An international exhibition could have value only in a world where trade restrictions of all kinds had been reduced to a minimum. These great exhibitions were the product of the liberal conception of economy: free trade, free communication, and improvement in production and performance through free competition.

The exhibitions also fostered a spirit of rivalry, a desire to equal or improve upon the last exhibition. Thus risks were taken in many departments, not least of all in architecture. Such a spirit of rivalry, together with the efficiency it promoted, is visible in the Crystal Palace world exhibition of 1851.

The history of exhibitions during the latter half of the nineteenth century constitutes at the same time a history of iron construction. Exhibition buildings were planned for rapid erection and dismantling: both were facilitated by the use of iron. Again, iron parts for such buildings could be fabricated in widely separated workshops. Finally, iron was everywhere regarded at this date as the medium of expression most truly appropriate to the period. But exhibition buildings did not simply call for the use of iron; the fact that they appeared at short intervals and were meant to be only temporary encour-

243

aged the experimental employment of iron in their construction. The exhibition became the trial ground for new methods. In all the great international exhibitions — from the first at Crystal Palace, London, in 1851 to the last at the end of the century — constructors attempted tasks that had never been faced before. When their experiments succeeded in this special field they became a part of standard building practice. It was in this way that the Eiffel Tower came to be erected in 1889, despite the most doleful prophecies of disaster.

New constructions demanded new aesthetic responses

The history of the exhibition shows not only the developments in iron construction during the period but also important changes in habits of aesthetic response. The new structural treatments of load and support demanded new aesthetic reactions. In the past people had grown to expect the basis of the equilibrium between load and support in a building to be visible at a glance, to lie open to inspection. But with the introduction of new methods of iron construction it became more and more difficult to differentiate between load and support: a new poised equilibrium of all the parts of a structure began to appear.

What the exhibitions symbolized

The optimism of the nineteenth century and its faith in the possibilities of industry are reflected in the great exhibitions. Industry would "unite the human race" — or so Prince Consort Albert dreamt in 1850. There seemed no limit to what industry could achieve at the start of its period of greatest expansion; people confidently expected it to solve all the ancient problems of the world.

Unparalleled concentration of human activities

The exhibitions sprang from and symbolize the urge to master the earth's resources and draw out all its wealth. In a manner which is unparalleled in earlier periods they served as a concentration point for human activities of every sort, the emphasis always falling on industry and its latest inventions. These exhibitions mark the points where the nineteenth century drew aside from the rush of production in which it was caught to survey the progress that had been made.

The concentration of the activities of the century in a single place attracted interested representatives from all over the world. The exhibitions became, naturally, the scene of all sorts of international congresses — of science, industry, finance, and labor. Beyond this, they attracted official observers from all those countries which were anxious to learn of and adopt the new developments. There are reports by Spanish, Italian, and Turkish observers which fill many volumes. The report of the United States Commissioner to the Paris exhibition of 1867 takes up six volumes, each of about three hundred and fifty pages.

The very complete surveys published by the countries where the exhibitions were held show a contemporary realization of their unique importance. They were edited with great care; later generations will find them the most satisfactory sources for a knowledge of what actually went on during the nineteenth century. These reports were often made under the supervision of men who possessed real foresightedness and initiative. Henry Cole was responsible for the first of these large-scale surveys — the *Official Descriptive and Illustrative Catalogue of the Great Exhibition* (London, 1851), in four big blue volumes. The thirteen-volume report on the Paris exhibition of 1867 was prepared under Michel Chevalier, a former Saint-Simonist. As an exile, Chevalier had traveled in the United States during the thirties; after his return to France he worked continually to promote industry.

Official reports: scope, and historical value

Exhibitions grew out of the old fairs, familiar to every century. The first French exhibition in 1798 was essentially a kind of people's festival, and all later exhibitions retained this festival motif.

The nineteenth century marks the point when leisure vanished from daily life. The ability to develop an original form for festivals vanished with it. During the second half of the nineteenth century the exhibitions remained the great festivals in the life of nations. Warehouses, department stores, and office buildings remained closely bound up with immediate practical needs. The exhibitions had their practical function to fulfill also, but they operated in an atmosphere far removed from the rush of everyday life and were able to sustain a festive character. There was always a sharp contrast between their festive and their practical or official aspects. The sureness which appears in the construction of their great halls is not

The great exhibitions, the nineteenth century's original form for festivals

245

carried over into the social arrangements in the interiors of the halls, for example. But, even so, they represent the closest approach of the period to an original form of group celebration.

Even in the nineteenth century, when architecture was rooted in the background of industrial development, it was in these buildings of a certain festive intent that the great solutions of the period to the vaulting problem were made.

Significance of the vaulting problem during the Renaissance, the baroque period, and the nineteenth century

From the beginning of architecture the vaulting problem has always brought forth the highest architectural expressions of every epoch. Thus the barrel vault painted by Masaccio during the early Renaissance was developed into a ceremonious expression of the full Renaissance and early baroque world. In the late baroque, changes in vaulting once again accompanied changes in the outlook of the age.

Solutions to the vaulting problem played the same important role in the nineteenth century. The *haut goût* of the nineteenth-century style in architecture requires — as we have already noted more than once — more careful study than it has yet been given. But, whatever results such a study may lead to, the constituent facts of architectural development will be found to be those original solutions of the vaulting problem which first took shape in the large halls of great exhibitions.

New vaulting problems of the nineteenth century solved in industrial buildings

Objections to this view could readily be advanced. It might be said that these exhibition buildings represented nothing but the answers to very sober practical needs, while the vaulting problem had possessed an almost metaphysical significance in earlier periods.

These objections cannot be ignored. Furthermore, it is obvious that such exhibition buildings were out of direct contact with human needs. But in a certain sense this remark applies to the period as a whole. Their indifference to human needs makes these constructions a true — if harsh — expression of the times. Nevertheless we may succeed in showing that behind this indifference a new feeling lies hidden.

The two most beautiful buildings of the period of the great exhibitions — the Crystal Palace of 1851 and the Galerie des

246

Machines of 1889 — have disappeared. The first was destroyed by fire in 1937; the second was senselessly torn down in 1910. Their loss is a typical consequence of the day-to-day mood that governs our period. Only photographs and etchings remain as witness that the overcoming of gravity in apparently floating constructions (which is the essence of any solution to the problem of vaulting) was achieved in magnificent form during the nineteenth century.

The Great Exhibition, London, 1851

The Crystal Palace (*fig.* **143**) had the impact of a fairy story on all those who saw it opened in London in 1851. Industry, after all the blight and disorder it had brought about, now displayed another and a gentler side, aroused feelings that seemed to belong only to the world of dreams.

The Crystal Palace housed an exhibition that was the first of its kind, one that reflected the courage and enterprise of the early Victorian period. The Prince Consort, Albert, and Sir Henry Cole [1] were its leading spirits, and it was the former who gave it a central theme. Cole relates a conversation he had with Prince Albert at Buckingham Palace on June 29, 1849: "I asked the Prince if he had considered [whether] the exhibition should be a national or an international exhibition. The French had discussed whether their own exhibition should be international, and had preferred that it should be national only. The Prince reflected for a minute and then said, 'It must embrace foreign productions' — to use his words — and added emphatically, 'International, certainly. . . . Where do you think it should be?' I answered, 'In Hyde Park.'" The prince's decision was by no means a casual reply. In 1850 he declared: "None will doubt that we are living in a most remarkable period of transition, laboring forcefully toward that great

The great exhibition initiated by the Prince Consort and Sir Henry Cole

[1] Sir Henry Cole (1808–1882) was an active influence upon English industry from 1845 on. Unlike the members of the movement begun by William Morris in the sixties, Cole tried to work with industry rather than to revive hand crafts. As he said in 1845, his aim was to develop "'art manufactures,' meaning fine art or beauty applied to mechanical production." His program included the founding of schools of design intended to raise the level of popular taste. As a part of this program he founded the first museum of decorative art, the Victoria and Albert Museum in South Kensington. More space will be devoted to Henry Cole in a book now in preparation.

143.   Crystal Palace, London, 1851.   *General view.   Lithograph.*

144.   Crystal Palace, London, 1851.   *Plan.   Ground area, eight hundred thousand square feet.   The Crystal Palace made no real contribution to the nineteenth-century problem of vaulting in iron, but it marks the first use on a grand scale of prefabricated parts, and it arrives at a new artistic expression through the use of the new material, plate glass.*

248

aim indicated everywhere by history: the union of the human race. . . . Gentlemen, the exhibition of 1851 shall give a vivid picture of the stage at which industry has arrived in the solution of that great task." [2]

The Crystal Palace had behind it the highly developed industry of England and is an application of the most simple and rational system of manufacturing — that of serial production. Its builder, Joseph Paxton, used the "ridge and furrow" construction employed in the greenhouses which were used to protect the tropical plants at Chatsworth in 1837. The design of the whole building was planned around the largest standard sheet of glass, which was only four feet long. Larger panes could not be made at this time. The panes used in the Palace were the work of the Chance Brothers' Birmingham plant. (The furnace used in this work is still in service.)

Crystal Palace based on prefabricated parts

It is astonishing to find Paxton able at this early date to dissect the whole building into a simple system of small prefabricated units. There are the wooden ridge and furrow frames for the glass, the iron lattice girders on which the panes rested, and the cast-iron supporting pillars — bolted together floor by floor. The wood and iron structural members were manufactured in various shops in Birmingham and fitted together on the site at London. In this manner a building with a ground area of some eight hundred thousand square feet — about four times that of St. Peter's, as contemporaries remarked with pride — arose within six months. Its length was 1,851 feet — to correspond with the date of its erection. But for all its architectural beauty, the Crystal Palace makes no contribution to the problem of vaulting as it concerns iron construction. The barrel vault in its transept had a wooden framework, and its span of seventy-two feet was less than that of many medieval buildings (*fig.* 144).

Small span

The Crystal Palace was the realization of a new conception of building, one for which there was no precedent. It was, in addition, the first building of such dimensions constructed of glass, iron, and timber over a framework of cast- and wrought-

"A revolution in architecture"

---

[2] Sir Henry Cole, *Fifty Years of Public Service* (London, 1884), I, 124–125.

iron girders accurately bolted together. The possibilities dormant in modern industrial civilization have never since, to my knowledge, been so clearly expressed. It was recognized at the time that this combination of wood, glass, and iron — incidentally a combination resulting in an admirably practical exhibition technique — had evoked a new kind of imagination which sprang directly from the spirit of the age. Only thus can we explain the confident prediction of contemporaries, since justified in all essentials, that "the Crystal Palace is a revolution in architecture from which a new style will date."[3]

---

[3] Lothar Bucher, *Kulturhistorische Skizzen aus der Industrieausstellung aller Völker* (Frankfort, 1851), p. 174.

Lothar Bucher wrote in 1851 that "the building encountered no opposition, and the impression it produced on those who saw it was one of such romantic beauty that reproductions of it were soon hanging on the cottage walls of remote German villages. In contemplating the first great building which was not of solid masonry construction spectators were not slow to realize that here the standards by which architecture had hitherto been judged no longer held good." [4]

An opinion of 1851

Bucher, a democratic political exile who was later to become Bismarck's right-hand man in the Wilhelmstrasse, then goes on to describe the interior (*figs.* **145, 148**). The description reads almost exactly like a present-day analysis of architecture: "We see a delicate network of lines without any clue by means of which we might judge their distance from the eye or the real size. The side walls are too far apart to be embraced in a single glance. Instead of moving from the wall at one end to

"All materiality blends into the atmosphere"

146. "The Favorites": popular sculpture of 1851. *It is important not to lose sight of what was really admired in the nineteenth century by officials, critics, and the public. A contemporary opinion of "The Favorites": "One of the most charming groups of the British Sculpture Court . . . lifelike, interesting and beautiful . . ."*

[4] Bucher, *ibid.*

251

that at the other, the eye sweeps along an unending perspective which fades into the horizon. We cannot tell if this structure towers a hundred or a thousand feet above us, or whether the roof is a flat platform or is built up from a succession of ridges, for there is no play of shadows to enable our optic nerves to gauge the measurements.

"If we let our gaze travel downward it encounters the blue-painted lattice girders. At first these occur only at wide intervals; then they range closer and closer together until they are interrupted by a dazzling band of light — the transept — which dissolves into a distant background where all materiality is blended into the atmosphere. . . . It is sober economy of

147. HECTOR HOREAU. First prize in the competition for the Crystal Palace, 1850. *Hector Horeau (whose project for the Grandes Halles we remember) won the first prize with a light iron construction of the basilica type. It may to some extent have influenced the committee's decision not to erect a monumental edifice, their original intention.*

language if I call the spectacle incomparable and fairylike. It is a Midsummer Night's Dream seen in the clear light of midday."

Counterparts in painting: the landscapes of Turner

Are there counterparts of the Crystal Palace among the paintings of the period — any paintings, that is, which give "no idea of the actual size or distance involved," and where "all materiality blends into the atmosphere"? There are none to be found outside the orbit of English painting. J. M. W. Turner's study of the Simplon Pass,[5] painted c. 1840 (*fig.* **149**), uses a humid atmosphere to dematerialize landscape and dissolve it into infinity. The Crystal Palace realizes the same intention through the agency of transparent glass surfaces and iron structural members. In the Turner picture the means employed are less abstract, but an equivalent insubstantial and hovering effect is produced. The deep hollows in the

[5] In the Fogg Art Museum, Cambridge, Massachusetts.

mountains — done in gray, brown, and blue — and the yellowish-brown road that winds up to the peaks in the background combine to eliminate every naturalistic feature: they seem precisely to make up parts of a dream landscape, "seen in the clear light of midday."

In the Crystal Palace an artistic conception outdistances the technical possibilities of the era — something which is very rare in the nineteenth century. The whole building reflects the careful hand of its builder, the landscape gardener Joseph Paxton, who was more accustomed to work with plants than with machinery. The curious association of an unmistakable grandeur with a certain gentleness was never again to be achieved.[6] From now on, development will come for decades at the hands of the engineer. He will achieve the new solutions.

The Crystal Palace: association of gentleness with grandeur

The Universal Exhibition, Paris, 1855

The exhibition was inaugurated in France as a national festival in 1798 and continued to develop along such lines throughout the first half of the nineteenth century. In 1849 the French Minister of Commerce proposed making the Paris exhibition of that year an international one. The French chambers of commerce, however, lacked sufficient courage to open their frontiers to foreign industry. It was not until 1855, four years after the international exhibition at the Crystal Palace, that the first "exposition universelle des produits de l'industrie" was held in France. But from 1855 on, all the great exhibitions, all those that had any historical importance, were held in France. During this period, as in Gothic times, France was the scene of the most audacious constructions. Both the public and the press adopted a certain waiting attitude toward the exhibition of 1855 which disappears with later French exhibi-

France the center of exhibitions after 1850

[6] During the fifties several attempts were made to construct a building exclusively of glass and iron — as in the New York exhibition of 1853, for example. The plan executed at New York in 1853 was a mediocre one which grafted a monumental dome upon Paxton's ideas. Paxton himself submitted a design, but it was unsatisfactory. The plan of James Bogardus — an original and genuinely American solution to the problem — was also rejected (cf. Fig. 111). The beginnings Paxton had made in the Crystal Palace suffered another setback in the London World's Fair of 1862. Its pseudo-monumental domes and triumphal arches followed in the path of the Palais de l'Industrie, Paris, 1855, but without equalling its constructive hardihood. For further details, cf. "Record of the Great Exhibition," *Practical Mechanic's Journal* (London, 1862).

148. Crystal Palace, Interior. *"We see a delicate network of lines without any clue by means of which we might judge their distance from the eye, or the real size"* (*Lothar Bucher, 1851*).

tions. At first people were anxious not to commit themselves; finally new applications for exhibition space were made in such numbers that the area originally fixed upon proved too small. The exhibition consequently ended by showing numerous additions.

Scheme for the exhibition of 1855

Ground plan (*fig.* **151**): The Palais de l'Industrie was a rectangular structure with a high center aisle which was surrounded by a double row of galleries. The low side aisles were supported by numerous cast-iron pillars. The center aisle connected with one of those circular panoramas so popular at the time and with the twelve-hundred-meter Galerie des Machines which extended along the Seine. The Galerie des Machines (*fig.* **152**), in spite of the narrow barrel vault which seems to link it with Fontaine's gallery in the Palais d'Orléans, was the starting point for that succession of *halles des machines*

149. J. M. W. TURNER. *Simplon Pass.* *Water color, c. 1840.* *Fogg Museum, Cambridge, Mass.* *The unsubstantial and hovering effect of the Crystal Palace is achieved here through a humid atmosphere which dematerializes the landscape and dissolves it into infinity.*

which produced the most daring solutions to the vaulting problem.

Span: The Palais de l'Industrie had a span of forty-eight meters. This was the widest vaulting attempted in the period. It represents a great advance over what was achieved in the Crystal Palace, with its span of about twenty-two meters.[7] Wrought-iron lattice girders, partially hand-forged, were used. It was the first time they had been employed for vaulting. The enormous areas of glass introduced into the vaulting almost blinded contemporary spectators, who were unaccustomed to the amount of light that was admitted. The form of the vaulting recalls the manner in which great halls and staircases were covered during the first and second empires. Even

Widest vaulting
of the period

---

[7] Long before this, Gothic builders had attained a span of twenty-nine meters in the wooden vaulting of the Salone at Padua.

150. International Exhibition, Paris, 1855. *Interior of the main building. Span of forty-eight meters very great for the period. No tie bars were used, but they were avoided artificially, through the use of heavy buttresses.*

151. International Exhibition, Paris, 1855. *Plan.*

152. The Hall of Machines, Paris, 1855. *A gallery twelve hundred meters long paralleling the Seine, the starting point for those Galeries des Machines which became more and more the pivotal points of the industrial exhibitions.*

at this early stage, the meaning of the new materials had been grasped; emphasis rests upon the opening-up of space rather than the walling-in of a volume (*fig.* **150**).

Construction: The round, high-swung arches of the center aisle show how much progress had been made. No tie bars encroach upon the free space, in spite of the bold span of nearly fifty meters. Still, one feels that the construction lacks a certain lightness which is familiar to us from present-day work. In order to counteract the lateral stress there was still no alternative to the imitation of Gothic principles of construction. The immense blocks of lead that were used as abutments were as expensive as they were wasteful of space. Hector Horeau had used the same principle in his unexecuted design for the Grandes Halles (1849).[8]

No tie bars; use of buttresses instead

In this exhibition a combination of a wide span with a light construction was attempted before the appropriate methods had been discovered. But there is also a dangerous retrogres-

Use of stone

[8] Cf. pp. 229–230.

sion from the advance which the Crystal Palace represents. The main building, the Palais de l'Industrie, was completely encased in heavy stone walls and included an immense triumphal arch. This monumental stonework was unhappily taken as a pattern for later exhibitions in London (1862) and in Chicago (1893).[9]

The Palais de l'Industrie stood in the Champs-Élysées — during the whole Second Empire a central point in Haussmann's project for building a new Paris. It was used for society gatherings and for shows of various kinds until 1897, when it was pulled down to make room for the exhibition of 1900.

Paris Exhibition of 1867

Ground plan symbolized the globe; director an economist

Ground plan: The external contour of the exhibition building was intended to symbolize the globe (*fig.* **154**). When the Champ-de-Mars was chosen as a site it became impossible to give the building a circular outline, and it was designed as an ellipse instead. The long axis was 490 meters (1,608 feet) and the short axis 386 meters (1,266 feet). Frédéric Le Play — the distinguished engineer, economist, and expert on European labor conditions whom Napoleon III appointed director of the exhibition — was responsible for the outline of its ground plan, and for its general program as well. From this time on, the Champ-de-Mars, the site in 1798 of the first of the small national exhibitions, was the accepted site for the great world exhibitions.

With regard to the ground plan, the question arose: How should the separate sections be arranged so as to give the spectator an ordered and undisturbed insight into the industry of all nations?

Organization of the elliptical exhibition building

Within the elliptical main exhibition building seven concentric galleries were placed, each conforming to the main outline of the grounds (*fig.* **156**). A garden was laid out inside the central ellipse of this *colisée du travail*. The galleries increased in size as one moved outwards from the center. The outermost

---

[9] Cf. pp. 273–275, 378–380.

gallery — the Galerie des Machines — was twice the height and width of the others (*fig. 157*). Industrial machinery was exhibited here. Clothing, furniture, and raw materials were displayed, in that order, in the next three galleries, counting toward the center. The two innermost and smallest galleries contained exhibits which concerned, respectively, *l'histoire du travail* and the fine arts. A palm garden with statues occupied the innermost oval (*fig. 102*).[10]

Transverse walks divided this building into separate segments. From each segment a spectator could trace without effort the developments within a single country and compare them with the displays of other countries occupying adjacent segments. This was an attempt at "living" statistics.

The aim of the exhibition can be gathered from a quotation taken from an official publication of 1867. "To make the circuit of this palace, circular, like the equator, is literally to go around the world. All peoples are here, enemies live in peace side by side. As in the beginning of things on the globe of waters, the divine spirit now floats on this globe of iron." The flowery language, somewhat reminiscent of Second Empire decoration, nevertheless reveals the essential motive.

153. Popular sculpture, "The Love of the Angels," 1867.

Construction: The iron skeleton of the Galerie des Machines — span thirty-five meters, height twenty-five meters — consisted of pillars twenty-eight meters high. The arches of the vault girders reached twenty-five meters into the air.

The pillars did not stop at the level of the vaulting but were allowed to continue straight up into the air. The chief constructor, J. B. Krantz, did this to avoid the use of tie bars, and because the lateral stress could only be supported by girders built out from the pillars to the basket arches. These pillars extending into the air were considered hideous, and an attempt was made to disguise them as flag poles.

Projecting pillars replace the bars

Hydraulic lifts with all the clumsiness of newborn monsters afforded communication between the ground floor and the roof,

---

[10] Cf. *L'Exposition universelle de 1867, illustrée, publication internationale autorisée par la commission impériale* (Paris, 1867).

around which there ran a platform giving a striking view of this city of galleries in corrugated iron and glass.

Behind the chief constructor stood the young Eiffel, who had founded his own factory a short time before. It was from him that the real inspiration for the Galerie des Machines came. In all sorts of ways — by the extensive use of new materials, by the employment of new devices like the elevator, by the provision of walks along the transparent glass surfaces of the *promenoirs* — the public was introduced not only to the new technical achievements but also to completely new aesthetic values.

155. MANET. View of the Exhibition of 1867. *Oil painting. Manet, whose pictures were denied entry to this exhibition, showed his whole output on the Pont de l'Alma. Manet has not only grasped externally the actuality of this building; he has set it forth in an adequate artistic language. The thing that is important here is dynamic relation between the masses of color.*

←
154. International Exhibition, Paris, 1867. *Air view.*

261

156. International Exhibition, Paris, 1867. *Section of the galleries of the main building. Seven concentric galleries were placed within the elliptical main building; the Galerie des Machines was twice the height and width of the others.*

157. International Exhibition, Paris, 1867. *Galerie des Machines. The entire span of thirty-five meters was achieved without visible tie bars.*

Paris Exhibition of 1878 [11]

Scheme   The exhibition of 1878 was intended to show the world that France had recovered from its defeat in 1870. The success of the exhibition of 1867 had been so great that in planning its successor a larger area was fixed upon. The exhibition was

---

[11] The Philadelphia exhibition of 1876 is of interest as the first example of the use of the pavilion system. This system was used again at Chicago in 1893 and at Paris in 1900. By the end of the century it had become the accepted method of organizing an exhibition. The increasing scope and complexity of industry made it necessary to segregate its different aspects in separate buildings. But all this falls outside the scope of our research. The Philadelphia exhibition brought no new solutions to the vaulting problem which was just on the verge of being solved in France.

158. International Exhibition, Paris, 1878. *The main entrance. The inflated sheet-metal architecture is of no importance as compared with the glass wall and the marquise vitrée. The latter so intersects the vertical elements that the relation between load and support can no longer be grasped at sight.*

divided into two sections: one part was devoted to a monumental building in stone, the palace of the Trocadéro on the far side of the Seine; temporary constructions made up the rest of the exhibition.

The main exhibition building follows the rectangular outline of the Champ-de-Mars. The ellipsoidal shape was abandoned because it had proved very difficult, after an exhibition ended, to find a use for the curved girders such a shape dictated.

Main building rectangular

A series of galleries in parallel formation extended over the length of the site, all of them flanked and dominated by the

Galerie des Machines. Along the shorter sides of the grounds ran two vestibules constructed by Eiffel (who was also responsible for the main entrance facing the Seine).

Transitory facts conceal constituent phenomena

The inflated sheet-metal architecture of the main entrance (*fig.* **158**) and of the pavilions on both sides is a transitory fact of little consequence. Even at the time it was regarded as of questionable merit, *fort discutable*. But if we carry our attention beyond the temporarily favored shapes it embodied, we shall find that the building exemplifies many important constituent phenomena. The courage shown in the glass wall at the front was important for the future. It was not until a half-century later, in the Bauhaus at Dessau, that the additional courage was found to juxtapose glass, iron, and concrete without any auxiliary pretexts, and thus to achieve an architectonic expression which stems directly from the unconditional use of pure materials.[12]

The glass wall and the *marquise vitrée*

Another constituent fact of later architecture appears in the projecting glass canopy, or *marquise vitrée*, which is carried the length of the glass front wall. This *marquise vitrée* constitutes a hovering, horizontal plane surface, intersecting the vertical elements in such a way that the relations between load and support can no longer be grasped at sight.[13]

From the very beginnings of architecture, a visible relation between load and support had been one of its outstanding facts. This sort of construction marks the beginning of a different kind of aesthetic feeling.

Construction: The main building of the exhibition of 1878 was flanked on both sides by the imposing Galerie des Machines (*fig.* **159**). The Galerie resembled in form the hull of an overturned ship. Its framework girders, meeting in the roof, were built up of separate parts, and already showed a differentiation between the specific functions that need to be fulfilled by iron vaulting.

---

[12] An intermediate step is to be found in a ferroconcrete loft building on Sutter Street, San Francisco, intended for wholesale merchandising, where a glass surface, covering the whole front, is suspended, cantilever fashion, in front of the supporting pillars.

[13] Eiffel seems to have been fond of this device. He used another canopy of plain glass and iron on the front of his Magasin au Bon Marché in Paris (1876). This canopy remained unchanged until very recently. (Cf. p. 239.)

264

159. International Exhibition, Paris, 1878. *Section and perspective of the Galerie des Machines. Span, thirty-five meters; height, twenty-five meters. Thanks to the engineer De Dion, it had become possible to lead all the forces at work on a building directly into the foundations, without employing tie bars.*

Girders: The girders used are of the De Dion type. The engineer De Dion was the real creator of girders fit for large spans. From a careful study of the tensile strength of materials he arrived at the proper form for a built-up girder capable of withstanding the various stresses put upon it without the assistance of tie bars. De Dion died shortly before the opening of the 1878 exhibition, while he was still engaged upon these calculations. (The arrangement of the framework girders shows a certain inner elasticity consequent upon the researches into the essential laws of materials.)

Toward new solutions of the vaulting problem

Stepped roof joists ran through the lattice girders and joined them into a continuous structure. On both sides, from the halfway point up, the walls were filled in with glass. (Such a union of glass and iron demands by its nature an extensive dematerialization of a building, which can be felt when one studies the Galerie des Machines. The contemporary architect Boileau defines with perfect precision the impression produced by this union: "The spectator is not aware of the weight of transparent surfaces. These surfaces are to him air and light, that is to say, an imponderable fluidity.") [14]

Glass walls: an "imponderable fluidity"

[14] *Encyclopédie d'architecture*, 1887–88, p. 97.

Thanks to the work of De Dion, it had become possible to conduct all the forces bound up in a building straight into the foundations, without taking up any of them through the use of tie bars. However, this foundation was still rigidly connected with the pillars and framework. The pillars are riveted into U-shaped iron sockets which are sunk in the foundations. But an iron skeleton is subject to temperature changes and cannot be rigidly bound together in the manner of a stone palace. De Dion was a pioneer in the study of the problems that follow from this fact. The matter was dealt with quite directly in the 1878 Galerie des Machines. Every sixty meters along the ridge of the roof where the pairs of lattice columns met, there was a complicated system of bolts set in oval holes which automatically provided for the expansion and contraction of the whole skeleton.

The rigid connection with the ground that is still maintained, together with the box-section girders and the canopy that rests on them like a capital, suggests that memory of the ancient column and its simple relation of load and support still lingered. But from this time on, with the rise of the truss girder, a new system sets in, a system that in the iron skeleton demands a hovering balance of the forces acting upon it.

Paris Exhibition of 1889

Climax of the development

The exhibition of 1889 marked at once the climax and the conclusion of a long development. In it great engineers like Eiffel reached the height of their powers. New conceptions in construction and new advances in industry united to give this exhibition expressive brilliance and an enormous influence. The long but humble Galerie des Machines of 1855, the huge circular Galerie which Krantz and Eiffel built in 1867, and the two great aisles of De Dion's Halle des Machines of 1878 are steps in a development which culminates in the Palais des Machines of 1889.

The exhibition of 1889 centered around the Eiffel Tower, which Eiffel and his engineers had raised on the bank of the Seine in the short space of seventeen months. The exhibition buildings were spread out behind the tower. There were two

266

160. International Exhibition, Paris, 1889. *Galerie des Machines. Span, 115 meters; length, 420 meters. The first time a span of such size had ever been bridged. It embodies constructional experience accumulated during almost a whole century. This building was wantonly destroyed.*

wings, one housing the *beaux-arts*, the other the *arts liberaux*, which were joined together by a section devoted to general exhibits. The immense metal bulk of the Galerie des Machines rose in the background to dominate the whole complex.

A kind of traveling crane — *les ponts roulants* — was erected within the Galerie des Machines (*fig.* **160**). It transported spectators over the length of the immense hall and enabled them to inspect all the machinery (much of it in operation) which was displayed on the floor below. On good days as many as a hundred thousand passengers rode on this crane.

For the last time industry aroused some of the wonder with which it was viewed at the time of its birth. Four years later at the Chicago World's Fair a display of machinery on view from *ponts roulants* could not have had this degree of success. But the progress made between 1878 and 1889 was so tremendous that visitors were stirred to the point of excitement by the boldness of the Galerie des Machines and the Eiffel Tower. These buildings attained a standard which has remained unexcelled.

Unprecedented dimensions

Construction: The constructor of the "Galerie des Machines" (actually named the "Palais des Machines") [15] was Cottancin; the architect, Dutert. The dimensions of the Galerie exceeded anything previously known. The largest vaulting attempted up to this time had been that of the St. Pancras Station in London, 1868, which had a span of seventy-three meters and a height of twenty-five meters.[16]

Its skeleton was composed of twenty trusses. Its length was four hundred and twenty meters. Huge glass walls enclosed the sides.[17]

A building not circumscribed within its real limits

The volume of free space included by the 1889 Galerie des Machines represented an entirely unprecedented conquest of matter. There is no earlier example that is comparable to it in this respect. But the glass end walls do not, strictly, close up the building; they constitute only a thin transparent membrane between the interior and outer space. And it is not as

---

[15] This building, one of the high points reached in the evolution of construction, was torn down in 1910 — out of "artistic sadism," as Frantz Jourdain correctly says.

[16] The St. Pancras Station is similar in form to the Galerie des Machines and, like it, contains no pillars. The girder framework, however, is rigidly connected with the ground by heavy anchors, and tie bars buried in the ground are used to take up the lateral thrust. It was constructed by Barlow.

[17] "The great enclosure has a daring and grandiose outline — everywhere the metal shapes are formed in such a way as to ensure their being inherently decorative" (*Exposition universelle de Paris de 1889: Monographie des palais, jardins, constructions diverses et installations générales*, by Adolphe Alphand, Paris, 1892–95, p. 521). Somewhat earlier, and in a more unassuming way, J. W. Schwedler had attempted a similar *Auflagerung* in his Central Railway Station, Frankfort on Main (opened in 1888). It is true that the girders of his three halls come together almost in a point along the peak of the roof. These halls, however, do not break away from the barrel shape, which is ruled out in the Galerie des Machines by the very nature of the triply articulated girders used. Dimensions of the Frankfort Station: length 186 m., width 56 m., height 29 m.

a building circumscribed within definite limits that the Galerie des Machines is important. The girders in its skeleton could have been either more or less numerous without thereby effecting any distinctive alteration. The aesthetic meaning of this hall is contained in the union and interpenetration of the building and outer space, out of which there grows a completely new limitlessness and movement in keeping with the machines it contains.

Each arched truss is made up of two segments. A pin unites them at a pivotal point high above the center line of the hall. Moving downward, the trusses become increasingly attenuated until they appear scarcely to touch the ground; moving upward, they spread and gain weight and power (*fig.* **161**). The usual proportions seem to be exactly reversed. These triply articulated arches disturb, or rather disrupt, traditional static feelings with regard to the rational relations of support and load. Elongated like immensely drawn-out cantilevers, the trusses embody movement in all their parts. Nothing remains of the quiet stone architecture of the barrel vault. A new sort of movement, penetrating space — as new in kind as that achieved in Borromini's cupolas — is created here.

Traditional static feelings disrupted

There is a further distortion of scale which must be noted: a section of these trusses would be about five times as deep as it was wide (three and a half meters deep by seventy-five centimeters wide). This is felt as a distortion, since the eye tends to take the dimensions of the stone architrave as its standard of comparison.

When trusses were enlarged to such proportions there seemed to be a lack of filling material. In addition these girders were unusually light, since this was the first time steel framework had been used to such an extent. The eye of the contemporary onlooker was confused by these strange dimensions. Even Anatole de Baudot, one of the first to open a path for contemporary architecture, declares that the proportions are a failure, and the Belgian constructer Vierendeel complains that "this lack of proportion produces a bad effect; the girder is not balanced; it has no base ... it starts too low. ... The eye is not reassured. ... The supports of the Galerie des Machines show another fault: they are too empty."

Contemporary criticisms

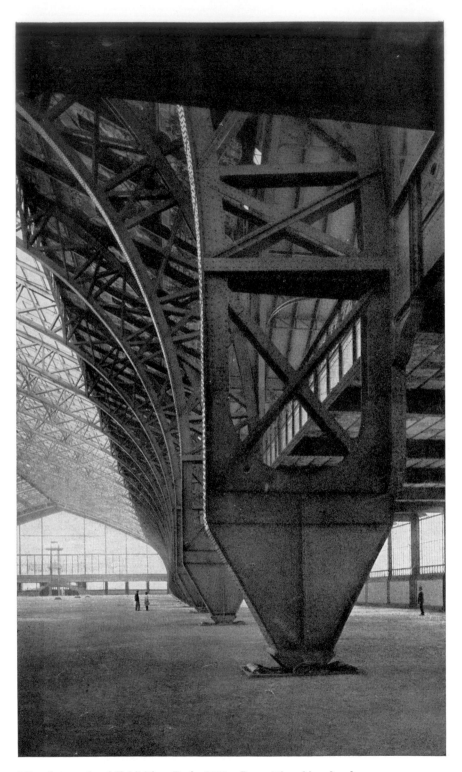

161.   International Exhibition, Paris, 1889.   *Base of three-hinged arch.*

162. EDGAR DE–GAS. "The Dancer." *Degas, the most daring experimentalist among the painters of the period and the exact contemporary of Eiffel, projects his dancers stripped of all erotic façade. He shows their distended nostrils and all the tenseness of straining effort. Max Liebermann remarks (in "Pan," the most "precious" of the German avant-garde reviews, p. 195) that "he seems to disguise his models and to see the nascent prostitute in the young dancer: no other painter has so completely subdued the novelistic element." This painting exhibits in its field the impersonal, precise, and objective spirit which produced constructions like the Galerie des Machines.*

It is precisely the features that are criticized which pointed to later developments. Here construction is unconsciously moving toward aesthetic feelings which did not find their equivalents in art and architecture until decades later.

Construction moves unconsciously toward new aesthetic feelings

In this hall the light pouring in from above swallowed up the thin latticework. So far as the optical impression is concerned, the vault attains a floating or hovering state.

The last hint of the antique column has disappeared. It is impossible to separate load and support.

Bent as though in the act of leaping, the vaulting starts at a very low level to take up its load. If we wish, we may regard this vaulting as our equivalent of the caryatid. It does not

271

163. Popular painting, "The Kiss of the Wave," 1889. *An immense woodcut filling two pages in no. 2 of "Le Courrier de l'Exposition," special edition, April 14, 1889. With its facile histrionics and its full share of erotic façade it met all the demands of its day.*

carry its burden with the dignity of the maidens of the Erechtheum nor does it break down under it like the nude giants on baroque portals. It springs up against its load to unite with it.

The ends of the girders, narrowing as they approach the floor (*fig.* **161**), are no longer rigidly connected with the ground but are left free to move. The girders transmit their own weight, plus the horizontal stress of 120,000 kilograms, directly through a hinged joint. With this system of support, even foundation movements could take place without setting up internal stresses.[18] This was the only means whereby the play of forces at all points of the system could be controlled.[19]

[18] This is an example of the way in which during the nineteenth century important results followed from the application to building of discoveries made in purely technological fields. Hinged joints were used in bridges around 1870 by Eiffel and others. (Cf. Erving Matheson, *Works in Iron*, London, 1873, p. 145.) The outstanding example is Eiffel's bridge over the Douro, in Portugal.

[19] "A single method of construction produced a mathematical determination of the distribution of the forces in different sections of the arch. This was the articulation at base and apex. The system ensured a rational and completely exact distribution of the stresses and of the materials used" (Alphand, p. 46).

The division between load and support which was still indicated in De Dion's halls of 1878 is here obliterated. Iron vaulting has found its true form. The play of enormous forces is held in equilibrium, an equilibrium that is floating rather than rigid.

It is the equilibrium of a balance beam daringly poised against continually varying forces.

A new oscillating harmony is created.

An elastic counterpoise is achieved which absorbs changes in the interior, the exterior, and the foundation.

This counterpoise adjusts itself to fluctuations of the ground.

An equilibrium is achieved against changes in the molecular structure of the building itself.

An equilibrium is achieved against external pressure, wind, and snow.

Construction passes over into expression.

Chicago, 1893

It is a curious illustration of the complex character of the nineteenth century that the great exhibitions should have begun their decline in Chicago. At this period Chicago was the place where the most daring and original work with office buildings and apartment houses was being done. While the Paris exhibitions — and especially that of 1889 — produced structures that opened up new ranges of feeling, the World's Columbian Exhibition at Chicago was the beginning of "mercantile classicism." The influence of its plaster architecture was widespread and tenacious. This was foreseen at the time by Louis Sullivan, who in his *Autobiography of an Idea* predicted that "the damage wrought to this country by the Chicago World's Fair will last half a century."

Chicago: advanced office buildings and "mercantile classicism"

Louis Sullivan's prediction

It is true that there were good things at Chicago in 1893: Louis Sullivan's own Transportation Building (his one contribution to the fair) and the covered piers that ran out into Lake Michigan. The contemporary Belgian constructor Vierendeel was nevertheless quite justified in saying that "the constructions were only imitations of what we have known in Europe for a long time. We expected better, much better, from the well-known audacity, initiative, and originality of the Americans. We have been profoundly deceived." The staff architecture enveloping the metal framework also lacked originality. "In a new world they dared no innovations. They had doubts of themselves." [20]

It was not the pure curves of the piers extending out into the lake that delighted the public but rather the gondolas and gondoliers that had been especially imported from Venice (*fig.* **164**). Louis Sullivan's building also failed to achieve a popular success, which went instead to those "marble" colonnades that were born out of the spirit of the French academicians — the very men who had done everything in their power to prevent the erection of the Eiffel Tower. At the Chicago World's Fair the architects believed that they were

[20] *La Construction architecturale en fer et acier* (Brussels, 1902), p. 249.

164. World's Fair, Chicago, 1893. *Venetian gondoliers.*

reviving the creative spirit of Medicean times and the public fancied that the radiance of Florence was being recalled for them to live in. These attitudes are easily understood; they represent only another one of those frequent and futile attempts to escape from the actual present, which — like financial crises — recur constantly throughout the industrial era.

New Forms — New Shapes

It would have been very interesting — had space permitted — to discuss everything that falls under the heading of "the Great Exhibitions," and to deal in some detail with their immense influence upon the industry and life of nations. The manner in which the "theme" of each exhibition found expression certainly merits some discussion too. Thus it would be possible to establish with complete accuracy the date when "the industry of all nations" came to be the inevitable theme for any great exposition — and also came to be accepted without any of the wonder and excitement that had attached to it in the beginning. At that moment the exhibition as a problem in building lost all its creative force. It became simply an organized show like many others, and its success or failure was a matter of no historical importance. A new theme, the needs and desires of man, is required to give a new impetus to the exhibition movement. People are no longer vitally concerned with the question, "How can we produce the greatest number of objects?" The great problem for us is, "How can production be regulated in the interests of the consumer?"

Influence and decline of the great exhibitions

GUSTAVE EIFFEL AND HIS TOWER

No other century in the history of the western world developed such hypertrophic building activity as the nineteenth, and none produced such a small number of creative architects. We do not think that this is due to any lack of talent, but rather believe the society gradually killed any creative impulse with the poison of its ruling taste.

Fate of architects and engineers

165. International Exhibition, Paris, 1867. *Iron skeleton. Probably the first pure skeleton construction was the elliptical main exhibition building of this world's fair. Behind the chief engineer stood the young Eiffel, the real inspirer. He calculated and verified the construction of the pillars and the wide span of 35 meters. The modulus of elasticity in a large construction was tested for the first time.*

When revolutionary architects such as Henri Labrouste were finally admitted to the French Academy, it was already recognized by their contemporaries that they had left behind them "la passion et l'espoir de confesser leur temps."[1] Architecture must stand up to wind and weather that it may have a chance to have its impact on man. Unlike painting, architecture that never leaves the paper fades away like an old photograph.

Sheltered in the shadow of industry and protected by the authority of science, engineers were not hampered in their development, for they did not have to play up to the ruling taste. Although their names were unknown in their day, they are noted in history and will not be forgotten. In the same way most of their work remained anonymous, like

[1] Émile Trélat, in *Encyclopédie d'Architecture* (Paris), 1880, p. 45.

276

Gustave Eiffel's elegant skeleton (1886) that carries the hammered copper skin of the Statue of Liberty at the entrance of New York Harbor. That Eiffel's name is familiar to the public is due only to the fact that the Eiffel Tower bore his name from the very beginning.

Gustave Eiffel (1832–1923) [2] came from Burgundy, the birth-place of many great constructors. He got the best training available, at the École Polytéchnique and the École Centrale. We encountered his name earlier in connection with his calculations for the arches of the Galerie des Machines (1867), the glass walls of the large entrance hall for the international exhibition of 1878, and the marvelously lit Bon Marché department store in Paris (1876), now deprived of its original charm through hopeless "modernization."

Gustave Eiffel

In the daring construction of bridges over deep rivers in Europe and Africa, and also over the enormous streams of Indo-China, he learned to master the elements of weather, water, and wind. By means of hydraulic pressure the piles of his first bridge near Bordeaux (1858), were driven twenty-five meters below the surface of the water. Later, when he had to span deep gorges, he erected columns (pylons) in the shape of slender pyramids, tapering toward the traffic-way they support. The large spans and the lofty heights of these latticed supports, designed according to the newest methods and with the greatest elegance, made him and his engineers familiar with the impact of the wind. Early he was interested in meteorological research, and in his later days he was one of the first to found — at his own expense — an aerodynamic laboratory. From the platform of his tower he dropped an apparatus he had invented for registering the influence of wind pressure on plane surfaces. Later, in his laboratory at Auteuil, he had a large wind tunnel built for experiments in the field of aviation. The action of moving air on rigid bodies continuously preoccupied him — an interest carefully registered in many of his publications.

Eiffel's foremost interest

Gustave Eiffel is the master of elegantly constructed iron towers — pylons — and airy two-hinged arches, which formed, connected by horizontal traffic-ways, bridges like that over

Arched bridges

---

[2] See Jean Prevost's small biography, *Eiffel* (Paris, 1929).

the Douro or the Garabit Viaduct. The grandiose display of equipoise which they offered had never been surpassed.

The river Douro [3] in northern Portugal, with its strong and changing currents, its depth varying between forty-five and sixty feet, in addition to a very unstable soil, made the use of piles in the river bed not possible. Eiffel bridged it in a single span of about five hundred feet — 160 meters — the longest at that time (*fig.* **166**), with exception, of course, of suspension bridges. Eiffel built the two-hinged arch from the

166. G. EIFFEL. Bridge over the Douro, 1875. *Span, 160 meters; height, 61 meters above the level of the water. In erecting the high pylons and assembling the arches in midair, Eiffel gained the necessary precision and experience to build the thousand-foot tower.*

high iron pylons without scaffolding, by means of suspended cables (1876–77). The Americans in bridging the Mississippi River at St. Louis used a similar procedure.

The most daring of Eiffel's bridges remains the Garabit Viaduct (1880–84).[4] Its total length is nearly half a kilo-

---

[3] G. Eiffel, *Notice sur le Pont Douro* (Clichy, 1879). Good descriptions, drawings and woodcuts.

[4] G. Eiffel, *Mémoire présenté à l'appui du projet définitif du Viaduc de Garabit* (Paris, 1889). The importance of this bridge is shown in a large portfolio with all stages of the calculation, the procedures of assembly, and photographs.

meter; it crosses the gorge 122.5 meters over the river Thuyère with an arch span of 165 meters (*figs.* **167, 168**). He used every possible graphic, analytic, and experimental means to design his parabolic arches, which touch the ground in point supports.

It was here that Eiffel and his engineers learned to master the difficulties of assembling precisely dimensioned parts, so that later the rivet holes of the factory-made members of the Eiffel Tower could coincide to the tenth of a millimeter when being erected on the site.

The Eiffel Tower

The one-thousand-foot Eiffel Tower, erected for the Paris exhibition of 1889, embodied in one single work all his experience with foundations and supports, against the intricacies of earth and wind.[5] Even Eiffel himself was at first afraid to shock the ruling taste with the erection of an uncompromising bare structure in the heart of Paris, but he was urged on by the head of his "Bureau d'études," the young Swiss engineer Maurice Koechlin (1856–1946), who had made calculations for the Garabit Viaduct.

In his artistic taste Eiffel was a true son of his time. His own residence was filled with "a mess of heteroclite and unbelievably ugly works of art." [6] As is well known, even the creative personalities of our time still suffer from the split between the methods of feeling and the methods of thinking. Eiffel does not differ in this respect from other great constructors, like Freyssinet and Maillart.

Viewed from the standpoint of construction, the whole tower is an adaptation of the lofty supports of iron bridges, increased to cosmic dimensions. It springs in three stages to its full height. Its large dimensions made it necessary to compose the structure of four members meeting asymptotically at the top and embracing an enormous space. The four pylons are anchored to separate foundations, for which

---

[5] In 1900 Eiffel published *La Tour de trois cents mètres* in two monumental folio volumes, describing the structure which will stand forever as a personification of "l'art de l'ingénieur moderne et le siècle d'industrie et de science." These are the words with which in 1885 he introduced his "Tower in iron" before the Society of Civil Engineers in Paris.

[6] Blaise Cendrars, *Aujourd'hui* (Paris, 1931), p. 148.

167. G. EIFFEL. Garabit Viaduct, 1880–84. *The most daring of Eiffel's bridges. Span, 165 meters; total length, almost half a kilometer; height above the water, 122.5 meters. A perfect example of coördination of vision, calculation, and experiment.*

168. G. EIFFEL. Garabit Viaduct. *Detail of abutment. In the late nineteenth century, pure forms — as far as structures are concerned — are found in the works of the great engineers. The plastic form of arch, hinged joint, and abutment transcend the realm of construction.*

169. G. EIFFEL. Decorative arch of the Eiffel Tower, 1889. *The arch is merely a decorative link, somehow a distraction for the eye from the heavy horizontal girders which connect the four pylons.*

170. G. EIFFEL. A pier of the Eiffel Tower. *Viewed from the angle of construction the Eiffel Tower is formed of four immense pylons, merging asymptotically together.*

Eiffel used, of course, the hydraulic press, as he had done for his bridges since 1858. Elevators run in the interior of the supports as far as the second platform. Another elevator runs within the core of the structure from the second to the third platform, 904 feet above the ground. The four arches which connect the supports (*fig.* **169**) are mainly decorative, reminiscent nevertheless of Eiffel's original intention of carrying the tower on four bridge arches.

The airiness one experiences when at the top of the tower makes it the terrestrial sister of the aeroplane. It is interesting that revenue from the entrance fees declined after the enormous success of the exhibition in 1889, to rise again steadily from 1904,[7] which corresponds with the time when the interest in flying machines began to arouse public curiosity. It was no accident that Santos-Dumont chose to circle about this tower on his spectacular flight in his airship.

To a previously unknown extent, outer and inner space are interpenetrating (*fig.* **171**). This effect can only be experienced in descending the spiral stairs from the top, when the soaring lines of the structure intersect with the trees, houses, churches, and the serpentine windings of the Seine. The interpenetration of continuously changing viewpoints creates, in the eyes of the moving spectator, a glimpse into four-dimensional experience.

Emotional content of the tower

The emotional content of the tower remained veiled during the next decades. The tower, which "stood up from Paris like a hatpin" for the generation coming to the fore around 1910, was of course for the representatives of the ruling taste a menace, a disgrace. In February 1887, a month after Gustave Eiffel had signed the contract with the French government and the city of Paris, the famous protest against the erection of the tower was handed to the chairman of the exhibition committee: "We, the writers, painters, sculptors, and architects come in the name of French good taste and of this menace to French history to express our deep indignation that there should stand in the heart of our Capital this unnecessary and monstrous Tour Eiffel." But, fortu-

---

[7] *Journal du Crédit Public*, April 25, 1929.

282

nately, the chairman was the farsighted engineer and landscape architect Alphand, the same man who had created, under Haussmann, the great parks of Paris.

Two decades later, an optical revolution shattered the static viewpoint of the Renaissance, and suddenly the hidden emotional content of the tower was revealed. It now became the symbol of the "Grande Ville." "Such was Paris, with her great tower from which every night streamed the blue tresses of the wireless telegraph."[8]

It was now that the great tower found its artistic revelation. The Parisian painter, Robert Delauney (1885–1947), found in its structure a possibility of showing what was going on below in the changing apprehension of the outer world (*fig. 173*). Indeed since 1910 the tower, portrayed in all its multi-sidedness, accompanied Delauney through all the different stages of his life. The poet Blaise Cendrars in his *Aujourd'hui* gives us insight into the new approach of this young generation.

No longer is the tower a hideous monster. It grows in its emotional significance, and its contemporary, the Sacré Cœur of Montmartre, with its white cupolas, becomes degraded to a sugarplum in the eye of the poet.

"I saw through my window the Eiffel Tower like a flask of clear water, the domes of the Invalides and the Pantheon as a teapot and sugar basin, and the Sacré Cœur a pink and white sugarplum. Delauney came almost every day to visit me. He was always haunted by the tower."[9]

"At that time there was no artistic formula that could claim to express the plasticity of the Eiffel Tower. Under the laws of realism it crumbled, and the laws of Italian perspective could not catch it. . . . But Delauney wanted to find a plastic interpretation. He dismembered the tower so that he might enter within its frame; he truncated it and inclined it to make it express the vertigo of its full three hundred meters; he took ten standpoints, fifteen outlooks; he looked at this part from

[8] For this and other quotations from contemporary poets, see C. Giedion-Welcker, "Robert Delauney," in *Das Werk* (Zurich), No. 8 (1946).

[9] Blaise Cendrars, *Aujourd'hui*, p. 136.

171. G. EIFFEL. Spiral staircases between first and second floors of the Eiffel Tower. *Ever-changing viewpoints and interpenetration of inner and outer space were experienced here decades before architects or painters realized the new conception of space.*

173. ROBERT DELAUNEY.
Eiffel Tower, 1910. $\longrightarrow$

172. G. EIFFEL. Eiffel Tower. *View from the second platform to the first. The photo is made in the elevator shaft. Right and left, the elevator tracks which penetrate into the ground floor.*

**174.   ARNODIN.   Ferry Bridge in the "Vieux Port" of Marseilles, 1905.   *Iron struc-
ture and stone architecture blend well together.*

**176.   ARNODIN.   Ferry   Bridge,   Marseilles,
1905.   *Height, 54 meters; length of carriage-way,
240 meters.* $\longrightarrow$

**175.   ARNODIN.   Ferry Bridge, Marseilles.   *View from upper platform to suspended
ferry.   Relation between fixed and moving parts.   Slender steel construction.   Observe plat-
forms of staircase, jutting boldly out into space.   (Cf. Bauhaus balconies, 1926.)*

below, that from above, the surrounding houses from the right, from the left, from the wings of a bird and from the bed of the earth." [10]

No doubt, in this hovering tower some of the spirit has materialized of the technical Utopianism of Jules Verne, who belonged to Eiffel's generation.

The rapid evolution from James Bogardus' unexecuted cast-iron tower for the New York World's Fair of 1853 (*fig.* **111**) to the Eiffel Tower, conceived only three decades later, when viewed in historic dimension is indeed fantastic.

After reaching this peak, the evolution slowed down and turned in other directions. During the following half-century the steel skeleton of the skyscraper developed in America. In France, nearest to the airy sensitivity of the Eiffel Tower were the elegant ferry bridges, especially that of the Vieux Port at Marseilles, 1905 (*figs.* **174, 175, 176**) heavily damaged toward the end of the second world war.

The engineer, Arnodin, was a specialist in these elegant structures, which he knew how to place excellently in French river ports as in Rouen (1889) or in Nantes, the latest having been erected in the late twenties in Bordeaux.

The ferry bridge at Marseilles, the Pont Transbordeur, which must transport vehicles across the river without hindering the passage of tall-masted ships, consists of two pairs of slender pylons touching the earth at two points. They support at a lofty height a carriage-way for the traveling crane from which the ferry, hovering over the water, is suspended by cables.

---

[10] *Ibid.*, pp. 145–148, translated by J.T.

PART **IV** **THE DEMAND FOR MORALITY IN ARCHITECTURE**

THE NINETIES: PRECURSORS OF CONTEMPORARY ARCHITECTURE

There are whole decades in the second half of the nineteenth century in which no architectural work of any significance is encountered. Eclecticism smothered all creative energy. Here and there — especially as the century wore on — voices were raised in protest, but they could do nothing to alter conditions.

It was just at this time that an unprecedented wave of building activity swept over Europe. Its cities took on the shapes from which we still suffer today.

The painter was able to withdraw from this overpowering environment. The men who did the important work at this period gave up all prospects of fame and an audience and practiced their art in seclusion. Cézanne and Van Gogh, for example, buried themselves in the solitude of Provence. The architect had no such course open to him; not a single one managed to escape from the atmosphere of eclecticism.

Dissatisfaction with this almost universal state of affairs reached its peak around 1890. Toward the end of the century H. P. Berlage was to produce a building which would serve to purify architecture all over Europe, his Amsterdam Stock Exchange. In the nineties he was already denouncing the prevailing architecture as "Scheinarchitektur, d.h. Imitation, d.h. Lüge" ("Sham architecture; i.e., imitation; i.e., lying"). "Our parents and grandparents as well as ourselves," Berlage wrote, "have lived and still live in surroundings more hideous than any known before. . . . Lying is the rule, truth is the exception."

The smoldering hatred of eclecticism came to a head in Europe with startling suddenness. In the same way, a fish net can be hauled for a long time quite uneventfully and then, in a single moment, the whole catch shows up all bunched together. This moment in the history of architecture did not arrive by accident: industry had at length reached its full development and the time was ripe for great changes. In the earlier part of the century decades go by with nothing achieved in architecture; toward the close of the century almost every year has importance. Ambition revives and brings with it courage and strength to oppose those forces which had kept life from finding its true forms. Developments come in one surge after another. The diversity of movements with their variety of experimental gropings indicates the vitality of the period. Individual failures and the mixture of transitory with constituent facts are of little importance. These are traits of every transitional period.

Much of what was attempted between 1890 and 1930 remained fragmentary and incomplete. This period, however, found the courage to undertake the building up of a tradition of its own.

What Were the Sources of This Movement?

According to the easy explanation that was advanced later, the movement developed as the application of two principles: the abandonment of historical styles, and — consequent upon this — the use of "fitness for purpose" as a criterion. The explanation is correct, inasmuch as both these factors were involved, but it does not go far enough. The movement took its strength from the moral demands which were its real source. The cry went up, "Away with this infected atmosphere!"

Moral demands behind the new movement

The young painter Henri van de Velde was among those who attacked the "infected atmosphere" most vigorously. In the late nineties he took the lead in the fight for *l'art moderne*. He campaigned for it first in his native Belgium, next in France, and then in a country which, at the time, lay wide open to any new movement — Germany. He has given the reasons why his development took the direction it did in his writings, where he preaches, explains, and defends his doctrines. But it may be that the moral impetus behind the *art moderne* movement appears more directly in some remarks which he made only a short while ago.

I met van de Velde in Brussels during the summer of 1938. A great leader during the nineties, he still remains extremely active; he had, in fact, just returned from laying the cornerstone of the Belgian Pavilion at the New York World's Fair. Knowing that he had begun his career as a painter, I asked him how he had come to turn to architecture. He answered by describing the situation that prevailed around 1890: "The

Van de Velde: what drove him into architecture

real forms of things were covered over. In this period the revolt against the falsification of forms and against the past was a moral revolt." [1]

He went on to tell how, shortly before 1890, a nervous breakdown had left him incapable of work. At this point he met a woman who gave him renewed courage to face life. Soon after, he wished to marry and establish his own household. "I told myself — this was in 1892 — that I would never allow my wife and family to find themselves in 'immoral' surroundings." [2] But at that date everything that one could buy on the open market was smothered under the *mensonge des formes* which van de Velde hated. He had to design for himself everything in his house, from cutlery to doorknobs. Then — since these articles demanded a setting which would "ward off ugliness" — he was led to build his first house. "You asked me how I became an architect. Well, this house pushed me into architecture."

"This house" was van de Velde's home on the Avenue van der Raye in Uccle, a suburb of Brussels.[3] It showed a remarkable freedom in the treatment of the roof and in the way in which the windows were cut out to meet the special requirements of each room. The revolution this house provoked when it was completed in 1896 derived from its pronounced simplicity, in strong contrast with the over-fanciful façades to which people were accustomed. In this respect van de Velde's earliest work pointed farther into the future than Horta's house in the Rue de Turin.

Parallel case of William Morris (1859)

A generation earlier the same disgust with the falsification of forms in all objects of trade had led William Morris to create and equip his "Red House" at Upton in Kent, England. According to one of Morris' biographers, Red House had much the same history as van de Velde's house in Uccle: "During the year 1858, William Morris plodded on as a painter with a

---

[1] "Toutes les formes étaient cachées. À cette époque la révolte contre les mensonges des formes et le passé était une révolte morale."

[2] "Je me disais — c'était en 1892 — jamais je ne veux pas admettre que ma femme et ma famille se trouvent dans un milieu qui est immorale."

[3] There are some excellent illustrations of this house in a book by van de Velde's biographer and Maecenas, Karl Ernest Osthaus: *Van de Velde* (Hagen i. W, 1920).

growing dejection over the work accomplished despite the fact that he sold one picture for £70. But Morris' wedding, in April 1859, turned his mind again and more intensely to those domestic arts which had attracted him at Red Lion Square. He now set his heart on building a home that should fulfill his conception of the 'house beautiful,' and secured Webb's services as architect. . . . The name of the house, which is built of red brick and tiles, expressed a revolt against the prevailing and tyrannous formula of stucco walls and slate roofs." [4]

Does this parallel mean that van de Velde simply followed the example Morris had already set? We do not think so. The parallel springs from the fact that the disorder introduced into human life by industry made itself felt in England more than thirty years earlier than on the Continent. Identical conditions led to identical reactions.

Brussels the Center of Contemporary Art, 1880–1890

Why was Belgium, rather than some other country on the Continent, the starting point of the new movement?

The pioneering spirit of Henri van de Velde can only be understood in relation to the background provided for it by Belgium in the eighties. Belgium was the first country on the Continent to become heavily industrialized. The problems that grow out of industrialization thus showed themselves first and most intensely in Belgium.

But there was another reason — at least as important as this one — why it was in Belgium that *l'art nouveau* first began to affect architecture and the industrial arts. Brussels between 1880 and 1890 was the one city in the entire cultural world which gave a welcome and a hearing to those creative artists who were despised or ignored by the great public. Painters like Seurat, Cézanne, and van Gogh, sculptors like Rodin and Meunier, musicians like Debussy and Vincent d'Indy, and poets like Verhaeren were invited to Brussels to present their work for exhibition and discussion. The courage and

---

[4] Montague Weekley, *William Morris* (London, 1934), p. 53. It was at Red Lion Square that Morris had established his first workshop, in conjunction with Burne-Jones.

artistic instinct required to establish such a policy cannot be overestimated. These exhibitions, lectures, and concerts represented the first systematic attack upon a public taste that for decades had been corrupted by the productions of an art entirely out of touch with life. The pseudo-monumental façades of the period and its *peinture à la mode* were both alike examples of the *mensonge des formes*.

The work of education in Belgium was carried on by two men who loved the arts, and who themselves wrote, painted, and composed in the time allowed them by their professions: Octave Maus (1856–1919) and Edmond Picard (1836–1924). Both were well-to-do lawyers who entertained extensively.[5]

L'Art moderne (1881) In 1881 Maus, Picard, and some others founded the weekly periodical, *L'Art moderne*. Each number contained only a few printed sheets; there were no illustrations, and the articles published were usually unsigned. One of these anonymous essays in the first issue of the magazine (dated March 6, 1881) announces a program directed not only against academic art but against fixed conceptions of all kinds:

"Art is for us the contrary of every recipe and formula. Art is the eternally spontaneous and free action of man on his environment for the purpose of transforming it and making it conform to a new idea."

L'Art moderne appeared regularly for over thirty years — extraordinary longevity in a review of this type — and served as a model for many of the later periodicals that took up the cause of the *avant-garde*. Its files offer a still unexplored mine of information to the historian of the period. It was this review that soon after its foundation brought together the group of young Belgian artists known as "Les XX" ("The Twenty"). Among its members were Ferdinand Knopff and A. W. Finch (who, according to Henri van de Velde, made the bridge between Morris and his circle and the Belgian *art nouveau*).

---

[5] Picard was perhaps the more versatile of the two. In his youth he interrupted his studies for some time to become a sailor. Later he studied philosophy and law and became a valued advocate at court. Over and above his professional work he was active as a critic. In his review, *L'Art moderne*, he defended the victims of popular disapproval, the impressionists and all the rest. Octave Maus was an initiator with a great range of interests. He had both the instinct and the tireless energy needed for organizing endeavors on a large scale.

294

Another member was James Ensor. Ensor was already prominent as a painter when the first exhibition in 1884 showed a large number of his pictures. (Most of these now hang in the Musées Royaux des Beaux Arts in Brussels.)

Maus was the secretary and the leading spirit of Les XX for as long as the society existed, from 1884 to 1893. He went on to found La Libre Esthétique, the association which replaced Les XX in 1894. The Libre Esthétique showed the work of William Morris and gave the young Henri van de Velde a chance to put his ideas before the public. In a lecture on the "déblaiement d'art" van de Velde told of what had been done in England and France and pointed to America as the land of the future.

Avant-garde exhibitions

Maus discerned in all countries the hidden forces that were at work, quite ignored by the public. He sought to persuade all those artists who — like Cézanne — were unwilling to show their work to exhibit at Brussels. At the first exhibition in 1884 the Frenchman Rodin (who exhibited his bust of Victor Hugo), the American Whistler, and the German Max Liebermann were represented. As year followed year, new names appeared on the list: in 1886 Auguste Renoir, in 1887 Georges Seurat (who showed one of his principal works, "Le Dimanche à la Grande Jatte," now in the Chicago Art Institute). Pissarro and Berthe Morisot were also included in the 1887 exhibition.

The Seurat "Dimanche à la Grande Jatte," arriving fresh from the artist's studio with its flat treatment of landscape and figures and all its *poésie aérienne,* caused a terrific uproar. This picture — whose value is no longer a subject for controversy — was attacked with umbrellas at its first showing, so van de Velde told me.

In 1889 van Gogh made his debut at Brussels. His feverish colors made the greatest impression on the young artists. Cézanne, who exhibited at the same time, was almost overlooked.

We have mentioned only one phase of the activity that went on in Brussels during these years and have noted only the high points in that phase. Even so, there is no need for further explanation of the sudden emergence there of so many talents. Henri van de Velde is one instance; Victor Horta and Paul Hankar are others.

The English
arts and crafts
associations of
the eighties

In Brussels between 1884 and 1894 the works of great contemporary painters and sculptors found display. In England during the same period a different kind of contribution to the arts was made. It was at this time that the work of Morris and his circle began to bear fruit, and that a serious attempt was made to reform public taste in the field of household furnishings. Meanwhile a younger generation of artists had grown up — men like Arthur H. Mackmurdo, Cobden-Sanderson, and C. R. Ashbee — who did not share Morris' hatred of modern techniques and business methods. The social point of view of Morris and Ruskin, however, was carried even further by this younger generation.

Numerous associations, like Mackmurdo's Art Workers' Guild of 1884, rallied together the artists and architects who were interested in art and handicrafts. Even the dilettantes joined together in the same year to form the Home Arts and Industries Association. The Arts and Crafts Exhibition Society organized great shows intended to prove that the so-called "minor arts" occupied as high a level as painting. This belief was — as is well known — taken up on the Continent about a decade later by the *art nouveau* movement, and vigorously argued by them.

As early as 1892 the Brussels exhibition had included examples of industrial art, specimen pieces of stained glass and ceramic work. In 1894, the year La Libre Esthétique was founded, there appeared the creations of the Morris group, as well as a typical contribution from a French artist — a studio interior.

So once more it was Brussels which was the starting point from which the arts and crafts movement spread over the Continent. Henri van de Velde — tireless both as an artist and as the evangelist of the *art nouveau* — carried his version of the findings arrived at in Brussels first to Paris (1896) and then to Dresden (1897). The few interiors which he exhibited created a sensation such as was rarely aroused at the time by

296

work of this nature. The demonstration stirred to full consciousness talents in both countries which had hitherto been uncertain in what direction to turn for an outlet. The impact of the arts and crafts movement upon the all-too-long dormant Continent dates from this time.

Victor Horta's Contribution

Considering the receptivity of Brussels to new work in the arts, it is not surprising that the first really daring Continental residence should have been built there. This was Victor Horta's house at 12 Rue de Turin (*fig.* **177**). Completed in 1893, before there were any signs of a new European architecture, the Horta house marked a turning point in the treatment of the private home. From that time on, new artistic principles were to be applied to the problem of the dwelling, and new human needs were to be allowed to affect its design. This house roused Continental architecture from its lethargy at one blow.

House in the Rue de Turin (1893): a starting point for new developments

Number 12 Rue de Turin stands in a row of conventional Brussels residences. Since it had to conform to the same conditions, it resembles them in being long and very narrow: the front is a bare twenty-three feet across. The ground plan developed within these predetermined proportions, however, is entirely original. In the typical Brussels house, Horta tells me, the whole extent of the ground floor is visible from the entry. Horta avoided this by breaking the floor up into different levels. Thus the drawing room is half a story higher than the entrance hall which leads into it. Differences in level represent only one of the devices which Horta employed to give new flexibility to the ground plan. He hollowed out the massive body of the house, introducing light-wells that provided new and unusual sources of illumination in so narrow an exterior. The photographs do not reveal the surprising interrelations into which these rooms at their different levels are brought. And all this was done within the smallest compass imaginable (*fig.* **178**).

Flexible treatment of the ground plan

Horta's house was soon famous in every European circle interested in restoring the vitality of architecture. It was ad-

Contemporary opinion

177. VICTOR
HORTA. 12 Rue de
Turin, Brussels, 1893.

178. VICTOR
HORTA. 12 Rue
de Turin, Brussels.
*Plan. Horta achieves
flexibility and some
independence between
floors through the use
of the internal iron
skeleton.*

179. St. Louis river front, 109–111 North First Street, 1849 or 1850. *An earlier American combination of those elements developed for industrial buildings which Horta translates into residential terms.*

mired chiefly for two things: its perfect adjustment to its owner (a Mr. Tassel), and its freedom from any trace of historical styles. Five years after it was built, the Austrian critic, Ludwig Hevesi, published an article which shows the value his contemporaries placed on Horta's work.

"There lives in Brussels now, in 1898, the most inspired of the modern architects, Victor Horta. . . . His fame is exactly six years old, and dates from the residence of Mr. Tassel in the Rue de Turin. This is the first of these famous modern dwellings which fit their owners like faultlessly cut coats. It houses the man for whom it was built in the most perfect manner conceivable — as perfectly as the mussel shell does the mussel. It is most simple and logical . . . altogether new and just as delightful. But — and note this — there is in it not the faintest echo of any of the historical styles. . . . No detail derives from anything at all in existence. It has the pure charm of lines, curves, and surfaces — and it is quite personal, as personal as if Horta, instead of simply drawing the parts, had handed them to the workmen all modeled in advance." [6]

John Nash, in the drawing room of the Royal Pavilion at Brighton (1818), had openly displayed the ornate cast-iron columns and girders that entered into its construction. No one before Horta had dared to follow this example and permit construction to intrude upon the intimacy of a private house. In Horta's house the staircase clearly reveals pillars and girders, which hold the eye by their shape and ornamentation (*fig.* **180**). The drawing room is even more notable in this respect; an I-section support is carried across its free space without any attempt at disguise.

The visitor receives his first impression of the interior of the house from the cast-iron column that rises from the elevated main floor next the staircase. Curved iron tendrils spring out of its vase-shaped capital. Their forms are partly like those of primitive plants, partly arbitrary creations. Their lines are freely continued on the smooth surfaces of the walls and vaulting and on the mosaics of the floor in wild and swirling curvilinear patterns.

The house in the Rue de Turin marks the first appearance of the *art nouveau* in the field of architecture. It is for this reason — not merely because of the qualities Hevesi admired in it — that it finds a place in all histories of art. In Horta's house the aims of the *art nouveau* were fully carried out in architectural terms at the very first attempt. There are no earlier examples in architecture of this transitional style. Indeed its best representative, Aubrey Beardsley, did not arrive at his own artistic language until 1893 — the date of the Rue de Turin residence. [7]

One source of the *art nouveau*

In Horta's house the point of origin of the *art nouveau* becomes patent: it is iron construction. What are these lines but the *unrolled* curls and rosettes that are to be found under the eaves of so many Belgian railway stations? They have simply stripped off their Gothic or Renaissance clothing (*fig.* **181**).

[6] *Wiener Tageblatt*, November 11, 1898.

[7] His drawings were included in the first volume of *Studio*, 1893.

180. VICTOR
HORTA. 12 Rue de
Turin, Brussels. *Iron
column and staircase.
At the end of the cast-
iron period, the cast-iron
column is once more
introduced into the
house — and brings the
art nouveau with it.*

181. ALPHONSE BALAT. Strap-
iron ornaments on the conservatory,
Laeken, 1879. *One source of the art
nouveau.*

The *art nouveau* was an interesting intermezzo between the nineteenth and twentieth centuries. It would be a digression, however, to go into the various theories of its origin.[8] In spite of the revolutionary intentions behind its fight against the use of historical styles, it succeeded only in matching shape against shape. It was essentially an "anti" movement, and this may explain its comparatively short life.

Significance of the façade

The front of the Tassel house is as original in its modeling as the interior. The bow window — a standard feature of every house in Brussels — is preserved, but Horta transforms it into a curved, glassed-in surface. The smoothly treated wall is blended into this undulating section. For all its fresh modeling, the façade is quite conservative in construction for the date it was built: it is simply the ordinary type of massive stone wall. Where a series of windows has been let in, horizontal supporting girders of wrought iron are introduced. These second-story windows run downward from the supporting girders to a point level with the floor. They are based on the principle of the display windows developed in the second half of the nineteenth century. The rivets in the girders are accentuated with the same fondness Otto Wagner shows in his handling of the aluminum bolts on the front of the Vienna Postal Savings Bank.

The revolutionary aspect of Horta's work consists in this: he took over elements which had appeared in business and industrial buildings of the fifties and incorporated them in a private house. Purely utilitarian structures erected in America between 1850 and 1870 — for example, the St. Louis river front commercial buildings with their cast-iron fronts — are based on a principle which Horta uses. There are the same slim iron columns erected in front of a continuous range of glass windows. These earlier buildings make an even simpler and more convincing use of this principle, as appears from the 109–111 North First Street establishment (1849–50) which we reproduce here (*fig.* **179**).[9]

---

[8] Cf. Fritz Schmalenbach, *Jugendstil* (Würzburg, 1935).

[9] Cf. also figs. 112, 113.

302

What remains of importance in the house at 12 Rue de Turin? From our later point of view, it is neither its perfect adjustment to its owner nor the first appearance in it of the *art nouveau*. It is rather the flexible ground plan in which the consequences of the new materials were drawn — the free disposition of the rooms at different levels, and the independence of the partitions one from another. This is one of the European beginnings of what Le Corbusier was later to call *le plan libre*.

In 1897 Horta built his Maison du Peuple at Brussels. Its curved glass and iron façade is one of the boldest achievements of the period (*figs.* **182, 183**). The youthful freshness of his house in the Rue de Turin reappears in it; in this building Horta really is the *chercheur* that one of his contemporaries named him.[10]

The Maison du Peuple (1897); glass and iron front, imaginative layout

The interior shows all the independence of his earlier work. Without waste of either space or time, one is brought immediately into the great dining hall, with its wide opening and its freely outspread iron structure. Horta did not hesitate to place the lecture hall — so seldom called into use — in the upper story. The Maison du Peuple reveals in its every detail the hand of a trained architect who is at the same time an ingenious inventor.

Horta had a brilliant career. Born in 1861, he was made head of the Academy at Brussels in 1913; later he became Baron Horta. He has built many important structures, and important tasks are still put into his hands. But comparatively soon he lost contact with youth and with the movement which continued his own efforts. This will concern us again when we speak of the competition for the League of Nations Palace (1927),[11] in which Horta played a decisive role as a juror.

Horta's later conservatism

During the summer of 1938, when I was in Brussels, I asked Baron Horta how he had come to build such a revolutionary structure as the house in the Rue de Turin.

When he was a young man, he explained, an architect at the beginning of his career had three courses open to him: he could

---

[10] *L'Émulation* (Brussels, 1895), p. 187.
[11] Cf. pp. 519–520.

establish himself as a specialist in Renaissance, classic, or Gothic modes. Horta found these restrictions illogical. "I asked myself why architects could not be as independent and daring as painters were." With that he pointed to a faded photograph which stood on his table: "This is my teacher, Balat, a classicist and a revolutionary — as well as the best Belgian architect of the nineteenth century.[12] I drew the milk of my youth from his instruction."

Horta went on to explain the real individuality of Balat's work. His museum in Brussels was an entirely independent masterpiece in spite of its classical façade. It was this building which determined Horta to follow his own bent.

"Its fine ground plan — thoroughly organic and independent of conventional formulae — was entirely of Balat's creation. Why then did he have to copy the classic in its façade? Why not make a modern elevation, too, and be as independent and individual as the painters were?"

Paul Hankar and the Belgian movement

Victor Horta did not work alone; he was simply the outstanding member of a group. "En Belgique," as a Parisian critic wrote at the time, "on a toutes les témérités." In the Rue de Facque, not far from the Rue de Turin, Paul Hankar also built a house in the year 1893. While he does not show Horta's imagination, Hankar was working in the same direction.[13]

But Hankar's masterpiece was the installation of the colonial exhibition at Tervueren (1897), where the perfect unity of the spirit behind the iron construction and the interior aroused the interest of artistic Europe. Finished two years before the opening of Horta's Maison du Peuple, the exposition was entirely the product of the younger generation in Belgium. At this exposition, intended by Leopold II to render the Congo problem more attractive (its motto was "New State, New Woods, and New Shapes"), the young innovators were

---

[12] Alphonse Balat (1818–1905), *architecte du roi*. Besides the Brussels museum, he was famous for his bell-shaped *jardin d'hiver* of the Residence of Laeken (1879). The iron construction here is exceptionally fine. The strap-iron ornaments on the trusses suggest Horta's *art nouveau* ornamentation of his house in the Rue de Turin.

[13] Hankar and Horta were among the first Europeans to attack the design and equipment of department stores as an artistic problem, and Hankar's solutions are sometimes the purer. Hankar had to his credit the Magasins de la Maison Claessen, Rue de l'Écuyer, Brussels (1896), and the Maison de Coumerie, Rue Lebeau, Brussels (1895–96).

182. VICTOR HORTA. Maison du Peuple, Brussels, 1897. *Exterior. The curved glass and iron façade is one of the most advanced productions of the period.*

183. VICTOR HORTA. Maison du Peuple, Brussels, 1897. *Second- and third-floor plans. An interior organized with great astuteness and independence, the little-used lecture hall relegated to the upper story.*

184. H. P. BERLAGE. Stock Exchange, Amsterdam, 1898–1903. *Wall treatment. This — the Damrak Street side, which contains the offices of the Exchange — is one of the first European façades to return to the wall as a plane surface.*

given charge of the equipment of the interior. Even in the great Paris exhibitions this had remained the work of the *tapissiers.* This unity in design of interior and exterior had a decisive influence upon later developments.[14]

Berlage's Stock Exchange and the Demand for Morality

Dutch architecture in the nineteenth century

Dutch painting and architecture in the nineteenth century exhibited considerable moderation. The cities of Holland succeeded in escaping much of the disfigurement that other Continental cities experienced. The Rijks Museum and Cuyper's railway station are examples of the mild eclecticism that governed large buildings in Amsterdam.

On the other hand, Holland failed to take effective part in the developments going on (under French leadership) in painting and construction, or in the arts and crafts movement which

---

[14] For a more extended discussion of Hankar, cf. Charles Courady and Raymond Thibaut " Paul Hankar, 1859–1901," *Revue la Cité* (Brussels, 1923).

185. H. H. RICHARDSON. Sever Hall, Harvard University, Cambridge, Mass., 1878.

grew up in England. The Dutch stood aside from this activity; they never quite lost sight of the great tradition they had to preserve. And the seventeenth- and eighteenth-century mansions that stood alongside their canals served as quiet and constant reminders of that past.

One man and a single building announced a new vitality in Holland — Hendrik Petrus Berlage (1856–1934) and his Amsterdam Stock Exchange of 1898. Even in his own lifetime Berlage's contemporaries recognized what his unique achievement had been. It was he who first succeeded in realizing, in an actual building, the demand for a purified architecture. Others had seen the need for morality in architecture, but his Amsterdam Exchange actually embodied the thoroughgoing honesty they had only called for.

New vitality introduced by one building

Berlage's career as an architect was a curious one. Like another leader of his generation, Chicago's Louis Sullivan, his early work in the middle eighties was confined to office buildings of various types. They were in the mixed style — half

186. H. P. BERLAGE. Stock
Exchange, Amsterdam, 1898–
1903. *Drawing.*

Romanesque, half Renaissance — which was favored at this
period.

Berlage was always very cautious in the use of new forms. He
received first prize in a competition for the Amsterdam Stock
Exchange as early as 1885.[15] If this plan for a quite conventional structure in Dutch Renaissance style had been followed, the Exchange would have failed entirely to influence
later architecture.

In his final version Berlage used forms slightly suggestive of
the Romanesque (*fig.* **186**). The Romanesque fascinated
Berlage, as it had Henry Hobson Richardson some twenty
years earlier. Berlage had carefully examined medieval
buildings and knew their laws of proportion. We shall
soon see, however, that Berlage's approach to the Romanesque differs from the transitory imitation of historical
shapes.

Conservative
methods of
construction

We should not expect to find Berlage's treatment of the
construction of the exchange embodying any revolutionary
advances. Holland did not possess the great tradition in constructional matters which stood behind French architects, for
example. It is nevertheless surprising that he did not avoid
visible tie bars in the great hall of his Amsterdam Exchange by
using the triply articulated girder. He is likewise very sparing

[15] He was not awarded the building contract until 1897, however. Cf. Jan Gratama,
Dr. H. P. Berlage (Rotterdam, 1925), p. 28.

308

in his use of glass and iron. All this just before the turn of the century, when elegance in iron construction had been taken for granted for several decades. The construction of the Amsterdam Stock Exchange does not go a significant step beyond Henri Labrouste's work in the Bibliothèque Sainte-Geneviève of 1843. There too the iron work had been enclosed in a self-supporting masonry shell which was quite independent of it structurally.

Much greater daring in this respect was shown at this time by Victor Horta, in his Maison du Peuple at Brussels (1897–99).[16] Horta broke the façade wide open, and filled it with glass and iron. It was Berlage's work, however, which had the deeper and the more widespread effect. By their own testimony, it acted upon his contemporaries like a revelation.

Comparison with Horta's Maison du Peuple, Brussels

The Amsterdam Stock Exchange is a brick building without stucco surfacing on either the interior or the exterior. Its ground plan, which includes three glass-roofed halls, is very compact. The largest of the halls is occupied by the Commodity Exchange and dominates the whole building (*fig. 188*). Through the open arcades which lead to the brokerage and committee rooms the actual exchange in the center of the hall can be seen.

The exterior is the final result of many separate designs. In the earliest schemes everything was in a state of turbulence. In the final plan all the sections have been cleanly fused into the flat surface of the outer wall; not even the tower is allowed to project. It is only at the monumentally treated corner of the building where the main entrance and the tower come together that a trace of the restlessness of European architecture appears. There is nothing restless in the treatment of the side that fronts on Damrak Street (*fig. 184*).[17] This wall of the Exchange has the aspect of a simple office building — and that is just what it is on that side. The windows are flush with the wall, which is held to a flat surface, broken only by the square fall-pipes and the window sills.

Flat surfaces outstanding in Berlage's treatment of its exterior

---

[16] Cf. p. 301.

[17] In the design of this front Berlage used as a module the Egyptian triangle with its sides in the ratio 5:8.

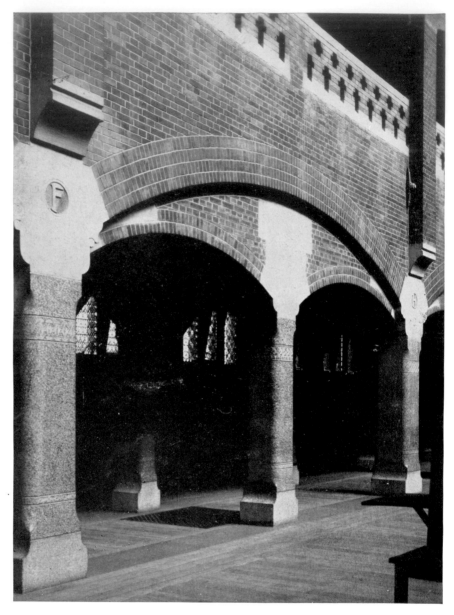

187. H. P. BERLAGE. Stock Exchange, Amsterdam, 1898–1903. *Interior.*

The brick walls of the loggias enclosing the Commodity Exchange also form a flat surface, from top to bottom (*fig.* **187**). Berlage, working with great discretion and smoothness, introduced several different materials into these walls: majolica, granite (in the square pillars), and various bright stones in the capitals of the pillars. But these capitals do not protrude in the

310

usual way; they are level with the wall, as though cut off with a razor.

This feature is by no means a casual one. In a lecture on style in architecture Berlage explains what he was aiming at: "Above all we should show the naked wall in all its sleek beauty.... Pillars and columns should have no projecting capitals: the joint should be fused with the flat surface of the wall."[18]

What is the source of the great influence exerted by the building? The secret lies in the unshakeable consistency with which Berlage strives for sincerity and purity in its architecture. The granite steps of the staircase are only coarsely chiseled out; they are still rough today. The brick arches of the ceilings in the committee rooms are shown entirely without disguise. The iron girders of the framework are emphasized with paint. The clean white joints of the brickwork in the unplastered walls stand out sharply. Used this way — as though for the very first time — these materials act as unexpected decoration.

Source of Berlage's influence

As he himself points out, Berlage sought to impart to this building something of "the quality which distinguishes old monuments from the buildings of today: quiet!" With the least compromise possible at the time, he gave the wall — until then either chaotically dismembered or deceptively patched together — the reconquered unity of the flat surface.

The reconquest of the flat surface

The wall as a flat surface was soon to become the starting point for new principles in architecture, not merely in Holland but everywhere.

Berlage's conscious asceticism — called barbarism by some of his contemporaries — joined with his fanatical zeal for truth at any price to produce in the Amsterdam Stock Exchange a building which served as a guidepost to many. He gave an example of the honorable treatment of a problem in building. No other building accords so well with the demand that lay behind the movement in architecture at that time — the demand for morality.

In Europe, where the entire previous generation had taken an altogether different line, the purity of the wall came with the

---

[18] H. P. Berlage, *Gedanken über Stil in der Baukunst* (Leipzig, 1905), pp. 52–53.

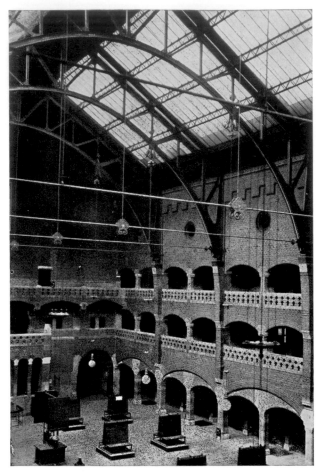

188. H. P. BER-
LAGE. Stock Ex-
change, Amsterdam,
1898–1903. *The great
hall. The Commodity
Exchange, the largest
of the three glass-roofed
halls.*

impact of a revelation. It is improbable that it would have had the same revolutionary effect in America at that time — for reasons that we shall discuss later in some detail. At this point, however, some related work by an American architect may be mentioned.

Berlage and Richardson: their leaning toward Romanesque forms not mere historical imitation

Henry Hobson Richardson was one of the first Americans in this period consciously to practice architecture as a fine art. His Sever Hall of 1878 (one of the Harvard College buildings, Cambridge, Massachusetts) has much in common with Berlage's work (*fig.* **185**). Berlage and Richardson both tend toward simplified Romanesque forms, forms which from the time of their inception have been bound up with the treatment of the wall as a flat surface.

312

It might seem that these two men, in taking over Romanesque forms, simply differ from others among their contemporaries in the direction of their choice. The majority of these eclectics appropriated classical and Gothic shapes. And certainly their followers — those of Richardson particularly — returned to the familiar path of historical imitation. The rows of little houses, each like a tiny Romanesque castle, which sprang up some years later in America and Europe demonstrate this.

But the history of the nineteenth century is complicated. The new aims derived from their study of Romanesque buildings, and not the fact that Berlage and Richardson used somewhat Romanesque shapes, are what matter. The time was not ripe for the outright invention of new forms derived from a new space conception, and they turned — very naturally — to history for help. Romanesque methods started them on the way toward the new forms their own period still awaited.

The same relation exists between the Romanesque and their best buildings that links modern painting with primitive art. Picasso did not copy the patterns of African masks; he learned from them a new way of looking at his subjects. There was an affinity between that art and the not fully conscious endeavor of his own period to compose in terms of planes. To a certain extent Berlage and Richardson also found in the Romanesque not simply another transitory fashion but an inner affinity which aided them in moving toward the still-veiled expressions of their own period.

When we penetrate to what is significant in the Amsterdam Stock Exchange we understand why Berlage became the admirer and the European advocate of American architecture, particularly that of Frank Lloyd Wright. Berlage came to America in 1911, after his Stock Exchange had been finished, on the invitation of George E. Elmslie, Louis Sullivan's partner. He found here in American buildings just those things he himself had been fighting for so passionately in complete isolation.

Berlage and the next generation

Berlage's influence upon the rising generation was very great. Even when the younger men took other directions than those he had indicated, they retained all their reverence for his

313

artistic integrity.   In Holland his influence and the image of the Amsterdam Stock Exchange appear behind an early project for a swimming pool by J. J. P. Oud (1915).   As one of the first to introduce Frank Lloyd Wright's work to Europe, Berlage unconsciously made sure that the generation after him in Holland would be stimulated to production.[19]

In Belgium, too, Berlage made a deep impression on the rising generation.   Victor Bourgeois, the Belgian architect whose Brussels garden settlement of 1922 — La Cité Moderne — gave the signal for the present-day movement, told me that around 1914, when he was a student at the Brussels Academy, only two names fascinated young men: those of Berlage and Frank Lloyd Wright.

Berlage was almost a recluse, so far as personal relations were concerned, but he valued objective connections.   He was the only representative of the older generation to take part in the founding of the C.I.A.M. (*Congrès internationaux d'architecture moderne*) at Château de la Sarraz, Switzerland, in June 1928.   At this first international rally of contemporary architects, the younger men discussed nothing except the new points of departure.   But Berlage, who, though he was the oldest participant, had not hesitated at the long journey from Holland, was the only one to read a carefully prepared paper, "The Relations between the State and Architecture." [20]

This small man — wearing the inevitable black cravat — sat in the Gothic chapel at La Sarraz quite isolated in the midst of a younger generation, and read his essay with imperturbable earnestness.

Otto Wagner and the Viennese School

Wagner's function as an educator

In the year 1894 Otto Wagner (1841–1918) was made professor of architecture at the Academy of Vienna.   The Academy at the time appeared to have lost its attraction for the younger generation, and Wagner seemed the man to restore it.   He was

---

[19] Curiously enough, Le Corbusier was first directed to Frank Lloyd Wright by a lecture Berlage delivered in Zurich (published *in extenso* by the *Schweizerische Bauzeitung*, vol. LX, nos. 11–13, 1912).

[20] This paper is preserved in the archives of the C.I.A.M., Zurich.

then just past fifty. He was a successful and energetic archi-
tect whose buildings in the manner of early Florentine and full
Renaissance work were celebrated for their excellent plans.
The Academy could expect to gain in luster from his presence.
Just at the moment of his election, however, a metamorphosis
which had long been preparing showed itself in his work.

It was in that year — 1894 — that he began a small book for
his students with the title *Modern Architecture*.[21] Soon translated into many languages, it became the textbook of the new
movement. In it Wagner asserted that "our starting point for
artistic creation is to be found only in modern life."[22] He goes
on to insist that new principles in construction and new materials are not isolated facts, but that they must lead to new
forms and be brought into harmony with human needs. The
effect of Wagner's writing was increased by the rare mixture of
sarcasm with confidence in the future that marks it. In addition, his readers felt that mature experience in architecture
stood behind his every word.

In this small book there is condensed the experience that
every nineteenth-century artist underwent from the moment
he set himself against accepted standards. Wagner makes it
plain that he no longer hopes for help from the state in any new
developments.[23] His disparagement of the layman's judgment,
"which always has been, and is, disastrous in its influence,"
reflects bitter experience of his own.[24] He holds with Goethe's
dictum: the artist must create what the public ought to like,
not what it does like.

This book speedily disillusioned the official circles responsible
for Wagner's appointment. "A fully developed architect has
become a mere experimenter with art — a sensation-monger,
a train-bearer of fashion" — this judgment appears in a
pamphlet of 1897.

In the year of his election to the Academy, Wagner built the
system of elevated and underground railways which encircles
Vienna on its outskirts. The elevated stretches were carried on

---

[21] *Moderne Architektur* (Vienna, 1895; 4th edition, 1914). "Architectural education
should educate the architect as an artist and not as a mere specialist."

[22] Page 115.   [23] Pages 133–134.   [24] Page 113.

heavy brick arches like a Roman aqueduct. Wagner carried out all the details involved in this railway, including the stations along the line. He made separate designs for each of these; those built earliest show some classical influence, while the later ones move in the direction of *l'art nouveau.*

Wagner's isolation In Brussels, as we have seen, untiring efforts were made to create an atmosphere favorable to new movements. In Vienna there was no trace of such endeavors. We miss the significance of Wagner's work if we do not realize what it is to work in complete isolation. In 1894 no one in Wagner's country was working along the same lines as he. The Austrians, Josef Hoffmann, Adolf Loos, and Joseph Olbrich, and the German Peter Behrens were of the generation of 1870, and at this date were just starting their activity.

The Karlsplatz station (*fig.* **189**) of the Vienna subway serves to show that Wagner was moving toward modern architecture. Its ornamental ironwork and the hemispherical roof are a prolongation of nineteenth-century usages. They are a further development of French iron architecture as it appeared in the domes and vaults out of which Eiffel formed the front for the main building of the Paris Exhibition of 1878.[25] Wagner's contemporaries seem to have recognized this: in one of the many vicious pamphlets directed against him, we read that Wagner "is an adherent of the brutal Gallic architectural materialism."

Wagner did not merely continue the work of the French: he introduced new elements of his own. In 1894 he prophesied that "the new architecture will be dominated by slablike, tabular surfaces and the prominent use of materials in a pure state."[26] In the Karlsplatz station he himself used thin marble slabs for the outer walls, securing them with angle irons which are left visible. This treatment shows the wall as simply a slablike screen, with no load to carry.

Ten years later in the Vienna Postal Savings Building (1904–06) he stressed still more the function of the wall as a plane surface. The façade of this bank is covered with marble slabs

[25] Cf. Fig. 158.

[26] *Moderne Architektur,* p. 136.

attached by massive aluminum bolts whose heads can be seen plainly.

The interior of the Postal Savings Building (*fig.* **190**) reveals an astonishing purity of design. It is without doubt one of the most uncompromising rooms of the first years of the twentieth century. It is very characteristic of the work of Wagner (and of his contemporaries as well) that this purity follows upon the contact with new materials. Wagner gave this bank a glass-roofed interior court. Such courts had been common since the middle of the nineteenth century. Here in the white hall of the Postal Savings Building, however, the glass and iron vaulting does not merely fulfill all functional requirements but also blends into and becomes a part of a whole architectonic expression.

In the pure and abstract forms of this glass and iron hall the touch of the architect is no longer apparent; yet his hand is everywhere present, in its curves, its colors, and the modeling of its space.

The Continental successes of these architectural pioneers were won mainly by surprise attacks. Wagner's experience followed the same pattern. A reaction against his early work in the new directions set in, and his later projects — for museums, public buildings, and towns — exist only on paper. Nevertheless, Wagner's influence on the younger generation in Austria was very strong. Although his students were men of talent, they never achieved work of his standard. One of his students was the architect Josef Hoffmann, who was the founder of the Wiener Werkstätte for handicrafts. Another, who died quite young, was Joseph Olbrich. Wagner showed these young men the direction they should take, but they were all more directly influenced by Charles Rennie Mackintosh and the Glasgow group. This was especially true of Hoffmann and the Werkstätte circle. This meant that in Austria around 1900 the movement was from handicrafts to architecture and not from architecture to handicrafts.

It resulted in the sort of overconcentration on decorative aims which appears also in Joseph Olbrich's "Secession" gallery in Vienna (1898). This was bitterly denounced by Adolf Loos.

Wagner and the Vienna school

317

189. OTTO WAG–
NER. Karlsplatz Sta-
tion, Vienna, 1894.
*Detail. "The new ar-
chitecture will be domi-
nated by slablike tabu-
lar surfaces and the
prominent use of ma-
terials in a pure state"
(Otto Wagner, 1895).*

190. OTTO WAGNER. Savings Bank, Vienna. *The hall. In this hall glass and iron
vaulting not only fulfills all functional requirements but also blends into and becomes a
part of a unified architectonic expression.*

This Viennese architect had lived in England and America,
and had learned to recognize the importance of the anonymous
work being done in those countries in the production of

articles of everyday life — from clothing to bathtubs and trunks.

As late as 1914 in Hoffmann's Stoclet house, Brussels, the influence of the cabinetmaker and of decorative art is still evident. The flat surfaces of this banker's home are made up of white marble slabs, but they are treated like framed pictures.

The influence of Wagner and his Austrian school can be detected in an entirely unexpected quarter — in the work of Antonio Sant' Elia (1888–1916), the young Italian futurist architect who was killed in 1916 in the war (*figs.* **191, 192**). His scheme for a skyscraper connected with subways and elevators, and with traffic lanes at different levels, brought together into

191. OTTO WAGNER. Drawing for bridge, subway, and different street levels, Vienna, 1906. *Part of a system of elevated and underground railway lines encircling Vienna along its outskirts.*

192. ANTONIO SANT' ELIA. Project for a subway, 1914. *Different street levels, combined with apartment houses and elevators. Sant' Elia's Nuova Città reflects the futuristic delight in intersecting streams of movement.*

one architectural unity, is quite in accord with the futurists' love of motion and interest in its artistic possibilities.[27] Sant' Elia cannot be called a disciple of Wagner; still, this unexecuted scheme points backward to a work of Wagner's which remains one of his plainest links with the present. Wagner showed the same interest in the interpenetration of different streams of motion in his drawings for the Vienna subway, with their different levels and their combination of railroads, streets, and bridges.

FERROCONCRETE AND ITS INFLUENCE UPON ARCHITECTURE

Late appearance of ferroconcrete

The *art nouveau*, in architecture at least, had its roots in the tradition of iron construction. At the beginning of the century, when this movement was spreading from Brussels, there appeared a new building material which achieved a surprisingly rapid influence upon architecture: ferroconcrete. It was at this time that architecture tore itself loose from the prejudices which had held it back for so long, and absorbed the new methods that had grown out of the period itself. It was this which promoted the use of ferroconcrete. Hardly had it been developed to the point where mills, silos, and reservoirs could be made from it than it was employed for more purely architectural purposes. Between 1910 and 1920 it became almost the trademark of the new architecture.

Although it was very late in reaching maturity, this material with its complicated composition has a past that goes very far back. There is no need to retrace its technical development, since there are many sources of information on the subject. We shall only consider a few matters that have a bearing on architecture.

Early rediscovery of concrete; Smeaton, 1774

John Smeaton, one of the great engineers of the eighteenth century, attained a triumph in the construction of the Eddy-

---

[27] Design for a " City of the Future," 1913.

193. JOHN SMEATON. Eddystone Lighthouse, England, 1774. *Etching from Smeaton's report on the lighthouse.*

stone Lighthouse (*fig.* **193**) in England. Previous lighthouses on this spot had been destroyed by storms, and the site was exposed to the full strength of the sea. But Smeaton used a system in the construction of his stonework which bound it together into an extremely tenacious whole. He locked the stones into one another, and for the foundations and the binding material he used a mixture of quicklime, clay, sand, and crushed iron-slag — concrete, that is. This occurred in 1774, five years before the first cast-iron bridge — the one over the Severn — was built. This — so far as we know — is the first use of concrete since the Roman period.

Smeaton's experiments are described in detail in the magnificent volume, illustrated by etchings, dealing with the lighthouse which he published.[1] These experiments began in the fifties of the eighteenth century, when he observed that quicklime containing clay would harden under water. As we have

---

[1] *A Narrative of the Building and a Description of the Construction of the Eddystone Lighthouse* (London, 1793).

194. HENNEBIQUE. Residence, Bourg-la-Reine. *Hennebique tries to display in one spot all the potentialities of ferroconcrete but finds no architectural language available beyond the common idiom of the late nineties.*

already seen, it was Smeaton again who first dared to use the new material, cast-iron, for pumps and other machinery.

The success of Smeaton's work on the Eddystone light led to numerous further experiments. In 1824 Joseph Aspdin of Leeds produced the first "hydraulic" binding material: Portland cement. (A hydraulic cement is one which hardens in water.) Smeaton had used the constituents as they occur in their natural state; Aspdin regulated the admixture himself.

Five years later, in 1829, a Dr. Fox developed a method of making concrete floors by using the concrete as a filling between iron girders. In 1844 this method came to be protected by patent. As we have seen, it was used (in a developed form) throughout the seven- and eight-story warehouses built by the Manchester engineer, William Fairbairn. This system of construction, using tie bars embedded in concrete, comes very close to true ferroconcrete construction. Nevertheless, fifty years went by before scientific analysis revealed the exact nature of the connections between the two elements in

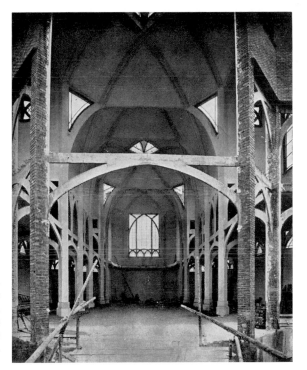

195. ANATOLE DE BAUDOT. Saint-Jean de Montmartre, Paris. Begun 1894. *The first church to be built with a ferroconcrete skeleton closed in by thin outer walls.*

ferroconcrete. During this interval all effort and attention were devoted to the development of the great iron constructions.

So far as can be discovered, the first extensive use of concrete was at the Paris Exhibition of 1867, where it was employed for the floors of the sub-basements of the restaurants in the great main building.

Ferroconcrete, taking the term in its strict sense, made its initial appearance in 1868, when the gardener Monnier began to use wire network for the cores of concrete tubs. This procedure involved nothing new in itself: Labrouste had made the vaulting in his Bibliothèque Sainte-Geneviève of interlaced wires covered with layers of plaster.

Reinforced concrete did not come into common employment on a large scale until the 1890's, when it was so used in America by Ernest Leslie Ransome (born in 1844, in Ipswich, England)[2] and in France by François Hennebique (1842–1921).

First large-scale use of reinforced concrete in the 1890's: François Hennebique

[2] The employment of ferroconcrete in America previous to the Leland Stanford Jr. Museum of about 1890 and the building of the Pacific Borax Company deserves more

François Hennebique had as his guide preliminary work carried out by a number of constructors. He knew the separate requirements of the iron and of the compressed concrete, how to apportion one to the other, and how to dispose the iron reinforcing rods — all the relevant laws, in short. But, beyond this, he was an excellent contractor and had built in every part of Europe: mills at Nantes, granaries at Genoa, silos at Strasbourg, sanatoria in Switzerland.

Use in residences

The villa which he built for himself during the nineties at Bourg-la-Reine (*fig.* **194**) served as a piece of propaganda for the use of ferroconcrete. The villa makes its possibilities obvious at once to any observer. The octagonal tower rests on two cantilevers which project four meters. Not content with this, the tower exhibits other projecting constructions higher up; these enclose a spiral staircase that leads to the uppermost roof garden (which is planted with trees). Roof gardens, terraces, freely projected building elements: a veritable architectural tightrope dance! Done entirely in the architectonic idiom of the nineties, it is a fantastic mixture, one calculated to win the heart of any Surrealist.

Use in a
church (1894)

French architecture of the nineties is not to be compared with its forceful Belgian counterpart: after reaching its high point in the 1889 Galerie des Machines it entered upon a decline. There are some achievements which are of interest, however, even if they failed of international influence. In 1894 Anatole de Baudot began work on the first church to have a ferroconcrete skeleton enclosed by thin walls, his Saint-Jean de Montmartre in Paris (*fig.* **195**). Anatole de Baudot in his official capacity was the "Protector of Ancient Monuments"; in his lectures, delivered over a period of twenty-five years, he stood for the regeneration of architecture. As soon as the new material, ferroconcrete, appeared, he used it for a church — a marked departure from outworn routine. In his "Architecture and Reinforced Concrete" [3] he informs us that he was

---

careful study, directed at the progressive stages of this early development. Shortly before this, Ransome had built the Academy of Sciences at San Francisco, using reinforced concrete floors and iron columns. For more details cf. Ernest L. Ransome and Alexis Saurbrey, *Reinforced Concrete Buildings* (New York, 1912), especially the first chapter, "Personal Reminiscences."

[3] *L'Architecture et le ciment armé* (Paris, n.d.).

awarded the contract because by using the new material he was able to underbid all his competitors.

The boldness of De Baudot's work was recognized, but for many reasons it failed to equal the great effect produced by Victor Horta's house in the Rue de Turin.[4]

By the first decade of the twentieth century reinforced concrete came into widespread use nearly everywhere. It was used in the Queen Alexandra sanatorium, built at Davos, Switzerland, in 1907 (*fig.* **196**). Robert Maillart was responsible for its construction; the architects were Pfleghard and Haefeli. The

196. PFLEGHARD, HAEFELI, and MAILLART. Queen Alexandra Sanatorium, Davos, 1907.

Queen Alexandra occupies a wide ledge halfway up a mountainside. Its three wings with their wide open terraces are carefully oriented to catch all the available sunlight.

In the same year work was begun in Chicago on a warehouse designed for Montgomery, Ward and Company.[5] Completed

---

[4] Quiet pioneer work was also done by Louis Bonnier, who was responsible for the construction of a civic building at Pas-de-Calais (devoid of the usual decoration). Dutert, who had been in charge of the architectonic part of the Galerie des Machines of 1889, erected a museum of uncovered brick for the Jardin des Plantes in Paris, a building which likewise honestly displayed the iron in its construction wherever it was used.

[5] Cf. Fig. 249.

in 1908, this warehouse was the work of R. E. Schmidt, Garden, and Martin — members of the Chicago school's second generation. Some eight hundred feet long, it has large windows of the horizontally elongated Chicago type and broad horizontal bands running without interruption the full extent of its façade. "It is a huge aggregation of storage lofts, nine stories high, a repetition of units of a monotony truly appalling. . . . It is entirely of reinforced concrete construction — foundations, columns, floors, and walls." [6]

Contemporary critics were thoroughly bewildered by this structure, one of the first in the United States, I believe, to use ferroconcrete with a clear recognition of its properties. "It is not intended to be an architectural monument . . . the qualifications are functional, structural, and economical . . . in this building architectural expression was not wanted." But "if it is not in itself beautiful or graceful, it is at least logical." [7] Actually this warehouse is one of the few late buildings in which the spirit of the Chicago school still survives.

The further advance in reinforced concrete construction and in the exploitation of its artistic potentialities took place in France.

A. G. Perret

Auguste Perret (born in 1873) remained an *architecte-ingénieur* throughout his career.[8] Perret came from Burgundy, from a town near the great monastery of Cluny. It was the Cluniac monks who initiated the great reform and purification of church architecture carried out during the twelfth century.

Rue Franklin apartment

Perret built his 25 *bis* Rue Franklin apartments in Paris in 1903 (*fig.* **197**), ten years after Horta's Rue de Turin house. This apartment house by no means embodies the pure forms of the Chicago office buildings, and it fails to match the strength of Frank Lloyd Wright's work of the same period. The familiar European restlessness is still present to a considerable degree.

---

[6] "On American Architecture," *Architectural Record*, XXII (1908), 115–120.

[7] *Architectural Record*, XXII, 115–120.

[8] See Paul Jamot, *A.-G. Perret et l'architecture du béton armé* (Paris and Brussels, 1927).

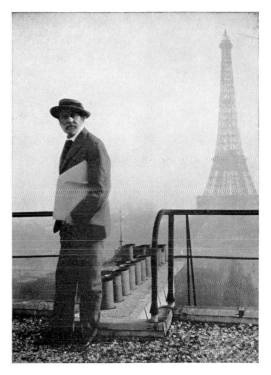

198. AUGUSTE PERRET on the roof of 25 bis Rue Franklin.

199. AUGUSTE PERRET. 25 bis Rue Franklin. *Plan. The flexible planning which the ferroconcrete skeleton makes possible.*

197. AUGUSTE PERRET. 25 bis Rue Franklin, Paris, 1903. *The ferroconcrete skeleton, instead of being disguised, is openly presented as a constituent element.*

327

Nevertheless, it represents the first employment of ferroconcrete as a medium for architectonic expression, and many of its features were to prove seeds for future developments.

The ferroconcrete skeleton is used without disguise; it stands out plainly as one of the constituent elements of the building. Earlier buildings in concrete — Hennebique's Rue Danton apartments, for example — made no architectonic use of the skeleton. The façade as a simple support for ornament has been almost abandoned. A series of delicate progressions and

200. AUGUSTE PERRET. 25 bis Rue Franklin. *Office on ground floor. The street floor has been almost dissolved into pure glass.*

recessions removes from it all associations with weight. This effect of lightness is reinforced by the way in which the seven upper stories are cantilevered out over the street. And the street floor (which at one time held Perret's office) has been almost dissolved into pure glass, broken only by a few narrow piers of reinforced concrete (*fig.* **200**). A thin, narrow slab surmounts this floor — to provide a small area of shade and a support for a balcony. The ferroconcrete joists of the skeleton are brought out into the open in the top stories.

The total effect is reminiscent of some iron structures: everything seems to grow lighter and lighter toward the ground, until finally only a few thin members connect the building with the earth. This impression of fragility had its financial consequences. Banks refused to take a mortgage on the apartment house, since the experts predicted its speedy collapse.

The flat roof, like several in Tony Garnier's projected "Cité Industrielle," exhibits a rudimentary roof garden (*fig.* **198**). The light-well has been done away with, and the walls for the staircase are executed in glass bricks, which leave it entirely open to the daylight. Perret told me that he used these bricks because his neighbors could legally have forbidden the cutting of windows on this side of the building. This, of course, does not at all detract from Perret's ingenuity in finding a new use for a familiar material. The same trait appears in his adoption of simple pipe railings to replace the usual elaborate hand-wrought affairs.

Interior: novel uses of materials and flexible planning

But Perret made his most important contribution to the younger generation of French architects in the flexible treatment of the ground plan (*fig.* **199**). Partitions are set in with complete freedom to connect separate ferroconcrete pillars. Perret was working here in the same spirit as Horta and, later on, Le Corbusier. Each story is planned as an independent unit.

A short time later Perret built what he himself regards as the "première tentative (au monde) de béton armé esthétique." This was his garage in the Rue Ponthieu. Here the reinforced concrete skeleton is given full opportunity to determine the character of the façade.

Garage in the Rue Ponthieu

There are other fine works of Perret's which, unfortunately, we shall be unable to discuss: his Théâtre des Champs-Élysées (1911–14), the source of so much controversy between him and Henri van de Velde; the docks at Casablanca (1916), with their eggshell-thin vaultings; his churches at Rancy (1922) and elsewhere, which exerted such influence upon contemporary church buildings; his private houses; and his latest works. Auguste Perret, with his sense for construction, gave Le Corbusier a decisive impetus toward his own work.

And the next generation of architects as a whole carried Perret's results still further. Perret's buildings follow the best nineteenth-century French tradition in construction. Like the earlier *architectes-ingénieurs*, he drew his inspiration from his materials. Perret did for ferroconcrete what Henri Labrouste had done for iron.

Classical
reminiscences

Like Tony Garnier, Perret preserved some connections with the classic past. But classical canons remained alive and flexible for the best French architects, just as they had for the French masters of baroque days — for Racine, Molière, and Descartes. Perhaps later on we shall come to see that something of the classic spirit is present even in the work of the men who came after Perret; that they too reflect the classic urge toward balance, symmetry, and repose.

201. TONY GARNIER. Central Station, 1901–04. *Project. At a time when railroad stations were customarily executed in the style of huge monuments, Garnier returns to actual functions and exploits the new materials: glass and reinforced concrete.*

Tony Garnier

Ferroconcrete
the basic material
in Garnier's work

The *architecte-constructeur* Auguste Perret was the first to find new architectonic means in the unexplored potentialities of ferroconcrete. This material was, indeed, peculiarly attractive to French builders. Concrete accorded perfectly with their traditional penchant for daring and extensively hollowed out structures.

Tony Garnier (born in 1869) made reinforced concrete the basis of all his work. In his "Cité Industrielle" (1901–04) this new material was used to organize a whole town along original

330

and strikingly farsighted lines. This is a scheme which we shall discuss in some detail later on.[9] The Cité Industrielle, planned when Garnier was only thirty, really laid down the outlines for his whole future output. The "grands travaux de Lyon," carried out under Édouard Herriot in Garnier's native city, were practical outgrowths of his youthful project. These "grands travaux" were very extensive; they included the Lyons stockyard (1909), the city stadium (1915), twenty-two pavilions of the Granges-Blanches hospital (begun in 1911, but erected over a period of some two decades), and part of a residential district — "Quartier des États-Unis" — which was begun in 1920. Garnier's later work included pavilions at several French exhibitions, his own house, and a number of villas along the Riviera. All these buildings can be regarded as developing out of his first serious work, and it is his foresighted planning of this Cité Industrielle which gives Garnier his place in the history of architecture (*fig.* **201**).

We are approaching the moment when European architecture could at last attain a mastery of contemporary problems through the means created by the engineers. By this time people could see that modern techniques offered the only means of expression for feelings stemming from modern life. But we have first to retrace developments in America, whose influence was to become effective only when this European architecture had begun to recover from its own maladies.

---

[9] Cf. pp. 689 ff.

PART V AMERICAN DEVELOPMENT

The colonial and the republican periods were of great importance to American development; they provided a solid foundation for future advance. But the period between 1850 and
1890 is more important for American influence on the outside
world. The preparations which made that influence possible
were completed during these decades. The years between 1850
and 1890 produced not only the great surge toward the unsettled lands in the West but also strong manifestations of a
new and specifically American spirit. This period has particular significance to foreign eyes. The new forms which grew up
in it had their roots in an organization of labor altogether different from that which prevails in Europe.

The illustrative material published here was often unearthed
with difficulty. Documents from this period are not readily
accessible, just because there is so little interest in it and so
little understanding of its importance. Material showing the
development of the life of the period and the daily habits reflected in it is very difficult to find. What is of more importance, there is the constant danger that it will be lost forever.

Manufacturers simply laugh when asked for specimens of their
early productions and for old catalogues. There is no time for
and — above all — no interest in the sources of the tradition
which governs the life of the man of today. In the future, historians who examine this period will certainly be more interested in uncovering the roots of the great anonymous productions of industry than they will be in the monumental or
official architecture of the time. But what institute tries, out
of a human rather than a technical interest, to collect the
documents dealing with the anonymous beginnings of our
period? We are too unaccustomed to considering interrelations between different realms of human activity to see clearly
the points at which they are connected. The danger is that the
material for reconstructing these relationships may be lost by
the time their importance has been recognized.

Europe Observes American Production

The European public had its initial contact with American
tools and furnishings at the first international exhibition — the

334

202. American clocks, c. 1850.

great London Exhibition of 1851. European observers were astonished by the simplicity, technical correctness, and sureness of shape revealed in American productions. The astute Lothar Bucher called attention to "the grandfather clocks with their excellently contrived works and simple walnut cases; the chairs — from simple wooden work benches to easy chairs — with their freedom from the gingerbread carving which tears at our hands and clothing, and the absence of the right angles of those currently popular Gothic chairs which are hunching everyone's shoulders. All that we see of American domestic equipment breathes the spirit of comfort and fitness for purpose"[1] (*fig.* **202**).

Similarly, Count Léon de Laborde, a French observer, saw in the Americans "une nation industrielle, qui se fait artiste" — an industrial nation which was becoming artistic. He added that "America would go her own way."[2]

[1] Lothar Bucher, *Kulturhistorische Skizzen aus der Industrieausstellung aller Völker* (Frankfort, 1851), pp. 146 ff.

[2] Léon de Laborde, *De l'union des arts et de l'industrie*, I, 312 ff.

335

The height of the lower part of the top of the desk, is just equal to the highest part of the back of the chair, so as to allow it to pass under.

The front edge of the seat is in a perpendicular line with the edge of the top of the desk, so that the scholar is required to sit erect, when engaged in writing or studying, and the same time that part of his back which requires support is fully in contact with the chair.

203.   Standards of American school furniture, 1849.

Gottfried Semper expressed a similar opinion. Semper was a German architect who (like Richard Wagner) had been exiled from his own country for revolutionary activities in Dresden. He was one of the founders of the first English school of design, organized at London in this same year — 1851. Semper writes that "although there is very little evidence of craftsmanship in America, nevertheless a real national art will spring up there first." [3]

American school furniture, c. 1851; advanced functional design

The Americans showed schoolroom furniture with cast-iron supports in which everything was carefully adjusted to the pupil's age, occupation, and anatomical structure (*fig.* **203**). This furniture — most of it produced in the New England area, around Boston — was the product of a twenty-year fight for better school equipment that had begun in 1830 with W. J. Adams' lecture, "Schoolhouses and School Apparatus," before the American Institute of Instruction. In 1838 Henry Barnard completed one of the pioneer works in this field, his essay on school architecture, for the Senate's Standing Committee on Education. Barnard was perfectly clear on the functional demands that such furniture had to satisfy: "Every pupil, young or old, should be provided with a chair just high enough to allow, when properly occupied, the feet to rest on the

---

[3] Gottfried Semper, *Wissenschaft, Industrie und Kunst* (Brunswick, 1852), pp. 73 ff.

floor without the muscles of the thigh being pressed hard upon the front edge of the seat. . . . The seats should be provided with a support for the muscles of the back, and, as a general rule, this support should rise above the shoulder blades, and should in all cases incline back as it rises, one inch in every foot." [4]

A quarter of a century later, at the Philadelphia Exposition of 1876, the European observers split into two camps. Those who expected to find European fashions in the American exhibits were disappointed. They found, as Jakob von Falke says, "neither furniture nor furniture covers, neither glassware nor fayence ware, which attracted us by reason of its taste, color-scheme, or beauty." Certain objects of daily use which, according to von Falke, ought to be richly decorated — grandfather clocks, for example — "show the sad state of American taste by their complete absence of ornamentation." [5]

In this instance a European observer condemned the characteristic which gave American industrial art its individuality and significance for the future: simplicity.

On the other hand, those observers who did not judge on the basis of preconceived standards were impressed with "the beauty of form in which the Americans cast their tools and machinery." F. Reuleaux, the well-known scientist who headed the German delegation to the exposition, comments on this in his "Letters from Philadelphia" of 1876: "The axes, hatchets, hoes, hunting knives, hammers, etc., are executed with such variety and beauty as cannot but excite admiration and astonishment. A constraint runs through all of them. They are designed so well for the purpose to be served that they seem actually to anticipate our needs." [6]

The Victoria and Albert Museum at South Kensington has preserved the catalogue of a Chicago hardware firm of the

---

[4] Henry Barnard, *School Architecture, or Contributions to the Improvement of School-houses in the United States*, 5th ed. (New York, 1854), p. 342. The Senate committee refused to publish Barnard's essay, which did not appear until 1841, and then only — as he relates — "through the strenuous effort of a few intelligent friends of school improvements," and with the author bearing a part of the expense.

[5] Jakob von Falke, "Vorbemerkungen zur Weltausstellung in Philadelphia," *Der Gewerbehalle*, XIII (1875), 144 ff.

[6] F. Reuleaux, *Briefe aus Philadelphia* (Brunswick, 1877), pp. 18 ff.

MAYDOLE'S CAST STEEL HAMMERS.

Nos. 81 to 83.

No.		Weight.	Per Dozen.
81	Engineer's Ball-Pein Hammers, Extra Cast Steel,	2 ℔.	$15 00
82	" " " " " " "	1 ℔. 9 oz.	13 00
83	" " " " " " "	1 ℔. 2 oz.	11 00

One-fourth Dozen in a Package.

Nos. 91 and 92.

91	Engineer's Hammers, Extra Cast Steel,	2 ℔. 4 oz.	12 00
92	" " " " "	1 ℔. 12 oz.	10 50

One-fourth Dozen in a Package.

Nos. 61 and 62.

61	Blacksmith's Hand Hammers, Extra Cast Steel,	3 ℔.	15 00
62	" " " " " "	2 ℔. 10 oz.	13 50

One-fourth Dozen in a Package.

The Weights given above are for Single Hammers, without the Handles.

204. Ball-peen machinist's hammer; blacksmith's hammers. Chicago catalogue of 1877. *Reuleaux remarked of tools like these that "they are designed so well for the purpose to be served that they seem actually to anticipate our needs" (1876).*

seventies. The precise and sensitive forms of the tools illustrated in it show why Europeans were so astonished by them (*fig.* **204**). Such articles as the "engineer's machine hammer" and the Yale lock were not even introduced into Europe until comparatively recent years (*fig.* **205**).

Julius Lessing, the first director of the Museum of Industrial Arts in Berlin, when he saw the exhibit of American tools at the Paris World's Fair of 1878, experienced — so he says — as intense an aesthetic pleasure from a display of American axes as from a real work of art. He remarked the beauty of line which was achieved without any ornamental embellishment, "simply by molding the axe to the human hand and to the movement of the human body as it is used." [7]

Lessing goes a step further. He points to the surprising parallelism between these tools and the most beautiful of primitive stone and bronze instruments. At the same time he regards as

[7] Julius Lessing, *Berichte von der Pariser Weltausstellung von 1878* (Berlin, 1878), p. 99.

338

a "lamentable retrogression every effort of the Americans to imitate European art forms."

The official French report on the exposition at Philadelphia in 1876 includes some comment on American furniture. Particular attention is called to the fact that American furniture, in contrast with European, is marked by its use of flat surfaces, of fewer surface planes. "The moldings are simple, with very little carving. The parts are thus easy to make separately and are easily assembled." [8] The French report argues that a new style has appeared on the other side of the Atlantic, a style which manifests itself in all forms of the industrial arts. To show how typically American these products were in their eyes, they called this the "Pullman car style."

Elaborate and costly furniture appeared at the exhibitions. Thus the Paris Exposition of 1867 featured a French sideboard, valued at twenty thousand dollars, which awed all beholders. Regarded as a museum piece at the time, it now presents a somewhat dreadful appearance. American exhibitors — especially after the seventies — preferred to display what was known as "patent furniture." A page from the official cata-

American "patent furniture" in the sixties

205. Yale lock, Chicago catalogue of 1877. *One early instance of the way machinery came to displace the skilled craftsman — here the locksmith.*

[8] *Exposition internationale et universelle de Philadelphie 1876* (Paris, 1877), pp. 185 ff.

206. Folding bed, Philadelphia Exhibition, 1876. *A specimen of the patent combination furniture which came into extensive use about this time.*

logue of American exhibits at Paris in 1878, headed "Cheap and Fancy Furniture, all Series Productions," lists "Perforated Veneer Seats," "Automatic Sofa-Spring Beds," "Folding Chairs" (they folded into a lounge), a "Swing Convertible Cradle," a "Child's Crib," a "Reclining Chair," etc. (*fig.* **206**).[9]

All these things were developed just at the period when European photomontages of historical styles were beginning to influence American production.

Innate beauty of American tools

By the time of the Chicago World's Fair of 1893 Lessing found the Americans awarding all the prizes to heavily ornamented European articles. "But we who went over with the will to

[9] Patent furniture had its origin in the early industrialized England of the beginning of the nineteenth century. Thomas Sheraton, known to the public for the style that bears his name, is perhaps more important today as one of the first cabinetmakers to be interested in producing "patent" furniture. (Cf. Sheraton, *Designs for Household Furniture*, third ed., London, 1812: easy and hunting chairs, chairs which may be converted into beds, tables which may be converted into high desks, movable bookcases, etc.)

American furniture-makers followed this trend, which nearly disappeared in Europe through the influence of "period" furniture, and consciously developed very original solutions. No research seems to have been done on this important branch of American furniture manufacturing.

learn," he writes, "have found other things more important for future development. We are bringing back to Europe smooth wooden chairs, polished doorknobs, and gracefully curved utensils entirely devoid of embellishment.

"Here we saw utensils and tools created in the same spirit as railroads, ships, and wagons. Here we saw objects of daily use developed clearly and without any preconception — objects appealing not so much to the calculating intellect as directly to the senses. They convey to the eye the satisfying sensation which only beauty can give." [10]

As the last of the European observers, Gropius may be quoted. In 1913, just after his completion of the Fagus works, he wrote an essay on the development of modern industrial buildings for one of the publications of the German Werkbund, which did so much to introduce contemporary ideas into Germany. For the first time he gives illustrations and speaks of the unintentional beauty of American industrial architecture:

"In comparison with the other countries of Europe, Germany seems to have gone far ahead in the field of factory design. But in America, the motherland of industry, there are great industrial structures which, in their unconscious majesty, are superior to even our best German buildings of that type. The grain elevators of Canada and South America, the coal conveyors of great railway lines, and the more modern industrial plants of North America are almost as impressive in their monumental power as the buildings of ancient Egypt. They present an architectural composition of such exactness that to the observer their meaning is forcefully and unequivocally clear. The natural integrity of these buildings resides not in the vastness of their physical proportions — herein the quality of a monumental work is certainly not to be sought — but in their designers' independent and clear vision of these grand, impressive forms. They are not obscured by sentimental reverence for tradition nor by other intellectual scruples which prostrate our contemporary European design and bar true artistic originality" [11] (*fig.* **207**).

---

[10] J. Lessing, "Neue Wege," *Kunstgewerbeblatt*, VI (1895), 1 ff.

[11] Walter Gropius, "Die Kunst in Industrie und Handel," *Jahrbuch des Deutschen Werkbundes* (Jena, 1913), pp. 21–22.

207. Grain elevator, Chicago, 1873.

The Structure of American Industry

American industry differs from European industry in its structure. These differences have to be kept in mind if one is to understand clearly the process of evolution which American industry has followed. Such structural differences are also the grounds for the dissimilar attitudes toward the crafts—and later toward the "arts and crafts" — which exist in these two areas.

Industrialization of complicated handicrafts

European industry, springing into existence on English soil in the late eighteenth century, substituted the machine for hand labor in the working of some simple raw materials — iron, and plant and animal fibers. The spinning and weaving machines which were invented in England at this time served as unsurpassed trail-breakers in the mechanization of industry.

American industry became robust at a much later period, around 1850. Naturally, European inventions were adopted and introduced into this country. Divergences appear at the points where problems inherent in a totally different situation demanded new solutions.

To this day skilled craftsmen persist in Europe. For comparatively low wages they make its bread and sausages, shoes, clothing, clocks and furniture, and build houses.

About 1850, in America, all these complicated crafts based on skilled labor became industrialized. The change came about partly through new inventions and partly through new methods of organization. The major emphasis, indeed, rested on a new organization. Very early this new organization even penetrated the household. New tools were introduced to lighten hand labor in cooking — the apple parer (1868), for example. Before 1850 the manufacture of men's and children's clothes had been largely a household industry, but the invention of the sewing machine transferred it to the factories. A team of three to five, or more, persons produced the finished garment.[12] By the 1840's the "Oak Hall" establishment in Boston was supposed to be the largest clothing store in the United States. It was housed in a building of the Gothic Revival style which resembled a medieval tomb.

From an author of the sixties we discover that "few are aware of the vast extent to which the sale of ready-made clothing is carried on at the present day. Probably no branch of business has so rapidly increased.

"But a few years ago it was confined to goods of very inferior quality, style, and make, worn mostly by laborers and seamen."[13]

By 1876 Wanamaker was producing ready-made clothing for men and boys on a great scale, and with all the knowledge of service, advertising, and price policies best calculated to attract the masses.

In the manufacture of boots and shoes, machinery did not come into use until nearly the middle of the century. At

---

[12] Walter W. Jennings, *A History of Economic Progress in the United States* (New York, 1926), p. 430.

[13] C. D. Goyer, *History of Chicago, Its Commercial and Manufacturing Interests* (Chicago, 1862), p. 170.

about the same time butchering was converted into the meat-packing industry, with stockyards, elaborate refrigeration methods, and the modern, endless-chain system of operation — including mechanical hog-scraping apparatus.[14] The first "mechanical bakery" was established in Brooklyn in December 1856. The second mechanical bakery was set up shortly afterwards in Chicago. It had "one oven passing from the basement to the third floor and within the oven . . . three endless chains supporting the cars containing the bread." [15]

To summarize: In America materials were plentiful and skilled labor scarce; in Europe skilled labor was plentiful and materials scarce. It is this difference which accounts for the differences in the structure of American and European industry from the fifties on. In America just about that date, mechanization began to replace skilled labor in all the complicated crafts.

This trend can be observed astonishingly early in the field of housing; mechanized methods appear even before the fifties. In this period James Bogardus was producing cast-iron buildings assembled from prefabricated parts which were forerunners of the skeleton frame. The encroachment of industrialization upon skilled hand trades is shown much more plainly, however, in the introduction of a new type of wooden construction, one used for some 60 to 80 per cent of all the houses in the United States: the balloon frame. The balloon frame in its technical aspects has little interest for us, but a study of its origins may yield us an insight into an important period in the American development.[16]

---

[14] Jennings, *op. cit.*, p. 734; H. T. Warschow, *Representative Industries in the United States* (New York, 1882), pp. 444 ff.

[15] Goyer, *op. cit.*, p. 122.

[16] Some of the quotations in this section are from Heinrich Waentig, *Wirtschaft und Kunst* (Jena, 1909). Waentig, as he remarks in his foreword, "gathered together out of life and the libraries" the materials for one of the few really penetrating studies of the arts and crafts movement in the nineteenth century. Anyone who has done similar research into nineteenth-century developments can understand his remark that he was more than once on the verge of abandoning the whole enterprise.

Waentig goes directly to the constituent facts of the period. He was not an art historian but a political economist — that is, he had been trained to concentrate on the problems of his own age at greater length than a final appendix to a study of some earlier period permits. His book has great value for anyone interested in the nineteenth century.

THE BALLOON FRAME AND INDUSTRIALIZATION

The balloon frame (*fig.* **208**) is closely connected with the level of industrialization which had been reached in America. Its invention practically converted building in wood from a complicated craft, practiced by skilled labor, into an industry.

The principle of the balloon frame involves the substitution of thin plates and studs — running the entire height of the building and held together only by nails — for the ancient and expensive method of construction with mortised and tenoned joints. To put together a house like a box, using only nails — this must have seemed utterly revolutionary to carpenters. Naturally enough, the balloon frame met with attack at the start: "The Balloon Frame has passed through and survived the theory, ridicule, and abuse of all who have seen fit to attack it. . . . Its name was given in contempt by those old fogy mechanics who had been brought up to rob a stick of timber of all its strength and durability, by cutting it full of mortices, tenons and auger holds, and then supposing it to be stronger than a far lighter stick differently applied, and with all its

208. Balloon-frame construction. *From G. E. Woodward, "Woodward's Country Homes" (New York, 1869).*

209. St. Mary's Church, Chicago, 1833. *The first building in balloon frame. Razed and reërected three times during its short life.*

210. Balloon frame. *From W. E. Bell, "Carpentry Made Easy" (1859). "If it had not been for the knowledge of the balloon-frame, Chicago and San Francisco could never have arisen, as they did, from little villages to great cities in a single year"* (Solon Robinson, 1855).

211. Windsor chair. *Parallels the balloon frame both in its use of thin structural parts to produce a light and strong construction, and in its anonymous development.*

346

212. R. J. NEUTRA. House in Texas, 1937. *Modern balloon-frame houses like this one reveal the elegance and lightness which are innate qualities of this type of skeleton construction*

capabilities unimpaired. . . . The name of 'Basket Frame' would convey a better impression, but the name 'Balloon' has long ago outlived the derision which suggested it."

The balloon frame marks the point at which industrialization began to penetrate housing. Just as the trades of the watch-maker, the butcher, the baker, the tailor were transformed into industries, so too the balloon frame led to the replacement of the skilled carpenter by the unskilled laborer.

"A man and a boy can now (1865) attain the same results, with ease, that twenty men could on an old-fashioned frame. . . . The principle of Balloon Framing is the true one for strength, as well as for economy. If a mechanic is employed, the Balloon Frame can be put up *for forty per cent less money* than the mortice and tenon frame." [1]

[1] The quotations are from G. E. Woodward, *Woodward's Country Homes* (New York, 1869), pp. 152–164.

Without machine-made nails the balloon frame would be economic nonsense. It was only when machinery had made nails cheaper, and "cut nails of steel and iron and nails made of wire could be furnished of excellent quality and at a cost much less than old-fashioned wrought-iron nails [that] the comparatively expensive system of house framing with mortise and tenon began to be supplanted by a more economic system dependent entirely upon the efficacy of nailing." [2]

The invention of the balloon frame really coincides with the improvement of sawmill machinery as well as with the mass production of nails (*fig.* **210**).

Several machines for cutting and heading nails were developed in both England and the United States toward the end of the eighteenth century. Thomas Clifford patented such a device in 1790, and about the same time a similar machine was invented by Jacob Perkins of Newburyport. A machine which cut, shaped, and headed tacks in a single operation at the rate of sixty thousand a day was patented by Jesse Reed in 1807. [3]

"When the manufacture of cut nails was first undertaken, wrought nails cost 25c a pound. . . . This made their use for houses and fences difficult." [4] All this changed with the introduction of machinery. The price of nails was suddenly reduced. "In 1828 the production was so brisk that the price was reduced to 8c a pound. . . . In 1833 the rapidity of production had brought prices down to 5c . . . in 1842, 3c." [5]

The Balloon Frame and the Building-up of the West

The balloon frame has an established connection with the conquest of the West from Chicago to the Pacific Coast.

Contemporaries knew quite well that houses would never have sprung up with such incredible rapidity — either on the

[2] Russell Sturgis, *Dictionary of Architecture and Building* (New York, 1902), III, 1125.

[3] *Great Industries of the United States* (Hartford, 1872), p. 1072.

[4] William E. Bell, *Carpentry Made Easy* (Philadelphia, 1859). Bell worked as a carpenter in Ottawa, Michigan. Writing in 1857 he claims (p. 53) to have had fifteen years' experience constructing and repairing balloon frame buildings.

[5] Albert S. Bolles, *Industrial History of the United States* (Norwich, Conn., 1889), p. 220.

348

prairies or within the big cities — had it not been for this construction.

"With the application of machinery, the labor of house building has been greatly lessened, and the western prairies are dotted over with houses which have been *shipped there all made*, and the various pieces numbered." [6] Another observer goes further: "If it had not been for the knowledge of the balloon-frame, Chicago and San Francisco could never have arisen, as they did, from little villages to great cities in a single year." [7]

At the period when the West was being built up, contemporaries called "the method of construction known as 'balloon framing' the most important contribution to our domestic architecture."

To me it seems very characteristic of the negligence with which contemporary history is treated that no dictionary of architecture or construction gives a precise answer to the question of who invented the balloon frame and when it was invented.

The Invention of the Balloon Frame

Even as far back as the fifties and sixties there seems to have been no certainty with regard to the invention of the balloon frame. One early witness, writing in 1872, relates that "when it was first used is not known with any definiteness, but it has within the last fifty years replaced the old method of construction." [8]

Woodward, in 1869, confesses that "the early history of the Balloon Frame, is somewhat obscure, there being no well authenticated statements of its origin. It may, however, be traced back to the early settlement of our prairie countries, where it was impossible to obtain heavy timber and skillful mechanics. . . . The Balloon Frame belongs to no one per-

---

[6] *Great Industries of the United States.*

[7] Solon Robinson in *New York Tribune*, January 18, 1855. Quoted in Woodward, *op. cit.*, p. 151.

[8] *Great Industries of the United States.*

son; nobody claims it as an invention, and yet in the art of construction it is one of the most sensible improvements that has ever been made." [9]

Nevertheless, the balloon frame does seem to have had an inventor and to have emanated from one particular town.

George Washington Snow, 1797–1870

The inventor of the balloon frame was George W. Snow.[10]   He was born at Keene, New Hampshire, September 16, 1797, of an old American family which traced back to the *Mayflower*.

He must have been rather a restless spirit, since he first left the family homestead for New York and afterwards went to Detroit with his wife.   Under rather primitive conditions he crossed the state of Michigan, and finally, in a canoe paddled by an Indian guide, he reached the mouth of the Chicago River, July 12, 1832.   The small community he found there — there were only two hundred and fifty inhabitants — pleased his pioneer temperament.   He took an active part in its affairs for many years: in 1833, when Chicago became a city, Snow was appointed its first assessor and surveyor; he was elected alderman in 1849, and made drainage commissioner the same year; he was at one time chief of the pioneer hook and ladder company.

As one of his descendants remarks in a letter, like many of the first settlers Snow was something of a jack-of-all-trades.   He was one of the earliest of the Chicago lumber dealers, purchasing "Carver's Lumberyard" in 1835.   He owned considerable land and conducted a real estate business.   He was a building contractor, as well as a general contractor and financier.

Snow was not merely a surveyor; he had been educated as a civil engineer in his youth.   This technical training may have led him to the invention of the balloon frame.   How this came

---

[9] Woodward, *op. cit.*, pp. 151–154.

[10] Until more exact researches have been made it cannot be taken as certain that no other men figured in the development of the balloon frame.   Solon Robinson (to whom we have already referred) writes that he was using the balloon frame as early as 1835. Walter Field in a Harvard thesis, "A Reexamination into the Invention of the Balloon Frame," shows how difficult it is to give George Snow full credit for the invention of the balloon frame.   Further investigation seems to be necessary.

about and what his struggles were we do not know. The tag, "balloon frame," was a mere nickname, a jocular reference to the lightness of this new type of construction.

There are several confirmations of the tradition in Snow's family that he invented the balloon frame. Its invention is credited to him by Andreas in his *History of Chicago*,[11] and in *Industrial Chicago*, the most important book on the development of Chicago, we read that "the balloon frame is the joint idea of George W. Snow and necessity."[12] Andreas' statement is based on the words of one of Snow's fellow townsmen, the architect J. M. Van Osdel, who arrived in Chicago in 1837. In an article, "The History of Chicago Architecture," published in a Chicago monthly of the early eighties, Van Osdel remarks that "Mr. Snow was the inventor of the 'balloon frame' method of constructing wooden buildings, which in this city completely superseded the old style of framing with posts, girts, beams and braces."[13]

George Snow's name is nearly unknown. There is no portrait of him in any of the local histories, but one was obtained from a family album which reveals a face at once full of puritan energy and of human sensitivity.[14]

The first building in balloon frame was St. Mary's Church in Chicago, the earliest of the Catholic churches of the city (*fig. 209*). "In July 1833 a number of men are found erecting a church on Lake Street near State Street."[15] Old builders prophesied its collapse. In the short term of its existence this church was razed and reërected three times.

Until the seventies the balloon frame was called simply "Chicago construction," as we learn from a report of United States Commissioner H. Bowen, published in Washington in

---

[11] I (Chicago, 1890), 504.

[12] I (Chicago, 1891), 51.

[13] *Inland Architect and Builder*, I, no. 3 (April 1883), 36. This magazine was the organ of the developing Chicago school of architects.

[14] I am indebted for this biographical material to Miss Marion Rawls, librarian of the Burnham Library of the Art Institute of Chicago, and to Mrs. George A. Carpenter of Chicago, Snow's granddaughter, who provided the portrait. I published this portrait in an article in the annual, *New Directions*, 1939.

[15] *Industrial Chicago*, I, 51.

1869. Bowen speaks of the western farmhouse which was forwarded in sections to the Paris Universal Exposition of 1867 as being of "Chicago construction."

The balloon frame, then, is associated with Chicago, like the skyscraper construction which, half a century later, was also called simply "Chicago construction."

The balloon-frame building with its skeleton of thin machine-cut studs and its covering of clapboards grew out of the seventeenth-century farmhouses of the early settlers. Snow was familiar with such houses in his home state of New Hampshire and his wife's home, Connecticut, where they were especially common. In these houses comparatively thin and narrow studs were used as intermediary framing, with the whole construction tied together by the clapboard covering.[16]

George Snow started with these traditional methods, changing and adapting them to meet the new possibilities of production in a way which was as simple as it was ingenious.

The balloon frame has kept its vitality for a whole century and is still used extensively. This simple and efficient construction is thoroughly adapted to the requirements of contemporary architects. Many of Richard J. Neutra's houses in Texas and southern California reveal the elegance and lightness which are innate qualities of the balloon-frame skeleton (*fig.* **212**).

The Balloon Frame and the Windsor Chair

The thin two-inch studs of the balloon frame stick up into the air apparently without weight in comparison with the traditional timber construction. Even today the European observer finds their thinness really daring.

The same idea, the use of thin structural members to produce a most efficient whole construction, had figured a century earlier in the development of the Windsor chair. The Windsor chair is as outstandingly important in the history of American

---

[16] Cf. J. F. Kelly, *The Early Domestic Architecture of Connecticut* (New Haven, 1935), p. 40. Here the "studs or intermediary framing members" are described as "generally measuring about $2\frac{1}{2} \times 3$ inches in section." Their height, however, was only equal to "the distance between the horizontal members of construction."

furniture as the balloon frame is in the history of American housing.

There is a familiar anecdote attached to the name of this piece of furniture. The Prince of Wales, toward the end of the seventeenth century, is supposed to have seen the original specimen in a peasant's cottage near Windsor Castle, and to have ordered it copied for his own use, though England never gave the artistic consideration to the Windsor chair that America did. Windsor chairs were the strongest type of chair made in the colonies and easily movable. Their construction was of spindles (*fig.* **211**), and the early ones were made by wheelwrights. It is very seldom that the vogue for furniture extends over a century, but that of the Windsor chair lasted from 1725 to 1825. No single chair-maker won individual fame for the design.[17]

For the historian it seems worth while to observe the curious interrelation existing between the development of the balloon frame and the Windsor chair in two different centuries.

There is the same tendency to counteract the American climate — wet and dry in turn — by assembling thin structural parts to produce a light type of construction. There is the same tendency toward anonymous work and toward serial manufacture, with lightness and efficiency achieved by the simplest means.

PLANE SURFACES IN AMERICAN ARCHITECTURE

In speaking earlier of architecture as an organism with its own continuing life, we remarked that nowadays we are chiefly interested in those persisting influences which give this life its continuity. The lines of force which spread and develop throughout several periods concern us more than the history of styles, for styles are those special aspects of periods which mark them off one from the other.

---

[17] See Marta K. Sironen, *A History of American Furniture* (New York, 1936), p. 18.

Historical styles are particularly uninformative with regard to what was actually going on in America. They arrived here fully grown and give little insight into the constituent facts of the native American development.

During the eighties European architecture lost more and more of its dignity. The closer it clung to historical forms in the search for security the more insecure it really became. In barely fifty years the whole architectural inheritance of the eighteenth and early nineteenth centuries was lost in a welter of transitory detail. The inner unrest and uncertainty of the period appears time and again in unbalanced treatments of the wall and of the ground plan. The whole organism of architecture was riddled by a fatal disease.

American independence of Europe showed itself in the development of new and logical forms for tools and furniture, and in the informal and flexible ground plan of the American house. In the same way the wall maintained its unity and balance in America throughout this whole period of European uncertainty and confusion. America produced its share of grotesque work during these years, but — in contrast to Europe — attention never entirely strayed from the basic elements of architecture. These elements always remained dominant in American work, taken as a whole. It may be that this is why new architectural solutions were reached in America earlier than they were abroad.

The plane surface: the brick wall

The plane surface — the flat wall of wood, brick, or stone — has always been a basic element in American architecture. In part this has been due to the simplicity which a scarcity of skilled labor enforced; in part it directly continues late eighteenth-century tendencies. The Georgian manner of treating the brick wall has been carried over into the nineteenth century; wooden houses have kept to traditions established by the first settlers.

The *brick wall*, to be cheap, must be kept flat and simple. All openings are cut very cleanly into the flat surface of the wall.

Such undisguised brick walls (*fig.* **213**) are familiar features of the American scene; they appear in New England mansions

354

213. Old Larkin Building, Buffalo, 1837. *Specimen brick building of a type omnipresent in the United States, with flat, undisguised walls and clean-cut openings.*

of the late eighteenth century, in small anonymous buildings on the main streets of all the cities, and in the big factories of the Civil War period. The plain brick wall was firmly established as a basic element in architecture when men like Henry Hobson Richardson began their work in the seventies. Richardson's Sever Hall was built in 1878. We found a European example of such scrupulously level surfaces in Berlage's Amsterdam Stock Exchange. But the Stock Exchange was built two decades later; flat brick surfaces, such as Richardson used, were almost unknown in the Europe of the seventies.

Frank Lloyd Wright, too, was able to use the brick wall, taken as a simple surface, from the very start. Unlike van de Velde and Horta, there was no need for him to begin by crusading against the mutilation and overcrowding of the wall, or to invent an *art nouveau* to compete with established modes of ornamentation. He was able to begin his work on a much higher level.

214. Longfellow House, Cambridge, Mass., 1759. *Clapboard wall of the sort which has been used continuously in America for three centuries.*

The wooden wall

The *wooden wall* has been governed by eighteenth-century American traditions to an even greater extent than the brick. The simple clapboard wall (*fig.* **214**) has remained a constituent element for three centuries, without any interruption, from the time of the first colonists to the present. Clapboards had been used in England, but only for unpretentious farmhouses. In America they dominated the whole field of wooden building. We find them everywhere, from the rudest huts to the finest mansions, churches, and town halls. Such a widespread and enduring authority for one type of wall treatment covering a period of three hundred years is entirely unknown on the other side of the Atlantic.

The use of clapboards automatically tends toward balanced and simple treatments of the wall. They are ill suited to breaks or interruptions in its flat expanse, and they discourage the use of applied ornament.

The stone wall

Stone walls were treated with the same simplicity in states where stone was used as a building material. Excellent workmanship was displayed in the New England states: in the flat

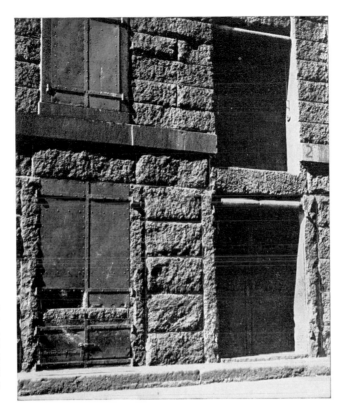

215. Stone wall, Union Wharf warehouse, Boston, 1846. *The granite posts and lintels for windows and doors were cut in one piece at the Quincy quarries.*

granite walls of the community houses of the Shakers (*fig.* **216**), in the granite warehouses along the Boston wharves (*fig.* **215**), and in the commercial buildings of Boston of the fifties and sixties (*figs.* **217, 218**).[1]

[1] Many of these buildings were designed by Alexander Parris, who also designed Quincy Market (the market buildings around Faneuil Hall, *c.* 1825). The earliest of the waterfront buildings date from the middle twenties; the wharf warehouses were built in the forties; the mercantile blocks on Commercial Street were erected in the fifties; the remainder were mostly completed by 1869, when Franklin Street was opened.

Many of these mercantile buildings are excellent examples of a well-proportioned and logical pre-Richardson architecture which certainly played a larger part in later developments than is generally believed.

In a seminar which I conducted during the summer of 1938 on Boston office buildings between 1830 and 1860 we endeavored to learn more about this work. An account of one of the earliest of the great commercial architects, Gridley J. Fox Bryant, was discovered in a copy of the *New England Magazine* ("An Architect of the Old School," vol. XXV, n.s., November, 1901). Between the fifties and the seventies, Bryant built hundreds of business blocks on the Boston water front, most of them granite buildings. According to the *New England Magazine*, he left all his papers to Henry Turner Bailey. One of my students, Miss Lydia Jones, wrote to Bailey's widow. This material has apparently disappeared, for Mrs. Bailey replied that her husband had "got rid of it one day."

216. Shaker Community House, Concord, Vermont, 1832. *A specimen of the excellent stonework that was produced by this religious sect.*

These commercial buildings with their rusticated walls display typical plane surfaces and economy of detail. Earlier warehouses, dating from the forties, are built of huge plain blocks of rough-hewn granite, but no reminiscences of Florence are involved. Their impressive austerity is easily explained: the granite came from the Quincy quarries near-by, and labor was saved by cutting out the window or door pillars on the spot, in one piece.

Richardson was a student at Harvard in the period when these commercial buildings were erected. Later on he went to Paris and came under European influences. These new buildings along the Boston water front must nevertheless have constituted his earliest architectural impressions.

The Marshall Field Store

Richardson's Marshall Field Wholesale Store in Chicago (1885–87) was his best work (*fig.* **219**). This building with its massive stone walls occupies a rather strange position in the Chicago development as a whole. For all that, it furnished a strong incitement to the work of the Chicago school, and something of its character was reflected in other buildings erected in the Loop during the eighties.

Louis Sullivan's criticisms of the architecture of his time were as uniquely severe as they were just. The Marshall Field Store, however, was to him an "oasis" in the midst of a desert of doubtfully sincere edifices. The "young man" to

217.   Commercial Block, 140 Commercial Street, Boston, Mass., 1856.   *Detail.   One example of the well-proportioned and logical pre-Richardson architecture that appeared in Boston during the fifties and sixties.*

218.   Commercial Block, 140 Commercial Street, Boston, Mass.   *From Boston Almanac, 1856.   A contemporary print of the building from which the detail in Fig. 217 was taken.*

219. H. H. RICHARDSON. Marshall Field Wholesale Store, Chicago, 1885. *Richardson here continues the American tradition of the plain and massive stone wall.*

whom he so describes it in his *Kindergarten Chats* interrupts him with ironic astonishment:

"'You mean there is a good piece of architecture for me to look at?'

"'No, I mean, here is a man for you to look at. . . . I mean that stone and mortar here spring into life and are no more material and sordid things . . . wholesomeness is there, the breath of life is there, an elemental urge is there.'" [2]

We break in upon this poetic vision only to ask, What is this building? Romanesque? Florentine Renaissance? [3] But need we go so far back? Would it not be simpler to look for its origin in the rugged stone walls which gave Richardson his first

[2] *Kindergarten Chats* (Lawrence [?], Kansas, 1934), p. 15.

[3] Henry Russell Hitchcock in his biography of Richardson makes a very careful effort to trace the stages by which Richardson arrived at his Romanesque style. The account (inevitably) presents large gaps.

architectural impressions? The plain and massive stone wall had been one of the basic elements in American architecture from the very beginning, from the fortifications of the Revolutionary period to the commercial buildings contemporaneous with Richardson's student days at Harvard. The sober impressiveness of this store could be Romanesque and at the same time thoroughly indigenous, an artistic transmutation of elements which had grown out of American life.

The Flexible and Informal Ground Plan

American architecture has been marked by one tendency since the arrival of the earliest settlers: the American house is given a ground plan which can be enlarged whenever new social and economic conditions make it desirable. This contrasts very sharply with European procedure. In Europe a farmhouse is planned as a solid, cubical unit from the very beginning. Sometimes the interior is left unfinished, to be fitted up by later generations when they come to need larger living quarters.

The American and the European farmhouse

The American practice of adding new units to the original one can be seen in those New England houses which survive from the seventeenth century.[4] All these heavily timbered houses began as one and a half or (at most) two-story structures, with a single room on the ground floor. The next generation, with improving circumstances, enlarged this ancestral nucleus both horizontally and vertically. A new roof was spread over all these additions, quite asymmetrically. But the important thing was the addition of wings, which was very general. The L-shaped ground plan, the beginning of the flexible and informal layout, developed from this sort of planning.

Houses were not invariably enlarged. Sometimes — as in the William Pepperell house at Kittery, Maine — they proved too big for a later generation and were cut down. "This family mansion was then much more imposing than at present, being 10 feet longer at each end and surrounded by a beautiful park. It was reduced after the American Revolution when the estate was confiscated in 1779." [5]

[4] For example, the Hancock house, Lexington, Mass. (1698, enlarged in 1734), the Jackson house, Portsmouth, N. H. (*c.* 1664), and the Whipple house, Ipswich, Mass. (1642).

[5] *The Portsmouth Guide Book* (Portsmouth, N. H., 1876), pp. 145–146.

In the late eighteenth century people did not hesitate to cut through the solid oak framework of a house and divide it into several portions. These were then moved to a new site and reassembled, with whatever changes and enlargements suggested themselves. The house at 34 Chestnut Street, Salem, Massachusetts (*fig.* **220**), is the product of such methods, although no one would ever suspect it. This charming residence, which seems to have been conceived as a unified whole, was really built in three sections. "It is the only house now standing on the street which was not built in its present location but

220. House at 34 Chestnut Street, Salem, Mass., 1824. *The two ends were originally part of another house and were moved on wheels to the Chestnut Street site; there the center portion was built.*

was moved to the street. . . . It was originally a portion of the house on the West Farm at Oak Hill, Danvers [miles away], and was moved on wheels to Chestnut Street, in two parts, about 1824." [6] The architect added the center with its Palladian window, and changed and adapted it to the so-called Palladian or academic ground plan which was in favor at this period.

The flexible treatment of the house which has been common practice in America since colonial days is one of the keys to

[6] Richard Hall Wiswall, *Notes on the Building of Chestnut Street* (Salem, 1939), p. 18.

its domestic architecture. Opinions are supposed to change oftener in America than elsewhere, but this is not true in the field of housing. Here there has been continuous growth. American developments show more continuity than we find in Europe, and more of the power to develop new elements for the future out of the existing architectural inheritance.

American publications of the sixties and seventies show the great variety of foreign influences which were at work in the country. England, Germany, France, Spain, the Orient — fashions from all these quarters came into favor. They remained, however, only the latest fashions at one season or another; they did not permanently infect American architecture. When Wilhelm Bode visited the Chicago World's Fair of 1893 he remarked that "in contrast to Germany, the modern American house is built entirely from the inside out. It not only corresponds to particular individual demands but above all to the peculiarities, customs, and needs of the Americans. That these customs are pronounced and distinctly marked gives domestic architecture in the United States a great advantage over our own German architecture." [7]

American interiors
of the nineties

It was precisely the things which still impress European observers that surprised Bode almost fifty years ago. He notes that "rooms along the hallway are fitted with sliding doors or partitions   often half as wide as their walls — and that these doors are nearly always left open.[8] In this way it is possible to look into the various rooms of the house." The Continental apartment houses to which Bode was accustomed, with their ridiculously high ceilings, dark and overcrowded rooms, and luxuriant wall-coverings, were in sharp contrast to American

---

[7] Wilhelm Bode, "Moderne Kunst in der Vereinigten Staaten," *Kunstgewerbeblatt*, V (1894), 115–117.

[8] To this day the European's house remains, more or less, his castle. Its doors are real doors, and they are usually kept closed. Sliding partitions never open upon the hallways; they are used only to connect interior rooms. In American houses there are not only these daringly placed partitions but even a lack of keys for half of the doors within the house, and a lack of locks in the case of closets and wardrobes. European windows are provided with both shades and curtains, and both — usually neither, in America — are drawn after nightfall. The American rarely even fences his house, and lately there are some signs that he may abandon the garage and take to leaving his car under a mere shelter. "A garage is no longer necessary, as cars are made," says Frank Lloyd Wright. "A carport will do, with liberal overhead shelter and walls on two sides" (*Architectural Forum*, January 1938, p. 79).

interiors. In America, Bode remarks, "the rooms, according to our notions, are somewhat low. They are not overcrowded with furniture, *and they have light-colored walls and ceilings.*" [9] (These are features which contemporary architects have finally established in Europe, after considerable struggle.)

Functional planning in the seventies

Bode's report of an advanced American domestic architecture is supported by popular literature on home building published as early as the seventies. Books like Gardner's *Illustrated*

221. E. C. GARDNER. Kitchen, 1882.

222. E. C. GARDNER. Country house, 1882.

Homes, Describing Real Houses and Real People (Boston, 1875) [10] did much to propagate sound housing. The way in which these books of the seventies approach the problem of the house is surprising, considering the period. Instead of the discussion of details which one might expect, the house is considered as a whole — as a unit which must vary in each special case. Their authors find this attitude so natural that the tone of the discussions is invariably light and easy and sometimes actually playful. They deal with houses planned not in some special style but for some special purpose: with houses for the newly married, doctors' houses, well-to-do business men's houses — even one-room houses for "old maids."

---

[9] *Op. cit.*, p. 117.

[10] Eugene C. Gardner (1836–1915) was one of the popular authors in this field. He was principal of the Talmadge Academy, at Talmadge, Ohio, and editor of the *Builder* from 1885 to 1887.

The old maid and her house (*figs.* **223, 224**) are particularly interesting. This is a lady who knows precisely what she wants: "I propose to build a house to live in, merely that and nothing more. . . . My house must have one room and of closets four; one for a little dressing room; one for my silk dresses, which will accumulate, as I have no one to give them to except to home missionaries' wives, and they ought not to wear silk; one for my china, and one for my umbrella and

223. E. C. GARDNER. One-room house for an "old maid."

224. The architect and his spinster client. *From Gardner, "Illustrated Homes" (Boston, 1875).*

overshoes." [11] The close-knit unity of the ground plan produced to satisfy these demands and the economy with which its space is put to use recall one of J. J. P. Oud's low-rental apartments of 1920.

The functional spirit which dominated Europe in the twenties is even more clearly apparent in the way the problem of the kitchen is handled. In another of his books Gardner proposes a space-saving treatment strikingly similar to the Frankfort kitchen of about 1920 (*fig.* **221**). The later design was supposed to derive from the space economies effected in the modern dining-car. Gardner achieved his solution through a direct approach to the working problems of the cook and the house-wife. The kitchen is made long and narrow "so that it may

[11] Gardner, *op. cit.*, p. 114.

have ample wall space and yet keep the distance between the range and the pantry as short as possible." It has windows at opposite sides "to admit plenty of light" and so that "the summer breezes may sweep through it and keep a river of fresh air between the cooking range and the dining room." [12]

The interior of the typical American house is subdivided as little as possible. This urge to unite the various rooms and to open the interior is occasionally reflected in the use of different floor levels, as in certain large Classical Revival houses of the nineties.

An anonymous development

Nineteenth-century Americans who could afford to be stylish had houses whose exterior forms reflected the styles in favor at the time — romantic, Victorian, French Renaissance, Romanesque, or classical. The ground plan, however, generally retained its soundness. The flexible and informal ground plan which was, on the whole, standard in America grew up without any great names being attached to it. Like tools and patent furniture, it remained strictly anonymous. It is the outgrowth both of the urge for comfort in the dwelling and of the American tendency to tackle problems directly. Frank Lloyd Wright found the basic elements of the flexible ground plan ready at hand in its anonymous development. Undoubtedly Richardson gave a new artistic intensity to this sort of planning in his houses of the early eighties — particularly those built around Chicago and in New England. But open planning itself, the flexible and informal ground plan — this is a product of the American development as a whole.

THE CHICAGO SCHOOL

Chicago in the eighties

During the eighties a whole colony of buildings suddenly sprang up in Chicago — to heights of twelve, fourteen, sixteen, and twenty-three stories. These buildings were erected not in

---

[12] *The House that Jill Built* (New York, 1882), p. 82. Kitchens with a highly differentiated organization and highly developed technical installations are first to be found in England in the forties. Cf. the interesting description of the great kitchen of the Reform Club in London (built by Charles Barry in 1837) in the Larousse *Dictionnaire du XIX siècle*, heading "Club."

isolation, as they were in other cities, but in close proximity to each other. Each had its own individual appearance and its own name, and yet the aggregate appearance was not chaotic.

American buildings are commonly so short-lived that in a few decades, perhaps, these buildings will all have disappeared. Many of the best specimens have gone already and many more are destined to go soon.

The strongest growth of the Chicago school is to be found between 1883 and 1893.[1] Two contemporary voices may inform us of the state of development at the beginning and at the end of this period.

"In no period since 1830 has the city experienced such wonderful development in increase of population, trade and building up as . . . in 1882. . . . The character of the buildings are [*sic*] monstrous and costly. . . . There is such a demand for business and office quarters that the permit to build a block is no sooner obtained than applications are made for renting apartments, and before the building is completed it is all rented and the renters are ready to step in with their implements of trade. Block after block mount up into the clouds overhanging the city from every street and avenue."[2]

---

[1] The works concerned with the Chicago school in its development between 1883 and 1893 are for the most part anonymous. The first two volumes of *Industrial Chicago*, 6 vols. (Chicago, 1891–96), published by the Goodspeed Publishing Company, treat the building interests. These two volumes, rarely found in American libraries, are the Vasari of the Chicago school. The volumes of the *Inland Architect* (Chicago) after 1883 also give some insight into the development of the school.

The best illustrations and plans (besides those in *Industrial Chicago*) are to be found in *Prominent Buildings Erected by the George A. Fuller Company, Chicago* (Chicago? 1893?) and *Fireproof Building Construction: Prominent Buildings Erected by the Geo. A. Fuller Company* (New York and Chicago, 1904), both published by the George A. Fuller Company. George A. Fuller (1851–1900), a Massachusetts man, went into business in Chicago as a builder. He was one of the first building contractors to work with skeleton construction, and he was connected with the erection of many buildings with which we shall deal — the Tacoma, the Monadnock, the Pontiac, the Fair, the Reliance, and the Marquette buildings, the Ashland Block, and the Carson, Pirie, Scott and Company department store as long as Louis Sullivan worked on it.

Not to be overlooked are several guides, such as L. Schick, *Chicago and Its Environs: A Handbook for Travellers* (Chicago, 1891). Others will be mentioned later. For illustrations see *Pictorial Chicago* (Chicago: Rand, McNally, 1893).

For the earlier period see T. A. Andreas, *History of Chicago* (Chicago, 1884), which contains rare statistics and illustrations.

[2] *Stranger's Guide* (Chicago, 1883).

In 1893, shortly before a great crisis affected Chicago and its activities, another contemporary witness traces the end of this period: "many times has it happened in Chicago that the morning papers have come out with accounts of the letting of the contract for the largest office building in the city and the evening papers of the same day have given news of other contracts for buildings far surpassing those told in the morning." [3]

In the eighties the Loop — the business center of the city — became the perfect illustration of American audacity in the direct assault that was made upon its problems. Whole streets were developed in a way that had never been seen before. Walking through the Loop, one is struck by the impression that Chicago is an outpost for the immense areas which are spread out behind it. At the time its great buildings went up, Chicago was the real point of concentration for the products of the West and Middle West, and not merely an enormous stock exchange, like New York. The rapid growth of this great center led to sudden enlargements of its needs. To meet them, the urge grew up to use the new potentialities of construction, potentialities which had hitherto been exploited only in bridges and industrial structures of various kinds.

Large office buildings for business firms and insurance companies were the first to appear. Buildings of equal power soon appeared to meet other demands — immense hotels for the travelers who passed through the city and combination office-theater-hotel buildings like the Adler and Sullivan Auditorium. At the same time the problem of the modern apartment house — which still remains unsolved — was attacked with great consistency and daring.

Office buildings as the starting point of the Chicago school

The Chicago school is bound up with the creation of the modern office building — in other words, with the creation of an administration center (*fig.* **231**). All sorts of engineering problems entered into the solution reached in the Chicago buildings, and the founder of the Chicago school, William Le Baron Jenney (1832–1907),[4] was an engineer before he was an

---

[3] *World's Fair Souvenirs* (Chicago, 1893).

[4] Cf. Charles B. Jenkins, "W. L. B. Jenney and W. B. Mundie," *Architectural Reviewer* (Chicago), February 1897.

architect. He had received a thorough technical grounding and had been a major in Sherman's corps of engineers. The future architects of Chicago received their training in Jenney's office. William Le Baron Jenny played much the same role in the training of the younger generation of Chicago architects that Peter Behrens did in Germany around 1910, or Auguste Perret in France. He gave young architects the preparation they needed to tackle the new problems for which the schools could offer no solutions.

Today William Le Baron Jenney's imagination and courage are not sufficiently recognized. Even Louis Sullivan describes him as rather a connoisseur than an architect, and in Chicago one of Sullivan's collaborators told me that Jenney had no sense for detail and ornament. Architectonic detail and stylistic remnants play, it is true, a negligible part in Jenney's work. For all that, he was the man whose Leiter Building of 1889 was the earliest solution of the problem of the great building in skeleton construction, a solution whose clarity and freedom from compromise were far above the average.

Jenney's background was excellent. He had received the best technical training available in this period at the École Polytechnique and the École Centrale in Paris. In Jenney's studio French engineering combined with the methods of his German specialists in ornament to produce a curious mixture. In 1873, as a young beginner, Louis Sullivan worked in this studio and had his eyes opened to "suppressed functions" in architecture. Besides Sullivan (who stayed here no longer than he did most places) Jenney's staff at one time or other included many of the future builders of Chicago: Martin Roche, Holabird, and even Daniel Burnham — later the partner of John Root.

Jenney's hand first showed itself clearly in a warehouse which he built at 280 West Monroe Street for Leiter in 1879 (*fig.* **225**). This building (which is still in existence) has brick pillars on its outer walls, and wide glass openings similar to the "Chicago windows" of a later date. The interior has the cast-iron columns which were standard during this period.

Jenney's first building of a type new both in respect to its height and its construction was erected for the Home Insur-

225. WILLIAM LE BARON JEN-NEY. First Leiter Building, Chicago, 1879. *Brick pillars on outer walls; cast-iron columns in the interior. The wide glass openings suggest the "Chicago windows" of a later date.*

ance Company in 1884–85.[5] In it a complicated construction was made to produce a thoroughly integrated whole.

Jenney, a leader in construction

Richardson planned the Marshall Field Wholesale Store and Warehouse (*fig.* **219**) while Jenney was at work on his Home Insurance Company building. This store showed Chicago architects how unobtrusively a great volume could be integrated. Richardson injected into this building something of the vitality of the rising city, in a treatment which was full of dignity. The dominance of the windows is emphasized, as it is in Jenney's Home Insurance offices, but the construction is rather conservative. Richardson's massive stone walls belong to an earlier period. When Adler and Sullivan came to build their Auditorium, they used similarly massive outer walls, even though the interior iron structure was very daring.

Architects did not at once follow Jenney in his adoption of skeleton construction. In 1889, however, three years after his

[5] Cf. p. 205. This building was still sound in 1929 when it was torn down.

226. WILLIAM LE BARON JENNEY. Manhattan Building, Chicago, 1891. *The bay windows of many different forms are intended to catch all the light available on this narrow street. They disappear entirely in the unobstructed upper stories.*

Home Insurance Company, Holabird and Roche put up the Tacoma Building, a twelve-story skeleton structure.[6]

Meanwhile William Le Baron Jenney kept to his own course. He erected his second Leiter Building in 1889. His Manhattan Building (*fig.* **226**) — at this period the highest building of pure skeleton construction — was finished in 1891.[7] The Manhattan is on Dearborn Street, which is comparatively narrow. In order to catch as much sunlight as possible, Jenney — like Holabird and Roche in the Tacoma Building — filled its front

---

[6] In a building of the Tacoma's dimensions, the gain in renting area through the use of skeleton rather than masonry construction was equivalent to the rent on an additional floor. It was for this reason that skeleton construction was used. A certain indecision is still apparent in the design of the Tacoma. The total window area is exceptionally great, but the individual windows themselves are quite small. The Tacoma was torn down in 1929.

[7] "The Manhattan, fronting on Dearborn Street, is the pioneer of the sixteen-story and basement building . . . 204 feet high . . . designed May 1890 and completed in the summer of 1891" (*Industrial Chicago*, vol. I, 1891, p. 69).

with bay windows.[8]   But these windows are very carefully diversified in shape, and they disappear entirely in the unobstructed upper stories.[9]

Jenney built "The Fair," one of Chicago's great department stores, in 1891.   With this nine-story building on Dearborn, Adams, and State streets, Jenney returned to his principle of making the skeleton the determining factor in the design.   The first two stories of The Fair are almost pure glass (*figs.* **227, 228**).   This feature was demanded by the owners of the store, who wanted the largest possible amount of display area.

The new potentialities change the aspect of the city

The spirit of the Chicago school, its impulsion toward the simplest and most self-evident solutions, soon dominated the entire Loop.   Its works sprang up one beside another.

Burnham and Root erected their Monadnock Block at the corner of Dearborn and Jackson streets in 1891.   This was the last of the high buildings with walls of solid masonry.   A contemporary critic — Montgomery Schuyler — called it "the best of all tall office-buildings," [10] but it is not too typical of the Chicago school.   Its expression derives more from architectonic refinements than from the new potentialities.[11]   And heavy masonry walls were not the solution to the problem of the many-storied building.   The rather small dimensions of the windows indicate the extent to which they hampered the architects.

Diagonally across the street from the Monadnock Block is another Burnham and Root building, the Great Northern

---

[8] "Light and space are preferred to any definite style" (*idem*).

[9] The Manhattan was reproduced in *Inland Architect*, vol. XIII (1889), no. 8.

[10] Harriet Monroe, *John Wellborn Root* (New York, 1896), pp. 141–142.

[11] At this period the taste of speculators and investment counselors was sometimes more advanced than that of architects — a rare phenomenon. "The Monadnock — 'Jumbo,' Root used to call it — was the last of the tall buildings to show walls of solid masonry. For this building Mr. Aldis [Owen F. Aldis, of Boston], who controlled the investment, kept urging upon his architects extreme simplicity, rejecting one or two of Root's sketches as too ornate.   During Root's absence of a fortnight at the seashore, Mr. Burnham ordered from one of the draughtsmen a design of a straight-up-and-down, uncompromising, unornamented façade.   When Root returned, he was indignant at first over this project of a brick box.   Gradually, however, he threw himself into the spirit of the thing, and one day he told Mr. Aldis that the heavy sloping lines of an Egyptian pylon had gotten into his mind as the basis of this design, and that he would 'throw the thing up without a single ornament'" (Harriet Monroe, *op. cit.*, p. 141).

227. WILLIAM LE BARON JENNEY. The Fair Building, Chicago, 1891. *The skeleton is made the determining factor in this design.*

228. WILLIAM LE BARON JENNEY. The Fair Building, Chicago, 1891. *Skeleton.*

229. HOLABIRD and ROCHE. Marquette Building, Chicago, 1894. *The front is exceptionally well-proportioned, imposing in its simplicity and its wide expanse of "Chicago windows."*

230. HOLABIRD and ROCHE. Marquette Building, Chicago, 1894. *Plan of one story with undivided offices. In most of these buildings large portions of every floor were left without partitions, so that they could be subdivided later to suit the tenants.*

Hotel (1891; *fig.* **232**). Its clean brick façades carried over to the hotel room the "Chicago windows" used for offices. The Fair, Jenney's department store, was also built around this time. Three years later, in 1894, Holabird and Roche constructed their Marquette Building farther down the street (*fig.* **229**).

The front of the Marquette is exceptionally well-proportioned, imposing in its simplicity and its wide expanse of "Chicago windows." It remains the typical Chicago office building of the nineties. The demand of the owners that not one inch of the interior be unlighted is exactly satisfied. From the street the Marquette looks like a closed block, but actually it is cut out at the back somewhat like a letter **E**. The middle bar of the **E** — relatively the darkest part of the building — is used as an elevator hall, with all the elevators massed together in it. As in most such buildings, large parts of its floor space were built without partitions so that they could be subdivided later on to suit the tenants (*fig.* **230**).[12]

The Apartment House [13]

In Chicago the problems of large-scale housing, of the hotel and the apartment house, were attacked with the same clearheadedness that appears in the office buildings of the city. During the seventies, just after the great fire, a trend away from the small private home and toward the big many-storied apartment house set in — this on the authority of the anonymous author of *Industrial Chicago*. As he puts it, "the modern flat is the palace of those who wish to be relieved of house owning and its cares." [14]

The interior organization and the architectonic details of some of these buildings are astonishingly daring and advanced.

---

[12] J. K. Freitag, *Architectural Engineering, with Special Reference to High Building Construction*, 3rd ed. (New York, 1912), p. 38. Freitag's book is one of the few technical publications dating from the most flourishing period of the Chicago school. It contains the ground plans of many important buildings as well as a wealth of technical details.

[13] Cf. *Industrial Chicago*, vol. I, chap. 7, on modern flats and other residences, and illustrations and comments in the following issues of the *Inland Architect:* August 1884, pp. 8, 15; January 1887, p. 101; December 1890, plate (Ricardi apartments); October 1897, plate (Cary apartments); March 1887, p. 28 and plate; February 1893, plate (the "Kenwood"); November 1893, plate (the "Omaha").

[14] *Industrial Chicago*, I, 254.

Solutions which today are still in process of being formulated appeared in outline in these flats and hotels of a generation back — just as contemporary business and civic centers were anticipated by the Chicago office blocks.

The Adler and Sullivan Auditorium marks one of the early stages in this development. This huge and complicated structure housed not only the actual auditorium and an office building but also a large hotel. The hotel is noteworthy in many respects: the staircase is modeled with an impressive strength; the great length of the bar is emphasized by a heavy beam carried along the ceiling parallel to its front edge in a clear span with no vertical supports; the top-floor dining hall (since converted to other uses) is developed as a broad barrel vault, thereby matching the auditorium proper.[15]

The Hyde Park Hotel on the south side of the city was built in 1887–91 by Theodore Starrett and George A. Fuller. Its site on Fifty-first Street, near the lake shore, was then almost rural; it has since been heavily developed. "The hotel has 300 rooms, finished in suites of 2 to 5 apartments, . . . 50 suites are furnished with private baths and incandescent lamps . . . and heated by steam."[16] The building was of eight stories, with broad windows, and — once more according to *Industrial Chicago* — "a very large verandah extending around the building."

Some of these apartment houses had removable partitions so that a suite of five rooms could be thrown together into one. This was the case in the Leander McCormick flats, later the Virginia Hotel, at the northwest corner of Ohio and Rush streets. Its architect was Clinton J. Warren, a product of the Burnham and Root offices.[17]

---

[15] For a detailed description of this theater, the best of the period, with plans, see Hugh Morrison, *Louis Sullivan* (New York, 1935).

[16] *Industrial Chicago*, I, 460.

[17] This building was torn down a few years ago; the site is now used as a parking lot. In its time the Virginia was one of the finest residential hotels in the city, on a par with the Drake. Cf. the illustration in P. T. Gilbert and C. L. Bryson, *Chicago and Its Makers* (Chicago, 1929), p. 529.

231. Chicago in the early nineties: Randolph Street about 1891. *The large buildings here are the Ashland offices, built by Burnham and Root in 1891.* →

232. Great Northern Hotel, Chicago, 1891. *Advances made in Chicago office buildings were taken over to create the type of hotel and apartment house suited to the industrial age.*

The Brewster apartments on Pine Grove Avenue, built during the early nineties, are still in existence. The architect, R. H. Turnock, had done his early work under William Le Baron Jenney. The main staircase has treads of plate glass so that the light can flow through the entire eight stories of the building from the skylight on the roof. As is well known, Le Corbusier came to a similar solution some forty years later in his Clarté apartments in Geneva (1932).

We have been able to do no more here than simply point to a few of the buildings which were included in the field of the Chicago development. It is a field whose importance has been overlooked for too long — so long, in fact, that buildings and documents alike may have disappeared before any real insight into what they represent has been gained. These Chicago apartment houses represent the first steps toward a kind of large-scale housing which is very different from anything we find in Europe. Progress in this direction was largely canceled in the next generation, however. A reaction set in against the big apartment house and the residential hotel, coupled with a fresh concentration of attention on the private, one-family dwelling. Frank Lloyd Wright is the outstanding figure in this later movement.[18]

In 1893 this Chicago architecture impressed a French observer — the novelist Paul Bourget — with "the simple force of need as a principle of beauty. . . . There is so little caprice and fancy in these monuments and these streets that they seem to be the work of some impersonal power, irresistible, unconscious, like a force of nature, in the service of which man has been but a docile instrument. It is this expression of the overpowering immensity of modern commerce which gives to the city something of tragedy, and, to my feeling, a poetry."[19]

The Chicago school has many claims to importance. Its members made the first expressive use of the new technical potentialities in buildings which were permanent and essential parts of the structure of Chicago's daily life. They produced not just a few isolated specimen structures but covered the whole business district with a new architecture. Their work changed the entire face of a great modern city.

TOWARD PURE FORMS

The architects of the Chicago school employed a new type of construction: the iron skeleton. At that time it was called quite simply "Chicago construction."

Innovations of the Chicago school

They invented a new kind of foundation to cope with the problem of the muddy ground of Chicago: the floating foundation. They introduced the horizontally elongated window: the Chicago window.

They created the modern business and administration building.

---

[18] For information concerning its course, cf. Purcell, Feick, and Elmslie, "The Statics and Dynamics of Architecture," *Western Architect*, January 1913, p. 1, and the article on Irving J. Gill's work in California on p. 35 of the issue of April 1913. The issue of August 1913 contains an account by Walter Burley Griffin of some of his own suburban developments (p. 66).

[19] Paul Bourget, *Outre Mer*, vol. I, chap. V, as quoted in Harriet Monroe, *op. cit.*, pp. 136–137.

The importance of the school for the history of architecture lies in this fact: for the first time in the nineteenth century the schism between construction and architecture, between the engineer and the architect, was healed. This schism marked the whole preceding part of the century. With surprising boldness, the Chicago school strove to break through to pure forms, forms which would unite construction and architecture in an identical expression.

Contemporary statement of its aims

These Chicago architects of the eighties were quite conscious of their own boldness. In 1890 John Root — the constructor of the Monadnock Block — said, speaking of modern business buildings, that "to lavish upon them profusion of delicate ornament is worse than useless. . . . Rather should they by their mass and proportion convey in some large elemental sense an idea of the great, stable, conserving forces of modern civilization.

"One result of methods such as I have indicated will be the resolution of our architectural designs into their essential elements. So vital has the underlying structure of these buildings become, that it must dictate absolutely the general departure of external forms; and so imperative are all the commercial and constructive demands, that all architectural detail employed in expressing them must become modified by them. Under these conditions we are compelled to work definitely with definite aims, permeating ourselves with the full spirit of the age, that we may give its architecture true art forms." [1]

The amount of work which came out of the Chicago school in the course of its development was very great. We shall take three buildings, each by a different architect but all showing clearly the inherent urge of the Chicago school toward purity of form.

The Leiter Building, 1889

The first building of pure skeleton type; its aesthetic significance

William Le Baron Jenney not only produced the first example of Chicago construction in his Home Insurance Building of 1884–85, but he also erected the first building in which there was not even one self-supporting wall, the Leiter Building.

[1] From a paper read at the Chicago Art Institute and published in the *Inland Architect*, June 1890. Quoted in Monroe, *op. cit.*, p. 107.

With it purity of constructional methods seemed to find its equivalent in architecture; the Leiter Building attains to an expression in which the lingering memories of historical styles play a negligible part.

The Leiter Building, planned in 1889, fills a whole block at Van Buren and State streets (*fig.* **233**).[2] Jenney dealt with and mastered a front four hundred feet long and eight stories high through the use of great and simple units. The skeleton furnishes the dominating accents of the building, appearing in the huge squares into which the outer wall is divided. These panels are filled by plate-glass windows which "are separated only by fireproofed metal columns." [3]

The spirit behind this employment of the skeleton as an architectonic means has received further development in contemporary architecture. Le Corbusier's Maison de Verre, a Geneva apartment house of 1932, represents a later stage in its evolution (*fig.* **234**).

Le Corbusier, 1932

Jenney's contemporaries seem to have recognized the significance of his work. Even the anonymous author of *Industrial Chicago* (1891) momentarily discards his accustomed sobriety in speaking of it: "It has been constructed with the same science and all the careful inspection that would be used in the construction of a steel railroad bridge of the first order. The severely plain exterior is grand in its proportions. The great corner piers are carried upward to a chaste cornice. Designed for space, light, ventilation, and security, the Leiter Building meets the object sought in every particular." With its building, he goes on to exclaim, "a giant structure . . . healthy to look at, lightsome and airy while substantial, was added to the great houses of a great city . . . a commercial pile in a style undreamed of when Buonarroti erected the greatest temple of Christianity." [4]

Contemporary reaction

Although the Leiter Building seems to be the first of the high buildings to exhibit the trend toward the use of pure forms, it

[2] "The building will be located on the East side of State Street and will extend from Van Buren to Congress Street. It will be eight stories; the three street fronts will be of light gray New England granite, the construction a steel skeleton, the masonry protecting the external columns. It is intended that the whole building should be one great retail store" (*Inland Architect*, vol. XIV, no. 1, August 1889, p. 10).

[3] *Industrial Chicago*, I, 205.

[4] *Industrial Chicago*, I, 204–205.

233. WILLIAM LE BARON JENNEY. Leiter Building, Van Buren Street, Chicago, 1889. *The skeleton becomes a means of architectonic expression.*

is today almost unknown, except to a handful of specialists. Its importance consists not in its height — which happens to be of eight, rather than twelve or twenty stories — but in the identity between what is expressed in its construction and in its architecture. The Leiter Building marks a starting point for this kind of architectural purity and should not be ignored in the history of architecture.

234. LE CORBUSIER. Maison Clarté, Geneva, 1930–32. *The properties of the skeleton used in the service of residential needs.*

The Reliance Building, 1894

John Root died in 1891; Daniel Burnham, his partner, swung over into the classical school and took his cues from New York.[5] But in 1894 one more building in the spirit of his dead partner emerged from Burnham's office, the Reliance Building

Experience of the Chicago school summed up in this glass tower

[5] Peter B. Wight, "Daniel Hudson Burnham and His Associates," *Architectural Record,* vol. XXXVIII, no. 1 (July 1915).

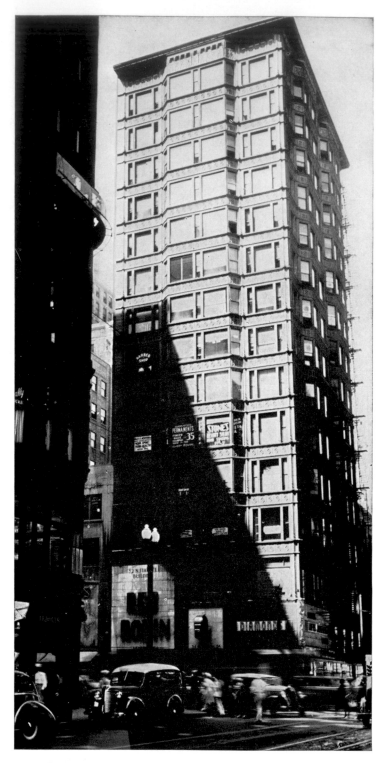

235.   BURNHAM and COMPANY.   Reliance Building, Chicago,
1894.   *In its airiness and purity of proportion, this building serves to
symbolize the spirit of the Chicago school, whose swan song it was.*

236. MIES VAN DER ROHE. Project for a glass tower, 1921. *A modern excursion into the realm of fantasy, something of whose spirit, nevertheless, had been anticipated in the Reliance Building.*

on State Street — the "swan song" of the Chicago school.[6] Speaking in a broader sense, it might perhaps be said to have grown out of the Chicago soil itself, to be a reflection of the high architectural level that has been reached in that city.

The Reliance Building is a glass tower fifteen stories high (*fig.* **235**). The base is formed from some dark and unobtrusive stone, in sharp contrast to the glass and glazed white tile tower which springs up from it. The eaves of the flat roof are only thin slabs, emphasized no more than they must be to serve as protections. There is no overbearing cornice of stone.[7]

Ten years' experience lies behind the understanding treatment of the horizontally proportioned "Chicago windows." In

[6] "The Reliance Building was the 'swan song' to the old traditions, based on independence of design, for which were noted the works of Burnham and Root. It stands today a symbol of our inconsistency and an ample proof that no sooner do we approach a common way of working than the promise of a truly expressive style of American architecture is broken by the capricious introduction of a new fashion" (A. N. Rebori, "The Work of Burnham and Root," *Architectural Record*, vol. XXXVIII, no. 1, July 1915, p. 62.

[7] In this respect it differs markedly from Burnham's Flatiron Building in New York (1902), with its immense cornice and its skeleton cluttered with heavy stonework.

earlier office buildings of the Chicago school (the now-destroyed Tacoma Building by Root and Burnham, for example) the bow windows tend somewhat to be independent and isolated parts of the design. In the Reliance Building they project no more than they are required to in order to pick up light. They are wholly incorporated into the glass body of the building.

This glass tower is still standing, and, although its glazed white tiles have become encrusted with dirt, its airiness and pure proportions make it a symbol of the spirit of the Chicago school. It is curious that this building too has been left unnoticed in the history of architecture. It has its place there as a witness to the best of the spirit of the nineteenth century.

Mies van der Rohe, 1921

Mies van der Rohe's scheme for a skyscraper of glass and iron is the dream of a European architect in the year 1921 (*fig.* **236**). The points of departure for dream projects of this sort should perhaps be sought in works like the Reliance Building of some three decades earlier. But it may be that this Chicago building is something more than an incentive for fantasy: an architectonic anticipation of the future.

Sullivan: The Carson, Pirie, Scott Store, 1899–1906

In 1899 Louis Sullivan began to remodel the Schlesinger & Mayer store at State and Madison streets, on the famous "World's Busiest Corner." The work was done in three sections, in 1899, 1903–04, and 1906.[8] In the summer of 1904 the establishment was taken over by the Carson, Pirie, Scott firm. The third unit was built for it by Daniel Burnham & Company, but Louis Sullivan's scheme for the first two sections was retained, with only a few unimportant changes (*fig.* **237**).

Unsurpassed strength and precision

In spite of its complexity Sullivan's building remains unsurpassed in its expressive strength. The interior is still of the warehouse type, with continuous, unbroken floor areas. The

[8] The first unit was nine stories high and three bays (some 60 feet) in width; the second was twelve stories high and 150 feet wide, but otherwise identical in design with the first. The final unit was 105 feet wide. Hugh Morrison (one of the first to recognize the architectural importance of this store) gives a detailed account of its building in his careful study, *Louis Sullivan, Prophet of Modern Architecture* (New York, 1935), pp. 197 ff.

386

237. LOUIS SUL–
LIVAN. Carson, Pi–
rie, Scott and Com-
pany, department
store, Chicago, 1899–
1904. *Built in three
units on State and
Madison streets, the
"World's Busiest Cor-
ner." The round tower
at the corner was in-
cluded at the insistence
of the owners.*

front is designed to fulfill its indispensable function, the ad-
mission of light. Its basic elements are the horizontally elongated "Chicago windows," admirably homogeneous and
treated to coincide with the framework of the skeleton. The
whole front is executed with a strength and precision that is
matched by no other building of the period. The slightest differences in proportion can be felt at once against a background
of this definiteness. The windows, with their thin metal frames,
are sharply cut into the façade (*fig.* **238**). The windows in the
lower stories are connected by a narrow line of ornament
pressed into the terra cotta. Too thin to be visible in the
photograph, this line nevertheless helps to accentuate the
horizontal organization of the front.[9]

Even when architects of Sullivan's generation pressed on
toward new solutions they sometimes found themselves held
back by nineteenth-century traditions. They suffered from the

*Intrusion of
the pavilion*

[9] George Elmslie, whom we have already mentioned as one of Sullivan's staunchest
collaborators, was the designer of most of the ornamentation on his buildings. It was
not influenced by the contemporary *art nouveau*.

sort of split personality which we spoke of earlier. The split personality of the nineteenth-century architect makes itself felt in Sullivan's Carson, Pirie, Scott building. The round tower at the corner with its narrow vertical ribs and glass panes suddenly introduces a motif quite out of character with the rest of the building. The owners had asked for this curvilinear addition (which we noted as a stylistic remnant in Eiffel and Boileau's Bon Marché of 1876) as a reminiscence of the pavilion attached to their old store. But this alone would not have affected the work of as strong-minded a man as Sullivan.

Contrast with
other Sullivan
buildings

Around 1900, on its completion, this store appeared old-fashioned to contemporaries. By this time they had lost their hearts and heads to the "commercial classicism" of the New York architects and its distortion of business buildings into mercantile palaces. For three decades the New York practitioners of the academic architecture ruled the whole country. The Carson, Pirie, Scott store, one of the late productions of the Chicago school, seems to be molded more by the anonymous spirit which ruled the work of that school than by Louis Sullivan's personal tendencies. In Sullivan's best-known buildings — from the Wainwright in St. Louis (1890–91) to the Prudential in Buffalo (1894–95) and the Bayard Building in New York (1897–98) — he continually increased the stress upon the vertical elements in the design, emphasizing the piers at the corners. He uses narrow pillars and gives the whole building a strictly upward orientation, a movement as marked as that which we encounter in the Gothic cathedrals.

The skeleton a
neutral network

But the skeleton — whether iron or steel or reinforced concrete — is essentially a neutral spatial network. Its "cage construction" bounds a certain volume of space with complete impartiality, and no one intrinsic direction. In his typical buildings Sullivan picks out and emphasizes the vertical lines of force in this network. In the Carson, Pirie, Scott store, however, it is the neutral and impartial equilibrium inherent in the skeleton construction which Sullivan chooses to project upon the façade of the building.

The influence of the Chicago school was cut short by the influx of eclecticism. Louis Sullivan — the great architect of the school — did leave his mark upon the next generation of architects in the Middle West. (Frank Lloyd Wright was to emerge as the outstanding figure in this generation.) And during the first decade of our century, the traditions of the Chicago school survived in works by some of its younger members: George Elmslie, Hugh Garden, George Maher, Griffin, Thomas Tallmadge, and a few others. Some of their buildings might have served as a revelation to the rising generation in Europe. They failed entirely, however, to influence the corresponding groups in their own country. A literary architectural education cut the younger men off from the principles of the Chicago school and destroyed their individuality as well. Left in isolation, the surviving members of the Chicago school grew discouraged, and many of them lost the force which they had shown in a more favorable period.

In the 1922 competition for the Chicago Tribune Building, the plans of a competent American architect — Raymond Hood — won the first prize. By this time, however, the confidence and belief in its own forces which had sustained the Chicago school had completely disappeared. The school might just as well have never existed; its principles were crowded out by the vogue of "Woolworth Gothic." [10]

The Chicago Tribune Tower; nullification of the Chicago tradition

The hundred thousand dollar international competition for the Tribune Building drew entries from everywhere. The projects submitted give an invaluable cross section of the architecture of this period.[11] One of the foreign entrants was Walter Gropius. Both the jury and the public must have considered his scheme quite unstylish and old-fashioned. There is no doubt, however, that it was much closer in spirit to the Chicago school

Foreign projects closer to the Chicago school

---

[10] Stemming from the Woolworth Building in New York, 1911–13.

[11] All these projects, with the exception of K. Lonberg-Holm's entry, were published in *International Competition for a New Administration Building for the Chicago Tribune* (Chicago, 1923), issued by the Tribune Company. The American entries fall tragically short of the level reached in Chicago during the eighties and nineties. Fashionable architects submitted typical specimens of the now dominant "Woolworth Gothic," and all the entries show a secondhand fancifulness instead of a sense for scale and proportion. The competition chiefly inspired an unhappy excursion into romanticism. An equally distressing helplessness appears in the European projects, with the exception of a few entries from the northern countries: Bruno Taut (project # 231), Max Taut (# 229), Bijvoet and Dujker, K. Lonberg-Holm, Walter Gropius, and Adolph Meyer (# 197). (The numbers refer to the plans published in *The International Competition.*) These men produced schemes which represented endeavors to escape from familiar routines.

than the Gothic tower which was executed. When we compare Gropius' 1922 project and Sullivan's Carson, Pirie, Scott store they seem like two stages in the development of the same set of ideas. In both of them the network of the skeleton is the basis of and inextricable from the architectonic expression. There are the same hovering and sharply cut surfaces. Gropius even

238. LOUIS SULLIVAN. Carson, Pirie, Scott and Company Department Store, Chicago, 1899–1904. *Detail. Outstanding for strength and purity of expression even in the work of Louis Sullivan. The neutral and impartial equilibrium inherent in cage construction is emphasized, rather than its vertical elements.*

employs the "Chicago window," with a fixed glass panel in the middle and narrow ventilating windows at the sides (*fig.* **239**). The whole plan seems an outgrowth of the Chicago school, but actually Chicago windows and the Chicago skyscraper were unknown in Europe. This coincidence, the way in which these two men arrived independently at similar solutions, shows that the Chicago school really was "permeated by the spirit of the age," in the phrase of one of its best representatives. It could therefore create constituent facts for architec-

239. WALTER GROPIUS Project for the competition on the Tribune Tower, Chicago, 1923. *Constituent facts developed by the Chicago school reappear independently in this European project.*

ture, facts that reappeared in later periods just as Borromini's undulating wall reappeared in English residential quarters.[12]

The Influence of the Chicago World's Fair, 1893

At the very moment when the Chicago school gained a mastery of the new means which it had created, its further development and influence were abruptly choked off. The event which di-

The World's Fair and the Chicago school

---

[12] Hood, whose Gothic Tribune Tower was completed in 1925, was himself on the verge of a change which achieved its full expression about 1930. In that year he built the McGraw-Hill building in New York, whose architecture recognizes in part the new European developments. He was to arrive at far more impressive solutions later on in the buildings at Rockefeller Center.

rectly effected this change was the Chicago World's Fair of 1893 (the World's Columbian Exposition), but influences working in this direction had set in long before in another section of the country.

American architecture came under many different influences during the nineteenth century, but none was so strong or came at such a critical moment as the rise to power of the mercantile classicism developed in the East.

Tremendous public success

The 1893 World's Fair elicited a variety of responses. The public and most of the architects were rapturous in their delight. While I was in Chicago, one architect who had worked on it quoted from memory the rather ironical comment of William James: "Everyone says one ought to sell all one has and mortgage one's soul to go there; it is esteemed such a revelation of beauty. People cast away all sin and baseness, burst into tears, and grow religious, etc., under the influence."

Some European observers were more sceptical. The extremely well-informed Belgian constructor Vierendeel found both its staff architecture and the construction it enveloped timid and secondhand — as we saw toward the end of our discussion of the great nineteenth-century exhibitions.

Sullivan's prophecy

The lonely American voices raised against the unexampled seduction of the public taste underlying the Fair's pseudo-splendor went unheard. Louis Sullivan said bitterly that "the damage wrought to this country by the Chicago World's Fair will last half a century." At the time this may have seemed only the exaggerated expression of an outraged artist; it turned out to be a precise prophecy of what was actually to follow.

Influence of the Beaux-Arts

Public, artists, and literary people believed themselves to be witnessing a splendid rebirth of the great traditions of past ages. The immense appeal of this re-created past in "the White City" can only be laid to a quite unnecessary national inferiority complex. It was the same feeling — reinforced by the prestige of the Paris exhibition of 1889 — which gave the French academicians a dominating role at this Chicago fair. The contemporary biographer of John Root expresses it quite clearly: "At that time few hoped to rival Paris; the

392

artistic capacity and experience of the French made us distrustful of ourselves. We should have a great American fair, but in points of grouping and design we must expect inferiority to French taste." [13] And it was to France that the builders of the Fair turned in their search for beauty. Its beauties were taken out of the preserve jars of the Académie des Beaux-Arts — where they had been laid up during what was certainly its worst period. *Grand prix de Rome* façades were copied, and men like Burnham (who had assisted in raising the Chicago school to a level much higher than the Academy's) acted like docile children in the presence of the French masters. All this is another instance of the split between thought and feeling in the nineteenth century. Only Louis Sullivan had sufficient inner strength to hold fast in the midst of a general surrender. But his Transportation Building for the Chicago fair marked the beginning of his unpopularity as an architect.

Mercantile classicism had been developing and gaining strength in New York since the eighties, but it won its country-wide ascendancy at the World's Columbian Exhibition of 1893.[14]

Eastern mercantile classicism

The spirit behind it had now come to possess authority for American architecture as a whole.[15] The Fair should, indeed, have stood in New York; it so thoroughly represented the influence of that city. But as soon as a Columbian exposition was proposed, the people of Chicago leaped at the idea. "The enthusiasm of the city was set on its mettle; an aggressive campaign was organized, and five million dollars pledged by private subscription before other cities had begun to act." [16]

The hypnotic spell which mercantile classicism exerted appears from some lines in Frank Lloyd Wright's *Autobiography*. Shortly after the close of the Fair (and after the completion of Wright's Winslow house), Daniel Burnham called on him.

F. L. Wright and the Beaux-Arts

---

[13] Harriet Monroe, *op. cit.*, p. 218.

[14] Immense and thoroughly businesslike New York building firms (McKim, Mead, and White) carried out the greater part of the Fair.

[15] Professor Hamlin observes that "by 1880 there were constantly a dozen or fifteen Americans in the Ecole of Paris. In all the schools, Paris-trained men were in demand as instructors. . . . The Ecole had furnished the model upon which all our American schools were shaping the teaching of design" ("The Influence of the Ecole des Beaux Arts on Our Architectural Education," *Architectural Record*, April 1908, p. 242).

[16] Monroe, *op. cit.*, p. 216.

"To be brief, he would take care of my wife and children if I would go to Paris, four years of the Beaux Arts. Then Rome — two years. Expenses all paid. A job with him when I came back. . . .

"'Another year and it will be too late, Frank,' said Uncle Dan. . . .

"'Yes, too late, Uncle Dan. It's too late now, I'm afraid. I am spoiled already.

"'I've been too close to Mr. Sullivan. He has helped spoil the Beaux Arts for me, or spoiled me for the Beaux Arts, I guess I mean.'

"'. . . The Fair is going to have a great influence in our country. The American people have seen the "Classics" on a grand scale for the first time. . . . I can see all America constructed along the lines of the Fair, in noble "dignified" classic style. The great men of the day all feel that way about it — all of them.'"[17]

FRANK LLOYD WRIGHT

Wright and the American Development

Preëminence as
an architect

Of all present-day architects whose span of work reaches back into the nineteenth century, Frank Lloyd Wright is without doubt the most farsighted, a genius of inexplicably rich and continuing vitality. He ranges the wide expanse of historical interrelations, drawing particularly upon the architecture of the Far East — not, however, in the manner of the last century, as a substitute for creative impulse, but, like Matisse with Negro or Persian art, from an inner sympathetic relationship. At the same time he springs out of the American soil and the American tradition more directly perhaps than any other of the great American architects. True insight into his work demands a somewhat subtle approach, for Wright's dominating personality, present in every touch of what he does, is not at all simple. He bears in himself the marks of the late

[17] F. L. Wright, *An Autobiography* (New York, 1932), pp. 123–124.

394

nineteenth century; yet isolated and singlehanded, without aid from his contemporaries among painters and sculptors, he has introduced the beginnings of a new conception.

American background

When he began work in 1887, he was — in Chicago — at the very center, the fountainhead, of architectural development. He was apprentice in the atelier of two of the best men, Louis Sullivan, "lieber Meister," he calls him, and Dankmar Adler, "the grand old chief," at the very time when they were on the ascendant creatively, working on the Auditorium Building. He had as the principal influence of his youth the culmination of the Chicago renascence. And yet when he began to work independently, Wright did not continue directly in the Chicago school; he did not carry over the use of the new materials — the iron skeleton and the great glass surfaces of the office buildings — into his own sphere: housing. Instead he was rather conservative; in many respects he followed Richardson more than Sullivan. It was not until as late as the thirties, when European architects were already utilizing the inherent possibilities of ferroconcrete to the fullest, that Wright, as he says himself, used it for the first time to any great extent for one of his houses.[1] This was due not to any lack of technical ability but to his own will and character.

In Europe Wright was very shortly accepted and understood by the generation which was responsible for the modern movement. In 1908 he was visited by Kuno Francke, then a German exchange professor lecturing at Harvard University on aesthetics. The result of this visit was the publication in Germany in 1910 of a monumental work on Wright's architecture.[2] This was supplemented in 1911 by a smaller work on the same subject, which enjoyed a very wide circulation.[3] These two books marked the beginning of Wright's foreign influence; the book published in 1910 has not since been approached in comprehensiveness.

What is the explanation of the fact that Wright is the only architect so far ahead of his own generation, a man who is even

---

[1] The Kaufman house, "Falling Water," Bear Run, Pennsylvania, 1937.

[2] *Frank Lloyd Wright, ausgeführte Bauten und Entwürfe* (Berlin, 1910), with a preface in German by Wright.

[3] *Frank Lloyd Wright, ausgeführte Bauten* (Berlin, 1911); foreword by C. R. Ashbee.

240. FRANK LLOYD WRIGHT. Charnley house, Astor Street, Chicago, 1892. *The Charnley house is from Wright's earliest period, designed while he was still an employee of Adler and Sullivan. (The extension of the right wing is of a later date.) In it he uses the flat surfaces of the American tradition, cutting in the windows sharply as if with an axe.*

today creating works that have a strong impact? The answer is rather simple: he had less debris to clear away than the Europeans. He had been born in the Middle West, within the shadow of the place possessing the greatest architectural vitality of the period: Chicago.

Devotion to housing

From the outset Wright devoted himself to the problem which was to be his life interest — the house as a shelter. He had at his disposal the anonymous American tradition, the example of Sullivan, and the conscious artistry which Richardson had cultivated in home building. The secret of Wright's work is that he saw in the tradition of the American house those elements which could be used as a basis for the future. He takes these basic elements and adds new ones, enlarging — with all the force of genius — the structure of the house delivered to him.

The objection may be advanced that the English had been working on the problem of the dwelling house since 1860. But the English at this time had no architects of the stature of Sullivan or Richardson. Philip Webb and Norman Shaw are not to be compared with the two Americans. The crux of the difference between the English and American architects lies in their point of departure: the Englishmen began with a reform, through handicraft, of furniture, rugs, wallpaper, and other small household objects which had been debased by industrial production. The Americans, on the other hand, started from the house as a whole, and were not seduced by an overemphasis upon handicraft.

It would be not without interest to make a comparative study of Frank Lloyd Wright and his Scotch contemporary, Charles Rennie Mackintosh,[4] who was born in the same year — to remark their differences and the traits they possess in common; to consider the way in which they treat wall surfaces, how they use and expose wooden posts and beams, and how they conceive their furniture. They both began by working in terms of their own generation, Mackintosh in Glasgow, Wright on this side of the Atlantic. Some of Wright's early peculiarities, especially in his furnishings, persist in his work up to the present time.

Wright and the English development

The Charnley house on Astor Street, Chicago (*fig.* **240**), with its projecting wings (executed in 1892 while Wright was still in the employ of Adler and Sullivan, and usually attributed to that firm) is not very different from the Mary Ward Settlement of 1896 in the Bloomsbury district of London.[5] In the final analysis the façades of European buildings cannot avoid restlessness and are to a certain extent split into details. Their architects never dare to use rigorously, as Wright did in the Charnley house, the flat surfaces of the American tradition, cutting in the windows sharply and clearly as if with an axe

---

[4] The Scottish architect, Charles Rennie Mackintosh (1869–1928), noted for his art school in Glasgow and especially for his country houses (e.g., the house of Dr. Blackie, Helensborough, 1902). Mackintosh had a direct influence on the *art decoratif* movement in Vienna, the Wiener Werkstätte. The founder of this institution took his artists to Scotland to show them how household furnishings and architecture should be designed. The influence was a complete one for the moment, but restricted to matters of taste. No new architectural vision came out of it. Nikolaus Pevsner, in his *Pioneers of the Modern Movement* (London and New York, 1937), gives an excellent survey of Mackintosh's work, with a bibliography (pp. 221 222). Pevsner may be consulted also on other questions concerning the British development. A sharply unfavorable attitude toward Mackintosh is taken by his close compatriot, P. M. Shand, in "Glasgow Interlude," *Architectural Review*, LXXVII (January 1935), 23.

[5] Cf. Pevsner, *op. cit.*, p. 157.

and molding the house with few but persistent accents.[6]   Yet as a whole Wright's earliest houses, even the first built on his own account, are not fundamentally different from the best English examples.   The change, however, was not to be long in coming.   England produced nothing more.   Europe was adrift, seeking solutions.   Frank Lloyd Wright went ahead.

The Cruciform and the Elongated Plan

Ground plan and interior space

Before I had seen any of Wright's houses, I stopped once for a rest in a hunting lodge in the Vermont hills.   It had an immense stone chimney which stood massively in its center, rising the entire height from the ground up through the roof.   The interior space was undivided, except for a partition which cut off the kitchen and the sleeping room.   There was no ceiling, but simply open rafters from which hung fox and bear skins. At that moment I began to understand the way Wright conceives his interior spaces.   He works fundamentally and as far as possible with the house as one room.   Its inner space is differentiated to meet special needs.   As he points out, he "declared the whole . . . floor as one room, cutting off the kitchen as a laboratory, putting servants' sleeping and living quarters next to it, semi-detached, on the ground floor, screening various portions in the big room, for certain domestic purposes — like dining or reading, or receiving a formal caller." [7]

Cruciform plan

In organizing his plans Wright goes back to the seventeenth century in the use of the large chimney in the center of the house as starting point for the whole layout.   He spreads out the different rooms from this massive kernel.   What first impressed European architects was his "windmill" plan, so called because of the way the rooms were extended outward from the center like the vanes of a windmill (*fig.* **243**).   This "windmill" plan is really cruciform, an interpenetration of two parts of the house, which cut each other transversely to

[6] Speaking of the Charnley house, Hugh Morrison, in his *Louis Sullivan* (New York, 1935), says that it was "broader in conception than any of Sullivan's other residences, with more feeling for the organization of plane surfaces, skillfully punctuated by window voids" (pp. 132–133).

[7] *Modern Architecture* (Princeton, 1931), Princeton Monographs in Art and Archaeology, p. 72.

form a cross. Often they are of different heights; then the effect is of one crossbar superimposed upon and penetrating the other.

This early American practice of using a central chimney as the core of the house, as the point about which the whole is organized, was kept alive also through the nineteenth century (*fig.* **241**). Again we may cite as evidence one of those unknown writers who reflect the common taste. In one of the small popular books on suburban and country houses in the early seventies, there is proposed a country house built completely around a fourfold, four-sided chimney, with rooms leading off in wings from each of the four sides. The author's reason for this cruciform arrangement is very close to Wright's own intention, both in the stress placed upon light — Wright emphasizes the fact that rooms in his layout can get light from three sides — and in the urge to treat the several rooms as a unit: "The design of this house was made for the purpose of giving each room a sunny southern exposure, and out of ten rooms nine have at least one lookout to the southeast. The principal floor is so managed that the spacious hall with winding staircase presents an attractive feature on entering. The chimney is in the center of the house and sliding doors connect each of the principal rooms so that when occasion requires, hall, parlor, library, and dining room may be thrown together, the octagon form of these rooms adding much to their beauty." [8] As always in this period, the exterior of the house has nothing of the precision of the plan (*fig.* **242**). Nevertheless, there are suggestions of the interpenetration of two volumes, for which in his Chicago period Wright was to find artistic solutions.

Most of Wright's houses, especially the smaller ones, are based on the cruciform plan issuing out of and produced by this interpenetration of two volumes of different heights. Such are the Hickox house, Kankakee, Illinois, 1900; the Ward house, Willett Park, Illinois, 1901; the Willitts house, Highland Park, Illinois, 1901; the small country house of Charles Ross at Lake Delavan, Wisconsin, 1902; the Robert Evans house in Long-

[8] George E. Woodward, *Suburban and Country Houses* (New York, copr. 1873), pp. 15–16.

241. G. E. WOODWARD. Plan of a cruciform country house, 1873. *From Woodward, "Suburban and Country Houses" (New York, c. 1873). Built around a fourfold, four-sided chimney with diagonally sliding doors to convert the house, to a certain extent, into a single room.*

242. G. E. WOODWARD. Cruciform country house, 1873. *As always in this period, the exterior has nothing of the precision of the plan. One of Wright's great accomplishments was to find an equivalent for the ground plan in spatial and exterior treatment.*

wood, Illinois, 1904; the Isabel Roberts house, 1907; the Horner house, Birchwood, 1908.

Of these, the Isabel Roberts house in River Forest, Illinois (*figs.* **243, 244**), one of the most charming of Wright's smaller houses, shows an interesting employment of the interpenetration of two volumes of different heights, in which Wright uses the higher volume to mold, not the hallway, but the space of the living room from the ground up through the whole height to the inner planes of the roof (*fig.* **245**). It represents an effort to satisfy the feeling of a need for the full height as living space. This feeling finds expression not only in the houses of American settlers of the seventeenth century but in many early civilizations, and it has reappeared in our own period. Wright was one of the first to recognize this feeling, to formulate it and give it expression. In the Isabel Roberts house the living room dominates, rising up to the gently sloping roof,

243. FRANK LLOYD WRIGHT. Isabel Roberts house, River Forest, Illinois, 1907. *Plan. Built late in the Chicago period, when Wright had found freedom of expression.*

244. FRANK LLOYD WRIGHT. Isabel Roberts house, River Forest, Illinois, 1907. *The slab roof and the low horizontal extension of the wings are interesting. This exterior shows Wright's clarification and purification of standard material.*

245. FRANK LLOYD WRIGHT. Isabel Roberts house, River Forest, Illinois, 1907. *Two-story living room. Wright uses the higher volume to mold the space of the living room from the ground up through the entire height to the inner planes of the roof.*

and divided in height by a gallery, so that there are recessed spaces both above and below. This gives an unaccustomed and new plasticity to the whole room, which is enhanced by the use of various planes in different materials — the brick face of the chimney, the several wall surfaces, and the slope of the roof.

Mies van de Rohe, the German architect — one of the few whose early work reflects Wright's influence without either being absorbed by it or reducing it to a merely decorative use — developed the "windmill" plan in several of his schemes.[9]

Wright himself never abandoned the idea of the house spread out from a central core. When in 1939 he built a low-cost four-family housing unit (Suntop Houses, Ardmore, Pa.; *figs.* **246, 247**),[10] he separated the different apartments by brick walls

[9] Project for a brick house in 1922.
[10] See *Architectural Forum*, August 1939.

402

crossing at right angles. At the central core he put not a chimney but all the utilities — plumbing, heating, electricity, and ventilation — so that they were concentrated in the darkest spot in the building.

When it is possible, Wright likes to spread his structures out freely over the ground. In the introduction to the study of his work published in Berlin in 1910, he points out that the first floor was often built principally as a cellar. The main living quarters lie in the upper story on one floor, as in the Coonley house (1911), where only the entrance hall and the game room are on the ground floor; in Taliesin, his own house, they are set into and connected with the ground. This led him to the flexible and informal ground plan so deeply embedded in the American architectural development from its beginning. As a consequence of this development Wright now let the different rooms flow out horizontally, just as, in houses like the Isabel Roberts house, he had molded them vertically.

Flexible and informal ground plan

By 1910 Wright had achieved a flexibility of open planning unapproached hitherto. In other countries at that time the flexible ground plan and the flexibly molded interior and exterior were almost unknown. Wright's realization of a flexible treatment of the inner space of a building is probably his greatest service to architecture. It brought life, movement, freedom into the whole rigid and benumbed body of modern architecture.

Plane Surfaces and Structure

The Japanese house impressed Frank Lloyd Wright as "a supreme study in elimination — not only of dirt, but the elimination, too, of the *insignificant*." For the American house he accomplished just such an elimination, a rejection of the confused and the trivial. But he did more than this. He took up those elements lying about everywhere unobserved — elements arising from purely utilitarian solutions — and discovered in this raw material its hidden expressiveness, just as the following generation was to discover the hidden expressiveness in engineering and construction. Wright brought forward these elements and changed them, opened our eyes to their

Use of native elements

403

PENTHOUSE   MEZZANINE

SUN TERRACE

Upper Part L.R.

D.R.

KIT.

BOU-DOIR

Upper Part Bath

B.R.

B

BOUDOIR   MAIN B.R.

BALC

HEAT R.   STORE RM

Scale in feet
0   5   10   15

CARPORT

Line of Mezzan above

UNEX

LIVING RM

FOUNDATION   GROUND FL

246. FRANK LLOYD WRIGHT. Suntop Houses, Ardmore, Pennsylvania, 1939. *Plan. In this low-cost, four-family housing unit, Wright separates the different apartments by brick walls crossing at right angles. At the central core he has put all the utilities — plumbing, heating, electricity, and ventilation, so that they are concentrated in the darkest spot in the building.*

247. FRANK LLOYD WRIGHT. Suntop Houses, Ardmore, Pennsylvania, 1939.

404

secret potentialities and their inherent beauty, revealing their symbolic strength as a poet does in showing forth what inner content of feeling the trees and mountains, the rivers and lakes, of his native land hold for him and for us.[11]

In the treatment of the house as a spatial unit he seized upon these elements wherever he could find them. He also sought to shape the whole house in terms of its own period. The earliest American houses — those of the settlers along the fron-

The porch

FRONT ELEVATION

248.   Central Park Casino, New York City, 1871.

tier — had to afford protection against attack, and consequently were meagerly supplied with openings on the first floor, being without rows of windows and open galleries like those that have given the peasant houses of Switzerland and southern Germany — at any rate since the early seventeenth century — so distinctive an exterior. Much later, with the

---

[11] Joseph Hudnut, in the foreword to the catalogue of Wright's first exhibition in New England (Institute of Modern Art, Boston, January–February 1940), emphasizes the fact that to understand Wright "we must think of him . . . as a poet."

appearance of the porch on the houses of southern rice and cotton planters, there was a corresponding opening up of the American house in the southern part of the country. In nine-teenth-century America the porch was used much more exten-sively as the recreation area of the home than the veranda of the European peasant house, even becoming a decisive ele-ment in the appearance of suburban and country houses. Sometimes it stretched out in long, unbroken horizontal lines,

249. R. E. SCHMIDT, GARDEN & MARTIN. Warehouse of ferroconcrete for Montgomery, Ward & Co., Chicago, 1908. *Immense warehouse built in the same year as the Robie house. With unbroken horizontal lines.*

covered with a slightly sloping roof. The appearance of the Central Park Casino, New York, 1871 (*fig.* **248**) — one of many anonymous examples — is due to an extension of this peculiarly American employment of the porch. Apparently Americans like a strong and unbroken horizontal line equally in their houses and in the Pullman car.

Wright adopts the porch for his houses — not, however, en-circling his buildings with it, but pushing it forward, in keep-

406

ing with his cruciform or elongated plans, as an extension of the wings. Very often it thrusts out into space as a pure canti-lever hovering above the earth. Such a treatment had never been attempted before. True, it is the old element of the porch, but it is not simply something attached to the house; rather it is an essential part of the structure, molded as an inseparable part of it. For several reasons, which he has explained over and over in his writings, Wright uses overhanging eaves. He

250. FRANK LLOYD WRIGHT. Robie house, Woodlawn Avenue, Chicago, 1908. *In this house, which has had far-reaching influence, Wright has used plane surfaces at different depths, advancing and receding. The Robie house, a town villa, is in close relation to the aims of the Chicago school.*

treats them, too, as horizontal planes — "broad protecting roof shelters," as he calls them — just as Burnham, before he turned classicist, roofed his Reliance Building with a thin slab (*fig.* **235**).

To these hovering horizontal elements Wright has added the plane of vertical surfaces. When he built the Charnley house in 1892 (*fig.* **240**), he used the clean-cut level surfaces of the

Treatment of the walls

American tradition. But soon he became more daring, especially in his elongated schemes, such as the D. D. Martin house in Buffalo (1904), and in the house which has had perhaps the most far-reaching influence of all his works, the Robie house, a town villa on Woodlawn Avenue, Chicago (*fig.* **250**). In the nineteenth century the exterior of the American house was not up to the level of the floor plan in quality and artistic expression. Wright brought about a change. He took the plane surfaces presented to him and organized them variously, multiplying them, intersecting them or placing them in different depths one behind another, incorporating the plane of the garden wall with the different advancing and receding planes of the house itself so that often its solid volume is not at all apparent. This handling is not without relation to what was being explored in space conceptions in France during the very years when Wright was building the Robie house. To speak of his houses of the late Chicago period as being in the "prairie style," as having been inspired by the long lines of the prairie, is a pat explanation, but it does not go to the root of the matter. The forms of the Robie house, the long horizontal bands, the series of windows, the garden walls, are sharply cut as if by a machine. These houses are to be explained as a pure artistic expression which is deeply connected with the anonymous aims of their period.

Chicagoans who did not like the Robie house, who were offended by the novelty of its appearance and its long stretched-out horizontal lines, sought to deride it by comparing it to a steamship, just as later Le Corbusier's critics were to refer similarly to his buildings. Without knowing it, they were implying that the house was built in the spirit of the age out of which it came, that, like the steamship, it had been born naturally out of its period. What is decisive in it is not a superficial and misunderstood similarity to a steamship but its inner relationship with the aims of its time. The warehouse of Montgomery, Ward and Company (*fig.* **249**), with its unbroken front of eight hundred feet and the undisguised expression of its structural body,[12] was built in the same year (1908) as the Robie house.

---

[12] Cf. the section on Ferroconcrete. The warehouse was built by Richard E. Schmidt, Garden, and Martin.

From the beginning Wright treated the inner as well as the Inner space outer wall as a plane surface. It never occurred to him to do what European architects did about 1896 — replace rococo decoration with the serpentine lines of the *art nouveau*. In his interiors, too, there is a constant endeavor to find interrelations between the various separate elements — walls, ceilings, windows, and door openings. Different ceiling heights are sometimes introduced into the same room, a treatment which parallels Wright's use of horizontal planes at different heights, such as cantilevered porches, overhanging eaves, and levels varying according to the grades of the site.

Correlative with the use of abstract plane surfaces is the use of Use of different structures various materials and contrasting structures. The broad brick wall of a chimney and light-colored walls with wooden partitions are often juxtaposed. Very early Wright introduced the rough structure of a rusticated wall into the house, bringing it unbroken from the outside, as in primitive times. In this feeling for different materials and the search to find a new quality of lighting, Wright has developed an even greater refinement as he has grown older. The buildings of the Johnson Wax Company at Racine, Wisconsin (1937–39), are lighted by means of Pyrex glass tubes (*fig.* **255**). In the winter home of the Taliesin fellowship in the Arizona desert (1939) many contrasting materials are used — desert stone, walls of rubble concrete, wooden trusses, and inclined canvas planes forming in one surface windows and ceilings, creating, as in the Johnson Wax Company buildings, a specific quality in accordance with the existing circumstances.

To use plane surfaces, on the one hand, and to give them force and expression by the frank use of undisguised materials, on the other, is to employ, as we shall soon see, one of the means of painting, which at this time in France was opening the way for our new spatial conceptions.

Wright had around him no painters and sculptors who were Aesthetic directions inspired by the same spirit. He is one of those rare exceptions, the architect who is in advance of the contemporary painter in his optical vision. In Europe, where the new spatial conceptions flowered about 1910, the case was just the opposite; there

251. FRANK LLOYD WRIGHT. Larkin Administration Building, Buffalo, 1904. *Details of capitals of pillars. These straight-edged, sharp-cornered forms appear at the top of great piers, occupying the place usually taken by capitals. Though they are decorative, nevertheless, like all Wright's work, they have another impact than the purely ornamental.*

252. FRANK LLOYD WRIGHT. Tennis Club, River Forest, Illinois, 1906. *Bench of concrete slabs. Wright's way of working with slabs and interpenetration of volumes may be observed even in small details, such as this bench, in which concrete slabs are used to elongate one level, pushing through the wall and hovering above the ground.*

the painter showed the way. But Wright had to do his work alone, design his own stained-glass windows, architectural details, and pictorial ornamentation. He did the capitals of the Larkin Building (*fig.* **251**) as "straight-edged and sharp-cornered groups of ornaments at the top of the great piers and directly below the skylights . . . strange masses of square-edge patterning." [13] The fresco of the Midway Gardens, a restaurant in Chicago, now lost with the tearing down of the building, he designed out of interpenetrating circles of different sizes and different colors. In its pictorial intention this fresco stands midway between the designs of the English group around Mackintosh and the new spatial treatments which Wassily Kandinsky was undertaking in Munich at about the same time.

In his houses Wright takes the traditional flat surfaces and dissects them in strips horizontally organized and in a juxta-posed play with solid volumes, his vertical chimneys pene-trating the roof in opposition to the horizontal planes of the cantilevered porches and overhanging eaves, thus giving the exterior of the American house an expression synonymous with its plan. He dissects the wall and puts it together again with an unprecedented — after all, we are in the first decade of the twentieth century — keenness of imagination. He is impelled unconsciously by the same forces that worked in Europe about ten years later; there, however, the concern was to explore new penetrations of inner and outer space rather than, as with Wright, to treat the house as an enclosed spatial unit.

Wright often uses the same elements as the Dutch architects of the "Stijl" group, Mondrian and Doesburg, or the Russian constructivists like Malewitsch — for example, the abstract quadrangle, which is still the hallmark of Wright's work. Male-witsch, however, used it as an absolute form, as a protest against academic *trompe l'œil*. The Dutch organized geometri-cal forms not for ornamentation but for the expression of pure and undisguised interrelations between surfaces and colors. Behind the European research lies, to a certain extent, another will and another spatial conception.

---

[13] Russell Sturgis, "The Larkin Building, Buffalo, N. Y.," *Architectural Record*, XXII (1908), 320.

The Urge toward the Organic

Throughout history there persist two distinct trends — the one toward the rational and the geometrical, the other toward the irrational and the organic: two different ways of dealing with or of mastering the environment. These contrasting approaches to the problem have been evident in all cultures, both early and late. Since the beginning of civilization there have been cities planned according to regular schemes and cities which have grown up organically like trees. The ancient Greeks put their mathematically proportioned temples on the top of rocky acropolises, outlined against their southern skies; the villages of the Greek islands, whitewashed on the crests of hills, are easily distinguishable far out at sea because of their clearly marked and periodically rewhitened walls.

The difference between organic and geometrical perceptions is present even today in contemporary painting and contemporary architecture. They are constantly recurrent ways of approach; one cannot be considered superior to the other. The artist has the right of choice, of saying according to his own point of view which pleases him and which he will follow. From the beginning Frank Lloyd Wright has faced toward an organic perception of the world.

Wright's whole career has been an endeavor to express himself in what he calls "organic architecture," whatever that may be. He likes to work within the shadow of this feeling. As recently as January 25, 1940, when he lectured in Jackson Hall, Boston, he devoted his entire discussion to this problem of his life. He tried by a sort of Socratic dialogue, a give-and-take between himself and his audience, to define and explain it. But his effort was futile. It was clear, finally, that no explanation was possible in words, that what he meant by organic architecture could be revealed only in his work.

Around 1900 Louis Sullivan, in his *Kindergarten Chats*,[14] sought to arrive at "the true meaning of the words 'Organic Architec-

---

[14] *Kindergarten Chats*, first published in 1901–02 in *Interstate Architect and Builder*, is the testament of Louis Sullivan to American youth. It is full of prophecies, some of which have already been fulfilled. Others, I believe, will be. The quotations are from the revised edition published in book form by Claude Bragdon (Lawrence [?], Kansas, 1934), pp. 46–49.

ture'" through contrast, by exploring "what the word 'organic' doesn't mean." Organic, he said, means living, means development, and not, as in the reigning American architecture of 1900, "pitiful in its folly, ... functions without forms, forms without functions; details unrelated to masses, and masses unrelated to anything but folly. . . ." Of this he adds: "Organic it is not. Inorganic it is becoming." "Organic" means for him the "searching for *realities*, — a word

253. FRANK LLOYD WRIGHT. Residence, Taliesin.

I love because I love the sense of life it stands for, the ten-fingered grasp of things it implies. . . ." "Organic," in the sense of Sullivan and of Wright, is a protest against the split personality, against a split culture. It is identical with "the ten-fingered grasp of reality" or with that development in which thinking and feeling approach coincidence.

On a deep blue day in July 1939 we stood on the top of the hill on which is built Wright's own home, Taliesin (*fig.* 253). The dome of the hill was so precise in shape, especially the hill-

Wright's organic treatment

413

crown which became a low-walled garden above the surrounding courts, reached by stone steps walled into the slopes,[15] that I asked if it had been built up in artificial regularity from below. "No, it is the natural soil," Wright said. "I never build houses on the top of a hill. I build them around it, like an eyebrow." And I saw that it was indeed the house itself which brought into consciousness the pure curve of the ground, that in a certain sense its many-layered and unobtrusive forms gave meaning and definition to the contours out of which it rose.

At the time when he was isolated in his profession and without public support, when America had turned against him, Wright even built houses in the folds of the earth, so that they seem to grow into nature and out of it. But even in his earlier houses, like the Coonley house of 1911, with its projecting eaves and its plants growing along and spreading over wooden cantilevers, we may see this tendency of the house to melt into its surroundings, so that it is often impossible to say where it begins. There are also contemporary sculptors, like Hans Arp, who would prefer to set their works in the midst of the forest so that, like a part of nature, they cannot be distinguished from other stones.

This urge toward the organic may partly explain why Wright prefers to use materials taken directly from nature, rugged stone walls, rough granite floors, and heavy unfinished timbers. Throughout his Chicago period he made no use of the skeleton either of iron or ferroconcrete; [16] he is most reticent in the use of glass and of white, and so cautious with openings that it is sometimes difficult even to find the entrance door. Likewise his urge toward the organic accounts for his developing his flexible, open plan — in the age of central heating — from the huge chimneys of the early colonial house.

---

[15] See Wright, *Autobiography*.

[16] When he did employ concrete, it was, as in the Oak Park Temple, in the form of concrete walls without glass surfaces. For his walls and porch pillars Wright prefers brick or small Roman brick such as was used by McIntire in the early and Richardson in the late nineteenth century. He avoids even clapboards and has used them — so far as I know — only in a single house in Chicago, designed when he was still working with Sullivan.

414

The usual criticism of the houses of his Chicago period — the Martin house in Buffalo (1904), for example, and even the Robie house (1908) — is that they are rather dark. They have overhanging eaves and deep, low rooms. It is not completely clear what he was trying to express with them, nor what his real motives were. It may be that, having grown up in Chicago's most vigorous period, he reacted against the big city and its heavily glassed-in areas. In his houses and even his administration buildings he seeks to make a spatial unit of the structure, but to seal it rather than to open it up.

Behind this cautiousness in the use of new materials and this hesitation about opening up the house with glass walls, as was done in the Chicago office buildings of the eighties and the European houses of the twenties, seems to lie a special conception of the needs of human nature. Wright binds the human dwelling to the earth as intimately as possible, introducing the earth into the house in the form of rough walls, and attached to it as if, in the words of Louis Sullivan, by "the ten-fingered grasp of reality." For Wright the house is a shelter, a covert into which the human animal can retire as into a cave, protected from rain and wind and — light. There he may crouch, as it were, in complete security and relaxation, like an animal in its lair. Is there back of this the desire for shadowed dimness that prevailed in the late nineteenth century, or is it an urge toward primitive eternal instincts which sooner or later must be satisfied? This we do not know. Always in the study of Wright's personality a distinction must be made between his use of elements belonging to his generation, on the one hand, and, on the other, his own genius, overleaping its natural frontiers.

The European development based on constructive means and the new visual approach had first to clear the atmosphere by pure functionalism. This was necessary, unavoidable, and healthful, but the moment the means of expression had been found, the clearing up accomplished, then again the urge to the organic could be felt. On another level and by other ways than Wright's it is moving toward the organic. In the northern countries the work of the Finnish architect Alvar Aalto indicates this — and not only there. On another level European and American architecture together may find a new and common path.

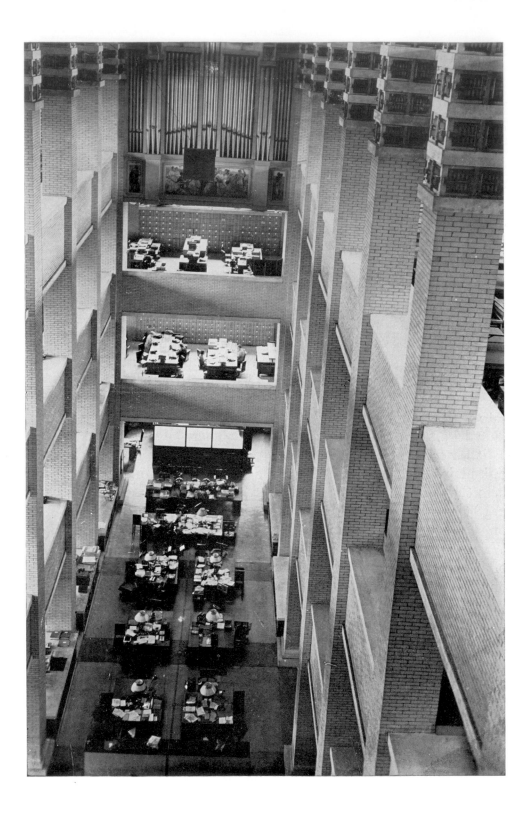

Office Buildings

Frank Lloyd Wright's distinctively individual feeling for the house as a shelter and his handling of it as an enclosed spatial unit are reflected in his two office buildings — the Larkin Soap

254. FRANK LLOYD WRIGHT. Larkin Administration Building, Buffalo, 1904. *Nave with surrounding galleries.*

←

255. FRANK LLOYD WRIGHT. Johnson Wax Company, Administration Building, Racine, Wisconsin, 1938–39. *Interior.*

Company administration building in Buffalo (1904; *fig.* **254**) and the Johnson Wax Company administration building in Racine, Wisconsin (1939; *fig.* **255**). Though they were erected a quarter of a century apart and are very different in appearance, they show the same spirit and give an equal insight into Wright's architectural treatment. Both are treated primarily as *one room;* both are separated from the outdoors; both are enclosed by massive walls and receive their light through skylights and high-placed windows or glass tubing. They are shells shutting out the outer world, isolated and self-contained units, and thus in the strongest contrast, on the one hand, to the buildings of the Chicago school of the eighties with their wide open glass areas and, on the other, to the designs of the European movement of the twenties.

Larkin Building

The Larkin Building stands a resolutely independent mass embraced by the extended wings of the much larger factory building of the company. There is an interplay between the volume of its spatial unit and the square towers at either end and flanking the entrance. These towers, which encase the stairways and rise starkly without interruption upward over a hundred feet, were the despair of contemporary critics, who protested that they thrust up so strongly that there was no play of light and shadow, and who thought that they should be relieved by moldings or softened by glazed tiles in a variety of color patterns.[17] The building itself had for these critics a grimness of aspect which repelled them. It was for them an "accumulation of strange sharp-edged solids, offering no modulation of surface," its features "the square corner, the right angle, the straight edge, the sharp arris, the firm vertical and horizontal lines, unbroken, unmodified, uncompromising in their geometrical precision."[18] Curiously enough, is not this very much the same sort of attack which Wright himself later made upon the right angles, flat surfaces, and triangles of the European architects of the twenties?

---

[17] Cf. Russell Sturgis, "The Larkin Building, Buffalo, N. Y.," *Architectural Record*, XXIII (1908), 319, 321. It is interesting to note how an earnest critic who appreciates the high quality of the plan and organization of the building cannot, however hard he tries, accept it emotionally.

[18] *Ibid.*, p. 319.

No skeleton was used in the Larkin Building. Just as in his small dwelling-houses, Wright employs brick; the towers are square brick shafts; the walls are a massive brick shell closed above by a flat roof pierced by skylights. The architect himself characterizes the structure thus: "Building sealed. . . . Furnishing and filing systems built-in of steel. . . . First air conditioned office building.[19] . . . First metal bound plate glass doors and windows. . . ."[20] Its inner core is a large space five stories high surrounded by galleries, forming a great nave open to the skylight. Square, sand-colored brick piers, rising with a Gothic strength, divide the nave from the galleries. That the owners later on placed an organ in this vast room is an indication of the serenity of the whole. Standing on the uppermost floor and looking down into the nave and the galleries, we can observe how the light falls upon the metal desk-tables from high-placed windows invisible to us.

The administration building of the Johnson Wax Company (1937–39) is also treated as a spatial unit, but primarily in one story. It soon became famous on account of its unusually formed columns. But the accent here again is on the manner in which the lighting is achieved. I had occasion to see the building just before it was completed, and I should like to give here my first impressions:

Johnson Wax
Company Building

"We come to Racine, thirty miles north of Chicago, one of those places which have neither an end nor a beginning. In the middle of the town is the Building Office for which we are looking, and in front of us there is a curved brick wall with strange, long glass strips let into the top, just visible in the winter light. . . . From a dark entrance, we arrive in a big hall filled with mushroom pillars. All the engineers have shaken their heads over these pillars which taper toward their bases and are fitted into steel shoes.[21] At the top there are

---

[19] Buffalo was the birthplace of air-conditioning.

[20] *Architectural Forum*, LXVIII (January 1938), 88.

[21] This type of column was challenged by the authorities. It "was 22 ft. high, carried about 12 tons, had a base 9 in. in diameter, flagrantly disregarding the code which called for a 30 inch thickness on a column of this height. To demonstrate the soundness of his design Wright poured a test column, let it stand seven days, and watched workmen load it with 60 tons of material. Convinced, doubters piled on no more, pulled it down. On the basis of the test the column would be good for a minimum of 80 tons at 28 days. Secret of its amazing strength is wire mesh, welded into a cone." ("Frank Lloyd Wright Tests a Column," *Architectural Forum*, vol. LXVII, August 1937, p. 10.)

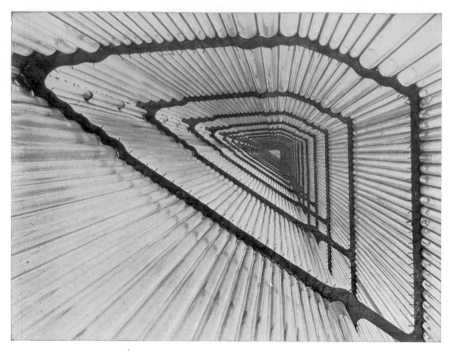

256. FRANK LLOYD WRIGHT. Johnson Wax Company, Administration Building, 1938–39. *Interior of cornice of glass tubing, outer wall.*

widespreading circular discs which seem to float like leaves of the *Victoria regia* among the tubes of heat-resisting (Pyrex) glass. Most of the pillars carry nothing but the air above them. This glass is manufactured in small lengths, and it is very difficult to fix. But it does not discolor, and that is what Wright wanted. The pillars are a luxury, and so is the special glass, but why should not an administrative building, which is a work-building, for once be based on poetry? The light that shimmers through the tubes is of a marvelous quality. The impression of the hall is magic. We look up into the light, like fish from the bottom of a pond, and the plates seem to swim in the flowing glass. The hall is the most fantastic thing that has been conceived in the architectural imagination for a long time. Its apparent pointlessness irritates many people [22]

[22] The Johnson Wax Company building has been harshly attacked by the younger architects not only for its streamlined exterior, but also because they say it lacks response to function and is theatrical in effect. Certainly, as in every one of Wright's buildings, there are to be found in the details many reminiscences of a bygone generation, but over against all these objections it seems to us necessary to set into relief the fact that the importance of this building lies in its experimentation with plastic forms and a new

— one could have spanned the whole space with a single truss. But the magic effect would have been lost.

"This building is said to have cost double the amount originally contemplated, but the firm is able and willing to afford this luxury. There have always existed buildings which satisfied this need for luxury, and they will exist again. The point that matters is what we are to understand by luxury. Luxury does not simply mean waste of material, but only makes sense when *it broadens emotional experience by means of new discovery*. Only a few can fulfill this. Frank Lloyd Wright achieves in this building by means of silver light and plasticity of form, a new spatial sensation without which it is not possible to think of architecture. He shows us here, after half a century of building, how luxury can still be creative in architecture" (*fig.* **256**).[23]

Influence of Frank Lloyd Wright

Frank Lloyd Wright is not only an architect. He belongs among the great preachers of his country; he has by nature the will and the courage to protest, to revolt, and to persevere. He carries on in architecture that tradition of sturdy individualism of which in the middle of the last century Walt Whitman and Henry Thoreau were the literary spokesmen. He regards this tradition as part of himself. As prophet, preacher, and agrarian individualist, he preaches hatred of the city and return to the soil and to the productive, self-sufficient community — in a land where man's relation to the soil is too often remote and impersonal; where at the same moment, according to the varying demands of the economic trend, forests are being changed into farms and acres of growing grain changed back into forests; where food to a great extent comes to the table out of tins; and where now it is even being advocated that tomatoes should be grown in water treated with chemical salts.

Wright, the preacher

---

quality of light, a new technical means, for broadening the emotional scale. Like a baroque church, the building cannot be judged without being seen, gone through, experienced.

[23] S. Giedion, "The Dangers and Advantages of Luxury," *Focus* (London), no. 3, Spring 1939, pp. 34–39.

Frank Lloyd Wright belongs, in one sense of the word, to a sacrificed generation. When he began building, he had every prospect of commercial success; he built more houses in his early period than any of his European precursors. But what he built was only for the individual client. Not that his houses — all of them erected in the Middle West and the West [24] — are purely local, limited by the region and the personal tastes and requirements of the single client; like any work of art, they embody something that overreaches all restrictions of place and personal ownership. But they have had no influence on the country; they have not become an impelling creative force.

The reason is that Wright began work at the very moment when American architecture was undermined by the most dangerous reaction since the time of its origin. The classic and Gothic fashions which in those years overwhelmed the constituent facts of American architecture had, of course, nothing to do with tradition. They meant nothing more than the giving of an artificial backbone to people who were weak in their emotional structure. Behind the screens of their houses — miniature Versailles, Tuscan villa, or medieval manor — or their skyscrapers in sacred Gothic shapes, these people could hide their inner uncertainty. This had its deplorable consequences for the business of architecture. The architect who wished to live by his profession had to conform to the vogue or give up.

During this dominance of classic and Gothic imitations, which became stronger and stronger between 1910 and 1925, Wright and Louis Sullivan had to live almost as exiles in their own country. In the last year of his life, so an older Chicago architect has told me, Sullivan received monetary assistance monthly from some of his colleagues. And Wright in 1940, speaking at his exhibition in Boston, summed it up when he said simply: "They killed Sullivan, and they nearly killed me!"

In this period he and Sullivan became, in the eyes of their contemporaries, the representatives of a lost cause. But actually it was not they who had lost the cause. Rather it was the country which had lost, for later on it was the country, and not Wright, which had to change. At this time, when Europe

---

[24] Not one house was built by Wright in the country's financial center, New York; not one in Boston.

was beginning to purify architectural means, when the demand for truth appeared in architecture, America had no organ with which to hear what was going on. All that was being expressed abroad was cut off like a silenced radio. The effects are still to be felt today.

The foundation bearing Wright's work is a strong tripod: the American tradition, his urge toward the organic, and his power to find an artistic language for his own period. By the time the definitive publication of his buildings appeared in Berlin in 1910, all this had been realized. At forty years of age Wright had already achieved a body of work great enough and influential enough to assure him his place in history.

Nature of
Wright's influence

What is to be grasped, what can be observed of his direct influence, is often only superficial and leads to misunderstanding. Whoever as an architect has tried to imitate or even to follow him, whether in Europe or America, has misused his work and misinterpreted his spirit. Much more important perhaps than Wright's direct influence is his significance as an index, as a sort of signpost of new directions, for no equivalent could be found for his work in Europe between 1900 and 1910.

After 1910 the best brains of Europe began to understand what he had achieved in America. One of the finest, H. P. Berlage, introduced Wright's work extensively into Europe through his own exhibitions and lectures. By his moral authority he ensured the next Dutch generation a stimulus to their own development.[25] The Dutch people were best prepared to receive help from Wright's impulse. In this connection we are not thinking so much of the work of Dudok in Hilversum, who in the early twenties had a great success with his sentimentalized buildings, but rather with such a sensitive and fine-spirited architect as Robert van t'Hoff, who built two massive concrete houses at Huisterheide in 1914–15. These houses, the only ones van t'Hoff ever built, were a direct reflection of Wright's ideas. Although they stood alone and isolated in Europe, nevertheless they performed a clarifying function there. They were made known to the European advance guard in 1919 by an article of Theo van Doesburg in his review, *Style*.

Influence in
Europe

[25] Curiously enough, Le Corbusier was also directed to Wright through an article which appeared in the *Schweizerische Bauzeitung* in 1912, and which was an extensive résumé by Berlage himself of a lecture he had given in Zurich.

In the early work of several Dutch architects, and also in some projects of J. J. P. Oud, it was undoubtedly the stimulus that was to be found in Wright's work which helped them to clear a way to self-realization. But it would be completely superficial and wrong to try to find detailed evidence of his influence on them, to refer in their case to models and pictures for similarities to his designs. For there are other elements in European architecture — as we shall soon see — which formed their specific character. No. Wright's real influence, his great and educative influence, cannot be shown in a few poor photographs; his real influence is that of his methods and ideas, as they are reflected in his work. We shall see how later on Wright's conception of space, coming into contact with the European movement, was developed and changed in the hands of its leading figures.

PART **VI** **SPACE–TIME IN ART, ARCHITECTURE, AND CONSTRUCTION**

THE NEW SPACE CONCEPTION: SPACE–TIME

Social, economic, and functional influences play a vital part in all human activities, from the sciences to the arts. But there are other factors which also have to be taken into account — our feelings and emotions. These factors are often dismissed as trivial, but actually their effect upon men's actions is immense. A good share of the misfortunes of the past century came out of its belief that industry and techniques had only a functional import, with no emotional content. The arts were exiled to an isolated realm of their own, completely insulated from everyday realities. As a result, life lost unity and balance; science and industry made steady advances, but in the now detached realm of feeling there was nothing but a vacillation from one extreme to the other.

The scope and strength of the emotions are both greater than we sometimes suppose. Emotion or feeling enters into all our affairs — speculation is never completely "pure," just as action is never entirely practical. And, of course, we are far from having free choice in this matter of feeling. Large tracts of our emotional life are determined by circumstances over which we have no control: by the fact that we happen to be men, of such or such a kind, living at this or that period. Thus a thoroughly integrated culture produces a marked unity of feeling among its representatives. For example, a recognizable common spirit runs through the whole baroque period. It makes itself felt in activities as distinct from each other as painting and philosophy or architecture and mathematics. This is not particularly surprising. Techniques, sciences, the arts — all these are carried on by men who have grown up together in the same period, exposed to its characteristic influences. The feelings which it is the special concern of the artist to express are also at work within the engineer and the mathematician. This emotional background shared by such otherwise divergent pursuits is what we must try to discover.

Do We Need Artists?

Some people question whether any pervasive unity of feeling is possible in a period like ours. They regard science and industry as inimical to art and feeling: where the former prosper, the latter decline. Or they see science taking over the arts, opening up new means of self-expression which make us independent of them. There is some basis for views like these. It is obvious that the serious artist plays no very important role in contemporary life — usually he cannot even make a living by his work. At the same time, this civilization is too intimately a part of us to be simply abandoned. Do we, then, really need artists any longer?

In any civilization, feeling continues to filter through every activity and situation. An environment whose chief aspects remain opaque to feeling is as unsatisfying as one which resists practical or intellectual control. But just this sort of emotional frustration has prevailed for a long time past. An official art has turned its back upon the contemporary world and given up the attempt to interpret it emotionally. The feelings which that world elicits have remained formless, have never met with those objects which are at once their symbols and their satisfaction.

Such symbols, however, are vital necessities. Feelings build up within us and form systems; they cannot be discharged through instantaneous animal outcries or grimaces. We need to discover harmonies between our own inner states and our surroundings. And no level of development can be maintained if it remains detached from our emotional life. The whole machinery runs down.

This is the reason why the most familiar and ordinary things have importance for the genuinely creative artists of our generation. Painters like Picasso, Juan Gris, the lyricist of cubism, and Le Corbusier have devoted themselves to the common objects of daily use: bowls, pipes, bottles, glasses, guitars. Natural materials have received the same attention: stones hollowed out by the sea, roots, bits of bark — even weather-bleached bones. Anonymous and unpretentious things like these scarcely figure at all in our normal consciousness, but they attain their true stature and significance under the artist's hand. They become revealed as *objets à réaction poétiques*, to borrow Le Corbusier's phrase. Or, to put it somewhat differently, new parts of the world are made accessible to feeling.

The opening up of such new realms of feeling has always been the artist's chief mission. A great deal of our world would lack all emotional significance if it were not for his work. As recently as the eighteenth century, mountain scenery was felt to exhibit nothing except a formless and alarming confusion. Winckelmann, the discoverer of Greek art, could not bear to look out the windows of his carriage when he crossed the Alps into Italy, around 1760. He found the jumbled granite masses of the St. Gotthard so frightful that he pulled down the blinds and sat back to await the smooth outlines of the Italian countryside. A century later, Ruskin was seeking out the mountains of Chamonix as a refuge from an industrial world that made no kind of aesthetic sense. Ships, bridges, iron constructions — the new artistic potentialities of his period, in short — these were the things Ruskin pulled down the blinds on. Right now there are great areas of our experience which are still waiting to be claimed by feeling. Thus we are no longer limited to seeing objects from the distances normal for earth-bound animals. The bird's-eye view has opened up to us whole new aspects of the world. Such new modes of perception carry with them new feelings which the artist must formulate.

The artist, in fact, functions a great deal like an inventor or a scientific discoverer: all three seek new relations between man and his world. In the artist's case these relations are emotional instead of practical or cognitive. The creative artist does not want to copy his surroundings, on the one hand, or to make us see them through his eyes, on the other. He is a specialist who shows us in his work as if in a mirror something we have not realized for ourselves: the state of our own souls. He finds the outer symbols for the feelings which really possess us but which for us are only chaotic and — therefore — disquieting, obsessive stirrings. This is why we still need artists, however difficult it may be for them to hold their place in the modern world.

Artist and public: how they have lost contact

But if the artist is so necessary to us, how is it that he seems to have lost contact with all but a small number of his contemporaries? Ordinary people make it almost a point of pride to insist that, so far as they are concerned, his vocabulary of forms is totally incomprehensible.

428

This is often said to be a consequence of the revolt against naturalism. Actually, however, it dates from quite another event: the *proclamation de la liberté du travail* of March 17, 1791, which dissolved the guild system. The abolition of all legal restraints upon the choice of a trade was the starting point for the tremendous growth of modern industry.

Cut off from the crafts, the artist was faced with the serious problem of competing with the factory system for his living. One solution was to set himself up in the luxury trades, to cater, quite unashamed, to the lowest common denominator of public taste. Art-to-public-order flooded the world, filled the *salons*, and won the gold medals of all the academies. With no serious aims and no standards of its own, the most such an art could hope for was a financial success, and this it often achieved. The most favored of these cultivated drudges — a Meissonier, for example — sometimes saw their canvases sold at a thousand francs the square inch.

As far as the public and the critics were concerned, this was art — and this the work the artist was meant to do. The half-dozen painters who carried on the artist's real work of invention and research were absolutely ignored. The constituent facts in the painting of our period were developed against the will of the public and almost in secret. And this from the beginning to the end of the century, from Ingres to Cézanne.

The same situation held for architecture. Here too the advances were made surreptitiously, in the department of construction. The architect and the painter were faced with the same long struggle against *trompe l'œil*. Both had to combat entrenched styles by returning to the pure means of expression. For some four decades painter after painter makes the effort to reconquer the plane surface. We have seen how the same struggle arose in architecture as a consequence of the demand for morality. Painters very different in type but sharing a common isolation from the public worked steadily toward a new conception of space. And no one can understand contemporary architecture, become aware of the feelings hidden behind it, unless he has grasped the spirit animating this painting.

The fact that modern painting bewilders the public is not strange: for a full century the public has ignored all the developments which have led up to it. There *would* be cause for surprise if the public could read at sight an artistic language elaborated while its attention was elsewhere, absorbed by the pseudo art of the *salon*.

THE RESEARCH INTO SPACE: CUBISM

In many places, about 1910, a consciousness that the painter's means of expression had lost contact with modern life was beginning to emerge. But it was in Paris, with cubism, that these efforts first attained a visible result. The method of presenting spatial relationships which the cubists developed has furnished the plastic principles of present-day visual approach.[1]

The half-century previous to the rise of cubism had seen painting flourish almost nowhere outside of France. It was the high culture of painting that grew up in France during this period which formed the fostering soil for our contemporary art. Young people of talent — whether Spanish like Picasso, or Swiss like Le Corbusier — found their inspiration in Paris, in the union of their powers with the artistic tradition of that city. The vitality of French culture served to the advantage of the whole world. Among the general public, however, there was no sympathetic response to this achievement. It was from a form of art which the public despised that nineteenth-century painting drew its positive strength. Cubism, growing up in this soil, absorbed all its vigor.

---

[1] We shall treat contemporary movements in art here only so far as their methods are directly related to the space conceptions of our period, and in order to understand the common background of art, architecture, and construction. For an understanding of these movements the elaborate catalogues of the Museum of Modern Art, New York, are very useful. Cf. Alfred H. Barr, Jr., *Cubism and Abstract Art* (New York, 1936). For a short survey with emphasis on historical relations, see J. J. Sweeney, *Plastic Redirections of the Twentieth Century* (Chicago, 1935); for the relation of contemporary art to education, industrial design, and daily life, see L. Moholy-Nagy, *The New Vision* (New York, 1938). The close relation of contemporary sculpture to primitive art, on the one hand, and, on the other, to an enlargement of our outlook into nature is stressed in C. Giedion-Welcker, *Modern Plastic Art* (Zurich, 1937).

Picasso has been called the inventor of cubism, but cubism is not the invention of any individual. It is rather the expression of a collective and almost unconscious attitude. A painter who participated in the movement says of its beginnings: "There was no invention. Still more, there could not be one. Soon it was twitching in everybody's fingers. There was a presentiment of what should come, and experiments were made. We avoided one another; a discovery was on the point of being made, and each of us distrusted his neighbors. We were standing at the end of a decadent epoch."

From the Renaissance to the first decade of the present century perspective had been one of the most important constituent facts in painting. It had remained a constant element through all changes of style. The four-century-old habit of seeing the outer world in the Renaissance manner — that is, in terms of three dimensions — rooted itself so deeply in the human mind that no other form of perception could be imagined. This in spite of the fact that the art of different previous cultures had been two-dimensional. When earlier periods established perspective as a constituent fact they were always able to find new expressions for it. In the nineteenth century perspective was misused. This led to its dissolution.

The three-dimensional space of the Renaissance is the space of Euclidean geometry. But about 1830 a new sort of geometry was created, one which differed from that of Euclid in employing more than three dimensions. Such geometries have continued to be developed, until now a stage has been reached where mathematicians deal with figures and dimensions that cannot be grasped by the imagination.

These considerations interest us only in so far as they affect the sense of space. Like the scientist, the artist has come to recognize that classic conceptions of space and volumes are limited and one-sided. In particular, it has become plain that the aesthetic qualities of space are not limited to its infinity for sight, as in the gardens of Versailles. The essence of space as it is conceived today is its many-sidedness, the infinite potentiality for relations within it. Exhaustive description of an area from one point of reference is, accordingly, impossible; its

431

character changes with the point from which it is viewed. In order to grasp the true nature of space the observer must project himself through it. The stairways in the upper levels of the Eiffel Tower are among the earliest architectural expression of the continuous interpenetration of outer and inner space.

Space in modern physics is conceived of as relative to a moving point of reference, not as the absolute and static entity of the baroque system of Newton. And in modern art, for the first time since the Renaissance, a new conception of space leads to a self-conscious enlargement of our ways of perceiving space. It was in cubism that this was most fully achieved.

Space-Time The cubists did not seek to reproduce the appearance of objects from one vantage point; they went round them, tried to lay hold of their internal constitution. They sought to extend the scale of feeling, just as contemporary science extends its descriptions to cover new levels of material phenomena.

Cubism breaks with Renaissance perspective. It views objects relatively: that is, from several points of view, no one of which has exclusive authority. And in so dissecting objects it sees them simultaneously from all sides — from above and below, from inside and outside. It goes around and into its objects. Thus, to the three dimensions of the Renaissance which have held good as constituent facts throughout so many centuries, there is added a fourth one — time. The poet Guillaume Apollinaire was the first to recognize and express this change, around 1911. The same year saw the first cubist exhibition in the Salon des Indépendants. Considering the history of the principles from which they broke, it can well be understood that the paintings should have been thought a menace to the public peace, and have become the subject of remarks in the Chamber of Deputies.

The presentation of objects from several points of view introduces a principle which is intimately bound up with modern life — simultaneity. It is a temporal coincidence that Einstein should have begun his famous work, *Elektrodynamik bewegter Körper*, in 1905 with a careful definition of simultaneity.

432

The Artistic Means

"Abstract art" is as misleading a term for the different movements which depart from the spatial approach as "cubism" is for the beginnings of the contemporary image. It is not the "abstract," it is not the "cubical," which are significant in their content. What is decisive is the invention of a new approach, of a new spatial representation, and the means by which it is attained.

This new representation of space was accomplished step by step, much as laboratory research gradually arrives at its conclusions through long experimentation; and yet, as always with real art and great science, the results came up out of the subconscious suddenly.

The cubists dissect the object, try to lay hold of its inner composition. They seek to extend the scale of optical vision as contemporary science extends the law of matter. Therefore contemporary spatial approach has to get away from the single point of reference. During the first period (shortly before 1910) this dissection of objects was accomplished, as Alfred Barr expresses it, by breaking up "the surfaces of the natural forms into angular facets." Concentration was entirely upon research into a new representation of space — thus the extreme scarcity of colors in this early period. The pictures are gray-toned or earthen, like the grisaille of the Renaissance or the photographs of the nineteenth century. Fragments of lines hover over the surface, often forming open angles which become the gathering places of darker tones. These angles and lines began to grow, to be extended, and suddenly out of them developed one of the constituent facts of space-time representation — the plane (*fig.* **257**).

The advancing and retreating planes of cubism, interpenetrating, hovering, often transparent, without anything to fix them in realistic position, are in fundamental contrast to the lines of perspective, which converge to a single focal point.

The planes

Hitherto planes in themselves, without naturalistic features, had lacked emotional content. Now they came to the fore as an artistic means, employed in various and very different ways, at times representing fragments of identifiable objects, at

433

257. PICASSO. "Still Life," c. 1914.

others such things as bottles or pipes flattened out so that interior and exterior could be seen simultaneously, at still others completely irrational forms equivalent only to psychic responses.

Around 1912 new elements entered; the planes were accentuated, assumed strength and dominance, and were given an additional appeal — to the tactile sense — by means of new materials (scraps of paper, sawdust, glass, sand, etc.). And when, though always meagerly, color was employed, it was often corrugated and roughened in order to strengthen the pigment. In such *collages* fragments of newspapers, fabrics, or handwriting, sometimes even single words, achieved the force of new symbols.

The process continued, from the grayish background of the first period through the *collage*, to the reappearance of color, which gradually became stronger and more varied, until its brilliant culmination in Picasso's and Braque's still-lifes toward and at the beginning of the twenties. In this period, perhaps cubism's happiest, color was used in pure strength. At the same time curvilinear forms were introduced, taken from such everyday objects as bowls and guitars, or simply invented. Color no longer had the exclusive function of naturalistic reproduction. Used in a spatial pattern, it was often divorced from any object, asserting a right to existence in itself.

Cubism originated among artists belonging to the oldest cultures of the western world, the French and the Spanish. More and more clearly it appears that this new conception of space was nourished by the elements of bygone periods. Its symbols were not rational, were not to be utilized directly in architecture and the applied arts, but they did give force and direction to artistic imagination in other fields. Following upon the first efforts of the cubists, there came, as has already been said, an awakening in various countries. In France appeared Le Corbusier and Ozenfant; in Russia, Malewitsch; in Hungary, Moholy-Nagy; in Holland, Mondrian and van Doesburg. Common to them was an attempt to rationalize cubism or, as they felt was necessary, to correct its aberrations. The procedure was sometimes very different in different groups, but all moved toward rationalization and into architecture.

When Ozenfant and Jeanneret (Le Corbusier) came together as young painters in 1917, they called their painting *Purisme* (*fig.* **307**). In comparison with the movements preceding it (constructivism in Russia or neo-plasticism in Holland), purism, coming out of French soil, was the closest of all to the aim of cubism and, at the same time, to architecture.

Two years after the exhibition of the cubists in the Salon des Indépendants, there appeared in Russia an abstract-art movement, fostered by Kasimir Malewitsch, which completely eliminated the object. It was a flight from and a protest against the naturalistic object, with painting reduced to a few signs of symbolic intensity. What its paintings achieve are fundamentally only pure interrelationships. Flatly extended rectangles and strips float in continuous interrelation in space for which there is no true human measure.

Interrelation, hovering, and penetration form the basis of Malewitsch's half-plastic architectural studies, which he calls

Purism

Constructivism

258. BRAQUE. Collage, 1913.

259. MONDRIAN.

"architectonen." These objects are not intended for a particular purpose but are to be understood simply as spatial
research. Interrelations are created between these prisms,
slabs, and surfaces when they penetrate or dislodge each other
(*fig.* **260**).

436

260. MALEWITSCH. Architectonics, c. 1920.

261. THEO VAN DOESBURG and C. VAN EESTEREN.
Scheme for a villa, 1923.

262. WALTER GROPIUS. The Bauhaus, 1926.

Neo-plasticism, an expression used by the Dutch painter Mondrian, signifies that three-dimensional volume is reduced to the new element of plasticity, the plane. Mondrian sacrifices every contact with illusionistic reproduction, going back to the fundamental elements of pure color, of planes, their equipoise and interrelations.

The small circle of young artists who gathered around Theo van Doesburg and his periodical, *Stijl*, after 1917 progressed much more radically than the French painters and architects. Van Doesburg and Mondrian sought "pure art" not in any way deflected by external motives. With them everything rests on the distribution and juxtaposition of planes of pure color: blue, red, yellow. To these are added black and various tones of white, all being placed in a network of panels.

The Belgian Vantongerloo, who also belongs to this circle, demonstrated with the prisms, slabs, and hollows of his plastic of 1918 that contemporary sculpture, like painting, was not to be limited to a single point of view.

Van Doesburg, the moving spirit of the circle, was painter, man of letters, and architect. Although he executed few buildings, he cannot be omitted from the history of architecture, since, like Malewitsch, he possessed the gift of recognizing the new extension of the space sense and the ability to present and explain it as though by laboratory experiments.

One of van Doesburg's drawings in which an attempt is made to present "the elementary forms of architecture" (lines, surface, volume, space, time) may very well have appeared to many at that time as so much disjointed nonsense (*fig.* **81**). The present-day observer, who has the advantage of being able to look back upon intervening developments, has a very different attitude toward these mutually penetrating flat surfaces. He sees how the enormous amount of contemporary architecture which has since appeared acknowledges this vision of space.

In 1923 van Doesburg, together with van Eesteren (*fig.* **261**), who later became a town planner of Amsterdam, produced a house that is bolder than any other building executed during the period. The breaking-up of the compact mass of the house, the accessibility of the roof, the horizontal rows of windows — in fact, all the features that were later to be realized in numerous examples were indicated in it. If a *collage* by Georges Braque (*fig.* **258**), produced ten years earlier, consisting of different papers, scraps of newspaper and fragments of planes, is placed alongside a reproduction of this house, no words are necessary to indicate the identity of artistic expression. An architectonic study of Malewitsch might be likened to it equally well. The effect is as if the blind surfaces of the Malewitsch sculpture had suddenly received sight. It is obvious that in the second decade of this century the same spirit emerged in different forms, in different spheres, and in totally different countries.

THE RESEARCH INTO MOVEMENT: FUTURISM

In the first decade of this century the physical sciences were profoundly shaken by an inner change, the most revolutionary perhaps since Aristotle and the Pythagoreans. It concerned, above all, the notion of *time*. Previously time had been regarded in one of two ways: either realistically, as something going on and existing without an observer, independent of the existence of other objects and without any necessary relation to other phenomena; or subjectively, as something having no existence apart from an observer and present only in sense experience. Now came another and new way of regarding time, one involving implications of the greatest significance, the consequences of which cannot today be minimized or ignored.

The notion of time

As was stated at the beginning of this book, it was in 1908 that Hermann Minkowski, the great mathematician, speaking before the Naturforschenden Gesellschaft, proclaimed for the first time with full certainty and precision this fundamental change of conception. "Henceforth," he said, "space alone or time alone is doomed to fade into a mere shadow; only a kind of union of both will preserve their existence."

Concurrently the arts were concerned with the same problem. Artistic movements with inherent constituent facts, such as

439

cubism and futurism, tried to enlarge our optical vision by introducing the new unit of space-time into the language of art. It is one of the indications of a common culture that the same problems should have arisen simultaneously and independently in both the methods of thinking and the methods of feeling.

Beginnings of futurism

During the Renaissance the common artistic perception, perspective, was expressed by one group of artists primarily through lines, and by another primarily through colors. So in our own day the common background of space-time has been explored by the cubists through spatial representation and by the futurists through research into movement.

For Jakob Burckhardt there reigned in Italy "the quiet of the tomb." The futurists were a reaction against this quietness; they felt ashamed that Italy had become simply a refuge for those seeking to escape from the demands and realities of the present. They called upon art to come forth from the twilit caves of the museums, to assert itself in the fullness of modern thought and feeling, to speak out in authentic terms of the moment. *Life* was their cry — explosive life, movement, action, heroism — in every phase of human life, in politics, in war, in art: the discovery of new beauties and a new sensibility through the forces of our period. Not without right did they claim to be "the first Italian youth in centuries." [1]

So, from the beginning, they plunged into the full struggle, carried their cause militantly to the public. The poet Marinetti, whose apartment in Rome even to this day bears the escutcheon of the "Movimento futurista," proclaimed in the Parisian *Figaro* of February 20, 1909, "We affirm that the splendor of the world has been enriched by a new beauty: the beauty of speed." And later, in 1912, in the "Second Technical Manifesto of Futurist Painting," the futurists developed their principal discovery, that "objects in motion multiply and distort themselves, just as do vibrations, which indeed they are, in passing through space." The most exciting of their paintings realize this artistic principle.

---

[1] For the literary intentions of futurism cf. the article of its founder, F. T. Marinetti, in *Enciclopedia italiana*, vol. XVI, 1932.

The productions of futurist painting, sculpture, and architecture are based on the representation of movement and its correlates: interpenetration and simultaneity. One of the futurists' best minds and without any doubt their best sculptor, Umberto Boccioni, who died much too early, in 1916, has most clearly defined their purposes. In an effort to penetrate more deeply into the very essence of painting, he sought terms for his art, terms which, now obscurely felt, now shining clear and immediate in his increasing creative experience, anticipated those that later appeared in the atomic theory. "We should start," he said, "from the central nucleus of the object wanting to create itself, in order to discover those new forms which connect the object invisibly with the infinite of the apparent plasticity and the infinite of the inner plasticity."

Boccioni tried in these words to circumscribe the sense of a new plasticity which conceives objects (as they are in reality) in a state of movement. This was reflected directly in his plastic, "Bottle Evolving in Space," 1911–12, with its intersecting spatial planes. One of the few sculptural masterpieces of the epoch, this sculpture expresses the inherent significance of an object of daily use by treating it with new artistic invention. Sometimes, as in this instance, cubistic and futuristic works are closely bound together on a common basis of the same spatial conception.

Futurism and cubism — common traits and differences

The French painter, Marcel Duchamp, who belonged neither to the futurists nor to the cubists, painted at the same time (1912) his "Nude Descending the Staircase," in which the movement is dissected mathematically and yet fully surrounded by the multi-significance of irrational art.

Usually the futurists present movement as such, as subject matter ("Elasticity," Boccioni, 1911; "Dynamisme musculaire, Simultanéité," Carrà, 1912; "Speed," Balla, 1913), or show objects and bodies in motion (Gino Severini's study of the dance as a movement in mass, "The Dance Pan-Pan," 1911; "Walking Dog," Balla, 1913; "Rattling Cab," Carrà, 1913).[2]

---

[2] For illustrations of this first and most important futuristic development cf. Boccioni, *Pittura, scultura futuriste* (Milan, 1914), a volume of over 400 pages, with bibliography of exhibitions, manifestoes, etc.

263. BOCCIONI. "Bottle Evolving in Space," 1911–12.

In both futurism and cubism this enlargement of the optical was achieved before 1914, before the first world war. The cubists were the more passive and less vocal. Not fighters in the futuristic sense, more purely research men in their work, they kept to their ateliers, preparing quietly and without fanfare the symbols of our artistic language. Braque and Picasso wrote no ponderous tomes expounding their theories. Even the name "cubist" was a label fixed upon them by outsiders. They did not try to paint "movement" itself, or the dynamism of muscles, or the automobile, but through their still lifes of things of daily use sought to find artistic means for our spatial conceptions. This is the reason cubism found extension into so many ramifications. This is why laboratory painters, who had no thought beyond their own artistic problems, could also give an impulse to the expression of the new spatial conceptions in architecture.

Architecture To try to introduce the principle of movement directly into architecture did not touch the fundamental problem. In his projects for his "Città Nuova," in his skyscraper apartment houses connected with subways, elevators, and traffic lanes at different levels, Antonio Sant' Elia tried, as we have already said, to introduce the futuristic love of movement as an artistic element in the contemporary city (*fig.* **192**). But we do not know how his talent would have developed. He died in 1916, at a time when his contemporary, Le Corbusier, was still far from self-realization. However, while Sant' Elia's schemes were not quite in the direction which was to be followed by later architecture, he did point the way in a period when everyone was looking for a signpost, for something by which to fix his point of view. In his manifesto of July 14, 1914, which he published in connection with the exhibition of his schemes in Milan, he demanded an architecture imbued with the utmost elasticity and lightness, utilizing all the newly developed elements of construction from iron and ferroconcrete to composite materials made by chemical processes, including textile fiber and paper. Behind these technical demands loomed his artistic aim: mobility and change. What he wanted to realize he condensed into the few words: "Every generation its own house!"

There are times when the man of the laboratory is compelled to go forth into the street to fight for his work. On occasion this may be advisable. But normally he endangers his work by so doing. The futurists were perhaps too much bound up

Difficulties

264. BALLA. "Speed," 1913.

in trying to apply their ideas to all kinds of human activities; the result was that their movement — which, it must be remembered, cannot be overlooked by the historian as one of the pivotal points in formulating any judgment of our period — had a comparatively short span of volcanic productivity. It was unfortunate in that some of its ablest exponents died too early and even more unfortunate in that others, often for very different reasons, ended in regrettable routine, bequeathing nothing to the future except the few years of their youth.

265.   EDGERTON.   Speed photograph of a tennis player, 1939.

Futurism did not have the opportunity of the cubist movement: to accumulate, through all the many-sided stages of modern development, the results of artistic research, until they should appear united and in full power in a single great work — *Guernica.*

PAINTING TODAY

Picasso's "Guernica"   Since the first decade of this century the research into space has broadened through various successive stages, never losing, how-

444

ever, its original and primary concern with the new conception. What it had arrived at in the late thirties may be comprehended in a single painting which in itself sums up the entire experience of three decades — the "Guernica" of Picasso. In it are embodied the principle of simultaneity, the penetration of inner and outer space, the working with curved planes and different textures.[1] Nevertheless, this mural of the Spanish war seems to be the first real historical painting since the beginning of the Renaissance and the work of Paolo Uccello. It is the

266. PICASSO. "Guernica," 1937. *Detail.*

tragedy of a country distilled to its full strength by an artist able to transmute physical suffering and destruction into powerful symbols — a mother with her dead child, a woman falling in a burning house, a spear-transfixed horse, fragments of a mutilated warrior, one severed hand clutching a broken sword, all triumphantly surveyed by a great bull and lit by a lamp held in an outstretched hand. Above the carnage shines

---

[1] A connection with earlier periods is likewise evident, the figure of the woman falling in the burning house being referable, as a French architect has remarked, to Raphael's "Fire of Borgo."

"the radiant eye of day with the electric bulb of night for a pupil."

In the course of its composition, the picture went through many variations and preliminary studies, but one detail remained unchanged almost from the beginning — the rush of flight condensed into a symbol of two elongated human heads with hair streaming back, chin and neck in one sweeping line, the faces as if enclosed in spherical triangles (*fig.* **266**). How charged with inner truth this symbol of Picasso's is has recently been revealed by the stroboscope of Edgerton, which is able photographically to disintegrate a movement into single parts which the human eye is incapable of grasping. A study of one of these stroboscopic photographs (*fig.* **265**) makes clear how closely connected are the realizations of the creative artist and those of the scientist. Out of the unknown, an artist like Picasso can produce intuitively symbols for a reality which, as in this instance, is afterwards confirmed by scientific techniques.

CONSTRUCTION AND AESTHETICS: SLAB AND PLANE

The Bridges of Robert Maillart

We spoke earlier [1] of the way in which the methods of science and the methods of art came unconsciously to parallel each other about 1908. Among other more spectacular instances, we noted that construction and painting arrived at similar basic elements in their search for solutions to problems that had not previously been attempted. With the bridges of the Swiss engineer Robert Maillart we are brought back to this topic They offer us the chance to compare these basic elements and to investigate the way in which the aesthetic effect produced by a new type of construction arises. [2]

---

[1] Page 439.

[2] This investigation appeared in more extensive form in *Circle, International Survey of Constructive Art*, edited by J. L. Martin, Ben Nicholson, and N. Gabo (London, 1937), pp. 220–236. It was published there under the title "Construction and Aesthetics" (English version by P. Morton Shand).

Those whose aesthetic sense has been formed or developed by the art of the present age can hardly fail to be stirred by Maillart's bridges, for their appearance may be trusted to arrest such observers before they can even ask themselves why. Maillart's surprising designs, which attract some as much as they repel others,[3] are the product of the uncompromising application of a new method of construction. They have almost as little in common with the solid arches, stout piers, and monumentally emphasized abutments of the usual "massive" type of bridge as an airplane has with a mail coach.

What, then, is the peculiarity of Maillart's methods of building?

Maillart's structural principles

In the early days of reinforced concrete the same methods of construction were used as were employed with timber and iron. Timber, being the trunks of trees, has length, just as iron has when rolled into long girders. One dimension always dominates, which is the one that transmits the load. As Maillart himself puts it: "The engineer was so accustomed to using those basic materials which provide only one-dimensional support that they became second nature to him, and restrained him from exploiting other possibilities. This was the state of affairs when reinforced concrete was introduced, and at first no change ensued."

Maillart was a pupil of Hennebique;[4] and Hennebique's reinforced concrete structures had beams and columns like timber-framed buildings. Following the model of timber construction,

---

[3] Although the first of his bridges have been standing these thirty years, and their adequacy for their purpose has long since ceased to be questioned, they still continue to arouse antagonism among local bodies, many of which regard them as positively hideous. It happened that most were built across remote Alpine valleys, where they were considerably cheaper to erect than other types and (an equally important consideration) where comparatively few people would see them. The stark, lean assurance of their construction belies the aesthetic lights of a wide section of the public through its elimination of emphasis on means of support and through the taut, weblike appearance of the arch-spans which results. "I am sick of these puff-paste bridges" was the way the chairman of one of these local bodies expressed his aversion. This remark is worth mentioning, since it shows what an influence aesthetic feelings exercise alike on those who commission the building of bridges and those who merely chance to look at them, and how often these feelings are the secret determining factor of decisions apparently dictated solely by questions of cost and efficiency.

[4] Early in his career Maillart was the engineer in charge of the construction of a concrete sanatorium at Davos for which Hennebique was the contractor.

his beams reached from wall to wall and from column to column, the roof stretching across them in the form of a flat, inert slab. This was the point where Maillart began his life's work. Like all great constructors, he has consistently followed a single line of thought which he has progressively developed and expanded in the course of his career.

In designing a bridge Maillart began by eliminating all that was nonfunctional; thus everything that remained was an immediate part of the structure. He did this by improving the reinforced concrete slab until he had turned it into a new structural element. What Maillart has achieved since then is based on one idea: that it is possible to reinforce a flat or curved concrete slab in such a manner as to dispense with the need for beams in flooring or solid arches in bridges. It is very difficult to determine the forces present in slabs of this nature by calculation alone. To obtain positive results entailed a complicated process which cannot be entered into here, except to say that it was based partly on calculation and partly on experiment.

Slabs had hitherto played a neutral or passive part in construction. Maillart transformed them into active bearing surfaces capable of assuming all forms of stress, and he subsequently developed this principle into a comprehensive system of support that is now adopted for types of building in which it had previously been considered impossible to use concrete. Whether engaged in perfecting a new form of flooring or in striking out new principles in bridge construction, he has always adhered to the same basic method of using reinforced concrete slabs as active structural elements.

Mushroom flooring   Maillart's experiments with beamless flooring date from 1908. He treated a floor as a concrete slab, converting it into an actively coöperative structural member by distributing the reinforcement throughout its whole area (*fig.* **267**). Since every part of the surface now became self-supporting, beams disappeared, their function being resolved into the floor itself. The heavier the load this homogeneous type of flooring is called upon to bear, the greater the practical inducement to adopt it. Consequently it is usually found in warehouses, factories, and other large, many-storied buildings.

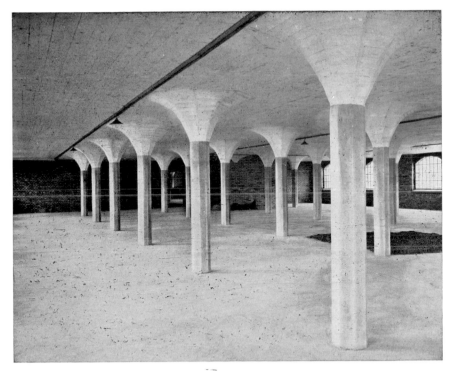

267. MAILLART. Warehouse in Zurich, 1910. *First mushroom ceiling in Europe. The important innovation is the disappearance of the beams: the whole floor is treated like a slab. A new element is the reinforced slab which supports the same amount of weight at each point of its surface.*

The appearance of the branching columns which support this type of flooring somewhat recalls certain traditional styles, for in the basements of warehouses they resemble the heavy pillars of a Romanesque crypt and in the upper stories they suggest the slender palmlike columns of late Gothic. In point of fact, however, mushroom-headed columns have nothing beyond these superficial resemblances in common with either, since the peculiarity of the system resides neither in the formation of the shafts nor in the extruded corbeling of the capitals that crown them, but wholly in forces in the ceiling above, which do not meet the eye.

As floors of this type provide a uniform bearing surface throughout their length and breadth, their ends can be cantilevered out to carry supplementary loads. They are therefore ideal in combination with nonsupporting walls, such as continuous expanses of horizontal fenestration. It is hard to

449

268. MAILLART. Tavanasa Bridge over the Rhine, Grisons, 1905. *Span, 51 meters; width, 3.60 meters; cost, 28,000 Swiss francs; system, three-hinged arch. Maillart for the first time achieved here a monolithic construction by integrating arch and roadway into a structural unit, and the creation of new aesthetic values — transparency and hovering lightness — by stripping the construction of all disguise. The bridge was destroyed in 1927 by a landslide.*

realize this in the obscurity of a warehouse, for the latent possibilities of mushroom slab construction can only find architectural vindication in buildings which are flooded with the light of day from all sides.[5]

The American engineer C. A. P. Turner had been experimenting with the mushroom system a year before Maillart, but the Swiss engineer had employed slabs as basic elements in bridges since the beginning of the century.[6] American designers have

[5] The first specifically architectural endorsements of this principle did not occur until twenty years after Maillart's initial experiments. Brinckmann and van der Vlugt's splendid van Nelle factory in Rotterdam (1927–28) is the outstanding example, although it embodies the ponderous American type of mushroom-headed columns.

[6] Cf. C. A. P. Turner, *Concrete Steel Construction* (Minneapolis, 1909). Turner's article, "The Mushroom System of Construction" (*Western Architect*, 1908, p. 51), gives an

269. MAILLART. Salginatobel Bridge, 1929–30. *Span, 92 meters.*

not rid themselves of the idea that a slab is subject to stress
in separate directions, and they embed their rods diagonally
across the floor like intersecting beams. American practice
has not fully grasped the structural role of the slab; consequently the forms of its mushroom-headed columns manifest a
certain characteristic heavyhandedness. They can be recognized at the first glance by the presence of an intermediate
slab introduced between the head of the pillar and the ceiling,
as in the Doric order of columniation. To the best of my knowledge, the Americans have not even yet thought of using the
slab as a basic element in bridge construction.

---

earlier account of his invention: "It was first used in the construction of the Bovey
Building in Minneapolis. . . . The essential feature of this new construction is the formation of a so-called mushroom at the top of each column, by extending its reinforcing rods
laterally, some four feet or more out into the slab in a radial direction and supporting on
these ring rods, which in turn carry the lighter reinforcement for the slab construction.
The top of the column is enlarged, forming a neat capital, which assists in taking the
additional stress, and is advantageous from the fact that there are no ribs to interfere
with light or to reduce the clear story height of the building."

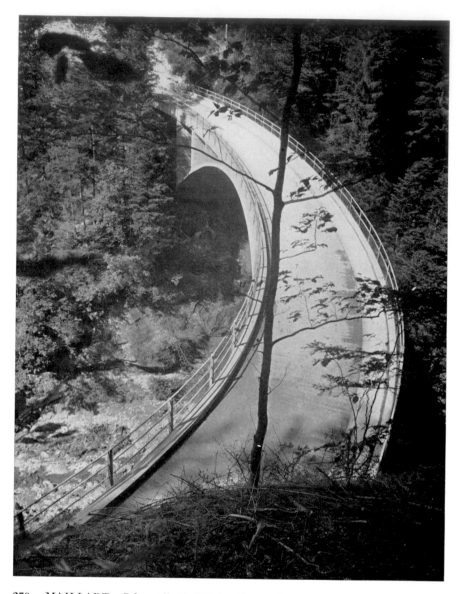

270. MAILLART. Schwandbach-Brücke, Canton Berne, 1933. *Air view. Maillart resolved bridge-building into a system of flat and curved slabs. In Maillart's hands the rigidity of the slab, hitherto an incalculable factor in construction, became an active bearing surface. The torsional strain that would have to be allowed for in a concrete bridge built on a curving alignment can be utilized only by this method of construction.*

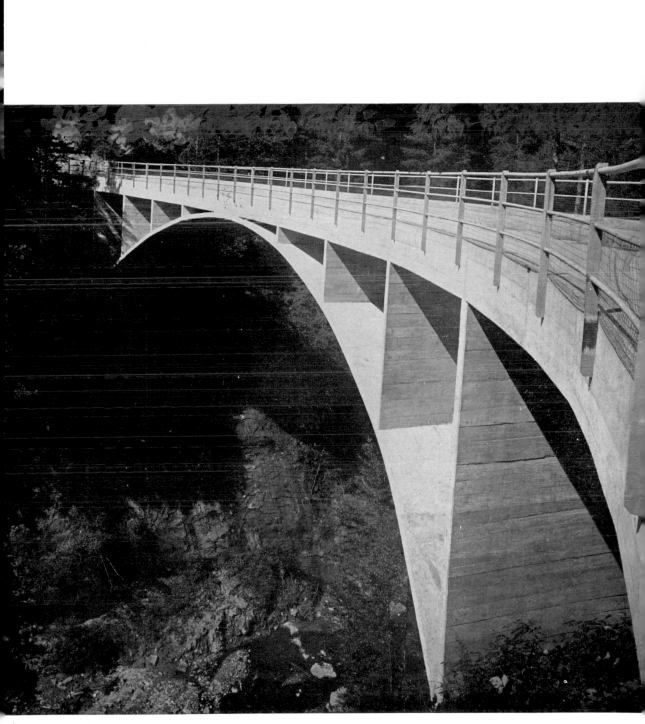

271. MAILLART. Schwandbach-Brücke, Canton Berne, 1933. *Slabs.*

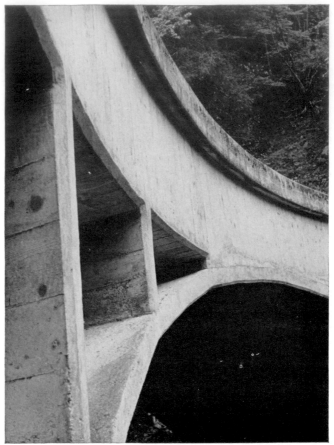

The slab as a
basic element for
bridge-building

Maillart had embodied this principle in a bridge as early as 1900; and in that over the Tavanasa (1905) he dared to strip his construction of all disguise. The Tavanasa bridge (span, 51 m.) represented a wholly unprecedented form, for in it Maillart discarded massive beams just as he was also shortly to eliminate the beams from floors. Instead, he employed a shallow, curved, reinforced concrete slab for the arch, which, with the horizontal slab of the platform and a series of stiffened vertical slabs used as ties to articulate them, constituted the entire structure.

Thus Maillart resolved bridge-building into a system of flat and curved slabs so juxtaposed as to achieve a positively uncanny counterbalance of all stresses and strains arising between them. The first realization of a stiffened elliptical concrete bridge with

454

273. Rainbow Bridge near Carmel, California. *The same problem — a narrow gorge — as in the Swiss valley. Using the normal construction, the approach had to be built in staggered sections; the alignment of the bridge could not be curved.*

an arch of eggshell thickness (his Valtschiel-Brücke) followed in 1925.

The elimination of all nonfunctional members has led Maillart during the last few years to dispense with the usual separate decking slab. In these later bridges trains and motor cars run directly upon their naked structural framework: that is to say, on the longitudinal slab of the platform itself.

In Maillart's hands the rigidity of the slab, hitherto an incalculable factor in construction, became an active bearing surface, which, being under initial tension, opened up possibilities that had remained a closed book for reinforced concrete engineering. Thus the torsional strains that would have to be allowed for in a concrete bridge built on a curving alignment had previously been deemed to defy calculation.[7] Maillart's Schwandbach-Brücke in the Canton of Berne, opened in 1933 (*figs.* **270, 271**), is the most beautiful example of a road bridge carried out in that material with a sickle-shaped platform.

---

[7] The problem of bridging mountain gorges with curved spans occurs in every mountainous country. When girders and arches are used in the ordinary fashion the bridge must be held to a rigidly straight line. At most, a curve can be produced by building the approaches in staggered sections, as in the Rainbow Bridge near Carmel, California (fig. 272).

One of the few large bridges which could pass an inimical jury carries the recently reconstructed main road between Zurich and Saint-Gall over the river Thur (*fig.* **274**) at a point where it traverses broken country with a flat-topped hill in the background. A single arch spans the river bed, flanked on each side by a short approach viaduct supported by remarkably slender pillars.

To appreciate the full plastic beauty of the form of this bridge — the flattened curves of the twin hollow ribs, and the manner

274. MAILLART. Bridge over the river Thur near Saint-Gall, Switzerland, 1933. *Single span, seventy-two meters; cost, $42,000.*

in which they are yoked together; their three-pin articulation on a level with the crown and at the abutments (the slightly ogival pointing of the summit of the arch which results should be noted); the upright slabs that act as vertical ties between the ribs of the arch and the platform, as also the interplay of the pattern of these members with that produced by the unusual section of the columns of the viaducts — it is necessary not only to go and see it, but to clamber down the shingle to the river bank so as to gain a view of the structure from beneath. There are few contemporary buildings in which the solution of the structural problem approaches so closely to pure plastic expression.

Before I throw out the question which underlies this analysis, one or two striking features of Maillart's bridges may be touched on without entering into the technique of his structural methods.

One of the problems in art in which research has not yet made much headway is the relation between sculpture and nature — and, beyond this, the interrelations between sculpture, painting, and architecture. It is easier for the constructor to find a convincing solution than the artist, because physical factors (like the width of the interval to be spanned, the nature of the foundations, etc.) dictate its conditions. All the same, there is something altogether out of the ordinary in the way Maillart succeeds both in expressing and in sublimating the breadth of a chasm cleft between two walls of rock (i.e., in his Salginatobel-Brücke, 1929–30; *fig.* **268**). His shapely bridges spring out of shapeless crags with the serene inevitability of Greek temples. The lithe, elastic resilience with which they leap their chasms, the attenuation of their dimensions, merges into the coördinated rhythms of arch, platform, and the upended slabs between them.

Sculpture and nature

A bridge designed of slabs of various shapes no longer resembles the ordinary kind of bridge either in its form or in its proportions. To eyes that are blind to the vision of our own day, slanting columns with grotesquely splayed-out heads, like those of the approach viaducts of the Thur bridge — a form imposed by purely structural considerations that enabled Maillart to make two columns do the work of four — are bound to appear somewhat ugly; whereas eyes schooled by contemporary art recognize in these shapes an echo of those with which modern painting has already familiarized them.[8]

New forms enforced by the use of the slab

When Picasso paints half-geometric, half-organic plastic images on canvas — forms which in spite of their apparently capricious projection somehow achieve a singular degree of equipoise — and the constructor (proceeding from purely technical premises) arrives at similar absolute forms by sub-

---

[8] Cf. the strangely formed pillars of the Arve bridge (fig. 275).

stituting two vertical supports for four, there is a clear inference that mechanical shapes and the shapes evolved by art as the mirror of a higher reality rank *pari passu* in terms of development.

Parallel methods in painting and construction

It is, of course, easy enough to retort that this is simply the result of chance, and that such resemblances are purely superficial. But we cannot afford to leave the matter there, for what concerns us is the question which must serve as our point of departure: Are the methods which underlie the artist's work related to those of the modern structural engineer? Is there in fact a direct affinity between the principles now current in painting and construction?

We know the great importance which *surface* has acquired in the composition of a picture, and the long road that had to be traversed — starting with Manet's light-fusion of paint, advancing by way of Cézanne's flat coloration and the work of Matisse, and ending with cubism — before this was finally recognized.

Surface, which was formerly held to possess no intrinsic capacity for expression, and so at best could only find decorative utilization, has now become the basis of composition, thereby supplanting perspective, which had triumphed over each successive change of style ever since the Renaissance.

With the cubist's conquest of space, and the abandonment of one predetermined angle of vision which went hand in hand with it, surface acquired a significance it had never known before. Our powers of perception became widened and sharpened in consequence. We discovered the interplay of imponderably floating elements irrationally penetrating or fusing with each other, as also the optical tensions which arise from the contrasts between various textural effects (the handling of color *qua* color, or the use of other media, such as sand, bits of dress fabrics, and scraps of paper, to supplement pigments). The human eye awoke to the spectacle of form, line, and color — that is, the whole grammar of composition — reacting to one another within an orbit of hovering planes, or, as J. J. Sweeney calls it, "the plastic organization of forms suggested by line and colour on a flat surface."

458

If Maillart, speaking as an engineer, can claim to have developed the slab into a basic element of construction, modern painters can answer with equal justice that they have made surface an essential factor in the composition of a picture. The slab long remained unheeded and unmastered: an inert inadaptable thing which defied calculation and so utilization.

275.   MAILLART.   Bridge over the river Arve near Geneva, 1936–37.   *Span, fifty-six meters; width, ten meters; cost, 80,000 Swiss francs.   This bridge on the outskirts of Geneva was built mainly by the private means of the landed proprietors.   It had to serve for heavy loads and yet be built at minimum cost.   This was a case where Maillart could realize unprecedented construction ideas.   The triple box-like arches as well as the rows of elastic supports are evident here.*

But just as a great constructor has transformed it into a medium for solving structural problems that had always been considered insuperable, so the development of surface into a basic principle of composition in painting has resulted in opening up untapped fields of optical expression.

This is no longer a fortuitous optical coincidence, as might be objected, but a definite parallelism of methods. By what mental

459

processes the constructor and the painter arrived at it defies analysis. We can only authenticate a particular phenomenon in a particular case: a new method of construction has found its simultaneous echo in a parallel method in art. But this proves that underlying the special power of visualization im-

276. MAILLART. Arve Bridge, 1936–37. *Support and reinforcement of the support. Instead of steel joints, Maillart shaped the cross-like elastic slab support to take up the changing loads and stresses. By tapering it in the middle and inserting an ingenious armament, he gave the rigid slab the properties of a flexible joint and approached organic form.*

plicit in each of these fields similar elements have emerged which provide a creative impetus for both of them.

If the constructor, who necessarily proceeds from quite different considerations, finds he has to adopt substantially the same basic elements as the artist in order to solve his own technical problems, this signifies that in each case similar methods have informed optical imagination.

Contemporary artists continually reiterate the claim that their work forms part of Nature. This they explain as follows: "Modern art has reached the same results as modern science

460

by entirely independent, intuitive steps. Like science it has resolved the shape of things into their basic elements with the object of reconstituting them in consonance with the universal laws of Nature." Now those forms in concrete which ignore former conventions in design are likewise the product of a process of "resolution into basic elements" (for a slab is an

277. MAILLART. Arve Bridge, 1936–37. *Supports and two of the box-like arches. Like archaic Greek idols, they stand in rows under the platform of the bridge.*

278. Dipylon Vase, seventh century B.C. *Detail. On archaic Dipylon vases the geometric abbreviations of human bodies are characterized by the triangular articulation of the hip joint. Maillart, on the other hand, is conceiving structural elements in approaching organic growth.*

irreducible element) that uses reconstruction as a means of attaining a more rational synthesis.

In this connection mention should be made of the "eggshell" concrete vaulting which Freyssinet used for some locomotive sheds he built at Bagneux, outside Paris, in 1929, though since then that particular branch of reinforced concrete engineering has produced forms of almost fantastic daring. On the same principle of using the slab as an active structural member, the

279. MOHOLY–NAGY. Painting, 1924.

280. ALVAR AALTO. Armchair.

281. FREYSSINET. Locomotive sheds at Bagneux, near Paris, 1929. *Eggshell-thin reinforced slabs which can be bent like cardboard, change the former straight shed into a vault, providing excellent lighting.*

282. MAILLART. Cement Hall, Swiss National Exhibition, Zurich, 1939. *Two stiffening ribs end in two pairs of supports. A connecting gangway — as in Maillart's bridges — is an active part of the structure.*

462

Finnish architect, Alvar Aalto, has struck out an entirely new line in furniture design. He uses thin sheets of plywood, which, like the concrete slab, was formerly regarded as useless for purposes of structural support (*fig.* **280**).

In the community of method which now prevails in so many departments of human activity we may read a presage of far-reaching developments. The growth of this spontaneous identity of approach and its repercussions on society are being separately studied in every branch of knowledge. That there is a remarkable analogy between recent departures in philosophy, physics, literature, art, and music is a fact which has frequently been commented on. In the light of the particular case we have just examined, it is worth considering whether the field of structural engineering cannot be included as well. New methods are new tools for the creation of new types of reality. The greater the degree of identity in respect to what is fundamental to each of the creative spheres, and the closer the extent of their approximation to one another in terms of achievement, the sooner will the requisites for a new phase of culture be forthcoming.

Robert Maillart was born in 1872 and died in April 1940. He died at the age of sixty-eight; nevertheless one feels that it was too early and that his life work was not accomplished.

His bridges, immaterially spun in space, belong through their supreme sensitiveness to the purest expression that our period has been able to achieve.

During his lifetime his country did not recognize his significance. He was often hampered and his intentions misunderstood, so that he did not give all that he might have given. We know that this is to be explained as a result of the difference between the advanced intellectual and the undeveloped emotional perception that exists today in so many of us — one of the factors that most effectively prevents the organic development of our culture.

Afterword

Maillart's life was a continuous fight against economic pressures and public apathy.

In 1912 he was called to Russia, where he constructed large factories and warehouses — most of which were Swiss investments — in Kharkov, Riga, Leningrad. After the revolution of 1917, he returned to his own country, penniless and heavily in debt to Swiss banks.

It is not the prerogative of the historian to speculate on what could have happened if developments had moved in another direction. But in the case of Maillart one cannot stop thinking what would have come about if a call from the United States instead of from the Czarist empire had reached him in 1912.

Like Brancusi, Maillart limited himself to a few forms and fundamental ideas which he never abandoned and which demanded a lifetime to be developed to their last crystalline shape. His main inventions, the bridge conceived as a single structural unit and the building conceived as a unit, were achieved before he was forty.

"Maillart's development in thirty years of research unfolds organically, springing from that inner power which enables every great artist or scientist to transcend the existing technical knowledge through his vision. One had only to talk with Maillart to realize at once that he was a man who had absolute confidence in his imagination. He often designed his bridges with a single curve on a scrap of paper while en route from his Zurich office to his Bern office. The specialist's simple calculations would have been too insufficient a guide toward new solutions where invention, in the fullest sense of the word, plays a more decisive part than calculation. It is significant of Maillart that he made calculation a servant and not a master. His bridges satisfy the feeling by the poetic expression which pervades them, and the mind by their delicate equipoise." [9]

---

[9] Since these lines were written in 1934 and two pages were devoted to a simple footbridge over a creek near Zurich (S. Giedion, "Nouveaux Ponts de Maillart," *Cahiers d'Art*, vol. IX, 1934, nos. 1–4), Maillart's name has acquired the weight denied him during his life and in his own country. The general public was introduced to his works through an exhibition initiated by the Museum of Modern Art, which commissioned us to assemble the material in Switzerland. For the first article on Maillart, see S. Giedion, "Maillart, Constructeurs des Planchers à Champignons," *Cahiers d'Art*, vol. V (1930), no. 3. For further information, see Max Bill, *Robert Maillart* (Zurich, 1949), a compilation of his work with pictures and drawings. Specialists may be di-

283.   MAILLART.   Cement Hall, Swiss National Exhibition, Zurich, 1939.   *Parabolic barrel vault of extreme thinness (six centimeters) touches the unsolved vaulting problem of our period.   A sturdy construction and yet hovering over the earth like a silken balloon ready to rise.   Span of the vault, sixteen meters;   height of the vault, twelve meters.*

Maillart's most important works, however, were nearly all accomplished during the last ten years of his life.   As he advanced in age, his bridges became more daring in their aspect and more imbued with the vigor of youth.

rected to the excellent monographs of Professor M. Roš, Federal Institute of Technology, Zurich, for research on text reports of some of Maillart's bridges.

A bridge is like a house. Each bridge and each house is a
special case; each must be constructed and shaped according
to the environment with which it must cope and the function
it is to have.

As we have seen, Maillart conceived different systems for the
construction of bridges. The stiffened arch, which is nowhere
more beautifully realized than in the curved Schwandbach-
Brücke (*figs*. **270, 271**) led to almost eggshell-thin members.
Unfortunately, none of his later projects employing the stiffened arch ever saw execution. It is the most daring of his
constructions, the least verifiable by calculation and the most
opposed to the ruling taste.

Another system which he used for narrow and long spans
with heavy loads is based on the principle of the continuous
beam. This he further enhanced by hollowing out the heavy
structure so that it gave an aspect of astonishing lightness. He
built several very interesting smaller bridges in this way (for
instance, the oblique river crossing at Gündlischwand, Berner
Oberland, 1937) but reached highest perfection in the bridge
over the Rhône at Aire-la-Ville-Peney in 1937. Here the
slablike column supports merge with the platform and the
arches, which seem to be imbued with the elasticity of a steel
spring and the suppleness of a willow branch. This bridge
was never executed. A jury incapable of judgment rejected it.

From his early beginnings — about 1901 — to his last bridges,
he developed the three-hinged arch with hollowed-out boxlike
sections. He gave an elasticity to this type such as was previously known only in iron bridges. The Tavanasa bridge of
1905 (*fig*. **268**) was the first conceived out of a pure form.
The Salginatobel bridge built in 1929–30 (*fig*. **269**) uses this
system under daring conditions.

The section of the arch takes on a more and more precise
U-sectioned form. In the bridge over the Thur, 1933 (*fig*.
273), two arches are placed parallel to one another. The Arve
bridge, 1936–37 (*fig*. **275**) uses three parallel U-sectioned
arches, combining them with utmost skill and sensitivity with
the elastic supports. The repetitive use of standardized elements is of great economical advantage, for the same scaf-

folding and shuttering can be used several times. From the viewpoint of aesthetics, the reëmployment of identical elements is even more decisive.

In Maillart's last bridges, the problems to be solved become more complicated but conversely the solutions more simple. The bridge over the Simme built in 1940 (*figs.* **286, 288**) and the bridge near Lachen (*fig.* **284**) completed in 1940 after his death are his solution to the problem of an oblique crossing. The bridge near Lachen with its twin arches forms a highway overpass on the Zurich-Arlberg railway line where highway and tracks intersect at an acute angle. Maillart used parallel U-shaped girders here as in the Thur and Arve bridges. According to the needs of this situation, the abutments and the arches start at different levels and one behind the other. Maillart was awarded this last contract because he was able to produce a design for this unusual situation within a few days, faster than any of his competitors.

In the Simme bridge, 1940 (*fig.* **288**) Maillart reaches his highest degree of simplification. The girders meet in the center like a pair of knives. The question cannot be wholly dismissed: Was this the limit? What would the next step have been?

Some hints, if only very fragmentary, should be given on the relation of Maillart's constructional methods with practical achievements and their aesthetic impact.

Arches and supports

Together with the lowering of the height of the arch between center pin and abutment goes the new shaping of the arch. The bridge over the Salginatobel (1929–30) still clings to the continuous masonry arch (*fig.* **269**) even if the construction is completely revolutionized. The bridge over the Thur (1933) shows how reinforcement of this type leads from the curved masonry arch to the pointed arch (*fig.* **273**). In the bridge over the Simme (1940), a straight line of enormous strength springs from the abutment to the center hinge (*fig.* **288**). It is as if one could see the unbent reinforcing rods embedded in the concrete. Nothing is left of the traditional arch; the ultimate simplification seems to have been reached.

284. MAILLART. Bridge at Lachan, 1940. *Span, 40 meters; width, 8 meters; system, three-hinged arch. The bridge forms a highway crossing over the railway line from Zurich to Arlberg. Highway and tracks cross at acute angles. The independently constructed box-sectioned arches start at different levels and one behind the other, thus solving the problem of the oblique crossing. This bridge was finished after Maillart's death.*

285. MAILLART. Bridge at Lachan. *The joint of the arch.*

286. MAILLART. Bridge over the Simme, Berner Oberland, 1940. *Span, 32 meters; width, 7.9 meters; system, three-hinged arch of two hollow rib girders. This bridge shows the highest degree of simplification. A straight line of enormous strength springs from the abutment up to the center pin. The girders meet in the center like a pair of knives. Nothing is left of the traditional arch. (Compare the girders of the Galerie des Machines, p. 289.)*

287.   MAILLART.   Bridge at Lachan, 1910.

288.   MAILLART.   Bridge over the Simme, 1910.

Maillart had a particular sensitivity, an almost intuitive understanding of the forces which act upon a structure. He felt, like a dowser discovering the course of subterranean waters, movements and forces running through it and tried to form it as the artist tries to reveal emotions through irrational curves. Steel rods and concrete were not dead materials to him.

What he formed out of an artifact — ferroconcrete — was an organism in which every particle throbs with life. He never permitted dead masses or excess weight where shrinkage-cracks easily develop. He hollowed out his girders, reduced the dimensions of supports to the utmost.

This requires an imaginative, flexible mind in close contact with nature, and not the bookkeeper's mentality of the mere calculator. Against such as these and their academic representatives, Maillart waged a lifelong struggle.

Every part of a construction had its active role. Even an aqueduct crossing a valley (Châtelard, Canton Valais, 1925–26) assumes under his hand an astonishing shape that strikes the senses immediately without the explanation that in this case the water conduit is formed like the box girders of his bridges and the inclined supports are so conceived that they form with the bottom of the conduit the active parts of a vault.

Maillart's almost organic formations can be best understood by means of the various ways he treats supports and the changes they undergo in accordance with the conditions with which they must cope. We only direct attention to the unusual form of the articulated supports of the triple arch of the Arve bridge of 1936 (*fig.* **274**). Maillart simply said he did not employ steel joints as elastic supports for reasons of economy. Using only ferroconcrete, he shaped the cross-like elastic slab supports (*fig.* **275**) which stand, like archaic Greek idols (*figs.* **277, 278**), in double rows of three under the platform of the bridge. By tapering the supports in the middle and inserting an ingenious armament, he gave the rigid slab the properties of a flexible joint (*fig.* **276**).

470

The system of these bridges, in which all parts are active, keeps them in a state of continual tension. The inexplicable urge of this period to impart the highest tension to people, material, and things is symbolized in Maillart's work.

Toward the end of his life, Maillart was at last given an opportunity of expressing himself, without the constricting necessity of solving practical problems, in the pavilion of the Swiss Portland Cement Company at the Swiss national exhibition of 1939 (*fig.* **283**). Here he could reveal the art and elegance that a ferroconcrete structure can display. This hall was destined from the outset to be destroyed for the sake of experiments in tensile strength. And yet this mere "test-tube building" became a part of history.

A parabolic barrel vault of extreme thinness (six centimeters) — the back part of it slightly conical — touches the earth by two pairs of slender supports in the middle (*fig.* **284**). Ascending and encompassing the vault, they form two stiffening ribs which, together with the connecting gangway spanning the interval between them, are all that Maillart needed to produce a sturdy construction hovering over the earth like a silken balloon about to rise.

Kurt Schwitters, the Dadaist poet and painter, once remarked: "When an artist spits, it is art." In the hands of a great engineer, this pavilion, conceived only to combine strength and the utmost lightness, became at once a work of art.

This light and solid barrel vault could easily be thought of as a part of a civic center. Maillart touches unconsciously on the unsolved vaulting problem of our period. With a very few exceptions — Le Corbusier, Aalto, and some others — the contemporary architect is rather hesitant as soon as he touches on the sphere of the ceiling, where he can let loose his imagination. The nineteenth-century genius gave form to the airy spans of the great exhibition buildings. But iron lattice girders are ephemeral in nature. The most brilliant halls have disappeared, and the Eiffel Tower will only stand as long as its rivets are continually checked and its structural members safeguarded from rust.

289. Japanese wooden bridge of the eighteenth century.

What will be the vault of our period in the great public buildings to come? Reinforced concrete and especially eggshell-thin slabs which can be bent like cardboard have both the buoyancy we like and the permanence we like. The slab with mesh reinforcement was used by Maillart and by Freyssinet (*figs.* **281, 282**) in the form of eggshells curved in one direction. It was employed in circular form in flattened domes for market halls in Algeciras, water tanks in the United States, and gambling casinos in Brazil.[10] The engineer Ove Arup, together with the Architects' Coöperative Partnership, roofed an English factory building (1947–48) with nine concrete shells, nineteen thirty-seconds of an inch thick and curved in two directions.

All that is needed are architects who know how to stir the imagination of the engineer. The engineer is capable of fulfilling emotional needs just as he is capable of solving the most intricate practical problems. Maillart's Cement Hall points in this direction. He, as the humble servant of architects, constructed a very large number of buildings which do not

[10] "Shell Concrete Construction," Dr. K. Hajnal-Kónyi, in *Architects' Yearbook*, vol. II (London, 1947).

reveal that he had anything to do with them. He never encountered an architect who fully knew how to integrate his genius. Where he was great, he was alone.

Maillart is not an isolated case. It belongs to the unhappy constitution of this period that engineers like Maillart, sculptors like Brancusi, Arp, or Pevsner, painters like Picasso or Léger, have to create their works in isolation. They do not find a concomitant receptiveness, and therefore this period has produced fragments, worthy entities in themselves, but an orchestration in an encompassing whole seems to be denied it.

WALTER GROPIUS AND THE GERMAN DEVELOP-MENT

Germany in the Nineteenth Century

Manual production methods are deeply rooted in the German temperament. Industrial liberty, proclaimed in France in 1791, was not adopted in Prussia until 1846. It did not come to the south of Germany until 1862. There was a great crisis in England during the second decade of the nineteenth century as a consequence of the change from hand to mechanized production. In France in 1835 hand weavers were declared to be "in the last spasms of agony." Gustav Schmoller, the economist, notes that this period in Germany witnessed an increase in the percentage of manual workers and a marked trend toward production by small artisans.

Belated industrialization of Germany

During the nineteenth century the number of power spindles in a country was an accurate index of its degree of industrialization. In the year 1865 there was one such spindle in Germany to three in France and eight in England. Other branches of industry showed parallel stages of development, including the steamship and the railroad, which, as Sombart says, entered Germany "on the crutches of English industry."

American industry was only in the first stages of its development in the first half of the nineteenth century. But, as later developments indicate, there was a fundamental difference between the two countries. From the start, the American spirit was orientated toward mechanized production.

Violent
industrialization
from 1870 on

But around 1870 a rapid transformation sets in and steadily gains speed. Germany, the country of the hand worker and the farmer, drives on with the aim of becoming not only an industrialized state but the leader of the industrial age.

This early indifference to the machine and the factory followed by a headlong acceptance had serious human and psychological consequences. The deep uncertainty that prevailed at this period in Germany is reflected in its architecture. Other countries were expanding, but their architecture shows nothing like so complete a loss of inner equilibrium and confusion with regard to fundamental principles as was seen in Germany. There was nothing that resembled William Morris' work in England during the sixties, nothing comparable to the Chicago school of 1880 or the Belgian movement in the nineties.

Increased efforts
in applied arts
after 1900

About 1900 there was another sudden change in Germany of quite a different kind. In the seventies there had been a great drive to catch up with the advance of industry; now there was the same kind of violent effort to overtake the developments in the realm of human feeling. It was at this time that Morris and Ruskin aroused the greatest admiration in Germany. Henri van de Velde was invited to exhibit there in 1897 and created a huge sensation. New movements sprang up in both Germany and Austria. For the next three decades Germany remained the country most hospitable to foreign ideas. The magnificent German edition of Frank Lloyd Wright's works that appeared in 1910 is only one among many instances of this receptivity. There were exhibitions by the advanced painters like those held in Brussels between 1880 and 1890, and the outstanding foreign architects were invited to build on an equal footing with their German colleagues.

New movements
in architecture

In the late nineties the impulse for new movements in architecture came first from Austria, from Otto Wagner and even from Adolf Loos, whose work held more hints for the future than that of the long-overestimated Alfred Messel (1853–1909). Messel's huge Berlin department store — built at the same time as Berlage's Amsterdam Stock Exchange — had only local influence.

474

Peter Behrens (born in 1868) epitomizes German architecture at the start of the twentieth century. He rapidly became famous as a result of approaching the industrial plant as an architectonic problem. Behrens consciously transformed the factory into a dignified place of work. Despite the classical severity and the Cyclopean forms of his buildings, Behrens trained the eye to grasp the expressive forces concealed in such new materials as steel and glass, as his Berlin turbine factory of 1909 shows.

Peter Behrens: industrial architecture

The atelier of Peter Behrens was the most important in Germany. Mies van der Rohe, Gropius, and even Le Corbusier worked there, the latter for five months.[1]

When a freshly industrialized Germany set out to make up lost ground in the realm of feeling, the effort produced several minor Renaissances in the courts of the small principalities.

The Maecenas of the movement

At Darmstadt, for example, the Grossherzog Ludwig von Hessen attempted to revive the spirit of artistic creation by forming a colony of artists and fine craftsmen.[2] The Grand Duke of Sachsen-Weimar called Henri van de Velde to his court — thereby following, with less energy and conviction, the example of Goethe's patron, his ancestor. Numerous German Maecenases appeared. There was K. E. Osthaus, who gave van de Velde his first chance to build in Germany and commissioned sculptors like Georges Minne and Aristide Maillol to execute work for his gardens and his museum. Then there were leading industrialists like Emil Rathenau, the president of the A.E.G. (the General Electric Company), who engaged Peter Behrens as artistic supervisor of everything from the trade-mark of the company to the design of street lamps and the erection of new plants.

All these endeavors of a country which had grown rich and self-consciously progressive during the past three decades

Deutsche Werkbund, 1907

---

[1] Le Corbusier's first, and now very rare, book is called, *Étude sur le mouvement d'art décoratif en Allemagne* (Chaux-de-Fonds, 1912). It was one of the first criticisms of the German movement.

[2] The houses which they produced for themselves (Peter Behrens' first house was one of them), together with their interior equipment and specimen works in the arts and crafts, were exhibited at the Mathildenhöhe, Darmstadt, in 1901. This was the first of those coöperative enterprises by German artists which were to prove so important in the future.

found their natural center in the Deutsche Werkbund, established in 1907.[3] Its chief aim was "the refinement of workmanship and the enhancement of the quality of production." Artist, workman, and industrialist were to collaborate in producing honest goods of artistic value.

The idea behind the Werkbund was not in itself a new one. Sir Henry Cole, one of the early English industrial reformers, founded "Art Manufacturers" in 1847 to "promote public taste" through "beauty applied to mechanical production." It was his efforts that led to the Great London Exhibition of 1851 and the Crystal Palace. The generation that followed William Morris made peace with industry and returned to Cole's line of attack with the formation of the arts and crafts guilds. In 1907, sixty years after the Art Manufacturers, the ground seemed to have been prepared for a final reconciliation: it seemed quite possible to bring art and industry into full collaboration.

The Werkbund; outlet for youthful talents in its exhibitions

The clash of opposed opinions marked the Werkbund almost from its inception. Throughout these controversies, however, the group worked steadily to create openings for youthful talents and found responsible roles for them at just the right moments. Both the rising generation and the generation that was at its height were represented in the Deutsche Werkbund's 1914 exhibition at Cologne. Next to works by Peter Behrens, Josef Hoffmann, and Henri van de Velde stood Bruno Taut's glass house and the office building by Walter Gropius. The Gropius building was the work most discussed at the exhibition, and embodied the most seeds for future development.

Even after the war years and the period of inflation, the Werkbund was capable of actions that ensure it a place in history. The Weissenhof settlement of 1927 is evidence of the group's steady efforts to bring the creative forces of the period to realization. Germany was impoverished, and there was a shortage of materials, when the magnificent gesture was made of inviting creative artists from every country to erect buildings at Stuttgart.

[3] There is an excellent account of its founding in Heinrich Waentig's *Wirtschaft und Kunst* (Jena, 1909), pp. 292 ff.

At about the same time the architect Ernst May was called in to organize the housing development on the outskirts of Frankfort-on-Main. May worked with Haussmannean speed and energy; he was not fortunate enough, however, to be granted a seventeen-year period for his operations. After a few years the whole enterprise was cut short — a familiar happening in German history. While the work continued, May showed the open-mindedness which marked the Deutsche Werkbund by employing foreign architects, several Austrians and a Dutchman, Mart Stam.

Housing development

In 1929 the government — through the Deutsche Werkbund — gave Mies van der Rohe full charge of the German pavilion at the Barcelona exhibition. In 1930 Walter Gropius was chosen to organize the first German exhibition at the Paris Salon since the war.

New prestige of the architect

The Werkbund period witnessed a complete change in the status of the architect in Germany. In this period he ceased to be subservient to clients and contractors, as he is in so many countries even now. It was recognized that the architect had a part in forming the spirit of his times.

290. WALTER GROPIUS. Fagus works, 1911–13.

Walter Gropius

Walter Gropius entered upon his career in the Germany of the Werkbund period. After finishing his studies he worked in the office of Peter Behrens. This was from 1907 to 1910, when Behrens was engaged on the turbine plant of the General Electric Company in Berlin. Gropius at the same time took part in discussions at the newly founded Deutsche Werkbund, which helped to crystallize his ideas "as to what the essential nature of building ought to be." [4]

The Fagus works: a new architectonic language

The first large commission which Gropius received after opening his own offices was from the Fagus works. The shoe-last factory which he built for them at Alfeld a.d. Leine in 1911 was a sudden and unexpected statement of a new architectonic language. While he was with Behrens, Gropius had seen his turbine plant — at that time "the modern building *par excellence*" — take form. The moment he set to work for himself he dropped his master's classical solemnity entirely and made the new aims of architecture clearly apparent. In the Fagus works, Gropius brought together the accomplishments of the past fifteen years, and in doing so he furnished an incentive for that "honesty of thought and feeling" which he himself values. [5] The break between thinking and feeling which had been the bone-sickness of European architecture was healed.

Plane surfaces predominate in this factory. The glass and iron walls are joined cleanly at the corners without the intervention of piers (*fig.* **291**). The contrast with the massive corners of Behrens' turbine plant of 1907 is marked. "The role of the walls [is] restricted to that of mere screens stretched between the upright columns of the framework to keep out rain, cold, and noise." It is "as a direct result of the growing preponderance of voids over solids" that "glass is assuming an ever greater structural importance." [6]

Balance between architectural and constructional means

The building still retains all its original freshness. It marks an outright leap over the transition period that usually precedes the crystallization in a building of a new architectonic concept. The American critic, Henry-Russell Hitchcock, is not

---

[4] Walter Gropius, *The New Architecture and the Bauhaus* (London, 1937), p. 33.
[5] *Ibid.*, p. 17.　　　　　　　　　　　[6] *Ibid.*, pp. 22–23.

478

291. WALTER GROPIUS. Fagus works (shoe-last factory), Alfeld a.d. Leine, 1911. *The glass and iron walls are cleanly joined at the corners, without the intervention of piers. "The role of the walls [is] restricted to that of mere screens stretched between the upright columns of the frame work."*

likely to be challenged when he calls it "the most advanced piece of architecture built before the war." [7] The hint of the theatrical in Behrens' work has disappeared. The new potentialities of iron, glass, and concrete, the cleaner treatment of the wall, the organic illumination of the interior — all these are brought into a clearly thought-out balance. Regarded simply as a structure, the building is part of a tradition that reaches back to the great iron constructions of Eiffel in the last quarter of the nineteenth century. The duality that marked the nineteenth century has been overcome, however; architectonic and constructional means contribute equally to a unified expression. The walls are developed as planes, and conceived as sheer curtains between inner and outer space. This view of their function "naturally leads to a progressively bolder (i.e., wider) opening up of the wall surfaces, which allows rooms to be much better lit." [8] The pillars are set behind the façade so that its curtain character is fully realized. It is undeniable that the way in which the volumes of the various

---

[7] Catalogue of the Museum of Modern Art, *Modern Architecture* (New York, 1932), p. 57.   [8] Gropius, *The New Architecture*, p. 22.

buildings are freely juxtaposed foreshadows the scheme for the 1925 Bauhaus at Dessau. It is not only the façade which gives the factory its novel brightness; glass walls instead of the normal closed partitions are used in the offices. Behrens made a factory which was like a monument; Gropius gave it a simple and more humane interpretation.

New elements in the Gropius model factory, Cologne, 1914

The "Fabrik," Gropius' model factory and office building at the Werkbund's Cologne exhibition of 1914 (*fig.* **292**), had a covered terrace for dancing on the roof, a hall of machinery and open garages at the rear. It has, however, some architec-

292. WALTER GROPIUS. Court elevation of the "Fabrik," Werkbund exhibition, Cologne, 1914. *Glass-walled offices and the covered terrace on the roof.*

tonic features which give it a new character. Before this, in the Fagus works, Gropius had discarded the normal stone enclosure of the staircase and replaced it by a shell of glass and iron. He repeated this practice in his Cologne building but handled it in an entirely new way. Here there were spiral staircases entirely encased in glass. They seem like a movement seized and immobilized in space (*fig.* **293**).

Our senses — slaves to habits built up during the centuries — automatically seek for the supports of projecting parts such as these staircases. The new conception of space, with its urge toward freely hovering parts and surfaces, leads one in exactly the contrary direction. It seeks the kind of aesthetic sensation that results when the relation between load and support is no longer traditionally obvious.

In the Gropius building at the Cologne exhibition (unfortunately destroyed by fire during the war years) it is notable that the roof was treated with the same care and skill that was devoted to other integral parts of the structure. The upper terraces provided space for the elevator and for dancing, with the whole area unified by a covered garden. Such details are never casual or accidental results; just because they outrun contemporary developments, they can only be created by minds unconsciously touched by the future.[9]

Post-War Germany and the Bauhaus

All the vigorous efforts of the decade before the war ended in disillusionment. The arts and crafts movement was seen to have worked itself out. It had, indeed, done much to eliminate fashions that were carry-overs from the previous period, but improvements in furniture and reforms in household taste opened up no real outlet for continued future development. In the German movement, architecture was swallowed up by the applied arts. This in itself shows that the movement produced reforms but no new positive conceptions, since without a new conception there can be no new architecture. Solutions such as the Fagus works (1911–14) were isolated exceptions that could not make their influence felt at the moment.

A state of widespread uncertainty once more prevailed. This uncertainty was, so to speak, the working-capital — not the object of attack — of the expressionist movement. German expressionism had its beginnings previous to the war, continued to develop while the war lasted, and reached its height in the years immediately after the war. The movement eloquently states the grievances of mishandled humanity and indicts a tragic situation. But there is a fundamental dif-

Expressionism

---

[9] Contemporaries were rather undecided about the "Fabrik." Cf. the critique of Walter Gropius by Theodor Heuss in *Die Hilfe* (Berlin), July 2, 1914.

293. WALTER GROPIUS. Spiral staircase on corner of the "Fabrik," Cologne, 1914. *These staircases entirely enclosed in glass seem like movements seized and immobilized in space.*

ference between expressionism and other movements we have encountered — cubism, futurism, and the rest. Faustean outbursts against an inimical world and the cries of outraged humanity cannot create new levels of achievement. They remain transitory facts — however moving they may be — and not constituent ones. The other movements had the spirit of invention in them: they did not weep over a time out of joint; they pointed to the way out, found — amidst the chaos — concealed patterns for a new life.

The expressionist influence could not be a healthy one or perform any service for architecture. Nevertheless it touched almost every German worker in the arts. Men who were later to do grimly serious work in housing developments abandoned themselves to a romantic mysticism, dreamed of fairy castles to stand on the peak of Monte Rosa. Others built concrete towers as flaccid as jellyfish.

This was the situation into which the Bauhaus came at its birth. The surviving ideals of the Werkbund proved its salvation: from the very beginning it set itself to unite art and industrial life and to find the keynote for a sound contemporary architecture. But even here, in the early productions of the Bauhaus and in some lesser works by Walter Gropius, traces of the literary, expressionistic approach appear. Expressionism infiltrated all German art.

Gropius was instinctively aware of the inadequacy of expressionism and of the need to escape from it. The war had left some vacancies on the staffs of the two schools at Weimar, the school of design and the school of applied arts. When Gropius united these schools to form the Bauhaus he tried to find teachers who had not worked in the field of applied arts. He gave the preliminary course to the young Swiss painter, Johannes Itten. Itten, while teaching in Vienna, had developed a completely new method for educating the tactile sense, the sense of color, and the sense of space and composition. It was this method of approach that baffled the public all through the Bauhaus period. The German sculptor Gerhard Marcks and the American-born Lyonel Feininger also came in with Itten at the beginning. Feininger was one of the few expressionists interested in problems of space.

Founding of the Bauhaus, 1919

The Swiss-German Paul Klee joined the staff in 1921. After this more and more men were recruited from the abstractionist groups: first Oskar Schlemmer, in 1921; then, in 1922, Wassily Kandinsky (who had been working on abstract compositions since 1911), and in 1923, L. Moholy-Nagy. The successive appointments of these men mark an ever stronger tendency toward the abstract movements and reflect the stages through which the Bauhaus passed.

Second stage in its evolution

Moholy-Nagy, a young Hungarian, was linked with the whole abstractionist movement by personal associations as well as through his own productions. His role in the Bauhaus has often been misunderstood. As editor of the Bauhaus books [10] he actively defended its ideas and gave the initiators of new movements in many countries the chance to address the Ger-

---

[10] Cf. *The Bauhaus, 1919–1928* (New York, 1938), pp. 222–223, edited by Herbert Bayer, Walter Gropius, and Ise Gropius. The bibliography by Beaumont Newhall embraces all the relevant literature on the subject. The book as a whole gives such an excellent account of the details of the Bauhaus development that there is no need in this discussion to retrace the same ground.

294. WALTER GROPIUS. Deutsche Werkbund exhibition, Paris, 1930. *Club lounge shown in cut-away section of a slablike many-storied apartment house.*

man public directly. Besides this, he helped through his own activities to overcome the lingering remnants of romantic mysticism.

Third stage The third stage in the development of the Bauhaus, bringing it into closer contact with industry, came about when it moved from Weimar to Dessau. At that time the Bauhaus showed its powers of self-renewal by adding to its staff from the groups of its former students. Among those who became masters in the school were Josef Albers, Herbert Bayer (typography), and Marcel Breuer.

The Bauhaus was soon well known all over Europe in those circles where the elements of a contemporary art were being sought — the Dutch "Stijl" group, for example. Theo von Doesburg himself came to Weimar in 1922 but, for various reasons, never acted as one of the Bauhaus teachers. The Stijl group's influence on the Bauhaus — underrated and overrated with about equal frequency — was on the side of the formal approach to aesthetic problems, of their reduction to basic elements and basic relations.

As far as public opinion was concerned, all the Bauhaus leaders were taken, in spite of their actual differences, as advocates of one artistic doctrine, a doctrine which was as cordially detested by the expressionists as it was by the conventional and the academic. Political divisions were likewise forgotten: Gropius and the Bauhaus came under attack by Left and Right wing elements equally. According to Leftist critics, "no art school, however good, could be anything but an anachronism at this time" (1928). Critics of the Right, seeing the Bauhaus program of education as only so many unrelated activities, and judging them from either the academic or the arts and crafts point of view, could see no sense at all to the venture.

The work of the Bauhaus can be grasped only when the conception behind modern painting has been understood. Without an understanding of the feeling which has developed out of the new sense for space and the new interest in textures and plain surfaces, the studies of the Bauhaus fall to pieces.

The École Polytechnique of 1797 was dedicated to the fusion of science and life. At the Bauhaus under Gropius the effort was made to unite art and industry, art and daily life, using architecture as the intermediary. Now that it is possible to see the whole Bauhaus institution in its historical relationships, we recognize what an important outlet it was for the German gift of teaching and organizing. The principles of contemporary art were there for the first time translated into the field of education. Dispersed tendencies were brought together and concentrated.[11] This treatment of the Bauhaus has been lim-

---

[11] Very early in his career Gropius saw that the exhibition could serve as an instrument for just such a coördination of new tendencies and conceptions. He wanted to use the exhibition systematically as a means for presenting ideas — that is, with all its features adjusted to one general point of view. He worked in this direction, at first quite alone, later with his old associates at the Bauhaus — Moholy-Nagy, Breuer, Bayer, and others. Their collaborative efforts developed a new type of exhibition in which every modern technique of display was called into service.

At the 1930 exhibition of the Salon des Artistes Décorateurs in Paris, the Werkbund was invited to participate. This was the first official foreign exhibition since the war to admit

295. WALTER GROPIUS. Project for an international academy of philosophical studies, 1924. *This advanced scheme was produced two years before the Bauhaus, which is foreshadowed in its open planning. Meant for the university town of Erlangen, it would have combined dormitories and common rooms. The idea of such an academy was typical of the internationalist spirit which prevailed in Germany during this period.*

ited to those of its aspects which have a bearing on our constant concern: the way in which this period has moved toward consciousness of itself. The vital and difficult development of the Bauhaus reflects that process in the circumscribed realm of education as no other institution of the period does.

The establishment of practical connections between industry and the Bauhaus and the manner in which these relations functioned fall outside our subject. We can only note how a system of education based upon fundamental conceptions of our period and conducted by genuinely creative artists supplied industry with a variety of models for its products. Experimental handiwork in the Bauhaus shops led to articles of

German entries. Gropius and Breuer showed a club lounge interior mounted in a section of a slablike modern apartment block (fig. 294) designed by Gropius. By this time the old animosities had subsided, and the French critics greeted the display with surprise and admiration. For many of them it was the first revelation of what had been accomplished in Germany during the post-war years.

Exhibitions in which Gropius participated are: World's Exhibition, Antwerp, 1912 (interior); Werkbund Exhibition, Cologne, 1914 (the "Fabrik," series of interior rooms; officers' quarters for warships, automobile bodies); Werkbund Exhibition, Paris, 1930, Building Exhibition, Berlin, 1931 (scheme for a many-storied apartment block, with Schawinsky); Berlin Exhibition, 1933 (display in nonferrous metals, with Joost Schmidt).

industry which were reproduced all over the world: lighting fixtures, carpets, fabrics, and the famous tubular steel furniture. Manufacturers in neighboring countries began to seek Bauhaus-trained supervisors of their productions.

The Bauhaus Buildings at Dessau, 1926

The building program for the new school at Dessau had to meet many different requirements. There was first the Bauhaus — the School of Design — itself; then the school of the city of Dessau for continuation courses in the trades; finally, combination studio and dwelling quarters for the students had to be provided. A dining hall, a stage, administration rooms, and a private studio for Gropius were also necessary. The instructors were given houses, also designed by Gropius, in a small pine wood. The architect's chief aim was to produce a clear separation of each of these functions from the others, at the same time not isolating them but bringing them together into efficient interrelation.

The chief accents fall on the Bauhaus, the nucleus of the whole school (*fig.* **296**). The Bauhaus combines "laboratories of design" with exhibition spaces, classrooms, and lecture halls. The laboratories of design were devoted to such various activities as cabinetmaking, theatrical crafts, dyeing, weaving, printing, wall coverings, and metalworking. On the third floor the lecture halls and the laboratories for metalworking and wall painting could be thrown together to make a single room. The Bauhaus is enclosed by the famous glass curtains. The section containing the pupils' studio-dormitory rooms rises six stories. The twenty-eight rooms it contains require the hyphenated title because each is intended not only for the student's residence but for his private work as well. Each has a small balcony, a concrete slab which juts out into open space. These slabs, hovering close to the massive wall, give the building its singular and exciting aspect. The students' building connects directly with the School of Design through a one-story wing. The wing ingeniously combines an assembly hall, the dining hall, and the stage of the school. These rooms can be thrown open to form a single hall accessible from the "aula," or main entrance hall of the whole school.

296. WALTER GRO-PIUS. The Bauhaus, Dessau, 1926. *Air view. This air view shows how the different units blend together. The eye cannot sum up such a complex at one glance.*

297. WALTER GRO-PIUS. The Bauhaus, Dessau, 1926. *Plot plan. This complex reaches out over the ground and expands into a kind of pinwheel with three hooked arms.*

A separate wing was reserved for the Dessau trade school. A short two-story bridge, supported by four pillars and crossing an intervening street, connects it with the School of Design. This *passerelle* or connecting bridge was reserved for administration rooms, meeting places for the masters' and students' councils, the architectural department, and the private atelier of Gropius.

The Bauhaus has a skeleton of reinforced concrete. Because of the German building ordinances, the supporting pillars are much heavier than they would have been in France or Switzerland. The continuous glass curtain is brought into abrupt juxtaposition with the horizontal ribbons of white curtain wall at the top and bottom of the building. An aerial photograph shows them plainly for what they are: mere ribbons, supporting nothing. In a bird's-eye view the whole cube seems like two immense horizontal planes floating over the ground.

Significance of the glass curtain

The glass curtain is not the limited and marked-off transparent area which Eiffel had already exploited in the 1878 exhibition: it flows smoothly around the building, the corners showing no vertical supporting or binding members. As in the Fagus works, the pillars from which it hangs are set behind the glass, making the curtain a specimen of pure cantilever construction. The glass curtain is simply folded about the corners of the building; in other words, the glass walls blend into each other at just the point where the human eye expects to encounter guaranteed support for the load of the building (*fig.* **299**).

Two major endeavors of modern architecture are fulfilled here, not as unconscious outgrowths of advances in engineering but as the conscious realization of an artist's intent; there is the hovering, vertical grouping of planes which satisfies our feeling for a relational space, and there is the extensive transparency that permits interior and exterior to be seen simultaneously, *en face* and *en profile*, like Picasso's "L'Arlésienne" of 1911–12 (*fig.* **298**): variety of levels of reference, or of points of reference, and simultaneity — the conception of space-time, in short. In this building Gropius goes far beyond anything that might be regarded as an achievement in construction alone.

Picasso and Gropius

298. PICASSO. "L'Arlésienne," 1911–12. *Oil.* "*In the head may be seen the cubist device of simultaneity — showing two aspects of a single object at the same time, in this case the profile and the full face. The transparency of overlapping planes is also characteristic*" (*Catalogue of the Picasso Exhibition, Museum of Modern Art, New York, 1939, p. 77*).

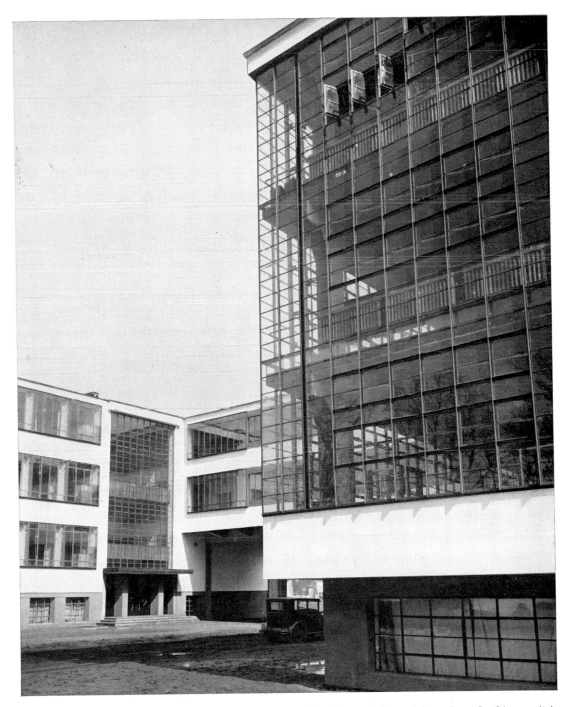

299. WALTER GROPIUS. The Bauhaus, Dessau, 1926. *Corner of the workshop wing. In this case it is the interior and the exterior of a building which are presented simultaneously. The extensive transparent areas, by dematerializing the corners, permit the hovering relations of planes and the kind of "overlapping" which appears in contemporary painting.*

491

The glass curtain wall is famous, but the really important function of the Bauhaus was fulfilled by it as a unit. When it was erected in 1926 it showed how the new space conception could be used to organize a great building complex; nothing comparable to this had until then been achieved in contemporary architecture.

There is no doubt that Frank Lloyd Wright, in the first decades of this century, worked with hovering vertical and horizontal planes in his houses. In this Chicago period he also realized open planning in some of his large houses — the Martin house in Buffalo (1904), for example, and the Coonley house at River Forest (1908). Their ground plans are extended and complicated, and the different parts are sometimes connected by bridges. But these wings are strongly attached to the ground, reach out over the plot like the exploratory tentacles of some earth-bound animal. They do not hover over the ground, and they embody no wish to do so. The whole treatment of the walls — their sudden structural changes, their overhanging eaves, their complicated relief — indicates this. This may explain why Wright is somewhat repelled by what has been done in Europe since his appearance.

By 1926 a new generation had set to work in architecture. They were in contact both with the artistic discoveries that had been made since 1910 and with the new methods and materials of construction. They brought these two formerly separate realms together and out of their conjunction developed what we know as contemporary architecture. The generation of Le Corbusier, Gropius, Mies van der Rohe, and the others knew the work of the artistic explorers and the new spatial feelings which they had discovered. Finally they were able to select from the accumulated developments in engineering just the means that were needed to give architectonic expression to this new space sense.

The Bauhaus complex is an arrangement of cubes, one juxtaposed against another — cubes differing in size, material, and location. The aim is not to anchor them to the ground but to have them float or hover upon the site. This is the reason for the winglike connecting bridges and the liberal use of glass. The glass was called in for its dematerializing quality; the

492

previous generation had used it either for practical purposes or (in private houses) had stained or painted it.

These cubes are juxtaposed and interrelated. Indeed, they interpenetrate each other so subtly and intimately that the boundaries of the various volumes cannot be sharply picked out. The views from the air show how thoroughly each is blended into a unified composition. The eye cannot sum up this complex at one view; it is necessary to go around it on all sides, to see it from above as well as from below. This means new dimensions for the artistic imagination, an unprecedented many-sidedness.

New organization of volumes

The ground plan lacks all tendency to contract inward upon itself; it expands, on the contrary, and reaches out over the ground. In outline it resembles one of those fireworks called "pinwheels," with three hooked arms extending from a center (*fig.* **297**). The impression one receives from it is similar to that produced by the glassed staircase in Gropius' exhibition building of 1914: it suggests a movement in space that has been seized and held.

The Bauhaus was the only large building of its date which was so complete a crystallization of the new space conception. Its appearance is in a way testimony to the irrational course of history. Germany in the second half of the nineteenth century showed a greater loss of architectonic honesty than any other country. But it was in this very country, after less than thirty years of effort, that the way was opened to new levels of accomplishment in architecture.

Architectural Aims

Gropius is happiest when he is planning on a large scale; he is the architect of buildings for whole social groups — factories, offices, schools, theaters of new types.[12] It was natural that he

Buildings for social groups

---

[12] His *Totaltheater*, for example, is completely adjusted to the new space conceptions. The stage is no longer a fixed focal point for every perspective in the body of the theater as it had been since Renaissance and Baroque times. It is placed in the middle of the building and fitted for circular and vertical movement, so that a many-sided spectacle is presented. Cf. W. Gropius, *Theaterbau* (Rome, 1934).

should take part in the building that went on in the twenties, when Germany set out to make up its shortage of middle- and working-class dwellings. Gropius built a large number of such apartments and housing colonies — in Berlin, Dessau, Frankfort-on-Main, Karlsruhe, and elsewhere. His most interesting work in this field was a scheme for a government institute for housing research.[13] The colony was eventually built, but not as Gropius had proposed. We shall discuss later on, in dealing with the new scale in city planning, the sort of slablike block unit which Gropius worked with in this scheme.

Designs in other fields: their advanced character

The fact that so many of his works — even those of his youth — have retained all their original freshness is evidence of Gropius' creative force. This holds true not only for his architectural productions — the Fagus works, for example — but for his work in other fields as well. Gropius designed a Diesel locomotive as far back as 1913. On a carefully studied functional basis he arrived at an artistic solution that was astonishingly advanced. He produced, in fact, a design which two decades later would have been recognized as "streamlined." [14] His 1932 memorial at Jena to those who fell in the Revolution — a composition of cement planes and prisms — has also remained completely timely, and shows no signs of "dating." [15]

The fact that a man's work had kept its contemporaneous character for two or three decades would have required no special comment in a period where thought and feeling moved in parallel channels. It is far from being a matter of course in periods like ours, however. Among us such sureness of production is — unfortunately — possessed by few artists.

Gropius, like many German artists, has a strong and solid rather than a quick imagination. But, working very quietly, he arrives at new and startling conclusions. Albrecht Dürer's ponderous figures lack the grace of the Venetian school; nevertheless, Dürer's conceptions are characterized by an inherent depth.

[13] The Reichsforschungsgesellschaft.

[14] Illustrated by S. Giedion, *Walter Gropius* (Paris, 1931).

[15] As a design, that is, since it was destroyed by the Nazis when they came into power.

494

WALTER GROPIUS IN AMERICA

What effect have his American surroundings had on Gropius, and how has Gropius influenced his American environment? There are delicate mutual reactions which obviously can only be very imperfectly gauged. Before attempting even the most summary analysis we shall have to consider a more general question: the significance of the post-1930 emigration from Europe to America.

The Significance of the Post-1930 Emigration

This emigration was the outcome of political pressure, but it was of an entirely different nature either from that of the European intellectuals driven into exile after 1848 or the mass exodus of peasants and artisans about 1860. At those periods America was still an only half-formed country. Wide stretches of its territory and many professional fields were just being opened up. Whoever went to America in those days became an American citizen almost automatically, and could acquire land either as a free gift or for a purely nominal price. But those who migrated in the 1930's were confronted with quite another situation; America was now believed to be settled and was defended by entry quotas; newcomers were regarded as aliens, whether they became American citizens or not. All the same, the influence of this emigration may in the long run prove to be deeper and more far-reaching than those of 1848 and the 1860's. For this did not consist of representatives of politics, business, or unskilled labor, but of representatives of cultural life — the most advanced scientists, humanists, and artists, who during the thirties had a direct impact in every domain of science and culture, from modern aesthetics to nuclear physics.

There are moments in the lives of nations when, like certain plants, they require extraneous fertilization in order to achieve a further phase of their cultural evolution. Just as, after the artistic exhaustion which followed the Gothic development, Italian artists of the Renaissance were called to France to incite a new development, so America, after a preponderant

495

role of business, needed a new spiritual orientation. The laws of chance made this need coincide with the exodus of many of the best European minds during the 1930's.

State of American architecture around 1930 After the structural forthrightness of the first Chicago School during the eighties, after Louis Sullivan's outstanding purity of architectonic expression and Frank Lloyd Wright's exciting example around 1900, the spirit of American architecture had degenerated into a mercantile classicism. The impulse to shake free from this disastrous development had to be initiated from outside. The time came in the late thirties.

As early as the 1920's a few modern-minded European architects had settled in the United States. It was at this time that Richard J. Neutra, for example, started his hard fight for contemporary architecture in Southern California, after earlier endeavors of Frank Lloyd Wright, Greene & Greene, and others had been submerged by sham Spanish imitations. In the twenties, American universities and similar institutions were all in the hands of representatives of the Académie des Beaux Arts. The modern spirit was excluded everywhere. But in the late thirties some far-sighted men in leading institutions felt the necessity of inviting men such as Mies van der Rohe, Moholy-Nagy, Walter Gropius, and later on, Alvar Aalto, to teach in America.

That the United States, unlike certain other countries, should have decided to employ some of Europe's most creative architects says much for that nation's intuitive sagacity. These appointments provided the rather devious retrospective means by which Americans were at last enabled to recognize their own pioneers. Even the American Institute of Architects began to reconsider its attitude toward Frank Lloyd Wright and awarded him its gold medal on his eightieth birthday in 1948. This recalls inevitably the honors with which the French Academy eventually loaded Ingres after having embittered his whole active career as a painter.

Walter Gropius and the American Scene

What did America do for Gropius and what has Gropius done for America? To begin with, there are definite points of re-

496

semblance to the functional type of American architecture in Gropius' own work, evidence of which can be found as far back in his career as the international competition for the Chicago Tribune Building in 1922. Though at that time Gropius did not know of the work of the Chicago School of 1890, the project he submitted was imbued with the selfsame spirit. Had his project been carried out instead of the pseudo-Gothic design that was chosen, it would be regarded today as a natural continuation of the Chicago School.

As it was, every rational design was laughed out of court, although there were names such as Duiker, Lönberg-Holm, and Bruno Taut among the other European architects who took part. In the library of Harvard University's Graduate School of Design there is a satirical pamphlet, issued by the "Celestial Jury" (1923), in which Gropius' design is referred to as that of "the man who invented the mouse-trap."

There were other points, too, in which, quite early, Gropius had shown a certain affinity with American building technique and its large-scale production and assembly. In 1910 — during the time he worked in the office of Peter Behrens — he laid before the German industrialist Emil Rathenau "A Plan for Forming a Company to Undertake the Construction of Dwellings with Standardized Component Parts." Gropius said at the end of this unpublished twenty-eight-page proposal, "It becomes today economically and technically possible to satisfy the justified demands of the client for individualized treatment of his dwelling by the use of the infinite possibilities for combination of these variable parts."

Standardized component parts

Thus in 1910 Walter Gropius perceived the pivotal problem, which forty years later has not yet been completely solved, of the part mechanization has to play in the mass production of houses. This problem consists in the reconciliation of individual needs with mechanical production to produce a solution that can satisfy varying human requirements.

As is well known, industry, trying first to mass-produce identical houses, like automobiles, had to learn the hard way that houses, unlike automobiles, demand respect for individual flexibility and that all that industry can do is to find out the best means of creating parts to be assembled in such ways that the necessary diversity may be guaranteed.

Since 1942, Konrad Wachsmann in collaboration with Gropius has developed a system of prefabricated houses (the "general panel system") based on Gropius' work with prefabricated corrugated-copper houses for Hirsch Kupfer, near Berlin, in 1931. The beveled edges of the frame were done there first and then taken over for General Panel. Its standardized wooden slabs or panels combine individual planning and architectural freedom with modern industrial methods.

Architectural Activity

Differing European and American views on academic teaching

European architects who emigrate to the United States are surprised that important jobs are nearly always placed in the hands of large firms with staffs running into hundreds; and that small architects' offices, such as they were accustomed to at home, have a hard struggle to keep going at all.

Another difference they find is that in Europe a teacher of architecture usually has to acquire a reputation in the field before being called to a chair, while in America a professor of architecture has been regarded until lately as someone estranged from reality, and best kept away from actual building activity, the teaching of architecture being regarded as a career in itself.

That Mies van der Rohe and Gropius did not accept this frustrating role was not the least of their accomplishments in bettering the standard of architectural training in America. All of us are convinced that an academic teacher can have a real influence on his students only as long as he is creative himself. To young people who are in a state of spiritual flux the close contact with a personality who is himself in a creative mood is the best means to liberate their own creative capacities.

That the prejudice that a creative personality may become too much absorbed by his own work is only slowly fading can be well explained by the fact that in America a university professor has about as many hours of lecturing a week as a high-school teacher in Europe. This is detrimental to the quality of the lectures as well as to his own scholarly work.

498

300. WALTER GROPIUS and MARCEL BREUER. Gropius' own house in Lincoln, Massachusetts, 1938. *View from the south and ground plan. This was the first modern house to be built in the vicinity of Boston.*

At the same time as he inaugurated his architectural teaching in America, Walter Gropius started to build himself a home at Lincoln, some twenty miles from Cambridge, Massachusetts. When I was staying with him in the autumn of 1938 crowds of visitors used to come over every weekend, and often on weekdays as well, to see the newly finished "modern house" (*figs.* **300, 301**); for up till then not a single example could be found within a radius of upwards of a hundred miles.

Yet neither its flat roof, its screened porch (though here designed as an extension of the dining-room, protruding from the house to catch eastern and western breezes during the hot and humid summers), its vernacular weather-boarding (in which, however, the boards were laid vertically instead of in the traditional horizontal manner), nor its large windows could be said to mark any notable divergence from the local New England building idiom.

Several country houses in the same area followed, all of which, like Gropius' own home, were designed in partnership with Marcel Breuer. Gropius always liked to have a partner at his side. During the first years of his American activity, 1938–41, he was associated with Marcel Breuer, whom he had called to Harvard and who had an excellent influence on the students. Breuer's hand can be felt in the particularly charming one-room Wayland cottage (1940) which hovers over the ground like a butterfly (*fig.* **302**). There were larger houses, too, less successful in design, which had to be planned for clients with exaggerated personal requirements.

The defense housing colony of New Kensington, near Pittsburgh, built in 1941 for the employees of an aluminum factory, caused quite a belated commotion in the Pennsylvania newspapers. The attacks in the local press must have reminded Gropius of those aroused by his Törten Siedlung at Dessau more than two decades earlier.

When Gropius and Breuer entered the competition for Wheaton College in 1938 — their first contribution to American college architecture — conditions were not ripe for them. No trustee could have been persuaded to vote the necessary funds. The consuming itch for representationalism still prevailed in the design of university dormitories. Yet this was just the time

500

301. WALTER GROPIUS and MARCEL BREUER. House in Wayland, Massachusetts, 1940. *This little house for an elderly couple is embedded in old pine trees.*

302. Graduate Center, Harvard University 1949–50. *Plan of the whole complex, including the Commons.*

when it began to break down and a year later, in 1939, it was possible for Mies van der Rohe to be commissioned to design the new campus buildings for the Illinois Institute of Technology. In 1947 Aalto was able to persuade the trustees of the Massachusetts Institute of Technology to allow him to carry out his revolutionary design for his dormitory on the Charles River, and in 1949 Gropius was entrusted with the building of the Harvard Graduate Center for "America's oldest and most respected educational institution."[1]

The Harvard Graduate Center was built in an extremely short time, 1949–50, by TAC (The Architects' Collaborative), composed of Walter Gropius and his young associates,[2] all of whom

---

[1] "Harvard Builds a Graduate Yard," *Architectural Forum, the Magazine of Building,* December 1950, pp. 62–71.

[2] The Architects' Collaborative: Jean Bodman Fletcher, Norman Fletcher, John C. Harkness, Sarah Harkness, Robert S. McMillan, Louis A. McMillen, Benjamin Thompson. Associate: Leonard Currie.

303. Graduate Center, Harvard University. *The Harkness Commons building, with passageways. In the background are some of the dormitory buildings.*

were trained in the spirit of the New American School. The funds available were rather limited compared to those used for former students' quarters or even for Aalto's new M.I.T. dormitory. This is not the only reason for the disappearance of a palatial type of building; it is also because another aspect of life is developing. Greater simplicity and deeper spiritual demands are to be found in the post-war generation.

The seven dormitories and the Commons Building brought into being by seven architects and their "job-captain" Gropius may provide a proper setting for this new orientation.

The dormitories for 575 students are spread informally. No enclosures separate them from the outside. All of the three- and four-story buildings are of reinforced concrete. Yellowish bricks, such as Gropius has liked ever since his Fagus works of 1911, form their curtain walls. Covered passageways

304. Graduate Center, Harvard University. *View of the Harkness Commons and detail of the entrance to a dormitory.*

connect the different buildings. Their long horizontals and slim, widely separated columns impart movement and smoothness. There is also a certain interplay with different horizontal planes: the flat-roofed three- and four-story dormitories, the two-story Commons, and the sunken garden before it.

Commons
Building

The Commons Building forms the social center for graduate student life at Harvard. Two-story structure, steel frame, limestone facing, large glass areas. It is delightful to observe how the carefully planned organization of this building gives an architectonic impetus to the whole structure.

Unusually placed on the second floor are the dining rooms and kitchen, which serves 1200 meals at a time. A cantilevered ferroconcrete ramp, forming a kind of backbone within the structure, leads directly to the cafeteria counters. The dining area is divided into four units to avoid the impression of mass feeding.

The ground floor, with its wide glass areas, serves as a social gathering place and the larger of its two lounges can easily be converted into a meeting hall.

305. Graduate Center, Harvard University. Grill Room, with wooden reliefs by Hans Arp. *It was a courageous experiment to invite creative artists — Hans Arp, Joan Miró, Josef Albers, and others—to reënforce the emotional content of the Commons building. Contacts between planner and artist are as important for future development as air conditioning.*

One thing should not be forgotten, that in spite of the rather limited means at their disposal, Gropius insisted that contemporary art should be present in the Commons Building. It was not an easy problem to solve. Not for reasons of money — a grandiose anonymous gesture later made everything possible — but for emotional reasons.

Commons Building and contemporary art

For one and a half centuries contemporary art and the public have lost contact. Belatedly and only after generations, the public responded. The banishment of creative art from public life had another effect: it estranged artists and architects from the habit of working together. This is the situation today.

It needed courage around 1920 to invite the most advanced painters to join the staff of a state institution like the Bauhaus. And the same intrepidity was necessary in 1949 to introduce the work of modern artists [3] within a university; not in the

---

[3] Mural paintings for the dining hall by Joan Miró and Herbert Bayer; wood reliefs by Hans Arp in the grill room; tile mural accompanying the ramp by Herbert Bayer;

form of an exhibition, but as a daily companion to the student's life.

At the Sixth CIAM Congress, at Bridgewater, England, in 1947, in which Gropius took part, the problem of aesthetics came to the fore and especially the question, is mutual coöperation between architect, painter, and sculptor possible? Everybody knew that this coöperation was not easy to accomplish because artists and architects had so long been separated by the circumstances. In the Commons Building it can sometimes be felt that the two did not work together from the beginning. In order to strengthen the emotional and symbolic content of community buildings the integration of art and architecture has again become an urgent demand. The Commons Building is a bold step toward this goal.

The TAC Harvard Graduate Center and the Aalto M.I.T. Dormitory are very different, just as Ingres and Delacroix are different in their means of expression. Which is to be preferred depends on the personal approach and the personal likes and dislikes of the individual; but one thing can be regarded as certain; the future will not forget that two distinguished institutions in the same city gave contemporary architecture a chance to mold itself into upgrowing generations.

Gropius as Educator

What predestined Gropius to become a teacher is that trait in his nature which makes him ready to listen to others and give them their full due. He might not have the temperament, or the eruptive inventiveness of other leading figures, but no one in the architectural movement possesses the far-sighted philosophical approach which enables him to perceive problems at a distance and correlate them within a broad framework.

Born teacher and organizer though Gropius is, much of his success in both capacities lies in his power to see his problems from every side. There is another quality he possesses: his mind is the reverse of rigid. It has nothing in common with the hidebound inflexibility of those sterile natures whose dim instinct of self-protection invariably makes them negate any-

a brick relief by Josef Albers; steel pylon by Richard Lippold in front of the Commons; world maps by Gyorgy Kepes in the dormitory lounges.

thing that might disturb the even tenor of their lives. Gropius is always prepared to consult and learn from others when he feels they have something of value to impart. He allows himself much time for his fellow man. His willingness to understand the minds of others liberates the creative capacity of his students and wins him friends.

He knows and likes the human side of life. This is the secret of his ability as a coördinator of diverging minds; it was quite the same whether he was dealing with the manifold personalities of his Bauhaus period, in the CIAM (Congrès Internationaux d'Architecture Moderne), where there is also no lack of individual opinions, with the Harvard students, or finally with the team of architects with whom he works.

That the Bauhaus managed to survive from 1919 until 1928 under his direction, during what were the most crucial years for the development of the new architecture, can only be ascribed to an act of faith which might be compared to building a house while one raging storm after another kept blowing away the mortar before it had time to set. And this miracle of tenacity was accomplished in a Germany crippled by inflation, where, under the mask of resurgent nationalism, the advent of the future Nazi state was ominously heralded.

It has often been said that the Bauhaus rationalized the teaching of modern art by a pedantic bottling of its various manifestations into neatly labeled compartments. But Gropius had something completely different in mind when he founded the Bauhaus in 1919. His leading idea then was: "The Bauhaus strives to coördinate all creative efforts in art into a new unity." In 1923 in its first large publication, *Staatliches Bauhaus in Weimar 1919–1923*, the idea was further evolved: "The guiding principle of the Bauhaus was the idea of creating a new unity of the welding together of many 'arts' and movements: a unity having its basis in Man himself and significant only as a living organism."

In Autumn 1947, speaking at the Sixth CIAM Congress at Bridgewater, England, after ten years of having directed the work for the master's degree in architecture at Harvard, Gropius summed up his experience in this field, and what he had to say was the natural outgrowth of the concepts of his youth. And it was not only relevant for the training of the architect but for the reform of educational methods as a whole:

"In architectural education the teaching of a method of approach is more important than the teaching of skills. . . . The integration of the whole range of knowledge and experience is of the greatest importance right from the start; only then will the totality of aspect make sense in the student's mind. . . . Such an educational approach would draw the student into a creative effort to integrate simultaneously design, construction, and economy of any given task with its social ends." This may be the reason that the Juniors at Harvard do not begin with detailing door-handles but are plunged at once into the problem of designing a neighborhood unit.

There are certain highly skilled mechanics in the Detroit automobile factories who work behind protective glass screens. It is their job to make the jigs and tooling which later on will be used for turning out millions of component parts needed for next year's models. In much the same way, a little body of picked architectural students is now being trained in some of the leading American universities and technical institutes to leave its impress on the life of the nation in the immediate future.

In February 1950 in a special number of *L'Architecture d'aujourd'hui* Chester Nagel wrote of Gropius: "[He] was the first man who interpreted the industrial revolution to us in terms of architecture, in terms of design, in terms of community planning. He constantly investigated the great potentialities of industrial society and showed us how to assimilate them to our ever-changing needs . . . looking back over the last twelve years, we, who have been Gropius' students, can say gratefully that he has shown us a place in society; that he has taught us that mechanization and individual freedom are not incompatible; that he has explained to us the possibilities and values of communal action and . . . I shall always doubt that a lesser human being could have given us that new faith in our world." [4]

---

[4] In *Walter Gropius — the Spread of an Idea*, edited by Paul Rudolph (Paris, 1950).

508

LE CORBUSIER AND THE MEANS OF ARCHITECTONIC EXPRESSION

306. LE CORBUSIER. The High Court of Justice, Chandigarh, under construction 1953. *Huge sloping eaves, pillars of the entrance hall, large water pools; in the distance the "open hand."*

Le Corbusier (Charles Édouard Jeanneret) was born at La Chaux-de-Fonds, in the French part of Switzerland.[1] His family, the Jeannerets, had been painters and engravers for generations. Le Corbusier himself learned to engrave watches.

Le Corbusier's spirit was never ground to a smooth specialization at a university. He showed the instinctive prescience of genius by turning up wherever new things were being done, or wherever a stimulating relationship to a bygone era could be established. From 1909 to 1910 he was in Paris, learning to use ferroconcrete in Perret's atelier. At Berlin he worked in the studio of Peter Behrens. His first published book — an examination and criticism of the German industrial art movement — was a product of this experience.[2] He saw Vienna and the Wiener Werkstätte, but made his excuses when Josef

Relations to his contemporaries and to history

---

[1] It was in this district that the marvelous automaton (fig. 86) originated.

[2] *Étude sur le mouvement d'art décoratif en Allemagne* (Chaux-de-Fonds, 1912).

Hoffmann (Otto Wagner's best-known pupil) asked him to come and work with him.

Instead, Le Corbusier set out — with empty pockets — to visit Athens and the Near East. St. Peter's in Rome, the Acropolis, the white houses indigenous to Mediterranean culture everywhere — from all these things he derived just the kind of assistance that was needed for the work of today.

Another influence must be mentioned: Le Corbusier's contact with (and share in) modern painting. Contemporary painting was at the high point of its development in 1917, the year Le Corbusier finally returned to Paris. He had the advantage not merely of living there at this time but of being himself a painter.

Our specialized period rarely produces a combination of painter and architect in the same person. Le Corbusier is one of the exceptions; in his scheme of daily work the morning is devoted to painting, the afternoon to architecture. Architectural creations come easily to him, but for twenty years he has been struggling with painting. The foundation of his work in both fields is his conception of space. Architecture and painting are merely two different instruments through which he expresses the same conception.

Interrelations between his architecture and modern painting

The spirit of Le Corbusier's houses shows an absolute identity with the spirit that animates modern painting. The floating transparency achieved in the works of modern painters finds its echo in Le Corbusier's own paintings (*fig.* **308**). He himself assures us in his *Peinture moderne* [3] that he has deliberately chosen the most uninteresting of objects — bottles, drinking glasses, and the like — so that attention will not stray away from the actual painting. A historian is not likely to view this choice as an accident, however. He sees in it a preference for floating, transparent objects whose mass and outlines flow into each other in a *mariage des contours* that leads us from Le Corbusier's pictures to his architecture (*fig.* **309**).

Around 1910 Picasso and Braque, as the consequence of a new conception of space, exhibited the interiors and exteriors of

[3] Amédée Ozenfant and Le Corbusier, (Paris, 1925).

510

307. LE CORBU-SIER. Ferroconcrete skeleton for a dwelling house, 1915. *Le Corbusier was able to transmute the concrete skeleton developed by the engineer into an architectural means.*

objects simultaneously. In architecture Le Corbusier developed, on the same principle, the interpenetration of inner and outer space. We have already observed gropings toward such an interpenetration in the seventeenth-century buildings of Francesco Borromini. But this interpenetration of space at large and space-particles could have further development only in an age whose science and art both perceived space as essentially many-sided and relational.

Le Corbusier takes ferroconcrete as the instrument for the expression in architecture of his ideas.[4] In this he joins the French tradition, continues the work of Perret and Tony Garnier. It was only in France that architects could use ferroconcrete unrestrictedly and without hesitation. Building legislators in Germany and England distrusted elegant constructions in reinforced concrete and insisted upon an unnecessary bulkiness. The French had always sought for lightness and precision in their buildings, and they made corresponding laws.

The concrete skeleton as an artistic means

The real starting point of Le Corbusier's career is a drawing dated 1915 (*fig.* **307**). It shows nothing but six reinforced concrete pillars and three horizontal slabs which are connected by a mere hint of a staircase. Le Corbusier was able — as no one before him had been — to transmute the concrete skeleton developed by the engineer into a means of architectonic expression. He knew how to bring out the secret affinity that existed

[4] For a survey of the output of Le Corbusier and Jeanneret, cf. *Le Corbusier et Pierre Jeanneret, Œuvre complète*, three volumes published, with slight variations in title, in Zurich, 1929, 1934, 1938.

between ferroconcrete construction and the human needs and cravings that were just coming to the surface.

To create houses of unprecedented lightness and to carry still farther the kind of "open planning" which Frank Lloyd Wright had begun, Le Corbusier used those properties of the supporting framework of reinforced concrete which make the disposition of the inner walls a matter of choice. This new interpretation of the concrete skeleton is the significant part of Le Corbusier's work.

308. LE CORBUSIER. "Still Life," 1924. *Oil. Like the cubists, Le Corbusier and Ozenfant were greatly interested in commonplace objects and in the problems of transparency. The "mariage de contour" between the different objects and outlines in this painting points ahead to the interpenetrations of inner and outer space which Le Corbusier achieved later in his buildings.*

The problem of the dwelling is the unequivocal center of Le Corbusier's activity, both theoretical and practical. His first house, built in the Swiss Jura in 1916, is externally of conventional form. It already shows, however, the reinforced concrete skeleton which appears in all its successors. The skeleton is actually turned to the purposes of housing.

Le Corbusier has laid down five points of liaison between contemporary architecture and contemporary construction:

1. *The pillar*, which is to be left free to rise through the open space of a dwelling.

Such a use of the pillar had been made early in the nineteenth century by John Nash. Henri Labrouste in 1843 had also used a free-standing cast-iron pillar in one of the rooms of his Bibliothèque Sainte-Geneviève. Le Corbusier uses the free pillar with a difference, however: through the girders of the

309. LE CORBUSIER and P. JEANNERET. Settlement houses at Pessac, near Bordeaux, 1926. *In this early experimental work, Le Corbusier plays with screens, volumes, light, shadow, and color. Soon to be followed by solutions of great plastic sureness.*

framework it takes up all the load in the structure and leaves the walls with nothing to support.[5] This leads directly to Le Corbusier's second principle.

2. *The functional independence of skeleton and wall*, in the case not only of the outer walls but of the inner partitions also.

---

[5] The machine shop which Walter Gropius built at the Fagus works in 1914 also placed the steel columns behind the outer wall.

William Le Baron Jenney, in the first true skeleton construction, his Leiter Building of 1889 (Chicago), also took advantage of the complete freedom this type of framework building permitted in the disposition of the nonsupporting inner walls. Victor Horta, in his house in the Rue de Turin (1893), and Perret, in his house in the Rue Franklin (1903), gave impetus to the flexible treatment of the ground plan which the mutual independence of the separate stories made possible.

3. *Le plan libre.* Le Corbusier converted the ferroconcrete skeleton from a technical device into an aesthetic means. Le Corbusier uses the partition walls to model the interior space of the house in the most varied manner, employing curved staircases and curving or flat partition walls for both functional and expressive purposes. The same means allow him to hollow out large portions of the house, and to bring about interpenetrations of outer and inner space which are unfamiliar and daring.

This whole treatment, the completely free and individualized organization of separate stories, is what is meant by "open planning" or *le plan libre.* By now the difference between the open planning of Frank Lloyd Wright and that of European architects should be apparent. The work of the latter is based upon the new conception of space as essentially many-sided which grew out of cubism.

4. *The free façade*, which is a direct consequence of skeleton construction.

5. *The roof garden.* Frank Lloyd Wright's houses demand that we go around them if we wish to understand their formation. Now a house can also be looked at from above or below; in a sense it presents a surface that opens on the sky. The flat roof is a recognition of that additional space-relation in the dwelling — although the flat roof can, of course, be used with many different intentions. Its employment by contemporary architects — often in conjunction with flat slabs that form free-standing dividing walls or hovering partial coverings — does not serve practical ends alone. Such treatments express the sense of space of our period.

The Villa Savoie, 1928–30

Since 1922, when he first began to build regularly, Le Corbusier has made use of and developed these five principles.[6] The experience gained in the construction of several private homes has enabled him to use them in his work in more and more clarified form. They appear at their purest, perhaps, in his Villa Savoie, built at Poissy in 1928–30.

All Le Corbusier's houses attack the same problem. He is always endeavoring to open up the house, to create new possibilities for connections between its interior and exterior and within the interior itself. We want rooms which can be thrown open or enclosed at will, rooms whose outer partitions fall away when we wish. Briefly, it is a question of achieving dwellings of a sort which, up to the present, have been beyond the reach of conception and execution alike. The armature construction is here in secret alliance with our half-realized desires; it anticipates them, in fact.

Previously to this, Le Corbusier's houses had been built on rather cramped plots, in more or less close proximity to their neighbors. The site of the Savoie house, on the contrary, was completely isolated (*fig.* **310**).

The problem involved here was one which affects every man when he leaves his work and seeks to regain contact with nature, with growing things, the countryside, and the sky. This attempt to renew our connections with nature raises the same fundamental questions wherever we build, by the seashore, in the mountains, or — as in this case — on the undulating expanses of the Seine valley just outside Paris.

At one period in his development Frank Lloyd Wright used to employ the smallest crevices in the rocks to help bind his houses still more closely to the earth. In the Savoie house Le Corbusier does exactly the opposite. The city-dweller for whom it was designed wanted to look out over the countryside rather than to be set down among trees and shrubbery. He wanted to enjoy the view, the breezes, and the sun — to experience that un-

The site

---

[6] Cf. S. Giedion, "Le Corbusier et l'architecture contemporaine," *Cahiers d'art*, V (Paris, 1930), 205–215.

310. LE CORBUSIER and P. JEANNERET. Villa Savoie at Poissy, 1928–30.

311. LE CORBUSIER and P. JEANNERET. Villa Savoie, 1928–30. *Cross section.
The hollowing out of the house from above and from below is accomplished with astonishing
sureness.*

516

312. LE CORBU
SIER and P. JEAN
NERET. Villa Savoie,
1928–30. *View of terrace and roof garden,
and ground plan. Large
glass areas of the living
room are directed toward
the great terrace, which
gives the landscape as
well as the sky only in
silhouette. The ramp
leads from the first to
the second floor inside
the house and from the
second floor to the roof
garden outside.*

hurried natural freedom which his work deprived him of. This is another instance of two eternally opposed responses to nature: a contemporary reflection of the difference between the Greek temple, sharply outlined against its background, and the medieval town, attached like a plant to the site on which it stands.

The structure — This house is a cube elevated on pillars. The cube part is not a solid mass; it is hollowed out on both the southeast and southwest sides so that when the sun comes up the light floods the whole interior instead of merely skimming the outer wall.

The entrance hall is on the northwest, but in coming in from the road one has to go all around the south side of the house to reach it. Of course there is really no façade and no back or front, since the house is open on every side.

The living room — five meters by fourteen — has horizontally sliding windows on two sides. The third wall (facing onto the terrace) is glass from floor to ceiling for some two-thirds of its length (*fig.* **312**). Half of this glass partition can be slid back by an easily manipulated lever. As a result, the room can be arranged quite freely, while the occupant is brought into connection with both the interior and the outdoors. The surrounding landscape, however, never appears in its full sweep. It is always shown in segments — framed, as it were — not only in the interior rooms but also on the terrace.

Since his La Roche house at Auteuil (1923–24), Le Corbusier has been preoccupied by the problem of the ramp in the interior of the house. When there is room enough, the elimination of the staircase permits an almost insensible transition from one level in the house to another. The ramp in the Savoie house is in two sections (*fig.* **311**): one wing is inside; the other wing continues along an outer wall to the roof garden. Besides the ramp, there is a spiral staircase which leads from the ground to the roof.

It is impossible to comprehend the Savoie house by a view from a single point; quite literally, it is a construction in space-time. The body of the house has been hollowed out in every direction: from above and below, within and without. A cross section at any point shows inner and outer space penetrating each other inextricably.

518

Borromini had been on the verge of achieving the interpenetration of inner and outer space in some of his late baroque churches. This interpenetration was first realized in our period, through the methods of modern engineering, with the Eiffel Tower of 1889. Now, in the late twenties, it had become possible to achieve it in a dwelling. This possibility was latent in the skeleton system of construction, but the skeleton had to be used as Le Corbusier uses it: in the service of a new conception of space. That is what he means when he defines architecture as *construction spirituelle*.

The League of Nations Competition, 1927: Contemporary Architecture Comes to the Front

The 1927 international competition for the League of Nations Palace at Geneva is one of the most illuminating episodes in the history of contemporary architecture. For the first time present-day architects challenged the routine of the Academy in a field which it had dominated for generations, the design of monumentally impressive state buildings. The Academy won this particular engagement, but its victory injured the prestige of its methods.

The conventional routines showed themselves incapable of producing architectonic solutions to problems of modern organization. The proof of that helplessness did much to break down popular resistance to modern treatments.

It was plain from the start that, among the 337 projects submitted, one — the work of Le Corbusier and Pierre Jeanneret — was peculiarly important and significant. Later developments verified this first judgment.

What made it important? It unexpectedly forced high officials from everywhere in Europe to consider seriously a kind of architecture which they had always dismissed as aesthetic trifling. For decades there had been an established style for the stately official building — an international style that hardly varied from country to country. Custom had made its validity seem guaranteed for all time, and the official element automatically turned to it when the matter of their Geneva setting came up. The scheme that came to the forefront, however, shockingly disregarded the stylistic approach in order to tackle specific problems.

Program

The idea of a league of nations is one which we encounter time and again in history. Its realization, however — the actual establishment of a neutral center where representatives of every country might meet to maintain the equilibrium of the world — was a completely new thing and brought a highly complex institution into being. Its varied functions required a division of its headquarters into three main parts: a secretariat, where the daily work of its administration could be carried on; a meeting place for committees of various sorts whose sessions occurred intermittently (the *Conseil* and the *Grandes Commissions*); and a hall for the yearly sitting of the *Assemblée générale*. Besides this, a great library was needed in the whole complex.

The scheme of
Le Corbusier
and Jeanneret

The outstanding fact about the scheme submitted by Le Corbusier and Jeanneret [7] is that they found the most compact and best-conceived solution to these needs (*fig.* **313**).[8]

The Secretariat (*fig.* **316**), the great administration building near the entrance to the grounds, was given a slender wing which paralleled the lake. The rows of horizontally sliding windows gave every clerk or typist an unimpeded view over water and mountains. A roof garden was available for rest periods. The building had a ferroconcrete skeleton and seemed to hover above its site on supporting pillars set back of the curtain walls. Le Corbusier had used the same treatment, a short time before and on a smaller scale, in his Villa Cook at Boulogne-sur-Seine.

The great Assembly Building was moved forward to the lake front. Two huge expanses of glass made up its side walls. The Grande Salle des Assemblées (*fig.* **314**), meant for twenty-six hundred auditors, was designed with the needs of a large audience as the determining factors. It had to be possible to hear and see perfectly from every one of its seats. To ensure this,

---

[7] Cf. Le Corbusier, *Une Maison, un palais* (Paris, 1928). Here the architect himself explains what he was aiming at in this scheme.

[8] At the suggestion of the Friends of Modern Architecture — an association connected with the International Congress for Modern Architecture (C.I.A.M.) — Le Corbusier's plans for the palace of the League of Nations were saved and purchased by the University of Zurich in 1939. The great view of the palace (fig. 312) hangs near the mathematics seminar of the University of Zurich. The other seventeen plans are preserved in the archives and are always available for study.

the ceiling was given a nearly parabolic curvature. This was on the advice of the specialist, Gustave Lyon.[9] But the ceiling is not simply introduced into the design as an acoustical aid: it is taken up into and influences the whole form of the hall. Le Corbusier converts what was offered simply as a technical expedient into aesthetic means.

In the treatment of the ceiling Le Corbusier unconsciously followed the example of earlier men. Thus Davioud in the seventies used a parabolic ceiling in a project for a theater of a capacity of five thousand. The Adler and Sullivan Auditorium of 1887 in Chicago — the finest assembly hall of its period — is similarly modeled by considerations of acoustics, but to an even greater extent than in the Grande Salle at Geneva.

Le Corbusier's plans show a thoroughly considered treatment of the traffic problem. The problem was acute when the General Assembly was in session, and it had to be possible to move great streams of cars in short order. The rear entrance of the Assembly Building accordingly took its form from an everyday solution to the same difficulty — the sheltered railway platform set between two transit lines (*fig.* **315**). But once again a purely utilitarian development is transmuted into an expressive means.

In the requirements of the Secretariat simply as an office building, in the need for making it possible to hear from every bench in the Grand Salle, in the traffic problems that arose at general sessions — in the needs of life, that is — Le Corbusier and Jeanneret found incentives to artistic creation.

But it was exactly those requirements which proved stumbling blocks to the architects who adopted the familiar monumental routine. As a consequence there is no need to consider which of these compositions was, as a whole, the best — for all alike were incapable of functioning. The requirements of a complex new social organism like the League of Nations could not be met by schemes whose general outline was determined in advance by the need for a certain type of impressive external

Program evaded academic solution

---

[9] Lyon had already constructed the Salle Pleyel at Paris. Le Corbusier's hall was designed before the loud-speaker came into use and simplified the problem of hearing. Such methods may be called for again in the future, however. We can reasonably expect a revived demand on the part of the public for the natural tones of the human voice, unaltered by electrical transmission.

appearance. Everything was smothered by the ostentatious exterior, as unsuitable here as plate armor for a man driving a car. And an architecture which cannot mold itself to the needs of its own time has lost its vital force.

The conventionally monumental schemes broke down in another respect. At Versailles, where a great building complex was first juxtaposed to nature, unlimited space was available, and the absolute will behind this endeavor stamped its own imprint upon the surrounding landscape. At Geneva the site

313. LE CORBUSIER and P. JEANNERET. League of Nations Palace, Geneva, 1927. *The first contemporary project for a monumental state building to gain serious attention from the public and the official element. Open planning in ferroconcrete achieved an efficient solution to a complex and variegated set of demands.*

was strictly limited. Moreover, in this period we no longer desire to *forcer la nature:* we seek to preserve it intact and to bring it and our buildings into harmonious unity. This the academic schemes were unable to do; they found no way of avoiding extensive terracing of the site, which destroyed its

314. LE CORBUSIER and P. JEANNERET. League of Nations Palace, 1927. *Cross section of the Grande Salle. The ceiling has the form of an acoustic shell with polished surfaces; it is hung from bridge girders in the roof. (The same problem was met and solved by Adler and Sullivan in their Chicago Auditorium of 1887.) Le Corbusier takes a technical device and converts it into an aesthetic expression.*

315. LE CORBUSIER and P. JEANNERET. League of Nations Palace, 1927. *Sheltered, platform-like entrance. The railroad platform has been purified in line and transformed into architecture with a classic sureness, just as the traffic ramp was in the Villa Savoie.*

natural contours and left the huge bulk of the Palace perched upon a ridiculously small pediment of lawn.

The Le Corbusier-Jeanneret project would have preserved the integrity of the plot. The flexibly arranged Assembly Building, the narrow Secretariat, the Library, and the elevated passageways connecting all three achieved a perfect adjustment to the actual site.

316. LE CORBUSIER and P. JEANNERET. League of Nations Palace, 1927. *Administration Building (Secrétariat général), rear view.*

Means developed during previous years are here brought together in the solution of a purely contemporary social problem. The plane surfaces which a long period of development had brought to a position of dominance are joined with the new lightness and charm achieved by construction. The result is a kind of informality and flexibility such as had been attained years earlier in the ground plan of the house. A building complex is evolved which goes beyond Renaissance conceptions of space and cannot be grasped by a view from any one point. In its entirety the Palace realizes the new conception of space-time.

The projects that were entered in the 1927 international competition permit an exceptionally wide survey of the state of architecture at that time. All the architectural fashions of the late nineteenth century are represented, together with all the experimental developments in contemporary architecture.

A confusion of architectural languages

The adherents of the Academy submitted beautifully executed schemes which treated the Palace as if it were a *prix de Rome* problem worked out in the quiet of the Villa Medici. From the northern countries and from Germany there came either smooth and placidly decorative projects or Faustean expressionistic sketches in soft charcoal. The work from Italy and from eastern Europe featured cupolas or mosque-like edifices — one of which had no fewer than twenty interior light wells to provide adequate ventilation. And from various countries the most radical experimentalists sent plans — not always ripe for execution — of structures imbued with Russian constructivism or of dream fantasies in glass. The jury was left to thread its way through this confusion of crosscurrents, a confusion that was reflected in its own composition.

In fact, the state of architecture in each of the European countries appeared in its choice of a distinguished man to represent it on the jury. Those countries which had witnessed genuine struggles for a new architecture rather than total neglect of *avant-garde* movements sent men who had stood in the midst of the fighting. The Dutch sent H. P. Berlage; the Austrians, Josef Hoffmann; the Belgians, Victor Horta. Switzerland was represented by Karl Moser, the man whose efforts have brought about the present high standard of architectural education in that country.

Divisions among the jurors

The opposition, not only on the jury but in political circles, came from countries which the thirty-year war for a new architecture had scarcely touched — countries like England and France, where the new movements had no influence upon the public or upon state functionaries. The English juror was Sir John Burnett; the French was M. Lemaresquier, one of the heads of the Académie. He was the most active and influential member of the academic party.

Berlage, Hoffmann, and Moser made up the group favoring the choice of a work in the modern spirit; with the support of Horta they would have constituted a clear majority. And there was an intimate connection between Baron Horta's early productions and the work of the younger architects. His house in the Rue de Turin of 1893 and his Maison du Peuple of 1896 had signaled the whole of Europe to abandon methods that were in opposition to the times. For all that, Horta joined the advocates of the conventions and made it impossible for a nonacademic project to be selected for execution. Le Corbusier's project was one of these. The task of making the final choice was passed on to the diplomatic arm.

The final compromise

The jury finally reached a verdict by awarding nine first prizes *ex aequo*. Not unreasonably, some of the diplomats regarded this action as an evasion of duty on the part of the jury. As a last compromise, the creators of four schemes in the established international monumental style were selected to collaborate in a final version.[10]

A new social organization of the type envisaged by the idea of the League of Nations cannot arrive at its proper framework by borrowing scattered features of an original scheme and executing the whole work in the opposed spirit of routine. This is certainly true in architecture; perhaps it is also true in politics.

We have paid particular attention to the League of Nations Palace because it served as the general public's first introduction to contemporary architecture. The same year also marked its introduction to modern solutions of the housing problem, solutions that in this case were executed. It was in 1927 that the Deutsche Werkbund put Mies van der Rohe in complete charge of the Weissenhof settlement at Stuttgart. Mies van der Rohe entrusted the design of the houses to those architects

---

[10] Further complications arose when a new and larger site was made available for the Palace. In the effort to satisfy the daily needs of the League while at the same time retaining a majestic interior, several plans were drawn up. In the end it was found that the only possible solution was to follow Le Corbusier's general layout. This general arrangement the architects treated in a spirit of routine that shows in their use of colorless historical shapes to produce a formal exterior appearance. In 1937, ten years after the competition was held, the building was opened and put into service. Everyone, from typists to diplomats, agreed that it was a failure.

from all over Europe who had been most active in the new developments. Le Corbusier's Geneva plan remained a project, but the principles embodied in it were partially realized in the Centrosoyus at Moscow (1928–34). The erection of the Centrosoyus — now the Ministry of Light Industry — was retarded partly by the requirements of the Five-Year Plan and partly by the emergence of an architectural reaction. It was one of the last modern structures erected in Russia.

Large Constructions and Architectural Aims

In Paris, at about the same time, two large constructions by Le Corbusier appeared in quick succession: the Salvation Army hospice (1929–33) and the Swiss Pavilion of the University City (1931–33). Both show additions to Le Corbusier's equipment of aesthetic means.

The pavilion of the Swiss dormitory is one of Le Corbusier's freest and most imaginative creations. The whole building is supported by immense ferroconcrete pillars which run deep into the soil to the underlying rock. One side of the building consists of the glass curtain wall of the studios; the other is modeled carefully in a curved wall of rugged stone and smooth slabs (*fig.* **317**).[11]

But what strikes one from the very first as extraordinary is the molding of volumes and space in the entrance hall. Although the room at his disposal was relatively limited, the imagination of the architect has created a space that is living, free, and vast. In the inventiveness it displays it is comparable to the work of the great periods. It is significant that the means employed are apparently very simple: the exact placement of the staircase, the unexpected undulations in the walls (the principle of the *plan libre*), and the use of microphotograph murals, set out checkerboard fashion. The incorporation into modern architecture of such imaginative elements is necessary to maintain its vitality.

Quite different inquiries and quite different solutions are involved in the Salvation Army hospice, the Cité de Refuge. The Cité de Refuge

---

[11] For further illustrations cf. *Le Corbusier et Pierre Jeanneret, Œuvres complète, 1929–1934*, vol. II (Zurich, 1934), with introduction by Sigfried Giedion.

This building — the largest Le Corbusier and his partner have yet built — is on the east side of Paris. Although there was a very limited budget and the building equipment had to be quite primitive, the hospice represents a really daring achievement. It is one of the first many-storied buildings in Europe to attempt a very simplified type of air conditioning.[12]

But here too the astonishing thing is the impression of grandeur produced by the interrelations between its volumes and space at large. It is such relations that give modern architecture its vitality. Notice how smoothly the entry leads into the semi-circular reception room, how smoothly the latter finds its continuation in the main hall, and how smoothly this in turn leads the men and women to their respective quarters. The building is a moving and unaffected assertion of the right of even the most humble to a human and dignified life.

At this point, however, we are obliged to cut short the examination of Le Corbusier's work. It has been published extensively, and he himself has discussed its principles in his writings.

Le Corbusier
as a writer

These writings — ranging in subject from painting to city planning — have had as much influence as his buildings, not only in Europe and the United States but in Latin America as well. Le Corbusier's literary connections are not even restricted to the arts. The articles in the periodical *L'Esprit nouveau* which Jeanneret (alias Le Corbusier) and Ozenfant published during the years 1919–25 deal with developments in every field which had a formative influence upon the thought of the period.

Le Corbusier has two great gifts: he can reduce a complicated problem to astonishingly simple basic elements, and he can summarize these results in formulas of lapidary clearness. But however summary the manner of treatment may be, basic concepts and principles are never lost sight of. The first three chapters of Le Corbusier's *Vers une architecture* (originally published in *L'Esprit nouveau*, 1920) cannot be ignored in any study of our time. In turning "les yeux qui ne voient pas" to the beauty of "les autos, les avions, les paquebots" he pointed out the bridge between the present age and its forgotten nineteenth-century forerunners.

---

[12] Frank Lloyd Wright's Larkin Building, Buffalo (1904) was, according to its architect, "the first air-conditioned office building."

317. LE CORBUSIER and P. JEANNERET. Swiss dormitory in the Cité Universitaire, Paris, 1930–32. →

On what does Le Corbusier's achievement rest? His constructions do not show Auguste Perret's precise engineering, and his houses do not match J. J. P. Oud's infinitely painstaking attention to detail. Le Corbusier, however, approached the house with a seismographic delicacy of perception and freed it from its inherited ponderousness. It has been his aim to incorporate in the house the floating counterbalance of forces, the lightness and openness, which nineteenth-century iron construction succeeded in expressing in abstract terms. He has shown us how to model all the surfaces of a house — above and below as well as at the sides.

The elements Le Corbusier uses are often to be found ready to hand in industry. The pillars on which his houses are poised occur in many warehouses; the elongated window — *fenêtre en longueur* — is a familiar consequence of methods of construction used in factories. The railroad platform which he incorporates in state buildings and the ramps he employs in some of his houses for an interpenetration of inner and outer space are used in many French railway stations (for example, the Gare Montparnasse).

Le Corbusier lifted these elements out of their everyday existence and changed them as the painters changed scraps of paper or pipes into art. He fused these elements on the basis of our spatial conception into a new architectonic language.

318. PICASSO. "Woman in an Armchair," 1938. *Detail.*

319. LE CORBUSIER. Project for exhibition at Liège, 1937.

LE CORBUSIER'S DEVELOPMENT
BETWEEN 1938 AND 1952

Le Corbusier has grown so greatly in his powers and in his outlook that the period between 1938 and 1953 cannot be passed over in silence.[1]   In this later development small structures and one-family-houses play no important role: Le Corbusier has become more and more the creator of large-scale designs.

These projects coincide with general signs that a new humanization of urban life is on the horizon.   Man is no longer satisfied to remain a mere onlooker, whether at a football game or a television screen.   His spontaneous relations can be seen in every part of the world during moments in which the passive spectator has become transformed into an active participant.[2] There is a world-wide trend toward creating centers of social activity, and this calls for far more from the architect than just technical capacity.   His task today is infinitely more complicated than that of his predecessors at the time when Versailles was built.   They had but to give concrete form to an exact program placed before them by a clearly stratified society.   Today the architect has to anticipate needs and to solve problems that exist only half consciously in the crowd. This involves a great responsibility.   The architect has to have the rare gift of a peculiar sensitivity that we would like to term *social imagination*.

Social imagination

This is the aspect of Le Corbusier's later work which will here be evaluated.

Le Corbusier has cast the net of his vision over the chaos of the contemporary metropolis.[3]   In his plans he has cut thoroughfares through vested interests, demolishing whole quarters and raising them anew.   Reality does not easily permit the

---

[1] For detailed information cf. Le Corbusier, *Œuvre complète*, 1938–1946, vol. IV (Zurich, 1949) and vol. V (Zurich, 1953).

[2] S. Giedion, "The Humanisation of Urban Life," in *CIAM, The Heart of the City*, edited by Tyrwhitt, Rogers, Sert (New York, 1952).

[3] S. Giedion, *A Decade of Contemporary Architecture* (Zurich, 1951), p. 201; e.g. Buenos Aires, 1938, and pilot plan for Bogotá with J. L. Sert and P. L. Wiener, 1949–50; Le Corbusier, *Œuvre complète*, V, 142–147.

realization of such radical operations, yet many of these plans — such as the second master plan for Algiers, 1942 [4] — will have more significance for future planners than the usual piecemeal rehabilitation.

Three landmarks stand out from Le Corbusier's work between 1938 and 1952. All of them are related to farsighted plans: The Core of St. Dié, 1945, the Unité d'Habitation, Marseille, 1947–52, and the Capitol of Chandigarh, India, 1951.

St. Dié   The civic center of St. Dié [5] displays in a masterly way a new kind of spatial relationship. The different buildings are designed and placed in such a way that each emanates its own spatial atmosphere and yet bears a close relationship to the whole core. The area is perforated by volumes of widely different shape that continually fill in or hollow out the space like contemporary sculptures.

People walking around or sitting in the cafe that forms a corner of the square, would have a continuously changing spatial experience. Theater, museum, administration center, all are freely placed in space, and the eye can even glimpse the distant old cathedral and on the opposite bank of the river green-girdled factories, *les usines vertes*, as Le Corbusier calls them. Medieval Italy knew how to place volumes in space: in the Piazza del Duomo in Pisa the cathedral, baptistry, campanile, and *camposanto* give an exciting display of volumes in space. The modest unrealized scheme of St. Dié develops a different spatial conception. The relationship in the Gothic period was the relationship of formally closed volumes. Today we are moving toward a more dynamic conception of space, created by solids and voids.

The whole area of the core of St. Dié is reserved exclusively for pedestrians and this, but not only this, relates it to the Greek Agora. St. Dié, for the first time in our period, would have presented a crystallization of community life which could have equaled the Greek meeting place. All political parties of the small French city of St. Dié, including those of

---

[4] See Le Corbusier, *Œuvre complète*, IV, 44–65. The story of this scheme has been told by Le Corbusier himself in a small booklet *Poésie sur Alger* (Paris, 1950), with most charming sketches.

[5] Le Corbusier, *Œuvre complète*, IV, 132–139.

the extreme left, incited by the academicians, shouted so effectively against the scheme that Le Corbusier's core was condemned to remain on paper.

Architecture cannot be confined to those buildings that have been erected. Architecture is a part of life and architecture is a part of art. As a part of life it is more dependent than any other form of art upon the will of the public; upon their desire to see or not to see a scheme come into being. In architecture the standard of values of the client is as important as the standards of the builder.

If in the time of the Parthenon, the Pantheon, Chartres, or St. Peter's the taste of those who had power to order the erection of public buildings had been as weak and debased as it is today, none of them would ever have been built. They were daring experiments, all of them.

One of the few instances where social imagination has been given three dimensional expression is the "Unité d'Habitation," 1947–52 — the residential unit — on the Boulevard Michelet in the outskirts of Marseille. The Marseillais call it simply "Maison Le Corbusier." That this daring building could be successfully completed during five difficult postwar years is due to the courage of M. Claudius Petit, the French Minister of Reconstruction, who defended it to the very last against violent attacks.

The housing problem begins to take on a wider meaning. Both, architect and planner, are now working to rebuild the broken relationship between the individual and the collective spheres.

The boldness of the Unité d'Habitation does not consist in housing some 1600 people under one roof or even in providing twenty-three different types for its 337 apartments varying from one room up to dwellings for "families with eight children." Its boldness consists in its social implementation. The most interesting experiment in this residential unit was to take the shopping center from the ground and from the street and to place it on the central floor of the building itself. From outside, this central shopping street — *la rue marchande* — can be immediately identified by its two-story louvers.

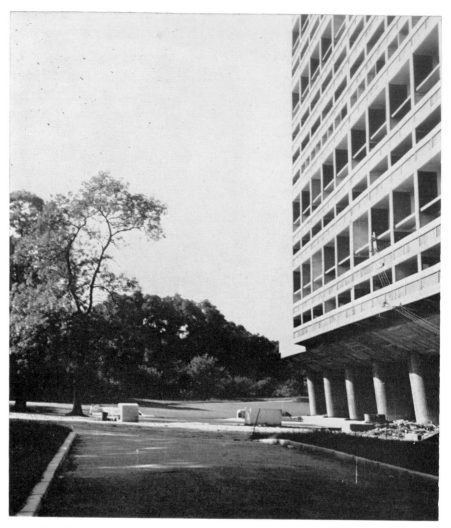

320. LE CORBUSIER. Unité d'Habitation, Marseille, 1947–52. *Detail.*

These, together with the vertical rows of square staircase windows in the middle of the block, vitalize and give scale to the whole front. The shopping street includes shops for groceries, vegetables, meat and fish, laundry and cleaning services, hairdresser and beautyshop, newspaperstand, post-office, cafeteria, and hotel rooms. On the seventeenth floor is placed the nursery for 150 children. A ramp leads directly to the roof terrace with its rest room on pilotis, its shallow pool, and some charming installations for the children, who are encouraged to decorate the walls with their own murals.

321. LE CORBUSIER. Unité d'Habitation, Marseille, 1947–52. *View, and cross sections.*

The other part of the 24 × 165 meter roof terrace is designed for social activities of the adults. There is an area for gymnastics, partly open and partly covered, and, at the north end of the building, a large slab which acts as a protection against the strong north wind — the *Mistral* — and also as a background for open-air theatrical performances. On July 26th 1953, when CIAM celebrated its twenty-fifth anniversary on the roof terrace of the Unité d'Habitation, it looked like a painting of Paolo Veronese, for all the different levels were filled with people, and architecture was vibrant with life.

In this building it depends on the individual inhabitant whether he prefers to remain a lost number in a huge building, or will participate in collective activities that can rouse him out of the melancholic isolation which is the common form of existence in every large city.

The features that make the Unité d'Habitation so rare an architectural spectacle are its plastic qualities. In the hands of Robert Maillart, reinforced concrete lost its rigidity and became almost an organic skeleton, where every particle throbbed with life. In the hands of Le Corbusier the amorphous material of crude concrete — *béton brut* — assumes the features of natural rock. He does not smooth away the marks and hazards of the form work and the defects of bad craftsmanship which, as Le Corbusier stated in his opening address, "shout at one from all parts of the structure." The use of the natural imprints of wooden boards to vitalize a concrete surface is far from new, yet it has never been used so consistently to give ferroconcrete the properties of "a natural material of the same rank as stone, wood or terra cotta." Le Corbusier continues: "It seems to be really possible to consider concrete as a reconstructed stone worthy of being exposed in its natural state."[6]

The rough concrete surface is employed wherever it can strengthen plastic intentions, as in the herring-bone pattern of the huge supporting pilotis, left by the narrow boards that composed their wooden form work. On the roof the rough surfaces of the ventilator shafts and elevator tower, on which every change in the strong Mediterranean light plays with a peculiar intensity, help to transform these utilitarian objects into exciting plastic elements.

Strong, pure colors are used in this building, but Le Corbusier, the painter, has refrained from using any colors directly upon the façade. He paints the side walls of the balconies red, green, yellow, but not the front. In this way they are made to gleam like vivid colors through gauze. Bright color is also used in all the artificially lit *rue-intérieures* and serves to lighten the dimness of these long corridors.

---

[6] Le Corbusier, *Œuvre*, V, 191.

The Unité d'Habitation rises beside the road which leads to the Riviera and faces east and west. Each two-story apartment looks to both sides. To the east their view embraces an arena of the limestone mountains that can be found everywhere in Provence. To the west lie the blue waters of the Mediterranean; while directly below the eye can rest on tree tops interspersed with red-tiled southern roofs. If Cezanne was able to seize the soul of Provence in his pictures, Le Corbusier has known how to capture it within an architectural frame.

Le Corbusier, as well as everybody else, knew that the Unité d'Habitation was a daring experiment both in the plastic sense and even more in the sphere of social imagination. Even after its successful opening in the fall of 1952 the French government remains skeptical and dares not even to take the risk of renting the apartments and shops but demands that they be sold outright, loading any risk upon the shoulders of the inhabitants and shopkeepers.

Yet there is no longer any doubt that this building will have an enormous influence in shaping the mind of the coming generation. It will help to liberate also the mind of the architect and planner from the conception of housing as a simple addition of single units and expand it to the wider frame of the human habitat.

The foundation of new towns is a sign of vitality and of an enterprising courage. New towns are often related to higher living standards or to the promise of them. This was the case during the Gothic period, when new towns suddenly sprang up in central and western Europe. The same phenomenon occurred during the last century in the United States, foreshadowing its industrial hegemony.

Toward the middle of the twentieth century we are witnessing the decentralization of western culture. New energy radiates from its former fringes: Finland, Brazil, Colombia, Venezuela, Canada, the African Gold Coast, to name only some areas of the centers of a new vitality. The Middle East is now also going ahead with an astonishing speed. Countries which have long been slumbering in their own lethargy or under oppression begin to awake and to become active participants in an evolution which is encompassing the entire world. In this process spirits of East and West are meeting together.

In the foreword to the Japanese translation of this book we tried to give some hint of this development: "Western civilization is actually in a state of transition. Experience is slowly showing us that the rationalist and exclusively materialistic attitude upon which the latest phase of western civilization has been grounded is insufficient. Full realization of this fact lead us slowly towards a new hybrid development."

New regional approach

This meeting of East and West may explain, why India — through the understanding of its leader Pandit Nehru — could choose a western architect for the new Capitol of Chandigarh. Yet there is also another reason. This is an inherent trend in contemporary architecture toward satisfying cosmic and terrestrial conditions and the habits which have developed naturally out of them. This explains why the forms of Brazilian architecture and Aalto's work in Finland, though so different, are both imbued with the spirit of the age. Both are regional contributions to a universal architectural conception. This attempt to meet cosmic, terrestrial, and regional conditions may be termed the new regional approach. This is the method of the best contemporary architects and is fully developed in Le Corbusier's boldest architectural adventure: the Capitol of Chandigarh.

When the Punjab was divided in 1947 between Pakistan and India, the ancient capital of Lahore was attached to Pakistan. A new capital became necessary for the East Punjab with its twelve and a half million inhabitants. On a sloping plateau at the foot of the Himalayas a superb site was discovered in 1950 through airplane reconnaissance by E. L. Varma, an eminent Indian government engineer.

The new capital city was called Chandigarh after a village on the site. When complete, it will house half a million people. The first section, now largely constructed, is for a population of 150,000. Neighborhood planning, housing, and schools are under the direction of Pierre Jeanneret and of Maxwell Fry and Jane Drew (whose building activities on the Gold Coast have been recognized) in coöperation with an entirely Indian staff of architects and engineers. The Capitol itself was entrusted to Le Corbusier, who has also been responsible for the final master plan of the whole city.[7]

A town planner, an architect, an artist, a sculptor, and a man with the grasp of a poet are surveying a wide empty space at the foot of the Himalayas. These five are united in one person. This is the spot where the Capitol of Chandigarh is to stand. There is nothing more thrilling for the truly creative mind than to turn a dream into reality here on this myth-soaked soil. To achieve this, it may be worth while to have accepted a lifetime of humiliations.

We can follow line by line in Le Corbusier's sketch-book how the vision of the new Capitol crystallized, how it became a mighty monument, in which, for the first time, eastern and western thought flowed into each other without a break. Western calculation, shell concrete vaulting and a butterfly roof of huge size which are normally associated with locomotive sheds and station platform, here change under our very eyes into some dream-building of the East (fig. **306**).

The program for the Capitol consists of a House of Parliament, a building for the Ministries, the Palace of the Governor, and the High Court of Justice. The most fantastic of these will probably be the Palace of the Governor,[8] designed in April 1952, with its roof terraces, the upper one concave in shape. The Court of Justice, with its seven chambers under construction in 1953, is under the shade of an enormous butterfly roof which provides an umbrella of reinforced concrete against tropical sun and monsoon rains, which last from July to October. The huge sloping eaves stretch far out from the building. Parabolic shell vaults stiffen the structure and span the wide open entrance hall, which reaches up to the full height of the building. In this strange Palace of Justice modern techniques comply with cosmic conditions, with the country and with the habits of its people.

---

[7] See Le Corbusier, *Œuvre*, V, 128–159. The first master plan, less regular in form, was designed by Albert Mayer and Matthew Nowiczky, 1949–50. See Otto Königsberger, "New Towns in India," *Town Planning Review*, XXIII, 116 (1952).

[8] Le Corbusier, *Œuvre*, V, 154.

What astonishes the European eye is the large distances between the buildings. Only reality will show whether these are not too grandiose, as has happened in India with government buildings erected under the British Raj. But there will be no dead surfaces between them. The sculptor in Le Corbusier has taken the opportunity to mold the enormous surface by varying levels, large pools, green lawns, single trees, artificial hills made of surplus material; and also by symbolic representations of the harmonic spiral, the daily path of the sun and other such. A dominant symbol will be the "open hand" which will be seen from everywhere and will "turn on ball bearings like a weathercock."[9] The impress of the human hand placed upon the rock was the first artistic utterance of man. This symbol is still alive in India, and at the marriage feast friends leave the red stamp of their hands — red is the color of good luck — on the white walls of the bridal pair.

A monument in form of an enormous hand can be found earlier in the work of Le Corbusier. It was then an aggressive and menacing hand. Now under an eastern sky it has quieted down like the hand of Buddha.

E. L. Varma, who discovered the site of Chandigarh, has given the Indian response to this symbol in a letter to Le Corbusier:

"We have a word, *Ram Bharosa*, which indicates deep faith in the ultimate — faith born of the surrender of the will to the Ultimate Source of Knowledge, service without reward and much more. I live in that faith and feel happy in the vision of the new city which is so safe and so secure in its creation in your hands.

"We are humble people. No guns to brandish, no atomic energy to kill. Your philosophy of 'Open Hand' will appeal to India in its entirety. What you are giving to India and what we are taking from your open hand, I pray, may become a source of new inspiration in our architectural and city planning. We may on our side, when you come here next, be able to show you the spiritual heights to which some of the individuals have attained. Ours is a philosophy of open hand. Maybe Chandigarh becomes the center of new thought."

[9] See Le Corbusier, *Œuvre*, V, 150, 151.

MIES VAN DER ROHE AND THE
INTEGRITY OF FORM

322. PETER DE HOOCH. Mother and Child, c. 1650. *Dutch interiors with their crystal-clear atmosphere have an inner affinity with Piet Mondrian as well as with Mies van der Rohe's balancing of plane surfaces.*

Mies van der Rohe grew up in Aachen, a residence of Charlemagne, the oldest center of German civilization. The town lies close to the Dutch border, and many of its inhabitants possess the calm, phlegmatic nature of the Netherlanders. This is not obtuseness, but rather a shield against the outer world — a withdrawal into an inner concentration. At least this is the way it is with Mies van der Rohe.

At all events, his work is closer akin to the Dutch than that of any other German architect. How these qualities are reflected in his buildings will be traced in the following pages. The spirit of Dutch seventeenth-century "interiors" with their crystal-clear atmosphere and precisely framed walls and open-

541

ings (*fig.* **322**), have an inner affinity with Mies van der Rohe's balancing of plane surfaces.

The correct placing of brick upon brick and stone upon stone was known to Mies van der Rohe from childhood in his father's workshop. His fanaticism for pure form and the great care with which he uses materials are probably derived from these early experiences.[1]

But these are merely general preliminary conditions. How does Mies van der Rohe's work stand in relation to his own period?

The Elements of Mies van der Rohe's Architecture

The secret of every creative architectural development is based mainly on three factors: a client with an instinct for quality; a master who, by his own work and personality, knows how to awaken the creative possibilities of a younger generation; and the existence of a rising generation, able to select the best place to provide the right nourishment for their needs.

Peter Behrens and Mies van der Rohe

In this instance, the client was Emil Rathenau, president of the General Electric Company of Berlin; the master was Peter Behrens; and the rising generation that found their way to Peter Behrens at this important moment included Mies van der Rohe, Gropius, and — for a short time as a visitor — Le Corbusier. Peter Behrens' atelier was the only one in Germany where this younger generation could find what it needed. Peter Behrens' turbine factory of 1909 showed that materials such as glass and iron possessed within them a secret strength of expression that could be brought out as soon as an artist understood how to develop their means and possibilities. Between this building of 1909 and the buildings of the forties lies the gulf created by the new conception of space. Nevertheless, the factories of Peter Behrens provided firmer foundations for Mies van der Rohe's means of expression than the country houses of the romantic German classicist Karl Friedrich Schinkel (1781–1840) or of Berlage, who, around 1900, brought the smooth wall surface back into European architecture.

---

[1] For further details see Philip C. Johnson, *Mies van der Rohe* (New York: Museum of Modern Art, 1947), with passages from the artist's writings and bibliography.

In 1910 Frank Lloyd Wright came into the European field of vision. During the time that Walter Gropius and Mies van der Rohe were working with Peter Behrens, the exhibition of Frank Lloyd Wright's work was shown in Berlin. "We young architects found ourselves in painful inner discord. The work of this great master presented an architectural world of unexpected force, clarity of language and disconcerting richness of form," Mies van der Rohe wrote much later.

The openness of the Wright ground plan, which grew out in all directions like a spreading plant (*fig.* **243**), and Wright's tendency to conceive the entire house as one flowing space brought the European architects to a sudden realization of their own stiffness. The man from the prairie taught them to return to living forms.

Among the elements of Mies van der Rohe's later work we can recognize the care in handling new materials that Peter Behrens had shown, and also the free ground plan of Frank Lloyd Wright's houses. The Fagus factory that Gropius was to build in the following year (1911) gives evidence of the altered outlook of the younger generation. Glass and iron were no longer enclosed by massive walls. They joined directly together at the corners, with effortless ease (*fig.* **291**).

Just as in Mies van der Rohe's well-known studies for glass skyscrapers between 1919 and 1921 [2] and in his scheme for a large office building in 1922,[3] artistic expression was given to the fact that the skeleton lies within the building or, as Mies

---

[2] These studies began in 1919 with a competition scheme for an office building in the Friedrichstrasse of Berlin. They should not be considered in isolation. In the office building for the Friedrichstrasse, while Mies van der Rohe's treatment of materials and the pureness of his form is far ahead of his competitors, his indented ground plan still reflects the expressionistic tendency of German architecture in the twenties. In the Dutch journal *Wendingen*, volume III, Series 5 (Amsterdam, 1923), there is an interesting article by H. Th. Wijdeveld and Dr. A. Behne on the romanticism of the skyscraper motif that was then sweeping through Europe. Here one becomes aware of the relationship as well as the difference between Mies van der Rohe's scheme and those by Hans Poelzig, Hugo Häring, and others.

[3] Johnson, *Mies van der Rohe*, p. 31.

van der Rohe puts it: "Columns and girders eliminate bearing walls. This is skin and bone construction."

A third impetus for Mies van der Rohe's creative development came from Holland. Around 1920 no other country was producing as many interesting developments in the field of housing as the Netherlands. The decisive outlet for expressing the new architectural vocabulary was neither in factories nor in retail stores, but in the human domain of the dwelling house and the housing group.[4]

It is therefore understandable that, following upon all the good work that was realized as well as some misguided efforts of the so-called Amsterdam school, Theo van Doesburg set forward an ideal clearing and purification program in his journal *Stijl* (1917).[5] The exhibition of the Stijl Group (painting, sculpture, and architecture) that was designed by Theo van Doesburg together with C. van Eesteren and G. Rietveld at Léonce Rosenberg's gallery in Paris (October 1923) exerted a great influence upon the leading talents such as Le Corbusier and Mies van der Rohe, particularly through its models and presentation of architectural material. This exhibition showed that the steps toward Frank Lloyd Wright's perception of the house as a flowing space bounded by vertical and horizontal planes had been fully taken and understood (*fig.* **81**).

Country Houses, 1923

Mies van der Rohe's studies for two country houses (**1923**), one in brick and one in concrete (*figs.* **323, 324, 326**)[6] are of

---

[4] No other country in 1920 could parallel J. J. P. Oud's workers' housing project in Rotterdam, Ir. J. B. van Loghem's Rosehaghe settlement in Haarlem (1920) and his concrete Watergraafsmeer houses in Amsterdam (1922), Jan Wil's Papaverhof dwellings in the Hague (1919–21), or, with reservations, M. de Klerk's apartment houses in Amsterdam between 1914 and 1923 (fig. 432) and W. M. Dudock's work in Hilversum around 1920. The sole forerunner was Robert van t'Hoff's concrete single-family houses in Huisterheide (1914–15).

[5] See above, pp. 438–439, and also J. J. P. Oud, *Hollandische Architektur*, Bauhausbücher Nr. 10, ed. by Walter Gropius and L. Moholy-Nagy (Munich, 1925); Ir. J. B. van Loghem, *Holland Built To Live In* (Amsterdam, 1932). Both books are written by leading architects and therefore particularly interesting in their selection of materials.

[6] Published first in *G*, Number II (Berlin, September 1923). This is a journal edited by Mies van der Rohe, Richter, and Graff, of which three numbers appeared. Its contents come near to *Stijl* and *Esprit Nouveau*.

inestimable importance for the development of modern architecture. The analytical spirit of Theo van Doesburg had enabled him to show by means of his transparent architectural drawings that the conception of the house as a self-contained cube had lost its meaning. In these two studies, Mies van der Rohe gives this conception a clear and concentrated artistic expression.

Under Mies van der Rohe's orderly hand the planes become assembly points for material and structure — plate glass, ferroconcrete, and, soon afterward, marble. Even more clearly than in the *Stijl* studies, these country houses of Mies van der Rohe give a realizable form to the floating character of the elements that make up the house. This is the period during which Le Corbusier built his La Roche house at Auteuil and G. Rietveld his stylized house at Utrecht (1924). Planes protruding from within the house do not halt at the outer walls, as with van Doesburg, but spread out into the landscape like the sails of a windmill. At the same time, the surface elements have become assembly points for the structural elements. Transparency is achieved by penetration through long window strips surmounted by a hovering roof slab (*fig.* **326**). All these elements, which are not individual inventions, are brought together with a masterly artistic control.[7]

In the houses Mies van der Rohe actually built about this time, he was unable to realize the daring that he had developed in his paper studies. His visions became a reality for the first time in his exhibition pavilion in Barcelona in 1929 (*fig.* **325**). With unsurpassed precision he used pure surfaces of precious materials as elements of the new space conception. Perhaps his most famous house is the Tugendhat House[8] in Brno, Czechoslovakia (1930), which achieves extreme generosity in its flowing interpenetration of space. Even so, one does not get away from the feeling of being exposed to an aquarium-like existence.

---

[7] In the introduction to R. J. Neutra's *Buildings and Projects* (Zurich, 1951), we have attempted to develop further the great influence which the unrealized schemes of both the Stijl Group and Mies van der Rohe had upon R. J. Neutra's own development.

[8] Johnson, pp. 76–86.

323. MIES VAN DER ROHE. Project of a brick country house, 1923.

324. MIES VAN DER ROHE. Brick country house, 1923. Ground plan. *Planes protruding from within the house do not halt at the outer walls, but spread out into the landscape like the sails of a windmill.*

325. MIES VAN DER ROHE. German pavilion at the International Exhibition, Barcelona, 1929. *Here his visions became a reality for the first time. With unsurpassed precision he used pure surfaces of precious materials as elements of the new space conception.*

326. MIES VAN DER ROHE. Project of a concrete house, 1923. *The plane surfaces have become assembly points for the structural elements. Transparency is achieved by penetration through long windowstrips, surmounted by a hovering roof slab.*

327. MIES VAN DER ROHE. Country house for a bachelor, Berlin Building Exhibition, 1931. *In the center of the great exhibition hall, Mies van der Rohe erected one of his glass-walled single-story houses. One of the last modern manifestations before the collapse of German culture.*

328. MIES VAN DER ROHE. Country house for a bachelor. Ground Plan. *The same trends are shown as in the brick country house, 1923. Planes protruding from within the house, as well as the flowing space of the interior, become reality.*

547

In 1931, when the Brownshirts were already filling the streets of Berlin and the country was in a state of crisis — five million unemployed, breakdown of industry in all fields, market difficulties of all kinds — a building exhibition on a grand scale was opened. In it the creative forces of Germany worked together. It was the last time. Walter Gropius, L. Moholy-Nagy, and Herbert Bayer of the Bauhaus, who were commissioned by the Coöperative Housing Society, attempted to show the public, with all the power of modern display techniques and artistic eloquence, what should be done to achieve a human approach to the housing problem.

In the center of the great exhibition hall, undisturbed by all the excitement, Mies van der Rohe erected a glass-walled single-story house with fine interiors, apparently for a bachelor, in which without any compromise he proceeded to develop the unity of space, plane, and structure which lay so near to his heart (*figs.* **327, 328**).[9]

Neither the propaganda appeal to the masses nor architectural achievement was able to have the slightest effect, however. Developments had to move in another direction.

In Germany, the architectural contribution was made in a terribly short time. The opportunity existed for only a very few years. No one who was present at the opening of the Weissenhofsiedlung in Stuttgart in 1927 could have foreseen that only five years later all would be over.

Mies van der Rohe and the Weissenhof Housing Settlement, Stuttgart, 1927

There was a moment in the middle of the twenties when the clear primary colors used by Picasso, Braque, Leger, and other modern painters seemed to radiate an optimism that had not been present before and was not to occur again. Once the war and the inflation had been overcome, it seemed that a new period was about to dawn in which the upsurge of a new way

---

[9] There were also family houses by the Berlin architects Luckhardt and Marcel Breuer, and a hall by Walter Gropius for one of his multi-story apartment houses. See Peiro Bottoni, "Berlin 1931," *Rassegna d'Architettura*, 15 September 1931.

of life, new art, and a new architecture could no longer be held under.

Germany was at this time more aware of the outside world than ever before. The *Avantgarde* were dragged out from their seclusion and plunged into active life. This explains the founding of the Bauhaus by Walter Gropius (1919) together with painters such as Paul Klee, W. Kandinsky, and Moholy-Nagy, as well as the appointment of Mies van der Rohe as first vice-president of the Deutscher Werkbund.[10]

The Weissenhof Housing Settlement at Stuttgart (*figs.* **329, 330**), which the Werkbund had entrusted to Mies van der Rohe, is perhaps the clearest indication of the change that had taken place within the all-too-thin layer of the elite. Invitations were issued, in the most generous manner, to young architects from other nations to execute their own buildings. From Holland came J. J. P. Oud and Mart Stam, both of whom built row houses following the custom of their own country. From France came Le Corbusier, who erected his two most-discussed houses on pillars. From Belgium came Victor Bourgeois. The young Swiss architects were given one of the flats in Mies van der Rohe's apartment home. At one end of the settlement, Peter Behrens, the veteran German architect, built his fortress-like apartment block; and around and between the German and Austrian architects established their single-family dwellings — Walter Gropius, Bruno Taut, Scharoun, Rading, Hilbersheimer, Doecker, J. Frank, and others.

No one who lived through these opening days will forget the optimism and the moral support produced by this event — achieved against apparently inflexible opposition.

A few paragraphs written in 1927[11] may convey a more immediate impression:

"The exhibition certainly gave us an insight into actual life. We believe that it has extraordinary significance because it has brought new methods of construction out from the secluded

---

[10] See pp. 475–476.

[11] S. Giedion, "L'Exposition du Werkbund à Stuttgart 1927," and "La Cité du Weissenhof," in *Architecture Vivante* (Paris, 1928).

329. Weissenhof settlement, Stuttgart, 1927. *In the foreground, Le Corbusier's two houses with roof gardens; to the left, J. J. P. Oud's row houses and Mies van der Rohe's apartment houses; to the rear, Peter Behrens' apartment house with tower; the two-story row houses in front of it are by Mart Stam.*

1-4	Mies van der Rohe	20	Hans Poelzig
5-9	J.J.P. Oud	21-22	Richard Döcker
10	Victor Bourgeois	23-24	Max Taut
11-12	Adolf G. Schneck	25	Adolf Rading
13-15	Le Corbusier ● Pierre Jeanneret	26-27	Josef Frank
16-17	Walter Gropius	28-30	Mart Stam
18	Ludwig Hilberseimer	31-32	Peter Behrens
19	Bruno Taut	33	Hans Scharoun

330. Weissenhof settlement, Stuttgart, 1927. Plan. *This settlement marks the moment when contemporary architects from different countries had an opportunity to show for the first time, not by words but by building together upon the same site, that a new approach to the housing problem had been developed.*

550

331. Weissenhof settlement, Stuttgart, 1927. *Mies van der Rohe's special contribution was the first adaptation of the steel skeleton to meet new needs in the housing problem. His large Chicago apartments are here foreshadowed.*

332. Ground Plan of the second floor. *Each floor had a different plan. The apartment to the left leaves the steel columns passing freely through the room.*

333. Steel Skeleton of Mies van der Rohe's apartment house.

laboratory of the *Avantgarde* and caused them to be put into operation on a broad scale. The new architecture . . . can never develop soundly without the active participation of the masses. Of course, the problems that have to be solved are not posed by any conscious expression of the masses. For many reasons their conscious mind is always ready to say 'No' to new artistic experiences. But if the unconscious mind is once directed into a new path, then the laboratory product will be broadened and adapted to meet the needs of real life. The Stuttgart exhibition appears to us as the nucleus of such a process, and herein lies its importance."

"The Weissenhof Housing Settlement gives evidence of two great changes: the change from handicraft methods of construction to industrialization, and the premonition of a new way of life.

"Mies van der Rohe's original plan was to interlock the house-plots so that a unified relationship could be created and the green areas would flow into one another. This plan unfortunately could not be realized for commercial reasons. Even so it is possible to experience how relationship and order are created by the level unassertive surfaces of flat roofs in places that would otherwise have been utterly chaotic. In flat towns, such as the Hague, one can observe how the flat roofs create wide interconnecting bands.

Mies van der Rohe's steel-framed apartment house

"The Weissenhof Housing Settlement is dominated by Mies van der Rohe's steel-framed apartment house (*figs*. **331, 332, 333**). Even the apartment house, which today usually takes the form of a palace or a castle, is here transformed into a more loosely articulated structure. The steel frame permits one to eliminate all rigid inner and outer walls. For the outside, an insulated filling wall with a half-brick thickness is sufficient, and the inner walls can be disposed according to the liking of the tenants, in whatever manner they choose. The wide and continuous window strips are the only limiting factors. These window strips are wide and continuous in order to enable good light to penetrate as deeply as possible into the building. The problem of the apartment house is today (1927) even further from solution than that of the single-family house.

552

Mies van der Rohe's steel skeleton shows a possible way of unraveling this problem.

"Many architectural critics found the continuous steel supports that ran freely through the houses of Mies van der Rohe and Le Corbusier very unsightly. It seems that it is especially difficult for the architect to free himself from the appearance of traditional structural methods in which the walls were the bearing members of the house. It is fundamentally organic to our present-day conceptions of space that complete expression is given to the inner construction of our houses. The continuous steel support is definitely not an aesthetic focal point. It may be allowed to run quietly through the space. Just as the columns of ancient architecture give the onlooker a feeling of security by means of their ordered play of load and support, so the continuous steel or concrete shaft gives today's onlooker an impression of a powerful energy that flows uniformly through the house. The free-standing visible column is thus given a new expressive quality apart from its constructive objectivity. Here is continuous energy at work: nothing in our life remains an isolated experience; everything stands in a many-sided interrelationship — within, without, above, below!

"Mies van der Rohe has followed the possibilities of his building through to the utmost detail. Plywood walls that can be screwed onto the ceilings enable the occupier to alter the disposition of his space at will. Doorless connections between rooms. One is continually amazed at the amount of space that this method makes possible within an area of 70 square meters (750 square feet). It acts upon us as a necessary stimulant — an impetus that can set industry into motion."

The Weissenhof Housing Settlement was, at the same time, a living manifesto of rational planning and organization of the house interior. We have described elsewhere how the general public was here, for the first time, introduced to the organization of work and space within the kitchen as well as to the cantilever tubular chair as developed by Mies van der Rohe and at the same time by Mart Stam.[12]

---

[12] *Mechanization Takes Command*, pp. 523–526, 493–503.

334. MIES VAN DER ROHE. Aerial View of campus of Illinois Institute of Technology, showing all proposed and completed buildings. *White outlines indicate buildings projected; asterisks in list below indicate completed buildings and dagger indicates building under construction, 1953. (1) Athletic field; (2) Gymnasium and swimming pool; (3) Field house; (4) Alumni Memorial Hall; * (5) Metallurgical and chemical engineering; * (6) AAR research building; * (7) Library and administration; (8) Chemistry; * (9) Liberal studies; (10) Mechanical engineering; (11) Civil engineering and mechanics; (12) Laboratory building; (13) Laboratory building; (14) Electrical engineering and physics; (15) Student Union and auditorium; (16) Architecture and applied arts; (17) ARF research and administration; (18) Institute of Gas Technology; * (19) Research laboratory; (20) Research laboratory; (21) Metals research; * (22) ARF engineering research; * (23) ARF engineering research; † (24) Heating and power plant; * (25) ARF engineering research.*

335. MIES VAN DER ROHE. Administration Building, 1944. *The pureness of form, juxtaposition of different structures, sensitivity of proportion, and discipline of outline — all previously indicated in his country house of 1923 — are here fully developed.*

336. MIES VAN DER ROHE. Chemical Engineering and Metallurgy Building, 1949. *Northwest view.*

Mies van der Rohe Builds

Scarcely anything is so much wasted today as creative energy in the field of the arts. This waste is aggravated by the fact that the dictatorships of our time — themselves without any awareness of contemporary art — detest everything which is not strictly reactionary in its means of expression.

If Mies van der Rohe, who — as we noted at the start — is well endowed with patience and tranquility, had not been invited to Chicago in 1938, what would have become of him? The subsequent fate of German architects and architecture — one of the most depressing spectacles of our time — gives sufficient answer.

Now his tall apartment houses spring up in the most beautiful parts of Chicago and he has been working since 1939 on the buildings for the Illinois Institute of Technology, whose completion may occupy a quarter of a century.[13] Usually an

The Illinois Institute of Technology since 1939

[13] For details see Hugo Weber, "Mies van der Rohe in Chicago," *Bauen und Wohnen*, No. 9 (Zurich, 1951), an excellent survey of the work of Mies van der Rohe.

337. MIES VAN DER ROHE. Minerals and Metal Research Building, 1943. South view. *The module of twenty-four feet as a basis for the planning of the whole campus, together with a careful balance within the plane surfaces, is evident in the south-front view of this laboratory.*

American building is completely amortised within this period. It would seem thus that Mies van der Rohe has somehow been able to transfer his own inborn patience to the American board of trustees.

The spatial disposition of the twenty-four buildings can be best understood when one looks back upon Mies van der Rohe's design for a country house in 1923. There the new relationship between the different fragments of the walls induced a feeling of an all-penetrating oneness of space. The same is true of the buildings for the Chicago campus. The twenty-four buildings stand in a rectilinear relationship to one another like that of the walls of the earlier project. At the same time, they are so disposed that an all-embracing space is created though not visible at one glance — a space that can only be slowly perceived by including the dimension of time, that is, by movement (*fig.* **334**).

Like an Egyptian sculptor working on a bas-relief, Mies van der Rohe stretches a network of squared coördinates across all the buildings on his campus. His module is 24 feet (*fig.* **337**). Without one's realizing it, this module is imprinted upon the spectator at every step.

Mies van der Rohe, with Le Corbusier, is among the very few architects who are again deliberately cultivating proportional relationships in their work. Both do this in the Pythagorean sense in which measurements are not merely measurements but possess qualitative as well as quantitative properties. Proportions

Care in handling proportions is allied with care in handling materials. The buildings for the Illinois Institute of Technology display none of the walls of onyx and columns of chromium of Mies van der Rohe's earlier period. But proportion, structure, and material are here related to one another with an even greater finesse.

The side walls of a laboratory or a factory, with their exposed skeletons of steelwork and brick infilling, are usually disregarded secondary factors, but with Mies van der Rohe they are transformed into elements of the highest artistic value.

This may not all be apparent to the casual observer. All the same, it is certain that — even without one's knowledge — an ordered environment of this sort has its effect upon one. Just as the Weissenhof housing settlement in 1927 was a manifesto which greatly influenced subsequent development, so the buildings of this Chicago campus make an appeal for greater artistic integrity in architecture.

In 1949, thirty years after his early skyscraper studies, Mies van der Rohe was building tall apartment blocks along Lake Michigan. One of these, the Promontory Apartments, stands in South Chicago, not far from the buildings shown in figure **449**. The view from the great glass windows over the limitless Skyscraper apartments since 1949

557

338. MIES VAN DER ROHE. Promontory Apartment, Chicago, 1949. East front. Detail of the entrance side. *Great care has been given to incorporate the ferroconcrete skeleton into the artistic expression of the façade. The photograph shows the distinct setback of the joists which grow slimmer as they gain height. This accentuation of the pillars together with the well-calculated setback of the window areas and filling walls is typical of Mies van der Rohe's integrating hand.*

339. Promontory Apartment, 1949. *The U-shaped ground plan together with the free planning of each floor was first used in Chicago office buildings (compare fig. 176); then for housing in the twenties, and toward 1950 for large apartment houses.*

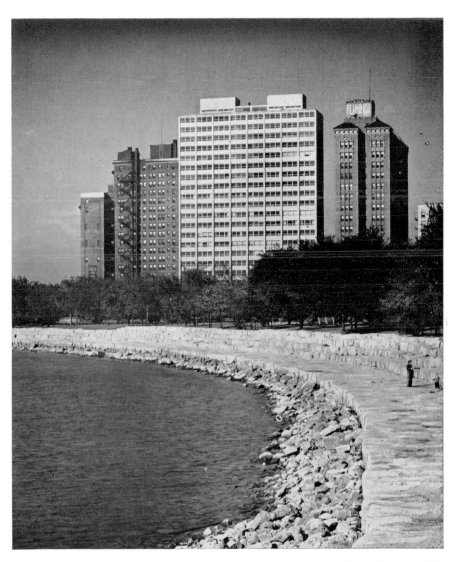

340. Promontory Apartment, 1949. East front. *This apartment house is situated in the South Side of Chicago, very near those in fig. 449. The windows overlook the broad expanse of Lake Michigan and the occupants enjoy a feeling of individual existence and contact with air and nature much greater than they can have in row houses on a side street.*

Lake is overwhelming. Twenty-two stories. Ferroconcrete skeleton. U-shaped ground plan, as in Holabird and Roche's Marquette Building, Chicago, 1894 (*fig.* **230**). The Promontory Apartments actually consist of two units joined as one, each containing its own elevators and stairway. The detailing is monastic in its austerity (*figs.* **338, 341**).

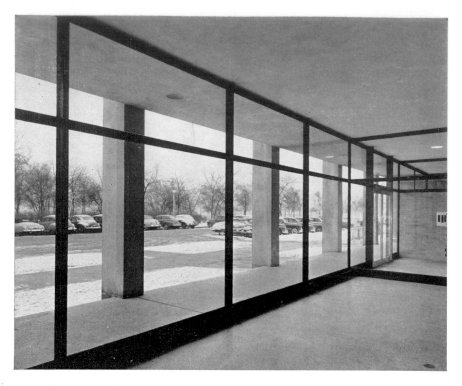

341. Promontory Apartment, 1949. *View from the lobby dividing the symmetrically built wings. Here too, the treatment of detail and proportion has a very stimulating effect.*

The hand of Mies van der Rohe can be felt in the ground plan of each of the apartments (*fig.* **339**) and particularly in the treatment of the façade (*fig.* **340**). These soaring ferroconcrete verticals, set back four times in their height, are handled with an extraordinary sensitivity and give a musical articulation to the whole façade.[14]

Mies van der Rohe's skyscraper apartments, now growing in the most prominent parts of Chicago, revive — after a dismal interval — the tradition of the Chicago School of the 1880's. In them a strange symbiosis has come about: an understanding between the creative powers of an artist and the gigantic organization of modern building industrialization.

[14] The following were connected with the Promontory Apartments: Associated Architects, Pace Associates and Mies van der Rohe; Consulting Architects, Holsman and Klekamp; Engineer, Frank J. Kornacker.

At the time of the Chicago School it was still possible for the architect to assume complete responsibility for carrying through his work. Mechanization of the building industry has now made this practically impossible, yet the creative artist who explores new ways can never be replaced by an organizational machine. When the creative architect knows how to play upon the stupendous keyboard of mechanization we need not feel troubled about the future of architecture.

None of Mies van der Rohe's buildings has had such an immediate influence upon his American contemporaries as his two largest and most radical apartment houses at 860 Lake Shore Drive, Chicago (1951; *figs*. **342, 343**). Here — as in his Farnsworth House at Plano, Illinois (1950) — integrity of form has become the supreme law to which everything else is subordinated. With uncompromising strength the architect permits not the slightest deviation from the clear-cut plane surfaces of the glass parallelepipeds or the glass box. Each detail seems to remind the spectator: Architecture is discipline; architecture is an artifact!

Lake Shore Apartments, 1951

On the Integrity of Form

There exist different types of creative spirits. Some conceive what they are destined to contribute to human culture once and for all at an early stage. Descartes perceived his philosophic system, as he has said himself, during the course of a single night. He elaborated it, but he never changed its structure.

There are other creative spirits who cannot be pinned down to what they thought in their youth, but who are continuously developing, continually in movement, throughout the span of their lives. Goethe is the prototype for this kind of eternally changing and developing spirit.

Confining our outlook to contemporary architecture, similar differences appear: Le Corbusier's development, for instance, undoubtedly reflects the second type, while Mies van der

561

Rohe belongs to those who, at an early stage, conceive what their temperaments will elaborate throughout their lives.

It was at the beginning of the 1920's that Mies van der Rohe came to realize his own innate mode of expression. At this time his schemes radiated out, as in the windmill plans of his country houses of 1923, or were multiform in outline, as in his glass tower of 1921.

What followed was a continuous pressure for the conquest of pure form. This has been accompanied by an ever stricter renunciation of all that seemed to the architect hampering or nonessential. It is this demand for the absolute that lies behind Mies van der Rohe's often deliberately misinterpreted saying: "Less is more."

He holds ever more strongly to one of the constituent elements of contemporary architecture, the plane surface, which he likes to use in its smoothest and most transparent form — the glass sheet.

342. MIES VAN DER ROHE. Lake Shore Drive Apartments, 1951. Plan. *One of the most advanced examples of building by assembling prefabricated parts.*

343. MIES VAN DER ROHE. Lake Shore Drive Apartments, 1951. *The use of glass may here have reached its zenith, unless industry creates the technical means for adjusting the different qualities of light without the use of curtains.*

He makes no distinction between his approach to a single-story dwelling, two-story buildings, or multi-story apartments. The attitude of the perfectionist controls the dimensioning of all surfaces, outlines, and details. Volumes are reduced to their simplest form — the glass towers of the Lake Shore Apartments, the glass-encased Mannheim Theatre (1952–53), the glass box of the Farnsworth House, the enclosed brick box of the Campus chapel, which develops a dramatic force by being reft open on its entrance side by an enormous glass screen through which the slim crucifix of stainless steel gleams from afar as two transverse beams of light.

This strict discipline has had a deep moral influence upon contemporary American architecture. Without it, it is possible that Eero Saarinen's delicately organized complex for the General Motors Technical Center (Detroit, 1951), would never have arisen in its present form; nor New York's purest skyscraper, the 24-story Lever House (Park Avenue, 1952),[1] which has a more socially welcoming attitude and spatial development than the monastic severity of the Lake Shore Apartments.

Mies van der Rohe and Le Corbusier

One becomes conscious of the creative diversity in architectural expression which has developed during a quarter of a century when one compares these Lake Shore Apartments with Le Corbusier's "Unité d'Habitation" in Marseille, whose plastic forms, which play so important a role in the whole conception, are made even stronger by the movement of light upon their deliberately rough concrete surfaces.

---

[1] Designed by Gordon Bunschaft of the firm of Skidmore, Owings and Merrill.

ALVAR AALTO:
ELEMENTAL AND CONTEMPORARY

Aalto is the strongest exponent of the combination of standardization with irrationality, so that standardization is no longer master but servant. The moral force behind the development of architecture in recent decades has had one supreme concern: to reëstablish a union between life and architecture. Aalto is the youngest of those architects who have created the present-day vocabulary.

Earlier, Frank Lloyd Wright evolved a language of forms, direct, as it would seem, from the prairie. His private houses of about 1900 emphasized the human aspect and stood in complete contrast to the skyscrapers the young Wright had watched as they grew.

The road that Europe had to take to free itself from the devaluated architectural language of the ruling taste proved to be a much more difficult one. When Walter Gropius put forward a new means of architectural expression in Europe about 1913, he could not begin directly with the home; he had to begin by confining himself to those forms of construction and types of buildings that had remained uncorrupted: frame structures, factories, exhibition buildings. In the early twenties, Le Corbusier shaped the house on the basis of a new space conception. His points of departure were the ferroconcrete skeleton and the means of artistic expression that had developed since cubism. At the same time, through the work of the *Stijl* group, Holland contributed theories of artistic fundamentals as well as practical solutions. The movement centered around Theo van Doesburg, Mondrian, Rietveld, van Eesteren, and others. J. J. P. Oud expressed its social concepts in the workers' quarters that he built from 1919 onwards, in which the marriage of function and aesthetics is handled in a masterly fashion. These means of expression and their elements — standardization, new methods of construction, and, above all, a new space conception — had developed so far by 1930 that an architectural language already lay at the disposal of anyone capable of using it.

The Complementarity of the Differentiated and the Primitive

About 1930 Alvar Aalto's name began to be known outside Finland. What part was he to play? At this time, painters like Joan Miró and Paul Klee, whose work is closely bound to the organic and the irrational, were coming to the fore. A similar event was about to happen in architecture.

As early as 1925, in Le Corbusier's Pavillon de l'Esprit Nouveau in Paris, natural objects — stones, shells, and grotesque roots — lay alongside mechanically formed objects which have acquired a perfect standard type through man's long experience with them, such as everyday drinking glasses, wine bottles, or laboratory equipment. It seems today to be requisite that we should live both with objects shaped by man and with objects of organic growth.

We have seen how the new architecture had first to develop out of those elements that had remained sound: iron construction and ferroconcrete. But by about 1930 the new means of expression had been attained. Now it was possible to strive for further development and to dare the leap from the rational-functional to the irrational-organic. This need already lay concealed within the functional conception. To avoid misunderstanding, let it be stated that this development toward the organic in no way approximates the German reaction of the 1930's, or certain Nordic evasions of the real problem curiously labeled "New Empiricism," which means, as has been pointed out, that "coziness is coming back into domestic work." The feeling for mass production and for standardization has not been discarded at all, only now we have at hand not only the necessary techniques but also perhaps an insight into the use of these from a human standpoint.

Alongside iron and ferroconcrete construction, the ancient material, wood, came again to the fore. By 1930 it appeared that wood had been squeezed by manufacturers of all its potentialities. It seemed as though the constellation under which Aalto was born predestined him to discover the new potentialities of this organic material.

Finland is with Aalto wherever he goes. It provides him with
that inner source of energy which always flows through his
work. It is as Spain is to Picasso or Ireland to James Joyce.
Part of the essence of present-day art is that its true representatives originate in a definite human environment and their
work is not created in a vacuum. But it is also part of its
essence that barriers between space and time, barriers between countries, and barriers between future and past are torn
down, and with a bold sweep our own period, the whole world,
and the whole of history are embraced. Georges Braque expresses this in a Bergsonian manner in his recently published
sketchbook: "L'avenir est la projection du passé, conditionée
par le présent." [1]

Perhaps later periods will observe that one of our good qualities was our endeavor to combine the technical with the
primeval. This same phenomenon appears in all the arts: out
of forgotten strata of consciousness the elements of primitive
man which are dormant in us are again brought to light, and
at the same time unity is sought with the present day.

Aalto is restless. He does not always remain in the pine and
birch forests of Finland. First he made contact with the
continent; since 1939 he has stood with one foot in America.
His nature leads him to come into contact with whatever
the place and the period have to offer for the forces of
artistic development. In addition, he has personal friend-
ships with such artists as Fernand Léger, Hans Arp, and
Brancusi, the sculptor. He recognizes modern art as a great
reservoir which, though often invisible, provides the decisive
power for his own creativeness. One senses this in his sanatorium, in his factories, in his Viipuri Library, as well as in
the simplest schemes that he sketches on the wall.

When Aalto was in the United States in 1939, building the
Finnish Pavilion for the New York World's Fair, he and I
were once sitting together with Brancusi, the sculptor. Bran-

---

[1] *Cahier de Georges Braque 1917–1947* (Paris, 1948.)

344. Finland, transportation of wood. *After drying in the forests, the logs start a year-long journey over lakes and rivers down to the sea, where they are converted into pulp at cellulose plants.*

cusi had been telling of some work that he had done for an Indian Maharajah when Aalto suddenly exclaimed, "I see now, Brancusi! You stand at the crossroads of Asia and Europe!" Finland is also at the crossroads of East and West, but for the moment we would only stress the fact that many remnants of primeval and medieval times still remain alive there and intermingle with modern civilization. This double nature is instilled in Aalto too, and gives creative tension to his work.

Finland

Finland is one of the countries that were longest covered with glaciers. Civilization, as it traveled over the earth, always reached this country very late — from the neolithic period onward to this century. Often eastern and western influences have intermingled here.

Of all the countries of Europe, Finland is in many respects one of the most peculiar. Its people have never risen to imperialistic power and splendor, like the Vikings of Norway in early days, the Danes in medieval times, or the Swedes in the seventeenth century. For hundreds of years, Finland formed a part of Sweden, till Napoleon delivered it, in a moment of rage, to the Russians. Each of the rulers left his imprint on the country; but not one of the invaders could really curb the people. The only way to get along with the Finns was to treat them in a friendly manner and, as far as possible, to leave them undisturbed. This has remained true throughout Finland's whole history. It is a unique mixture of smoothness and friendliness, with an imperturbable firmness in the depths of their soul, that makes up the strength of these people.

Finland, covered with its network of lakes and forests, suggests in its structure the days of the Creation, when water and earth were first separated. It is a country of vast dimensions and solitudes: although ten times the size of Switzerland, it contains only the same number of inhabitants. Metals, timber, water — these are its principal resources. Finland is favored in that its ten thousands of lakes are connected in four or five systems and have outlets to the sea, not to the frozen north as in Russia, but to the west and to the south.

Finland's chief raw material is wood. The trees are felled in the north during the summer season. After drying in the forests for six months, they start a year-long journey over lakes and rivers, hundreds of miles, down to the sea. There in large cellulose plants at the rivers' mouths they are converted into pulp (*fig.* **344**).

Finnish Architecture before 1930

Shortly before the first world war, Central Europe and Scandinavia, including Finland, all experienced a period of prosperity. It was the result of long years of peace. The efforts that Finland made at this time to establish a strong architectural expression of its own were immediately noticeable.[3]

---

[3] *Architecture in Finland* (Helsinki, 1932), published by the Finlands Architektfoerbund, is the only book which gives an insight into Finnish development up to that time.

345. ALVAR AALTO. Pavilion for an exhibition of forestry and agriculture in the village of Lapua, North Finland. *Exterior. This structure of unhewn logs seems rather a palisade fortress against Indians than an exhibition building for forestry and agriculture. Built in 1938 in a Northern Finnish forest, it shows in its roughness that Aalto had not become conventional through his contact with Western Europe.*

346. ALVAR AALTO. Pavilion for an exhibition of forestry and agriculture in the village of Lapua, North Finland. *Interior.*

Lars Sonck, a man of over eighty when I met him in the autumn
of 1948 at a luncheon in the Liberal Club of Helsinki, is doubt-
less the strongest personality among the older Finnish architects. Himself resembling a block of unhewn granite, he built
the best churches of the whole Art Nouveau movement in the
first decade of this century. Their expressive directness and

347. ALVAR AALTO. Orchestra platform for the 700-year Jubilee of Turku, 1929.

the manner in which granite, concrete, and space are treated
still immediately capture the onlooker of 1949.[4]

Long before Eliel Saarinen left Finland for America, he was
known outside his own country for his railway station in
Helsinki (1906–14). In this celebrated building it is very easy
to be reminded of South German influences; but, just like its
architect, it is more elegant and flexible than its prototypes.

J. S. Sirén's House of Parliament in Helsinki, built in the late
twenties, is an example of Swedish classicism (especially that

---

[4] Perhaps we are considering his rough granite church in Tampere, the Finnish Manchester, more than the Kallio Kirk (1908), a kind of landmark in Helsinki.

of Ivar Tengboom and his circle); yet from this building there does not emanate that over-perfumed flavor which makes Oestberg's Town Hall in Stockholm unsupportable after a time.

Aalto's First Buildings

Alvar Aalto's active life coincides with the most consistently agitated period of Finland's existence. First came liberation, followed by only a short span of undisturbed freedom, and then two wars. By normal reasoning, either of these should have been sufficient to wipe out Finland once and for all. After these catastrophes very little money remained for the rebuilding of the damaged instruments of production. Housing had to be reduced to the utmost, and there were no funds at all for town halls, museums, civic centers, and other such signs of financial prosperity. Great public buildings will not be found in Aalto's work, and such schemes as the sanitorium at Paimio, the factory complex of Sunila, the luxury of Mairea, were created during the short period before Finland's two great fights for its very existence.

In Finland, architects and foresters have a much higher social standing than in other countries, and they form a kind of aristocracy, to which Alvar Aalto's forebears (who were foresters) belonged. Aalto himself was brought up in a village, Alajarvi, close to the northwestern end of the most densely populated region of Finland. He had an early start in his career, and while still a student at the Institute of Technology in Helsinki he built his first house, for his parents, in Alajarvi.

In these early days, Aalto had much to do with several Finnish exhibitions, but only one of these temporary buildings shall be mentioned here: the Orchestra Platform in the exhibition that celebrated the 700-year Jubilee of the founding of Finland's old capital of Turku (Åbo). This slightly curved wooden sound box (*fig.* **347**), reduced to the utmost in all its parts and delicately outlined, works, together with the inclined orchestra floor, to assure perfect sound transmission, and reveals simultaneously its plastic finesse. It was con-

348. ALVAR AALTO. *Turun Sanomat* building, Turku, Printing room, 1928–30.

349. ALVAR AALTO. Building for the *Turun-Sanomat*, Exterior, 1928–30.

ceived at the same time that Aalto was marrying ceiling and wall in his Viipuri lecture hall.

In the mid-twenties, three young Finnish architects began work: Aalto, Bryggman, and Huttunen. They all used the ferroconcrete skeleton in the way that had been developed in France and elsewhere. It is difficult to distinguish their artistic handwriting at the time when Huttunen built his excellent flour mills, Bryggman his hotels, chapels, and insurance offices, and Aalto his first large block for an Agricultural Cooperative, containing offices, flats, and a theater for 600 persons. This was in 1928, in Turku, where Aalto had opened his own office.

Then, in 1928–30, came the office building for the *Turun-Sanomat* in Turku, the first of Aalto's buildings to become known outside Finland. Here can already be seen a coalition of western technique with an artistic language all his own: the ferroconcrete skeleton, bands of horizontal windows, roof terrace, and, especially, the mushroom ceiling of the subterranean hall that houses the printing press. The tapered columns of this skylight-illuminated hall, with their sensuous one-sided mushroom capitals, show Aalto's hand at its best (*figs.* **348, 349**). Soon, in Paimio, the whole man will come to the fore.

Aalto started between the years 1927 and 1929. Before he was thirty he had been commissioned to execute the Agricultural Coöperative, the *Turun-Sanomat* building, the Viipuri Library, the sanatorium at Paimio — all of them as a result of winning competitions. These facts are mentioned more to give an insight into Finland's atmosphere than to give proof of Aalto's genius. Had Aalto grown up in one of the other democratic countries, Switzerland for example, or the United States, he could never, as early as 1929, have been given first prize for a scheme such as the sanatorium at Paimio. His wings would have been broken before he had flown, or have been crushed down by compromises. Nothing reveals more clearly the spiritual leadership of a country than the capacity of its administration to recognize the best talents right from the start, and to trust them.

350. ALVAR AALTO. Tuberculosis Sanatorium, Paimio, 1929–33. *Rest hall on top of patients' wing.*

Paimio: The Sanatorium, 1929–33

As far as we can see, there are three institutional buildings inseparably linked to the rise of contemporary architecture: the Bauhaus at Dessau by Walter Gropius (1926); the League of Nations Palace at Geneva by Le Corbusier (1927); and Alvar Aalto's sanatorium at Paimio (1929–33) in the southwest part of Finland, not far from the former capital Turku.

This institution is a medium-sized tuberculosis sanatorium with accommodation for about 290 patients. The main building, an unbroken line of six stories, is oriented to the south-southwest; the solarium with its cantilevered balconies adjoins it at a slight angle (*fig.* 351). At the end of 1928, when Aalto won the competition for this public sanatorium, courage was needed to rest the solarium on a single row of ferroconcrete pillars, to close it at the back with one flat wall, and to let seven rows of balconies protrude in an unbroken line. In a

351. ALVAR AALTO. Tuberculosis Sanatorium, Paimio, South Finland, 1929–33. *View of the entrance.*

sanatorium we have been accustomed to conceive room and balcony as a single unit, to allow the patient direct access to the open air. There are no balconies connected with the rooms at Paimio. But this separation between room and balcony is intentional. Physicians considered it as a very important factor in the rest cure that patients be brought

353. ALVAR AALTO. Tuberculosis Sanatorium, Paimio, 1929–33. *Ground plan.*

together in small groups — according to their own choice, their own preference. To avoid the impression of endless rows of patients, small partition walls have been introduced so that the patients can be divided up into these small groups (*fig.* **352**). The top floor is used as a rest hall and runs the whole length of the building (*fig.* **350**). At the point where the main building and the rest hall intersect, Aalto links them together by giving the shelter an undulating curve. From the lounge chairs one can look into the tops of near-by fir trees and see the forests beyond them. But Aalto also planted pine trees in tubs along the balconies, to soften the concrete planes. When I saw them, in the autumn of 1948, they looked strong and healthy in their stout green growth.

The human side also comes into consideration in the basic layout of the individual rooms. This is made clearly evident by the position of the electric light near the bed, by the oval-shaped plywood doors of the small closet, by the simple arrangement at the window to provide fresh air without causing drafts, by the specially designed wash basins which permit a noiseless flow of water, and by the early use of ceiling heating. These illustrate the minute elaboration of details.

Set at a right angle to the main building which houses the patients is a short wing with staircases and elevators which forms the link to the dining and social rooms. Slightly lower wings for clinic and administration and still lower sections for kitchen, laundry, and power station radiate therefrom (*fig.* **353**).

Wherever you stand, new aspects enrich the space–time conception of this complex. Each of the walls has its own existence and is formed according to the function of the rooms behind it, but all are modeled and related to each other by a strong plastic vision. At the time of its construction no building in the northern countries could compare with the sanatorium at Paimio in its purity of form and boldness of conception. As in Le Corbusier's League of Nations Palace, as in the Bauhaus, the various parts are fully integrated — like the organs of a body — each having its distinct functions and yet being inseparable from the others. Only by encompassing the whole compound can one perceive its space–time planning and its relation with earth and woods.

The Undulating Wall

Viipuri Library One of the few buildings in which Aalto could freely express himself was the Viipuri Library, built with difficulty between 1927 and 1934. It was damaged in the first Russo-Finnish war and almost razed to the ground in the following conflict.

354. ALVAR AALTO. Viipuri Library, 1927–1934. *Undulating ceiling of the lecture hall.*

It consisted of the library proper, which had carefully constructed circular overhead lights, and an unusually shaped lecture hall with a spacious connecting vestibule.[5]

Aalto's treatment of the undulating wooden ceiling of the lecture hall is of great historical importance. The architect today appears nowhere so hesitant as in the region of the ceiling, above the reach of everyday functions. Here, to a large extent, is a freedom of opportunity to excite the plastic imagination of an artist. The solution of the problem of spanning space has always been an indication of the creativeness of a period.

Alvar Aalto is, like Le Corbusier, one of the few architects who in our times has tried anew to attack the vaulting problem in a way peculiar to this period.[6] In the intimate hall of the Viipuri Library the irrational curves of the ceiling glide through space like the serpentine lines of a Miro painting

[5] For a complete description see Alfred Roth, *The New Architecture* (Zurich, 1940), pp. 181–194.

[6] E.g., Le Corbusier's original plan for the large assembly hall of the United Nations building (New York, 1947), which linked ceiling, wall, and floor by consecutive yet segmented parts.

355.   ALVAR AALTO.   Finnish Pavilion, World's Fair, New York, 1939.   *Undulating wall in the interior.*

356. Finnish lakes and forests, Aulenko.

357. ALVAR AALTO. Finnish Pavilion, World's Fair, New York, 1939. *Ground plan.*

358. ALVAR AALTO. Glass vases.

(*fig.* **354**). From the floor behind the speaker, narrow strips of redwood sweep upward, curving irrationally along the glass wall. Of course, the architect himself can prove, with meticulous acoustic diagrams, that the undulating form he gave the ceiling enables sound to reach the human ear more perfectly. Here, therefore, scientific reasoning and artistic imagination have merged to free architecture from that rigidity which is today an ever-present menace.

Finnish Pavilion
New York, 1939

Aalto treated the walls of his Finnish Pavilion with even greater freedom. This was without doubt the most daring piece of architecture in the New York World's Fair of 1939: an inclined wooden screen three stories high embraces the interior space in a freely drawn curve. The screen consists of three sections, each cantilevered over the other; at the same time the whole structure leans forward, intensifying thereby the impression of continuous movement. A series of vertical ribs and the rhythm of their changing shadows animate the surface of the huge screen (*fig.* **355**).

Each detail has a well-reasoned explanation. In the technique of poster display, the undulating surface provides more space for large photographs; the forward tilting brings the uppermost pictures closer to the angle of vision; the series of vertical ribs thrust the photographs forward; the cantilever of the upper stories, which so intensifies the impression of hovering movement, provides room for a concentrated display of objects.

The outstanding feature is the new modeling of inner space that is involved in this experiment, which to many still appears rude and almost barbaric (*fig.* **357**).

Dormitory
M.I.T. 1947

Having given flexibility to the ceiling and to partition walls, Aalto then attacks the outer wall in his Dormitory for the Massachusetts Institute of Technology (Cambridge, 1947).

The sober program of a dormitory is given a new interpretation. All means are employed in the attempt to avoid the ant-hill atmosphere often emanated by such buildings. Aalto gives the individual his personal rights through a great variety of means: by the way he arranges the staircases, by the blending of spaces, by alternating the capacity, form, and

359. ALVAR AALTO. Dormitory (Baker House), Massachusetts Institute of Technology, 1947–49. *Air view.*

arrangement of the bedrooms. He dares to free the façade in an undulating wall so that, as he explains, every student has a clear view of the Charles River without being made aware of the large expanse of the building (*fig.* **359**).

In March 1947 Aalto showed me the scheme, but I have not as yet had an opportunity to see it in construction, and architecture can only be grasped by direct contact. Therefore, I may be permitted to quote some first impressions from a letter of an English observer.

"I went over the [unfinished] dormitory building. . . . It is itself so full of life that it literally makes one feel oneself more consciously alive.

". . . The great curving walls are made of small bricks and these too he brings to life. A small brick can go this way or that way, or it can be laid very smoothly as though it were poured concrete. It has variety in colour and also, within the limits of its function, in size and shape.

"Then the great curve is no sudden anachronism . . . just down the road is a row of rippling Boston bay windows, and Aalto has kept the same semicircular curve, only projecting it into the twentieth century.

"Perhaps the most exciting aspects of the building to me were the half-glimpsed end view where the windows, projecting as

361. M.I.T. Dormitory. *First floor plan, with asymmetrical projection.*

FIRST FLOOR

584

362. M.I.T. Dormitory. *Lounge with terrace, and basement dining hall.*

363. M.I.T. Dormitory. *Balcony lounge and stairway to dining room.*

364. M.I.T. Dormitory. *View from athletic field, showing entrance and projecting staircases.*

a series of buttresses, form a wonderfully rich linen paneling in the foreshortened view; then, the great main entrance (past a Maillart support) when one sees immediately, transparently, through the whole building: through to the great playing fields to the right, to the sweep of the river in front, the curve of the interior space and the (future!) hubbub and life of the students."

365. ALVAR AALTO. M.I.T. Dormitory. *Three-man study, with bunks to save space. Unplastered brick walls.*

Aalto's attempt to free architecture from the threat of rigidity points, like every constituent work, forward and backward, and is rooted at the same time in its own soil. He continues what Le Corbusier had attempted in the curved walls of the Swiss Pavilion in the Cité Universitaire (Paris, 1930–32), and in his project for Algiers (1931). As we have pointed out earlier, these continue the tradition of the undulating wall as a means of modulating space from Francesco Borromini's façade of San Carlo alle Quattro Fontane, 1662–67 (*fig.* **82**), to the serpentine windings of English crescents in the late eighteenth century (*fig.* **83**).

Aalto's endeavor to imbue things with an almost organic flexibility has another source: the nature of his country. As Joan Miró is rooted in the Catalan landscape, as the cubists transmitted the experiences — tables, glasses, bottles, newspapers — of a Parisian café into a new conception of space, so Aalto found a direct incentive in the curved contours of the Finnish lakes, shaped with astonishing smoothness by nature itself and set in high relief by forest masses pressing on all sides down to the water's edge (*figs.* **356, 358**).

Sunila: Factory and Landscape, 1937–39

Aalto's main activity in Finland is industrial planning, from the factory itself to the resettlement of whole industrial areas. This was the case in the Vuoksi river valley development (1947), where the left bank, annexed by the Russians, had to be abandoned, and all industry, settlements, and community centers transplanted and a new road system laid out.

Aalto has built several cellulose factories [7] and sawmills.[8] Theirs are not the grand dimensions of American industrial plants, nor the elegant luxury of the van Nelle factory in Rotterdam (1927). Yet Aalto knows how to raise a plant from a purely professional instrument up to a piece of architecture in which the site, the use of different materials, and the organization of volumes in space are given as much attention as the production line. Nowhere is this more apparent than in Sunila (1937–39).

Sunila, with a yearly output of 80,000 tons of cellulose sheets, was built jointly by five Finnish wood concerns. Good factories are taken for granted today, and production figures often provoke alarm rather than amazement. But Sunila is not merely a factory. It is a complex of homogeneous living zones and production areas. The living quarters were started before the factory itself and are strewn around in the fir forest, together with their *saunas* and laundries (*fig.* **369**).

Sunila stands on an island in a small bay. Its aspect is defined by the long horizontality of the warehouse, extending along

---

[7] For instance, the Toppila pulp mills at Oulu (1933), where the suggestive form of the flake bins is not completely mastered.

[8] Sawmills, with their flat boarded walls, generally recall the lifelessness of barracks. In Aalto's Warkhaus sawmill (1947), the usual dreariness of a sawmill is imbued with vitality just by the use of carefully profiled round timber and by giving the wall a lively contour.

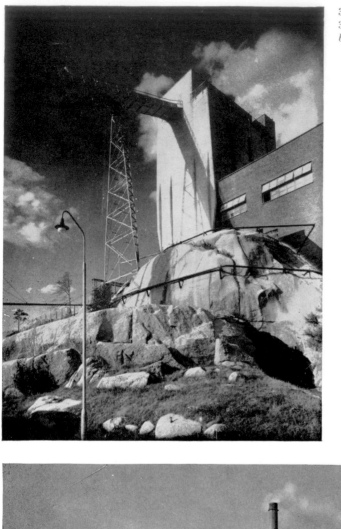

366. ALVAR AALTO. Sunila, 1937–39. *Conveyors, factory, and granite blocks.*

367. ALVAR AALTO. Sunila, 1937–39. *Warehouse, conveyors.*

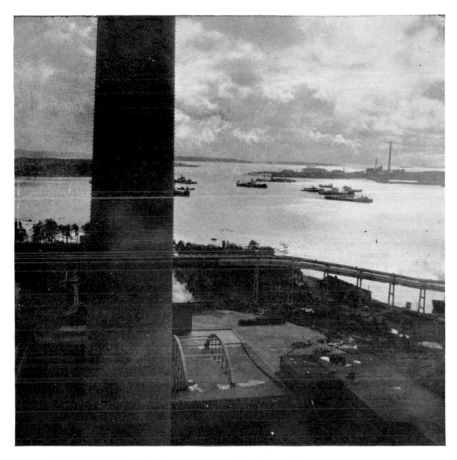

368. ALVAR AALTO. Sunila, 1937–39. *View toward the open sea.*

369. ALVAR AALTO.
Sunila, 1937–39. *Plan of
factory and living quarters.*

589

370. ALVAR AALTO. Mairea, 1938–39. *Exterior.*

371. ALVAR AALTO. Mairea, 1938–39.
Ground plan.

the seashore (*fig.* **367**), and the vertical accents of the different coördinated buildings of the plant. The inclined diagonals of the conveyors, leading to and from the storage towers, aggressively penetrate the whole complex.

Aalto took care that the rounded granite rocks on which the factory stands were not blasted to the level of the shore (*fig.* **366**). He knew how to use the contrast between the massiveness of these granite rocks on the one hand and the delicate steel structure of the row of pylons which support the conveyor and the different texture of the flat brick walls on the other.

Sunila has a most perfect production line. In the interior there are immense containers, boilers and digesters. There are pipe tunnels through which fluids and wood pulp flow, and a large machine for drying cellulose standing isolated in a spacious hall. But no men are to be seen. Only forty-five men are required to supervise the daily transformation of 30,000 logs into wood pulp; but more than three thousand men work in the forests to keep the plant supplied. No one is to be seen on the stairways connecting the different levels or in the numerous halls. There is an atmosphere like that in Captain Nemo's *Nautilus* in *Twenty Thousand Leagues under the Sea.* The problem of the production line here reaches a perfect solution. Here no human being is misused to become an adjunct to a machine.

One stands finally on the top level, on the flat roof-terrace of the high brick-clad storage building, from which the material, obeying the law of gravity, is conducted into the production process. Below radiates the organism of the factory, the large covered flake conveyor mounts almost to the terrace, and the eye passing over the granite rocks meets the Finnish landscape (*fig.* **368**): water, water, trees, and a vast expanse of space.

Close to the shore is an island of logs which have been floated down the river from distances of hundreds of miles. A cable crane picks them out to feed the machines. Ships wait in the bay to carry the brown cellulose sheets overseas. It is a Faustian prospect.

Mairea

Aalto's genius cannot be apprehended in a single piece of furniture, a living room, or a house. These must be seen together with his large-scale planning and the structure of the country. In Finland in these unsettled times there has been no opportunity for one-family houses and luxury villas. Aalto built a small house for himself and a larger one for his friend Gullichsen, president of one of the Finnish wood concerns. Gullichsen's house, named "Mairea" in honor of his wife, was built in 1938–39 in a clearing hewn out of the pine forest on the crown of a hill not far from the coast. Behind the house are a garden and a swimming pool with a group of gray silver willows in the background. It is a large mansion, yet it is intimate.

Mairea is a house poured, as it were, from a single crucible, for architect and client worked together, as in the eighteenth century. They had the same will and the same inclinations, a rather rare coincidence in this period when the architect has to spend most of his energy convincing a hesitating client in whom the last century still lingers. Moreover, nothing leads the modern architect farther astray than building for a client of large financial means, whose main concern it is to invent extravagant needs and an endless series of superfluous gadgets.

Even one accustomed to judge immediately the qualities of a building will not easily comprehend the architectural instrumentation of Mairea. It is architectural chamber music which demands the strictest attention to perceive the subtleties in the resolution of its motifs and intentions — and especially to grasp fully the handling of space and the extraordinary handling of materials. The broad windows permit the interpenetration of inner and outer space; the forest seems to enter the house and find its concomitant echo in the slender wooden poles employed there.

The use of textures — The spatial organization can perhaps be experienced to a certain extent from illustrations. It is otherwise with the use of the many materials and the lyricism which results from their juxtaposition. This is already apparent from the outside. The rough-hewn slabs of black slate beneath the window —

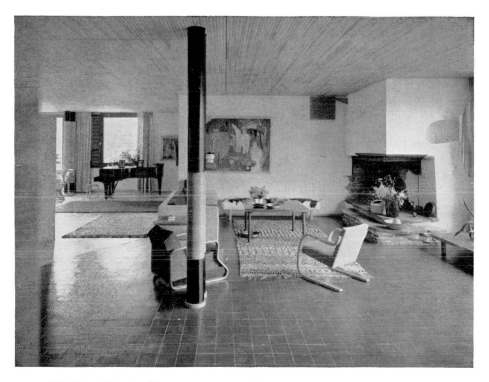

372. ALVAR AALTO. Mairea, 1938–39. *View toward the Finnish fireplace and drawing room.*

whose texture it is impossible to recognize in the illustration (*fig.* **370**) — are combined with the warm brown of the teak-wood shutters and the yellow band of birch of the parapet running above.

The interior has a more delicate use of texture. In conjunction with the spatial accentuation, the vestibule has large tiles of a curious brown, set diagonally — tiles used normally for the restoration of churches. In contrast to these, smaller reddish tiles cover the floor of the drawing room with the heavy Finnish fireplace and continue into the dining room, placed at right angles in the other wing. The four steps leading from the vestibule to the slightly raised level of the rooms opening from it are of a wood with a strikingly lucid quality. I asked Aalto later what kind of wood he had used here. It is rather rarely used, he said — a kind of white beech, the same as that used for the small strip which runs around the hull of a yacht. To indicate that the different parts of the main living room blend into each other, the tile zones merge with the wooden floor in an undulating curve.

A subtle juxtaposition of materials appears everywhere. The shiny twin columns of the living quarters are of an ebony black which is relieved by small bands of wickerwork, placed at varying heights around the columns, sometimes individually wrapped, sometimes bound together (*fig.* **372**). The large Finnish fireplace (Finnish because it follows the old tradition of the country of building the hearth about on table level) has cantilevered granite shelves above the floor level so that one may stretch out along them. In contrast to the American custom, the granite blocks are not continued in the surrounding wall, which is left white and smooth. One has to observe very precisely to apprehend the textual effect of the contiguous wall of roughly whitewashed brick.

This use of different textures has the same meaning as the use of the rocaille in the eighteenth century; it helps to modulate spaces in flux.

Spatial organization

It is the spatial organization which interests us most here. You enter the vestibule. The undulating wall of eye-level height that faces you gives a hint of other rooms to the right. Four steps lead to the level of the main living room, which unfolds in different directions. Diagonally in the background expands the area of the fireplace, and, on stepping toward it, you are drawn, diagonally again, into the depth of the large music room with its black wicker-clad columns and generously dimensioned windows. Only the library is granted complete privacy.

The moment you are on the level of the main living room, the slender poles arranged at irregular intervals on both sides of the wooden staircase captivate you by the way they separate it and yet permit space to penetrate. Incidentally, it is often the manner in which the staircase is integrated into the spatial organization of a house that betrays the architect's capacity for handling space. In this case, the light wooden staircase flows into the main room, announces the existence of other rooms and yet preserves its own identity. It is treated like a transparent sculpture (*figs.* **373, 374**).

594

In this house a rare thing has been achieved; the feeling of an uninterrupted flow of space throughout the house is never lost, and yet the feeling of intimacy is preserved, wherever you are.

Organic Town Planning

Town planning is only another term for integration. In this heyday of narrow-minded specialization, nothing is more dif-

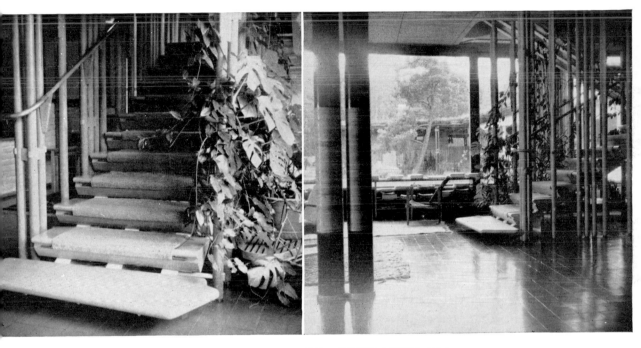

373. ALVAR AALTO. Mairea, 1938–39. *Details of the staircase.*

374. ALVAR AALTO. Mairea, 1938–39. *Staircase, drawing room.*

ficult than to conceive or to build up a whole from a number of difficult parts.

The ability to integrate is normally developed toward the end of a period, when it is at its cultural peak. This is particularly true in relation to town planning.

We are now at the beginning of a period; yet, it is already necessary for us to possess those qualities that normally develop much later. As far as I know, this situation is unique. But it exists, and we must act accordingly. We are confronted here and now with the necessity of finding a solution to the complex problems of the city, although specialists are still sharply discussing what kind of city it should be, and although we ourselves are perhaps not even quite sure what a town hall should look like. Let us not forget the present situation: that our imagination begins to freeze as soon as problems of integration are involved.

What is Aalto's contribution in the field of town planning? We can only touch on a few points here. The same qualities which enliven his buildings are even more obvious in his planning schemes. With the same freedom that he has employed to loosen up the structure of walls and ceilings, he loosens up the rigid framework of the human settlement. Rows of houses scattered in all directions seem to have been strewn by the wind, and yet they are held together by an invisible force, like filings in a magnetic field.

Sunila 1937–39 In the layout of Sunila, 1937–39 (*fig.* **369**), Alvar Aalto's approach to town planning is already manifest. The whole sequence of his later schemes will reflect the same principles. These may be briefly described as establishing an equipoise between the primary demands for a human environment: an equipoise between the living area, the center of production, and nature.

To secure the right of the individual to privacy, to a simple community life, and to the most intimate contact with the earth is today the preoccupation of every planner. This aim is no longer original. Today these demands have become a matter of course. What is still lacking is their realization.

We will not easily find, as early as 1937, many achievements like Sunila, where both the production area and the living area have been conceived in such a way that each has been given its necessary rights without disturbing the other. The grasp of a town planner can be felt in the layout of one-family houses upon the narrowest strip of the available land; in the grouping of row houses freely in the forest; in the slight variations of the engineers' row houses, which lie nearer to the waterfront and are arranged in a slight curve, to ensure the utmost privacy for each dwelling. It goes without saying that

375. ALVAR AALTO. Project for an experimental town, 1940

the necessary social facilities (especially several *saunas* — communal bathing houses) are located at strategic intervals.

Aalto's integrated approach enables him to have the structural completion of the whole community in his mind, even when he begins with only the first few cells. Together with other architects, he has been working, since 1944, on the solution of the large-scale problem of the reconstruction of Rovaniemi, the principal town of Finnish Lapland, which was completely destroyed at the end of the second Russo-Finnish war.

In his scheme for "An Experimental Town" which Aalto published in 1940, he had already indicated how he would synchronize, from the very beginning, the simultaneous growth of the single house, the town, and the processes of production (*fig.* **375**). Taking an area of hilly woodland scattered with lakes, so typical of the Finnish landscape, he laid out the various types of dwellings in the freest possible way.

Experimental town 1940

597

The terraced houses (f) circle about the hilltops in amoebic spirals, so that the structure of the landscape breaks through; the apartment houses (e) are turned at a slight angle one to another and sited at right angles to the slope of the hillside; the wood infiltrates into the area of the one-family houses (d); public buildings, schools, and sports grounds (b, c) are close to every part of the town, though each is laid out to its own advantage. The standardized and the irrational here flow together, as in all Aalto's works.

In 1940, this scheme was only a scrap of paper, designed for the students of M.I.T. When I went to Finland, in the fall of 1948, the Finnish government had just granted the necessary funds for the erection of several such experimental towns in Finland.

Kauttua 1938

But by 1938, Aalto had already planned Kauttua. Well hidden, in a narrow valley cut by a creek and about three to four hours' drive from Turku, lies a paper mill called Kauttua. On the opposite side of the valley, Aalto built, amidst the forest, a row of workers' houses. These climb the steep hillside in four great steps (*fig.* **377**). The flat roof-terrace of one house forms the large veranda of the next. It may well be that Aalto remembered the peasant houses on the Greek isles. Here, too, the children play on their neighbor's roof — something that is only possible in countries where people do not immediately become anxious if they have to share something. As on the Greek island of Santorin, the houses of Kauttua use the natural slope to avoid the expense of staircases (*fig.* **378**). In their form and shape they express man's relation to the soil from which he springs.

The wars interfered. Up to 1948, only one row of houses had been built, owing to lack of money and materials.

The matter of real importance here is not this single row of houses, but the realization of the whole plan, one of the best proposals for the shaping of a rural settlement (*fig.* **376**). Four rows of these terraced houses have been planned, each placed so that the natural forms of the slope are perfectly utilized. The brow of the hill is, as Frank Lloyd Wright likes to see it, untouched. Connected with these units, there are a

598

376. ALVAR AALTO.
Kauttua. *Ground plan.*

377. ALVAR AALTO.
Kauttua. *Terraced houses.*

378. ALVAR AALTO. Kauttua.
*Terraced houses showing entrances on
different levels.*

379. ALVAR AALTO. Oulu, 1943. *Model.*

380. ALVAR AALTO. Oulu, 1943.
The city with the new civic centers.

school and a small community center, and, further down the
slope, close to the river, is a steam bath, the *sauna*, built as
usual together with the communal laundry — the only fa-
cility that is already erected. This corresponds to an old
habit of the Finns, to start the small bath hut before building the dwelling.

Oulu 1943 Rapids rush through the city of Oulu, situated at the mouth
of the river Oulu in northwestern Finland. An architectural
problem here had to be solved: How could one make full use
of the water power without destroying the beauty of the

600

marshy islands that lie at the mouth of the river? Aalto
wanted to create a Venetian-style development (*fig.* **379**).
He accomplishes this by taking the hundreds of thousands of
cubic meters of stone and rubble resulting from excavation of
a canal and the necessary dredging of the river and using this
material to enlarge the islands and to raise their ground level
a few inches.

The islands nearest to the power plant will then support the
dwelling quarters of the workers. An administrative civic
center and a sports center will be created on the now desolate
isles that face the open water. A large highway will connect
all with the two parts of the existing city of Oulu (*fig.* **380**).
In front of the public center, a number of fountains will spring,
geyser-like, from the surface of the water.

Finally, there is the immense scheme for the transplantation
of industry from the left bank of the Vuoksi river, now occupied by the Russians, to the right bank, and the concomitant opening of new highways, the building up of rich industries, villages, and community centers, freely strewn into the
depths of the countryside. Both in size and in coördination,
this great regional enterprise will stimulate all planning activity in our period, provided that circumstances permit its
completion.

Vuoksi

Furniture in Standard Units

In Alvar Aalto's opinion, a house is not only a far more complicated organ than an automobile; there is also a real difference between an object which one may live in for a generation and a vehicle of transport which one may conveniently
exchange every second season. Furthermore, no two sites are
the same. Above all, the house reaches too far into the psychic
to admit of total mass fabrication.

Only elements of it should be standardized: doors, windows,
mechanical equipment, and constructional members, whether
they consist of skeleton or panel. The important matter is
that architectural freedom should be preserved. The standardized elements should awaken, not destroy, architectural
vision.

601

Both house and furniture today are composed of machine-made parts. The comparison can be taken no further, however. The type house, the prefabricated house, kills the phantasy of the architect and administers a deathblow to organic town planning. But furniture is predestined to be conceived in standardized types. I have discussed this question at length elsewhere,[9] yet I cannot close these remarks upon Aalto without mentioning his stimulation of furniture design in the middle thirties. The cause lies once again in his integration of the regional element with the latest mechanical processes and his full awareness of contemporary means of expression. The substance which he took in his hands and made flexible, as he had made walls, ceilings, and town planning flexible, was that organic material wood.

The constituent element of Aalto's furniture, like the slab in a bridge by Maillart or the plane surface in a modern painting, is a sheet of plywood. Aalto received the impetus for his first experiments when he had to furnish the Paimio sanatorium from top to bottom in 1929. Here can be found the first mass-produced plywood chairs, consisting of a ribbon-like wood frame, within which is suspended the undulated plywood seat (*fig.* **280**). About 1935, Aalto dared to do away with the closed plywood frame and built the chair as a free cantilever, a construction that, till then, had only been expected of steel.

Like all those who succeed in taking the plunge into the unknown, Aalto possesses the gift of seeing things as freshly as though they had never been touched before. This is the kind of talent that is urgently needed today, to discover an emotional equivalent that may rescue us from drowning in the flood of technical processes that is being poured over us.

Aalto now announces a new development in the manufacture of furniture. By a special suction process it is possible for wood to acquire such suppleness and flexibility that the architect may twist it and turn it as he pleases. Further, chemists have found a method of forming a cable-like structure from a number of small rod-like pieces of wood tapered at both ends — "wood macaroni" Aalto calls them. A physician, on

[9] *Mechanization Takes Command* (Oxford University Press, 1948).

602

seeing them, was at once reminded of certain organisms within the large intestine.

The Rococo developed the greatest mastery and finesse in wood carving. The skeleton of the chair was then reduced to astonishing slenderness and shaped in elegant forms. Today, entirely new possibilities have been opened up from within, through the aid of chemical changes. We wonder whether this chemical processing will be assimilated emotionally.

The Human Side

One cannot speak about Aalto the architect without speaking about Aalto the man. People are at least as important to him as architecture. Aalto is interested in every human being, in each of their particular desires and experiences, no matter where they come from or to what social class they belong. He draws incentive and stimulation from contact with men of varied callings, much as James Joyce did. Indeed, Aalto cannot set foot outside his door without becoming involved in some human episode. He approaches people directly and without inhibitions, in the same way that he approaches the organic material wood.

When Aalto first appeared, unknown to the rest of us, within the circle of the newly formed CIAM, in Frankfurt in 1929, he did not talk about his buildings but instead told us of a delicate adventure that had befallen him at nine o'clock that morning, on his way from the station to the hotel. In 1933, when he was traveling from Finland to the Athens Congress by plane, rail, and automobile, to take part in the formulation of the Charte d'Athènes, the long conversations that he had on his journey were of the greatest interest to him. Traveling with him was an elderly woman in a plaster cast — a grandmother, as he told us — whom he attended and assisted from train to train.

Aalto came to America for the first time in 1939 to build the Finnish Pavilion at the New York World's Fair. His English vocabulary was far from extensive, yet he lectured to the pampered public of the Museum of Modern Art in New York. The way that he stood there, the way in which he was able to express what he had to say with his fragmentary vocabulary and a few "okay"'s, captivated his audience from the start.

Aalto's call to a professorship at the Massachusetts Institute of Technology was a natural consequence of his personality, the success of the Finnish Pavilion, and the approval accorded to his furniture. Thus Walter Gropius and Alvar Aalto are at work in the same town.

Aalto divides his time and his work, as is well known, between the rebuilding of Finland and his American professorship. The dormitory that he has just erected for M.I.T. is a particularly bold undertaking when one considers that American college architecture has traditionally been decked with pseudo-gothic or colonial forms.

Aalto's relationship with man in his completeness cannot be defined on a rational basis. His personality radiates in direct contact. But, when he is gone, there does not seem to be any possible means of contact with him. It is probable that he has never carried on a regular mail correspondence in his life. However, immediately he appears, his tales, flavored by a whimsical understanding of human situations, and the radiance of his whole being, make it seem as though he had only left the day before.

There are certain architects whose work develops almost of itself. Aalto's work is of a different kind. Each line tells of his close contact with human destiny. This may be one of the reasons why his architecture encounters less difficulty in overcoming the resistance of the common man than that of others of his contemporaries.

I agree with Ernst Cassirer, the philosopher, who, in his last work,[10] demands so fervently that history should be written only with an intimate knowledge of the human side.

While these lines were being prepared for the press, a cable arrived from Helsinki on January 13, 1949, announcing the premature death of Aino Aalto.

---

[10] E. Cassirer, *An Essay on Man* (New Haven, 1944), p. 181.

All Aalto's exhibitions and his work have been signed "Aino and Alvar Aalto." It was not a gesture of chivalry that induced him to place the name of his wife before his own. This marriage was as singular as everything else related to him. Its steadfastness was based upon common sharing of all struggles and successes ever since their joint student days. But its real secret lay more likely in a profound reciprocation of human contrasts. Aalto is restless, effervescent, incalculable. Aino was thorough, persevering, and contained. Sometimes it is a good thing when a volcano is encircled by a quietly flowing stream.

Aino's name will always be connected with the work of Alvar Aalto. Yes, he always put her name before his own, but Aino herself always insisted, "I am not creative, Alvar is the creative one." This is not the moment to determine the extent of Aino's influence on Aalto's production. But we know that she had her quiet say as an architect at all stages of his work and life. She never appeared in the foreground or admitted what had really been designed by her. She was always at work behind the scenes, as when I last saw her in the fall of 1948: by day, director of Artek, the corporation engaged in the designing and manufacture of Aalto's furniture; in the evening, hostess at a dinner party for Finland's intellectual elite, sitting relaxed in a white gown among her guests, quiet as the Finnish lakes and forests from which she had sprung, active only in an unobtrusive way, as Nordic women often can be.

THE DEVELOPMENT OF CONTEMPORARY ARCHITECTURE

It would be a complete misunderstanding to suppose that contemporary architecture has been evolved by a few isolated geniuses. Vigorous artists, creative spirits strong enough to push beyond the dominant conventions without these, of course, nothing could have been achieved. But contemporary architecture is no longer dependent upon a few individuals; it has its roots deep in the life of our day. It grows more and more anonymous; innumerable workers in every part of the world contribute to its nourishment and progress.

The emphasis falls increasingly upon solutions, rather than upon the individual architect. This is the difference between the generation of the pioneers and the generation that has come after them. Individual creative work remains necessary, but the complicated problems which have to be solved (along with a growing unity of expression) are leading to more and more collaborative work. Architects are collaborating not only with other architects but also with specialists of every description — landscape gardeners, physicians, statisticians, and many others.

The CIAM   This inspired a new collectivity and united the leading architects of many countries in the CIAM (the Congrès internationaux d'architecture moderne).[1] The CIAM sets itself to analyze and work out problems which no solitary worker could handle. It dealt first with the problem of dwellings for the lower income classes (Frankfort, in 1929), went on to the treatment of block units (Brussels, 1930), and then to town planning (Athens, 1933).

The principles governing the attack upon these problems were always the same. To gain a universal insight into actual facts and conditions, groups in various countries carried out careful analyses. The same methods were used by each group, the same modes of representation, the same scale. Low-cost housing, block units, and town layouts were studied in Europe and elsewhere.

Architecture a moral problem   Architecture has ceased to be the concern of passive and businesslike specialists who build precisely what their clients bargain for. Architecture has cast off this passivity; it has gained the courage to deal actively with life, to help mold it. It starts with intimately vital questions, inquiring into the needs of the child, the woman, and the man. It asks, "What kind of life are you leading? Are we responsible for the conditions you have to put up with? How must we plan — not just in the

---

[1] June 1928, at the instigation of Mme Hélène de Mandrot de la Sarraz, who offered the association every possible help and made available the old Château de la Sarraz for its first meeting.

606

case of houses, but clear through to regional areas — so that you may have a life worthy of the name?"

When we go to the bottom of questions like these, we see that contemporary architecture takes its start in a *moral* problem. Architecture has emerged from the realm of narrow specialization to plunge into the realities of ordinary life. And by taking off his specialist's blinders, the architect has greatly extended his influence. Architecture is a highly complex activity; it works in the boundary area halfway between the regions of aesthetic feeling and practical doing. But this is just the reason why we look to it to give us the kind of surroundings that will express the life of our period.

Modern painters have enlarged our visual experience by working with relations between objects which we had never taken cognizance of in our ordinary, half-automatic seeing. Contemporary architects have been just as willing to anticipate public understanding. They too have refused to wait until they could be sure of universal approbation for their work. Following an impulse which was half ethical, half artistic, they have sought to provide our life with its corresponding shell or framework. And where contemporary architecture has been allowed to provide a new setting for contemporary life, this new setting has acted in its turn upon the life from which it springs. The new atmosphere has led to change and development in the conceptions of the people who live in it. This is understandable enough if we regard architecture as Louis Aragon does painting: as a language, and not as a mere matter of taste.

In the past (and to some extent even now) really creative art has met with resistance from a public whose conceptual development had outdistanced its emotional growth. The fight which contemporary architecture in Europe had to wage to establish itself was due to just this gap between thinking and feeling. That fight would never have succeeded if architecture had waited for other branches of knowledge to arrive at a coördinated and universal outlook. Builders, sociologists, economists, political theorists — none of these have as yet fulfilled all their aims. Meanwhile the architects have worked with whatever means were at hand — sometimes very primitive ones, with which completely satisfactory solutions were impossible — to establish the contours of a new kind of life.

Universal trends and local problems

Many different countries have contributed to the development which we have been discussing. It would be interesting to observe the spread of the new movements, through Holland, France, Germany, Sweden, England, and elsewhere; to see what direction was taken in each of these countries and the special dangers which each involves; to note the influence of environment and tradition upon the solution of architectural problems. Such local differences have a more than superficial importance. Those countries which accepted contemporary architecture as a kind of universal coinage — a collection of particular shapes which retained their full value wherever they were transplanted — invited architectural bankruptcy. Modern architecture is something more than a universally applicable means of decoration. It is too much the product of our whole period not to exhibit some universal tendencies, but, on the other hand, it is too much concerned with problems of actual living to ignore local differences in needs, customs, and materials. Finland, under the leadership of Alvar Aalto, has shown how contributions can be made to architecture universally through solutions adapted to the specific conditions of their native setting.

We must break off here, however, in spite of the interest and importance of these branches of the main movement. As always, our purpose is to follow developments only to the point where full consciousness of their import and direction has been reached. Today the most urgent and unsettled problems arise in another field, in that of town planning. To gain some insight into these problems, to become aware of what lies behind present conditions, to see if there is any escape from the desolate city of our times: these are things we cannot avoid attempting.

PART **VII** **CITY PLANNING**
IN THE NINETEENTH CENTURY

Once again we must turn back to the nineteenth century. We can appreciate what is required in the sphere of town planning today only if we understand how the present situation has come about.

A universal attitude basic in town planning

If a universal attitude is needed anywhere at all in architecture, then it is in town planning. Apart from a wide survey, a far-sighted point of view, there can be no urban order. Periods incapable of arriving at a consistent outlook on the world are also incapable of carrying out the kind of town planning that goes beyond mere patchwork. And armies of specialists are no help when what is missing is a universal attitude covering the whole of life.

Reign of the specialist in nineteenth-century town planning

On the contrary, specialists who lack the universal attitude are incapable of grasping real relationships. Valuable and precise as their work may be, its results will be limited and out of balance — perhaps even harmful, since one task is overstressed at the expense of another. Periods which depend on specialists are incapable of successful town planning. What happens in such times is something like the case of a man who reads a book, and from extreme exactitude never manages to get beyond the first ten pages. He loses the meaning of the whole in attending to the details. The situation nowadays is an analogous one. In spite of the existence of many conscientious town-planning associations and of trained specialists in the planning and administration of towns, there prevails a shocking lack of direction and an inability to remove the most obvious inconveniences.

The penalty cannot be evaded when, for a hundred years, there has been almost nothing but chaos in town planning. Regulations alone offer no solution, for the regulations also bear the stamp of the men who make them; a new universal vision is needed.

It would be unreasonable to expect new solutions to town-planning problems from a period like the nineteenth century. A century which (especially in its later course) was so dominated by the spirit of laissez-faire, and so much under the rule

610

of specialists, was no time for town planning, which by its very nature must come out of broad vision and foresight.

There is no doubt that the charm of many of the personal expressions and forms of living of the last century will be more and more fully recognized in the near future. But its town planning will not be included in this coming revaluation.

Our interest in town planning can be reduced to three questions: Was the highly developed late baroque art of town planning continued during the nineteenth century? What arose to take its place afterwards? Finally, what new solutions has the twentieth century to offer?

In times when there is a universal vision resting on a long and solid tradition, town planning is taken as a matter of course. We have considered some eighteenth-century solutions which were interesting for their farsightedness and for the feeling for space which they manifest. Many of an amazingly high quality are the work of anonymous architects, even of speculators. It is important to notice that solutions which come out of the universal vision of the eighteenth century still remain valid long after the death of the society — or the ideal of a society — for which they were formulated, and after changes in circumstance which the designers could never have foreseen. But when the vision of a period is predominately influenced by specialists, the solutions arrived at do not even satisfy the needs of the time of their creation.

Late baroque town planning: summary

The late baroque showed a magnificent power of dominating outer space. This period was thoroughly aware of the different relationships that held between one building and another and between buildings and nature: between constructions and organisms.

The feeling from which baroque town planning sprang — one made natural by its social life — limited attention to the connections between palatial residences and to the spatial treatment of the beautiful plazas of the great towns.

Late baroque town planning is the expression of two absolutisms: the first produced by the Counter Reformation, the second by monarchy. All the constructions which benefited from the great fund of experience of the period were built for the Church, for the king, or for those who helped these two to rule.

The lodgings of the common people did not enter into these schemes; they were not thought of as presenting any problem. The people formed the invisible foundation and support of the state; all that rose above the ground was meant, without question, for the ruling class. People of great experience and wide vision — like Vauban, Louis XIV's great military engineer — saw the danger in a system which put such burdens upon the people. But Vauban's *Projet d'une dixme royale* (1709) cost him the monarch's favor by its assertion that "what is wrongly called the dregs of the people" merited the "celestial king's" serious attention. "This mass is . . . very important," Vauban continued, "in view of its numbers and the services it renders to the state." The system itself inevitably dictated the rejection of Vauban's main proposal that the nobility and clergy should be taxed (to the extent of one-tenth of their incomes) as well as the people.

In this way it came about that a great town, as far as the mass of the people was concerned, was simply a crowd of houses, neglected in every respect. On the other hand, historical justice forces us to state that great towns in the eighteenth century in no way played the part they did in the nineteenth. The eighteenth-century city lay outside the interest and attention of the chief forces in the period. After the departure of Louis XIV for Versailles, town planning was entirely neglected except in so far as it concerned the building of *places* and great avenues of communication.

A specimen city tenement in the eighteenth century: Mercier's *Tableau de Paris*, 1786 — Everything that affected the people was either abandoned to disorder or arranged merely provisionally. The confusion and filth, the neglected approaches to the houses, and even the tragicomedy of the city-dweller's longing for flowers and greenery appear in an etching of 1786 (*fig.* **381**). The etching, bearing the title *Pot de fleurs*, is from Mercier's *Tableau de Paris*, a book which so fascinated Diderot that he described it as "pensé dans la rue et écrit sur la borne." The illustration shows the ordinary houses of Paris and the misfortune of one of the fifth-story tenants who has just seen his aerial garden

612

381. MERCIER. *Etching from Tableau de Paris, 1786.*

tumble into the dirty disorder below. But such houses were sparsely populated and cannot be compared with the slums created by the nineteenth century.

During the century between Versailles (1668–84) and Lansdowne Crescent in Bath (1794) [1] the residential group was placed in direct contact with nature. It belonged at first to the monarch, next to the nobility, then to anonymous wealthy citizens. The increased stress in the eighteenth century upon the connection of the dwelling with nature may be laid in large part to the trend of the times toward the Rousseauistic cult of the "natural man."

Space is necessary if houses are to be disposed facing greenery; it would have been impossible in the old walled towns. In the seventeenth century Vauban moved the defenses of Paris

Contact with nature of late baroque residential groups

[1] Cf. p. 157.

382. Tuileries, gardens laid out by Lenôtre. *Engraving by Mariette. The avenue of trees to the right, leading to the royal stables, still exists, and borders the Rue de Rivoli along one side.*

much farther out in order to protect it against new developments in armaments. It was this which permitted the eighteenth-century *places* in Paris to grow up.

It will be recalled that, in the north and south alike, baroque architects of the second half of the eighteenth century took pains to preserve the association of architecture and greenery. This new phase of town planning continued and was extended for a long while in the nineteenth century. Just because town planning is the last department of architecture to take form in any period, this phase remained in evidence in the nineteenth century until daily life, long under the influence of industrialization, was seriously altered. It is true, of course, that the industrial towns grew up around slums from the very start, and show no traces of this tradition.

Now we should like to demonstrate how long baroque knowledge of town planning lasted — it continued even into the nineteenth century — and when it came to an end.

614

383. Rue de Rivoli, Paris, c. 1825. *The part of the Rue de Rivoli first built by Percier and Fontaine for Napoleon I, looking toward the Place de la Concorde. Its single row of houses facing across the roadway onto greenery inspired the Regent, later George IV, to develop the Regent's Park terraces shortly thereafter.*

384. PERCIER and FONTAINE. Elevation of a house on the Rue de Rivoli, 1806. *This charming and unified façade is a basis for Haussmann's boulevards half a century later. Shops are hidden behind the arcades. Thus this street of Napoleon I has already, in germ at least, that mixture of residence and business functions which the English avoided.*

The Rue de Rivoli of Napoleon I

Late baroque
tradition in the
Rue de Rivoli
(1801)

When Napoleon I commissioned Percier and Fontaine, the founders of the Empire style, to design the Rue de Rivoli, the main outlines of the design were established in advance by existing conditions.

The Rue de Rivoli of Napoleon I, still the most beautiful street in Paris, is not a *rue corridor*. It has only *one* wall, and this faces upon the gardens of the Tuileries and, what is more important, upon an avenue. The avenue had been laid out under Louis XIV (as an eighteenth-century engraving by Mariette plainly shows), and at first led to the royal stables (*fig.* **382**). These stables occupied the site upon which the Rue de Rivoli was built.

The Place de la Concorde, where the Rue de Rivoli begins, was built under Louis XV and Louis XVI, and the bridge over the Seine was built just at the beginning of the Revolution, in 1790.

Louis XIV laid out the park, Louis XV the square, and Napoleon the street. It was quite typical of the building programs of the period that Napoleon should have commanded the building of a street (this was at the time of his consulate, in 1801). The street was intended for the rich bourgeoisie and offered a view of the royal gardens.

In marked contrast with the English practice of making business and residential streets entirely separate, the Rue de Rivoli was both in one.[2] Continuous pillared arcades protected shoppers from the weather and at the same time prevented the shop fronts from diminishing the dignity of the street. Placards and grocers' shops were excluded. These arcades continue the tradition of the seventeenth-century Place des Vosges.

In working out their new task Percier and Fontaine used a form which is as neutral as it is appealing (*fig.* **384**). It goes without saying that the houses were treated as a unit. To preserve the effect, there are but few accents. The pillared

---

[2] This separation appears in the Bloomsbury section of London, built up around the same time.

385. Rue de Rivoli, view toward the Louvre, 1840.

arches of the ground floor are in strict alignment; the balconies of the first, third, and attic floors are continuous; the walls are smooth-surfaced.

The Rue de Rivoli of the time of Napoleon I is a part of the late baroque tradition (*fig.* **383**). Its single row of houses permits as free an outlook as the brothers Adam provided for the occupants of their splendid Adelphi Terrace, built in 1768, overlooking the banks of the Thames. The Rue de Rivoli, at this stage of its development, inspired John Nash and his employer, the Prince Regent, in their plans for the laying out of Regent's Park and its terraces.

The various continuations of the Rue de Rivoli — the last completed as a part of Haussmann's *percement de Paris* — changed its whole character and made it over into one of those "endless streets" born out of the nineteenth century (*fig.* **385**).

THE DOMINANCE OF GREENERY: THE LONDON SQUARES

In the garden squares of London we have for the first time since the Middle Ages the outward appearance of the city as conditioned by the building activities of the upper middle classes. These classes created a residential style as self-confident as it is lasting. Like the Flemish towns of the fifteenth century, these London squares of the early nineteenth will bear witness for generations to the sureness with which the middle classes set about providing a framework for their living — that is, unless they are quite destroyed in the meantime by insensate building.

To understand the true nature of their development we must remember first of all the English preoccupation with the idea of comfort, the Englishman's insistence especially upon comfort in the home, all the way from the comfortable chair before the fire to the undisturbed privacy of the individual house. This strong urge toward *bienséance* does not appear for the first time in the eighteenth century. To see how far back it goes and how early it influenced the organization of the dwelling, one need only compare the English manor houses, with their spacious settings and arrangement, with their Continental counterparts. It is to this desire for comfort and privacy that the garden squares owe their particular pattern. Indeed, if the development of London may be said to follow any rule, it is an unwritten one — like so many in England which carry most weight — deriving from the democratic insistence that a man shall not be disturbed in his private life. The rule runs roughly as follows: The residential quarters of a city should, as far as possible, merge into the greenery. They should be as inconspicuous as possible.

London's irrational growth

If any city can be accused of having grown irrationally, that city is London. It developed with an almost total disregard for definite axes. Instead, it was at the mercy of the divisive influence of the great landowners, of the Crown, the nobility, the Church. Because of its lack of such guiding axes as those which make Paris so easy to survey, it is almost impossible to orient. On the other hand, the small districts into which it

618

386. WREN. Plan for the reconstruction of London, 1666.

resolves itself are all refuges from the sheer immensity of a city which has outgrown the human scale.

The comprehensive unity sought by the baroque was not acceptable to seventeenth-century England. The coördinated plan of Christopher Wren for the general rebuilding of London following the great fire of 1666 was rejected by Charles II after only three days' consideration (*fig.* **386**). And this just at the time when Bernini was laying out the Piazza in front of St. Peter's, and Le Nôtre the gardens of Versailles! The sweep of Wren's scheme — half baroque, half Renaissance in character — was too thoroughgoing to permit its execution,[1] but for a reason more fundamental than the one usually given. The popular belief is that Wren's plan was not used because it was impossible to reach agreements with the owners of a half-dozen burned-over sites through which Wren's axes inconveniently ran. But it was not merely a complicated question of ownership which blocked the lining out of axes in the Renaissance or baroque manner; there was also an inner repugnance to them. This same repugnance operated to prevent any

---

[1] London was self-governing and independent of the Crown. Neither Wren nor any other architect would have thought of using the Continental idea of arranging London about the Royal Palace. Wren's intended point of accent lay — almost in the Renaissance manner — in the center of the town, at the Stock Exchange. All his lines of force radiated outward from that point to penetrate the whole body of London. St. Paul's stood near the town gates, at the confluence of two main arteries; in the same fashion, two decades later, Rainaldi placed twin churches facing the Piazza del Popolo.

619

systematically related arrangement of terraces, squares, and streets in those areas where it could have been most easily achieved — within the great estates. The Crown and the Duke of Bedford ignored such schemes in the Covent Garden district; the Earl of Southampton did likewise in Bloomsbury. The way in which these squares are irrationally scattered over a site, separated and yet not quite cut off from each other, is

387. Queen Square, Bloomsbury, London, 1812. *Around 1800 the open spaces in the middle of the London squares were laid out with freely planted trees and lawns, the beginning of that luxuriant greenery which natural growth brought in due course of time. "Queen Square, situated to the eastward of Bloomsbury Square, is a handsome area, surrounded on three sides by good houses, having an extensive garden in the center. . . . The north side formerly commanded fine views of Hampstead and Highgate." ("Ackermann's Repository of Arts," September 1812.)*

like the pattern of an Oriental carpet or a painting by Paul Klee.

Nature of a square "The square," according to a *Dictionary of Architecture* published in 1887, "is a piece of land in which is an enclosed garden, surrounded by a public roadway, giving access to the houses on each side of it." For all its brevity, this definition is an excellent statement of the nature of the London squares. It very properly begins with the "piece of land"; next it stresses as an essential feature the enclosed garden (enclosed because it is only for tenants, who have keys); last of all, it mentions the houses which invariably surround it. It does not specify the shape of the square, which may be four-sided, three-sided, regular or irregular. There is no rule requiring that the square must bear any certain relation to neighboring squares, *places*, streets, or crescents.

The squares of the seventeenth and eighteenth century have great significance for the town planner. In them for the first time the countryside was built upon without being obliterated beneath masses of stone and networks of streets. As living flesh gleams warmly through sheer material, so the one-time gardens of the Duke of Bedford still disclose themselves beneath the residential developments of Bloomsbury with which they have been overlaid. Modern architects often boast of the attention they pay to trees; indeed, they sometimes build a house around one. In the best of the London squares a whole district is composed architecturally around the existing countryside. Herein lies the prescience of the squares.

The main constituent of all the London squares is a central garden of grass and plane trees (*fig.* **387**). When newly planted, the rows of plane trees did not achieve the effect of a romantic garden which they were intended later to produce. Such a picture required the predominance of a wall of greenery, which, grateful both to eyes and to lungs, had also the advantage of ensuring one's privacy from one's neighbors. The gardens were treated as a unit, just as the houses were. Here is no ridiculous breaking up into small allotments. There are wide expanses where the residents may stretch themselves out on the grass on sunny days or play tennis on the green lawns in front of their own houses.[2] And all this within five minutes' walk of the surging traffic of Tottenham Court Road or Oxford Street.

Central garden

---

[2] Onions and cabbages have been seen growing in the garden of one crescent near Euston Road, but this is a crescent that has degenerated into a slum.

These areas by no means began as garden spots. "Originally these open spaces were neither so aesthetically pleasing nor so healthful as they might have been, owing to the fact that it was the inevitable fate of open ground in every European city of the seventeenth century to become a dumping place for filth of all kinds. This was prevented only when the inhabitants of squares applied for powers to enclose, clean, and beautify them; St. James's Square, in 1726, was one of the first to seek such permission." [3]

388. Grosvenor Square, Mayfair, in the early eighteenth century. *"The square is a piece of land in which is an enclosed garden, surrounded by a public roadway, giving access to the houses on each side of it."*

Houses serial and inconspicuous

The architecture of the houses in these squares is also affected by the unwritten rule that residential quarters shall be as inconspicuous as possible. They are arranged serially in apposition, a treatment which was used for more than half a century in the newly erected parts of London without ever

[3] W. R. Davidge, "The Planning of London," *Journal of the Royal Institute of British Architects*, March 10, 1934, p. 433.

becoming either tiresome or antiquated. Everything is avoided that might obtrude; there are simply smooth, continuous surfaces with as little subdivision as possible. The building material — brick, without stucco — is admirably suited to conditions. Plain brick, instead of suffering from the dampness and fog of London, becomes mellowed and dignified with the passage of time, like a well-smoked meerschaum pipe. Paint is used only, and then sparingly, in places where weather cannot harm it and where it can be easily renewed: on the inside

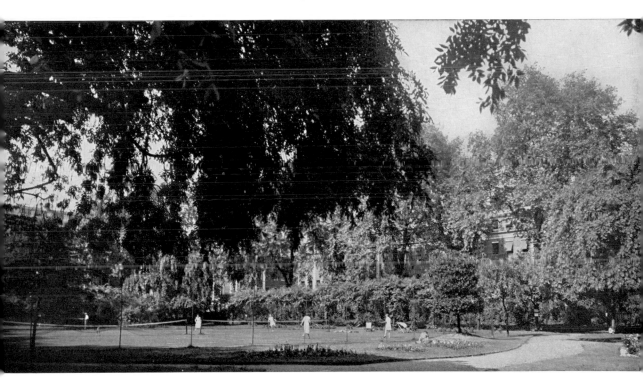

389. Square in the Bloomsbury district, c. 1825. *Although Bloomsbury was originally a suburb, even then the separation of traffic and residential quarters was carefully observed. The result is that even today, only a step from the most congested London traffic, the houses are intimately and directly related to their pleasure grounds.*

of the window casements, along the narrow molding at the entrance, and on the pediment of the house. Nash's use of stucco in Park Crescent, London (begun in 1812), shows a Continental influence which has already departed somewhat from the main tradition.

How did the London squares originate? This question requires
an answer only in so far as it will help us to understand better
the architectural inheritance which is theirs. The desire for
green spaces within London reaches back to Gothic times. In
the fifteenth century the court of Lincoln's Inn was laid out
as a lawn and converted into walks. At the same time a piece
of land outside the town, Moorfields, was being used by the
inhabitants as a recreation ground for archery and other
sports. As early as the seventeenth century, the most important of the popular parks, Hyde Park — far out of London, and
the property of the Crown — was opened to the public.[4]

It was in the seventeenth century also that the first squares
were built. They originated in the desire of various noble
landowners to build up portions of their estates. These constructions followed the baroque pattern of *places* rather than
streets. About 1630 the Earl of Bedford gave over seven acres
of his land to building purposes. The result was the first
London square: Covent Garden. It has often been pointed
out that this first square — never quite completed, by the
way — resembles the Place des Vosges in Paris (1612). Both
are typical seventeenth-century *places*, rectangular, and with
arcades running through the ground floor of the houses. As a
matter of course they were open to the public and devoid of
lawn or trees. The application to them and other such spaces
of the name "piazza" clearly shows a recognition of their
Italian origin.

The Earl of Bedford's example was soon followed by the Earl
of Leicester. Leicester Square, in front of Leicester House,
was laid out by him on the same principles in 1635. It is a
business center today and has been totally disfigured. In
1665 the Earl of Southampton "was building a noble square
or piazza, a little town,"[5] which became a fashionable quarter.
This later became Bloomsbury Square. Several other squares
followed: Soho Square in 1681, St. James's Square in 1684, and
Grosvenor Square (Mayfair) in 1695 (*figs.* **388, 390**).

From this brief account the pertinent point emerges that as
early as the late seventeenth century London, unlike Paris,

[4] Steen Eiler Rasmussen, *London, the Unique City* (New York, 1937), pp. 86, 92.
[5] *The Builder*, July 28, 1855, p. 349.

was becoming attractive as a residence for the upper classes. Furthermore, the London squares were separate, widely scattered areas like the French and Italian *places*.

There was increased building activity during the eighteenth century. About fifteen squares in all appear to have come into existence during this century.[6] To some extent this activity was devoted to completing the seventeenth-century squares. Thus Grosvenor and Hanover squares were completed in 1720, and Berkeley Square around 1730. Then building took an-

390. Grosvenor Square, London, begun in 1695. *An eighteenth-century square set in the midst of open fields with the enclosed area laid out as a formal garden. The gardens behind the houses stretch out into the fields.*

other spurt just as the century began its last quarter: the Adelphi Terrace on the banks of the Thames was built by the brothers Adam around 1770, Manchester Square in 1774, Bedford Square in 1775, Portland Place in 1778, and Fitzroy Place in 1790. The greatest activity went on in Bath from about 1730 — the time of the emergence of the elder Wood — until the construction of the Royal Crescent in 1767. What is

---

[6] *The Report of the Royal Commission on London Squares* (London, 1928).

important at Bath is the interrelations between the various squares and crescents, relations so much more subtle than the purely axial ones employed in French town planning. Such carefully thought-out relationships were arrived at in London only toward the end of the eighteenth century.

THE GARDEN SQUARES OF BLOOMSBURY

That harmonious interrelation of squares, *places*, and crescents upon which alone rests London's claim to a high level of urban planning came about during the years between 1775 and 1850.[1] On such sites as Bloomsbury, well-ordered spaces of every shape — oblong, circular, square, elliptical — accumulated to form a new and composite organism. In them the late baroque inheritance was carried on in a completely native manner, perfectly adapted to the conditions peculiar to London.

Bloomsbury's human scale

The development of Bloomsbury occupied more than a century and a half, approximately from the time Louis XIV began planning the removal of his court to Versailles down to the rise of great industrial cities like Manchester. It is the one known instance over such a long period of urban development to a constantly increasing perfection. As an architectural composition, Bloomsbury is, in its way, fully the equal of such different organizations as the monumental baroque squares before St. Peter's and, later on, the Place de la Concorde. There is no doubt that, playing with the whole orchestra of monumental voices, they are much the more impressive, but the Bloomsbury district has its place beside them. For although it employs shapes of an anonymous and humble character, they are right with a timeless validity, and the way in which they were successively added together to form ever-larger units — *places*, squares, terraces — produced a district which for its human treatment remains unsurpassed to this day.

---

[1] *The Report of the Royal Commission on London Squares* (1928) places the building peak between 1800 and 1850: "The activity in the development of the squares reaches its height in the early part of the nineteenth century. By 1850 practically all the well-known squares were completed" (p. 11).

626

391. Bloomsbury at the end of the eighteenth century. *Part of the estates shown on a 1795 map. This shows the original boundaries of the district just before the period of its greatest development, when it was still largely composed of estates of the Duke of Bedford.*

392. Bloomsbury in 1828. *Map of James Wyld, engraved by N. R. Hewitt. The whole plan follows late baroque tradition in emphasizing the squares, but they are laid out flexibly and informally. In their careful, yet irrational planning they resemble the pattern of an Oriental carpet or a painting by Paul Klee more than they do the rigid French axes.*

627

It is all of a piece, a simple and democratic fabric in which any touch of the monumental is a violation. The comparatively small mansions of the Bedfords and Montagues, around which it grew up, were no intrusion upon this unity, but the building of the British Museum early in the nineteenth century introduced an element harshly out of scale. Today the huge, artificially gigantic buildings of the University of London (as yet uncompleted) threaten to destroy Bloomsbury utterly.[2] Dominating them is a monstrous three-hundred-foot tower which thrusts itself upward like an explosion to shatter forever the serenity and cohesion of the district lying below.

However, the tower does serve one good purpose. It affords a unique vantage point from which to survey Bloomsbury and trace the pattern of its squares. From no other place can the disposition of the squares be comprehended. Laid out so that there are no extended vistas, their relationship to each other is not discernible from any one of them. Only from above is it possible to see the balanced proportion between building and open space, a balance so nicely maintained as to give every resident an equal sense both of his privacy and his freedom (*fig*. **393**).

Boundaries of Bloomsbury

The great thoroughfares that bound Bloomsbury are also easily distinguished from the tower — Holborn and New Oxford streets on the south, and Tottenham Court on the west; Bloomsbury itself stretches away to the east, to the gardens of Gray's Inn and the squares beyond, until it fades out of sight in the distance. The original boundaries of the district, as shown on a map of 1795 (*fig*. **391**),[3] were Tottenham Court Road, New Road, Southampton Row, and Holborn Street. This map defines Bloomsbury just before the period of its greatest development, when it was still largely composed of the estates of the Duke of Bedford, with Bedford House and its gardens the conspicuous architectural organization.

---

[2] "Artificially gigantic" not only because the skyscraper tower in the center is entirely false to the prevailing scale, but also because it is a misunderstood imitation of an American model. This unfortunate tower was meant to house the stack rooms of the university library. In 1938 the majority of the upper stories were entirely vacant; it had been discovered that the building laws forbade their use.

[3] University of London, *The Bloomsbury Site* (c. 1933), a pamphlet by Eliza Jeffries Davis. Cf. also *London Topographical Record*, XVII, 78 ff.

The beginnings of the Bloomsbury district date back to Restoration times. Southampton Square — later called Bloomsbury Square — was laid out in 1667 by the Earl of Southampton along the axis of Bedford House, his town mansion in Bloomsbury. Bedford House, with its *cour d'honneur* and extensive grounds and gardens, dominated the square. Thus the houses and the green but treeless areas of Bloomsbury Square were dependent, like any French *place* or Italian *piazza*, on a noble residence. Bedford House was still standing when new and greatly increased building activity began in the late eighteenth century.

Bloomsbury Square (1667)

The first of the new squares was Bedford Square. It was located at some distance from the gardens of Bedford House and on an axis at right angles to Bloomsbury Square. On the 1795 map it appears isolated and treeless and completely independent of its surroundings. Executed about 1775, this noble square, with its oval enclosure, is one of the few associ-

Bedford Square (1775)

393. Bloomsbury; air view of Russell, Bedford, Bloomsbury, and adjacent squares. *Only from above is it possible to see the balance between buildings and open spaces and the relationship of the squares to each other.*

394. Bedford Place, from Bloomsbury Square to Russell Square, begun in 1800. *This street, lined by houses the neutral architecture of which is the result of an old and highly refined tradition, is not a long extended street in the Continental sense but a short connecting link between two places. It is purely residential and without shops.*

ated with the name of an architect — in this instance, Thomas Leverton.[4]   Montague House, the town mansion of a family related to the Bedfords, also appears on the map of 1795.   It resembled Bedford House and had, like it, a *cour d'honneur.* In 1753 the British Museum was housed in it.

Thus at the end of the eighteenth century, Bloomsbury had three points of accent: Bloomsbury Square, Bedford Square, and the British Museum with its gardens.

Bedford Place
(1800)

The third and decisive stage in the evolution of Bloomsbury occupies the first quarter of the nineteenth century.   The fifth Duke of Bedford pulled down his house in Bloomsbury Square in 1800; its groves and avenues fell with it.   On the site arose

---

[4] Even this attribution has been questioned recently and, pending more evidence, is not to be taken as established.   Cf. John Summerson, *Journal of the Royal Institute of British Architects*, March 6, 1939, p. 440.

Bedford Place with its magnificently coördinated houses (*fig.* **394**). What was left of the gardens was also turned over to residential development; the largest and most lordly of the squares, Russell Square, was really the very heart of the gardens cut out and preserved intact in the midst of its new buildings.

The Duke did not undertake these projects himself. Instead he leased his lands to James Burton, a speculator and builder, who planned, designed, and executed Russell Square (1800–14)[5] and at the same time carried out work on several streets that open off that square — Keppel Street, Montague Place, and Southampton Row. Burton constantly pushed farther eastward, always striving to evolve appropriate dispositions of large open spaces.[6] He planted the land behind the houses on Bedford Place, which runs between Bloomsbury and Russell squares, with lawns and shrubbery. The result was particularly pleasing, for the low mews or stables behind the houses did not obstruct the view, and the openings at the ends of the rows of houses linked the parallel areas of greenery so that there were no closed blocks.

After 1820 Burton's work in this district was taken over by Thomas Cubitt (1788–1855). "He was thirty-two and already famous in the building world for his great workshops in Gray's Inn Road where he was doing what had never been done before — employing all the trades on a permanent collective basis. To keep his organisation going he took land and built wherever a good opportunity occurred."[7] Cubitt completed Torrington Square in 1827,[8] using a greatly elongated quadrangular pattern which, although it maintained sufficient distance for privacy between the opposite rows of houses, wasted no land. The intentions of its unknown architect are shown by a map of 1828, only one year after its completion, on which

Thomas Cubitt

---

[5] These dates are the result of John Summerson's recent researches. Earlier sources — for example, Henry Clutton, "The Squares of London," *Builder*, July 28, 1855, p. 349 — give the date as 1804.

[6] The segmented North and South crescents and Alfred Place (the broad connecting link between them) represent some of the solutions at which he arrived.

[7] Summerson, *Journal of the Royal Institute of British Architects*, March 6, 1939, p. 442.

[8] According to Summerson. According to Davis (*London Topographical Record*, XVII, 92), it was completed in 1829.

already there is indicated a row of trees planted along the middle axis of the enclosure (*fig.* **392**). This central garden has remained till today one of the most attractive in the district.[9]

Single-family house the basic unit

In every particular Bloomsbury is imbued with the architectural tradition of the eighteenth century. The delicacy and imagination which marked its town planning are here continued and very graciously united with the naturalistic landscape gardening of the early nineteenth century. The basic unit is the single-family house. The dwellings were intended for the professional upper middle class, for the lawyers and judges of Gray's Inn near-by, for writers and others of similar intellectual pursuits. The houses are treated like the gardens, in homogeneous units. Here again is the exercise of a wise distinction between what must be private and what is best held in common.

The architecture has that timelessness, that independence of fashion, so often found in farmhouses. Yet every detail of these buildings has refinement, from their apparently paper-thin slate or cast-iron balconies to the graceful sweep of their interior staircases. Sometimes the balcony is overhung with a small canopy which is carried on slim, cast-iron trellis work so delicate that it is more like the veining of a leaf than a design in metal.

The ground plan of the individual houses follows late eighteenth-century practice. At the core of the house is a stairway rising in spaciously curved flights through the entire height of the building to a skylight. This arrangement, first employed by the brothers Adam in their Adelphi Terrace (begun in 1768), leaves the exterior walls unblocked. Thus every room receives direct outside light. The rooms themselves are per-

---

[9] Cubitt was a pioneer in the construction of great building units, one of the few contractors to undertake works on a large scale and carry them through successfully. But it is perhaps of more interest that, although he was essentially a builder of streets, squares, and *places* in the late baroque tradition, he had nevertheless a definite connection with the new potentialities. In 1839 he became a member of the Institution of Civil Engineers. One of his two contributions to its proceedings was a paper entitled, "Experiments on the Strength of Cast-Iron Girders." Toward the end of his life, when the Crystal Palace Exhibition was being undertaken with doubtful success, Cubitt did everything possible to promote it and was among those who offered to guarantee the necessary funds.

395. Bloomsbury district, Woburn Square, row of houses, c. 1825–30.

fectly proportioned, being neither too large nor too small. It can only be said of their dimensions that they are human.

The location of the servants' quarters in the basement where they are exposed to the dust of the street has often been thought callous. Certainly it is a defect in planning. Even so, it is more humane than the Continental use of cramped attic stories.

The light-well, used later on with disastrous effect by Continental speculators, is in these houses happily avoided. Ample space both at front and back gives every room, whether opening on the court or on the street, its full amount of light. And the location of the stables and coachmen's quarters in one-story buildings at some distance to the rear of the houses removes any possible obstruction to openness of view. This combination of tall houses and low mews back of the gardens appeared as early as the late sixteenth century. Up to the sixties of the nineteenth, it sometimes appeared in duplicate,

Mews

396. Kensington, London, 1830–40. Air view. *Though comparatively modest in area, the squares of Kensington show a fine freedom of planning and the achievement of new organic shapes toward the end of the development.*

with twice the ordinary amount of space between the backs of two rows of houses. Occupying the wide distance between the houses were the two mews, forming a service street exclusively for coaches.

Controlled development   These London quarters condense and continue architectural experience going back to Renaissance times. Nevertheless, they were as much the products of speculation as those later Continental residential blocks which brought chaos into the structure of the city. The difference was one of control. The contractors active during the reconstruction of Paris had to build façades according to Haussmann's requirements, but that was all. What lay behind was subject to no real control, and they adopted the quickest means to the largest profits. In their hands buildings became part façade and part light-well. In London a much more careful control was exercised by the great landowners on whose estates the buildings were erected. These owners were accustomed to reckoning in terms of hundreds of years. The land and everything on it usually reverted to them in not more than ninety-nine years. Knowing very well that estates could be destructively exploited, they retained in their leases control over the utilization of the ground, and their trustees had the power to undertake maintenance work in cases of neglect.

Wandering through London, one frequently comes upon squares built between 1830 and 1860 in the most diverse and unexpected parts of the town.[10] Some of these almost unknown places (for example, Lloyd Square of about 1840) were laid out for people of small means; though simpler in execution than those of Bloomsbury, they too were treated in a manner that adapted them to human living.[11] Others, like the squares of Kensington (1840), are also comparatively modest in area, but show a fine freedom of planning and achievement of new organic shapes (*fig.* **396**). All of them, whatever their location and proportions, are the products of a town planning which strives for a plastic modeling of space. They continue the eighteenth-century tradition of towns like Bath and Edinburgh. They achieve a unity at once charming and reassuring, and demonstrate the vitality which can be introduced into the structure of a city through the laying out of quite freely formed complexes.

Other Squares

There is an obvious degeneration in the treatment of the houses after 1860, particularly in their architectonic features. The

Decline after 1860

[10] In 1858 *Building News* is still able to announce new work: "At present there are ten new squares in actual progress in the suburbs of London." It lists Kensington Gardens, Leinster Square, Bayswater Square, with its "first-class dwelling houses," Princes Square, and Norfolk Square. All these are in Bayswater and Paddington. (*Building News*, May 7, 1858, p. 479.)

[11] Cf. Christopher Hussey, "Georgian London, the Lesser-Known Squares," *Country Life*, LXXXV (January 28 and March 4, 1939), 91–94, 224–225.

hitherto discreet front becomes loud; the windows are over-loaded with detail; the whole house disintegrates into separate and conflicting parts. In addition, other influences were at work. The uniformly treated square was being supplanted by the semidetached suburban house with its miniature garden. There were also growing up along the great roads settlements consisting of endless rows of tiny houses lining the thorough-fares like boxes, merging into other settlements without distinction. Devastating in themselves, they are the ruin of all comprehensive town-planning schemes.

LARGE–SCALE HOUSING DEVELOPMENT: REGENT'S PARK

John Nash and Regent's Park

During the last stages of the development of Bloomsbury, John Nash was commissioned to design a scheme of buildings and gardens for what was then Marylebone Park, a large, irregularly shaped tract of meadow land belonging to the Crown at the north edge of London. The Regent wished it developed for residential purposes, though without being crowded with buildings. He particularly desired the creation of a large new park accessible to the inhabitants of the city. Nash drew up his first plan in 1812 (*fig.* **399**); after some modification and delay, the project was carried out during the twenties. The result was Regent's Park and its terraces.

In making his plan Nash "declared his aims to be threefold: firstly, to assure the greatest possible revenue to the Crown; secondly, to add to the beauty of the Metropolis; and thirdly, to study the health and convenience of the public." [1] His work was another essay in the free disposition of large building complexes facing nature. It followed not so much the example of the London squares as that line which begins with Versailles and continues through the Bath crescents and the arrangement of some other English towns.

Regent's Park lies along the axis of the Adams' Portland Place (1778). Connecting it and Portland Place with Piccadilly

[1] W. R. Davidge, "The Planning of London," *Journal of the Royal Institute of British Architects*, March 10, 1934, p. 443.

636

397. JOHN NASH. Park Crescent, London, begun in 1812. *The individual houses are treated as parts of a unit, organized in a single semicircular block behind a façade of a unified design. Park Crescent was the beginning of the large-scale housing development of Regent's Park.*

Circus in the heart of London is Regent Street, also Nash's work. This imposing London business street was built around 1820, being finished just as the Regent's Park terraces were begun. The two are the English counterpart of Napoleon's Rue de Rivoli. Nash had started his Park Crescent in 1812 (*fig.* **397**) at the end of Portland Place. The time, however, was not yet ripe; Napoleon was still unbeaten, commercial conditions were unsettled, bankruptcies were frequent. But by 1825 everything had been set straight, and a new wealthy class had sprung up.

It was for this new class that the Regent's Park residences were intended. An opulent and anonymous class who had been made rich by industry, the development of trade with the colonies, or the exploitation of English victories in the field,[2] they were quite able to afford the magnificent houses which

---

[2] It is said that observers sent by the London financiers followed all Wellington's campaigns and reported everything of importance by carrier pigeon.

Nash designed for them. Almost overnight there appeared in 1825 those long rows of terraces which, starting from Park Crescent, embrace Regent's Park like a pair of giant lobster claws. Set well back from the road encircling the park, most of the houses are on raised plots with the ground between them and the road terraced to separate them from it. They face directly on the park, which they overlook without dominating.

In Park Crescent the individual houses are once again treated as parts of a unit — a unit often consisting of fifty separate houses (*fig.* **398**). But this regard for the effect of the whole does not achieve the completely neutral result attained in

398. JOHN NASH. Large-scale housing adjacent to Regent's Park.

Bloomsbury. The terraces were consciously conceived as attenuated houses with an accent on monumentality. They remind one of the Royal Crescent at Bath, but in their pilastered central portions they already reveal the seeds of late nineteenth-century form.

Boldness in treating outer space

Definitely more important to us than the actual execution of the park and terraces is Nash's original plan of 1812, which unfortunately was not carried out. For in that plan are shown a boldness of imagination and a daring treatment of outer space which are highly significant today. The simple sketch of it which appears in Summerson's biography proves the originality and sweep of Nash's thought.[3] Its boldness of conception is illustrated by several striking details.

[3] John Summerson, *John Nash, Architect to George IV* (London, 1935), p. 113.

399.   JOHN NASH.   A terrace of Regent's Park.

400.   JOHN NASH.   First project of the housing development in Regent's Park, 1812. *This plan, which was not carried out as designed, is an essay in the free disposition of large building complexes in open spaces.   It followed not so much the example of the London squares as that trend which begins with Versailles and continues through the Bath crescents and the arrangement of some other English towns, and has its continuation in our period.*

401. View of Birmingham, 1850. *The squares of Bloomsbury do not give a full picture of what happened during the first half of the century to the English cities which endured the impact of mechanization. Its devastating effect on the urban pattern appears in this bird's-eye view of Birmingham. Living quarters and industry are inextricably mixed; inner courts are choked with chimneys and factories.*

For one thing, Nash planned to erect two huge semicircular crescents in the north of the park, which would have stood like two enormous half-cylinders in the midst of a sea of greenery. He also wanted to place a double circle in the center of the park. The houses of its concentric rings were to face in opposite directions, those of one inward, those of the other outward.[4] But even more interesting is his proposal to enclose the eastern side of the park with a series of terraces. He planned to push great complexes of buildings into the park, with a liberty of disposition that would be daring even today. At the southeast corner, supporting the main entrance,[5] an open square, intended by Nash to be larger than Russell Square, joined with the open space of the park. Near the short upper arm of this square he placed a long building, parallel to it and receding still further, and at right angles to that a single unit which, quite asymmetrically, extended half the length of the park. (See *fig.* **400.**)

---

[4] Summerson has discovered that the huge double circle was not entirely original with Nash. He finds in a scheme of 1794 what "was obviously the prototype for Nash's plan" (*Journal of the Royal Institute of British Architects*, vol. XLVI, March 6, 1939, pp. 444–445). This was the work of quite obscure architects — more evidence that town planning was within the reach of everyone at this period, as machine design is now.

[5] On Nash's plan the main entrance lies at the south of the park, as it does today. It was given the form of a circle which led into Portland Place. As is well known, only the southern half — Park Crescent (1812–19) — was completed.

Such an organization of exterior space, with advancing and receding complexes which cannot be embraced in a single glance, was never actually realized during this period. However, the free disposition of large building units in contact with nature that appears in this first plan of Nash's was a premonition of what we are venturing today. Just as Francesco Borromini in the late seventeenth century extended building frontiers by seeking to accomplish an interpenetration of inner and outer space, so Nash in this project approached in the realm of town planning that freedom of spatial organization which we are now exploring on even a larger scale.

We have seen that the fundamental requirement for town planning is the maintenance of one controlling authority, with no dispersion among independent owners of control over the ground. But perhaps as important is the necessity for this controlling authority to possess an instinct for town planning. At the present time enormous blocks of residential or business premises have been thrust into the beautiful late baroque squares — Berkeley Square, for example — and are destroying everything. Business is not alone the offender. The University of London is steadily reducing the noblest district of the city to insignificance. Various influential London groups have raised the cry of "Save the Squares!" A Royal Commission has been set up and a Preservation Act passed.[6] None of these efforts is likely to accomplish much. Thanks partly to Continental, partly to American influences, London seems to have lost that instinct for scale which was responsible for Bloomsbury.

London today

THE STREET BECOMES DOMINANT: THE TRANSFORMATION OF PARIS, 1853–68

The London squares antedate the railroad; the transformation of Paris, on the other hand, took place during the feverish middle years of the railway age. The London squares were designed primarily to be lived in, with busy thoroughfares excluded. Thus the traffic of London — at this period a city

Contrast between London and Paris

---

[6] Cf. "The London Squares Preservation Act," *Journal of the London Society*, no. 169 (March 1932), p. 39.

three times as big as Paris — circled the Bloomsbury district at a distance, and the same thing was true of many other sections of the town. Residential quarters were kept intact and systematically isolated from traffic routes.

The situation in the Paris of Napoleon III was quite different. One element dominates all others: the street, the "cannon-shot boulevard," seemingly without an end. The great town of the latter half of the nineteenth century, the metropolis of the industrial era, suddenly takes its typical form in Paris between 1850 and 1870. In no other city of this period do the changes consequent upon the development of industry proceed with such impetus.

Paris in the First Half of the Nineteenth Century

Alterations begun by Napoleon III

A large map of Paris hung on the wall of Napoleon III's study at Saint-Cloud. With his own hand — "his own august hand," Haussmann prefers to say — he plotted on it the alterations he intended to make in the city. These proposed alterations were marked out in red, blue, and green, in descending order of urgency. For the most part, those sketched in green were never executed.

The original and all but one of the copies later made of it were lost in a fire. The surviving copy was found quite recently in the library of the castle in Berlin by a French historian.[1] The King of Prussia had been presented with this copy by Napoleon III on the occasion of the German monarch's visit to the Paris Exhibition of 1867 — the apogee of the Second Empire. It is not quite identical with the original, as certain works — the extension of the Rue de Rivoli, for example — are prematurely shown as existing (*fig.* **402**). Nevertheless it affords at one glance an idea of the vast amount of town planning that was compressed within the short span of seventeen years.

---

[1] André Morizet, *Du vieux Paris au Paris moderne* (Paris, 1932), p. 130.

402. Map of Paris by Napoleon III. *The Emperor's own project for the transformation of Paris.*   →

Motives for this work	At first sight, the thick lines crisscrossing through the dense confusion of houses in the center of the city suggest not so much town planning as the layout of a trench defense system for some difficult piece of terrain. And in fact it was a kind of trench system, erected with an internal foe in mind. According to a French authority,[2] during the quarter century between 1827 and 1851 the streets and alleys of Paris had seen barricades thrown up on nine separate occasions. This called for drastic remedies, and wide, unbroken lines of streets were the best means of controlling incipient riots.

But since history refuses to progress in straight lines or in accordance with rational schemes, these streets and boulevards of the Second Empire never proved of service in its defense. The enemy which overthrew Napoleon came elsewhere than from the interior of his capital city.

Industry and the growth of cities	The rapid growth of big cities — the increase in their number as well as the violent expansion of their populations — is the outstanding phenomenon of nineteenth-century urbanism. It was in the second half of the century, just when there was the greatest uncertainty about how life should be organized to meet new conditions, that the major part of this growth took place. This speed and uncertainty were responsible for the heaviest of the tasks town planners of the next period found themselves confronted with. We have already argued that the social disorder which is clearly reflected in mid nineteenth-century town planning is connected with the break between methods of thinking and methods of feeling during the period.

The increase in the numbers and the populations of cities and the spread of industry are interrelated events. Thus the evolution of London into a great nineteenth-century city precedes the similar change in Paris by, roughly, a half century. The same interval lies between the industrialization of England and the industrialization of France.

Paris under Louis-Philippe	As a consequence of the French Revolution the population of Paris fell off by a hundred thousand. But between 1801 and 1848, after this first decrease, the population doubled, rising from a half million to more than one million. During the

---

[2] Morizet, p. 133.

eighteen years of Louis-Philippe's reign, a total of only forty-one and a half million francs was spent on street undertakings for Paris. This averaged somewhat less than half a million dollars per year. Over the same interval — 1831 to 1848 — the population grew from three-quarters to more than one million.

The guiding formula of Count Rambuteau, prefect under Louis-Philippe, was to give the Parisians water, air, and shade — "donner aux Parisiens de l'eau, de l'air, de l'ombre." He cannot be said to have been entirely successful in his endeavors, since at the end of them twenty thousand water-carriers still patrolled the streets of Paris — and they still depended on the Seine to supply their stock in trade. And in general the achievements of this Burgundian nobleman have not been given a very high rating. A French historian regards him as a half-ridiculous figure who conducted his work in petty-bourgeois fashion, never undertaking anything which threatened to exceed the amount of spare cash on hand.[3] On the other hand, an English authority regards him as the forerunner of Haussmann, one who anticipated him as a maker of modern Paris.[4]

Rambuteau, a forerunner of Haussmann

Rambuteau (earlier a prefect under the first Napoleon) was in fact a most amiable person. Tactful and considerate, possessed of a social conscience and regard for his fellows, Rambuteau genuinely loved nature as well. As prefect of the Swiss Department of Valais under Napoleon I, he imported the vintage grapes of Burgundy to these valleys, so favorable to their growth. In exchange he took back to Burgundy the pine trees of the Valais district. During the fifteen years of his prefecture in the Department of the Seine (terminated by the collapse of the July Monarchy) he leveled and paved the Boulevard Saint-Denis and the Boulevard des Bonnes Nouvelles, carefully planting them with trees and imparting to them the aspect which they wear today.

Rambuteau worked untiringly to humanize institutions for the unfortunate — prisoners, the sick, the insane, and the destitute. His name remains associated with the model prison

---

[3] Morizet, pp. 104 ff.

[4] O. F. Abbott, "A Maker of Modern Paris," *Contemporary Review* (London), no. 873 (September 1938), pp. 350–356.

of Mazas, the hospital of Lariboisière, and the Salpêtrière, whose barbarous methods and equipment for treating the insane were changed at his initiative. He founded playgrounds, and placed benches in the squares and public parks, where before his time there had been only chairs for hire.

In short, Rambuteau was neither ridiculous nor the maker of modern Paris: he simply typified the July Monarchy as Haussmann did the Second Empire. Achievements on a grand scale are possible only under regimes that ask for them and seek out the proper instruments for the work. Under Louis-Philippe, Haussmann would have remained a provincial prefect for life, and would never have found an opening for his talents.

The "Trois Réseaux" of Eugène Haussmann

Paris the first city to conform to the industrial age

Time after time, in many different fields, Paris had been the center of Europe. The guiding spirit of every age is crystallized in its monuments — from the Sainte-Chapelle to the Rue de Rivoli. But this splendid heritage was set in the midst of a thoroughly disorganized town, the monuments surrounded and isolated by a tangle of streets. The herculean efforts of Georges-Eugène Haussmann (1809–91), Préfet de la Seine under Napoleon III, drastically altered this situation. It was his desire to provide a splendid framework for the great tradition preserved in Paris. And he wished at the same time to make Paris the first of the great cities to be brought into conformity with the industrial age.

We have already mentioned the fact that Napoleon III had outlined the transformation of Paris before Haussmann was called in. He had even begun actual operations on some of his projects: the extension of the Rue de Rivoli, the Boulevard de Strasbourg (whose starting point, the Gare de l'Est, was in process of construction), the preparatory work on the Bois de Boulogne, and the erection of the Grandes Halles (for which there had been a demand since the late thirties).[5]

Napoleon's unsuccessful beginnings

Napoleon was none too successful with these undertakings, however. He proposed, for example, to lead a river through

---

[5] Cf. the account of Horeau's design, p. 229.

646

the Bois de Boulogne, in the style of Hyde Park. The bed for it had already been dug, under the direction of an old *jardinier-paysagiste* who had worked on the estates of Napoleon's father — when Haussmann arrived on the scene. He discovered that the water would have had to run uphill in one section. The old gardener "avait commis une erreur, sinon un complet oubli de nivellement." [6] There was nothing for it but to substitute two lakes on different levels for the projected river. A similar neglect of the elementary rules of surveying in the work on the extension of the Rue de Rivoli led to serious difficulties later on. The start on the great markets was not much more encouraging. We have already seen that the first stone pavilion had to be torn down.

In these matters Napoleon behaved as he did in politics: he drew up great schemes, but when serious difficulties arose he tried to twist his way through by making numerous petty concessions. This instinctive attempt to bargain his way out at the cheapest price was what undermined his regime from the beginning. In a similar way Napoleon allowed Haussmann to rule Paris, while things went smoothly. As soon as he became a political storm center, Napoleon to all intents and purposes abandoned him. But except for Haussmann's energy and determination, the transformation of Paris would never have been carried through — certainly not in the short space of seventeen years.

Between 1853 and 1869 Haussmann expended on his works some two and one-half billions of francs in "extraordinary expenses," about forty times what had been spent under Louis-Philippe. Easily the largest portion — nearly one and one-half billions — was spent on street construction and on the demolition program that the decision to run new streets through closely packed quarters made necessary. Paris in Haussmann's time was adapted to the totally changed conditions of the nineteenth century (*fig.* **403**).

Haussmann's aims

The fundamental aims behind Haussmann's schemes — communicated by him to the city council as he began his duties

---

[6] Georges-Eugène Haussmann, *Mémoires* (Paris, 1890–93), III, 122.

403. The transformation of Paris by Haussmann. *Map by Alphand.*

— are strongly colored by the fear of street fighting.[7] The latest outbreak of such rioting had occurred in 1852, shortly before his appointment.

The first of these aims was "to disencumber the large buildings, palaces, and barracks in such a way as to make them more pleasing to the eye, afford easier access on days of celebration, and a simplified defense on days of riot."

The second fundamental principle aimed at "the amelioration of the state of health of the town through the systematic destruction of infected alleyways and centers of epidemics." The central part of Paris was littered with these dreadful alleys. Many of them (including the one in which Gérard de Nerval, the romantic poet, hanged himself) were photographed by Atget.[8] Haussmann never really succeeded in cleaning up these areas, and the middle of Paris is still in bad condition.

The third point was "to assure the public peace by the creation of large boulevards which will permit the circulation not

[7] This policy is summarized in E. M. Bouillat, *Georges-Eugène Haussmann* (Paris, 1901), pp. 8–9.

[8] One of the early photographers.

648

only of air and light but also of troops. Thus by an ingenious combination the lot of the people will be improved, and they will be rendered less disposed to revolt." This point shows even more clearly than the others why the Second Empire took such pains to build wide streets.

Haussmann's fourth principle was "to facilitate circulation to and from railway stations by means of penetrating lines which will lead travelers straight to the centers of commerce and pleasure, and will prevent delay, congestion, and accidents." Here the traffic problem was the main consideration.

Haussmann's operations were conducted in three sections — *en trois réseaux*, to use his own terms. These *réseaux* do not constitute topographical units; the "first," "second," and "third" refer to different methods of financing. Thus works forming parts of the third *réseau* might be located in the areas of the first or second and might be completed before these were.[9]

Haussmann's réseaux

The first *réseau* was in full swing when Haussmann took office. It was financed, without any difficulties, by the state and the city of Paris jointly, under the act for the *prolongement* of the Rue de Rivoli (1849). The chief work under this act was the extension of the Rue de Rivoli from the Place de la Concorde to the Bastille. This operation, which provided for cross-town, east to west communication in Paris, was carried out in the years 1854–55.

Haussmann began with the Rue de Rivoli. Demolition and construction went on piece by piece, first as far as the Pavillon de Marsan, then to the Louvre. Forty-seven houses were pulled down, then twenty more, then a group of one hundred seventy-two (to clear the Palais-Royal and the Louvre on both sides of the Rue de Rivoli). If we consider in this connection the entirely new market halls (*fig.* **131**) which were constructed near by, it may be said that a new district and not merely a new street was organized.[10]

Extension of the Rue de Rivoli (1853–54)

---

[9] Haussmann, *op. cit.*, III, 55.

[10] Cf. pp. 228 ff.

The Rue de Rivoli was next carried to the Hôtel de Ville — the starting point of all Parisian revolts. The confusion of narrow streets in front of the Hôtel de Ville was cleared away; on their site appeared the Place du Châtelet (*fig.* **405**), soon to connect with the Boulevard Sébastopol (1858).

Bois de Boulogne

The first *réseau* also included the transformation of the Bois de Boulogne into a place of recreation for the elegant world. In connection with this there were also built the Longchamp race track and the magnificent approach to the Bois de Boulogne, the Avenue de l'Impératrice, today the Avenue Foch (*fig.* **407**).

404. Square de la Tour Saint-Jacques, 1855. *One of Napoleon III's endeavors to imitate the London squares. The great difference is that it is set in the midst of traffic.*

Haussmann was responsible for its great width of nearly four hundred feet, three times as wide as its architect had proposed making it.

The second *réseau*

In the second *réseau* the city was required to provide the greater part (three-quarters) of the cost. A decree of March 18, 1858, authorized the state to pay the remaining fraction, provided that the total amount did not exceed a hundred and eighty million francs, and that all the work was finished within ten years. This particular piece of legislation became known as "the decree of the hundred and eighty millions."

650

With the second *réseau* north to south communications received further extension: Haussmann led the Boulevard Sébastopol across the Seine to the Île de la Cité and the Latin Quarter on the Left Bank. From there it was continued as the Boulevard Saint-Michel (*fig.* **406**). The extension transformed the Île de la Cité into an administrative center. The adaptation to working-class use of the Bois de Vincennes (1860) — the eastern counterpart of the Bois de Boulogne — was financed under the same arrangements. Another of the works in this *réseau* was the *percement de l'est;* the interlacing of the working-class quarters with wide, straight roads — *à plan*

405. Place du Châtelet.

voyant — proceeded from 1858 onward, and was more carefully carried out here than in any other district. By it the last likelihood of really dangerous rioting was removed. As a result of this clearance, the Hôtel de Ville seems almost to float in space, but it remains isolated and unrelated to its neighbors. The Napoleon Barracks were erected next to the Hôtel to ensure its safety.

The final stage was the extension of the Rue de Rivoli decided upon in 1854. Crosswise communication in Paris was achieved in this extension. It embraced those points at which the political regime was most sensitive — the Hôtel de Ville and the Louvre — and formed the first of those streets reaching beyond the compass of the eye which were soon to determine the picture of Paris.

The route of east to west communication — the Rue de Rivoli — joins the north to south route; the Boulevard Sébastopol was Haussmann's prolongation of Napoleon's Boulevard de Strasbourg. All this work by which *la grande croisée* of Paris was achieved had to be carried on in a densely populated section.

Haussmann now turned to what he called the *Westend du nouveau Paris.* In spite of the strongest resistance, the Boule-

406. Boulevard Saint-Michel, 1869.

vard Malesherbes was cut through from the Madeleine. This work involved the demolition of several luxurious houses which had been built quite recently, in the time of Louis-Philippe. This final part of the second *réseau* was opened with great pomp and ceremony on the fourteenth of August, 1861.

Haussmann took this opportunity to complain that the moment he interfered with the "habits of the people who have been favored by fortune" he found himself assailed by a storm of complaints. He observed, rather pointedly, that the merchants, shopkeepers, and workmen had borne with great patience the "highly penalizing removals" made necessary by the work on the Boulevard Sébastopol.

The second *réseau* was affected by a development of great moment — the decree of June 16, 1859, which incorporated the suburbs into the city of Paris. The area of Paris was thereby increased by more than half. The incorporation was essential for the future, but it seriously handicapped Haussmann in his calculations of the moment and set him his most extensive task. Eighteen communities were spread out about Paris and had to be incorporated, with all their chaotic agglomerations of buildings and their neglected street systems.

407. Avenue de l'Impératrice (Avenue Foch), 1862. *The great width (nearly four hundred feet) of this approach to the Bois de Boulogne was insisted upon by Haussmann. His architects' original version was only a third as wide.*

Great additional expense could not be avoided; the budget estimate was exceeded by a hundred and sixty million francs. Napoleon and Haussmann did not stop at simple incorporation. Although the expression did not exist at the time, Haussmann arrived at the notion of regional planning. According to his *Mémoires*, he wanted to make the entire Department of Seine-et-Oise a single unit. This would ensure control over the smaller communities and over the course of development of the great city, in so far as it related to them.

Attempted belt
of greenery; defeat
of the project

A belt of greenery was to be created all around Paris, following the line of its fortifications. The project adopted by the Emperor in June 1859 used the land attached to these fortifications, and a strip, two hundred and fifty meters wide, of the terrain that lay beyond them. This latter area was subject to military restrictions and had greatly depreciated in value as a consequence. The Emperor wished to acquire this land for a boulevard and to provide "vast plantations" with walks for the residents of the new faubourgs and of the contiguous communities. The belt would have completely encircled the city, connecting its two great parks in the east and west, the Bois de Boulogne and the Bois de Vincennes.

But when Napoleon left for the Italian battle front his own *Conseil d'Etat* found opportunity to defeat his intentions. Haussmann, the implacable enemy of all shortsighted politicians, gives this account of what happened: The president of the council, M. Baroche, "a bourgeois full of the narrow and hidebound ideas of the Parisian middle class and opposed at heart to our great works," fought and defeated the whole project.[11]

Paris never got its belt of greenery. After his return from Italy Napoleon hoped to find a chance to repair this shortsightedness, but he never did. Public parks in this area would have prevented the erection of the seven- and eight-story tenements which stand there now and continue to be added to. These enormous buildings — magnificent slums, in effect — stand much more in the way of the possibility of replanning Paris than fortifications would.

The third *réseau* had to be supported in its entirety by the city: the deputies wanted nothing more to do with the building or the financing of Paris. Haussmann was left standing alone; in financing these works he had to manipulate the machinery of credit singlehanded. It was these financial operations (the whole cost of the third *réseau* had not yet been raised when he left his post) which enabled the deputies to bring about his downfall.

---

[11] Haussmann, *op. cit.*, II, 233.

Haussmann's operations over a seventeen-year period had called for eight hundred million francs in excess of normal expenditures. The sum had been raised without creating any new taxes or increasing the old ones. And was not Paris becoming more prosperous daily? Its population was growing at an unheard-of rate: within a bare two decades it had almost

408. Boulevard Richard-Lenoir, 1861–63. *Planned by Haussmann to cover an old canal. Behind the regular and endless street fronts a tremendous disorder is crammed, as though in a wardrobe.*

doubled. The five or six hundred million francs beyond what was actually on hand would certainly be found. The cost of the work could be paid off through annuities based on the increasing revenues of the city. Nothing was involved except time.

Two parks — Montsouris in the south and the Buttes-Chaumont in the north — were created by the third *réseau.*

Both were conversions of useless and neglected areas; the Buttes-Chaumont replaced an abandoned quarry.

The suburbs needed more and more streets. Streets leading out from Paris were extended, and new crosswise roads were made. In this manner the budget for the suburbs increased to double the amount estimated.

Haussmann pressed rapidly on with the development of Paris as though he knew there was no time to be wasted. To the west was a field for new town planning. The old toll barriers marked the western edge of the city; beyond them stretched the open country. The Champs-Élysées led up to the toll barriers. Just behind them stood the Arc de Triomphe de l'Étoile in its circular *place*. From the thirties on, the Champs-Élysées was one of the places where Parisians with any claim to smartness were expected to make an appearance.

Creation of the Champs-Élysées district

Haussmann could work with a free hand in this district. There was open land for the twelve avenues which he led out from the Place de l'Étoile; no demolition was necessary. His enemies accused him of running these avenues out into the open country and destroying the grainfields of Passy. But once more Haussmann's foresight was justified; the Paris of 1900 was to stand on this area.

Rue Lafayette

The interconnection of the various streets that pierced Paris greatly occupied Haussmann. Thus he insisted that the Rue Lafayette should reach a length of five kilometers so that it might lead travelers from the north and east railway stations to the Opéra and the Grands Boulevards in the heart of the city.

The Avenue Napoléon, now the Avenue de l'Opéra, is his master work in town planning. Besides being a magnificent street in itself, it functions as a traffic bridge between several main thoroughfares. The Rue de Rivoli and the opposite bank of the Seine achieve direct contact, through this avenue, with the Grands Boulevards and the northern parts of the city.

Avenue de l'Opéra

None of Haussmann's schemes appeared so foolish to his contemporaries as this comparatively short street. So far as they could see, it could only serve to connect the Théâtre Français with the Opéra — and who could possibly want to attend both on the same evening? Actually, if it were not for this street, the circulation of traffic in Paris in the present day would be impossible (*fig.* **409**).

Haussmann built only the beginning and the end of this thoroughfare. Between the two sprawled a network of streets which was not cleared away until much later. The whole length of the Avenue de l'Opéra was opened to traffic in 1879. This was under the Third Republic, long after Haussmann had left office.

If Haussmann anywhere succeeded in leaving a monument to himself and to that Second Empire in which he believed so thoroughly, it is in this avenue and its opera house. The grand staircase of the Opéra never served its original purpose, never furnished a background for the gliding train of the Empress Eugénie. Designed in 1861, when the Second Empire was at its zenith, the Opéra was not completed until 1875. It remains, nevertheless, the purest expression of the transitory glories of the Second Empire.

Squares, Boulevards, Gardens and Plants

We have observed the interrelations since the seventeenth century between groups of buildings and nature, and since the eighteenth century between squares and greenery. It is true that in the transformation of Paris other questions are in the foreground, but we must not overlook the great efforts made to save the city from becoming simply a vast acreage of asphalt and masses of stone. In discussing this work it is necessary to distinguish between the layout of squares with their gardens and the old and new parks and pleasure grounds.

As a refugee in London, Louis Napoleon was much impressed by the English squares and parks. When he came to power, he desired to provide his capital with similar open green spaces — immense romantic parks and squares planted with trees and shrubs. Both were unknown in Paris. From the point of view of town planning, too, the squares of Paris differed from those of London in one important respect: the London squares were isolated from traffic, whereas those in Paris were no more than the enlargement of streets. For example, the Place des Arts-

London and
Paris squares

657

409. Avenue de l'Opéra, from the Opéra to the Louvre and the Rue de Rivoli. *Haussmann's masterpiece, carried through against great opposition. Few people could see how necessary it would be later on as a traffic bridge.*
←

410. Grand staircase of the Tuileries. Imperial Ball, 1860.

et-Métiers was a broadening of the Boulevard Sébastopol; that around the Tour Saint-Jacques (*fig.* 404), of the Rue de Rivoli. The houses were so placed in straight, continuous lines along the streets as to permit no free spaces apart from pavements and traffic passages.[12] It was inevitable that the small parks created out of these squares, quite unlike those of London, should be set amidst the noise and dust of traffic.

No innovation in urban planning was more generally imitated in the years immediately following than this arrangement of squares filled with greenery in the midst of traffic. Especially pleasing and completely new to people was the fact that they were open to the public. W. Robinson, the English landscape gardener, whose books had had great influence up to this time on English landscape gardening, expresses the contemporary

---

[12] The evils inherent in the "block system" of houses were recognized about two decades later by the critic of straight-line thoroughfares, Camillo Sitte (*Der Städtebau*, Vienna, 1901, p. 203; first edition, 1889).

reaction to one bit of Haussmann's work: "The first thing that strikes the visitor in this square is its freshness, perfect keeping, and the number of people who are seated in it, reading, working, or playing." He recognized also the social significance of squares created for and open to the public: "but while we still persist in keeping the squares for a few privileged persons, and usually without the faintest trace of any but the very poorest plant ornament, they make them as open as our parks and decorate them with a variety and richness of vegetation." [13]

Boulevards

"Boulevard" means literally a walk on the walls of a fortified town, the word going back to the German *Bollwerk* (bulwark). The first boulevard in Paris was opened by Louis XIV in 1670 and extended from the Porte Saint-Denis to the Bastille, occupying the site of the ancient walls leveled by Vauban. These boulevards were formal footways, designed like gardens for the *promeneur* — not, like Haussmann's boulevards of the nineteenth century, intended as lanes for heavy traffic.

"If not already the brightest, airiest, and most beautiful of all cities, Paris is in a fair way to become so; and the greatest part of her beauty is due to her gardens and her trees." Such was the impression on Robinson of the Paris of the new boulevards at the height of their splendor (1869), and he continues: "What would the new boulevards of white stone be without the softening and refreshing aid of those long lanes of well-cared-for trees that everywhere rise around the buildings, helping them somewhat as the grass does the buttercups? . . . In Paris, public gardening assumes an importance which it does not possess with us. . . . It follows the street builders with trees, turns the little squares into gardens unsurpassed for good taste and beauty . . . presents to the eye of the poorest workman every charm of vegetation." [14]

The speed with which these boulevards were created was amazing. They seemed to come into being overnight — great thoroughfares lined with thirty-year-old trees in full leaf. Indeed, "the chief gardeners and the city architects were often called upon to extemporize shady avenues in a few days." [15]

[13] W. Robinson, *The Parks, Promenades, and Gardens of Paris* (London, 1869), pp. 82, 85.

[14] Robinson, *op. cit.*, pp. 1, 2.

[15] Édouard André, quoted by Robinson, *op. cit.*, p. 551.

They were able to accomplish such extraordinary tasks by the use of a tree-lifting machine which they invented, a cart by which in a simple and ingenious way they were able to transplant trees as much as thirty feet high (*fig.* **411**).

Like the squares with their greenery, these tree-lined streets leading to the heart of the city were accepted and copied everywhere. But they represented a solution of the problem which forced town planning to take a very dangerous direction that could not continue.

The great range of Haussmann's talent as an organizer is evident even today in the system of parks which he created on a large scale and in the grand manner. They derived from that class of English landscape gardens which imitated nature, often with romantic aim, encompassing within their limits mountains, valleys, lakes, and brooks in miniature. Their function was to give Paris the lungs that were lacking. They were designed for the *promeneur*, for the workman on his day off, for the Sunday stroller, who was thus enabled to take the air along their broad paths like a seigneur walking in contemplation through his estate. They were made to be looked at, to be enjoyed for their wide vistas and the massing of their herbage. And into them plants were introduced which had not appeared before in public gardens.

The parks

As a result, the old masters of gardening, the English, now came to Paris to learn how "a new aspect of vegetation" could also be given to English gardens. These new plants were hardy subtropical species (*fig.* **413**) which Jean Alphand and his collaborators discovered and brought to Europe in the greatest variety. They were large, vigorous, and easily grown. Some of them attained a height of ten or twelve feet (*Centaurus babylonius*); others, like pampas grass (*Gynerium argentium*), were remarkable for the "rapid vigor and great size of their herbaceous vegetations," or, like a type of the common tobacco (*Nicotiana macrophylla*), were "readily raised from seeds and [grew] luxuriously in rich soil." [16] It was a characteristic of them all that their enormous leaves and the grandeur of

Types of
new plants

[16] Cf. W. Robinson, *op. cit.*, chapter on "Subtropical Plants for the Flower Garden," pp. 182 ff., and chap. XI, "Hardy Plants for the Subtropical Garden," p. 210.

411. Tree-lifting machine for transplanting full-grown trees. *Through the use of such contrivances, thirty-year-old trees sprang up along the boulevards overnight.*

412. Place de la Concorde and Champs-Élysées. Air view, 1855.

413. Hardy subtropical plants: Wigandia. *These huge-leaved and impressive plants which Alphand introduced stood out at great distances.*

their aspect could be perceived from greater distances than usual, so that they were not lost when planted in spacious lawns.[17]

The two great parks in the west and east of Paris, the Bois de Boulogne (1853–58; *fig.* 414) and the Bois de Vincennes (1857–64; *fig.* 415), look on the map of Paris like the two lungs of the city. If Haussmann's idea had been carried out properly, they would have been connected with one another by a wide green belt around the girdle of fortifications. Each contains about two thousand acres. To them, besides the already existing

Parks for *promeneurs*

---

[17] Herein lies the principal reason for their choice by Alphand and his gardeners, and for their general use in European gardens up to the beginning of this century. Then they seem to have been forgotten. Today we are rediscovering in them a charm and vigor of growth which commends them to our own period.

parks, which were reorganized, must be added the Parc Monceau in the center of Paris, the charming Parc Montsouris in the south, and in the north the Buttes-Chaumont for the laboring classes. In keeping with the taste of the period, they were laid out on the most extensive scale as leisure grounds for the *promeneur*. The next step in development was not reached until more than three decades later, when the park of the *promeneur* gave way to the playground system, as in the south parks of Chicago.

414. Bois de Boulogne, 1853–58.

The City as a Technical Problem

Haussmann stands as a symbol of the faith of the nineteenth century in production.

It took Borromini nearly thirty years to erect a small church, and even then it was not quite complete. Louis XIV spent a lifetime in building Versailles, despite the fact that he had all the resources of France at his disposal. In seventeen years, by a mixture of determination and foresight, Haussmann created the great nineteenth-century city. The speed of the work reflects the tempo and enterprise of the industrial expansion which occasioned it.

To solve the problems connected with the city of the industrial age, Haussmann brought together the first precisely coördinated staff of technicians.[18] He could rely on very little assistance from the quarters one would have expected to furnish it. There were at that date no town planners to aid him in avoiding mistakes. The architects were of singularly little help. They could not even adjust themselves to the scale of his projects; on many occasions he had to send their work back and insist upon its enlargement. He remarks that the

415.   Bois de Vincennes, from Plateau de Gravelles, 1857–64.

Second Empire was unfortunate in not producing a single artist equal to the problems of the *temps nouveaux*. Haussmann seems to have resigned himself to this fact. The Bureau of Architects with its staff of academicians and celebrities was the one department which he left almost undisturbed when he took over the administration. His problems were too novel and too extensive for these men to handle; as Henri Labrouste had already seen, their training left them completely out of touch with their own period. This detachment from reality had gone so far that they could no longer even figure the costs

---

[18] Haussmann gives a lively account of the way this staff was built up in his *Mémoires*, vol. VII, chaps. IV, VIII, IX, XI, XIV–XVI.

on their own projects. "As artists . . . [they] had little concern for expenses. I might add that in general they possessed neither the knowledge required for drawing up an estimate nor the careful and detailed attention which is needed for checking a bill." [19] Estimates and bills alike had to be referred to two special commissions which Haussmann created for this purpose. Such men could have no understanding of the new and pressingly practical problems which town planning involved. They were prepared at best to design single buildings, for erection on sites pointed out by someone else. Architects at this period were like those old-style tragedians who would not have thought they were acting if they had been given prose parts to read.

Haussmann's staff of "unknowns"

Haussmann had to look in other fields for his helpers. And in any case buildings were for him only the *décor de la vie*. From the beginning he looked on his work as a technical problem and carried his real difficulties to the engineers, his closest collaborators. Most of these men were relatively unknown when he engaged them, but he was very astute in his choice, and his assistants grew up with him and with the work. Haussmann had been prefect of the Yonne and later of Bordeaux; he knew the able men in these southern districts and looked for his helpers there. Belgrand, for many years a subordinate engineer in a small provincial town, constructed in a faultless manner the enormous sewer system of Paris and the aqueducts which, for the first time in its history, provided Paris with an adequate water supply, drawn from the reservoirs of the Yonne and the Dhuis. Belgrand was of the inventor type; "a man of genius," he was always "modifying his original ideas in some respect or other." As engineer-in-chief and inspector-general of the bridges and highways department "he took upon himself all the work connected with the projects which he had most at heart, even though he had his choice of the most competent collaborators." This trait, Haussmann remarks, was "no doubt due to his long service in the inferior grades." [20]

---

[19] Haussmann, *op. cit.*, III, 511.

[20] Haussmann, *op. cit.*, III, 118–119.

666

To replace Napoleon's *jardinier-paysagiste* (whom he had dismissed after the fiasco in the Bois de Boulogne) Haussmann found a *jardinier-ingénieur* — Jean Alphand. Haussmann had known him in Bordeaux, where he had been an engineer in the bridge and highway service, and recognized him as a technician who possessed "le sentiment de l'art." Made head of the Service des Promenades et Plantations, Alphand transformed the old leisure grounds in Paris and laid out new ones: the Bois de Boulogne, the Bois de Vincennes, the Champs-Élysées, the Parc Monceau, the Buttes-Chaumont, and the Parc Montsouris. These kidney-shaped systems of walks in Paris — so different from contemporary English models — reflect his workmanship.

An engineer creates the Paris park system

Haussmann provided Alphand with — as he puts it — "a right and left hand" for his work: Davioud and Barillet-Deschamps, respectively. Davioud, a young architect (later, in 1878, the builder of the Trocadéro), had one of the rare clear heads in his profession, owing in part, perhaps, to his long training under Alphand. Barillet-Deschamps, an excellent horticulturist, remained comparatively obscure (in marked contrast to Alphand, who came to head the service, and was made *commissaire général* of the 1889 exhibition).[21]

Haussmann had found an engineer and a landscape gardener; he still needed a man to plot the lines of the streets which he proposed to cut through the body of Paris. This time he found his collaborator among the specialists employed by the city, in Deschamps, its chief surveyor. Haussmann thought enough of his work to say afterwards that "le Plan de Paris, c'était M. Deschamps." When the suburban zone was annexed in 1859, Haussmann created a new municipal service, the Direction du Plan de Paris, and made Deschamps its chief. Deschamps and his assistants in this service constituted the general staff for the planning as a whole and were largely responsible for its outcome.

A surveyor takes charge of the *Plan de Paris*

[21] It was Barillet who selected the plants that decorate the various public gardens in Paris. His choices were admirably suited to the purposes they were intended to serve. He was able to induce all sorts of foreign plants to grow in the city soil. One variety with enormous leaves (*Colocasia esculenta*) is particularly adapted to produce an impression at a distance. Universally popular during the eighties, this plant is once more coming into favor for just the uses Barillet put it to.

These three departments—the Service des Eaux et des Égouts, the Service des Promenades et Plantations, and the one just named — were Haussmann's chief instruments for his work. They could have been brought into being only in France, where, since its foundation, the École Polytechnique had been systematically training engineers with an unexcelled theoretical background. The first transformation of a great city to adjust it to the changes brought by industry was carried through by engineers.

Haussmann's Use of Modern Methods of Finance

The technical aspects of town planning had never been so systematically and precisely organized. It was necessary for Haussmann to attempt a similar control over the complex machinery of credit and finance. Parliament opposed his program (the parties of the Left and the Right agreed in this respect) and so did the landowners (whose privileges the regime was pledged to support). In these circumstances it took a real mastery of the complications of finance, as well as extraordinary address on Haussmann's part, to push the scheme through. He had also to find new sources of credit, based on the rise in values which work already accomplished had brought about.

"Productive expenditure" In the course of these manipulations Haussmann endeavored to persuade the legislative bodies concerned that the budget of a nation must find a place for those "extraordinary expenditures" which — when they are managed with intelligence — have the remarkable effect of enriching rather than impoverishing the country. This was his *théorie des dépenses productives* — of productive expenditure, that is. His point that some expenditures which are not strictly necessary can be justified as leading to "a general increase in revenue" is probably sound. And he went on to observe that "these 'productive expenditures' which ordinarily meet with economic censure" can really be incurred with little risk, "since they are optional, and are less trouble to cut down again than the others." [22]

---

[22] Haussmann, *op. cit.*, II, 265.

Haussmann ruled Paris from its city hall, the Hôtel de Ville. His city council was appointed by Napoleon; as Haussmann puts it, it was not subject to "the accident of the vote." After the decree of the hundred and eighty million francs in 1858, he established a fund for public works in Paris — *la caisse des travaux de Paris* — which was under his own control. The *caisse* was the financial instrument which made his huge operations possible. But the Cour des Comptes still rendered the final judgment on all revenue and expenditure. The members of this board had been appointed under Louis-Philippe. In 1868 they reported adversely on a loan made directly to Haussmann by the Crédit Mobilier. It was this report which, half a year later (March 1869), made Haussmann's expenditures in excess of budgeted amounts [23] the subject of debate in the Chamber of Deputies.

He frankly admitted that the *caisse des travaux* had been made to carry an entirely unauthorized debt of a hundred and fifty-nine million francs, but promised that such high-handed practices would be abandoned. In spite of the violent opposition of Adolphe Thiers, the Chamber passed the laws needed to regularize this affair, and the Senate confirmed them by a vote of 110 to 1.[24]

But the *caisse des travaux* had to be liquidated, and this meant the curtailment of Haussmann's liberty of action and the beginning of his downfall. He did not resign, since he hoped to find other ways of continuing his work. Political developments were against him, however. The new elections were a triumph for the Republicans, and the Emperor, trying to maintain his regime, took as his prime minister Émile Ollivier, a man who proposed to "concilier l'empire et le libéralisme."

Haussmann, the dictator of the Hôtel de Ville, saw quite clearly the mendacity of *l'Empire libéral:* "L'Empire Parlementaire, ah! oui. C'est celui-là que je repoussais de toutes

---

[23] The budget for the first *réseau* was exceeded by seventy million francs, the second by two hundred and thirty million francs, and the third by a hundred and eighty million francs. Haussmann's virtues as a town planner — the ability to carry projects through in the shortest possible time and to build them up to the proper grand dimensions — had their consequences.

[24] There is an excellent account of the episode in Morizet, *op. cit.*, p. 298.

mes convictions, auquel j'entendais ne participer en rien, tant je sentais qu'il allait nous mener fatalement aux abîmes!"[25] Napoleon III permitted him to fall away, and in January 1870 he resigned his place in the Hôtel de Ville. The same year was to see the Second Empire eliminated.

The bourgeoisie overthrew Haussmann, in spite of the fact that he had protected that class better than any of his predecessors. Even the Commission for Expropriation which fixed the compensation for houses that had to be demolished was made up of house-owners themselves. One of Maxime du Camp's anecdotes sums up the situation: when he asked a certain *nouveau riche* how he had arrived at his present prosperous state, the man replied simply, "I was expropriated."

The bourgeoisie, however, could not forgive Haussmann for disturbing their peace. What he achieved was achieved against the will of the majority.

The Basic Unit of the Street

To obtain an insight into Haussmann's Paris let us take a typical house, and see how it was occupied.

A tenement house and its sociological background

Boulevard Sébastopol, 1860: a tenement house (*figs.* **416, 417**) of normal type with shops on the ground floor, a mezzanine floor, three main floors, and two attic floors. The three main floors have the same plan. They are apartments intended for upper middle-class tenants. The three-windowed bedroom for Monsieur and Madame takes up the space at the corner. To its left is the living room, to the right the dining room. Further along to the right are the other bedrooms. There is a nursery which receives almost no light. The kitchen and the servant's room look onto a narrow light-well.

These narrow light-wells are an evil characteristic of Continental dwelling houses of this period, and of the years after it as well.

---

[25] Haussmann, *op. cit.*, II, 537. "Ah yes! The parliamentary empire! It is just that which I rejected with all my convictions and meant to have no part in; I was convinced that it would infallibly lead us into disaster."

416. House on the Boulevard Sébastopol, Paris, 1860. *Façade and section. Typical tenement house of the period (shops on ground floor, middle-class apartments above them, servants' quarters in attic). The basic unit of Haussmann's street. It exhibits an intermingling of functions which had been possible earlier but would not work in an industrial age.*

417. House on the Boulevard Sébastopol, 1860. *Plan of second, third, and fourth floors.*

The attic floors are the most densely overcrowded parts of the building. Here bed is placed next to bed, in the most confined space possible, for the accommodation of servants, night lodgers, and the lower classes generally.

The uniform façade of this house of 1860 covers a living unit in which the most diversified functions of daily living swirl

671

together. Business takes over the ground floor, and often encroaches on the mezzanine, in workrooms connected with the various establishments. The three main floors are given over to apartments for the well-to-do. The attic floors are congested slums.

Intermingling of
different functions

In earlier times the association of production with dwelling quarters was quite natural, but this connection could not be carried over into large towns. Tenement houses artificially bring together functions which, in an industrial society, should be kept strictly separate. It is absurd in an age of industrial production to permit residence, labor, and traffic to intermingle. It is not merely the endless streets that are inhuman but the units that go to make them up as well.

Haussmann is not alone to blame for this mixture. The same phenomenon appears in all countries. Behind it lies a failure that is peculiar to the nineteenth century, a marked inability to control the available resources.

It is true that there are fine houses which offer excellent rooms and the best of locations to the more prosperous. But just as poison gas cannot be stopped at the window, so the general disorder cannot be avoided by these luxurious dwellings. They stand in the midst of airless routes of heavy traffic, cut off from natural surroundings and exposed to every noise and disturbance.

If in an industrial age the various functions of daily life cannot be clearly separated, that fact alone spells the death sentence of the great city.

Uniform façades

Haussmann showed his sagacity in refusing to allow any tricks to be played with façades. Simply and without discussion, he spread a uniform façade over the whole of Paris. It featured high French windows, with accents provided by lines of cast-iron balconies like those used in the Rue de Rivoli under Napoleon I. He employed, unobtrusively, Renaissance shapes of a pleasantly neutral nature. A last touch of the unity which marked baroque architecture can still be felt. The neutral façades and the general uniformity make Haussmann's enormous work of rebuilding better than any other executed in or after the fifties of the nineteenth century.

The Scale of the Street

Haussmann's reorganization of Paris demonstrates the French fondness for the *culte de l'axe*. Wherever possible, he tries to introduce "grand prospects," usually without success.[26] Because of the great length of the streets, a building put at the head of a boulevard is soon lost in the blue distance. Thus the Gare de l'Est, out of which the Boulevard Sébastopol stems, sinks down from its dominating position long before one reaches the end of this thoroughfare. The street, and not the square or the single building, determines the impression. These Parisian streets were sometimes as much as three miles long. This is a new phenomenon in the history of architecture. (Several decades later, in Los Angeles, streets were to reach lengths of more than thirty miles.)

The boulevard developed out of the baroque avenue. The baroque idea was to have long avenues planted with trees but devoid of houses. In the nineteenth century this idea was taken up again and transmuted. It reappears in the form of endless streets lined by uniform houses.

We are likely to forget that during these seventeen years Paris was also sprinkled with buildings of the most various types: great exhibition halls, churches, schools, markets, the Bibliothèque Nationale, and so on.[27] All these are buildings which cannot be overlooked in the history of the nineteenth century. This is quite understandable, since the street dominates the new picture. *(marginal note: Miscellaneous building activity)*

To most of his contemporaries Haussmann seemed a dangerous *démolisseur*, a man who was mortgaging the future of the city and a financier who was inclined to play fast and loose with the law. All his projects were repugnant to "common sense" — with the exception of the work on the Rue de Rivoli, which had been under consideration from the time of Napoleon I. There would have been no objections if he had confined himself to enlarging streets already in existence. But to cut new ones was to disturb the settled scheme of things *(marginal note: Two units of scale for the street: the* promeneur *vs. the vehicle)*

26 Haussmann, *op. cit.*

27 Haussmann cites an impressive list of buildings put up during his transformation of Paris. Cf. *Mémoires*, II, 524–528.

and to show a lack of respect for the rights of property. With these new developments "on tombe dans ce que j'appelle la fantaisie, on est dans l'imaginaire et on marche vers la ruine financière." [28] So it seemed to Haussmann's bitterest opponent, the historian Adolphe Thiers, whose political career began under Louis-Philippe and — unlike Haussmann's — continued after 1870 under the Third Republic.

In taking the city as a technical problem, Haussmann came to view it primarily as a problem in traffic and transportation — this before the railway and the city street had been given their heavy contemporary burdens. His contemporaries, lacking his vision, could not understand Haussmann's passion for new lines of communication through the center of the city, and even into the suburbs, where no such counterrevolutionary measures were needed. "Pour les promeneurs," Thiers inquired, "quelle nécessité avait-il d'aller de la Madeleine à l'Étoile par la voie la plus courte? Mais les promeneurs, au contraire, veulent allonger leur promenade et c'est pour cela qu'ils font trois ou quatre fois le tour d'une même allée." [29]

Traffic receives primary consideration

The remark can be taken as revealing, quite unconsciously, the grounds for Thiers's criticisms. The town planning he understood worked from the point of view of the *promeneur*, while Haussmann's took the demands of an industrial age for its guide. The first effect of approaching the planning of a city as a transportation problem on a large scale is the endless street, the street that stretches beyond the range of the eye. Haussmann's preoccupation with traffic tended to force the residential problem into the background. The boulevards dismember the city. That housing was definitely secondary can be seen in the contemporary etchings which illustrate Alphand's large publication, *Les Promenades de Paris* (Paris, 1867–73). The Boulevard Richard-Lenoir (*fig.* **408**), for example, shows a wide highway covered with lawns and planted with trees in the center, but behind the uniform outer walls formed

[28] "We fall into what I call fantasy, we are in the realm of the imaginary and on the march toward financial ruin." Quoted in Morizet, *op. cit.*, p. 297.

[29] "Do people out walking need to go from the Madeleine to the Étoile by the *shortest* route? On the contrary; *promeneurs* want to prolong their walks. That's the reason they will take three or four turns up and down the same street." Quoted in Morizet, *op. cit.*, p. 297.

by its houses the most appalling disorder lies concealed.[30] The street dominates Alphand's bird's-eye view of the city; the houses which do not front on it have plainly been allowed to spring up in a huddled confusion. Haussmann uses the uniform façade as a kind of wardrobe into which all the disorder can be crammed. All other aspects of the life of the city are sacrificed to the problem of traffic.

One can recognize easily enough the mistake involved in considering only the problem of transportation and ignoring the residential problems. But at the stage of social and industrial development that existed in Haussmann's day not even the beginnings of a solution to housing problems in great cities had been found.

Haussmann's later critics have concerned themselves mainly with the aesthetic evaluation of his work. This is obviously a difficult undertaking, and it is not made any easier by comparing his "merely straight and convenient" [31] thoroughfares with "rhythmically articulated aesthetic compositions" by Renaissance masters. Haussmann himself was devoted to the *culte de l'axe*, but the enormous scale of his work made certain things impossible. The street cannot have "organic unity . . . as part of a dominant building" when it is required to serve as an artery for huge volumes of cross-town traffic. To criticize Haussmann for breaking with Mansard and Le Nôtre is to say nothing about his transformation of Paris.

Difficulties in the aesthetic evaluation of Haussmann's work

It is likewise true that "the wall of houses around the Place de l'Étoile is so broken that one hardly feels it as circular,"[32] and that, indeed, it "has no right to be called a 'place' in the sense of the word established by the French architects of the seventeenth and eighteenth centuries." But this is no more than a dispute about definitions. And in any event this is not a failure peculiar to or characteristic of Haussmann's planning. Outside of London, badly organized squares are common dur-

---

[30] Haussmann planned the Boulevard Richard-Lenoir (1861–63) to cover a canal. The avenue and its rows of trees are supported by the "roof" of the canal.

[31] This and the following quotations are taken from Elbert Peets, "Famous Town Planners: Haussmann," *Town Planning Review*, XII, no. 3 (June 1927), 187–188.

[32] Haussmann himself saw this defect in the work of his architect and planted trees before the small houses which were completely out of scale.

ing the nineteenth century and reflect a general loss of the baroque ability to model space.[33]

Haussmann worked at a time when architecture was in a very unsettled state. The best he could hope for — and at the time it was a considerable achievement — was to give his street fronts the most neutral character possible. Nobody else of his day or later in the century managed to equal the sure and inoffensive neutrality which the uniform façades of Paris display. Finally, aesthetic judgment of Haussmann's work is bound to place undue emphasis upon the transitory facts that appear in it. Granted that there is "a silk-hat slickness" to everything, a reflection of the artistic standards of "the bank-president and the midinette," this does not touch the main issue. Haussmann was in fact the first man to view the great city — the capital with millions of inhabitants — as a technical problem. Hence his distant relations with architects and his close collaboration with expert technicians.

Haussmann's Foresight: His Influence

Haussmann took extraordinarily long steps toward the solution of the traffic problem, steps far in advance of the needs of his time. The influx of automobiles, which came after Haussmann's death at eighty-two, made this problem still much more urgent and complex.

Anticipates development of the suburbs

The work of Haussmann points toward the future in another respect; every great town planner has been driven on to attempt — at whatever cost to himself — realizations that only the future can justify. The Préfet de la Seine was no exception, and ran into disaster through schemes whose anticipations exceeded the calculations of the majority. Haussmann's work on the incorporation of the *banlieue*, the suburban zone of Paris, was just such a *coup de génie*.

This enterprise, begun, as we have noted, under the second *réseau*, was still incomplete when Haussmann left the Hôtel de Ville. It was meant to give the great mass of the people a chance to live outside the city. It was, however, an undertak-

---

[33] This point is discussed with reference to some German squares in the author's *Spätbarocker und romantischer Klassizismus* (Munich, 1922).

676

ing whose extent could not be estimated in advance.[34] Haussmann's "illegal borrowings" from the *caisse des travaux* were carried out to finance suburban works whose scope constantly widened. His critics, taking the scale of the *promeneur* as final, could not have been expected to understand such arrangements, intended as they were for generations yet unborn. They could not have foreseen that these roads, carried clear over the horizon, would prove to be the most "productive" of the prefect's "expenditures," and would constitute the future living space of Paris.

It was useless for Haussmann to point out that in the years during which this network of suburban streets had been in process of development, the population of the zone had risen from 258,000 to 368,000. Since Haussmann's time, the population of Paris has increased seventy per cent, the population of the suburbs five hundred per cent.[35] This trend of growth in the whole greater Paris area has justified his schemes to an extent he himself could not have foreseen. The same phenomenon can be observed in the case of other large cities.

The later expansion of Paris proceeded without a hint of order; there was no one who had the power either to carry Haussmann's arrangements further or to adjust them to the growing need for a careful separation of residential and industrial areas. The chaotic mixture of villages suddenly inflated into cities, tiny houses scattered at random over the countryside, and new industrial centers sprang from the inability of the declining century to master and give form to its life.[36]

The later expansion of Paris

---

[34] The final cost was over three hundred and sixty million francs — a hundred and sixty million more than had been allotted for this purpose.

[35] Albert Demangeon, *Paris, la ville et sa banlieue* (Paris, 1934?), p. 20.

[36] Cf. *Les Banlieues urbaines* (Paris, 1920) by Henri Sellier, Conseiller général de la Seine. Sellier, who knows the Paris region intimately, gives a true picture of how immense agglomerations of high tenement houses were built along unpaved village roads, often without sewers, in the midst of old peasant houses, and became thickly populated slums, entirely lacking in sanitary facilities.

The result, as Professor Duguet revealed in his reports to the Commission of Hygiene, is a shocking death rate from tuberculosis in the Department of the Seine. For every hundred people dying of tuberculosis in the rest of France, a hundred and fifty die in the Department of the Seine. (Cf. *Revue des deux mondes*, July 15, 1923, p. 444.)

The chaotic growth of American cities since the sixties has often been attributed to a lack of tradition. Yet in the *banlieue* of Paris, a city with a history of twenty centuries, a similar disorganization occurs. The reasons for it are the same in both cases.

The wide scope of Haussmann's activities was not due solely to the autocratic powers given him by the regime of which he was so firm an adherent. He belonged to a generation — that *génération forte*, as he himself called it — which showed, in all fields, extreme initiative and an irrepressible urge to do all those things which had never been accomplished before.

Haussmann's enemies referred to him derisively as the *Louis quatorze municipal*. There was more truth in this than his contemporaries recognized. To be sure, his work lacked the unity of conception which underlay the great Louis's schemes. The split personality of the nineteenth century appears in its almost inextricable mingling of constituent with transitory facts. On the one hand there is its foresight and energy; on the other there are those dangerous expedients which reflect the uncertainty of Haussmann's period.

But the huge scale of this work is genuinely overwhelming. Haussmann dared to change the entire aspect of a great city, a city which had been sacred for hundreds of years as the center of the civilized world. To build a new Paris, attacking all ramifications of this problem simultaneously — this was work on a scale which none of the projects we shall discuss have ever equaled. The indomitable courage of the Préfet de la Seine has also remained unequaled. Haussmann allowed no group to block his schemes: he cut directly into the body of the city in his transformation of Paris.

Haussmann's influence

Haussmann's direct influence was immense. In every country where industrialization was late in developing, one encounters details imitated from the transformation of Paris, particularly from the early accomplishments of the first *réseau*. There are few cities without a main street directed toward the axis of the central station, like the Boulevard Sébastopol and the Gare de l'Est. The Parisian boulevards find many an echo in monumental streets built up along the line of razed fortifications. But it was only details which were imitated. There was no one with Haussmann's power to attempt a general attack upon the new problem of the city.

Countries like Germany, in which the expansion of industry was delayed until 1870, achieved markedly inferior results in reconstructing their big cities. Even the unity of the street was lost. Instead of the neutral continuity of Paris, there appeared in each of the four- or five-story blocks a pseudo style, pseudo individuality, and pseudo materials. The result was an aesthetic sewer.

PART **VIII** **CITY PLANNING AS A HUMAN PROBLEM**

From 1870 on, the great cities developed continuously toward what they are today — unserviceable instruments. No one knows when this tremendous waste of time and health will be cut down, when this pointless assault on the nerves will end, when this failure to achieve a dignified standard of life (a standard reached by every peasant) will be remedied.

Cities cannot simply be discarded, like worn-out machinery; they have too large a part in our destiny. But by now it is plain that the life which they have abused is increasingly exacting its revenge, and that this fundamentally provisional and feverish institution must soon be brought within narrower limits. Whether the work will be done by intelligence or by brute disaster cannot be foreseen.

Camillo Sitte's return to the city of the Middle Ages (1889)

Unsuccessful attempts at change and reform have been going on for a long time. As early as 1883 the Society of Arts — the body which organized the Great Exhibition in London in 1851 — offered twelve hundred pounds as prize awards for essays on the best ways of rebuilding central London and housing its poor.

On the Continent there was an early reaction against the degenerate and omnipresent imitations of Haussmann's work. In 1889 the Viennese town planner, Camillo Sitte (1843–1903), suggested — like the handicrafters of four decades earlier — that the remedy was to be found in a return to methods of the medieval period.[1] Sitte saw in the organic growth of the medieval town a way of humanizing the contemporary city. He made sensitive analyses of these towns — northern and southern, Roman, Gothic, Renaissance, and baroque. What concerned him was the sense for the organization of outer space which is expressed in their layout. He found it in the way the streets flow into the squares, in the relations between the square and the church or town hall, and in the free and well-pondered equilibrium of all the elements in these urban organisms.

Camillo Sitte felt, as everyone must, that the laws of town building are summed up in Aristotle's laconic statement:

---

[1] Cf. Camillo Sitte, *Der Städtebau* (Vienna, 1889).

PLAN OF A PROPOSED RURAL TOWN, TO BE CALLED *HYGEIA*,
The Property of Wl. Bullock
on the RIVER OHIO, KENTUCKY, in the UNITED STATES of AMERICA,
DESIGNED BY I. B. PAPWORTH,
Architect to the King of Wirtenberg &c. &c.

418. J. B. PAPWORTH. Scheme for "Rural Town" on the banks of the Ohio River, "Hygeia," 1827.

Towns should be built so as to protect their inhabitants and at the same time make them happy.

Most of us nowadays share Sitte's further conviction that the artistic problems raised by urban developments are fully as important as the technical ones.

Camillo Sitte's intentions were of the best. He sought to overcome the monotony and the artistic lifelessness of the typical late nineteenth-century city. Its defects he saw very clearly, but the measures he suggested to correct them were no more than palliatives. Clearing the centers of squares and placing all statues and monuments at the corners, locating gardens in the courtyards of apartment blocks instead of in busy public places, building high walls to isolate public parks from street noises — all these were surface reforms.

Such proposals show the extent to which the town planner had lost contact with his period. He was a kind of troubadour,

683

ineffectually pitting his medieval songs against the din of modern industry.

In the late nineteenth century the urbanist, like the popular painter, lost himself in the composition of idylls. Neither was able to work on the scale that was necessary. Life moved on along a different track.

Other measures were proposed by various specialists, but they can be found in any history of town planning, and we shall not deal with them here. We propose instead to ask a general question: What attitude did really creative artists around 1900 — men like Wagner, Garnier, and Berlage — take toward the problems of urbanism? This may lead us to some insight into the amount of mastery over town planning which was possible at this period.

Otto Wagner's faith in the big city

Otto Wagner (1841–1918) belonged to a generation which retained the hopeful attitude of the nineteenth century toward industry. He could never have imagined that the great city — then at the full tide of its growth — would in time come to find its prosperity seriously threatened.

When Wagner began formulating his ideas, Sitte's influence was at its peak. The garden city scheme had just been advanced as the solution to the residential problem. Wagner saw from the very beginning that the garden city could not solve the housing problem of the great towns. Much later, the pressure of facts forced people to acknowledge that Wagner was right.

The architectonic vision and energy which appears in so much of Wagner's work seems to be overcome by a sort of paralysis when he enters the field of town planning. In the endeavor to avoid the usual haphazard and chaotic development, Wagner drew up plans for a whole quarter in Vienna (*fig.* **419**).[2] His scheme provided for a sizable open area in the middle — "a center for air" — but the layout as a whole is rigidly formal and a great deal more static than Haussmann's arrangements in Paris. The governing unit of his design is the closed, five-story block, the basic element in almost every large

---

[2] Cf. Otto Wagner, *Die Groszstadt, eine Studie über diese* (Vienna, n.d.). These studies date back to the nineties.

419. OTTO WAGNER. Scheme for a district center in Vienna, c. 1910.

Continental city of the time. Wagner could not seem to hit upon any alternative to this kind of planning. In the late nineteenth century it would seem that town planning had exhausted all its possibilities and that no new solutions could be reached. The ability to organize space in accordance with actual problems had been lost.

But there did arise in this period the realization that it was the needs of its inhabitants which ought to govern the planning of the modern city. Otto Wagner was among the first to see this clearly.

Wagner's chief interest was the creation of a healthful environment for the man of ordinary means. He was one of the earliest to recognize that a great city embraces many different types of people, each type requiring a different kind of dwelling. He saw too that the residential needs of the average city-dweller changed with his circumstances.

Wagner called for community ownership of those areas which would be required for the future growth of the city. Only in that way could the city regulate land prices and maintain control over its own development. (Amsterdam had already adopted this system.)

Wagner perceived very clearly what was responsible for the diseased state of the big city: "The expansion of cities can no longer — as in the past — be abandoned to blind chance, with artistic influences regarded as superficial and the development of great towns left to detestable usury."

More than thirty years later, at its congress in Athens in 1933, the CIAM [3] laid down the same requirements (in less violent language):

"It is of the utmost urgency that each town establish an urban program, and that it create the laws necessary for its realization."

Ebenezer Howard and the Garden City

The idea of the garden city was advanced as a solution to the many dwelling problems of the late nineteenth century. The essence of the plan was that the community should control the ground (i.e., be its own landlord), and that all profits through increases in the value of the land should be returned to the community in order to discourage speculation of any sort.

The idea of the garden city as it was formulated by Ebenezer Howard is quite different from the forms the idea took in actual practice. Howard's book, *Tomorrow, a Peaceful Path to Real Reform*, first appeared in 1898. As the title indicates, it was no mean achievement at which Howard aimed. He aspired to nothing less than the abolition of the evils of the industrial revolution, the elimination of slums and overcrowded industrial districts. All this was to be accomplished without arousing the antagonism of any group, even the landlords. He expected to create new forms of public wealth through a complete transvaluation of values, without even waiting till some party sympathetic to his views was in power.[4]

One is reminded of Frank Lloyd Wright's "Broadacre City" when one reads in Ebenezer Howard of the migration of an industrial population into the country, the colonization of the land, and the setting down of factories in an unspoiled landscape.

---

[3] International Congress for Modern Architecture.

[4] Dugald Macfayden, *Sir Ebenezer Howard and the Town Planning Movement* (Manchester, 1933), p. 29.

686

Ebenezer Howard was an expert stenographer working in the London courts when the idea of the garden city came to him. That was in 1898, and he had just finished reading Bellamy's *Looking Backward*, published not long before in America, which a friend had lent him. He responded to the book with such enthusiasm that he immediately set to work to promote its publication in England. This book presented a graphic picture of the whole American nation organized on coöperative principles, and in reflecting on it Howard "was led to put forward proposals of his own for testing out Bellamy's principles, though on a very much smaller scale — in brief, to build by private enterprise an entirely new town, industrial, residential, and agricultural." [5]

This was how the garden-city idea got its start. It grew out of the same soil as the general problem of a coöperatively organized society.

Howard conceived of his city as a set of concentric circles. The center consists of a group of civic buildings grouped about a common. Midway between the center and the outermost circle is a circular grand avenue, four hundred feet in width, with trees and greenery. The outermost circle is an agricultural belt. An area set aside for manufacturing is anticipated. In the circular park at the center, surrounded by gardens, stand the larger public buildings, each in its own ample grounds: town hall, concert and lecture hall, theater, library, and so on. The "Crystal Palace" encircles a public park and recreation ground. It consists of a glass arcade, opening on the park, where manufactured goods may be exposed for sale. One part of it is used as a winter garden, a place of resort in bad weather. [6] The fundamental idea of this scheme — which, as Howard cautions us, is a diagram only, the plan necessarily depending on the site selected — was developed in the Renaissance. It came to be repeated under many different forms, and there are proposals made in the early nineteenth century which do not differ markedly from Howard's conceptions.

Howard's scheme

[5] Macfayden, p. 20.

[6] Ebenezer Howard, *Garden Cities of Tomorrow* (London, 1902), p. 23.

As early as 1827 proposals were made by the English architect J. B. Papworth for what he called "rural-towns." [7] Hygeia (*fig.* **418**), a settlement that was never brought into being, was to be on the Ohio River in Kentucky. He conceived of it as having community buildings in the center, with broad areas given over to gardening and with zoning regulations. The whole conception was very close to the late baroque urban tradition of John Nash.

It is often said that Howard treated his idyllic garden city as an isolated phenomenon unrelated to reality. He knew quite well, however, that overcrowded cities had "done their work" and that the great cities of the future would have to be constructed on another pattern.

He remarks at the end of his *Tomorrow* that "a simpler problem must first be solved. One small Garden City must be built as a working model and then a group of cities. . . . These tasks done, and done well, the reconstruction of London must inevitably follow. . . ."

Failure of the garden-city idea

But execution and idea were, as is so often the case, quite different. No "Crystal Palace" in a garden city ever appeared.[8] The idea of a garden city never exerted any influence on the rebuilding of a great modern capital. The most that resulted was the creation of new suburban settlements by coöperative societies and the introduction of better architectural schemes,[9] but for the most part the idea degenerated into the building of conglomerations of small houses in small gardens.

After the lapse of four decades it is easy to see why the idea of the garden city, "where town and country are married," was doomed to failure. The example of the "working model"

[7] The greater part of Cheltenham remains as a memorial to his powers as a town planner. Cf. R. P. Ross Williamson, "John Buonarroti Papworth, Architect to the King of Wurtemburg," *Architectural Review*, vol. LXXIX, 1936. Cf. also R. G. Thwaites, *Early Western Travels, 1748–1846* (Cleveland, 1904–07), vol. XIX, map preceding Bullock's "Sketch of a Journey through the Western States of North America."

[8] Letchworth, in 1903, attempted the first "model" but failed to attract much over half of its intended population.

[9] For example, the scheme of Peter Behrens in 1918; Vreewyke's garden city at Rotterdam; Radburn, N. J. (in connection with automobile traffic); and Neubühl in Zurich (1932).

shows that it offers no solution to the problems of today. A partial solution is impossible; only preconceived and integrated planning on a scale embracing the whole structure of modern life in all its ramifications can accomplish the task which Ebenezer Howard had in mind.

Tony Garnier's Cité Industrielle, 1901–04

In 1898 a young man named Tony Garnier was installed in the Villa Medici as the current holder of the *grand prix de Rome*. At about the same time Frank Lloyd Wright was building his early houses in the suburbs of Chicago, and Ebenezer Howard was vigorously urging his garden-city scheme. To satisfy the prize requirements, Garnier sent the Academy in Paris a reconstruction of the plan of Tusculum, Cicero's home. As with Henri Labrouste before him, however, the work he did on his own account was of a different character. This holder of the *prix de Rome* had set himself the task of planning a complete town — not merely its general layout, but all the rooms of every building. His Cité Industrielle was intended for some thirty-five thousand inhabitants (*fig.* 420).

First example of contemporary town planning

According to Garnier, the general layout was exhibited in 1901, and the detailed plan in 1904. It was not until 1917, however, that Garnier's ideas found publication in book form.[10] The deep influence of this book was not restricted to France; it circulated from hand to hand wherever new solutions were being sought.

Garnier had taken a great step forward in treating a whole town without losing himself in masses of detail, as many of his contemporaries did. His projected houses, schools, railway stations, and hospitals likewise represented a great advance.

Architecture begins in construction and ends in town planning; Garnier's work is based on both. His Cité Industrielle grew out of a broad understanding of social requirements. The balance of its layout is not destroyed by concentration on single issues, on the specialized problem of traffic or the more or less specialized problems of housing which absorbed the

---

[10] Garnier, *Étude pour la construction des villes* (Paris, 1917).

advocates of the garden city. Garnier sought for an organic interrelationship between all the functions of his town.

Ferroconcrete was the material Garnier chose for his constructions. Around 1900 its potentialities were just beginning to be appreciated, especially by the traditionally alert French constructors. It was quite natural that it should fascinate a young architect, even an "ancien pensionnaire de l'Académie française à Rome." With ferroconcrete Garnier could realize more adequately than with any other material his intention of providing an appropriate frame for industry, public services, and the life of the average man.

Ferroconcrete Garnier's primary material

There is a clear separation of all the different functions of the town: work, residence, leisure, and transport. Industry is cut off from the town proper by a green belt, as it was later in the Russian schemes for stratified cities. The health center occupies a protected site on the slope of an outlying hill and is oriented toward the south.

Clear distinction between different functions

The middle of Garnier's elongated town is reserved for a civic center, a high school district, and very complete and elaborate athletic fields.[11] This sports area adjoins open country, which gives it room to expand and a fine view as well.

Main-line railway traffic enters the city terminal (*fig.* **201**) through a subway. (This terminal, like some other buildings in the Cité Industrielle, is extraordinarily advanced for its date; the simple and functional exterior is genuinely revolutionary.) Garnier even includes an autodrome or speedway, as well as testing grounds for *moteurs d'aviation*.

The town site is divided into long, narrow lots, running east and west to facilitate proper orientation of the rooms in the buildings which stand on them. These lots — the basic units of the Cité — are thirty by a hundred and fifty meters. These stretched-out plots give a new aspect to the town and represent an extreme departure from the centralized Renaissance type of layout.

Most of these lots are placed at right angles to the main arteries of traffic. Contemporary urbanists have adopted a similar

---

[11] This is rather curious; at that time the French paid little attention to sports.

←   **691**

420. TONY GARNIER. Cité Industrielle, 1901–04.
General map. Designed for 35,000 inhabitants.

arrangement to avoid the *rue corridor* and to isolate residential sections from routes of heavy traffic. Garnier was quite aware of what he was doing: "On traverse la ville indépendamment des rues" (*fig. 421*).[12] The closed blocks and light-wells of Haussmann's time are completely eliminated. There are open spaces between all Garnier's blocks, the "community blocks" on the main thoroughfares, with their roof gardens.

421. TONY GARNIER. Cité Industrielle, 1901–04. *Air view of houses and gardens. Traffic is, for the most part, routed away from the houses. The attempt is made to solve the residential problem through the use of low houses set in the midst of communal gardens.*

422. TONY GARNIER. Cité Industrielle, 1901–04. *Plan of a dwelling unit; terraces.*

[12] This is not to be taken with complete literalness, but it would have held true for the small volume of traffic usual around 1900. The germs of later solutions are certainly present in Garnier's layout.

Each individual dwelling has a large central living room and small but well-organized bedrooms, bath, and kitchen (*fig.* **422**). The open areas between the houses are filled with greenery. The schools, low and open in their planning (*fig.* **423**), are distributed throughout the town to add their lawns and shrubbery to the green areas around the houses. Later on, the newer suburbs of Amsterdam were developed along similar lines.

423. TONY GARNIER. Cité Industrielle, 1901–04. *School, with open and covered terraces. An attempt is made to blend the surrounding open spaces with those around the houses so that they will form a neighborhood unit.*

Tony Garnier felt an attraction to the classical, as the modeling of his buildings shows. He broke through this attachment, however, in many of the details of his Cité Industrielle. Its houses, with their terraces and the gardens on their flat roofs (*fig.* **424**), are a sound combination of modern construction and the old tradition of the Mediterranean culture.

Garnier's scheme was partially realized later on at Lyons, where he built hospitals, stockyards, athletic stadia, and a residential district.[13] People looked to Howard's scheme to solve the problems of urbanism, though in reality it offered nothing more than

---

[13] Cf. Garnier, *Les Grands Travaux de la ville de Lyon* (Paris, 1924).

424. TONY GARNIER. Cité Industrielle, 1901–04. *Ferroconcrete houses with open staircases and roof gardens. Through the use of ferroconcrete, Garnier arrives at solutions which reappear later on.*

a soporific. The garden-city idea did not answer the questions raised by the large city; it only quieted them temporarily.

Garnier's plan clearly separated the different functions of the city: work, housing, traffic, and recreation. In allotting them their places, Garnier arranged things so that a future expansion of any one of them would leave the others undisturbed. These long blocks with their greenery are often planned to constitute neighborhood units and have their own schools and all necessary services. The drawings for every building are complete down to the last details of construction and layout, and often foreshadow future developments in an astonishing manner. Garnier's chief material, ferroconcrete, is employed to reach unexpected solutions in his schools, railway stations, sanatoriums, and residences.

The Cité Industrielle has directly influenced those men whose work of today is serving to outline the city planning of the future. This influence is understandable, since Garnier's scheme contains the germs of contemporary methods. Developments often take unpredictable courses: the lost instinct for town planning was recaptured by a young *pensionnaire de l'Académie à Rome.*

694

425. LE CORBUSIER. Settlement at Pessac, near Bordeaux, 1926.

AMSTERDAM AND THE REBIRTH OF TOWN PLANNING

We turned to London to gain an insight into the state of town planning between 1800 and 1850. Our example for the years between 1850 and 1870 was Paris, and for the period between 1900 and our own day it will be Amsterdam. There are other cities where, over a short interval, a more rapid advance was shown — for example, Frankfort on the Main in the late twenties. And in some respects Rotterdam went beyond Amsterdam, where, if building activity was more extensive, it was also sometimes carried on without coördination. It was at Rotterdam (from 1919 on) that J. J. P. Oud built his carefully planned tenements for lower income groups, and that van Tijen experimented (after 1930) with tall slablike apartment houses to meet the special requirements of a modern European city.

But Amsterdam is one of the few cities of our times which shows a continuous tradition in town planning, unbroken since 1900. This uninterrupted building activity is particularly important for our purposes, since it affords us a view over a long period of development and eliminates the necessity of

Continuous tradition at Amsterdam

695

collecting individual examples from all corners of the world. Amsterdam is thus the city best adapted to a study of the main currents working through the period.

Town planning in Amsterdam operated within the realm of what was really possible. There were no erratic developments, no Utopian enterprises, but a steady progress. The method behind the work might be called analytic. It admirably suited the temperament of the Dutch, who disliked daring speculations like those that went on in England around 1820. Both progress and mistakes were made by slow stages at Amsterdam.

For a long time the population of Amsterdam remained stable, but in 1875 it began to rise steeply. The rise followed the opening of the canal which gives Amsterdam its outlet into the North Sea. Between 1875 and 1900 the population doubled, and in the interval between 1900 and 1920 there was another increase of almost fifty per cent. It was in this second period (barring the war years) that the maximum building activity took place.

Amsterdam builds for the lower and middle classes

For what classes were these buildings raised? The early London squares and crescents were for the gentry and the richest members of the middle class. The middle classes were the chief objects of Haussmann's boulevard-building in Paris — with the poor often crowded into slumlike apartments on the top floors of the buildings. In Amsterdam building activity was carried on in the service of the lower middle class and the working people.

Traveling in Holland during the twenties one encountered brand-new housing settlements in every part of the country — variable in quality, but all marked by clean surfaces in brick, big windows, and a visible intention of giving the Dutch scene the imprint of the best contemporary architecture. Nowhere else was modern architecture given such an opportunity to change the whole face of a country.

Impetus furnished by Dutch Housing Act of 1901

The impetus for this entire development came from the Dutch Housing Act of 1901. "This enactment," to quote from the Harvard City Planning Studies, "is perhaps the most comprehensive single piece of legislation ever to be adopted in this

696

field. Its eleven chapters provide the essentials of a complete attack upon the national housing problems. Some amendments have been made since its passage, but the basic structure of the law remains and is the authority for the greatest part of all governmental intervention in housing in the Netherlands." [1] The act required every town of ten thousand or more inhabitants to draw up a scheme governing its future expansion. Detailed as well as general plans were required, and the general plan had to be revised every ten years. The process of expropriation was also regulated by the act, and was made easier for the cities to carry through.

This act came just when the northern countries were entering upon a new stage in the treatment of the housing problem. Up to this time, the ideal dwelling for the lower class family had often been displayed at the great exhibitions, but it had never formed a recognized part of building activity. The Housing Act of 1901 was shrewdly drawn to encourage just such constructions for the use of people of small means.

The city becomes a landowner

Coöperatively organized building societies received building credits on very easy terms from the state, the credits being guaranteed by the community. Thus the whole tendency of the act was to make the city a decisive influence upon all building activity. At the same time the city made intensive (though not always successful) efforts to constitute itself a great landowner and to acquire the land for its housing settlements before speculation forced up prices. And, like the nobles who were the landlords in London, the city of Amsterdam leased the ground instead of selling it.

Many cities have attempted to use a similar land policy. Amsterdam, however, actually succeeded in building whole districts which were homogeneous and met the demands of the community. Building contractors were forced to submit to the judgments of what was called a "commission for beauty," which saw to it that uniform façades were erected. This com-

[1] Richard Ratcliff, in Mabel U. Walker's *Urban Blight and Slums* (Cambridge, 1938) p. 398 (vol. XII of Harvard City Planning Studies). Ratcliff examines in detail the effect upon slums and blighted areas of the eleven chapters dealing with construction standards, housing and population surveys, closure and demolition of unfit structures, expropriation, town planning, slum clearance and redevelopment, financial assistance by municipalities and by the state, etc.

426. H. P. BERLAGE. Plan of Amsterdam South, 1902. *A mixture of influences is evident here, along with the uncertainty that accompanied Berlage's attempt to break with old formulas.*

mission formed the basis for the building activities of de Klerk and the other architects of the Amsterdam school in the twenties.

Land tenure and the character of the façade were pretty thoroughly controlled by the community; regulations governing ground plans were not set up until later.

Berlage's first plan for the Amsterdam South district, 1902

Besides the 1901 ordinances, individual creative forces were at work in bringing about at Amsterdam a kind of city planning that broke loose from routine. Such energies were not confined to this Dutch city; they could have been found elsewhere as well. There was, for example, Otto Wagner in Vienna — and he was conducting a long, bitter, and ultimately unsuccessful fight with the city administration. Amsterdam, by contrast, afforded remarkable freedom to a private architect of real genius by handing over the development of the Amsterdam South district to Hendrik Petrus Berlage (*fig.* **426**). Berlage drew up his first plans for this development in 1902. The Stock Exchange Building which was to make his name the

427. French landscape gardening, 1869. *The kidney-shaped windings of the paths are recalled in Berlage's 1902 plan for the Amsterdam South district.*

center of discussion in all parts of Europe was just then nearing completion.

Berlage assumed the responsibility for laying out a whole residential district — Amsterdam South — in complete independence of the city officials and the Department of Public Works. The results form an ideal test case for our purposes; nowhere else could we derive a better insight into the actual level of town planning at this period, and of the real limits to what could be accomplished. Conclusions from the Berlage development apply very closely to architecture in general, without the necessity of charging anything off to the narrowing effects of specialization or to interference by some cautious officeholder.

Furthermore, Berlage's schemes reflect the central difficulty at that date: the inability to arrive at new means of expression in the solutions offered for the problems peculiar to the times. In the 1902 plans particularly (and to some extent even in the later version of 1915) we sense the struggle involved in Berlage's attempted break with the formulae of previous decades, his spasmodic efforts to attain modes of expression suited to his purpose — the humanizing of the residential district.

Romantic charac-
ter of the plan

At first glance the 1902 drawings suggest a diagram of the convolutions of the brain more than the layout of a city. The oval windings of the streets embody curves which an English observer of 1869 recognized as the favorites of French gardeners (*fig.* **427**), and which are familiar in Haussmann's public parks of the sixties.[2] These outlines are quite in keeping with the generally romantic character of Berlage's first plan.

Another influence shaping the layout was a horror of the forced and artificial axis, and of the whole gridiron system. Camillo Sitte's sermons had made it seem that the remedy for this cheerless aspect of contemporary cities was a return to the medieval town, with its natural patterns of growth.

The specific problem was to construct a residential quarter for middle and working class tenancy; essentially it was a problem in housing. But how could houses be brought together without becoming sources of mutual annoyance? Berlage's concern with this question is evident in every line of his work, and with it a horror of relapsing into the cruel and banal solutions that guided average practice.

Uncertainty
revealed in it

Actually, a real solution of this difficulty was impossible at the moment. Though the garden-city idea had been advanced some years earlier, Berlage had perhaps not yet heard of it. It was, at any rate, irrelevant to the task at hand: he was planning a district which was expected to be rather densely populated. In this period of uncertainty as to the direction it was proper for town planning to take, Berlage fell back on the Renaissance system, with every district dominated by some prominent public building. The dwelling houses which should have given this section its character are thereby reduced to mere satellites. And the centers of force about which they cluster — markets, theaters, auditoriums — are arbitrary crea-

---

[2] "In the plans of the best French landscape-gardeners it is quite ridiculous to see the way the walks wind about in symmetrical twirlings, and, when they have entwined themselves through every sweep of turf in the place, seem to long for more spaces to writhe about in" (Robinson, *The Parks, Promenades and Gardens of Paris*, p. 64).

700

tions, with no reason for existing in suburbs on the outskirts of a great city. They are the artificial backbone upon which the whole scheme is pegged out, and the way in which they are brought into relation with each other (by patching or building out) suggests a jigsaw puzzle. Finally, these residences are not sufficiently oriented with regard to human needs; they are not even properly related to the play of sunshine.

The example may serve to show that in 1900 even the most progressive minds were affected by a tendency toward an artificial monumentality — an artificial or pseudo monumentality because it was used to hide the uncertainty and perplexity with which the organization of a town was approached, even when carte blanche had been given to the planner.

Berlage's second scheme for the Amsterdam South region, made in 1915 (*fig.* **428**), provided merely a general framework for its development. This time the city asked only for a plan which would cover the broad aspects of any later expansion, without specifying details of execution. These could be filled in to satisfy whatever necessities should arise. Berlage still had a free hand in his work, and the site was unobstructed meadow land, cut only by some small irrigation canals.

Berlage's second scheme, 1915

Berlage's original map for this area (a beautifully executed drawing) still hangs in the office of the Department of Public Works at Amsterdam. One's first and decisive impression is derived from the network of streets which appears upon it.

Dominated by the street

This network is so dominant that at a casual glance one would suppose the plan to deal with a business center rather than a quiet residential quarter occupying undeveloped land on the outskirts of town. The most prominent feature is the enormous Y formed by three streets which lead up from the bank of the Amstel River. This part of Berlage's scheme was later carried out, but a good deal of the remaining area is still open land.

The Amstellaan, the boulevard which forms the base of the Y, is the backbone of the 1915 layout. It is unusually wide for Holland, and comparatively short, splitting into the streets that constitute the branches of the Y. Its shortness is perhaps

428. H. P. BERLAGE. Final plan for Amsterdam South, 1915.

intended to prevent the destruction of residential-quarter intimacy by so broad a thoroughfare.

The Amsterdam South district — especially around the Amstellaan (*fig.* **429**) — was built up by the so-called Amsterdam school some years after the war. Before his early death, the leader of this group, de Klerk, played a major part in the work (*fig.* **432**). During the twenties this section with its uniform façades was the best-known example of the possibility of making a residential area both attractive and well-adapted to human living.

The street
humanized

The Amstellaan does not owe its unusual width and the trees and greenery down its center to any attempt at traffic control. Nor did it — like the Boulevard Richard-Lenoir in Paris (1861–63) — come about as the covering for a canal or any other break in the ground (*fig.* **430**). Its landscaping was something more than a tasteful screen for the light shafts and ventilation ducts required to keep the old canal under the Boulevard Richard-Lenoir operable. Width and greenery were both intended to produce a better living space, to give more air and freedom to the residents (*fig.* **431**). And its front walls are not used like the doors of a wardrobe to hold in a tangle of houses jammed together behind them. To the rear of the houses fronting on the Amstellaan are spacious courtyards, planted

429. Amsterdam South, North and South Amstellaan in the thirties. *Air view.*

430. Boulevard Richard-Lenoir, 1861–63.

with lawns and shrubbery.[3]   The 1915 plan as a whole, however, was not preceded by sufficient research into the housing requirements of the Amsterdam South area.[4]

It is doubtful whether Berlage was familiar with the garden-city movement in 1902, but in 1915 he flatly rejected it.   He wrote then that the residential block was the only available expedient, pending the arrival of an original style in architecture which would be capable — as in earlier periods — of binding together all the individual houses.   Building authori-

Berlage's opposition to the garden city

---

[3] It was J. J. P. Oud who first used the interior courtyard as a means of humanizing the tenement blocks in his Tusschendiyken settlement (1919).

[4] Later architects pointed out that this plan — as was usual at the time — pays little regard to traffic needs.   Thus a main artery (Rijn Straat) crosses the Amstellaan just before the latter opens out into a square.

431.　Amsterdam South, the Amstellaan.　*This was one of the first projects in which the street was dealt with as a unit.　It remains, however, essentially the street of the nineteenth century, though considerably humanized and with garden areas behind the houses.*

432.　　　Amsterdam South, the Amstellaan. *Apartment houses by de Klerk, 1923.　This district was built up by the Amsterdam school, especially by its leader, de Klerk.*

ties should not pass on single dwellings but on whole streets or parts of streets, so that their unity might be extended to include the residences that were parts of them.　"The building of dwellings is becoming a work of mass production. The block building must be used again, and to an even greater extent than formerly, to provide a solution." [5]

Berlage's reaction not only against the hopeless street fronts so common at the time but also against the romantic ideal of the garden city is easily understandable. In his plans for the district he proposes as remedies the employment of a unified surface and an arrangement that is quiet and unemphatic. These are precisely the qualities we find in his Stock Exchange Building. But at the same time his historical position is made quite plain. The demand for the erection of whole streets with unified fronts is a demand for the reinstatement of Haussmann's neutral façade. In effect, Berlage was trying to regain a historical level which had passed for good. This attempt, however, left the atmosphere cleared for new developments.

The streets throughout the Amsterdam South sector are wide and extensively planted with flowers and trees, handled with the great pains that the Dutch take in their gardening. It is much more human and dignified than the nightmarish town planning of the preceding decades. But this plan, like architecture in the years before 1900, still fails to break through and arrive at a genuinely contemporary expression based on a new conception of life. It succeeds only in reforming the streets and weakening their authority over the total arrangement. They remain residential streets, and that kind of street is not the solution to the problems of residence in a great city. This is not to deny that the district possesses a marked grandeur; no one can tour the Amsterdam South region without feeling it. And nowhere else on the Continent at this period was greenery brought so graciously into combination with uniform rows of buildings.

Berlage displayed here the courage needed to formulate a genuinely impressive system of streets and to conceive a whole district of a city as a unit. Individualized house façades disappear, and uniform street walls — treated as surfaces — take their place. These walls, despite their monumental and much-

---

[5] The remarks are from the foreword to his 1915 scheme, "Memorie van Toelichting," *Gemeenteblad von Amsterdam*, March 9, 1915.

433. Master plan for Amsterdam South, 1934. *An extension plan based upon coördinated scientific research. It is intended to be flexible and to lay down the general outlines for the city's expansion, and not to be taken as a rigid scheme.*

censured elevation at the street corners, never completely surrender their plane effect.

When we regard the Amstellaan from the point of view of later developments, we perceive that it belongs in the main line of nineteenth-century town planning: the street dominates the whole. The Amstellaan, moreover, is representative of the whole scheme; there is reform but no new conception.[6]

THE GENERAL EXTENSION PLAN
OF AMSTERDAM, 1934

The general extension plan of Amsterdam is a collective achievement carried out by the Department of Public Works. It represents the close-knit collaboration of an entire staff of specialists. The layout of the scheme as a whole exhibits an approach bearing an inner relation to that contemporary art which is a response to the world of today.[7]

Our main concern is the way in which our age is becoming conscious of its own nature, and we have therefore largely avoided technical detail. But in the case of the extension of Amsterdam it is impossible to understand the tendencies at work in the guiding plan — its inner structure — unless we know the problems that had to be solved by this scheme.

The general plan (*fig.* **433**) for the future development of the city, prepared by the Department of Public Works,[8] is based

[6] Berlage had a great influence upon the development and the increase of town planning in Holland. He himself planned extensive projects for several Dutch cities: The Hague (1908), Rotterdam (1914), and Utrecht (1921). He was responsible for the execution of some squares of a monumental character — Mercatorplain in Rotterdam, for example. Connected accounts of Berlage's activity as a town planner are still lacking, but see the article by the distinguished contemporary architect, K. P. de Bazel, in *Dr. H. P. Berlage en zihn werk* (Rotterdam, 1916), a symposium produced in honor of Berlage's sixtieth birthday.

[7] Cf. the two volumes published by the Amsterdam Department of Public Works, November 1934: *Algemeen uitbreidungsplan*. A complete understanding of the scheme and the methods employed in it can be derived from this publication and the maps which illustrate it. These volumes should be in the hands of every town planner.

For short references in English, cf. *Town Planning Review* (Liverpool), vol. XVII, no. 1 (June 1936), and *Architectural Review* (London), vol. LXXXIII (June 1938), "A New Plan for Amsterdam," by Arthur Korn.

[8] Ordered by the city, prepared by this public department, and approved as the master plan for the extension by the Amsterdam City Council. Research, planning, and exe-

on a careful correlation of all those factors which determine the social make-up of a community. All measures proposed have their foundation in the figures that come under the heading of vital statistics: birth and death rates, immigration and emigration totals, etc. Statistics more difficult to obtain also enter into the planning: calculations of the number of people who can make their living in the district, the rate and direction of population changes, and forecasts of the probable course of the business cycle.

Vital statistics and livelihood statistics

From a consideration of all these factors it was concluded that before long population growth in Amsterdam would cease. (The same inference has been made with regard to other European and American cities.) The population of Amsterdam in 1939 was about 750,000; it is calculated that this will continue to increase throughout the century, until the 900,000 mark is reached (although the figure of 1,000,000 is not beyond the range of possibility).[9] Accordingly, the plan for the extension of Amsterdam is based on the supposition that 250,000 additional inhabitants will have to be accommodated between 1934 and the close of the century.

Extent of the plan

The expansion is directed westwards, toward open land which requires years of preparation to make it fit for building purposes. The key area is the western edge of the harbor, and the big industrial plants that lie beyond the docks. The southern part of the development is a residential area for workers employed around the dockyards and in the neighboring industrial plants. At present there is not sufficient accommodation for these people within reasonable proximity of their places of work. This quarter will eventually extend to the limits of Berlage's Amsterdam South district of 1915.

Distribution of greenery

The general extension plan does not propose to destroy the rural belt around the city. The market gardeners on its outskirts will not be dispossessed this time, and the natural aspect of the Amstel's banks on the southern boundary will be preserved.

---

cution are in the same hands. The situation is vastly different in some other cities: New York, for example. Here the extensive regional survey of New York and its environs is supported by a group of civic-minded private citizens and has no official character.

[9] Cf. D. T. J. Delfgaauw, "A Study of the Future Growth of Population in Amsterdam," *Journal of the Town Planning Institute* (London), February 1933, pp. 79–80.

In the southwest, great parks — planned with extreme care — are already being developed. (One, the magnificent Amsterdam Bosch, has an area of 2,135 acres, about that of Haussmann's Bois de Boulogne.) This park system takes up land which is often unsuitable for building purposes and converts it into wooded areas.

The recreational needs of the future population have been studied in detail. It has been found that people make little use of any parks farther than a quarter of a mile from their homes. The maximum distance between any two parks has therefore been limited to a half mile. Such planning is consciously proportioned to the human scale, to the scale of the *promeneur*. It moves in the direction of those "playgrounds at the doorstep" which Le Corbusier has proclaimed as one of the fundamental requirements in town planning.

From the aesthetic point of view, this planning is important because of the new structure for the town which results from it. The unbroken spread of dense masses of houses has been done away with. This thick growth is everywhere broken up by strips of greenery of various dimensions.

Major unit of ten thousand dwellings

The project to accommodate 250,000 additional inhabitants is planned to be carried out by the building of successive units comprising ten thousand dwellings (*fig.* 434). The dwellings provide, on the average, quarters for three and one-half inhabitants each, a figure which is the result of careful investigations.

The method of forecasting the future needs and composition of its population was developed very early in Holland. As far back as 1920, the city of Rotterdam put into use a carefully differentiated method for accurately determining not only the number of dwellings needed but the kinds of people who would occupy them and the sort of dwellings they would require.[10]

The decision to provide for three and a half tenants per unit-dwelling in the Amsterdam extensions is the result of this sort

---

[10] Cf. T. K. van Lohuizen, *Zwei Jahre Wohnungs-Statistik in Rotterdam* (Berlin, 1922). The engineer Lohuizen is also responsible for important researches in the plan for the extension of Amsterdam (the present scene of his work).

of research. The planning authority knows what different categories of tenants have to be provided for, as well as their various needs, and the proportion of each type to the population as a whole.

The composition of the major unit of ten thousand dwellings reflects these varying needs. The majority (sixty-five hundred) have two rooms and a kitchen; fifteen hundred are of three rooms, eleven hundred of four rooms. Four hundred and fifty are designed for families with six children, and two hundred and sixty are especially designed to meet the needs of older people.

Municipal control over site, ground plan, and façade

The actual building of these major units is carried out by private enterprise and by coöperative societies alike. The city, however, exercises control over the ground plan and the façade, and determines where each house of a given type — two, three, or four rooms, etc. — is to be located. Both private contractors and coöperative societies must build on a site approved by the city as maintaining the organic unity of the whole unit of ten thousand dwellings.

Row-housing basic

Present-day town planning must be controlled by the needs of the people who, on the basis of preliminary researches, will make up the population of the district. In Amsterdam four-story houses in continuous rows predominate. These rows, made up of individual apartments with a volume of two hundred cubic meters, are left open at the ends, not formed into closed blocks (*fig.* **434**). High buildings, houses of eight stories, are rarely encountered.[11] Single-story houses facing south are planned for the use of elderly people. This follows an old Dutch tradition. The difference in the height, the location, and the space between houses establishes unexpected interrelations in the layout.

Execution of the extension plan: "Het Westen"

As on other occasions, when we dealt with urban developments at different periods, it will help us to gain a notion of the special character of this work if we study some of its smaller units rather carefully. How does such a theoretical study work when it is put into active practice?

[11] Van Tijen's experience with them at Rotterdam revealed that they did not suit Dutch habits, and this discouraged their use.

434. Amsterdam, master plan, district Bosch en Lommer, with detail of model, 1938. *A single unit of the general extension plan. Designed for 35,000 inhabitants. The neighborhood unit shown in the model makes the most economical use of open spaces and greenery.*

We shall take a small part of the Amsterdam West region, with its various building complexes and the school at their southern edge.[12] In this quarter the extension plan still called for residential blocks of three and four stories (*fig. 435*). The architects (different men were responsible for the various blocks) proposed an open layout, at right angles to the traffic thoroughfare (*fig. 437*). They oriented the blocks in such a way that space was left in the south, at their open ends, for the smaller residences of the elderly. This scheme was perfectly adapted to the general layout, whose effect is intensified by the better orientation of the buildings and the gain in free space around the school in the south. It is one of the chief advantages of a flexible general layout that it can easily be brought into harmony with changed circumstances.

This settlement, which provides seven hundred flats for the low-income classes, was erected by several coöperative building societies. We shall make another subdivision and consider only that part of it built by the "Het Westen" society, a group of two hundred and eight apartments carried out by the architects Merkelbach and Karsten in 1937 (*fig. 436*).

The unit of the single dwelling

The architects aimed at offering the tenants the greatest possible amount of comfort (*fig. 438*). The living room is given broad French windows at the front, so that the house can be thrown wide open in the summer time, and to facilitate moving. The coöperative societies maintain gardens and play areas in the courtyards. The whole settlement gives the impression that the apartments were created to meet existing demands. That they really meet them is shown by the sixteen hundred applications that poured in for these two hundred and eight apartments at the time they were opened.

Interrelations of Housing and Activities of Private Life

Housing must offer something more than privacy. It must provide for access to parks, playgrounds, schools, recreation centers, stores, and places of business. Such needs have always been recognized, but the problems they offer have been solved

---

[12] For a detailed account, cf. *Tijdschrift voor volkshuisvesting en stedebouw* (Amsterdam), vol. XVIII, no. 9 (September 1937).

435. Master plan of Amsterdam West, proposal for "Het Westen." *Such proposals do not have to be followed exactly. The architect is permitted certain liberties in developing his scheme, provided it remains in harmony with the larger unit.*
←

436. MERKELBACH and KAR–STEN. Low-cost housing settlement, Amsterdam West ("Het Westen"), 1937. *An element in the 1934 plan as executed.* ↓

437. Changes of the master plan by the executive architects of "Het Westen."

438. MERKELBACH and KARSTEN. Low-cost housing settlement, "Het Westen." *Apartment with living room, two bedrooms for parents and children, kitchen, balcony, and shower. The Dutch have succeeded in reconciling very low rentals with a high standard of living. The means that have been employed trace back to J. J. P. Oud's early tenement blocks in Rotterdam (1919) with their careful utilization of the space available.*

in isolation and apart from a comprehensive system. Until now town planning has not dealt in any carefully preconceived way with the interrelations between residence and the other activities. In the Amsterdam West development the chaotic methods of the late nineteenth century are discarded; provision is made in advance for such activities, and for their complex interrelations. And the preliminary research and calculation had to be guided by the need for a flexible final plan, one that could be changed when necessity arose.

The task of the town planner is to avoid mutual interferences in the various functions of a section, uniting or separating them as the case may require. Thus he will separate traffic arteries from residential streets, which will be closed to traffic and devoted exclusively to housing. He will concentrate stores in one area and avoid the random dispersion of workshops necessary to the inhabitants. Schools, playgrounds, and athletic fields will be so related to the rows of houses that greenery will penetrate the body of the town to the greatest extent compatible with its economic life.

Planning such as this results in an alteration of the structure of the city. The ground plan of the modern house has been made flexible and informal: the layout of the modern town tends in the same direction.

Caution in planning the extension

In Holland all measures toward this end have had to be carried through with great caution. Land is very expensive and must be used with strictest economy: pile foundations have to be driven for every house; an elaborate engineering service has to be maintained; and greenery and open areas require years of preparatory work. All these factors contribute to raise the price of land to forty-four florins the square meter.

In addition, rental rates are fixed at extremely low levels. In this situation there is no room for free flights of genius; advance is possible only by one careful step after another.

Dutch experience in such developments during the last twenty years is scrupulously collated and checked with that of contemporary architects in other countries. The town-planning authority is a clearinghouse for such data, which is carefully studied and guides the layout of the city. Practice has continued to justify the measures these experts have adopted.

It has sometimes been objected that houses in Amsterdam are too closely massed together, that more open space and greater individual freedom are needed. The scheme as a whole, however, operates under circumstances which put this beyond the power of the planner. As one of the Amsterdam officials has remarked, "It is not really the architect who makes these plans — it is society."

The kind of technical staff needed for large-scale urban developments was first brought together by Haussmann in the fifties for his transformation of Paris. In our period the tasks such staffs must deal with have changed. It is not merely engineering works in the service of the population as a whole that are needed — streets, traffic arteries, parks, sewer systems, aqueducts, etc. — but works to make possible an integrated life on the part of the individual citizen. The focal point of present developments is the single inhabitant and the interrelation of his activities with the total life of the city.

The technical and the human approach

The scheme for the extension of Amsterdam presupposes a continuance of the city's growth; though this growth is expected to decline in speed it is not thought that the city will actually begin to lose inhabitants. And the project for humanizing the city is joined to the belief that all population increases will be taken up by an expansion of the limits of the present city. No satellite towns are being projected. Units of ten thousand dwellings and some thirty-five thousand inhabitants will continue to be joined onto the existing city for as long as its growth persists.

In the steady process of realizing this scheme, only conditions actually in force — and those which calculation establishes as most probable in the near future — can be taken into consideration. All measures so far adopted have been approved by the later course of events. Life has filled out and diversified the original plan in the way a river occupies and shapes its bed.

It may be that the range of the normal Dutch traffic vehicle — the bicycle — has constituted the basic unit of scale for the development, and it might, therefore, prove unsuited to other countries. But, even so, the value of what has been achieved at Amsterdam would remain undiminished. It is the methods employed in these developments and not their specific successes which are important. There are cities ten times as large as Amsterdam — cities like London and New York — which are far behind it in methods of planning. The attempt is still being made to restore the sick bodies of these immense towns by operations performed on isolated subsections. Slum areas are selected here and there, re-housing is carried through — and the existing disorder in the city as a whole is simply increased. Research and statistics are not enough in themselves. They must be backed by vision, by a general understanding of the course of development today's cities must take.

The plan of Amsterdam involves no attempt at clearing out slums in the center of the city: it establishes a new town on its outskirts. And the freedom and flexibility of the scheme are not hopelessly constricted by the *rue corridor* or the gridiron system. The conception of space-time — the basis for a contemporary town planning — can already be felt in the layout of the new Amsterdam.

PART **IX** SPACE–TIME IN CITY PLANNING

Contemporary Attitude toward Town Planning

What is the general attitude of the town planner of today? What does he seek to achieve? From what concepts does he proceed to his work? Questions such as these are of the utmost importance in any consideration of our subject. For town planning is first and foremost a human issue: its problems are by no means exclusively technical and economic. It can never be carried on satisfactorily without a clear understanding of the contemporary conception of life.

Town planning and contemporary life

Nowhere else in architecture do we encounter the influence of the prevailing outlook so strongly as in town planning. Very little of it can be expressed in shapes and structure; often its participation in a given project can only be felt, an adumbration without explicit accent. But even when not visibly defined, it acts to unite the organism which is a town, much as the hidden skeleton of steel supports the modern building. Whenever town planning lacks such organic integrity, it must fall back upon artificial expedients, just as a building of faulty design requires buttresses.

In the future the town planner will need to advance further and further beyond the limits of the purely technical. The reconquest of the unity of human life is nowhere more urgent than in his work. Representative of present-day approaches to the problem is that of the Dutchman C. van Eesteren,[1] who, as chief architect, has conducted the general extension plan of Amsterdam since 1929. At various times he has outlined in conversation the attitude of the contemporary town planner toward the problems confronting him. From his comments, here paraphrased somewhat freely, we may perhaps get a more personal insight into the mind of the town planner.

Van Eesteren's idea of the town planner

The town planner, as van Eesteren sees him, is not concerned primarily with architecture. Nor does he believe that the town is essentially either an object of financial speculation or, as in the Russian formula, one of the instruments of production.

---

[1] Van Eesteren, who was trained as an architect, decided very early to concentrate upon town planning. He used a traveling scholarship to establish contacts with the leading European artists. As we have already noted, he collaborated with Theo van Doesburg; as a young man, his training under such modern architects as the members of the Stijl group laid the foundations for his later development.

He seeks to discover how the town came into being and how it has reached its present stage of growth. He wants to know as much as he can of the site (a matter of peculiar importance in Holland) and of its relations to the surrounding region and the country as a whole. Above all, he studies the different categories of people who have to be accommodated, each according to his manner of life; he finds out whether they are young or old, married or single, with few or many children. He must consider where these people work, the routes traffic must take, the distance there should be between residential and industrial sections. He must also establish a control of the relation between the communications of the city and its living quarters. He thinks no longer in linear terms of street and axis, but in terms of population densities. His approach to the town is conditioned by this population ratio, which at Amsterdam, for example, is allowed to range between 110 and 550 inhabitants per hectare.

The task before the town planner is to form his plans on the basis of widespread inquiries, so that they are adjusted to existing conditions and, so far as that is possible, to those of the future. But he will not adopt a rigid and definitive system; he must handle each section in such a way that unforeseen changes can be met. There must be a vital and mutual relation between the desired and the existing reality, between goals and facts. Moreover, he will not attempt to force the functions of residence, work, and leisure into conformity with tight and final arrangements; he makes only generalized distributions, leaving their ultimate shape to the interplay of circumstances. Yet these arrangements are not left to develop haphazardly; his aim must be to find the forms best suited to every special condition. The town planner knows what functions have to be provided for; his task is to create a whole out of the existing potentialities and conditions.

Flexibility of contemporary town planning

The foundation of town planning is the conception of life that holds for our time; without it order cannot be brought into the enormous mass of factual material that confronts the planner. This conception of life is molded and expressed in many different ways. Modern traffic, for example, educates and sharpens our sense of space. City-dwellers moving across

Conception of life the foundation of planning

congested avenues seem almost to know what is taking place behind them. This kind of spatio temporal awareness was unknown in baroque times; it may be a case of the redevelopment of a primitive sense.

The plan of a modern town must be developed in a more complicated way, take account of a tighter net of relations than ever before. Planning merely in terms of the two dimensions of the drawing board — the method of the last century — will not suffice, nor will the three-dimensional planning of the baroque. A town plan must bring all its constituents into a measured and living balance. A different feeling is required in the work of a present-day planner. When he is seeking, for instance, the proper location of a cemetery or a market hall, he must be able to go over his plan with almost tactile perceptiveness, sensing the contrasting character of its districts as plainly as though they were velvet or emery beneath his fingers.

In the modern city — only fragments of which have been realized so far — there exist interrelationships which are more than merely spatial. These subtle values are the elements from which the charm of the city must be derived. Upon them likewise rests the proper coördination of the various functions of the community. None of these, the technical and industrial included, can be allowed to dominate at the expense of the others. Technical and industrial factors should not complicate the development (as in the nineteenth century), but should help to overcome difficulties. In this manner the town may pass from a static condition to the free equilibrium of an organism.

DESTRUCTION OR TRANSFORMATION?

Reasons for structural change

Again and again we have tried to point out how in the various domains of construction, painting, and architecture — all independent each of the other — there has arisen a certain identity of method. We have observed that contemporary architecture can be explained in terms either of functions or of sociological patterns. But such explanations are not enough;

they are intellectual only; they do not comprehend and reveal the quality of feeling which underlies our architecture. It is the same with town planning. Cities have always, in every period, been essentially agglomerations of social, political, and economic interests. Consequently, changes in urban structure have been difficult to realize. Sometimes, as we well know, they have been forced by entirely independent processes exerting pressure from the outside. For example, the evolution in warfare and arms which rendered the older city helpless against attack forced changes in its structure for the sake of protection. Even today the threat of attack from the air demands urban changes.[2] Great cities sprawling open to the sky, their congested areas at the mercy of bombs hurtling down out of space, are invitations to destruction. They are practically indefensible as now constituted, and it is becoming clear that the best means of defending them is by the construction, on the one hand, of great vertical concentrations which offer a minimum surface to the bomber and, on the other hand, by the laying out of extensive, free, open spaces.

How serious the dangers of war will prove in the future there is, of course, no way of knowing. It is quite possible that there are many countries and cities which will never be threatened from the air. We may well hope so. However that may be, the city today still is profoundly menaced in all countries and without exception — not by any outside danger, but from within, by an evil shaping within itself. This is the evil of the machine. Because of the confusion of its different functions, its growing mechanization, the omnipresence and anarchy of the motorcar, the city is at the mercy of industrial machines. If it is to be saved, its structure must change. This change, which will be forced by machinery just as in other days it was

[2] Lewis Mumford's *The Culture of Cities* (New York, 1938), so far as it is concerned with the change of the structure of the city, is based on social, political, and economic developments, and points out especially the influence of arms and defense on the growth of the city.

A volume prepared under the auspices of the International Congress for Modern Architecture (*Can Our Cities Survive?* edited by J. L. Sert, Harvard University Press, 1942) contains a general analytical survey of the conditions of life in the cities of today based on the principles formulated by leading town planners of eighteen different countries. It is the first time that the problems of our cities have been worked out in a comparative way by means of maps, photographs, and statistics, so that everyone has an opportunity to see what the actual state of these great agglomerations is.

brought about by implements of war, is inevitable, whether it comes through insight or through catastrophe. The city must be changed or it will perish, and our civilization with it.

However, it is not of these facts that we wish to speak at the moment. Rather we wish to deal, as we did in discussing construction and architecture, with the city (today in the nascent state) in so far as its formation is emotionally conditioned, to look for the interrelations between its composition and the plastic tendencies of our time. Resistance to change in structure springs not only from the play of private interests but also from emotional sources. Complete freedom in the development of an area is not enough in itself. Even in countries where the authority of the state over the ground is absolute, planning still goes forward according to nineteenth-century ideas whenever those in power are not moved by the new artistic conceptions.

Future of the city   But first we must consider briefly a problem which is becoming more and more pressing and still resists solution: What is to be the future development of the great city? Opinions as to the destiny of the metropolis have changed considerably in the last decade. Around 1900, when Ebenezer Howard was advocating the garden city as a check to "depopulation of the country district and the overcrowding of our large cities," [3] the general belief was that the city would continue just as it had, but in ever-increasing accumulation; the curve of population would continue to rise in the same sharp ascent as in the immediate past. Architects like Otto Wagner also believed in the constantly enlarging city as a permanent phenomenon.

Approximately at the same time, as if in refutation, the population curve as it concerned the center of the city began to change — first in Europe, later on in America. A decline of the population in the center both of London and of Paris began in 1901. In New York it did not set in until a decade later, in 1910, but then quite strongly. [4] The question then arises whether the large city as it has been inherited from the nineteenth century, with its chaotic intermingling of functions, should not be allowed to die.

---

[3] *Garden Cities of Tomorrow*, p. 142.

[4] Manhattan decreased from 2,331,542 in 1910 to 1,662,195 in 1939. This sharp decline clearly shows the natural trend, the solution for which certainly does not lie in any artificial revaluation.

722

On this question the division is clear and sharp, especially in Two opinions the United States, where mechanization is so much more advanced than in Europe. One opinion is that the metropolis cannot be saved and must be broken up; the other that, instead of being destroyed, the city must be transformed in accordance with the structure and genius of our times. Understandably enough, the most radical advocates of the first position have appeared in America, because it is here that the large cities have been most completely subjected to the machine; here their density of population is greatest; here the motorcar is most numerous, as well as least successfully regulated in its chaotic development, any attempt at control being regarded an infringement of civil rights.

Several suggestions have been made as to how the break-up of the city is to be accomplished. Differing as they do in details, it is significant that they possess one tendency in common — an urge toward the organic, which has become increasingly strong in our time as a kind of self-protection against the evils of civilization. The difference between these proposals lies in how the organic may be realized.

One of them is that instead of concentrating the population Agricultural decentralization in gigantic blown-up agglomerations called cities, the whole country should be colonized in small tracts of one or two acres. Such a decentralization would change our entire life from that of the city dweller to that of the country dweller living on a single mechanized farm unit which would maintain a balance between rural and industrial occupation. It is the complete and conscious destruction of the idea of the city. It also undermines to a large extent that differentiation in society which is the basis of our civilization, for in it the small, self-sufficient landowner is predominant. Such schemes go back to the doctrines of Charles Fourier, the most thoroughgoing of the French utopian economists, who, in opposition to the existing industrial system, wanted to achieve the fullest development for human nature by the creation of a social and organic life in which the individual would find the greatest satisfaction. Such a life he envisioned in a decentralized society in which agriculture would be the staple industry. Since Fourier developed his ideas in the twenties of the nineteenth century, there have appeared many social thinkers who have followed them in an effort to deal with the evils produced by industrialization. Frank Lloyd Wright, with his "Broadacre City," has been one of the most vocal among the theorists. He bases his program, as he himself admits, on the ideas and experiments of Ralph Borsodi.[5]

There is no doubt that self-sufficient units have a proper place in economic life, but there is also no doubt that this primitive form of society can neither replace nor complete that differentiated organization which, whatever the political system, is basic to our culture. It would change the country into a forlorn hybrid, something neither rural nor yet urban, but with the limitations of both. In any case, a proposal to parcel the inhabitants out in small communities, with agriculture the staple industry, is completely out of scale with the problems which today demand solution.

Transformation of the city

The opposing point of view — that the city must be transformed but need not be destroyed — holds likewise that men cannot be separated from nature, and consequently that the city cannot continue to exist in its present form. But it immediately points out that the city is more than a contemporary and passing phenomenon. It is a product of many differentiated cultures, in many different periods. Thus the question of its life or death cannot be settled simply on the basis of present-day experience or conditions. The city cannot be damned to extinction merely because it has been misused since industrialization or because its whole structure has been rendered impotent by the intrusion of a technical invention, the motor-car. The question has to be considered from a broader view and extended into other queries: Are cities connected with every sort of society and civilization? Are they only to be explained as agglomerations first for defense, later for production, or is the institution of the city deeply a part of man

---

[5] A former economic consultant who realized his program of decentralization or "distributism" by means of small-owner units and mechanized home production (small tractors, small-scale labor-saving machines, etc.), first in Dayton, Ohio, and since 1935 in Bayard Lane, near Suffern, N. Y., only an hour's drive from New York City. Cf. John Chamberlain, "Blueprints for a New Society: Borsodi and the Chesterbelloc," *New Republic*, January 1, 1940. Borsodi's book, *This Ugly Civilization* (New York, 1929), is an attack upon the entire factory and industrial system. In his *Flight from the City* (New York, 1933) Borsodi tells of his experience with the self-sufficient small community, which performs all functions from canning food to making cloth.

himself? Are cities a temporary phenomenon, a stage in development, the difficulties of which we have to overcome by
means of mechanical inventions, radio, television, the motorcar, and the like? Or are they an eternal phenomenon based on
the contact of man with man despite the interference of any
mechanization? For myself, I believe that the institution of
the city is one native to every cultural life and every period.

Those who hold that the present state of the metropolis is inhuman and cannot continue are preëminently right. The only
question is whether this means the end of the city as such.
Can the unworkable disorder of today's giant cities be eliminated without destroying the institution itself? Those who believe that the city has been a component of every succeeding
human civilization see its existence menaced if its whole structure is not brought into harmony with the needs and requirements of present-day life. Clearly, small means are of no aid;
they serve merely — and in this Frank Lloyd Wright is quite
correct — to prolong its existence artificially without any real
hope of recovery. Nothing can be really accomplished by
sowing the streets with more and more traffic lights or by
clearing slums and simply erecting new buildings on the same
sites. Destroying all the slums in existence will not make the
city any less the unworkable instrument it is today.

When Haussmann in the fifties undertook the transformation
of Paris, he slashed into the body of the city — as a contemporary expressed it — with saber strokes. Cleanly he drew the
blade, cutting keen, straight thoroughfares through the congested districts, solving his traffic problems by single daring
thrusts. In our own period even more heroic operations are
necessary. The first thing to do is to abolish the *rue corridor*
with its rigid lines of buildings and its intermingling of traffic,
pedestrians, and houses. The fundamental constitution of the
contemporary city requires the restoration of liberty to all
three — to traffic, to pedestrians, and to residential and industrial quarters. This can be accomplished only by separating them. Haussmann's endless streets belonged not only
in their architectural features but also in their very conception to the artistic vision born of the Renaissance: perspective. Today we must deal with the city in a new aspect,

dictated originally by the appearance of the motorcar and based on technical considerations, and belonging to an artistic vision born out of our period — space–time.

The residential structure

Cities have to be modeled around human needs. In them human rights must be restored. Up out of the past comes a reminder of our architectural inheritance, the tradition of placing large groups of buildings in natural surroundings, which extends all the way from the Versailles of Louis XIV down to the London squares. In the Paris of 1850 the functions of traffic and housing were intermingled for every class of society, in contrast to the London squares, which wisely remembered that man demands for his existence quietude and the companionship of growing things. Now in contemporary architecture, in the new formation of city planning, there arises again the old demand that men should not be separated from the great outdoors, from nature.

How is this to be accomplished? How can the eternal law of urban life be realized, that cities must be more than masses of stone, that they must be joined to the living soil, either by their small scale, as in the Middle Ages, or by their intermingling with greenery, as in the late baroque?

When we briefly outlined the attitude of the town planner of today, we stated as a fundamental requirement that town planning can never be conducted without due consideration of the present conception of life and its expression through contemporary artistic means. There is a prevailing unity unconsciously underlying all technical, engineering, social, and aesthetic problems. As in the nineteenth century, however, too often those who have influence on the shaping of cities are experts in all practical and engineering questions but without any certainty, understanding, or feeling in what is the artistic equivalent of their practical creations. There persists that same difference between methods of thinking and feeling which was so disastrous during the last century. They do not see, for instance, that the *rue corridor*, which life itself condemns, at the same time naturally belongs to the optical vision of another day. Instead, they clear up large slum areas and erect new buildings on them, religiously following the old pattern of the *rue corridor*. They act without any understanding of the

726

real trend of development, of how the new city must be planned, of the fact that large areas should not be rebuilt on the old urban principles but should be changed into open green spaces according to a plan which gives the city a chance to survive.

THE NEW SCALE IN CITY PLANNING

The Parkway

We have found that in the nineteenth century construction was ahead of architecture in expressing, often unconsciously, the true constituent forces of the period. Even today in town planning the work of the engineer is often nearer to future developments than that of the town planner, who is too frequently concerned exclusively with the reorganization of the body of the city itself. The American parkways as they have developed since the early nineteen twenties — coincident, by the way, with the flowering of contemporary architecture in Europe — reveal in their whole treatment the fact that they are already one of the elements of the contemporary town, one of those born out of the vision of our period.

The definition of "parkway" is not yet exactly established.[1] The "definite legal definition of a parkway," as H. V. Hubbard points out, "is an attenuated park with a road through it. That is, a parkway is primarily for traffic, but mostly or exclusively for pleasure traffic." [2] In this sense the parkway is not new.[3] But considered in relation to the contemporary city,

What is a parkway?

[1] Professor Hubbard comments on this confusion of definition in his *Parkways and Land Values* (Cambridge, 1937), vol. XI of Harvard City Planning Studies: "What is a parkway? How does it differ from a boulevard or an avenue, or a highway beautified with trees? These terms . . . have been so loosely applied and have crystallized by custom as the names of such different things in different places, that nothing but specific local knowledge will make it safe to apply to a 'parkway' in one town what has been learned about a parkway in any other town" (p. xii).

[2] *Ibid.*, p. xii.

[3] The green belt by which Haussmann intended in the sixties to surround Paris and to connect the Bois de Boulogne and the Bois de Vincennes, the boulevards linking the south park system in Chicago in the early nineties, the layout of parked drives in Minneapolis by Professor Cleveland in 1883 — all these belong in the category of parkways. The device of passing one road under another to avoid the confusion of cross traffic, commonly applied to railways and even to overcrossing streets, is an established practice of the nineteenth century.

the modern parkway, as it has developed in America since the early thirties, is clearly to be distinguished from that of the normal legal definition. As an element of the future town it restores the rights both of traffic and of the pedestrian; it harmonizes the functions of both; in separating them definitely from one another, it gives full freedom to each. Out of this separation has come the fundamental law of the parkway — that there is to be unobstructed freedom of movement, a flow of traffic maintained evenly at all points without interruption or interference. To secure this steady flow, no direct crossing is permitted, nor do the owners of abutting property have the right of direct access; at intersections the conflicting or converging lines are disposed separately through the use of overpasses with their cloverleaves of connecting roads. It is interesting to note that, whether by tradition or coincidence, the first parkway in this sense was realized in the same area where in our period the large modern parkway systems have been created — in New York. America's great landscape gardener, the elder Olmsted, in his plan for Central Park in New York about 1858,[4] provided underpasses for vehicular cross traffic, cutting his roadbed through rock (*fig.* **439**).

Parkway and terrain

Up to this point the parkway may be said to be identical with the European *autostrade*, the highway without grades. But it is not, like certain Continental highways laid out for military purposes, driven through the country in rigid and dangerously straight lines. Nor is it built, as are railways, for the sake of the most direct and rapid transit. Instead it humanizes the highway by carefully following and utilizing the terrain, rising and falling with the contours of the earth, merging completely into the landscape.[5] The road is laid into the countryside, grooved into it between gentle green slopes blending so naturally into the contiguous land that the eye cannot distinguish between what is nature and what the contribution of the landscape architect. In the middle, separating the opposing move-

[4] *Third Annual Report of the Board of Commissioners of the Central Park* (New York, 1860).

[5] It is probably no accident that the first complete parkway system in Westchester County (1913–25), just north of New York City, followed in several of its branches the courses of rivers. Cf. Jay Downer, "Principles of Westchester's Parkway System," *Civil Engineering*, IV (1934), 85; Stanley W. Abbott, "Ten Years of the Westchester County Park System," *Parks and Recreation*, XVI (March 1933), 307 ff.

ments of traffic, are garden strips (often planted with cypress trees) which widen and contract as the course of the road requires. Sometimes the traffic lanes flow together in approaching a bridge, join as they pass under, and then separate again, drawing apart to restore the landscaped space between them. Air views may show the great sweep of the highway, the beauty of its alignment, the graceful sequence of its curves, but only at the wheel of the automobile can one feel what it really means — the liberation from unexpected light signals and cross traffic, and the freedom of uninterrupted forward motion, without the inhuman pressure of the straight-line layout pushing one on to dangerous speeds. Confidence is given the driver by the way in which the road fits into the earth between its sloping sides and by the protection which the dividing green and wooded strips afford against the hazards of contrary traffic. Yet he is held to a natural speed limit by the adaptation of the roadbed to the structure of the country, by its rise and fall, the smooth swing of its curves, its clear open runs before creeping under a cross highway or bridge. Full realization is given to the driver and freedom to the machine. Riding up and down the long sweeping grades produces an exhilarating dual feeling, one of being connected with the soil and yet of hovering just above it, a feeling which is like nothing else so much as sliding swiftly on skis through untouched snow down the sides of high mountains (*figs.* **440, 441**).[6]

There are other sections of the road where, in technical contrast, it crosses rivers and islands by great links of bridges with broad drives leading up to them (*fig.* **442**). These bridges, their mounting drives, and the modern sculpture of numberless single or triple cloverleaves prove that the possibilities of a great scale are inherent in our period. As with many other creations born out of the spirit of this age, the meaning and beauty of the parkway cannot be grasped from a single point of observation, as was possible when from a window of the château of Versailles the whole expanse of nature could be

---

[6] The Merritt Parkway, continuing the Hutchinson River Parkway from New York through Connecticut, opened 1939, is a masterpiece of organic layout. The State Highway Commissioner was authorized to undertake a layout of the route in 1931. Unfortunately, as in most other parkways, the architectonic detail used to embellish the overpasses is much below the high level of the scheme.

439. F. L. OLMSTED. Overpass in Central Park, New York City, 1858. *This early employment of the overpass by Olmsted, the great American landscape architect, had no real influence. Only the traffic confusion of recent times has forced its adoption.*

embraced in one view. It can be revealed only by movement, by going along in a steady flow as the rules of the traffic prescribe. The space-time feeling of our period can seldom be felt so keenly as when driving, the wheel under one's hand, up and down hills, beneath overpasses, up ramps, and over giant bridges.

The parkway and the city

It was Chicago which in the late eighties introduced the new potentialities in architecture. To New York in turn must go credit for the creation of the modern parkway. More than three hundred miles of parkways have been constructed in recent years in the metropolitan area. At first they all ended at the outskirts of the city. One of them, the Henry Hudson Parkway (1934–37), which is a continuation of the Westchester park system, has now been extended for thirteen miles down the west side of Manhattan, almost to the tip of the island (*fig.* 444). On the other side the Long Island system, of which

730

440. Merritt Parkway, Connecticut, 1939. *A masterpiece of organic layout exemplifying the arrangement of the modern parkway — adaptation of the roadbed to the structure of the country, careful alignment of traffic lanes, separation of vehicular and pedestrian traffic, and overpasses for crossing.*

441. Merritt Parkway, Connecticut, with overpass.

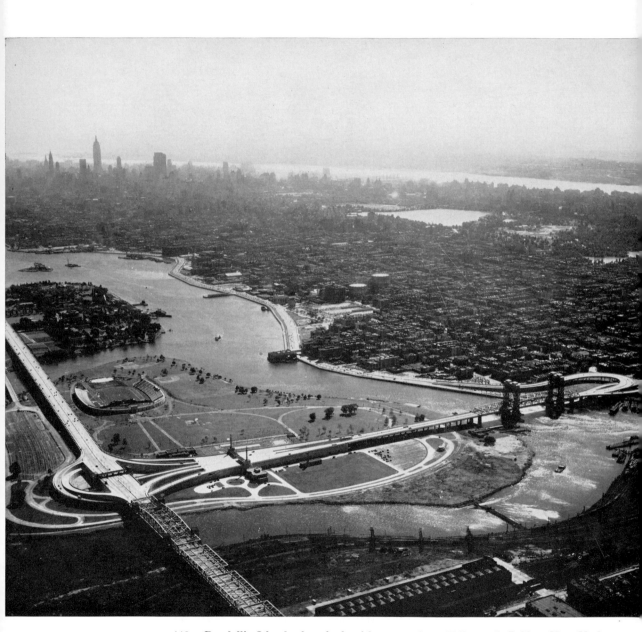

442. Randall's Island, cloverleaf, with approach to Triborough Bridge, New York City, 1936. *Such bridges, with broad drives leading up to them and the modern sculpture of numberless single or triple cloverleaves, prove that the possibilities of a great scale are inherent in our period. Expressive of the space-time conception both in structure and handling of movement.*

732

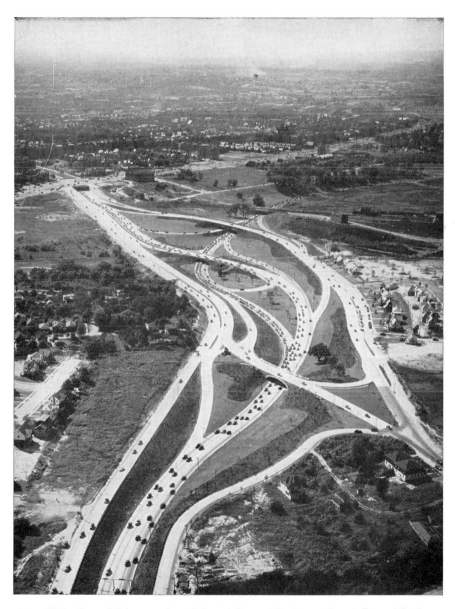

443. "The Pretzel," intersection of Grand Central Parkway, Grand Central Parkway Extension, Union Turnpike, Interboro Parkway, and Queens Boulevard, New York City, 1936–37. *One of the most elaborate and highly organized of all recent solutions of the problem of division and crossing of arterial traffic.*

444. West Side development, including Henry Hudson Parkway, 1934–37. *The park-*
way of today cannot penetrate the city, but can only go along its boundaries. Thus the Henry
Hudson Parkway, leading down from the northern suburbs as a continuation of the West-
chester park system, follows the Hudson River side of Manhattan almost to the tip of the
island.

the Northern State Parkway (1931–34) is the main artery, has been continued through open spaces, along and over rivers and through parks to the eastern entrances of Manhattan (*fig.* 443).[7] With the completion of several new recreation centers and their linking highways, a great circumferential parkway will surround the metropolis. This will constitute the forerunner of the city on a new scale.

But the problem of the city itself has scarcely been touched. The parkway ends today, and obviously must end, where the massive body of the city begins. It has not been able to penetrate the city because the city has persisted in remaining an inflexible structure, tightly bound within itself and immovable. We can well believe Robert Moses, Commissioner of Parks of New York, who has shown in his work for parks and parkways the enthusiasm and energy of Haussmann, when he points out that at the very time his program was being carried through, "planners were producing one scheme after another for taking care of the traffic within the city limits," and all of them to no effect. "Some were impractical, others over-elaborate, and others proposed such costly rights of way that they had to be tossed out of the window." [8] The parkway is not an isolated traffic lane independent of the organism of the city. It simply has a different scale from that of the existing city with its *rue corridor* and its rigid division into small blocks. No facilities of approach can really accomplish anything unless the city changes its actual structure.

Why may the parkway be called an element of the city which is now in the building? For one thing, it fulfills a fundamental law of the nascent town: it separates the intermingled functions of vehicular and pedestrian traffic. At the same time it delivers the death blow to the notion that the highway is an isolated track running through the countryside but unrelated to it. It is conceived in terms of its surroundings, being itself a part of nature. Perhaps most important of all, it is controlled in its entire layout by regulations governing all construction along

---

[7] By the great Central Park extension (1937) and the Triborough Bridge (1936), which is approached by one of the most elaborate of arrangements for the division of traffic arteries—the "Pretzel."

[8] Robert Moses, "The Comprehensive Parkway System of the New York Metropolitan Region," *Civil Engineering*, IX, no. 3 (March 1939), 160.

its borders, even limiting the number of gasoline service stations and restricting them to side roads. Entirely forbidden are residences, business houses, and factories.[9] Property owners have learned that their civil rights are not infringed when they are not allowed direct access to the parkway, but that it is useful in a wider sense to them as well as to the community. Only when the same truth has become recognized by the population at large will it be possible to attack the chaotic state of the cities. Finally, the parkway is the forerunner of the first necessity in the development of the future town: the abolition of the *rue corridor*. There is no longer any place for the street with its traffic lane running between rows of houses; it cannot possibly be permitted to persist. And the parkway is the first realized step in this clear separation of traffic and housing. It looks ahead to the time when, after the necessary surgery has been performed, the artificially swollen city will be reduced to its normal size. Then the parkway will go through the city as it does today through the landscape, as flexible and informal as the plan of the American home itself.

Tall Buildings in Open Space

Between those who believe that the city will disappear and those who try to preserve it by changing its structure, there is no disagreement on the point that the intricate disorder of the present day cannot continue, that man cannot live forever on asphalt. In Europe those who have made creative efforts to find a solution for the problems of contemporary urbanism have revealed by the projects they have set up that they believe in the continued existence of the city. But they have seen that, in order to achieve in densely populated districts the placement of living quarters amidst greenery which is imperative, there must be concentration in groups of high buildings which will stand in parks or, at any rate, in open spaces. Only in such a way can the necessary distances between buildings be secured. Thus the basic principle on which they have worked has been

---

[9] The ribbon development, cheap houses erected for speculation along new highways to economize street building, especially in England, has had a disastrous effect upon the countryside.

736

to condense great dwelling units into high buildings so as to gain free open spaces and thus be able to place them in gardens and recreation grounds.

There appeared in Germany during the early twenties pro- Slablike housing
posals for slablike eight- to twelve-story residential blocks units
standing at considerable distances from one another, yet having at the same time a density of population equal to that of lower blocks covering the same area but placed close together.

This type (*fig.* **445**), which was first conceived by Walter Gropius and Marcel Breuer,[10] proved to be an important factor in changing the structure of the existing city. It involved the breaking up of the solid rows of houses along the street into units placed at right angles to the public road and parallel to each other, facing the landscaped areas between. The realization of this sort of slablike apartment house came in Rotterdam about 1934, by the Dutch architect W. van Tijen, in collaboration with Brinckmann and van der Vlugt, in blocks nine and ten stories high, for low-cost apartments of two and three rooms. The two blocks are located in different parts of the outskirts of Rotterdam in districts where the buildings are not more than two or three stories high. The earlier one, the Bergpolder (1933–34), is a steel skeleton and lies amidst a densely populated district. The Plaslaan (1937–38; *fig.* **447**) is situated near parks and an artificial lake, surrounded by a large amount of open space, much as we imagine the town of the future may be. These slablike buildings (*fig.* **446**)[11] appear also in the extension plan of Amsterdam (1934), where large green areas were available, so that they could be built far enough apart.

---

[10] It was first introduced to the public in a scheme of Marcel Breuer's on the occasion of a competition in low-cost housing conducted by an architectural review (*Bauwelt*, 1924). Such buildings became popular through the careful research and comparative studies of Walter Gropius, especially his work in the large competition for a low-cost housing project for three thousand dwellings at Haselhorst near Berlin in 1929. He won first prize with his entry of three different projects — for low, medium, and high houses — and his comparison by means of layouts and calculations of the respective effectiveness of each. He proved that the best conditions are achieved, both as to light and economic requirements, when the same number of dwelling units are used, twelve-story blocks rather than two- or five-story units. Cf. Walter Gropius, "Das Ergebnis des Reichsforschungswettbewerbes," *Bauwelt*, 1929, no. 8, pp. 158 ff.

[11] Fully described in their various details, as well as with research into their efficiency, in Alfred Roth, *The New Architecture* (Zurich, 1940), pp. 91–104.

ansicht aus süd

445. WALTER GROPIUS. Slablike block units, 1930. *This type of slablike block was proposed in Germany about 1924 as a development of parallel rows of houses. To achieve more open space, the low, closely packed buildings are replaced by tall, slablike structures.*

446. WALTER GROPIUS. Model for the settlement "Haselhorst," Berlin, 1929. *One of the studies in which slablike buildings were used in experimental form and to a small extent. The influence of such German layouts of the twenties had their effect also on the extension plan of Amsterdam of 1934.*

About the same time Le Corbusier used it for one of his most gracious and human town-planning schemes — the small colonial town of Nemours in Morocco, where the blocks are freely located on a slope. Similar slablike blocks on a luxurious scale were built in England at Highpoint, London (*fig.* **448**),

447. W. VAN TIJEN. The Plaslaan, Rotterdam, 1937–38. *Situated near parks and an artificial lake, these slablike units are surrounded by a large amount of open space, giving an effect somewhat comparable to the structure of the future town.*

by the Tecton group (1936–38). The Highpoint project returns at the same time to the old English tradition of the house surrounded by and in immediate connection with recreation grounds.

These slender buildings encountered great opposition. The reason is that their form, being based on purely functional calculations, is an expression coincident with the new space conception of today. They seem very strange to a public accustomed to massive, earth-bound residential blocks. Stand-

448. Apartment house at Highpoint, London, by the Tecton group, 1936–38. *To a certain extent similar to the slablike block unit, this building, on a luxurious scale, represents at the same time a return to the early English tradition of combining houses and pleasure grounds.*

ing like rectangles on end, without the spread and heavy volume of the usual building, they appear all too immaterial to those whose feeling is only for the sprawling solid mass. They have been met by an emotional resistance which has been responsible for their slow acceptance.

Zigzag blocks   Another solution for the problem of highly populated districts — the use of zigzag blocks (*maisons à redents*) — was worked out by Le Corbusier after 1922, in his scheme for a contemporary city of three million people, exhibited in the Salon d'Automne in Paris. His adaptation of this project to Paris, the so-called Plan Voisin, exhibited in 1925 in his Pavillon de l'Esprit Nouveau on the outskirts of the Exposition of Decorative Art, followed the same idea, which was still further developed in his *La Ville radieuse* (Boulogne, 1935), a volume comprising his studies in town planning. These buildings, about a hundred and fifty feet high, with glass walls, and standing on pillars, Le Corbusier placed in green areas, with a distinct separation of traffic and pedestrians and with the business district located in cruciform and later in Y-shaped skyscrapers far from the residential quarters.

Le Corbusier projected schemes for the reorganization of the city all the way from Moscow and Stockholm to Rio de Janeiro, sometimes being magnificently inspired by the site of a certain city — as, for example, Algiers, for which he proposed a daring combination of various levels utilizing the natural contours of the land.[12] But always his thought swung back to Paris; again and again he returned to that city with new and still more advanced ideas.

Out of Le Corbusier's work we shall take a single scheme, that of Paris, 1937, to show how the new scale to be employed in town planning would work, restricting ourselves to a consideration only of the reorganization of residential areas. Le Corbusier and Pierre Jeanneret, who always work together, concentrated on a section in the east of Paris in the Faubourg Saint-Antoine which is designated by officials an *îlot insalubre*,[13] an unhealthful area. In their plans they united for the first time the solution of the modern traffic problem with the solution of slum clearance as it could be carried out today. Their scheme is one which could be realized immediately because it eliminates the old street system only as far as the boundaries of the section treated, and replaces it by free-standing building groups of about the height of the early Chicago skyscrapers of the eighties.[14] These building groups are disposed freely in green spaces. Their long wings are L-shaped or composed according to the demands of the site and their orientation to the sun. When at the end of our discussion of the London squares we spoke of the unexecuted scheme of John Nash for the Regent's Park housing development of 1812, with its advancing and receding building groups which cannot be em-

Îlot insalubre, No. 6

---

[12] Cf. p. 159.

[13] Le Corbusier discussed his idea in *Des Canons, des Munitions?* (Paris, 1938), pp. 67–82.

[14] Their height depends on the density to be given to the district. The density Le Corbusier favors is that of about eight hundred persons per hectare, which seems rather too high for the city of the future. It may be observed that in most of the European projects, especially in those of Le Corbusier, there persists the old belief that the existing level of population will remain the same, an optimism which is not in accordance with the observations of the last thirty years.

braced in a single glance, and felt it a premonition of what we are venturing today, we had in mind projects like Le Corbusier's *îlot insalubre, no. 6* (*figs.* **451, 452**).

The large building groups stand on pillars so that the ground is unobstructed for the pedestrian. The open space rescued by this concentration in height and in great units is used for landscaping, nurseries, cinemas, sports. Even the twelve per cent of the ground covered by the buildings is available for recrea-

449. Skyscraper apartment houses in open space near Lake Michigan, Chicago, c. 1929. *The problem of surrounding the human dwelling by greenery, present since the baroque, has to be met at any cost in our own period as well. These many-layered skyscrapers stand with good orientation, with a view of Lake Michigan and surrounded by open space. They were planned before the depression of 1929.*

tion, for the flat roofs are transformed into playgrounds and solaria. The single dwelling units, the individual apartments, are of various sizes. As in the American apartment house, even as in one of the rare projects of Frank Lloyd Wright for a skyscraper apartment building in 1929, they are duplex, built to the height of two stories. They are adapted to the old human

742

scale of approximately seven feet which Le Corbusier found in farmhouses all the way from Switzerland to the Greek islands. Parts of the units are in this height; in other parts the space is left undivided, extending to its full height of fourteen feet.

Along with slum clearance went an attack on the traffic problem. Le Corbusier's dream of an elevated express highway

450. LE CORBUSIER. Skyscraper amidst greenery; project for Buenos Aires, 1929. *What in the case of the Chicago apartment houses was perhaps due to the pressure of economic circumstances is here proposed as a principle.*

running from east to west through Paris would be much harder to realize. This is not because it is too extreme. It is not so much ahead of its time as Haussmann's *percement* of the city; indeed, it is a parallel to Haussmann's projects, being simply adjusted to present-day requirements. But circumstances have changed. It is a curious coincidence that the width of the proposed speed highway of Le Corbusier is the

743

same (a hundred and twenty meters) as Haussmann's broadest street, the Avenue Foch, which, as we pointed out earlier, Haussmann made three times as wide as the architect proposed. When Haussmann was transforming Paris, he once remarked bitterly that there were no architects living to match the "temps nouveaux." In the Paris of today the situation seems to be just the contrary: there are architects, but no directing official equal, as Haussmann was, to the opportunities and needs of the period.

The difference between the slum clearance of the Le Corbusier scheme and the methods customarily employed — for example, as in Paris, the miles and miles of H.B.M. (low-cost housing) seven or eight stories high and densely massed along the outer boulevards, or, as in America, the usual procedure of cutting slum areas out of the body of the city and replacing them with better buildings but at the same time scrupulously preserving the old street system — that difference, it must be noted, is a difference of scale. The use of a new and larger scale in town planning which would coincide with the scale already being used in the parkway system is an imperative necessity for the salvation of the city. This scale must permeate all urban projects. It is closely connected with the space-time conception of our period.

A Civic Center

In the great city of our age there will be a civic center, a public place which, like the agora of Athens, the Roman forum, and the medieval cathedral square, will be community focus and popular concourse. According to the highly differentiated requirements of present-day social life, this center will be concentrated in tall buildings freely placed in open spaces, surrounded and defined by greenery. What it will be like in spatial organization and plastic treatment may be largely foreseen in a recent great urban development — Rockefeller Center in New York City (1931–39; *fig.* **453**). Such an anticipation is the rare exception in our studies: it is not often our privilege to be able to discuss the new conceptions of our period in terms of actual construction. They have seldom achieved

451. LE CORBUSIER. Plan for "îlot insalubre, no. 6," 1937. *This large-scale housing development, with its open spaces and concentration on slablike buildings, has not yet achieved realization.*

452. LE CORBUSIER. "îlot insalubre, no. 6," housing development.

expression beyond schemes drawn on paper, because those in control of building seem usually to lack the vision necessary to provide what our period demands.

Rockefeller Center is a group of fourteen buildings located in midtown New York, between Fifth and Sixth avenues and Forty-eighth and Fifty-first streets. It stands in a cleft of the chaotic city, nearly three blocks (twelve acres) cut out of the narrow-scale gridiron system of New York and organized in a completely new and independent manner. It introduces for the first time into a contemporary city the large scale that is to be found in the parkways and great engineering works. Its buildings, which instead of facing existing streets are conceived in coördination as a unit, introduce correspondingly new and original plastic elements.

First, let us consider what these plastic elements are and what they involve architecturally. In Chicago the office buildings of the eighties, with their fifteen to twenty stories, had dignity, strength, and scale. They were so organized as to provide light everywhere, often in open planning, usually with a U-shaped inner court.[15] In New York from the beginning the skyscraper had none of these qualities. It lacked scale, dignity, and strength, becoming simply a tower rising to extreme heights. Louis Sullivan, who created some of the purest examples of what should have been followed in later developments, points out that "the architecture of lower New York became hopelessly degraded in its pessimistic denial of our art and our civilization." Where the New York skyscraper went astray was in the exaggerated use of the tower, with its intricate mixture of pseudo-historical reminiscences and its ruthless disregard of its surroundings, as well as of the entire structure of the city.

Plastic elements of Rockefeller Center

---

[15] Cf. the ground plan of the Marquette Building (1891), fig. 230.

←

453. Rockefeller Center, New York City, 1931–39. *Air view. The various buildings spread out openly from the highest, the R. C. A. Building, like the vanes of a windmill. Their slablike form represents a revolt against the old type of skyscraper, the imitation of the Gothic tower or the enlargement of the normal four-story block to extreme height, without consideration of new conditions.*

After the passage of the New York zoning law of 1916, the chaotic state of building development was reduced somewhat by the use of the setback and the application of other zoning regulations, but fundamentally no real order was achieved until an entirely new architectonic form was explored, a form for the high structure which was adapted to the requirements of its unusual height and to its internal necessities. This change did not come about until nearly four decades after the skyscraper problem had presented itself. How this new form developed step by step, here and there in various cities, cannot be outlined here.[16] We can only note the final image of the skyscraper as it eventually came into being in the R.C.A. Building of 1931–32 (*fig.* **454**).

"Its huge, broad, flat north and south fronts, its almost unbroken mass and its thinness," according to the *New York City Guide*, "are the features that impelled observers to nickname it 'the Slab.'"[17] To adopt the popular name, this slab, so close to our own investigations, stands on its site like an immense rectangle — a form impossible of realization in any other period. The shape grows naturally out of purely technical and economic considerations of how to give normal lighting to every spot of utilized space, based on a module arrived at for obtaining twenty-seven feet of optimum light and a proper location of elevator shafts. Raymond Hood explains the design thus: "Grouped in the center are the elevators, and the service facilities, and surrounding them on each floor we have stretched the 27 ft. of lighted space that experience has proved is the maximum to be allowed to provide adequate light and air to all parts of the building."[18] The

[16] Steps on the way to this overthrow of the tyranny of the tower, with its medieval echoes, are, for example, the Civic Opera House in Chicago (1928–29), by Graham, Probst, and White, three slablike wings, yet without any new spatial relationships; the Daily News Building in Chicago, by Holabird and Root (1929), with its blunt, obtuse T-shaped plan in the upper stories; and also to a certain extent Hood's McGraw-Hill Building (1930), which, perhaps unfortunately, had no influence on the architectural features of Rockefeller Center. The Daily News Building, with its upthrust of piers, in which there lingers a last implication of the Gothic, is much more clearly reflected in Rockefeller Center.

[17] Federal Writers' Project, *New York City Guide* (New York, 1939), p. 336.

[18] Raymond Hood, "The Design of Rockefeller City," *Architectural Forum*, January 1932, p. 5. Rockefeller Center was executed by three architectural firms: Reinhard & Hofmeister; Corbett, Harrison and MacMurray; Hood and Fouilloux.

748

454. The slablike skyscraper: R. C. A. Building, Rockefeller Center, New York, 1931–32. *Seventy stories and 850 feet high, this slab is based on the principle of 27 feet of optimum light for working area around a core containing the elevators and service space.*

455. R. C. A. Building, Rockefeller Center. *Floor plan.*

result is an immense slab born out of mathematical calculations for utilizing ground and space to the best advantage, in an effort to accomplish a form proper to our age; it is an employment of the same basic element as that used by the painter in his hovering planes or by an engineer like Maillart in the building of bridges out of reinforced slabs, both achieving solutions which would not have been possible with the usual means. The skyscraper slab form of today is as significant and expressive for our period as the monolithic obelisk of Egypt and the Gothic cathedral tower were for their periods.

The walls   The walls of the R.C.A. Building rise up unbroken eight hundred and fifty feet. In such a dimension the architectural form, when it is not spoiled by details inappropriate to the large scale, is not of decisive importance. All the strength and power lie in the curtain walls, in which the windows are reduced to mere lineations like the ribbing in the texture of a fabric. Preliminary to the final design of the R.C.A. Building, several studies of fenestration were made, among them the use of horizontal crossings and of compartmentation corresponding in a certain degree to the rectangularities of the steel cage,[19] before the associated architects at last returned to the pier system, which in such a dimension is automatically flattened into stripes.

Even the staggered setbacks of the curtain walls are at least in some respects justified, as Hood explains, by practical considerations. "We have," he says, "carried the principle [of providing light and air to all parts of the building] to its logical conclusion. As each elevator shaft ended we cut the building back to maintain the same 27 feet from the core of the building to the exterior walls." [20] What is startling to the human mind is the idea that planes quite usual in the horizontal sense should be pulled into the vertical. Nor can it be denied that when with the great scale there is combined the thinness of the structure, a certain feeling of hovering, of suspension, emanates from the surfaces — and, as a matter of fact, the immense surfaces of the curtain walls and the whole skeleton can move, flexible in the wind.

[19] *American Architect*, April 1931, pp. 34–35.
[20] *Architectural Forum*, January 1932, p. 5.

Nothing new or significant can be observed in looking over a map of the site. The ground plan reveals nothing. The gridiron runs through it, as everywhere else in the city. Even the first designs for the grouping of the buildings do not show a special approach; they were entirely conventional. Among the great number of studies which were made separately by the different firms, one still shows an attempt to build up a sort of ideal pyramid composed of the five main buildings; in spatial terms this would have meant a centralized unit. But from the beginning the schemes must have had for eyes accustomed to former conceptions something aggressive and intriguing.[21] It is a credit to the spirit of the planning architects that a celebrated designer of American Gothic churches has attacked their scheme as being a conglomerate of "sprouting amorphous and cubicular mushrooms." Is not this curiously reminiscent of the protest of Charles Garnier, the builder of the Opéra in Paris, against the erection of the Eiffel Tower for the exhibition in 1889, and of his belief that this huge, hideous iron structure would destroy the skyline of Paris forever?

Thus it is apparent that it was not through vision but through an effort to adjust design to changing necessities that the development gradually took its final shape — from the module of twenty-seven feet as optimum for well-lighted rooms to the organization of the volumes around the plazas, which for the first time realize open planning on the new scale — accomplishing now for town planning what the small Chicago houses of Frank Lloyd Wright in the nineties accomplished for the free and open planning of the single house.[22]

In their placement the fourteen buildings of Rockefeller Center are more closely grouped on the western half of the area, toward

Arrangement of Rockefeller Center

---

[21] The scheme, whose architectural shape is far from being revolutionary, stirred up public opinion nevertheless. The newspaper columns of the *Herald-Tribune* and the *Times* were filled with discussions in the form both of editorials and of letters from readers. *Pencil Points* brought out an article with the headline, "The Functionalist Design for Radio City Has Aroused Public Indignation" (May 1931).

[22] We cannot enter here into the history of Rockefeller Center, which started with the search of the Metropolitan Opera for a new home and which because of the depression of 1929 was changed into a radio and theatrical city-within-a-city. Cf. Frederick Lewis Allen, "Radio City: Cultural Center?" *Harper's Magazine*, April 1932, and "Look at Rockefeller Center," *Harper's Magazine*, October 1938.

Sixth Avenue. Here is Radio City, with its enormous Music Hall, its Center Theater, and its slablike seventy-story R.C.A. Building, which contains the broadcasting studios. On the eastern portion, toward Fifth Avenue, the buildings are not so densely massed. Placed there are the lowest of the structures, the comparatively small six-story buildings dedicated to foreign nations. They stand with their narrow fronts lined up on the avenue, so that coming along the street from the north one gets the effect of a series of truncations behind which rise the higher units of the center. Nearest, and standing a bit aside, is the forty-one-story International Building; then in the background, clearly separated from the lower buildings by the open space of the Plaza, rises the narrow slab of the R.C.A. Building. As one proceeds south, different dimensions in heights and depths are perceived by the observer, a succession of impressions like visual impulses recorded in time — the depth of the Plaza, the soaring reach of the R.C.A. Building, the narrow streets running through, and glimpses in fragments of the broad side of the thirty-six-story Time and Life Building.

The actual arrangement and disposition of the buildings can be seen and grasped only from the air. An air-view picture reveals that the various high buildings are spread out in an open arrangement from the highest, the R.C.A. Building, like the vanes of a windmill, the different volumes so placed that their shadows fall as little as possible upon one another, some of them in parallel relation, others at right angles. This is all quite rational, but the moment one begins moving in the midst of the buildings through Rockefeller Plaza, where the three largest structures rise in different directions and to different heights, one becomes conscious of new and unaccustomed interrelations between them. They can then be grasped from no single position nor embraced in any single view. There becomes apparent a many-sidedness in these simple and enormous slabs which makes it impossible to bind them rationally together. The Time and Life Building, completed in 1938, has through its free orientation the decisive force of planes separated by air but moved and combined unconsciously by the observing human eye. Out of these well-calculated masses one becomes aware of a new fantastic element inherent in the space-

456. The towers of Asinelli and Garisenda, Bologna, thirteenth century. *These leaning towers of two noble families of Bologna are private patrician fortresses of great height which can yet be embraced in a single view.*

time conception of our period. The interrelations which the eye achieves between the different planes give the clearly circumscribed volumes an extraordinary new effect, somewhat like that which a rotating sphere of mirrored facets gives to a ballroom when the facets reflect whirling spots of light in all directions and into every dimension.

Such a great building complex presupposes not the single point of view of the Renaissance but the many-sided approach of our own age. The difference can be indicated by comparing it with such thirteenth-century structures as the leaning towers of the two noble families of Asinelli and Garisenda in Bologna (*fig. 456*). Private patrician fortresses, they rise up magnificently into the sky, but they can be embraced at a single glance, in a single view. There is no uncertainty in the observer concerning their relation to each other. On the other hand, nothing of the essential character of an organism like Rockefeller Center is revealed in a view restricted to its central axis.

Space-Time and
Rockefeller Center

753

457. Rockefeller Center. *Photomontage. Expressions of the new urban scale like Rockefeller Center are forcefully conceived in space-time and cannot be embraced in a single view. To obtain a feeling for their interrelations the eye must function as in the high-speed photographs of Edgerton.*

It possesses symmetries which are senseless in reference to the aesthetic significance of the whole. It requires comprehension in space and time more closely analogous to what has been achieved in modern scientific research as well as in modern painting.

In Edgerton's stroboscopic studies, in which motion can be fixed and analyzed in arrested fractions of 1/100,000 of a second, a whole movement is shown separated into its successive components (*fig.* **458**). At Rockefeller Center the human eye must function similarly (*fig.* **457**); it has to pick up each individual view singly and relate it to all others, combining them into a time sequence. Only thus are we able to understand the grand play of volumes and surfaces and perceive its many-sided significance.

Rockefeller Center embraces many different activities. Leisure and entertainment, which were the initial motive in projecting the Center, are provided in Radio City, with its music hall, theaters, broadcasting studios, and night clubs; international trade is represented in the foreign buildings, journalism in the headquarters of the Associated Press, which gives its name to one of the buildings, and in the offices of two popular magazines,

458. EDGERTON. Speed photograph of golf stroke. *In Edgerton's stroboscopic studies, in which motions can be fixed and analyzed in arrested fractions of 1/100,000 of a second, a whole movement is separated into its successive components, making possible comprehension in both space and time.*

the Time and Life Building. In addition there are a variety of offices and establishments more or less connected with these activities, an underground shopping center, and a six-story garage built into one of the most recent structures (1939) with three of its stories below street level.

Obviously it can be objected that such a commercial composition does not constitute a civic center. It is a private enterprise arising from private initiative and carried out as a private speculation, based, as Raymond Hood says, on pure calculation of cost and return. What might have been a new home for the opera was changed by force of economic circumstances into the largest music hall in the world, where every night the world's longest line of shapely and well-trained girls' legs is on display. It may also be pointed out that, standing amid the chaos of midtown New York, it is not surrounded by greenery but instead is confined by the limitations of street and traffic.

A visitor wishing to stop there cannot step from his automobile without being warned by the police that he can park only from two to five minutes. Moreover, the Center dominates, indeed tyrannizes over, the entire vicinity — Fifth Avenue, the neighboring churches, all the surrounding buildings.

How then does it differ from the downtown district — from Wall Street and lower Broadway, which Louis Sullivan regarded as a center of infection, as "a plague spot of American architecture"?

The difference lies in one thing only: in the new scale of city planning inherent in Rockefeller Center, which coincides with the scale of modern bridges and parkways.

When Rockefeller Center was projected, there was objection on the part of eminent critics to the increased congestion which would inevitably result from its location in the midst of the city. To offset this threat of traffic congestion, proposals were made to widen the street fifteen feet. To have done so would have helped very little. What really needs to be changed is the entire structure of the city. The parkway and Rockefeller Center are only small beginnings, isolated new growths in the immense body of New York, like the young branches of a tree.

756

But it must not be forgotten that tiny new branches properly grafted can change the whole inner structure of a plant. Rockefeller Center simply is in advance of its period in the urban scale. What must change is not the Center but New York itself. The city must adopt the new scale which is identical with that of its bridges and parkways. Only then will the civic center stand amidst greenery. Until then it will stand as a reminder that the structure of the city must be transformed, not in the interest of single individuals but for the sake of the community as a whole.

We have chosen New York for an insight into the ultimate problems of city planning because New York is the one among the largest cities which still has the power to cope with new needs. There is the same inheritance from the nineteenth century as in Paris or in London: there is the distortion due to an artificially assimilated body, and the disorganization due to a chaotic intermingling of functions which should be clearly separated.

Along with the most intensive mechanization underground and above ground, there are blighted areas which appear directly in the shadow of the skyscrapers of Manhattan; extreme fluctuations in the value of land, population, and depopulation follow one another with disturbing rapidity. There is a street system completely inappropriate in scale, which cuts off the organic development of the city like an iron ring around a tree. The tree grows larger and larger, and the ring remains rigid and inflexible. There is no occasion for surprise when the city, like the tree, becomes completely deformed under these conditions. It may even be that the iron ring must burst or the tree die.

Yet simultaneously with this there exists in New York the initiative to cope with some of the problems that have to be solved; there is vision enough to create leisure centers for the masses, parkway systems, and the skeleton of a civic center on an appropriate scale.

Possibilities for the future and the danger of disaster are inextricably interwoven in the structure of New York, but its fundamental transformation will never be accomplished by the town planner alone. His schemes — though they are in harmony with the problems of the period — will never be executed unless those who are governing are imbued with a similar spirit.

The contemporary city, as the most visible symbol of human interrelations, can only be built when the methods of human organization are not opposed to but in conformity with those which have enabled science and art to make men aware of undiscovered spheres.

IN CONCLUSION

All we have been able to do has been to trace incompletely, in fragments, an image of our period. Perhaps at the present stage of our development this is all that is possible, thus to touch here and there at isolated points what is going on under the surface. Certainly to have aspired to any exhaustive or comprehensive treatment would have been futile. The time for that is not yet.

Architecture as finite organism
We have restricted our observations to architecture and its interrelations. We have pointed out why architecture reflects the inner tendencies of the time and therefore may properly serve as a general index. We have regarded architecture as a finite organism, isolated it, just as the scientist must isolate certain phenomena in order to determine their interior processes. We have not been at all interested in establishing in the organism of architecture any fixed or permanent laws which should manifest themselves at all times. Nor have we sought either to chart closed cycles of rise and fall or to define the manner in which these laws might apparently repeat themselves in different cultures.

What has interested us throughout the periods we have observed has been the growth and change in the architectonic organism and, especially, the development of those constituent facts which form the substance of its true history. Only by isolating architecture as an organism in itself, and by obtaining in consequence understanding of its nature and growth, have

758

we been able to seek out and fix its relations to other and cognate activities.

We must not forget also the relations between social develop- Politics and architecture ment on the one hand and architecture on the other. But, as it happens, very often these relations have been too much simplified. Historical space has many dimensions. It is many-sided. It does not permit the observer a single point of reference by which to interpret its phenomena. There appears — as in modern physics — no exact causality, no determination. Identical causes do not lead absolutely to identical effects.

Modern physicists, when they attacked the Newtonian system, called this uncertainty between cause and effect "semi-causality." This semi-causality prevails as well in the historical as in the subatomic. There are no definite rules, no simple causality which determines reciprocal dependence between political events and those human activities which explore thought and feeling. The irrational interferes. To draw these flexible relationships too tight would be to plunge us into inextricable disorder.

No preëstablished point of view is possible. Works rich in constituent facts and works of the most pernicious influence have appeared again and again under the same economic system. Speculators during the eighteenth and early nineteenth centuries were responsible, as we have seen, for housing developments which achieved the highest in human and urban values. Speculators also were responsible in the later nineteenth century for the destruction of the very structure of our cities, engulfing them in hopeless living quarters which destroyed human dignity.

It is possible even in the same political system, at the same time, and in the same country, to produce works full of power to invigorate the future, and along with them works of confusion and decadence. For example, during the eighties and nineties investment and land speculators erected the great office buildings and department stores of Chicago; at the same time, under the same economic conditions, the same category of buildings raised in New York became the "plague spot of American architecture."

759

We do not doubt that in some periods there has existed a unity of culture. In those periods imagination and the external world flowed into one another. Then the spirit was not condemned to go its way alone, and reality had not the single meaning of struggle for existence. Those were the happy hours of mankind, but they have been rare and of tragic brevity. So it was in Athens under Pericles; so it was in Rome during the lustrous reign of Augustus. It is a question among modern historians, for example, whether Augustus was formed by the great spirits who surrounded him and who represent today the glory of Roman literature or whether it was his own personal influence which called forth their creative power.

These periods, with their unity of intellectual, emotional, and political culture, are those in which life has been able to manifest such splendor as is possible to man. We cannot aspire so high. We must proceed more humbly. Before demanding in a disorganized world such a unity of emotional, intellectual, and political culture, we must first understand how far the emotional and intellectual are today interrelated, how nearly we have approached that vital preconception of every culture: the affinity between its methods of thinking and of feeling.

Sciences and arts belong to that group of activities which, by exploring the unknown of the human mind, directly enlarge our consciousness. Every scientist, every artist, is part of a long line of tradition. When he is a creative spirit, however, it is his function to go forward, beyond the limits of that tradition, to explore what before him no one has known, no one has seen, no one has felt. By means of intuition, imagination, mystical impulse — what you will — he must open up new spheres of the unconscious. These spheres are distinguished from the organization of the outer world in that their essential work is done directly, personally, without interference by any external power. They grow only in liberty, for no command can open the way to the unexplored.

We know also that the spirit is bound up with earth and social environment. It does not grow in air-tight tins. We do not deny the primary impulses of hunger, love, and self-esteem. We do not deny the influence upon research of good and bad conditions. Adverse ones may kill the creative effort before

760

it halfway reaches realization; favorable conditions may stimulate its growth suddenly, like leaves springing forth overnight.

At the moment, however, it is not so important in this case to establish the conditions of growth as it is to have an understanding of its real structure — that is, to become aware of *what kind of growth* is going on within the depths of our period. We cannot grasp the constitution of this growth without knowing what *methods of approach* underlie explorations in the different realms of thought and feeling.

In this respect our enlightenment is more than limited. The walls existing between the disciplines and the fact that people are so educated as to be submerged and confined by their special problems have resulted in their not being interested in, and in many cases even unable to give account of, their methodological principles. Consequently, there has been practically no comparative study of methods in the different realms, whatever they may be, from biology to music. The methods of approach underlying creative research form the *écriture automatique* of this age. They open the way for objective insight into its spirit by making plain how close we are to the preconception of culture: the identity of methods.

We do not deny the fundamental importance of the social and political in the structure of a period. There is an extensive literature dealing with the influence of the social order on architecture and on our environment. However, what we wish to emphasize is still another factor, the influence of which on human life is not so obvious and cannot always be fixed at a given time, but which achieves weight and importance by reaching more deeply into the present state of culture: the influence of feeling.

Influence of feeling

The influence of feeling on practical decisions is often regarded as unimportant, but it inevitably permeates and underlies the decisions of men. The chaos of our cities, from Soviet Russia to the United States, cannot be explained as a result of social and economic conditions alone. In the rebuilding of Moscow, in the slum clearance of New York, there is the same lack of scale, the same schism between retrogressive feeling and advanced technical means. Actions are released by social and economic impulses, but every human act is affected, is formed unconsciously, by a specific emotional background. Without exception, every human being is adjusted both mentally and emotionally to his profession, whether he be laborer, artisan, merchant, or scientist.

It is the same with politics and government. Behind any political system there are single individuals whose actions reflect their mental and emotional equipment. At the moment when there is a schism, the inner kernel of personality is split by a difference of level between the methods of thinking and those of feeling. The result is the symbol of our period: the maladjusted man.

It is possible that it may not be long before this situation will be recognized everywhere, and the schism may then disappear. But just now it is much easier to forward the most difficult scientific theory than the simplest of new artistic means. The education of the individual is today directed toward intellectual specialization. In contrast to this, the education of the emotions is neglected. At any rate, its level does not correspond to the level of knowledge which is to be mastered. Thinking is trained; feeling is left untrained.

Mentally trained people are capable today of following the most difficult scientific research, but the same people are lost when they are faced with new artistic means which force them to an enlargement of their inner natures. The reason is that most of them can rely in feeling on nothing equivalent to their mental training. Knowledge and feeling are isolated from each other. So we arrive at the curious paradox that in our period feeling has become more difficult than thinking.

In periods of equilibrium between thinking and feeling no one needs to speak of the training of feeling. It goes its own way, but it forms an inseparable unity with the act of thinking. As with freedom, so with emotion. When freedom exists, it is taken for granted, it is reflected in every action; no one thinks it necessary to mention it. But the moment freedom is suppressed, life is deprived of its tonic, its invigoration, and men become aware of its loss.

Science and art, in so far as they explore the unknown or anticipate the future, reflect the real level, the true being, of our age. They are the real moral forces; they will speak for us to later generations when the horror of the outer world of the present has faded away.

We may even go a step further. How explain the disorder which rules in all spheres concerned with human relations? How explain that disturbance which has involved the most primitive laws of human life? In addition to the many reasons which are always given for the present chaos, there is a fundamental one that is often forgotten: *factual knowledge has not been reabsorbed and humanized by an equivalent feeling.*

Reality, in so far as it is mirrored in the organization of the external world, has the power to destroy every one of us. This reality, which crushes down more and more people every day, menacing our culture just at the moment when it has begun to be conscious of itself, cannot be identified with the true being of our period.

What is this reality?

It is opposed to the methods of approach which prevail in the creative researches of our time. Its energy and external power are nothing but vain attempts to cope with the many-sided and complex problems of the day by means of a ruthless simplification.

In the nineteenth century the means of production were mechanized, and unrestricted production became an end in itself, bringing disorder into human relations for a century. In the twentieth century the means of destruction were mechanized, and unrestricted power became an end in itself. The façades of the last century were erected in many diverse shapes and styles, but these styles, as they were used, were not an avowal. They functioned merely as curtains disguising what was behind them. So mankind today has many different political systems. Most of them do not reveal — are even in contrast to — what is going on in the depths of the period, with its urge toward the organic. They serve only to hide the fact that in the outer world political power has become an end in itself.

The social disorder delivered to us is an inheritance from the Industrial Revolution. To restore order in this unbalanced world, we must alter its social conditions. But experience shows us that this is not sufficient. It would be a fundamental mistake to believe that today's maladjusted man, the product of a century-long rupture between thinking and feeling, would disappear as the result of a socio-political change. The unintegrated person is today multiplying everywhere and in every class; he is to be found equally among employers and employed, among high and low. His acts reflect his inner division. For though he may organize his affairs with the greatest care, his organizations will not fit with those of other organizers in other fields. However good these special organizations may be in themselves, the whole is crumbling into bits.

One of the most impressive political thinkers of the last century recognized about fifty years ago a central problem of our period when he demanded that the division of labor, the dominant fact in modern life, should be replaced by what he called "the integration of labor." "To integrate" means, according to the dictionary, "to make a whole out of different parts." Desirable, however, as such integration of labor is, it would not be enough, for it would be simply the treatment of a symptom. At the base of everything is the single man. He is often forgotten today. It is he who must be integrated — integrated in his inner nature, without being brutalized, so that his emotional and intellectual outlets will no longer be divorced by an insuperable difference of level. To bring this fact into consciousness and to try to overcome it is closely connected with the outstanding task of this period: to humanize — that is, to reabsorb emotionally — what has been created by the spirit. All talk about organizing and planning is vain when it is not possible to create again the whole man, unfractured in his methods of thinking and feeling.

Yes, we are going now through the test period of our civilization. The existence of each of us is menaced. Yet at the same time there is being revealed in different spheres of activity an affinity in methods of approach, which, though developed independently in each sphere, yet underlie all that is significant in our thinking and feeling. It is as if unconsciously and out of

764

its own forces our period were moving toward a cure of its fatal disease by a still unrealized process.

Some unpredictable event may change the situation, and all these isolated, drifting efforts may coalesce at once into an inner sureness. In this moment our period will master reality.

In a letter long believed to be apocryphal but now regarded as genuine, the philosopher Plato announced that no statement of a certain one of his doctrines existed in his own hand and that he would never write one. Nevertheless, his doctrine, so he said, would never be lost. In the human soul, as a result of "being absorbed by these things and by being in permanent contact with them," it would suddenly arise, "as a fire is kindled by a leaping spark and blazes forth into a bright flame." We think that it is the same today with the formation of our cultural consciousness. It may awake suddenly, but never if we do not begin to become "absorbed by these things," never without the strong will to an inner change, and never without forward-looking preparation.

INDEX

INDEX

Einstein, Albert, *Elektrodynamik bewegter Körper*, 432
El Chasne, 112
Elevators, 197, 206–209, 234, 259–261
Elmslie, George, 313, 387n, 389
Emulation, 303
Engineering, and architecture, *see* Science
Ensor, James, 295
Euclid, 431
Exhibitions, 241–275; influence of, 275; Barcelona (1929), 477, 545, 546; Champ-de-Mars (1798), 242; Columbian (Chicago, 1893), 262n, 268, 273–274, 340, 363, 391–394; Deutsche Werkbund, 476; London (1851), 184, 225; 230n, 243, 244, 246–253, 335; New York (1853), 196 197, 206, 253n; New York (1939), 291, 567, 580, 582; Paris (1855), 253–258; Paris (1867), 186, 208, 236, 258–261, 277, 323, 339, 642; Paris (1878), 262–266, 316, 338, 487; Paris (1889), 266–273, 392; Paris Salon (1930), 477; Philadelphia (1876), 262n, 337, 339; Salon des Indépendants, 432, 435; Stuttgart (1927), 548ff; Zurich (1939), 471, 472
Expressionism, 481–483

Factories, Birmingham, 249; Bolton, 182; Fagus works, 478ff, 489, 494, 513n; Manchester, 182, 234, 311; Massachusetts, 182; Noisiel-sur-Marne, 202–205; Salford cotton mill, 189–191; Soho foundry, 189–191, 216; Sunila, 587–592; van Nelle, Rotterdam, 450n
Fairbairn, William, 189–192, 234, 322; *On the Application of Cast . . . Iron*, 167n, 192
Falda, Giovanni Battista, 76, 80, 81n
Falke, Jakob von, 337
Faraday, Michael, 15
Feeling, importance of, 761ff
Feininger, Lyonel, 483
Ferroconcrete, 25, 264n, 320–331, 395, 470–472, 511–512, 545, 691, 694
Filarete, 43, 45, 46, 47, 48, 49, 54
Finch, A. W., 294
Finland, 566–567, 568–569, 571
Flachat, Eugène, 230–231
Floor plates, gridiron, 224
Flooring, beamless, *see* Maillart, Robert
Florence, workshop of Renaissance, 30ff; Leonardo's plans, 52, 53, 73, 74; cathedral, 32; Innocenti, 33, 38–39, 224; Pazzi Chapel, 39–40, 110, 225; Piazza della Signoria, 52; San Lorenzo, 33; Santa Maria del Fiore, 41; Santa Maria Novella, 33, 34, 39, 112; Uffizi, 59

Fontaine, 177, 615, 616
Fontana, Domenico, 87, 88, 89, 90, 91, 93, 94, 95
Foundation, floating, 379
Fouquet, Nicolas, 135
Fourier, Charles, 723
Fox, Dr., 322
Francesco di Giorgio, wedge-shaped bastions, 43; and *città ideale*, 47, 51, 52; versatility, 51; paintings of piazzas and streets, 51, 53, 54, 57, 58, 66
Francke, Kuno, 395
Frankfort-on-Main, 477, 594; Central Railway Station, 268n
Franklin, Benjamin, 170
Freitag, J. K., 375n
French Revolution, 644
Freyssinet, 461, 462, 472
Friends of Modern Architecture, 521n
Fry, Maxwell, 538
Fuller, G. A., 367n, 376
Furniture, Alvar Aalto's, 463, 601–603; Bauhaus, 487; chairs, 220, 352–353; "patent," 339; in England, 397; in United States, 335, 336–341
Futurism, 14; research into movement, 319–320, 439–444; and cubism, 441–442; and expressionism, 481

Gabriel, Jacques-Ange, 143, 148
Garden, Hugh, 389
Garden city, *see* Town planning
Gardens, public, *see* Parks; Squares; Paris; Haussmann, etc.
Gardner, Eugene C., *Illustrated Homes*, 364, 365
Garnier, Charles, 751
Garnier, Tony, 329–331, 511, 684, 689–694
Gautier, Théophile, 213
Giacometti, Alberto, 66
Giedion, Sigfried, 421n, 464n, 515n; *Spätbarocker und romantischer Klassizismus*, 2, 173n, 676n; *Walter Gropius*, 494n; *Mechanization Takes Command*, 602n
Giedion-Welcker, C., 283n, 430n
Gill, Irving J., 379n
Glasgow group, 317
Glass, use of, 177ff, 195, 223–225, 229, 236–239, 309, 317, 331, 383–386, 419–420, 479, 480, 487–489, 740. *See also* Gropius; Le Corbusier; Mies van der Rohe; Windows; Lighting; Exhibitions

Goethe, Johann Wolfgang, 315
Gogh, Vincent van, 290, 293, 295
Golden Book of the Wanamaker Store, 236
Goldsmith, Oliver, 147
Gothic, 32, 42, 55, 56, 108, 122, 180, 255n
Graham, Probst, and White, 748n
Greenough, Horatio, *Travels . . . of a Yankee Stonecutter*, 214n
Griffin, W. B., 379n, 389
Gris, Juan, 427
Gropius, Ise, 483
Gropius, Walter, 27, 150, 341, 389, 391, 473–509, 513, 543, 548, 549, 565, 604, 737, 738
Ground plan, eighteenth-century, 632; flexible, 297, 303, 329, 361–366, 398–403, 511–513, 543, 546, 547
Guarini, Guarino, 121–127, 132, 133, 138; *Architettura civile*, 131
Gullichsen, 592
Gurlitt, Cornelius, 109; *Geschichte des Barockstils*, 111n, 127n

Haefeli, 325
Hague, The, 593n
Hammond, J. L., and Barbara, *Rise of Modern Industry*, 167
Handicrafts, 317, 397; in Germany, 481ff. *See also* Arts and crafts movement
Hankar, Paul, 296; house in Rue de Facque, 304; Tervueren exhibition, 304
Hardouin-Mansard, Jules, 137, 143, 675
Haussmann, Georges-Eugène, transformation of Paris, 646–679; mentioned, 90, 228–229, 635, 641, 642, 645, 696, 715, 725, 735, 743, 744
Hempel, Eberhard, *Francesco Borromini*, 111n, 113n
Hennebique, François, 323–324, 328, 447
Herriot, Édouard, 331
Heuss, Theodor, 481n
Hevesi, Ludwig, 299, 300
Hildebrandt, Lucas von, 131
Hitchcock, H. R., 360n, 478–479
Hittorf, Jacques, 217n
Hoffmann, Josef, 316, 317, 476, 509, 525
Holabird, William, 371, 374, 748n
Home Arts and Industries Association, 296
Hooch, Peter de, 541
Hood, Raymond, 389, 391n, 748n
Horeau, Hector, 229–230, 231, 257
Horta, Victor, 200, 296, 297–306, 309, 325, 326, 329, 355, 514, 525
Housing, 500, 533–536, 548–553, 596–600, 670–672, 674, 692–694, 696–697, 700, 701, 704, 710–712

Howard, Ebenezer, 686–689, 722
Hubbard, H. V., *Parkways*, 727
Hugo, Victor, 231
Hussey, Christopher, 635n
Huttunen, 571
"Hygeia," *see* Papworth

Industrial Chicago, 351, 367n, 375, 376, 381
Industrial Revolution, 163ff
Industry, history of, 9ff; effect on architecture, 160, 232, 241–243, 341; social effects, 165, 334ff, 429, 493–494, 672ff, 677, 721–722; American, 341–344
Indy, Vincent d', 293
Invention, 163–165
Iron, 165–206, 218ff, 227ff, 243ff, 479
Itten, Johannes, 483

James, William, 392
Jaquet-Droz, Pierre, 164
Jeanneret, Charles, *see* Le Corbusier
Jeanneret, Pierre, 520ff, 538, 741–745. *See also* Le Corbusier
Jefferson National Expansion Memorial, 199n
Jenney, William Le Baron, 204n, 206, 236; and the Chicago school, 368–375, 378; Leiter Building, 369, 380–383, 514
Jennings, W. W., *History of Economic Progress*, 343n, 343–344
Jensen, E. C., 204n
Jobard, 212–213
Jourdain, Frantz, 268n

Kandinsky, Wassily, 411, 483, 549
Karlsruhe, 54, 144
Karsten, 712
Klee, Paul, 483, 549, 566
Klerk, de, 698, 703
Knopff, Ferdinand, 294
Koechlin, Maurice, 279
Krantz, J. B., 259, 266

Labrouste, Henri, 27, 185, 216–226, 237, 309, 323, 330, 513, 665, 689
Laugier, Abbé, 148
League of Nations, building competition, 303, 519ff
Le Corbusier (Charles Édouard Jeanneret), 27, 158ff, 215, 238, 303, 314n, 329, 378, 381, 408, 427, 430, 435, 443, 474n, 492, 509–540, 542, 545, 549, 550, 553, 565, 575, 578, 586, 709, 738, 741–744
Léger, Fernand, 473, 548, 567

773

Neutra, Richard J., 352, 496, 545n
New York City, parkways, 728ff, 731; potentialities, 756–757; population decline, 722; "Washington Stores," 233; A. T. Stewart store, 235; Bayard Building, 388; Central Park Casino, 405, 406; Flatiron Building, 385n; Harper and Brothers Building, 195, 232; McGraw-Hill Building, 391n, 748n; Woolworth Building, 389n; Museum of Modern Art, 430n. *See also* Rockefeller Center; Parks
New York City Guide, 748
New York Herald, 3, 194
Newhall, Beaumont, 214n, 483n
Newton, Isaac, 22, 432
Nineteenth century, 160ff, 763; architecture of, 179ff. *See also* Architecture
Nystrom, R. H., *Economics of Retailing*, 232n

Office buildings, 193, 206, 246, 326; Johnson Wax Company, 409, 415, 417–421; Larkin Building, 411, 417–419. *See also* Chicago; Chicago School
Olbrich, Joseph, 316, 317
Ollivier, Émile, 669
Olmsted, F. L., 728
Osthaus, Karl Ernest, *Van de Velde*, 292n, 475
Otis Elevator Company, 10, 207, 208
Otis, Elisha Graves, 207–208
Oud, J. J. P., 314, 365, 424, 530, 549, 550, 695, 703n
Ozenfant, Amédée, 435, 528; *Peinture moderne*, 510n

Paine, Thomas, 169–172, 188
Painting, Dutch, 542; Renaissance, 32, 252, 426ff; twentieth-century, 409ff, 444–446, 457–461, 510, 607. *See also* Cubism; Futurism; Expressionism
Palmanova, Italy, 43, 53
Panizzi, Sir Anthony, 220, 224n
Papacy, 76. *See also* Popes
Papworth, J. B., 688
Paris, 75, 77, 90; seventeenth-century, 135; changes in nineteenth century, 641–679; boulevards, 142, 657ff (*see also* Streets); squares, 142, 143, 148, 154, 616ff, 624, 626 (*see also* Squares; Parks); Le Corbusier's *îlot insalubre*, 741–744; Bastille, 649, 660; Bibliotheque Nationale, 220ff, 673; Bibliothèque Ste.-Geneviève, 185, 218–219, 309, 323, 513; Champs-Élysées, 140, 143, 148, 656;

Eiffel Tower, 209, 213, 244, 266, 274, 275, 279–284, 432, 519, 751; Étoile, 656, 675; Galerie d'Orléans, 177–178; Gare de l'Est, 229, 646, 673, 678; Granary, 174–175; Grandes Halles, 228–231, 257; Hôtel de Ville, 650, 651; Hôtel Lambert, 134; Ile de la Cité, 651; Jardin des Plantes, 179, 325n; Latin quarter, 651; Louvre, 134, 137, 138, 649, 652; Madeleine, 652; market hall, Madeleine, 227; Palais Royal, 177, 649; St.-Jean de Montmartre, 324; Ste.-Chapelle, 646; Théâtre-Français, 173–174, 189, 329, 656; Tour St.-Jacques, 659; Trocadéro, 263, 667; Winter Garden, 240
Parks: Hyde Park, 624, 647; Central Park, 728, 735n; in Paris, 650, 654, 655, 661–664, 667, 727n. *See also* Squares; Plants
Parkway, 727–736
Parris, Alexander, 357n
Pascal, Blaise, 108
Patte, 143
Paxton, Joseph, 197, 230n, 249, 253, 253n
Pérac, Étienne du, 61, 64, 80n, 84
Percier, 177, 615, 616
Perino del Vaga, 63
Perkins, Jacob, 348
Perret, Auguste, 330, 369, 509, 511, 530; Casablanca dock buildings, 219; Rue Franklin apartments, 326–329, 514; Rue Ponthieu garage, 329
Perspective, linear, 31ff, 109, 431–439; Renaissance, 43, 45, 54, 59, 60, 61, 431, 440; Baroque, 54. *See also* Space
Peruzzi, 115n
Peterson, C. E., 199n, 200n
Pevsner, Nikolaus, 397n, 473
Pflegard, 325
Philadelphia, Wanamaker's "Grand Depot," 235–236; exhibition (1876), 262n, 337, 339
Picard, Edmond, 294
Picasso, Pablo, 28, 115, 313, 427, 430, 434, 442, 457, 510, 548; "Guernica," 444, 445; "L'Arlésienne," 473, 489
Pillars, free, 513; mushroom, 419–420, 448–450, 571; novel use of, 742
Pinder, Wilhelm, *Deutscher Barock*, 127
Pissarro, Camille, 295
Plan libre, see Le Corbusier
Plants, for parks, 661–663, 667n
Plato, 765
Plywood, 602

Pollack, Oscar, 111n
Polonceau tie system, 231
Popes: Gregory XIII, 84, 85, 88, 92, 99, 101; Julius II, 57, 62, 63, 80, 92; Julius III, 80n; Leo X, 74, 76, 92; Nicholas V, 76, 80, 99; Paul III (Alessandro Farnese), 56, 70, 78, 81, 92; Pius IV, 64, 92; Pius V, 85, 88. *See also* Papacy; Sixtus V
Porch, 405–407
Practical Mechanic's Journal, 253n
Prefabricated parts, 194, 235, 243, 249ff, 311; Wright's experiments, 409. *See also* Bogardus; Gropius; van der Rohe
"Pullman car style," 339
Purisme, 435

Radburn, N. J., 688n
Radio City, *see* Rockefeller Center
Rainaldi, Carlo, 152, 619n
Rambuteau, Count, 645–646
Ramp, in houses, 519
Ransome, Ernest L., *Reinforced Concrete Buildings*, 323
Raphael, 44, 62, 76, 445n
Rathenau, Emil, 475, 497, 542
Reed, Jesse, 348
Rembrandt, 111
Renaissance, 30–75, 198, 431, 440
Renoir, Auguste, 295
Repton, Humphry, 172
Residences (i.e., houses), Chicago, 366; eastern United States, 361–362; Amsterdam, 708ff; London, 632ff; Paris, 670ff; of the future, 725ff, 744; influence of industrial buildings, 302; Aalto (Mairea), 592–595; Gropius, 499–501; Mies van der Rohe, 546–548; smaller houses by Wright, 399; Bourg-la-Reine, 324; Charnley house, 397–398, 407; Coonley house, 403, 414, 492; D. D. Martin house, 408, 415, 492; Kaufman house, 395n; La Roche house, 518; "Red House," 292; Roberts house, 400–402; Robie house, 408, 415; Rue Danton house, 328; Rue de Facque house, 304; Rue de Turin house, 200, 292, 297–303, 326, 513; Stoclet house, 319; Suntop Houses, 402; Taliesin, 403, 413–414; Taliesin Fellowship winter home, 409; Uccle house, 292; Villa Cook, 520; Villa Savoie, 515ff. *See also* Apartment houses; Housing
Reuleaux, F., *Briefe aus Philadelphia*, 337
Richardson, Henry Hobson, 200, 308, 312, 313, 366, 394, 396, 414n; Sever Hall,

312, 355; Marshall Field Wholesale Store, 10, 358, 360, 370
Rietveld, G., 545
Rivière, Georges Henri, 199n
Robinson, Solon, 349n, 350n
Robinson, W., 659–660, 661n, 700
Roche, Martin, 369, 371, 374
Rockefeller Center, 391n, 744–758; plastic elements, 747ff
Rodin, Auguste, 293, 295
Roebling, J. A., 176
Romanesque, 200, 308, 312–313, 360–361
Rome, maps of, 76, 80–81n; developments under Sixtus V, 75–107; Palazzo Farnese, 135; Piazza del Popolo, 150–154; Piazza Obliqua, 141; Pincio, 152; St. John Lateran, 121; St. Peter's, 35–38, 110, 619, 626; San Carlo alle Quattro Fontane, 110–114, 143; Santa Maria del Popolo, 152; Sant' Ivo, 113–116, 120
Rondelet, J.–B., *Discours*, 211
Roofs, 329, 481, 514, 534–535, 539, 545, 547, 742
Root, John Wellborn, 10, 369–383 *passim*, 748n
Roth, Alfred, *The New Architecture*, 737n
Rotterdam, 449n, 688n, 707n, 709, 737
Rouhault, 179
Ruskin, John, 4, 166, 296, 428, 474
Russia, stratified cities, 691. *See also* Moscow

Saarinen, Eliel, 570
Saarlouis, 53n
St. Louis, river-front area, 194, 198–202, 233, 302; Gantt Building, 200–202; Wainwright Building, 388
Saint-Simonists, 210, 231
San Francisco, Golden Gate Bridge, 177; Academy of Sciences, 324n
Sangallo, Antonio, 56–57, 70
Sant' Elia, Antonio, 319; Città Nuova, 443
Saulnier, Jules, 202–205
Saurbrey, Alexis, *Reinforced Concrete Buildings*, 324
Scamozzi, Vincenzo, 43, 54
Schinkel, K. F., 2, 216n, 543
Schlemmer, Oskar, 483
Schmidt, Garden and Martin, 326, 408n
Schmoller, Gustav, 473
Schönborns, the, 130
Schuyler, Montgomery, 372
Schwedler, J. W., 268n
Schwitters, Kurt, 471
Sédille, Paul, 237